LET'S GO:
LONDON

is the best book for anyone traveling on a budget. Here's why:

No other guidebook has as many budget listings.

In and around London we list twenty hotels and hostels for less than $26 a night. We tell you how to get there the cheapest way, whether by bus, plane, or thumb, and where to get an inexpensive and satisfying meal once you've arrived. There are hundreds of money-saving tips for everyone plus lots of information on student discounts.

LET'S GO researchers have to make it on their own.

Our Harvard-Radcliffe researchers travel on budgets as tight as your own—no expense accounts, no free hotel rooms.

LET'S GO is completely revised every year.

We don't just update the prices, we go back to the places. If a charming restaurant has become an overpriced tourist trap, we'll replace the listing with a new and better one.

No other budget guidebook includes all this:

Coverage of both the city and daytrips out of the city; directions, addresses, phone numbers, and hours to get you in and around; in-depth information on culture, history, and the inhabitants; tips on work, study, sights, nightlife, and special splurges; detailed city maps; and much, much, more.

LET'S GO is for anyone who wants to see London on a budget.

Books by Harvard Student Agencies, Inc.

Let's Go: London
Let's Go: New York City
Let's Go: Washington, D.C.

Let's Go: Europe
Let's Go: Britain & Ireland
Let's Go: France
Let's Go: Germany, Austria & Switzerland
Let's Go: Greece & Turkey
Let's Go: Italy
Let's Go: Spain & Portugal
Let's Go: Israel & Egypt

Let's Go: USA
Let's Go: California & Hawaii
Let's Go: The Pacific Northwest, Western Canada & Alaska
Let's Go: Mexico

LET'S GO:

The Budget Guide to

LONDON

1992

Stephen Blyth
Editor

Maya Fischhoff
Assistant Editor

Written by Harvard Student Agencies, Inc.

ST. MARTIN'S PRESS
NEW YORK

Helping Let's Go

If you have suggestions or corrections, or just want to share your discoveries, drop us a line. We read every piece of correspondence, whether a 10-page letter, a tacky Elvis postcard, or, as in one case, a collage. All suggestions are passed along to our researcher/writers. Please note that mail received after May 5, 1992 will probably be too late for the 1993 book, but will be retained for the following edition. **Address mail to:** *Let's Go: London;* **Harvard Student Agencies, Inc.; Thayer Hall-B; Harvard University; Cambridge, MA 02138; USA.**

In addition to the invaluable travel advice our readers share with us, many are kind enough to offer their services as researchers or editors. Unfortunately, the charter of Harvard Student Agencies, Inc. enables us to employ only currently enrolled Harvard students.

Maps by David Lindroth, copyright © 1992, 1991 by St. Martin's Press, Inc.

Distributed outside the U.S. and Canada by Pan Books Ltd.

ISBN: 0-312-06396-2

First Edition
10 9 8 7 6 5 4 3 2 1

Let's Go: London is written by Harvard Student Agencies, Inc.,
Harvard University, Thayer Hall-B, Cambridge, Mass. 02138.

Let's Go ® is a registered trademark of Harvard Student Agencies, Inc.

Editor	Stephen Blyth
Assistant Editor	Maya E. Fischhoff
Managing Editor	Jamie Rosen
Publishing Director	Zanley F. Galton III
Production Manager	Christopher Williams Cowell
Researcher/Writers	Maura A. Henry
	Nick Hoffman
	Jonathan Taylor

Sales Group Manager	Michael L. Campbell
Sales Group Representatives	Julie Barclay Cotler
	Robert J. Hutter
President	Robert Frost
C.E.O.	Michele Ponti

ACKNOWLEDGMENTS

Here's to the team that produced this book: researcher/writers Jonathan Taylor, Nick Hoffman and Maura Henry; assistant editor Maya Fischhoff; and managing editor Jamie Rosen.

If anyone has ever "done" London, it is **Jonathan Taylor.** He immersed himself in the city, investigating its many facets with the utmost dedication. Nothing escaped him. Jonathan came from Oklahoma, but handled London like a native. His immaculate copy batches, full of gentle wit and remarkable insight, were a joy to receive; we paraded them through the office, eliciting envious glances from other editors. Jonathan was at once committed and unassuming; indeed, his constant modesty was one of the most endearing aspects of the summer.

Nick Hoffman was equally impressive. From whole body donation to polo, from Sting to Edward the Confessor, Nick knew. His research was meticulous, his writing was flawless, and his marginalia kept Maya and me entertained all summer. Nick's very presence in London inspired fear in hotel proprietors. Jonathan, Maura and I all appreciated Nick's hospitality during the summer; it was his inspired idea to make the historic Team London visit to *Rock Circus*. Nick must be cool—his favorite footballer is John Barnes.

Maura Henry displayed her fine historical knowledge as she deftly circumnavigated London. She eliminated *Let's Go's* innumeracy regarding Kings Henry and burrowed deep into the ancient monuments of southern England. Reliving her youth as she passed through the great university towns, she kept cool amidst oppresive summer crowds, sending in thorough and objective copy. I was charmed by her deference to a certain researcher of last year.

Maya Fischhoff was the Alan Hansen of assistant editors: competent, poised, graceful, and blessed with remarkable ability. Her sterling efforts enabled *Let's Go: London 1992* to be the first book in *Let's Go* history completed one week ahead of schedule. She was magnificent. I would continue with the superlatives—but she would only cut them as bad style.

Jamie Rosen, the jungle-painting managing editor, provided encouragement and support throughout the summer; his enthusiasm for this book was most heartening. It was James's drive early on that got us cranking at a terrific rate. Ever entertaining, Sir James soon taught me that size is no indicator of wrestling ability.

Team London—Rosen in goal, Hoffman, Taylor and Henry up front, Blyth and Fischhoff in the middle of the park—was a winner.

—SJB

These acknowledgments are largely an ode to Steve, my ideal working partner and editor *extraordinaire.* Blyth, Blythee, Nigel, Andrew, Ted—under all aliases, he reorganized the book with his analytical flair and revitalized it with his stellar sense of humor. Steve's abundant optimism and sense of perspective resisted basement gloom and made sifting through our glorious copy (thanks, Jonathan, Nick, Maura) even more of a pleasure.

Miranda Spieler brought Marxism, magical realism, and a much-needed sense of irony to the general office flurry. Her sterling humor kept me laughing throughout the summer. Lev Grossman's deadpan wit made us wax appreciative. And although Jamie's initial spray-painting campaign bore only brief fruit, his gentle humor and charming edits proved more lasting.

Zan's and Chris Cowell's superior organization beat the proverbial *Let's Go* monster into a cowering pup; no all-nighters stalked the London book. Other people brightened my extra-office hours. Scones of appreciation to my housemates—Eva, Emily, Tamar, Talene, Karen, Blythe, and Alison—and to the friends whom I visited: the Hockensteins, the Zasloffs, Sarah Stein, and Blanche and Mainey. Most of all, buckets of love to my family, whom I adore, and who took me to London first, these many years ago.

—MEF

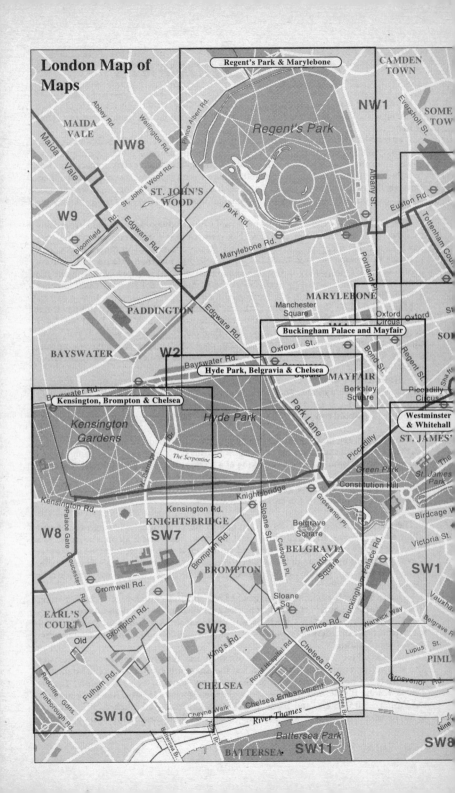

London Map of Maps

Regent's Park & Marylebone

Buckingham Palace and Mayfair

Hyde Park, Belgravia & Chelsea

Kensington, Brompton & Chelsea

Westminster & Whitehall

CAMDEN TOWN

NW1

SOME TOW

MAIDA VALE

NW8

ST. JOHN'S WOOD

Regent's Park

Abbey Rd.

Wellington Rd.

Prince Albert Rd.

Albany St.

Eversholt St.

Euston Rd.

Tottenham Cou

Maida Vale

W9

St. John's Wood Rd.

Bloomfield Rd.

Edgware Rd.

Park Rd.

Marylebone Rd.

MARYLEBONE

Portland Pl.

PADDINGTON

Edgware Rd.

Manchester Square

Oxford Circus

Oxford

St

SO

BAYSWATER

W2

Bayswater Rd.

Oxford St.

Bond St.

MAYFAIR

Regent St

Shaft

Bayswater Rd.

Kensington Gardens

Hyde Park

Park Lane

Berkeley Square

Piccadilly Circus

ST. JAMES'

The

Westminster & Whitehall

St. James Park

The Serpentine

Piccadilly

Green Park

Constitution Hill

Birdcage W

Kensington Rd.

Knightsbridge

Grosvenor Pl.

Victoria St.

W8

Palace Gate

Gloucester Rd.

Kensington Rd.

KNIGHTSBRIDGE

SW7

Sloane St.

Belgrave Square

Buckingham Palace Rd.

SW1

Cromwell Rd.

Brompton Rd.

BROMPTON

Cadogan Pl.

BELGRAVIA

Eaton Square

Vauxha

EARL'S COURT

Old

Brompton Rd.

Sloane Sq.

Pimlico Rd.

Warwick Way

Belgrave R

King's Rd.

SW3

Lupus. St.

PIML

Redcliffe Gdns.

Fulham Rd.

Royal Hospital Rd.

CHELSEA

Chelsea Br. Rd.

Grosvenor Rd.

Finborough Rd.

SW10

Cheyne Walk

Chelsea Embankment

Chelsea Br.

River Thames

Nine

Battersea Park

SW11

SW8

BATTERSEA

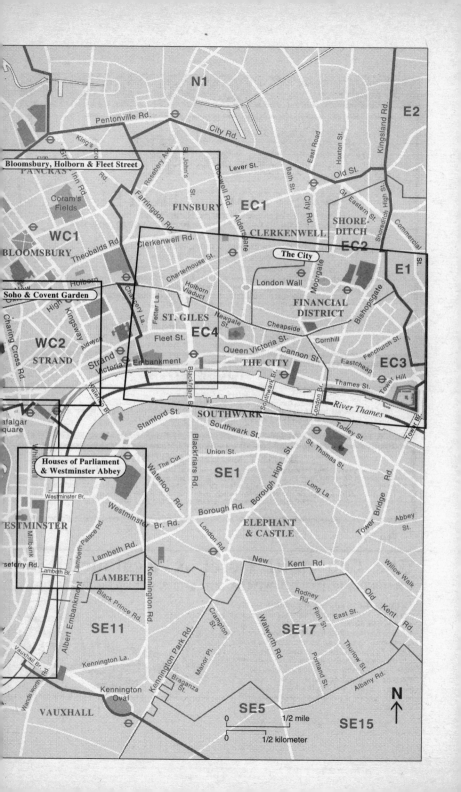

CONTENTS

xii   Contents

LIST OF MAPS

About Let's Go

A generation ago, Harvard Student Agencies, a three-year-old nonprofit corporation dedicated to providing employment to students, was doing a booming business booking charter flights to Europe. One of the extras offered to passengers on these flights was a 20-page mimeographed pahmplet entitled *1960 European Guide,* a collection of tips on continental travel compiled by the HSA staff. The following year, students traveling to Europe researched the first full-fledged edition of *Let's Go: Europe,* a pocket-sized book with tips on budget accommodations, irreverent write-ups of sights, and a decidedly youthful slant.

Throughout the 60s, the series reflected its era: a section of the 1968 *Let's Go: Europe* was entitled "Street Singing in Europe on No Dollars a Day." During the 70s *Let's Go* gradually became a large-scale operation, adding regional European guides and expanding coverage into North Africa and Asia. Now in its 32nd year, *Let's Go* publishes 15 titles covering more than 40 countries. This year *Let's Go* proudly introduces two new guides: *Let's Go: Germany, Austria & Switzerland* and *Let's Go: Washington, D.C.*

Each spring 80 Harvard-Radcliffe students are hired as researcher/writers for the summer months. They train intensively during April and May for their summer tour of duty. Each researcher/writer then hits the road on a shoestring budget for seven weeks, researching six days per week, and overcoming countless obstacles in a glorious quest for better bargains.

Back in a basement deep below Harvard yard, an editorial staff of 30, a management team of six, and countless typists and proofreaders—all students—spend four months poring over more than 70,000 pages of manuscript as they push the copy through a rigorous editing process. High tech has recently landed in the dungeon: some of the guides are now typeset in-house using sleek black desktop workstations.

And even before the books hit the stands, next year's editions are well underway.

At Harvard Student Agencies, CEO Michele Ponti and President Robert Frost graciously presided over the whole affair.

A Note To Our Readers

The information for this book is gathered by Harvard Student Agencies' researchers during the late spring and summer months. Each listing is derived from the assigned researcher's opinion based upon his or her visit at a particular time. The opinions are expressed in a candid and forthright manner. Other travelers might disagree. Those traveling at a different time may have different experiences since prices, dates, hours, and conditions are always subject to change. You are urged to check beforehand to avoid inconvenience and surprises. Travel always involves a certain degree of risk, especially in low-cost areas. When traveling, especially on a budget, you should always take particular care to ensure your safety.

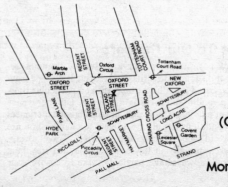

LET'S GO: LONDON

Life and Times

History

> *London; a nation not a city.*
>
> —*Benjamin Disraeli*

In the aftermath of the Great Fire of 1666, as most of London lay an ashy wasteland, ambitious young architect Christopher Wren presented his blueprints for a new city to Charles II. Always a dreamer, Wren envisioned broad avenues and spacious plazas: London would no longer be a medieval hodgepodge of streets and buildings. But the pragmatic king was well aware that the plan, which took no account of existing property lines, would have incensed local landowners. So he vetoed Wren's design and the city was rebuilt in the same piecemeal way that it had arisen: reflecting a host of private interests and individual desires.

Personal enterprise and ownership have defined London from its founding as the Roman Empire's farthest outpost. Although Roman officials laid out merely the skeleton of a town in 43 AD—a bridge, roads, a mint—the city soon became a thriving purchase and shipping hub for wool, wheat and metals. Within a few years, Tacitus described the new Londinium as "a great trading center, full of merchants." Relying on the Romans for protection, the locals concentrated their attentions on commerce. But in 61 AD, the Romans failed to prevent Queen Boudicca and her Iceni warriors from attacking, looting, and burning the town. The Romans built a large stone fort on the edge of the city to protect it from future raids. In 200 AD, they added a wall around three sides of the city and a wooden stockade on the fourth. But in 410, with Rome in decline, they left altogether.

London slipped into a period of decay. The city was largely abandoned and the Celts, Saxons and Danes squabbled over it until 886 AD, when King Alfred the Great of Wessex recaptured the city and strengthened its defenses. The Danes harassed Alfred's successor, Ethelred the Unready, and managed to seize the city. In response, Ethelred enlisted the help of his better-prepared friend Olaf (later a saint), who led a fleet up the Thames to the bridge in 1014. Inventive Olaf used wickerwork to protect his ships from Danish defenders, tied ropes to the bridge supports and rowed away, pulling the rickety bridge into the river. The Danes fell into the Thames—and the nursery rhyme "London Bridge is Falling Down" was born.

William the Conqueror arrived in town after his brief engagement at Hastings in 1066, and promptly made his mark, building the White Tower both to protect and govern his citizens. Under a more stable government, the city began to rebuild itself economically and politically. It gained a municipal government under Richard I, and the right to elect a mayor under John I. The merchant guilds, which arose after the Norman Conquest, took charge of the elections as well as a host of other municipal functions; they regulated the quality of goods, trained apprentices and took care of sick or elderly workers.

Overseas trade and inland culture gained new momentum under the astute guidance of Elizabeth I. Joint stock ventures like the Virginia Company sent the British flag across the seas. Playwrights and poets amused commoners in outdoor theaters. Coffeehouses cropped up, brewing business deals alongside literary and political discussions. The city was ravaged by natural disasters—the Plague in 1665 and the Great Fire in 1666—but Londoners energetically rebuilt and reproduced.

In the 18th and 19th centuries, the city became increasingly crowded. Its population multiplied sixfold. Rampant growth worsened structural problems that the

1

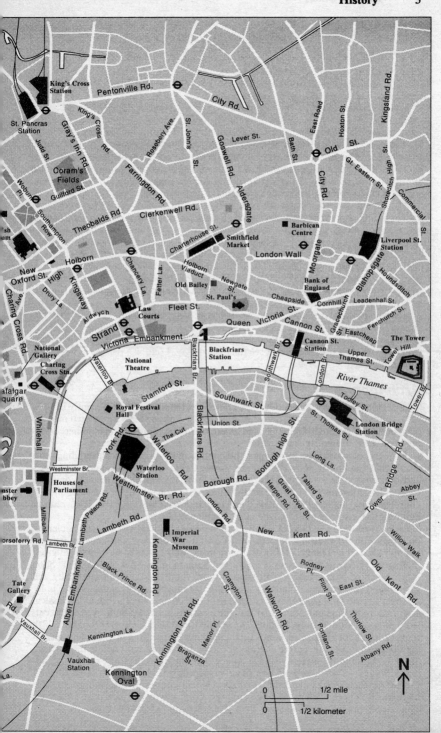

weak government was unable to address: most notably, horse-drawn traffic jams and street pollution. Private enterprise stepped into the gap; the first underground tube line was financed entirely by private backers. But the London County Council, created in 1889, provided a more substantial solution to expansion woes. It developed public motor-buses to reduce congestion and passed the Clean Air Act in 1935. The grimy, foggy streets that Holmes and Watson once rattled down in hansom cabs would never be the same again.

London's historic focus on economic profit by no means dooms it to a lack of common spirit. Londoners rally together against outside foes, most notably during World War II. "We would rather see London laid in ruins and ashes than that it should be tamely and abjectly enslaved," Winston Churchill declared in 1940. During the Battle of Britain, the city endured bombing every night but one for three months. But most Londoners held out, and many of those who had initially fled the city returned. When Hitler finally transferred the Luftwaffe to the Russian front, London emerged battered but still defiant.

After the war, some once again had great plans for the city, and they were more successful than poor Christopher Wren. By an act passed in 1944, the city gained the right to purchase all areas razed by the bombing, building hundreds of blocks of towering Council housing. In 1947 the Town and Country Planning Act provided for the provision of a green belt on the outskirts of the city. Office blocks sprouted in central London as the population grew. These days Londoners have grown concerned about the excesses of high-rise development, regarding the "dream homes" in post-war blocks of flats as blighted slums. The council, overhauled in 1965 to become the Greater London Council, was abolished amid controversy under Mrs. Thatcher, leaving London with no elected governing body. V.S. Pritchett has observed, "The merchants have always beaten down the planners. The mercantile mind cannot tolerate either vista or perspective." Wren's vision of the city—or anything like it—will probably never see the light of day. London's perspective remains essentially private.

Architecture

"London is not ugly," artist Gustave Doré repeated fondly and frequently in 1870 as he toured the city. London may not be ugly, but it often seems a confused muddle of structures. Gracious buildings from all architectural trends jostle together, creating a madcap but endearing skyline.

The Angles and the Saxons began the confusing story of English building with a style that combined severe Roman and simple Celtic. They built small monasteries and churches with several towers, an odd number of aisles and wooden or stone roofs. The Normans brought the first distinctive national style in the 11th entury: churches with endlessly long naves and rectangular east wings. Indeed, church building has inspired many of the city's architectural trends.

In the Middle Ages, Gothic architecture became the design of choice for clerical buildings. Ribbed vaulting, pointed arches and flying buttresses became immensely popular. But after Henry VIII broke with Rome and confiscated the monasteries, Gothic architecture—so strongly associated with religion—fell out of favor. Soon English manor houses had less gloom and more room, laid out symmetrically and surrounded by manicured gardens. The Italian influence had begun to take hold.

Court architect Inigo Jones was primarily responsible for introducing classical architecture to England. Jones first saw the classical buildings built by Andrea Palladio on a vacation in Italy. Inspired, he spread the Palladian style throughout 17th century England. He coated James I's Banqueting House in Whitehall with gleaming Portland stone; the marble was an especially refreshing sight beside the disorganized Tudor muddle of Henry's brick palace. The Banqueting House remains standing, although its brick adjunct has since burned down. Jones constructed the airy Covent Garden Piazza and built the first classical church in England for Charles I's Spanish fiancée. The royal pew cunningly connects to the palace by a passage. The chapel proved more pleasing than the marriage, which fell through.

The destruction of the city by the Great Fire of 1666 provided the next opportunity for large-scale construction. Christopher Wren, inspired by a visit to the Louvre, jumped at the chance. He built 51 new churches, covering the skyline with a sea of spires leading up to St. Paul's, his masterwork. Wren built St. Paul's last, having used the other churches as experiments to work out anticipated design problems. His final creation stands as a centerpiece for the city.

The lyrical styles begun by Jones and Wren continued to shape London's architecture for much of the next century. Other designers, like James Gibbs, Colin Campbell, and William Kent refined their styles and integrated them with the new Baroque trend sweeping the Continent. Gibbs, encouraged by the devout Queen Anne, built churches like St. Mary-le-Strand, a many-angled beauty. The tower and steeple plan of St. Martin's in the Fields, designed by Gibbs, proved a popular model for numerous colonial churches, particularly in the United States. Kent, a painter, designed the walls and pseudo-Pompeiian ceiling of Kensington Palace, while Campbell built early mansions such as Burlington House.

By the late 1700s, builders yearned for something more exotic. Tired of London's stout brick face, John Nash covered the town with fanciful terraces and stucco façades. He wanted to create a massive garden city for the nobility. His vision was never realized in full, but the romantic pediments, triumphal arches and sweeping pavilions of Regent's Park still provide a rich and sugary vision.

Archeological discoveries in the Mediterranean prompted the next trend. After diggers discovered Pompeii and Lord Elgin stole part of the Parthenon, Londoners became enraptured by ruins. James Stuart published a pop architecture tract, *Antiquities of Athens,* in 1751. Architects Robert Adam, William Chambers and John Soane went on columnic rampages, grafting Doric, Tuscan, Ionic and Corinthian pillars onto a variety of unlikely structures. London designers grew so inspired by the neoclassicism that they even printed Elgin marbles wallpaper.

Neoclassicism faded under the sober reign of Victoria. Even the Romantic poets disliked it; it was too restrained, too subtle, they complained. Victoria's dark propriety and the Romantics' flair combined to usher in a spirited Gothic revival. Suddenly, Gothic buildings sprouted even in the remotest London suburbs. Pubs, villas and banks were oddly festooned with Italian Gothic pillars. The design contest for the new House of Commons in 1894 required that the style be Gothic or Elizabethan. And an immense pink Gothic cathedral rose at St. Pancras Station.

Inevitably, all the dark wood and brooding sculptures came to seem rather overpowering. Aesthetician John Ruskin, who had previously championed the Gothic trend, wrote remorsefully: "There is scarcely a public house near the Crystal Palace but sells its gin and bitters under the pseudo-Venetian capitals copied from the Church of the Madonna of Health or Miracles of Morades...My present house is...surrounded everywhere by the accursed Frankenstein monster indirectly of my own making."

But Victorian London couldn't make up its mind. While many architects insisted on bringing back Gothic, others ushered in Italianate Renaissance, French and Dutch forms, still others latched onto Tudor, and some lonely pioneers discovered new building possibilities in iron and glass. Sir Joseph Paxton created the splendid Crystal Palace for the exposition of 1851. The inspirational building burned down at the time of Edward's abdication.

After World War II, the face of building in London, perhaps exhausted by the demolition of the war, took a harsher turn. Hulking monoliths now neighbor Victorians door pillars and spiraling chimneys. And the medley of building continues: modern, neoclassical, post-modern. Contemporary London continues to be the city planner's nightmare and the art historian's dream—the urbanscape that can't make up its mind.

Literary London

> Dear, damn'd distracting town, farewell!
> Thy fools no more I'll tease:
> This year in peace, ye critics dwell,
> Ye Harlots, sleep at ease!
> —Alexander Pope, "A Farewell to London in the Year 1715"

In the beginning, English literature was written in Latin. But in the 14th century, Geoffrey Chaucer and a few other brave souls began to write in a language that resembles the one spoken today. Since then, English literature has flourished and London has become its intellectual center.

Chaucer, the son of a well-to-do London wine merchant, initiated the tradition that British tales commence in London. The pilgrims in *Canterbury Tales* set off from Tabard Inn in Southwark on the south bank. Today, the writer rests in Poets' Corner at Westminster Abbey. Indeed you can visit many of your favorite dead poets in that choice corner. Especially note the unfortunate misspelling of Ben Jonson's name in the plaque that reads: "O rare Ben Johnson."

Jonson, as yet unmaligned, held sway in the English court scene of the early 17th century. He planned balls for Queen Elizabeth and her friends, creating original music, choreography and special effects. Meanwhile, William Shakespeare catered to the common folk in the circular theaters across the river in Southwark. Southwark was beyond the city's legal jurisdiction and was therefore the heart of the red light district; theaters were considered similarly sordid. Shakespeare had a number of fellow London dramatists: Nashe, Lyly, Marlowe. Most of them are now forgotten, or appear only in literary thrillers as possible identities for the "real" Shakespeare. But the Bard's plays live on, offering a vivid (if possibly erroneous) picture of historical London.

Many writers found the actual London—their present-day city—a degenerate, morally disturbing place. John Donne, who became Dean of St. Paul's Cathedral in 1621, wrote poetry while meting out advice to his parishoners. He set his first and fourth satires in London, drawing attention to urban evils. And John Milton held public office in an effort to eliminate those ills and fashion the city into an earthly paradise.

But even those who stayed out of politics agonized over the moral nature of the city. London society welcomed Alexander Pope as a prodigy at the age of 17, but his disillusionment came quickly. In London, "nothing is sacred . . . but villainy," he wrote in the epilogue to his *Satires.* Pope drank away his gloom with professional genius Samuel Johnson in the Cheshire Cheese Pub, while Boswell scurried about looking for crumbs.

Daniel Defoe, Henry Fielding, and Samuel Richardson also explored themes of urban injustice, using journalism, satire and sermons as their tools. They frequently let their characters stay in the countryside for a rest, and in the 1720s Defoe himself escaped to write the first *Let's Go* guide, *A Tour Through the Whole Island of Great Britain.*

Everyone complained about London, and poets of the Age of Reason fantasized about a classic city different from the crime-ridden one that they inhabited, but no one really moved away. London remained a haven for publishing and literary cliques still wrestling with ideas of social justice. In the early 18th century, Joseph Addison and Richard Steele attacked urban ills from a new perspective by creating a new literary genre: the *Tatler* and *Spectator* carried political essays written by the likes of Pope and Swift.

The Industrial Revolution provided a focus for discontent. As a grey haze settled over the city's houses and the beggars on the streets swelled into an army, the wretched state of the city became inescapably apparent. Charles Dickens followed his characters through 19th century London's backstreets and prisons. Even these fictional people began to notice that too much time in industrialized London did wretched things to one's nerves, and the Romantic poets had the same idea. They abandoned the classical idealization of the urban and left the city. Keats and Wordsworth lived in Hampstead and Westminster, both distant suburbs. Shelley wrote, "Hell is a city much like London," while Blake decried the factories as "dark" and "satanic."

By the end of the 19th century, however, the spirit of reform was mitigating industrialization. Soon some writers turned to purely aesthetic issues. In the 1890s, W.B. Yeats joined the London Rhymers' Club, writing light love poetry. Relentlessly quotable Oscar Wilde made life seem a comedy of manners, proclaiming that art could only be useless. Fellow dramatist George Bernard Shaw had a politically aware vision of art and wrote plays more didactic than decadent. A Fabian soialist, Shaw moved to London from Dublin at the age of 20 and was supported by his doting parents for nine years.

The First World War left London devestated and many poets tried to capture the traumas of war. In 1921, T.S. Eliot turned London into his angst-ridden modern *Wasteland,* an "Unreal City." The poem follows a crowd over a bridge, wondering how many of them the war has "undone".

Both Eliot and Yeats, dedicated modernists with an interest in mysticism, were not above joining fun literary cliques, and both of them did their time in the Bloomsbury group. This notorious crowd included Virginia Woolf, Vanessa and Clive Bell, economist Maynard Keynes and novelist E.M. Forster. Meanwhile, a penniless George Orwell was meeting street people and telling yarns of urban poverty in his ultimate tale of budget travel, *Down and Out in Paris and London.*

Orwell's depiction of a warped future society in *1984* cast a shadow of gloom into the second half of the 20th century. But aside from the disturbing visions of Anthony Burgess, much of London's modern literature is bright and often witty. Kingsley Amis and his son Martin Amis write deft satirical novels. And with the political breakdown of the British Empire, more ethnic writers, such as Anglo-Indian Salman Rushdie and Anglo-Chinese Timothy Mo, have appeared on the literary scene. Short story virtuoso V. S. Pritchett has added to the great tradition of travel narratives in his insightful *London Perceived.* And writers keep coming to the damn'd distracting town—as a publishing center and an inexhaustible topic, they seem unable to avoid it.

Royal London

In 1989, the government's annual allocation to the Queen for her royal homes and trappings came to some £4.6 million. It is a figure that many British citizens consider money well-spent. The monarchy symbolizes political stability. Besides, the royal presence enhances the mystique that draws millions of tourists, and tourist pounds, to London each year.

Although the British tabloid press sometimes presents the royal family as players in a soap opera, visitors may well find Londoners unaware of the outrageous royal gossip printed in foreign publications. Still, the royal personalities keep London entertained: Princess Diana singlehandedly galvanizes the British fashion industry; Prince Charles talks to his plants, and espouses Green as well as architectural views; Princess Anne, the Princess Royal, has won admiration for her strenuous worldwide efforts on behalf of "Save the Children" fund; Prince Andrew (Randy Andy) cavorts with his wife Sarah on TV game shows; the Queen revels in a quite royal dowdiness.

The role of the royal family has changed significantly from the time when their words caused heads to fall and armies to march. Now, the royals play a largely ceremonial role and the Queen keeps a resolute silence on controversial issues. Under Charles, however, the role of the monarch may well evolve differently. He recently sparked debate by criticizing the British architectural establishment. (Among other comments, he called the proposed extension on the National Gallery a "monstrous carbuncle.") Although some believe that Charles is overstepping his authority, much of the public now regards him as a champion of the views of the common people.

Having a tete a tete with the Queen may be difficult to arrange, but her public engagements are legion. They—a mere 420 in 1989—are published daily in the Court Circular in *The Times, The Daily Telegraph,* and *The Independent.* If receptions for the High Commissioner of Nauru do not grab you—and don't expect invitations even to them to be easy to come by—you can see the Queen at one of the numerous annual pageants she attends, such as "Trooping the Colour." In October, at the **State Opening of Parliament,** the Queen gives a speech prepared by the government outlining new legislation for the upcoming session. The Queen rides to Parliament via the Mall in one of her fleet of coaches. You can stand, cheer, wave a flag and admire the back of the basketball player in front of you. The **Remembrance Day Service,** held in Whitehall in November to honor the war dead, is also attended by many royals. **Maundy Money,** which dates back to the 12th century, is held on the day before Good Friday, at varying locations. The Queen distributes special silver coins to selected pensioners, the number of whom equals her age (66 in 1992). Originally, this ritual involved the monarch washing the feet of the poor, but the Plague made such an operation significantly less advisable. The Queen does not make an appearance for the **Changing of the Guard,** in front of Buckingham Palace; though she may peek out from behind a curtain. Guards also change regularly and ceremoniously at the **Horse Guards Parade.**

London's buildings bear testimony to the historic splendor of royal life. **Buckingham Palace,** where the Queen, Prince Philip, and the Duke and Duchess of York live, has been the official residence of the sovereign since Queen Victoria's reign. The Royal Standard flying indicates that Queen Elizabeth is at home. Prince Charles, Princess Diana and the Queen's sister Margaret live in **Kensington Palace,** W8. **Marlborough House,** SW1, and **Lancaster House,** SW1, are particularly gracious buildings. **St. James's Palace,** Buckingham Palace's predecessor, lies between them. The Queen mum lives in adjacent **Clarence House,** although she still gets out quite a bit—she recently showed the style that has always made her popular by having an impromptu half at an East End pub. (See The Mall, St. James's, and Buckingham Palace under Sights, and the Royal London Appendix.)

Politics

> *London is the epitome of our times, and the Rome of today.*
> *—Ralph Waldo Emerson, English Traits*

When the French have a revolution, they throw their furniture into the street. English reform, on the other hand, has stayed relatively calm ever since a few barons bullied King John into agreeing to the *Magna Carta* in 1215. England's 1688 revolution was "Glorious" and bloodless. When Parliament passed a badly needed reform bill in 1832 it became a "Great Reform Bill." British reforms have generally passed in a measured, polite way and, as the British are fond of pointing out, often seem to predate those of other countries.

English politicians do honor to the civilized tone of parliamentary politics. Artists, writers, and philosophers have traditionally served in politics. William Pitt, Benjamin Disraeli, and Winston Churchill chastised opponents and praised friends with eloquence and grace. While American politicians essentially have to be convicted of grand theft before they'll leave office, British politicans will resign over matters of honor or principle.

When a minor sex scandal does arise, the press tracks it for weeks. The steamy Profumo affair, on which the film *Scandal* was based, involved some high-profile House of Lords types and a few call girls.

As political power gradually transferred from the House of Lords to the House of Commons during the 19th century, Parliament increasingly became a voice for the whole nation. It granted suffrage in grudging increments, but made social welfare a priority by the beginning of the 20th century. After World War II, the Labour Party introduced a national health system and nationalized industries.

Politics took on a less humanistic tone in the 1980s, when Margaret Thatcher brought the country's movement towards socialism to an abrupt halt. She claimed to revitalize the nation's economy, increasing competitiveness and creating a new style of affluence for the money-managers, but she left growing social tensions, staggering dole lines and a tattered educational system in her wake. Thatcher's eleven year sway ended last year, amidst deep Conservative divisions over the move towards European monetary and political union. The question of how far Britain wishes to integrate herself into the European Community still plagues the government; Thatcher's replacement, John Major, follows a more pragmatic approach. A product of the state school system, the new PM promises a new, caring attitude to government, typified by his call for a "classless society."

Media

The Press

Ambitious English journalists aspire to finish their apprenticeships in the provinces and join the ranks of the "hacks of Fleet Street" (who now habitate Wapping). With the exception of the Manchester-born *Guardian,* most national papers originate from London.

Serious readers have an enviable choice of quality dailies from which to choose, each covering domestic and international news, business, sports, and the arts, as well as printing theatre, TV, and radio listings.*The Times,* for centuries a model of thoughtful discretion and mild infallibility, has recently turned Tory under the leadership of Rupert "Buy It" Murdoch. The correspondence section still carries on eccentric and excruciatingly annoying exchanges for weeks on end (on topics such as hedgehog hutches). The *Daily Telegraph* under editor Max "Hitler" Hastings has discarded much of its fuddiness yet still toes a fairly conservative, but rigorously fair, line. *The Independent* is. *The Guardian* veers to the left of center and prints some incisive features and a mean bridge column. *The Financial Times,* printed on pink paper, does more elegantly for the City what the *Wall Street Journal* does for Manhattan. No comment.

On Sundays, *The Sunday Times, The Sunday Telegraph, Independent on Sunday* and the highly polished *Observer* publish multi-section papers with glossy magazines and detailed arts, sports, and news coverage.

A screaming array of tabloids sits next to the qualities. *The Daily Mail, The Daily Express, Today* and *The Evening Standard* (the only evening paper) make serious attempts at popular journalism, although tend towards the gossipy. *The Sun,* more famous for its page three pin-up than for its reporting, specialises in thoughtful headlines such as "Gotcha!" *The Star* and Robert Maxwell's leftwing *The Daily Mirror* are as bilious as *The Sun.* On Sundays, *The Sunday Mirror* and *The News of the World* fight it out. *The Sunday Sport* defies description.

The magazine *Punch,* dating from the days of Dickens, continues to parody England and the world with eccentric delight. Subversive and snide, *Private Eye* carries gossip on media and law and pokes fun at prominent personalities and fellow magazines. Often threatened by exorbitant libel settlements, *The Eye* maintains a remarkable reader loyalty. Even those who don't get the in-jokes will keep reading. The immensely popular *Viz* parodies modern prejudices and hypocrises with unashamedly outrageous comic-strips. *The Economist* covers world affairs with subtle wit. *New Statesman Society* on the left and *The Spectator* on the right cover art and politics with weekly verve.

Radio

The BBC strives to maintain its reputation for scrupulous fairness, amidst Conservative complaints of bias. The "Beeb" established said reputation with its radio services. Pop music channel Radio1 features rock-and-roll critic John Peel on weekdays from 8:30-10pm. Radio2 plays easy-listening tunes and light talk shows. Superbly programmed Radio3 broadcasts classical music. During cricket matches, it also puts out the incomparable *Test Match Special,* a national institution that features idiosyncratic ball-by-ball commentary. In addition to excellent news coverage and intellectual tidbits, Radio4 plays "The Archers," a radio drama that dates to 1951. Brand new Radio5 covers sports and children's programming. The BBC World Service broadcasts 24 hr.—"This is London." Program times are usually published Greenwich Mean Time; in summer you will have to add an hour.

Local stations abound. Capital Radio sponsors a music festival each summer, runs the Capital Help Line and Flatshare Line, and broadcasts local news and pop music round the clock. Recently legalised KissFM competes. LBC puts out 24-hr. news and comment. BBC Radio London mixes news and music. JazzFM is cryptically named. Pirate stations sometimes swashbuckle between channels, although new regulatory practices are allowing yesterday's buccaneers to become today's radio entrepreneurs. Know your notation. AM is sometimes called Medium Wave (MW) in England.

Television

TV owners in England pay a licence fee that supports the advertisement-free activities of the BBC. Its quasi-governmental associations have not hampered innovation. Home of *Monty Python's Flying Circus,* BBC TV broadcasts on two national channels. BBC1 carries news at 1, 6, and 9pm plus the more mainstream of the BBC's dramatic, sporting and entertainment offerings. More alternative cultural programs are telecast on BBC2, ranging from sheepdog trials to *Open University.* ITV, Britain's established commercial network, carries an equally impressive schedule of programming. Under the recent Broadcasting Act, the ITV franchises are put up to auction—the highest bidder (subject to quality safeguards) wins the right to broadcast. Channel 4 has highly respected arts programming and a fine news broadcast at 7pm on weeknights—Salman Rushdie once worked for them. The high-tech satellite channels of BSkyB beam down films, sports, news and American imports. Look for a dish on your hotel. Both *Radio Times* and *TV Times* have listings for BBC1, BBC2, ITV, Channel 4, and satellite programs.

Teletext, an electronic information service broadcast alongside the TV signal, provides remote control news, sport, travel and weather information. The BBC's version is called *Ceefax,* ITV's *Oracle.* Don't miss it if your hotel manager has invested in a decoder.

Manners and Mores

> *One should always eat muffins quite calmly. It is the*
> *only way to eat them.*
> *—Oscar Wilde, The Importance of Being Earnest*

Although to a visitor Londoners' concern for formality may take an occasional turn for high farce, manners here are a serious business. Try to treat everyone as you would an endearing old uncle. While handshakes in Britain tend to be slightly more robust than the limp-wristed, continental sort, you should still be careful not to go around pumping peoples' arms as you might in Dallas or they'll think you're a thug.

American tourists still have a reputation for rudeness by British standards and should avoid glaring mistakes like bringing food into a church, snapping pictures during services, or whooping at cricket matches. And be as polite as possible when asking for something—bar staff at London pubs have been known to complain that with Americans it's always, "I want, I'll have, give me, more, another . . . "When down the pub, the British invariably buy rounds of drinks for their companions, even if they're recent acquaintances. This remarkable generosity is expected to be reciprocated; if you see empty glasses and drumming fingers, you know what to do. During conversation, refer to people as British as opposed to English (or Scottish or Welsh). And don't knock the Royal Family (except Princess Michael of Kent)—the Brits adore them.

It's hard to feel improperly dressed in London. Punks stripped away most remnants of clothes snobbery. However, American men doing business here should stay away from striped ties as they are often copies of old school ties or English regimentals; they care about such things here. Academic allegiance is always understated in Britain; no graduate would dream of sporting a sweatshirt with their alma mater emblazoned on the chest. You can dress up or down for dinner or for the theatre. Tuxedos are only really seen at the opera.

Tipping

Where tipping is expected, 10-15% is the norm anywhere in London. A small number of restaurants may automatically add a service charge (usually around 10%) to your bill. If you are dissatisfied with the service, you can legally deduct this charge, but to do so you must make your complaint to the manager. If your service has been exceptional, a small tip above and beyond the flat charge is appropriate and should be left at the table.

Do not tip bar staff in pubs. If you do, they will think you're either crazy or making untoward advances. If one has been particularly good to you, you might discreetly offer to buy him or her a pint of ale. This gesture is generally welcomed and, when shrewdly timed, it can also increase your chances of a free refill.

Don't tip in theatres or cinemas, and only tip doormen if they hail a cab or go out of their way to do something for you. But do tip cocktail waiters and waitresses in hotels, restaurants, and nightclubs, as well as barbers, hair stylists, tour guides, parking valets, porters (50p per large bag), and cab drivers (10-15%, but never less than 40p). And eat those muffins calmly.

Planning Your Trip

> It is difficult to speak adequately or justly of London
> . . . it is not agreeable, or cheerful, or easy, or exempt
> from reproach. It is only magnificent. You can draw
> up a tremendous list of reasons why it should be insup-
> portable. The fogs, the smoke, the dirt, the darkness,
> the wet, the distances, the ugliness . . . You may call
> it dreary, heavy, stupid, dull, inhuman, vulgar at
> heart and tiresome in form . . . But for one who takes
> it as I take it, London is on the whole the most possible
> form of life.
>
> —Henry James

Useful Addresses

The amount of information available to travelers can seem overwhelming. Don't get lost in the whirlwind of tourist-office pamphlets and brochures. Choose your information carefully and develop a clear idea of what you want to see. Remember that the mission of a tourist office is to lure you to a particular sight, not to assess its virtues objectively. Never plan ahead so thoroughly that you will have no freedom to wander and explore. Below, we list British consulates, better equipped than embassies to handle tourist inquiries.

Tourist Offices

British Tourist Authority (BTA), 40 W. 57th St. #320, New York, NY 10019 (tel. (212) 581-4700). In Canada, 94 Cumberland St. #600, Toronto, Ont. M5R 3N3 (tel. (416) 925-6326). U.S. branches in Chicago and Los Angeles; also in Sydney, Wellington and 11 European cities. Publishes some useful vacation guides, including *Stay With a British Family* and *The Bed and Breakfast Guide.* The **British Travel Bookshop,** on the third floor of the New York office, will send you their mail-order catalog of accommodations upon request.

Consulates and High Commissions

British Consulates: In **U.S.,** British Consulate General, 845 Third Ave., New York, NY 10022 (tel. (212) 745-0200); Marquis One Tower #2700, 245 Peachtree Centre Ave., Atlanta, GA 30303 (tel. (404) 524-5856); 33 N. Dearborn St., Chicago, IL 60602 (tel. (312) 346-1810); 1100 Milam #2260, Houston, TX (tel. (713) 659-6270); 3701 Wilshire Blvd., Los Angeles, CA 90010 (tel. (213) 385-7381); and 3100 Massachusetts Ave. NW., Washington, DC 20008 (tel. (202) 462-1340). In **Canada,** British High Commission, 80 Elgin St., Ottawa, Ont. K1P 5K7 (tel. (613) 237-1530). In **Australia,** British High Commission, Commonwealth Ave., Canberra, (tel. (62) 706 666). In **New Zealand,** British High Commission, Reserve Bank of New Zealand Bldg., 9th Floor, 2 The Terrace, Wellington 1 (tel. (4) 726 049);and 17th floor, Faye Richwhite bldg., 151 Queen's St., Auckland (tel. (9) 303-2970 or -2971).

Hostel Associations

U.S.: American Youth Hostels (AYH), P.O. Box 37613, Washington, DC 20013-7613 (tel. (202) 783-6161). IYHF cards, hostel handbooks, information on budget travel. Hires group leaders for domestic and foreign outings. Must be 21 and complete a 9-day training course. Compensation includes travel expenses and a small stipend. Membership for 1 year: $25, over 54 and under 18 $10, families $35.

Canada: Canadian Hostelling Association (CHA), National Office, 1600 James Naismith Dr. #608, Gloucester, Ont. K1B 5N4 (tel. (613) 748-5638). IYHF cards and hostel handboooks.

Australia: Australian Youth Hostels Association (AYHA), Level 3, 10 Mallett St., Camperdown, New South Wales 2010 (tel. (02) 565 1699).

New Zealand: Youth Hostels Association of New Zealand, P.O. Box 436, corner of Manchester and Gloucester St., Christchurch 1 (tel. 3 79 99 70; fax 3 65 44 76).

England and Wales: Youth Hostels Association of England and Wales (YHA), 14 Southampton St., Covent Garden, London WC2E 7HY (tel. (071) 240 5236). Also at Trevalyn House, 8 St. Stephen's Hill, St. Albans, Herts, AL1 2DY (tel. (0727) 552 15).

Budget Travel Services

Council on International Educational Exchange (CIEE/Council Travel), 205 E. 42nd St., New York, NY 10017 (tel. (212) 661-1414; for charter flights (800) 223-7402); branches in a host of other cities. In addition to issuing the YIEE International Youth ID and International Student Identity Card (ISIC), CIEE publishes information for budget travelers and those planning work or study abroad. Write for their free and invaluable *Student Travel Catalog,* or pick it up at any CIEE office. Offices also in Amherst, Ann Arbor, Atlanta, Austin, Berkeley, Boston, Boulder, Cambridge, Chicago, Dallas, Davis, Durham, Evanston, Long Beach, La Jolla, Los Angeles, Milwaukee, Minneapolis, New Haven, New Orleans, Portland, Providence, San Diego, San Francisco, Seattle, Sherman Oaks, Tempe, and Washington DC.

Educational Travel Centre (ETC), 438 N. Frances St., Madison, WI 53703 (tel. (608) 256-5551). Provides flight information, IYHF (AYH) membership cards, BR and Eurail passes. Write or call for their free pamphlet, *Taking Off* ($1 postage), for tour and flight information ($1 postage).

International Student Travel Confederation (ISTC), ISIC Association, Gothersgade 30, 1123 Copenhagen K, Denmark (tel. 45 33 93 93 03). In U.S., CIEE (address above); in Canada, Travel CUTS (address below); in Britain, London Student Travel, 52 Grosvenor Gardens, London WC1 (tel. (071) 730 3402); in Ireland, USIT Ltd., Aston Quay, O'Connell Bridge, Dublin 2 (tel. (01) 778 117); in Australia, SSA/STA, 220 Faraday St., Carlton, Melbourne, Victoria 3053 (tel. (03) 347 6911); in New Zealand, Student Travel, 2nd Floor, Courtenay Chambers, 15 Courtenay, Wellington (tel. (04) 850 561). These organizations all issue the ISIC.

Interexchange Program, 356 W. 34th St., 2nd floor, New York, NY 10001 (tel. (212) 947-9533). Write for their catalogs about low-cost camping tours for U.S. students and working abroad.

Let's Go Travel Services, Harvard Student Agencies, Inc., Thayer Hall-B, Harvard University, Cambridge, MA 02138 (tel. (617) 495-9649). Sells Railpasses, AYH memberships (valid at all IYHF youth hostels), International Student and Teacher ID cards, YIEE cards for non-students, travel guides (including the *Let's Go* series), maps, discount airfares, and a complete line of budget travel gear. All items available by mail. Call or write for a catalog.

STA Travel, over 100 offices worldwide. In the U.S., 17 E. 45th St., New York, NY 10017 (tel. (800) 777-0112 or (212) 986-9470). In Britain, 74 and 86 Old Brompton Rd., London SW7 3LQ (tel. (071) 937 9921 for European travel, (071) 937 9971 for North American travel, (071) 937 9962 for the rest of the world). In Australia, 222 Faraday St., Melbourne, Victoria 3053 (tel. (03) 347 6911). In New Zealand, 64 High St., Auckland (tel. (09) 390 458). Sells ISICs and Eurail passes; offers a variety of travel services, including low-cost flights to those under 26 and full-time students under 32.

Travel CUTS (Canadian Universities Travel Service), 187 College St., Toronto, Ont. M5T 1P7 (tel. (416) 979-2406). In Britain, 295-A Regent St., London W1R 7YA (tel. (071) 255 1944). Other offices throughout Canada. Issues the ISIC, IYHF, and FIYTO cards to Canadian citizens. Also sells discount travel passes and arranges transatlantic charter flights from Canadian cities. Prints a complimentary newspaper, *The Canadian Student Traveler,* available at their offices and on campuses across Canada.

Bed and Breakfast Agencies

Auntie's (Great Britain) Limited, 56 Coleshill Terrace, Llanelli, Dyfed, Wales, UK, SA15 3DA (tel. (0554) 770 077). £13-20 per person (under 13 half price) for family B&Bs. Covers London suburbs and other areas of the United Kingdom. Specializes in catering for vegetarians.

Bed and Breakfast (GB), P.O. Box 66, Henley-on-Thames, Oxon, England RG9 1XS (tel. (0491) 578 803). The most comprehensive service, covering all of Great Britain and even parts of France for £9 and up per night. Write for their brochure and rate schedule.

The Independent Traveller, Dinneford Spring, Thorverton, Exeter, England EX5 5NU (tel. (0392) 860 807). Offers cottages, houses, and apartments for rent. Various price ranges, short or long stays.

London Home-to-Home, 19 Mt. Park Crescent, Ealing, London W5 2RN (tel. (081) 567 2998). B&B in 40 homes in West London and Southwest London. Daily rates for singles £20, doubles £32-42; family rooms available.

Books

Ford's Travel Guides, 19448 Londelius St., Northridge, CA 91324. Sells *Ford's Freighter Travel Guide & Waterways of the World* ($8.95, $15 for a subscription that sends you semi-annual copies), a listing of freighter companies that will take passengers for transatlantic crossings. Also sells *Ford's International Cruise Guide* ($9.95, $34 for a quarterly subscription), a listing of ships, destinations and dates of departure.

Forsyth Travel Library, 9154 W. 57th St., P.O. Box 2975, Shawnee Mission, KS 66201 (tel. (913) 384-3440 or (800) 367-7984). Well-stocked mail-order service with a wide range of European city, area, and country maps, as well as rail and boat travel guides. Sells the *Thomas Cook European Timetables* ($23.95 plus $4 postage) and Thomas Cook's *Rail Map of Europe* ($9.95).

Michelin Travel Publications, Davy House, Lyon Rd., Harrow, Middlesex, England HA1 2DQ (tel. (4418) 61 2121). Guides and maps for Britain. Available in most bookstores; in the U.S., write or call Michelin Travel Publications, P.O. Box 3305, Spartanburg, SC 29304 (tel. (803) 599-0850).

North American Vegetarian Society, P.O. Box 72, Dolgeville, NY 13329 (tel. (518) 568-7970). Distributes the *International Vegetarian Travel Guide* ($15.95 plus $2 postage), published by the Vegetarian Society of the United Kingdom, Parkdale, Dunham Rd., Altrincham, Cheshire, England WA14 4GQ (tel. (061) 928 07 93). About half of the book deals with organic Britain, listing restaurants.

Sepher-Hermon Press, 1265 46th St., Brooklyn, NY 11219 (tel. (718) 972-9010). Distributes *The Jewish Travel Guide,* edited by Danny Koffman and published by the London Jewish

Chronicle ($11.50). Updated annually, the guide lists synagogues, kosher restaurants, and other Jewish institutions in cities and towns throughout Britain. In England order from Jewish Chronicle, 25 Furnival St., London EC4A 1JT.

Superintendent of Documents, U.S. Government Printing Office, Washington, DC 20402 (tel. (202) 783-3238). Publishes *Safe Trip Abroad* ($5).

Documents and Formalities

Entrance Requirements for Britain

Travelers must have a valid passport to enter Britain. Citizens of the U.S., Canada, Australia, and New Zealand may enter without a visa. If your travel plans extend beyond Britain, remember that some countries on the European continent do require a visa. When entering the country, dress neatly and carry proof of your financial independence (such as a visa to the next country on your itinerary, an air ticket to depart, enough money to cover the cost of your living expenses, or a letter from someone back home promising financial support). The standard period of admission is six months. To stay longer, you must show evidence that you will be able to support yourself for an extended period of time. Admission as a visitor does not include the right to work.

Passports

U.S. passports may be obtained at any passport agency; many post offices and federal and state courthouses also issue them, though at a snail's pace. For the nearest agency, check the telephone directory under "U.S. Government, State Department," or call your local post office. Processing usually takes two weeks through a passport agency, three to four weeks through a courthouse or post office. If you have proof of departure within five working days (an air ticket, for example), the Passport Agency will provide a rush service while you wait; call ahead and ask what time of day you should arrive for fastest service.

A passport application must include: proof of U.S. citizenship (a birth certificate or certified copy, naturalization papers, or a previous passport), a valid photo or descriptive ID, and two identical photographs (2 in. square on a white background). Passports remain valid for 10 years (five years for those under 18). The fee is $42 for adults, $27 for those under 18. Parents must apply in person for those under 13. A 10-year renewal costs $35 and can be obtained by mail by those whose most recent passport was issued after their sixteenth birthday and within 12 years of the date of new application. For a recorded message, call (202) 647-0518; for further information contact the Washington Passport Agency, Department of State, 1425 K St. NW, Washington, DC 20522-1705 (tel. (202) 326-6060; open Mon.-Fri. 8am-4:15pm).

Canadian passports may be obtained by mail from the Passport Office, Department of External Affairs, Ottawa, Ont. K1A 0G3. You can also apply in person at one of 19 regional offices. The fee is CDN$25, and processing requires about two weeks if you mail your application, three to five working days if you make a personal appearance. Passports remain valid 5 years.

Australian passports may be obtained at a Passport Office or at any post office; every applicant must show up in person. (Those who find it impossible to do so may be eligible for a temporary passport.) The fee is AUS$76 (valid 10 years) for those over 18, otherwise AUS$31 (valid 5 years). Your guarantor must have known you for at least one year. For more information, consult your local post office or call tel. (008) 026 022 (toll free in Australia; open Mon.-Fri. during working hours). Australian citizens age 12 and over must pay a departure tax of AUS$10 before leaving the country.

New Zealand passports may be obtained at a local passport office or consulate. The application must be accompanied by evidence of citizenship; the fee is NZ$50. The passport stays valid for 10 years (5 years for tykes under 18, but it can later

be extended for five more years, free). Allow three weeks for your passport to be processed.

Before you leave, record your passport number and keep it separate from the passport. If you lose your passport while traveling, notify the local police and the nearest consulate of your home government immediately. Carry an expired passport or a copy of your birth certificate in a separate part of your baggage; at the very least, carry a photocopy of the page of your passport that has your photograph and identifying information on it. With one of these, your consulate will be able to issue you temporary traveling papers or replace your lost passport.

Student and Youth Identification

The **International Student Identity Card (ISIC)**, the most widely recognized proof of student status throughout the world, gets better and better. Last year, the card merged with that of the International Union of Students (IUS), incorporating a new array of benefits. The $14 card offers access to over 8000 discounts on train, ferry, and airfares, museum admissions, theater tickets, transportation and accommodations. Present the card wherever you go and ask about discounts even when none leaps out from an ad. If purchased in the U.S., the card also includes limited medical insurance and access to a hotline. You must provide current, dated, unambiguous proof of your student status (a letter on school stationery signed and sealed by the registrar, a copy of your bursar's receipt, or a photocopied grade report); and a 1½ × 2-in. photo with your name printed in pencil on the back. You must be at least 12 years old to obtain the card, which remains valid until the end of the calendar year in which you purchase it. (See Useful Addresses above for student travel offices which issue the ISIC card.)

Customs

Persons entering Britain must declare at the point of entry the three great aromatic luxuries: alcohol, tobacco, and perfume. Duty must be paid on excessive quantities of these substances. Britain does not limit the amount of currency you may bring into or out of the country.

Upon returning home, you must declare all articles acquired abroad. It may be wise to make a list (including serial numbers) of any valuables that you take with you from home, particularly if you register this list with customs at the airport office before you depart. This seemingly odd practice will prevent greedy homeland customs officials from charging duty when you bring them back. **U.S. citizens** may bring home a maximum of $400 worth of goods duty-free; the next $1000 is subject to a 10% tax. Duty-free goods must be for personal or household use and cannot include more than 100 cigars, 200 cigarettes (1 carton), or one liter of wine or liquor (you must be 21 or older to bring liquor into the U.S.). All items included in your duty-free allowance must accompany you; you cannot ship them separately. You may mail unsolicited gifts back to the U.S. from abroad duty-free if they are worth under $50, but you may not mail liquor, tobacco, or perfume. Mark the accurate price and nature of the gift on the package; as the customs service will continually remind you, "honesty is the best policy." If you mail home personal goods of U.S. origin, mark the package "American Goods Returned." For more information, consult *Know Before You Go*, available from the U.S. Customs Service, 1301 Constitution Ave., Washington, DC 20229 (tel. (202) 566-8195).

Similar regulations apply to **Canadian citizens.** After you have been abroad for at least two days, you may bring in up to CDN$100 worth of goods duty-free. Once every calendar year, after you have been abroad at least a week, you may bring in up to CDN$300 worth of goods duty-free. Duty-free goods can include no more than 200 cigarettes, 1kg of tobacco, and 50 cigars (for those 16 or older). You may not bring in more than 1.1 liters of alcohol. Anything above the duty-free allowance will be taxed: 20% for goods that accompany you, more for shipped items. You can send unsolicited gifts worth up to CDN$40 duty-free, but again, you cannot mail alcohol or tobacco. For more information, write or call the Revenue Canada Customs and Excise Department, Communications Branch, Mackenzie Ave., Ot-

tawa, Ont. K1A 0L5 (tel. (613) 957-0275), for the stirring pamphlet *I Declare/Je Declare.*

Australian citizens aged 18 or older may bring in up to AUS$400 worth of duty-free goods; for those under 18, the limit is AUS$200. Duty-free allowances include no more than 1 liter of alcohol (for those over 18), and 250 cigarettes. Personal property being sent home is not subject to duty as long as it is 12 months old or older. Unsolicited gifts may be sent back to Australia duty-free as long as they are under AUS$200 and are bona fide gifts (e.g. wrapping paper and card). Aussie bureaucracy prohibits the export of more than AUS$5000 without permission from the Reserve Bank of Australia. These and other restrictions may be found in *Customs Information for All Travelers,* available from fun-loving local customs offices.

New Zealand citizens can bring in NZ$500 of duty-free goods. Those 16 or older are allowed 250g of tobacco in any of its forms; 4.5 liters of beer and wine; and one 1125-ml bottle of liquor. According to customs regulations, however, New Zealanders will have to leave behind their birds' nests, dead bees, raw eggs, azaleas, and (gulp) homemade noodles. New Zealand Customs' *Guide for Travellers,* available from any Customs Office, makes fascinating reading.

The U.S. Customs Service has proclaimed that "a vital part of Customs' role is screening out items injurious to the well-being of our nation." The U.S., Canada, Australia, and New Zealand all prohibit or restrict the import of firearms, explosives, ammunition, fireworks, plants, animals, lottery tickets, obscene literature and film, and controlled drugs. To avoid problems when carrying prescription drugs, make sure bottles are clearly marked, and have a copy of the prescription ready to show the customs officer.

Money

Currency and Exchange

Even those fortunate enough to have money may have trouble holding on to it as they make their way through the sticky web of commissions and conversion rates. To minimize stress, follow the fluctuation of rates for several weeks while planning your trip. The exchange rates of August 1991 are listed at the end of this section. If your crystal ball or financial know-how tells you the pound is on the rise, you may want to exchange a significant amount of money at the beginning of your trip. Converting at least $50 before you go will allow you to breeze throught the airport while others languish in exchange counter lines. Observe commission rates closely when abroad. Banks will unfailingly offer better rates than those of travel agencies, restaurants, hotels, and the dubious *bureaux de change*. Since you lose money with every exchange transaction, it's wise to convert large sums (provided the exchange rate is either staying constant or deteriorating).

US$1 = 0.60 British pounds	**£1 = US$1.67**
CDN$1 = £0.52	**£1 = CDN$1.92**
AUS$1 = £0.47	**£1 = AUS$2.13**
NZ$1 = £0.34	**£1 = NZ$2.94**

The British pound sterling (£) is divided into 100 pence (100p). Coins are issued in denominations of 1p, 2p, 5p, 10p, 20p, 50p, and £1; notes are issued in denominations of £5, £10, £20, and £50. The old 5p coin has been replaced by a new, smaller coin. You may come across coins held over from Britain's previous monetary system such as the two-shilling "florin" (10p). These are still legal tender. The terminology used in the old system still lingers in street markets. A "shilling" is 5p, "Half-a-crown" is 12½p; a "quid" or "nicker" is £1; and a "guinea" is £1.05.

Most banks close on Saturday, Sunday, and all public holidays; Britain enjoys "bank holidays" scattered throughout the year—Jan. 1 (New Year's Day), Good Friday, Easter Monday, the first Monday in May (May Holiday), the last Monday in May (Spring Holiday), the last Monday in August (Late Summer Holiday), Dec. 25 (Christmas Day), and Dec. 26 (Boxing Day). Usual weekday bank hours are Monday through Friday 9:30am to 3:30pm.

Traveler's Checks

You've seen the commercials. Traveler's checks are the safest way to carry money. The major brands can be exchanged at virtually every bank in Britain, sometimes without a commission. Traveler's checks are also accepted at some B&Bs, shops, and restaurants, though smaller establishments, especially in remote towns, will not honor them. Furthermore, if lost or stolen, traveler's checks can be replaced, often within a matter of hours.

While American Express traveler's checks are the most well-known worldwide and the easiest to replace, Barclay's and Thomas Cook's are more widely recognized in Britain, and their branches in London are easier to find. If you will also be visiting countries other than Britain, do yourself a favor and buy your checks in U.S. dollars—few currencies are as easily exchanged worldwide, and you will save yourself the cost of repeated currency conversions. If you are visiting only Britain, however, be aware of the exchange rate trend prior to your departure. If the dollar is going up, buy your traveler's checks in dollars—if plummeting, buy in pounds. The following companies offer checks in U.S. dollars, British pounds, or both:

American Express: Traveler's Check Operations Center, Salt Lake City, UT 84184. In the U.S., call (800) 221-7282; in England, call collect collect (27) 369 3555. Purchase commission 1%. American Express Travel Offices will cash their own checks free. The **American Automobile Association (AAA)** and the **American Association of Retired Persons (AARP)** offer American Express traveler's checks to their members with no commission charge.

Barclay's: Call (800) 221-2426 in the U.S. and Canada; from abroad, call collect (212) 406-4200 or (071) 937 8091. Purchase commission 1%. Barclay's branches cash Barclay's-Visa and other Visa traveler's checks free Mon.-Fri.; charge levied on Sat.

Thomas Cook: Call (800) 223-4030 in the U.S.; from Canada and abroad, call collect (212) 974-5696. Purchase commission 1%, but since checks must be purchased through an affiliated bank, an additional commission may be levied. You can buy Thomas Cook-Mastercard

Don't forget to write.

If your American Express® Travelers Cheques are lost or stolen, we can
hand-deliver a refund virtually anywhere you travel. Just give us a call.
You'll find it's a lot less embarrassing than calling home.

traveler's checks at any bank displaying a Mastercard sign, and cash them free at Thomas Cook locations.

Bank of America Traveler's Office: P.O. Box 37010, San Francisco, CA 94137. Call (800) 227-3460 in the U.S.; from Canada and abroad, call collect (415) 624-5400. Checks in US$ only. Commission usually 1%. Checkholders may use **Travel Assistance Hotline,** offering, among other services, free legal assistance and urgent message relay. In the U.S., call (800) 368-7878; from abroad, call collect (202) 331-1596.

Citicorp: Call (800) 645-6556 in the U.S. and Canada; from abroad, call collect (813) 623-1709 or (071) 438 1414. Purchase commission 1%. Checkholders automatically receive access to **Travel Assist Hotline,** at (800) 523-1199.

Mastercard International: Call (800) 223-7373; from abroad, call collect (609) 987-7300. Commission, from 1-2%, varies with issuing bank. Checks available only in US$.

Visa: Call (800) 227-6811 in the U.S.; from Canada and abroad, call collect (415) 574-7111 or (071) 937 8091. Visa doesn't charge a commission, but the bank that sells the checks usually does—1% on purchases by non-customers. Any Barclay's branch will cash these traveler's checks for free.

Credit Cards

Even Bridget the budget traveler should consider bringing the plastic along; credit cards can come in handy in London, especially for financial emergencies or major purchases such as travel tickets. Credit cards are accepted in most places in the city. **Visa** and **Mastercard** (MC) are the most widely recognized, followed by **American Express** and **Diner's Club.** Until recently, virtually all credit cards in England were **Barclaycards** (Visa cards) or **Access** cards (Mastercards), but with the proliferation of similar credit cards issued by other institutions, the terminology "Access and Barclaycards accepted" has been more or less replaced by "Mastercard and Visa accepted." Banks associated with a credit card will give you an instant cash advance in local currency as large as your remaining credit line. This arrangement follows the policy of the bank that issued the card and enables you to avoid paying exorbitant rates of interest. You can often reduce conversion fees by charging traveler's checks. Visa and Mastercard currently do not levy commissions on purchases made in foreign exchange with their card, although they threaten to change this policy. Some automatic teller machines will accept credit cards for cash withdrawal (use your usual personal identity number) but will charge conversion fees, other service fees, and interest. For example, Barclaybank and Midland Self Service machines accept Visa cards. Note that some U.S. cash networks have associates in Britain; the Abbey National Building Society's AbbeyLink ATMs belong to the Plus network.

Through ExpressCash, American Express cardholders may use ATMs throughout Europe to withdraw money from a personal checking account. They can also employ the services of Global Assist, a 24-hr. helpline offering legal assistance and other services (in the U.S. call (800) 554-2639; from abroad, call collect (202) 783-7474).

Sending Money

Sending money overseas is a complicated, expensive, and often extremely frustrating adventure. Do your best to avoid it; carry a credit card or a separate stash of emergency traveler's checks. To have money sent quickly and cheaply, have someone **cable** money through a large commercial bank network. To pick up the money, the recipient must present proper ID, such as a passport or driver's license. **Bank of America's Global Sellers Network** (tel. (800) 227-3333 or 3460) has a Worldwide Delivery system that delivers to any Seller location in three to five working days, charging a 1% fee plus $15 telex charge ($25 buys you $1000). Unfortunately, the service is being phased out, probably in Jan. 1992. For $10, **Barclay's** (tel. (212) 412-3838) will deliver money within one day. The sender must have a Barclay's account.

Western Union offers a convenient but expensive service for cabling money abroad. Using a major credit card, the folks at home can send any amount up to

Gain 500 pounds within minutes.

Sometimes there's no such thing as unwanted pounds. At those times it's nice to know that with Western Union you can receive money from the States within minutes, in case the situation arises. Plus it's already converted into pounds.

So just call either the toll-free number in London, 0-800-833-833, or the United States, 1-800-325-6000, and then pick up your money at any Western Union location.

Traveling can be a lot easier if you're packing a few extra pounds.

WESTERN UNION | WORLDWIDE MONEY TRANSFER®

their remaining credit limit; call (800) 325-6000 or 4176. A sender without a credit card must journey to one of Western Union's offices with cash or a cashier's check (no money orders accepted). The money will arrive within 15 min. in London or at any Western Union Agency and within 24 hrs. elsewhere in Britain. Fees are immense ($13 to send $50), but become slightly more reasonable for larger amounts ($50 to send $1000, $225 to send $5000).

You can also turn to omnipresent **American Express** (tel. (800) 543-4080) for help; expect to wait 15 minutes for a money transfer to London. Limitations are similar to those imposed for cash advances: the first $200 can be received in cash; anything beyond that will be issued either in traveler's checks or as a money transfer check cashable at a bank. AmEx charges $70 for sending $1000, $80 for sending $2000.

Citibank (tel. (800) 248-4007) will also transfer money in 24-48 hrs. The Citi never sleeps. A fee applies to all amounts sent. In addition, the receiving bank will probably charge a commission.

If you find yourself destitute and desperate, you can usually have money sent through your government's diplomatic mission in Britain. Desperate American citizens should turn to a U.S. Consular Office, which will assist by contacting friends or family in the U.S. and arranging for them to send money. Senders at home should contact the State Department's Citizens Emergency Center, Department of State #4811, 2201 C St. NW, Washington, DC 20520 (tel. (202) 647-5225). The State Department renders this service only to those faced with destitution, hospitalization or death. Jim Baker will levy a $15 service charge.

VAT (Value-Added Tax)

Britain charges value-added tax (VAT), a national sales tax, on most goods and some services. VAT is 17.5% on many services (such as hairdressers, hotels, restaurants, and car rental agencies) and on all goods (except books, medicine, and food). The prices stated in *Let's Go* include VAT unless otherwise specified. Visitors to the United Kingdom can get a VAT refund through the Retail Export Scheme. Ask the shopkeeper for the appropriate form, which immigration officials will sign and stamp when you leave the country. Once home, send the form and a self-addressed, British-stamped envelope to the shopkeeper, who will then send your refund (in theory). In order to use this scheme, you must export the goods within three months of purchase.

Packing

Don't schlep. Pack light. Leave the Dick Tracy action figures, the CD collection, and the suit of chain mail where they belong—at home. The more ground you're planning to cover, the lighter you ought to travel. One tried and true method of packing has always been to set out everything you think you'll need, then pack half of it—and twice the money. Save room that one-liter bottle of Glenfiddich.

For an extended stay in London you might prefer a suitcase to the conspicuous backpack that traditionally hallmarks the budget traveler. If you'll be on the move frequently, go with the pack. Bring along a small daypack for carrying lunch, a camera, some valuables, *Let's Go: London* and other masterpieces of world literature. Keep your money, passport, and other valuables with you in a purse, neck pouch, or money belt. Label every article of baggage both inside and out with your name and address. For added security, purchase a combination lock for your main bag and for London hostel lockers.

Nothing will serve you more loyally in London than comfortable walking shoes and a folding umbrella. Try to bring warm clothing and a raincoat, Gore-Tex if possible. Throw in a travel alarm clock and a single-sheet sleeping sack: many hostels require them. If you're coming from the U.S., bring color film; it's significantly cheaper than in Britain.

A self-assembled medical kit should suffice for minor health problems. You might include aspirin, bandages, antibiotic ointment, tweezers, an elastic bandage, a protected thermometer, and some sunscreen. If you wear glasses or contact lenses, take an extra pair along. Most common brands of contact lens solutions can be purchased at drugstores in London. If you take prescription drugs, bring extra medication and have an explanatory note from a physician ready to show customs officials.

Finally, those North Americans unable to live without a beloved electrical appliance (including contact lens disinfection systems) will need an adapter and a converter. The voltage in England is 240 volts AC, which is enough to fry an unsuspecting North American appliance (110 volts AC) thoroughly. Converters and adapters suitable for most appliances are available worldwide in department and hardware stores.

When To Go

Traveling during the off-season is a great way to minimize the damage to your bank account. Airfares drop considerably and domestic travel becomes less congested. You won't have to compete with squadrons of fellow tourists crowding hotels, sights, and train stations, taking pictures of themselves, driving up prices, and inflaming local tempers.

Climate

> *A duller spectacle this earth of ours has not to show than a rainy Sunday in London.*
> —Thomas De Quincey (1785-1882), The Pains of Opium

When choosing clothing, remember that London weather, while often damp, stays mild, with an average temperature in the low to mid-60s in the summer and in the low 40s in the winter. May and June are the sunniest months, July and August the warmest, and October and November the rainiest. December and January have the worst weather of the year—wet, cold, and cloudy. Throughout the year, you should expect unstable weather patterns; a bright and cloudless morning sky often precedes intermittent afternoon showers. For weather information in London, call 246 8091.

Time

Though Greenwich Mean Time (GMT) is the standard by which much of the rest of the world sets its clocks, the British have a system of their own, with Winter Time (GMT) and British Summer Time (late March-late Oct.; 1 hr. later than GMT). This time change is a week out of sync with Continental and American daylight savings time changes.

Drugs

Beware of drugs. If you're caught with any quantity of illegal or controlled drugs in Britain you can be arrested and tried under British law or immediately and summarily expelled from the country. Home governments can not shield offenders from the judicial system of a foreign country. Consular officers can visit anyone jailed for drug possession, provide them with a list of local attorneys, and inform family and friends. For more information on the subject of drugs overseas, send for the brochure *Travel Warning on Drugs Abroad* (Publication 9558) to the Bureau of Consular Affairs, U.S. Department of State, Washington, DC 20520 (tel. (202) 647-1488).

Insurance

The firms listed below offer insurance against theft, loss of luggage, or injury. You may buy a policy either directly from them, or in some cases, through a travel agent. Additionally, some traveler's check and credit card companies offer free insurance to their checkholders. **American Express** cardholders, for example, receive automatic rental-car and flight insurance on purchases made with the card. Check with your bank or issuing company. Remember two basic points when buying insurance. First, beware of unnecessary coverage. Check whether your homeowner's insurance (or your family's coverage) provides against theft during travel. Most homeowner's plans will provide up to $500 against loss of travel documents. University term-time medical plans often include insurance for summer travel. Canadian citizens may be covered by their home province's health insurance plan up to 90 days after leaving the country. Second, insurance companies generally require that you submit documents relevant to the loss (and only upon returning home) before they will honor your claim. Keep all appropriate receipts, doctor's statements, police reports, and anything else that might prove useful, and check the time limit on filing to make sure you will be returning home in time to secure reimbursement.

Access America, P.O. Box 90310, Richmond, VA 23230-9310 (tel. (800) 851-2500). A subsidiary of Blue Cross/Blue Shield. Covers trip cancellation or interruption, on-the-spot hospital admittance costs, and emergency medical evacuation. Also maintains a 24-hr. hotline.

ARM Coverage, 120 Mineola Blvd., P.O. Box 310, Mineola, NY 11501 (tel. (800) 323-3149 or (516) 294-0220).

Edmund A. Cocco Agency, 220 Broadway #201, Lynnfield, MA 01940 (tel. (800) 821-2488). Globalcare Travel Insurance covers travel, accident, sickness, and baggage loss, as well as on-the-spot payment for medical expenses, trip cancellation and trip interruption insurance, and medical insurance for foreign visitors.

Healthcare Abroad: Wallach and Co., Inc., 243 Church St. NW, #100D, Vienna, VA 22180 (tel. (800) 237-6615 or (703) 281-9500).

WorldCare Travel Assistance, 1150 S. Olive St., Suite T-233, Los Angeles, CA 90015 (tel. (800) 253-1877). Annual membership ($162) covers an unlimited number of trips under 90 days. Shorter-term policies also available, as well as a **ScholarCare** program tailored to students and faculty spending a semester or year abroad.

If you have no medical insurance, or if your policy does not extend overseas (Medicare, for example, does not cover European travel), you may want to purchase a short-term policy for your trip. The **International Student Identification Card (ISIC)** and **Teacher's International Card,** offered by the CIEE (see Useful Addresses above), provide accident and sickness coverage if purchased in the U.S. ID cards also provide a 24-hr. Traveler's Assistance Service for legal, medical, and financial aid. In addition, CIEE sells a moderately inexpensive plan called "Trip Safe," which doubles cardholders' insurance and can provide coverage for travelers ineligible for CIEE ID cards. Trip-Safe includes coverage for situations ranging from medical treatment, hospitalization, accidents, and lost baggage, to charter flights missed due to illness. This plan is available only to U.S. citizens traveling outside and foreign nationals traveling inside the U.S. Holders of major credit cards may have insurance plans available to them at no charge.

Additional Concerns

Senior Travelers

The following is a list of places and publications where senior citizens can obtain information about the discounts and special services available to them. You might also be able to pick up some helpful tips from the British Tourist Authority or your local travel agent.

American Association of Retired Persons (AARP) Travel Service, P.O. Box 92964, Los Angeles, CA 90009 (tel. (800) 227-7737, membership information (800) 441-7575); or AARP, Special Services Department, 1909 K St. NW, Washington, DC 20049 (tel. (202) 662-4850). Holidays, tours, and cruises for AARP members. Discounts on car and RV rentals, air travel, lodging, and sight-seeing for members traveling independently as well. (Members must be over 50; annual membership fee includes spouse.)

Bureau of Consular Affairs, Superintendent of Documents, U.S. Government Printing Office, Washington, DC 20402. For information on passports, visas, health, and currency, send for their free *Travel Tips for Older Americans* ($1). Allow 4 weeks for delivery.

Elderhostel, 75 Federal St., Boston, MA 02110 (tel. (617) 426-7788). Residential programs in universities. Participants spend a week to four weeks studying subjects ranging from bee-keeping to music appreciation. Four week programs in Britain costs $900-$5000. Fee covers airfare, room, board, tuition, and extracurricular activities. Those who enroll must be 60 or over, but may bring a spouse or companion over 50. Scholarships available. Also publishes a newsletter, *Between Classes.* Write for a free catalog.

Gateway Books, 13 Bedford Cove, San Rafael, CA 94901 (tel. (415) 454-5215). Offers *Get Up & Go: A Guide for the Mature Traveler* ($10.95 plus $1.50 postage), by Gene and Adele Malott. General hints for seniors.

National Council of Senior Citizens, 1331 F St. NW, Washington, DC 20004 (tel. (202) 347-8800). For $12 a year or $150 a lifetime, an individual or couple of any age can receive hotel and auto rental discounts, a senior citizen newspaper, and use of a discount travel agency.

Pilot Books, 103 Cooper St., Babylon, NY 11702 (tel. (516) 422-2225). Distributes *The International Health Guide for Senior Travelers,* by Dr. W. Robert Lange ($4.95, plus $1 postage).

Gay and Lesbian Travelers

Attitudes towards gay and lesbian people in London are fairly progressive, although people in rural areas tend to be less tolerant. Below are resources specifically for the gay or lesbian traveler.

Gaia's Guide, $12.95. Available in the U.S. from Giovanni's Room (see below); in Britain at 412 Archway Rd., London N6 (£7). From Australia and New Zealand, order at the London address (£20). Annually revised "international guide for traveling women" that lists local lesbian, feminist, and gay information numbers, publications, bookstores, cultural centers and resources, restaurants, and accommodations.

Gay's the Word, 66 Marchmont St., London WC1N 1AB (tel. (071) 278 7654). Widest stock of gay and lesbian literature in England; mail order service available. Noticeboard and coffee area. Open Mon.-Fri. 11am-7pm, Sat. 10am-6pm, Sun. and holidays 2-6pm.

Giovanni's Room, 345 S. 12th St., Philadelphia, PA 19107 (tel. (215) 923-2960). The best source for gay and lesbian travel books; also distributes feminist literature. Book post shipping charge $3.50.

Spartacus International Gay Guide, $27.95. Available from **Bruno Gmuender, publisher,** 100 E. Biddle St., Baltimore, MD 21202 (tel. (301) 727 5677) and from **Renaissance House,** P.O. Box 292, Village Station, New York, NY 10014 (tel. (212) 674-0120). Lists bars, restaurants, hotels, bookstores, and hotlines throughout the world. Specifically for men.

Disabled Travelers

Transportation companies in Britain are remarkably conscientious about providing facilities and services to meet the needs of disabled travelers. Notify a bus or coach company of your plans ahead of time, and they will have staff ready to assist you. BR has a discounted railcard for disabled travelers, only available to British citizens. If you don't have a railcard but are traveling in your own wheelchair or are blind and traveling with a companion, you are still eligible for certain discounts and services. With advance notification, BR will set aside a convenient spot for your wheelchair. Not all stations are accessible; write for the pamphlet "British Rail and Disabled Travellers." National Express (bus travel) also offers some discounts. Several car rental agencies can have hand-controlled cars available provided you give them advance notice. Britain imposes a six-month quarantine on all animals entering the country which includes seeing-eye dogs. The owner must also obtain a veterinary certificate (consult the nearest British Consulate for details). You can write to the British Tourist Authority for free handbooks and access guides. Other helpful sources of information are:

Access to the World: A Travel Guide for the Handicapped, by Louise Weiss ($12.95). Provides information on tours and organizations. Available from Facts on File, Inc., 460 Park Ave. S., New York, NY 10016 (tel. (800) 322-8755).

Evergreen Travel Service, 4114-198th SW, Suite #13, Lynnwood, WA 98036-6742 (tel. (800) 435-2288 or (206) 776-1184). Its "Wings on Wheels" tours provide charter A short walk up Parkway brings you to the northeast edge of buses with on-board, wheelchair-accessible facilities. Other services include White Cane Tours for the blind (1 guide for 3 travelers), tours for the deaf, and "Lazy Bones" tours for slow walkers.

Flying Wheels Travel, 143 West Bridge St., P.O. Box 382, Owatonna, MN 55060 (tel. (800) 535-6790; in Minnesota (800) 722-9351). Arranges trips and cruises for groups and individuals.

The Guided Tour, 555 Ashbourne Rd., Elkins Park, PA 19117 (tel. (215) 782-1370). Year-round travel programs for developmentally and learning-disabled adults, as well as trips for those with physical disabilities. All expenses except lunch included in most tour prices.

Pauline Hephaistos Survey Projects Group, 39 Bradley Gardens, West Ealing, London W13 8HE (tel. (081) 997 70 55). Distributes access guides to London (£4).

Mobility International, P.O. Box 3551, Eugene, OR 97403 (tel. (503) 343-1284; voice and TDD). International headquarters in Britain, Columbo St., London SE1 8DP. Contacts in 25 countries. Information on travel programs, international work camps, accommodations, access guides, and organized tours. Membership $20 per year. Publishes *A World of Options for the 1990s: A Guide to International Educational Exchange, Community Service, and Travel for Persons With Disabilities* ($14, nonmembers $16, postpaid).

Royal Association for Disability and Rehabilitation (RADAR), 25 Mortimer St., London W1N 8AB (tel. (071) 637 5400). Information on traveling in Britain; publishes the annual handbook *Holidays in the British Isles—A Guide for Disabled People* (£4.50 postpaid).

Society for the Advancement of Travel for the Handicapped, 345 Fifth Ave., Suite 610, New York, NY 10016 (tel. (212) 447-7284). Publishes quarterly travel newsletter *SATH News* and information booklets (free for members, $2 for nonmembers). Offers advice and assistance on trip planning. Membership $40 per year, seniors and students $25.

Travel Information Service, Moss Rehabilitation Hospital, 1200 W. Tabor Rd., Philadelphia, PA 19141-3099 (tel. (215) 329-5715). Information on accessibility in international travel: send for their brochures on tourist sights, accommodations, and transportation (nominal postage fee).

Twin Peaks Press, P.O. Box 129, Vancouver, WA 98666 (tel. (800) 637-2256). Operates a worldwide travel nurse network and publishes 3 books: *Directory of Travel Agencies for the Disabled* ($19.95); *Travel for the Disabled* ($14.95); and *Wheelchair Vagabond* ($9.95). Postage $2 for first book ordered, $1 for each additional book.

Bringing the Kids

Traveling overseas with children, especially to London, is not particularly difficult. And if you take them along on your travels, they will have more interesting memories of early childhood than endless afternoons spent playing with multicolored Play Do.

If you do decide to bring the tots, these books may be helpful. *Travel With Children,* by Maureen Wheeler, is packed with user-friendly tips and anecdotes ($10.95). Order from 155 Filbert St., Suite #251, Oakland, CA 94607 (tel. (415) 893-8555). The *Kidding Around* series of illustrated books *for* children includes one about London that might prove educational and distracting on long trips ($9.95; postage $2.75 for the first book, 50¢ thereafter). Write to John Muir Publications, P.O. Box 613, Santa Fe, NM 87504 (tel. (800) 888-7504).

Diet and Drugs

Travelers with dietary concerns should consult Books in Useful Addresses above for vegetarian and kosher guides. Alcoholics Anonymous (tel. (071) 352 3001) and Narcotics Anonymous (tel. (071) 351 6794) have chapters in many areas.

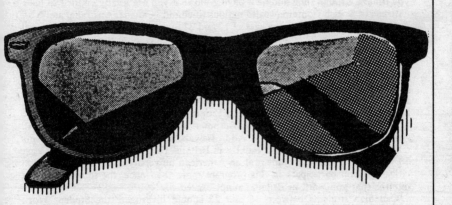

Alternatives to Tourism

Work

Becoming a part of the economy may be the best way to immerse yourself in a foreign culture. You may not earn as much as you would at home, but you should manage to cover your living expenses and possibly your airfare. A range of short-term opportunities are available, although obtaining a work permit may be difficult.

Permits

Unless you're a citizen of a Common Market or a British Commonwealth nation, you'll have a tough time finding a paying job that you are legally entitled to take. Citizens of British Commonwealth nations (including Canada, Australia, and New Zealand) who are between the ages of 17 and 27 may work in Britain during a visit without permits if the employment they take is "incidental to their holiday." And Commonwealth citizens with a parent or grandparent born in the United Kingdom may apply for a patriality certificate, which entitles them to live and work in Britain without any other formalities. If you do not fit either of these categories, you must apply for a work permit to be eligible for paid employment in Britain; contact a British consulate (or High Commission, in Commonwealth countries) for details before you go, and the Department of Employment when you arrive.

In cooperation with the British government and the British Universities North America Club, CIEE (see Useful Addresses above) can issue American students a $96 work permit valid for six months in Britain. To qualify, you must be at least 18 years old, a full-time student at an American university or college, and a U.S. citizen. If you participate in this program more than once, the total number of months that you work in Britain cannot exceed six.

Canadian students between 18 and 25 should investigate the Student Work Abroad Program of Travel CUTS (see Useful Addresses above). *Au pair* jobs, temporary volunteer positions, and jobs at work camps and farm camps do not require a work permit; you'll need only an entrance card or letter of invitation from the organization concerned. This letter does not permit you to undertake any other kind of paid employment during your stay.

Finding A Job

> *So poetry, which is in Oxford made*
> *An art, in London only is a trade.*
>
> *—John Dryden*

More practical, if less poetic, advice can be found at a local university's work-abroad resource center. The following organizations yearn to supply further information:

CIEE (see Useful Addresses above). Publishes *Work, Study, Travel Abroad: The Whole World Handbook* ($10.95 plus $1 postage; available from CIEE and at many bookstores). For individual job listings, consult *Summer Jobs in Britain* ($9.95 plus $1 postage). *The Teenager's Guide to Study, Travel, and Adventure Abroad* ($9.95 plus $1 postage) describes over 150 travel and study programs abroad. *The Student Travel Catalog* (free at any CIEE office) contains a "Work Abroad" permit application. In London, publications like *TNT* and *Southern Cross* (free magazines targeted at Australians and New Zealanders) list lots of student-type job openings.

Peterson's Guides, 202 Carnegie Center, P.O.Box 2123, Princeton, NJ 08543-2123 (tel. (800) 338-3282, in NJ (609) 243-9111. Vacation Work's *1991 Summer Jobs in Britain* ($13.95) lists 30,000 jobs in Scotland, Wales, and England, including openings for office help, farm laborers, chambermaids, and lorry drivers. For some light reading, try *Work Your Way Around the World*, a useful compendium of information and tips ($16.95), or the resourceful *1991 Directory of Overseas Summer Jobs* ($14.95).

Other Work Programs

American Youth Hostels (AYH) (see Useful Addresses above) hires tour group leaders for trips abroad. You must be 21 years of age and undergo a nine-day training course ($295) to partake of this adventure. You must lead a group in the U.S. before going abroad; leaders receive expenses and a small stipend. **The Experiment in International Living** offers similar employment opportunities but has stiffer requirements; you must be 24, a former resident of the country in question, fluent in the language, and experienced at working with high-school and college-aged people. Contact this organization at P.O. Box 676, Kipling Rd., Brattleboro, VT 05301 (tel. (802) 257-6161 or (800) 451-4465).

Au pair positions are officially reserved for unmarried female nationals of Western European countries whose primary aim is to improve their English. However, native English speakers can sometimes obtain these jobs. Check the help-wanted columns of the *International Herald Tribune* for possible positions. Generally, *au pairs* help a host family by taking care of the children and helping with light housework for about five hours per day (1 day off per week); in return they receive room, board, and a small monthly stipend. Applicants should determine the details of pay and obligation before settling in with their family.

The **Association for International Practical Training (AIPT)**, the umbrella organization for the **International Association for the Exchange of Students for Technology Experience (IAESTE) Trainee Program,** 10400 Little Patuxent Parkay, Suite 250, Columbia, MD 21044-3510 (tel. (301) 997-3069), offers on-the-job training in agriculture, engineering, computer science, math, and natural/physical sciences. You must have completed sophomore year at an accredited four-year institution, although most people accepted into the program have completed junior year. Internships generally last 8-12 weeks in the summer; apply by December 10.

Volunteering

Opportunities range from working on an archeological dig to arranging a community play group for children. You can join a local community volunteer group—look in the local telephone directory under Voluntary Work Information Services, Volunteer Bureau, or Citizens Advice Bureau.

At the 2000 **work camps** across Europe, established after World War I as a means of promoting peace and understanding, you can spend one to four weeks doing manual or social work. Expect to pay a registration fee (anywhere from $25-70), arrange your own travel, and sometimes contribute to your food and accommodation costs. For information, write **International Voluntary Service,** Rte. 2, P.O. Box 506, Innisfree Village, Crozet, VA 22932 (tel. (804) 823-1826). **Volunteers for Peace** publishes a directory of over 800 work camps in over 34 countries ($10 ppd.). Membership is $100. For information and a free newsletter, write to 43 Tiffany Rd., Belmont, VT 05730 (tel. (802) 259-2759). Finally, CIEE (see Useful Addresses above) would love to send you their book *Volunteer! The Comprehensive Guide to Voluntary Service in The U.S. and Abroad* ($6.95 plus $1 postage).

For information on working on archeological digs, write to the **Council for British Archaeology,** 112 Kennington Rd., London SE11 6RE (tel. (071) 582 0494; fax (071) 587 5152). They publish *British Archaeological News* (annual subscription; send self-addressed, stamped envelope for details). In addition, **The Archaeological Institute of America,** 675 Commonwealth Ave., Boston, MA 02215 (tel. (617) 353-9361), publishes an *Archaeological Fieldwork Opportunities Bulletin,* listing 210 field sites throughout the world. It's available in January for the following summer.

Study

Spending a year studying in London under the auspices of a well-established year-abroad program is relatively easy. But if you're interested in enrolling as a full-time student in a British university, things get a little trickier. Their requirements for admission can be hard to meet unless you attended a British secondary school, and some of the more selective universities take only a handful of foreign applicants each year. A good place to start investigating different study programs is *Work, Study, Travel Abroad: The Whole World Handbook* (see Work above). High school students might look into CIEE's *The Teenager's Guide to Study, Travel, and Adventure Abroad,* which describes over 150 travel and study programs (see Work above). For initial information on studying in Britain, contact the British Council office in your home country. The following organizations can also deluge you with information:

American Institute for Foreign Study (AIFS), 102 Greenwich Ave., Greenwich, CT 06830 (tel. (800) 727-2437 or (203) 869-9090; Boston office (617) 421-9575, (800) 888-2247, or (800) 825-2437; San Francisco office (800) 222-6379). Helps arrange study programs, transportation, room, and board for both term-time and summer courses at Richmond College in London. Participants must make arrangements for credit at their home institutions. Rolling admissions. Academic programs generally for high school graduates. The American Council for International Studies (ACIS), a subdivision of fellow acronym AIFS, administers educational travel and study programs for high school students.

Association of Commonwealth Universities (ACU), John Foster House, 36 Gordon Sq., London WC1H 0PF (tel. (071) 387 8572). Publishes the *British Universities Guide to Graduate Study* (£25, postpaid) and provides information on study at institutions throughout the Commonwealth.

British Information Services, British Consulate General, 9th floor, 845 Third Ave., New York, NY 10022 (tel. (212) 752-5747). One of the best sources of information in the U.S. about study in Britain. They understand the massive confusion outsiders may feel in the face of university application regulations. They care. Write for their free pamphlet, *Study in Britain.*

Institute of International Education (IIE), 809 United Nations Plaza, New York, NY 10017-3580 (tel. (212) 883-8200). Publishes several annual reference books on study abroad. The hefty *Academic Year Abroad* ($31.95 plus $3 postage) and *Vacation Study Abroad* ($26.95 plus $3 postage) detail over 3200 study programs offered by U.S. colleges and universities, as well as by foreign and private sponsors. They also offer a free lightweight pamphlet, *Basic Facts on Study Abroad.*

Universities Central Council on Admissions (UCCA), P.O. Box 28, Cheltenham, Gloucestershire, England GL50 3SA (tel. (0242) 222 444). Offers excellent information and handles applications for admission to every single full-time undergraduate course in universities and their affiliated colleges in Britain. Write for an application and the handbook *How to Apply for Admission to a University* (sent free and slowly by surface mail). These people are sticklers for procedure; don't even think about sending in any application materials until you've read the pamphlet and fully understand the application process.

Degree Programs

The first step in the multi-tiered process of applying to British universities is to send for the handbook, *How to Apply for Admission to a University* and an application form from UCCA, above. Generally, U.S. students must have completed two years' study at a U.S. university or college; British Information Services' pamphlet *Study in Britain* lists some schools that accept high school students. Applications for full-time undergraduate study in Britain must be made to UCCA and should arrive by December 15 of the year preceding admission (by Oct. 15 for applicants who wish to be considered by Oxford or Cambridge). For Oxford and Cambridge, separate applications must also be made to the affiliated colleges (check details in the UCCA handbook). Regulations vary for students who already have a BA and wish to study in Britain; write directly to the school concerned to find out its preferences. (Graduate applications should be filed by mid-March of the year preceding admission.)

British tuition costs. "Home students" (British students, or students from other EC countries who have lived in the EC for three years immediately preceding the year of their admission) pay reduced, subsidized rates, but "overseas students" are hit with the real thing. In the 1989-90 academic year, you could expect to pay around £5000 for a year of humanities courses and £4000-6000 for other expenses, not including plane fare. The ACU states that it is not possible for a student to work his or her way through college and warns that a student may have to produce evidence of financial security to gain admittance. (Only after arriving may foreign students apply to the British Department of Employment for permission to work; strict regulations rarely allow students to work enough to pay for tuition and expenses. See the BIS pamphlet listed above for more information.) For outside funding, your best bet is to apply for international scholarships and fellowships; contact your university's study-abroad office. The book *Higher Education in the United Kingdom 1991-92: A Handbook for Students and their Advisers* ($32.95), revised every three years, rigorously discusses financial and other aspects of the British university experience. (Stocked in many college libraries in the U.S.; published by Oryx Press for the ACU, 4041 N. Central Ave. #700, Phoenix, AZ 85012; tel. (800) 279-6799 or (602) 265-2651).

The **British Council** (tel. (071) 930 8466) and **The U.K. Council for Overseas Student Affairs,** at 60 Westbourne Grove, London W2 5SH (tel. (071) 229 9268) can advise those enrolled in British programs on a wide range of student welfare topics.

Non-Degree Programs

Inter-study Programmes, 42 Milson St., Bath, England BA1 1DN (tel. (0225) 464 769 or 464 096), offers four accredited programs at universities in London and will help you arrange a transfer of credit to your school at home. **Beaver College Center for Education Abroad,** Beaver College, Glenside, PA 19038-3295 (tel. (800) 767-0029) offers a similar service. These organizations will make your experience significantly more expensive, but the red tape that you will avoid, and the extras that you will receive (tours and orientation programs), may be worth the additional cost.

Summer Programs

The organizations listed above—CIEE, IIE, and AIFS—offer a wide array of schemes for summer study. The IIE, with the Universities of Birmingham, London, and Oxford, administers a "British Universities Summer School" program in literature, drama, and history. CIEE's *Work, Study, and Travel Abroad,* as well as IIE's

Study in

London, England

Emphases in Liberal Arts, International Business and Criminal Justice

Mainstream classes with British students, plus specially designed courses just for American students

All courses approved by UW-Platteville and validated on an official UW-Platteville transcript

$4200 per semester for Wisconsin and Minnesota residents
$4550 per semester for non-residents

Costs include:
> Tuition and Fees
> Home-stay accommodations and meals
> Fieldtrips

All financial aid applies

For further information contact
Study Abroad Programs
308 Warner Hall
University of Wisconsin-Platteville
1 University Plaza
Platteville, WI 53818-3099
(608) 342-1726
University of Wisconsin-Platteville

Vacation Study Abroad, list further programs. AICS (a branch of AIFS) offers "Educational Trips and Academic Programs," both academically and travel-oriented. These include "Yuletide in London," "London Theaterland," and "London, the Lake District and Scotland."

Long-term Stays

Accommodations

Finding a flat in London is easy. Finding a nice one, however, requires some effort. Consider renting a **bed-sit,** anything from a studio apartment to a small room in a private house, with access to a kitchen and bathroom. Bed-sits run at very least £40 per week, and most landlords won't lease for less than a month. The **University of London Accommodation Office** puts out lists of accommodations for summer stays (after about June 15), and at Christmas and Easter. Visit the office at the University of London Senate House, Malet St., WC1 (tel. 636 2818; Tube: Russell Sq.; open Mon.-Fri. 9:30am-1pm and 2-5:30pm), with a valid student ID. They list a range of studios, flats, and flatshares (from about £40-50 per week), and all University of London residence halls.

Accommodations agencies generally charge one or two weeks' rent as a fee; it's in their interest to find high-priced accommodations, and in your interest to avoid their services whenever possible. **Jenny Jones Accommodation Agency,** 40 S. Molton St., W1 (tel. 493 4801; Tube: Bond St.) and an affiliated branch, the **Derek Collins Agency,** Panton House, Panton St., SW1 (tel. 930 7986; Tube: Piccadilly Circus), off the Haymarket, charge the fee to the landlord instead of the tenant, and have bed-sits starting from £50 for something suburban. You may have to check several times for a central location (£65 and up). Check which zone the flat is in; this will determine your transport costs for your stay. (Both open Mon.-Fri. 9:30am-2pm and 2:30-5:30pm.) **Flatsearch,** 68 Queensway, W2 (tel. 221 6335; Tube: Bayswater), has bed-sits from £40-50, charging a full week's rent as commission. (Open Mon.-Fri. 9:30am-5:30pm.) **Universal Aunts,** 250 King's Rd., SW3 (tel. 351 5767; Tube: Sloane Sq.) has central locations for £65-70 plus a service charge. For a price, they will also offer advice and sympathy, meet children or the elderly at airports, and inform you of local customs and etiquette. The **Hillel House** at 1-2 Endsleigh St., WC1 (tel. 388 0801), opposite John Adams Hall, assists Jewish people seeking accommodations in London and its suburbs for periods ranging from one month to one year.

Various **independent landlords** lease blocks of flats to tourists throughout London; a short list of such landlords appears in the London Tourist Board's *Where to Stay in London* (£2.50). The BTA's free leaflet *Apartments in London* leans to the more expensive holiday apartments, but has some budget listings. Bulletin boards in small grocery shops frequently list available rooms and flats; keep an eye open for these. Check the classified sections of *Time Out, City Limits, LAW, The Guardian, The Times, Gay Times, Loot, Dalton's Weekly* (Thursday), *The London Weekly Advertiser* (Thursday), *Capital Gay* (weekly, free in gay clubs and bookstores), and *The Evening Standard* (first edition appears Mon.-Fri. at 10:45am at 118 Fleet St., near Blackfriars Tube). Call as early as possible when responding to advertisements in one of the larger papers. Call the publisher to see when and where you can pick up an early edition. On Tuesdays at 11am, **Capital Radio** comes out with a list of about 100 flatshares at the Capital Radio Foyer, Euston Centre, Euston Rd., NW1 (tel. 388 1288; Tube: Warren St.). Beware of ads placed by accommodations agencies; they sometimes try to sell you something more expensive when you call.

Opening Bank Accounts

For a long stay in London, an English **sterling bank account** may be a more convenient way of managing finances than carrying around trunkfuls of traveler's checks. But opening an account can be difficult. Those working or studying in London will probably find it easier than tourists, to whom banks may be reluctant to issue checks or check guarantee cards. The four main English banks—Barclay's, Lloyd's, Midland, and National Westminster—all have oodles of branches in London, with the following head offices: Barclay's Bank, 54 Lombard St., EC3 (tel. 626 1567); Lloyd's Bank, 71 Lombard St., EC3 (tel. 626 1500); Midland Bank, 27 Poultry, EC2 (tel. 260 8000), National Westminster Bank, 41 Lothbury, EC2 (tel. 606 6060). Procedures vary somewhat from bank to bank; in all cases you should contact your home bank before coming to London. They can send funds to a London bank, to await collection on the production of suitable identification. And they may be able to act as references in establishing a bank account in London. If possible, investigate the services of your home bank a couple of months before departure. Once in London, it may be harder to have your home bank help you open an account. Start by going to one of the larger central branches, where the staffers should be more plentiful and clueful. Most banks will require one or two references from holders of U.K. bank accounts who know you personally. Foreign references may be unacceptable, or may take months to check. Positive ID plus funds to start the account will also be necessary; foreign checks can take weeks to clear. Details of your plans while staying in London and particulars of a foreign bank account (bankbook or statement) can help convince the bank manager of your honorable character.

Once you have made your way through all the red tape, the bank will issue you a checkbook, a check guarantee card (vouching for checks of up to £50 or £100), and a cash machine card. They may be rather reticent about handing out credit cards to temporary visitors—which should not matter as long as you can arrange to have your own credit card bills paid back home. Note that Barclaycard acts as both a Visa card and a check guarantee card for Barclay's checks. "Free while in credit" banking has become more widespread in England; full-time students' accounts are particularly sought-after by banks.

Getting There

> Our travellers were at a great loss and difficulty how to get the
> horse over, the boat being small and not fit for it: and at last could
> not do it without unloading the baggage and making him swim
> over.
> —Daniel Defoe, A Journal of the Plague Year (1722)

From North America

Budget air travel began inauspiciously with Icarus, whose no-frills flight to the center of the solar system experienced technical difficulties. Survival rates have risen dramatically since then, but the situation has become somewhat more complicated. Use the following suggestions as a base for research, but above all, plan ahead and shop around.

Making reservations far in advance gives you access to cheaper fares and a wider choice of dates. Also, try to be flexible. Direct, regularly scheduled flights are notoriously expensive. If possible, leave from a travel hub; major cities—such as New York, Atlanta, Dallas, Chicago, Los Angeles, San Francisco, Seattle, Montreal, Toronto, and Vancouver—foster more competition for flights than others. Off-season travelers will enjoy lower fares and face much less competition for inexpensive seats, but you don't have to travel in the dead of winter to save. Peak season rates begin on either May 15 or June 1 and run until about September 15; warm weather can still be found outside that spectrum.

Begin by calling student travel organizations such as Council Travel, Travel CUTS, or Let's Go Travel (see Useful Addresses above). They cut special deals for students not available to regular travel agents, and are often significantly cheaper. If you are not eligible for their fares, look for a knowledgeable, sympathetic travel agent. Some travel agents won't be eager to help you find the cheapest option, since budget flights earn them only a small commission. Another option is the Sunday travel sections of *The New York Times* and other newspapers, where Sunday travel sections of *The New York Times* and other newspapers, where fare brokers advertise incredibly cheap but erratic fares.

Charter flights make the most economic sense, especially in the high season. You can book charters up until the last minute, but most flights during the summer fill up months in advance. Later in the season, companies have trouble filling their planes and either cancel flights or charge special fares. Charter flights allow you to stay abroad for as long as you like and often allow you to mix and match arrivals and departures from different cities. Once you have made your reservations with a charter company, however, flexibility, that fickle deity, flies away. You must choose your departure and return dates when you book the flight, and if you cancel your ticket within 14 to 20 days of departure, you will lose some money.

Be aware, however, that charter flights are often inconvenient and require long layovers. Also, ask a travel agent about your charter company's reliability, since such companies reserve the right to cancel flights until 48 hours before departure.

CIEE offers flights from the U.S. to destinations all over the world through their subsidiary, **Council Charters.** Reserve early for these extremely popular flights. Call 800 223-7402 or write to CIEE (see Useful Addresses above). Other major charter companies include **Council Travel** (for students and teachers only; (212) 661-1450); **DER Tours** (tel. (800) 782-2424); **Let's Go Travel Services** (tel. (617) 495-9649); and **TRAVAC** (tel. (800) TRAV-800 (872-8800) or (212) 563-3303). In Canada, try **Travel CUTS** (see Useful Addresses above).

Last-minute **discount clubs** and **fare brokers** offer savings on European travel, including charter flights and tour packages. Organizations that act as clearing houses for unsold airline, charter, and cruise tickets include **Access International** (tel. (800) 825-3633 or (212) 333-7280); **Airhitch** (tel. (212) 864-2000); **Discount Travel International** (tel. (800) 334-9294 for reservations or (215) 668-7184 for membership information; $45 membership); **Last Minute Travel Club** (tel. (800) LAST-MIN (527-8646) or (617) 267-9800); **Moment's Notice** (tel. (212) 486-0503, hotline (212) 750-9111); **Traveler's Advantage** (tel. (800) 548-1116); and **Worldwide Discount Travel Club** (tel. (305) 534-2082). Clubs generally charge a yearly subscription fee of $30-50; fare brokers like Access International do not. Both sell empty seats on commercial carriers and charters from three weeks to a few days before departure. Their often Byzantine contracts bear close study—you may prefer not to stop over in Luxembourg for 11 hours. London's **bucket shops** offer similar deals; these travel agencies sell leftover tickets on commercial flights at unofficially discounted prices.

Go-getters who don't mind traveling light might consider flying to England as a **courier.** A company hiring you as a courier will use your checked luggage space for freight, leaving you with only the carry-on allowance. Fares vary wildly, depending on proximity to departure date, but are usually standby level or lower—often dramatically lower. **Now Voyager** (tel. (212) 431-1616) couriers fly to London from New York. **Halbert Express** (tel. (718) 656-8189) and **TNT Skypack** (tel. (516) 745-9000) advertise similar opportunities. Check the travel section of a major newspaper for other courier companies.

From Continental Europe

As a rule, air travel is prohibitively expensive across much of Europe. In high season, however, budget fares make flights between London and the Continent quite affordable. Look for student discounts and holiday charters available through budget travel agents and local newspapers and magazines. **STA Travel** and **CIEE** offices are good contacts for inexpensive flights throughout Europe.

Sealink (tel. (071) 836 9421) and **P&O European Ferries** (tel. (071) 734 4431) offer extensive ferry service across the channel between France (Calais or Boulogne) and England (Dover or Folkestone). Summer crossings are usually very crowded, but if you cross between midnight and 6am (to Dover), you may have the ferry to yourself. Other routes between the Continent and England (4-6 hr.) include Cher-

bourg to Weymouth, Portsmouth, or Southampton; Dieppe to Newhaven; Le Havre to Portsmouth or Southampton; and Zeebrugge to Hull. **Sally Line** (tel. (071) 409 2240) sails from Ramsgate to Dunkirk. **Brittany Ferries** (tel. (0705) 827 701) has service between Plymouth and Roscoff, Portsmouth and St. Malo, and Portsmouth and Caen. These ferries are relatively inexpensive, especially for those armed with an InterRail pass.

Speed-racers will like the hovercraft (35 min.), but should book it eons in advance. **Hoverspeed** (tel. (081) 554 7061) services depart from Boulogne for Dover, with extra craft operating to Ramsgate during the summer. The service is suspended in rough weather; you might have to wait for the ferry. Hoverspeed offers combination rail/coach and hovercraft service between London and Paris, Brussels, Amsterdam, and points in southwestern France. Channelers under 26 travel at youth rates.

Going overland combines train and bus connections with the cross-channel voyage. Those under 26 can use Eurotrain's **BIJ** tickets, which cut up to 55% off regular second-class rail fares on international runs. You can only buy the tickets once in Europe, but contact CIEE or Travel CUTS for information, or get in touch with Eurotrain directly at 52 Grosvenor Gardens, London SW1 0AG (tel. (071) 730 8518). CIEE and Travel CUTS explain routes and sell vouchers for BIJ tickets to and from Britain. Tickets from points elsewhere on the Continent must be purchased at Eurotrain offices abroad.

The cross-Channel services await with dread the birth of Chunnel, the undersea road-and-rail connection which has been dreamed and planned since the 19th century. A recent Anglo-French agreement has laid the groundwork for the realization of the Chunnel project, and excavations are underway.

Once There

Safety

Travelers can feel much safer in London than in large American cities. After all, even the police are unarmed. Reasonable precautions and common sense will ward off most bad fortune; sleepless vigilance and twitching paranoia accomplish little.

When you're on the street, be careful with your possessions. Clasp your handbag tightly and drape its strap across your chest. Be wary of pickpockets, who are considerably less charming than Fagin's minions. Unattended packages will be taken, either by thieves or by the police. And take special care of bicycles— few valuables tempt thieves more than those that provide a built-in getaway.

London is a tourist-friendly city; it's hard to wander unwittingly into highly unnerving neighborhoods. Most of the more unpleasant areas, in parts of Hackney, Tottenham, and South London, lie well away from the West End and Chelsea. But avoid all parks and heaths after dark—even those in gentrified areas can be dangerous.

Late trains on the tube out of central London are usually crowded and noisy. Waiting late at night at less central stations, on the other hand, can be unsettling. On night buses, sit on the lower deck next to the driver,who has a radio.

When walking after dark, stride purposefully on busy, well-lit roads. Keep to the right, facing oncoming traffic. Avoid shortcuts down alleys or across wasteground. Women may want to carry a rape alarm or whistle. For more safety tips, get a copy of *Positive Steps,* a Metropolitan Police leaflet, from the Positive Steps Campaign, P.O.Box 273, High Wycombe, Bucks. HP12 3XE (tel. (0494) 45 05 41), or order Maggie and Gemma Moss's *Handbook for Women Travellers* (£7) from Judy Piatkus Publications, 5 Windmill St., London, W1P 1HF.

In an emergency, call 999, a free call from any pay or card phone. The operator will ask whether you require police, ambulance, or fire service.

EUROPE BY YOURSELF

WITH THE YOUTH & STUDENT TRAVEL SPECIALIST

FROM LONDON TO

		by plane return	by train return
Amsterdam	£	72	56
Athens	£	240	246
Berlin	£	118	122
Madrid	£	114	163
Munich	£	119	136
Paris	£	65	68
Rome	£	108	165
Venice	£	153	153
L. Angeles	£	336	-
New York	£	209	-

FROM PARIS TO

		by plane return	by train return
Berlin	ff	1200	1064
Rome	ff	900	948
Venice	ff	1580	894
L. Angeles	ff	3850	-
New York	ff	2590	-
Bombay	ff	4950	-

FROM ROME TO

		by plane return	by train return
Athens	L.	368.000	269.000
Cairo	L.	594.000	-
London	L.	310.000	274.000
Tunis	L.	302.000	-
Istanbul	L.	344.000	289.000
L. Angeles	L.	1.094.000	-
New York	L.	834.000	-

Domestic and international tickets. Discounted and regular international train tickets. Hotel reservations. Tours and pocket holidays worldwide.

CTS YOUTH & STUDENT TRAVEL CENTRE

LONDON	**W1P 2AD - 44, Goodge Street - Metro Goodge Street**
	Tel. (071) EUROPE 5804554 - USA 6375601- LONG HAUL 3235180
PARIS V°	20, Rue des Carmes - Tel. (1) 43250076 Metro Maubert Mutualité
ROME	16, Via Genova - Tel. (06) 46791
	297, Corso Vittorio Emanuele II - Tel. (06) 6872672/3/4
FLORENCE	25/R, Via dei Ginori - Tel. (055) 289721/289570
MILAN	2, Via S. Antonio - Tel. (02) 58304121
NAPLES	25, Via Mezzocannone - Tel. (081) 5527975/5527960
VENICE	3252, Dorso Duro Cà Foscari - Tel. (041) 5205660

CARTAVERDE OFFERS DISCOUNT ON ITALIAN RAIL FARES

If you are under 26 years you can buy CARTAVERDE at all CTS offices in Italy. It costs about $7, is valid for a year and offers you up to 30% discount on domestic rail fares.

Language

Confusion abounds when foreign English speakers come to England, expecting to be understood perfectly. The English have unique uses of language, both subtle and coarse, that will probably pass over or below many visitors. Listed below is a brief glossary of English English which may help prevent some of the more common misunderstandings.

aubergine	eggplant
bangers and mash	sausage and mashed potato
bap	a soft bun, like a hamburger bun
bedsitter, or bedsit	one-room apartment, sometimes with kitchen
bill	check (in restaurants)
biro	ball-point pen
biscuit	if sweet, a cookie; if not, a cracker
"bladdered," "blitzed"	drunk
bobby	police officer
bonnet	car hood
to book	to reserve
boot	car trunk
"boozer"	pub
brick	a sport, a good person
brilliant	nifty, "cool"
brolly	umbrella
caravan	trailer, mobile home
car park	parking lot
cheers, or cheerio	goodbye, sometimes thank you
chemist	pharmacist
chips	french fries
circle	theatre balcony
coach	bus
courgette	zucchini
court shoes	women's pumps
crisps	potato chips
crumpets	like English muffins only different
dicey, or dodgy	problematic
digs	lodgings
dinner	lunch
"dosh"	money
dual carriageway	divided highway
dustbin	trash can
first floor	first floor up (second floor)
flannel	washcloth
flat	apartment
fortnight	two weeks
grotty	grungy
ground floor	first floor
hire	rental
hoover	vacuum cleaner
iced lolly	popsicle
interval	intermission
in the high street	on Main Street
jam	jelly
jelly	Jell-O
jumble sale	yard sale
jumper	sweater
"kip"	sleep
knackered	tired, worn out
lavatory, "lav"	restroom
lay-by	roadside turnout
leader (in newspaper)	editorial
leaflet	pamphlet, brochure, flyer
to let	to rent
lift	elevator
loo	restroom
lorry	truck
mate	pal
motorway	highway
"naff"	uncool

nappies	diapers
"narg"	geek, nerd
off-license	retail liquor store
pants	underwear
pavement	sidewalk
petrol	gasoline
phone box, or call box	telephone booth
"piss" (take the piss out of)	make fun of
"pissed"	drunk
plimsolls	sneakers
pudding	dessert
"pull"	to "score"
quid	pound (in money)
queue up	line up
repeat	rerun (on TV)
return ticket	round-trip ticket
ring up	telephone
roundabout	rotary road interchange
rubber	eraser
self-catering	(accommodation with) kitchen facilities
self-drive	car rental
single carriageway	non-divided highway
single ticket	one-way ticket
sixth floor	seventh floor
sleeping policeman	speed bump
sloane	An affected individual attending a fine English school, or feigning attendance. Given to saying "ya."
smarties	M&Ms without the M
spotted dick	steamed sponge pudding with raisins
stalls	orchestra seats
stone	14 pounds (in body weight)
subway	underground pedestrian passage
sultanas	raisins
sweets	candy
swish	swanky
ta	thank you
ta-ta	good-bye
tights	nylons
toilet	restroom
torch	flashlight
trainers	sneakers
trunk call	long-distance telephone call
Tube, or Underground	London subway
verge	edge of road, shoulder
vest	undershirt
way out	exit
wellies	boots
W.C. (water closet)	restroom
wing mirror	rear view mirror
zed	letter "Z"

Cockney Rhyming Slang

Only a few words of this neat and amusing slang are in common use in London, although "dictionaries" of slang may try to persuade otherwise. It can occasionally be useful to be aware of the more widespread rhymes, especially when watching reruns of *Minder.*

word	example	rhyme	meaning
dog	"I'm on the dog"	dog and bone	phone
trouble	"the trouble's at home"	trouble and strife	wife
butcher	"Take a butcher's at her"	butcher's hook	look
pen	"You bloody pen!"	pen and ink	stink
porky	"Don't tell porkies"	pork pies	lies

Place Name Pronunciation

There is no LIE-sess-ter Square in London. Nor is there a MAGG-da-lean college at Cambridge. BERK-lee is in California.

Berkeley	BARK-lee
Beauchamps	BEECH-am
Dulwich	DULL-idge
Ely	EEL-ee
Gloucester	GLOS-ter
Greenwich	GREN-idge
Holborn	HO-burn
Leicester	LES-ter
Lincoln	LINK-un
Marylebone	MAR-lee-bun
Magdalene	MAUD-lin
Norwich	NOR-idge
Peterborough	PETER-brer
Salisbury	SAULS-bree
Southwark	SUTH-uk
Woolwich	WOOL-idge

Staying in Touch

> *It pleased him . . . to be able to go there from time*
> *to time when he was in London and to think, as he*
> *sat in solitude before his gas fire, that there was liter-*
> *ally not a soul in the universe who knew where he was.*
> *—Aldous Huxley, Antic Hay*

Mail

Air mail from London to anywhere in the world is speedy and dependable. A letter will reach the East Coast of the U.S. or urban Canada in about a week and may arrive in as few as three days. **Surface mail,** while much cheaper than airmail, takes up to three months to arrive. It is adequate for getting rid of books or clothing you no longer need in your travels. (See Customs above for details.) Post offices carry a free pamphlet on international mail services, including rates and regulations.

If you have no fixed address while in Britain, you can receive mail through the British post offices' **Poste Restante** (General Delivery) service. Mark the envelope "HOLD," and address it like this (for example): "Jonathan Taylor, c/o Poste Restante, Glastonbury, Somerset, England BA6 9HS." Include the county and the postal code if you know them. Try to have your Poste Restante sent to the largest post office in a region; smaller offices may be mystified by them French words. When in London, send mail to **Poste Restante, Trafalgar Square Post Office, 24-28 King William IV St., London WC2N 4DL** (tel. 930 9580; Tube: Charing Cross; open Mon.-Sat. 8am-8pm). If you don't specify a post office, mail will automatically be sent to **London Chief Office, King Edward Bldg., EC1** (tel. 239 5049; Tube: St. Paul's; open Mon.-Tues. and Thurs.-Fri. 8:30am-6:30pm, Wed. 9am-6:30pm). Canadian visitors are encouraged to have mail sent to Visitor Mail, Canada House, Trafalgar Sq., London SW1Y 5BJ (tel. (071) 629 9492). American Express Travel Offices will hold mail free for their traveler's check and cardholders. (See American Express card listing in Money section.)

When writing abroad for information, you may have to send an "International Reply Coupon" with your request. This coupon, available from all post offices, can be exchanged for postage stamps and will cover charges on bulk packages sent back to you.

Telephone

London's telephone code changed in 1990 from 01 to 071 (or, in the suburbs, to 081). If you are dialing from one 071 number to another, you don't need to dial the prefix. If you are dialing from 071 to 081 or vice versa (or from another phone code in Britain), you do. If you are dialing from outside Britain, you need only dial 71 or 81. In *Let's Go: London,* **numbers have 071 codes unless otherwise noted.**

The newer, more polite British pay phone lights up with the words "Insert Money" as soon as you lift the receiver. Insert money; most pay phones now accept all but the 1p coin. When the initial time period is exhausted, a series of annoying beeps warns you to insert more money. For the rest of the call, the digital display ticks off your credit in penny increments so that you can watch and plan ahead when to insert more money. Unused coins are returned. The dial tone is a continuous purring sound; a repeated double-purr means the line is ringing. Fans of the cinematic masterwork *Local Hero* mourn the passing of the older type of phone, infamous for its redness, its rudeness and, now, rareness. In the unlikely case that you run across one, dial before inserting any coins; when the connection is made, desperately feed your 10p coins down the slot. When your money is running out the beeps will resume; at this point, you have 15 seconds to feed the beast before your connection is bitten off. You may hear Madness playing in the distance.

A convenient alternative to carrying tons of oversized English change is the handsomely decorated British Telecom **Phonecard,** available in denominations of £2, £4, and £10. Phonecard phone booths (look for the green sign) are extremely common, except in rural areas. Cards are available everywhere; main post offices and almost any newsagent, W.H. Smith, or John Menzies (the ubiquitous stationery chains) stocks them. Newsagents also sell the **Mercury Phonecard,** for use on the snazzy blue Mercury designer phones, usually located around Tube stops. Mercury, Telecom's upstart competitor, charges somewhat less for its calls. Mercury phones and some Telecom phones accept credit cards.

For international calls, dial the international code (010), the country code and (if necessary) the city code, and then the local number. The country code for the U.S. and Canada is 1; Australia 61 and New Zealand 64. British Telecom publishes a simple pamphlet telling visitors how to call Mom from any phone (available at tourist offices and most hotels, printed in several languages). Consider calling through U.S. long-distance companies, which offer significantly cheaper rates. To access a U.S. AT&T operator from Britain, dial their "USA Direct" number, (0800) 89 0011. You can then call collect or with an AT&T calling card. Calling collect costs much, much more. Call AT&T in the U.S. at (800) 222-0300 to order a card and garner more specific information about prices. Using an MCI calling card will also reduce your costs; from Britain, access an operator at (0800) 89 0222. You can only use this service if you have an MCI calling card; call MCI to get one (in the U.S., (800) 444-3333). U.S. Sprint customers can dial the "Sprint Express" number, (0800) 89 0877. For Canadian Calling Card Holders, "Canada Direct" is (0800) 89 0016. Antipodeans should direct their inquiries to "Australia Direct" ((0800) 89 0061) or "New Zealand Direct" ((0800) 89 0064).

Reduced rates for most international calls from Britain apply from 8pm to 8am Monday through Friday, and all day and night on Saturday and Sunday. The low-rate period to Australia and New Zealand is from midnight to 7am and 2:30 to 7:30pm daily. Within Britain, three rate periods exist: the lowest rates are from 6pm to 8am Monday through Friday, and all day and all night Saturday and Sunday;

calls are slightly more expensive from 8 to 9am and 1 to 6pm Monday through Friday, and most expensive on weekdays from 9am to 1pm.

Important numbers in Britain include **999** for police, fire, or ambulance emergencies, 100 for the telephone operator, 142 for London directory inquiries, 192 for directory inquiries elsewhere, 155 for the international operator, and 153 for international directory assistance. Directory assistance is free from public phones only. Area codes for individual cities in Britain are listed in telephone directories. *Let's Go: London* provides codes under Practical Information in the Daytrips section. Telephone area codes range from three to six digits, and local telephone numbers range from three to seven. The rarely-seen code (0800) indicates a toll-free number. Before you call an advertised number beginning with 0898, 0836, or 0077, be aware that you will be charged at the highest, nay extortionate, rate.

Weights and Measures

1 kilogram (kg) = 2.2 pounds
1 meter (m) = 1.09 yards
1 kilometer (km) = 0.621 mile
1 liter = 1.057 U.S. quarts
1 liter = 0.88 Imperial quarts
1 Imperial gallon = 1.193 U.S. gallons
1 pint of beer in the U.S. = 0.84 pints of beer in London

Orientation

Getting Into and Out of London

By Air

With planes landing every 47 seconds, **Heathrow Airport** (tel. 759 4321), in Hounslow, Middlesex, is the world's busiest international airport. The banks in each terminal are open daily: Thomas Cook, Terminal 1 (open 24 hrs.); International Currency Exchange, Terminal 2 (open 6am-11pm); and Travellers' Exchange Corporation, Terminals 3 and 4 (open 24 hrs.). The easiest way to reach central London from Heathrow is by **Underground** (about 70 min.), with one stop for terminals 1, 2, and 3 and one for terminal 4. A single ticket into the city costs £2.30, but if you plan on making more than one tube ride in a day, invest in a Travelcard for £3.10. To reach **Victoria Station,** transfer at Earl's Court or Gloucester Rd. to a District Line or Circle Line train heading east. At Victoria, you'll find a blue **Tourist Information Centre** with an accommodations service, a currency exchange office, and information about transportation connections (see Getting Around London below).

London Regional Transport's **Airbus** (tel. 222 1234) makes the one-hour trip from Heathrow to central points in the city, including hotels (departures every 30 min. 6am-3pm, every hr. 3pm-6am; £5, children £3). A **National Express** bus (tel. 730 0202) goes from Heathrow to Victoria coach station approximately every half hour until 9pm (1 hr., £6.75). A **Green Line** bus (tel. 668 7261) also makes the trip. After midnight, you can avoid the £30 taxi fare to Central London by taking night bus #N97 from Heathrow bus station to Piccadilly Circus (every hr. just before the hr. until 5am). National Express makes the 1-hr. trip from Gatwick to Heathrow every hour for £6.75.

Most charter flights land at **Gatwick Airport** in West Sussex (tel. 668 4211 or (0293) 228 22). From there, take the BR **Gatwick Express** train to Victoria Station (30 min., £7). Taxis take twice as long and cost almost five times as much. National Express coaches (#777) run hourly between Gatwick and Victoria from 6am to 8pm (75 min., £6).

Flights from the US go into both Gatwick and Heathrow. During the summer of 1991, airlines were crazily buying and selling landing slots at the two airports. Before you leave, double check which airport your flight serves.

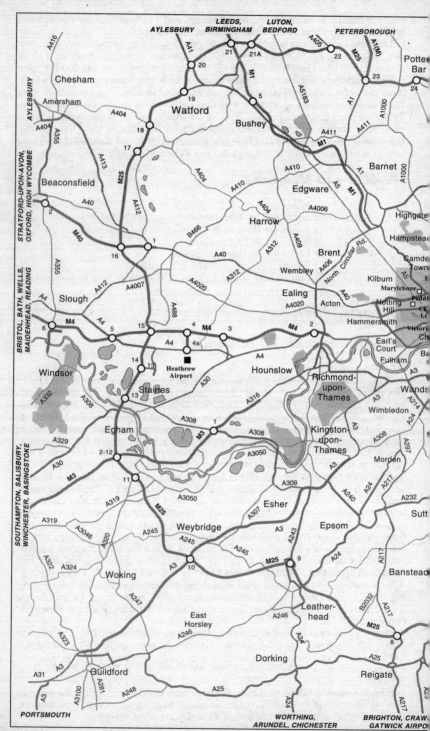

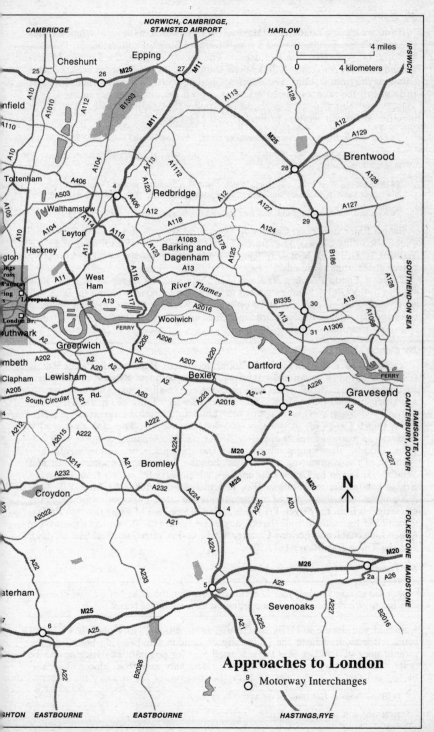

Approaches to London

○₉ Motorway Interchanges

By Train

˙ If you are leaving London by train, find out from which of the eight major stations (Charing Cross, Euston, King's Cross, Liverpool Street, Paddington, St. Pancras, Victoria, or Waterloo) you will depart. The subway system, the **London Underground** or **Tube,** conveniently links these stations, and the tube stops bear the same names as the train stations. For information about particular destinations in Great Britain, call the numbers listed below or consult the display pages in the British Telecom business and services phonebook (under the heading "British Rail"). For inquiries about rail services to Europe, call 834 2345.

To East Anglia, Essex, Southern England, Northeast, East, and South London: Tel. 928 5100.

To the South Midlands, West of England, South Wales, West London, and Republic of Ireland via Fishguard: Tel. 262 6767.

To the East and West Midlands, North Wales, Northwest England, Scotland via West Coast, Northwest London, Northern Ireland, and Republic of Ireland via Holyhead: Tel. 387 7070.

To East and Northeast England, Scotland via East Coast, and North London: Tel. 278 2477.

British Rail runs **Travel Centres** at its mainline stations and at 12-16 Regent St. (Tube: Piccadilly Circus); The Strand (Tube: Charing Cross); Victoria St.; and King William St. (All open Mon.-Fri. 9am-5pm.) For **lost property,** check the property offices at mainline terminals.

To get a **Young Person's Railcard** (£16), you must be under 24 or a full-time student in the UK. A **Senior Railcard** for persons over 60 also costs £16. Both will save you 1/3 on off-peak travel for one year. A **Network Card** (£8) gives the same discount for travel in the Network South East area. Further details can be obtained from any mainline station.

By Coach

Victoria Coach Station (Tube: Victoria), located on Buckingham Palace Rd., is the hub of Britain's denationalized coach network. **National Express** coaches service an expansive network which links cities big and small. Coaches are considerably less expensive than trains but also take longer. (See Day Trips for rates and frquency of train and coach services to towns near London.) National Express offers a **Discount Coach Card** (£5) to students, disabled, and elderly. The card gives a 30% discount off normal fares at any time. Other coach companies compete with National Express; their routes often overlap and their prices are almost identical.

Much of the commuting area around London, including Hampton Court and Windsor, is served by **Green Line** coaches, which leave frequently from Eccleston Bridge behind Victoria Station. (For information, call 668 7261 Mon.-Fri. 8am-8:30pm, Sat.-Sun. 9am-5pm; or try the information kiosk on Eccleston Bridge.) Purchase tickets from the driver. Prices are higher before 9am Monday through Friday. Green Line discounts include the one-day **Rover** ticket (£5.50, valid on almost every Green Line coach and London Country bus Mon.-Fri. after 9am, Sat.-Sun. all day); and the **Three-Day Rover** (£12.50)

By Thumb

Let's Go strongly urges you to seriously consider the risks before you choose to hitch. We do not recommend hitching as a means of travel.

Should you decide to hitch, the Tourist Information Centre publishes a list of route suggestions. Check the University of London Union's ride board, on the ground floor of 1 Malet St. (Tube: Russell Sq.) for possibilities. Hitching can be quite difficult within central London and reasonably easy from places like Cambridge and Oxford to the city. If you're heading out of the city, try these routes:

To Bath: Same as Heathrow to the M4, then to the A4.

To Brighton: Same as Gatwick to the A23.

Contiki Holidays, the ultimate travel experience for 18-35 year olds

Get ready for the most exhilarating travel experience of a lifetime. With Contiki, you can explore Europe, Australia, New Zealand, North America or Russia with 18-35 year olds from around the world. You stay in unique places like our Beaujolais Chateau in France or on board our three mast Schooner in the Greek Islands. You can enjoy activities from bungy cord jumping, white water rafting, cycling to hot air ballooning in Australia's outback. You have more time to discover the heart and soul of the countries you visit because Contiki sorts out the time-wasting hassles. Half our clients are travelling by themselves; we handle the room sharing arrangements. Unique accommodation, most meals, land transport, ferries, sightseeing and the time of your life start at just US $58 per day. Contiki combines all of the above to give you the ultimate travel experience. Why settle for anything less. Get your brochure and video today.

Contact Contiki's International Offices below:

Contiki Holidays
for 18-35s

Contiki Holidays
Suite 1616
415 Yonge St.
Toronto, Ontario
Canada M5B 2E7
Tel: (416) 593-4873
Fax: (416) 581-1494

Contiki Travel Inc.
1432 E. Katella Ave.
Anaheim, California
92805 U.S.A.
Tel: (714) 937-0611
Fax: (714) 937-1615

Contiki Holidays Pty. Ltd.
Level 7
35 Spring St.
Bondi Junction, NSW 2022
Australia
Tel: (02) 389-0999
Fax: (02) 387-8360

Contiki Services Ltd.
Wells House
15 Elmfield Road
Bromley, Kent
BR1 1LS
England
Tel: (081) 290-6777
Fax: (081) 290-6569

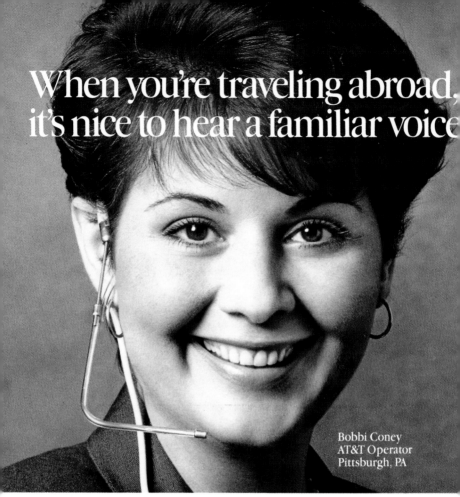

When you're traveling abroad, it's nice to hear a familiar voice

Bobbi Coney
AT&T Operator
Pittsburgh, PA

The language may be difficult.
The food may be different.
The customs may be unfamiliar.
But making a phone call back to the States can be easy.

Just dial the special *AT&T* **USADirect®** access number for the country you're in.

Within seconds, you're in touch with an *AT&T Operator* in the U.S. who can help you complete your call.

Use your *AT&T Calling Card* or call collect. And not only can you minimize hotel surcharges but you can also save with our international rates.

Only *AT&T* **USADirect** *Service* puts you in easy reach of an *AT&T Operator* from over 75 countries around the world.

And it's just another way that AT&T is there to help you from practically anywhere in the world.

So call **1 800 874-4000 Ext. 415** for a free information card listing *AT&T* **USADirect** access numbers.

And see how making a phone call from distant lands can become familiar territory.

AT&T USADirect® Service
Your express connection to AT&T service

AT&T
The right choice.

To Cambridge: Piccadilly Tube to Turnpike Lane, bus #144, 217, or 231 to Great Cambridge Roundabout, then the A10.

To Canterbury: Bus #53 to Blackheath (Shooters Hill Rd.), then the A2 to the M2.

To Dover: Same as Canterbury to the A2.

To Gatwick: BR from Victoria to Norbury, then the A23. Or bus #109 to Brighton Rd., #159 to Streatham Garage, or #68 to South Croydon.

To Heathrow: Bus #27 from Marylebone Rd. to the A4 (Great West Rd.) then M4. Or District Tube to Chiswick Park; walk along Chiswick High Rd. (the A315) to the A4.

To Oxford: Central Tube to Hanger Lane; west along Western Ave. (the A40) to the M40.

To Salisbury: District Tube to Richmond; walk out Twickenham Rd. to Chertsey Rd. (the A316), which leads to the M3; eventually the A30.

To Stratford-upon-Avon: Same as Oxford to the A40 and the M40; eventually the A34.

Layout of Greater London

> *Mr. Weller's knowledge of London was extensive and*
> *peculiar.*
> —Charles Dickens, *The Pickwick Papers (1836-7)*

Greater London is a colossal aggregate of distinct villages and anonymous suburbs, of ancient settlements and modern developments. As London grew, it swallowed adjacent cities and nearby villages, chewed up the counties of Kent, Surrey, Essex, and Hertfordshire, and digested all of Middlesex. Names such as the "City of Westminster" are vestiges of this urban imperialism. "The City" now refers to the ancient, and much smaller, "City of London," which covers but one of the 620 square miles of Greater London. London is divided into boroughs and into postal code areas. The borough name and postal code appear at the bottom of most street signs. Areas or neighborhoods (like Mayfair or Holborn) are more vaguely delineated, but correspond roughly to the numbered postal areas; the district names are used frequently in non-postal discourse.

Most of the sightseer's London falls within the five central boroughs: the **City of London,** the **City of Westminster, Kensington and Chelsea, Camden,** and **Islington.** This central region, north of the river Thames, is bounded roughly by the Underground's Circle line. The center of most visits to London is usually the West End, an area primarily within the borough of the City of Westminster. The West End incorporates the elegant Georgian façades of Mayfair, the crowded shopping streets around Oxford Street, the seedy labyrinth of Soho, and the chic, rehabilitated market in Covent Garden. All distances in London are measured from **Charing Cross,** the official center of London just north of Westminster. The West End also includes London's unofficial center, **Trafalgar Square.**

East of the West End, toward the City of London, lies Holborn, the center of legal activity, and Fleet Street, until recently the center of British journalism. Though the City of London is no longer the hub of central London, it continues to function as the financial heart of the metropolis. Here St. Paul's Cathedral is skirted by newer, taller, and certainly less impressive buildings. The Tower of London, at the eastern boundary of The City, stands between central London and the vast Docklands building site stretching down the Thames.

Northeast of the West End, Bloomsbury harbors the British Museum, the core of London University, and scores of bookshops and art galleries. North and northwest of the West End, tidy terraces cling to the streets bordering Regent's Park in the districts of Marylebone, Camden Town, and St. John's Wood. One stage farther north, Hampstead and Highgate are separated from each other by the enormous Hampstead Heath. Two of London's most desireable residential areas, they command exceptional views of the city. Lying rather ominously west of the West

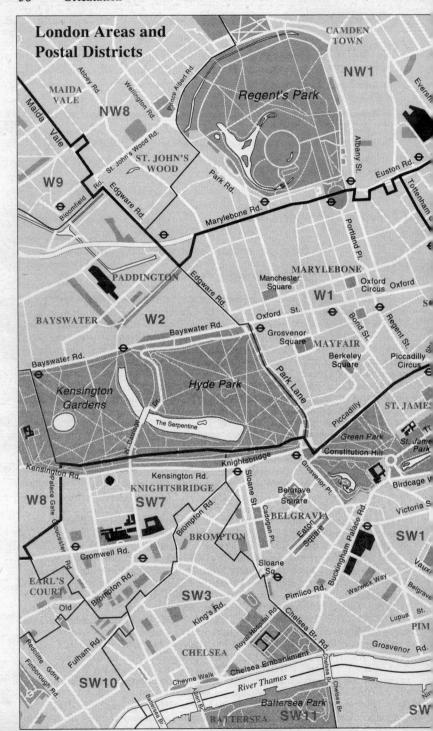

London Areas and Postal Districts

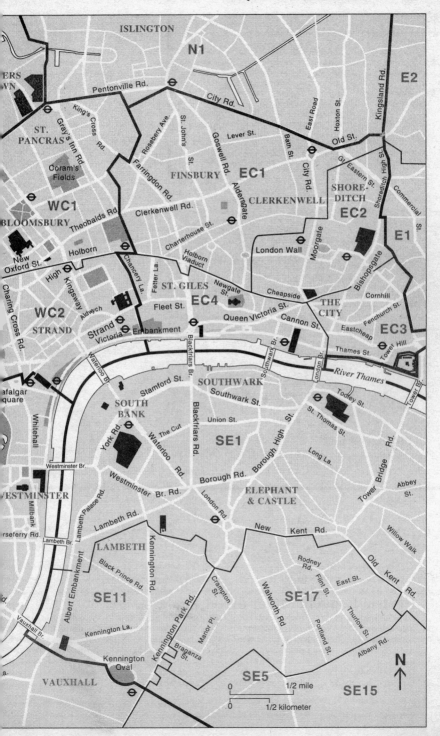

ISLINGTON

N1

Pentonville Rd.

City Rd.

ERS
WN

E2

King's Cross Rd.

Gray's Inn Rd.

ST.
PANCRAS

Rosebery Ave.

St. John's St.

Lever St.

Goswell Rd.

East Road

Old St.

Hoxton St.

Kingsland Rd.

E1

Coram's
Fields

FINSBURY

EC1

Bath St.

City Rd.

SHORE-
DITCH

Gt. Eastern St.

Shoreditch High St.

Commercial St.

WC1

Theobalds Rd.

Farringdon Rd.

Aldersgate

CLERKENWELL

Moorgate

EC2

E1

BLOOMSBURY

Clerkenwell Rd.

Charterhouse St.

London Wall

Bishopsgate

New
Oxford St.

Holborn

Chancery La.

Holborn
Viaduct

Cheapside

Cornhill

Fenchurch St.

THE
CITY

High

Fetter La.

Newgate
St.

EC3

Charing Cross Rd.

Kingsway

ST. GILES

EC4

Queen Victoria St.

Cannon St.

Eastcheap

WC2

Aldwych

Fleet St.

Tower Hill

STRAND

Strand

Victoria Embankment

Blackfriars Br.

Southwark Br.

Thames St.

London Br.

Tower Br.

afalgar
quare

Whitehall

Waterloo Br.

River Thames

Stamford St.

SOUTHWARK

SOUTH
BANK

Southwark St.

Tooley St.

St. Thomas St.

York Rd.

Waterloo Rd.

The Cut

Blackfriars Rd.

Union St.

SE1

Long La.

Tower Bridge Rd.

Abbey
St.

Westminster Br.

WESTMINSTER

Millbank

Westminster Br. Rd.

Borough Rd.

Borough High St.

ELEPHANT
& CASTLE

London Rd.

Willow Walk

Lambeth Palace Rd.

Lambeth Br.

Lambeth Rd.

New Kent Rd.

Old Kent Rd.

rseferry Rd.

LAMBETH

Kennington Rd.

Black Prince Rd.

Rodney
Rd.

Flint St.

East St.

Thurlow St.

SE11

Albert Embankment

Crampton St.

Manor Pl.

Walworth Rd.

SE17

Portland St.

Kennington La.

Kennington Park Rd.

Albany Rd.

Vauxhall Br.

Braganza
St.

N

VAUXHALL

Kennington
Oval

SE5

0   1/2 mile

0   1/2 kilometer

SE15

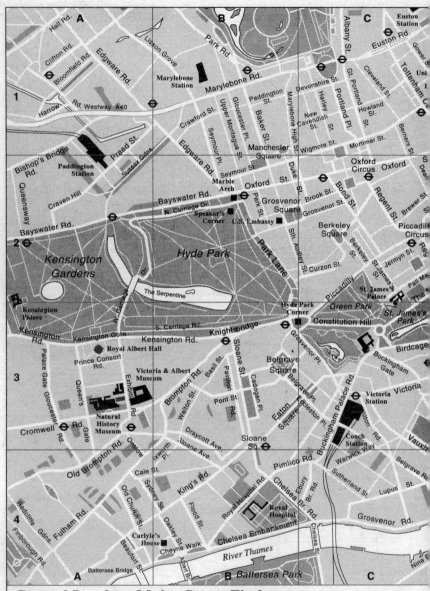

Central London: Major Street Finder

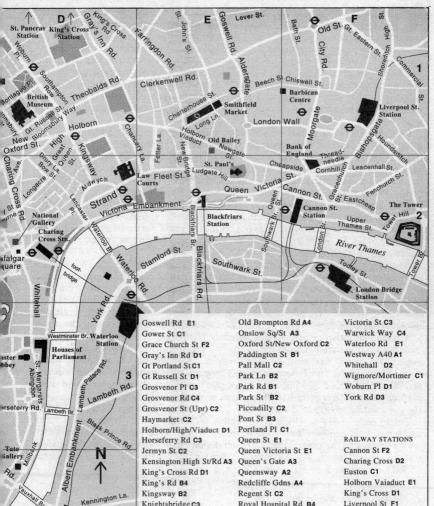

End, the tired, faded squares of Paddington and Bayswater give way to Notting Hill, home each August bank holiday to the largest street carnival in Europe.

South and southwest of the West End, still in the borough of Westminster, is the actual district of Westminster. This is England's royal, legislative, and ecclesiastical center, home of Buckingham Palace, the Houses of Parliament, and Westminster Abbey. Belgravia, packed with embassies, nestles between Westminster and the semi-gracious borough of Kensington and Chelsea. The excellent museums of South Kensington, the punk rockers and less flamboyant "posers" stalking the King's Road in Chelsea, and the Australians in Earl's Court ensure this borough has no single image.

London's galaxy of suburbs extends for miles in all directions. Some pockets of delight can be found in these generally drab outskirts. To the southwest, Kew luxuriates in its exquisite botanical gardens. In adjacent Richmond the expansive deer park brings wildlife to the capital. Towards the southeast, Greenwich takes pride in its rich navigational and astronomical history, as it lies on the privileged path of the Prime Meridian. The common at nearby Blackheath was the site of the world's first golf club. Brixton, just south of the river, is home to a large Afro-Caribbean community. Farther south lies the residential suburb of Wimbledon, site of the famed tennis tournament. Far out on the fringes of northeast greater London, ancient Epping Forest manages to preserve a degree of wildness and straddles the eastern and western hemispheres.

At times you'll need the ingenuity of Sherlock Holmes to find one of London's more obscure addresses. Some homeowners favor names rather than numbers, and the owner of a house on a corner is free to choose either street name as an address. Numbering starts at the end of the street nearest the center of London, but note that house numbers on opposite sides of large streets increase at different rates; house #211 may face #342. Numbers occasionally go up one side of the street and down the other. Some streets abruptly change names, disappear, and then materialize again after a hundred yards, while others twist through and around greens. You might find yourself in a tangle of Eaton Mews, Eaton Square, Eaton Gate, Eaton Place, and Eaton Terrace. There are 31 variations on Victoria Road, and 40 streets named Wellington. To navigate this mess, get a comprehensive street map or guide with a complete index, such as Nicholson's *London Streetfinder* or the compact *London A to Z* ("A to Zed," as streetwise Londoners call it; £2-5.50).

Postal code prefixes, which often appear on London street signs and in street addresses, may help you find your way. The letters stand for compass directions, with reference to the central district (itself divided into WC and EC, for West Central and East Central). All districts that border this central district are numbered "1." There are no S or NE codes.

EC1: Farringdon, Clerkenwell. **EC2:** Barbican, The City. **EC3:** Tower of London. **EC4:** Blackfriars, Fleet St., Temple, St. Paul's.

WC1: Bloomsbury. **WC2:** Charing Cross, the Strand, Holborn.

E1: Whitechapel. **E14:** Limehouse, including much of Docklands.

W1: Mayfair, Piccadilly, Oxford St., Soho, Marylebone. **W2:** Paddington. **W6:** Hammersmith. **W8:** Kensington. **W9:** Maida Vale. **W10:** North Kensington. **W11:** Notting Hill. **W14:** West Kensington.

SE1: South bank of the River, including Southwark and Waterloo. **SE3:** Blackheath. **SE10:** Greenwich. **SE11:** Lambeth.

SW1: Victoria, Westminster, Belgravia, Pimlico, The Mall. **SW2:** Brixton. **SW3:** Chelsea, Brompton. **SW4:** Clapham. **SW5:** Earl's Ct. **SW6:** Fulham. **SW7:** South Kensington. **SW8:** South Lambeth. **SW10:** West Brompton. **SW11:** Battersea.

N1: Islington. **N6:** Highgate.

NW1: Camden Town. **NW3:** Hampstead. **NW5:** Kentish Town. **NW8:** St. John's Wood.

Touring

Seeing all of London? Guess again. You'll never finish. London is a city of details and discovery. Don't try to "see it all," or feel that you must visit every monument of Western Civilization; they'll all still be there when you come back. Some tours can breeze you through the highlights enabling you to decide where to focus your energies.

The **London Transport Sightseeing Tour** (tel. 222 1234), provides a convenient and reasonable overview of London's maze of attractions. Tours lasting 1½ hrs. depart from Baker St., Haymarket, near Piccadilly Circus, Marble Arch, and Victoria St. (near the station), and include Buckingham Palace, the Houses of Parliament, Westminster Abbey, the Tower of London, St. Paul's, and Piccadilly Circus. (Tours daily every ½ hr. 10am-5pm; £8, under 16 £4, or £7 and £3 in advance from the British Travel Centre, a London Tourist Board Information Centre, or a London Transport Information Centre.) Longer day trips are also available. For half the price and a different perspective, London Transport also operates **London by Night**, which whizzes by London's floodlit landmarks. It departs 9pm from Victoria Station, 9:10pm from Park Lane, 9:15pm from Lancaster Gate, 9:20 pm from Paddington Station, and 9:35 pm from Piccadilly Circus (£3.50, under 14 £2).

A walking tour can fill in the hidden nooks that bus tours run right over; with a good guide, it can be as entertaining as it is informative. **The Original London Walks** (tel. 435 6413; £4, £2.50 for students, accompanied children under 15 free) conducts 2 hr. walks in the morning, afternoon, and evening. They have two different tours each for Shakespeare and Dickens and for Sherlock Holmes's London, as well as "Ghosts of the City" and others. **City Walks of London** (tel. 837 2841) allows you to discover "Beatles London" or revisit some of the more horrific aspects of the late 1880s in "On the Trail of Jack the Ripper." Tours cost £4, students and YHA members, £2.50. **Historical Walks of London** (tel. 668 4019), offers the usual jaunts (Dickens, Ripper, et al.) (£4, concession £3). In any case, ask around for opinions from veterans of the tours. The quality of the walks can vary widely, even within the same company.

The **London Silver Jubilee Walkway** map (available free at any LTB tourist office) circles central London in a ring of sights. Follow the map (and the round silver plaques in the pavement along the way) from Trafalgar Sq. to Westminster, along the South Bank to Tower Bridge, then back through the City and Bloomsbury to Trafalgar Sq. The 12-mile walkway easily breaks up into smaller sections for less ambitious types.

Touring Tips: The Secrets of Landmarks

Whether you tour alone or with a group, pay attention to the user-friendly landmarks around you. Kind-hearted souls have conveniently labeled and catalogued the unwieldy city. Since 1867, the historically minded (first from the Royal Society of Arts and then from the London County Council, the Greater London Council, and finally English Heritage) have been marking the houses of prominent personages with Blue Plaques (see below). A few local societies have joined in. Oval plaques divide the city into administrative wards. Insurance companies used to put firemarks on houses to identify insured houses to firemen; you can still see a few of them, for example in Goodwins Court. Keep your eyes up for decorative ironwork, stylized balconies with the crest of their owner, ornate lampposts, doorway carvings, brass door trappings, public clocks, old-fashioned telephone booths, weather vanes, and rooftop statues, such as Justice over the Old Bailey. Keep your eyes on the ground for coal-hole covers (used in old terraced houses to deliver coal from the basement without soiling the threshold), and boundary marks. The boundary bollards of some London parishes can still be seen; the most distinctive ones lie in the City of London. At the west end of Fleet Street, a boundary marks the spot where even the Queen herself must receive permission to enter the City. Since London has had a few growth spurts in its time, outside of central London, you can still see milestones marking the distances to what used to be London; look at Kensington Court or along Kensington Gore. Polite landscape history fanatics could spend weeks asking for permission to London's secluded and private gardens in and around Kensington and Chelsea. London's public squares (Covent Garden, Lincoln's Inn, Bedford Square), shopfronts (near Jermyn St., Old Bond St., and Artillery Row), drinking fountains, and even wooden benches (bearing the carved name of their donors) capture a fascinating record of the city's history.

Blue Plaque Houses

Matthew Arnold (1822-1888)	poet and essayist	2 Chester Sq., SW1
John L. Baird (1888-1946)	TV pioneer	22 Frith St., W1
Sir James Barrie (1860-1937)	novelist, playwright	100 Bayswater Rd., W2
Aubrey Beardsley (1872-1898)	illustrator	114 Cambridge St., SW1
David Ben-Gurion (1886-1973)	Israeli statesman	75 Warrington Crescent, W9
Hector Berlioz (1803-1869)	composer	58 Queen Anne St., W1
James Boswell (1740-1795)	author	8 Russell St., WC2
Elizabeth Barrett Browning (1806-1861)	poet	99 Gloucester Pl., W1
Beau Brummell (1778-1840)	dandy	4 Chesterfield St., W1
Sir Edward Burne-Jones (1833-1898)	painter	17 Red Lion Sq., WC1
Thomas Carlyle (1795-1881)	essayist and historian	24 Cheyne Walk, SW3
Frederic Chopin (1810-1849)	composer	4 St. James's Pl., SW1
Sir Winston Churchill (1874-1965)	statesman, soldier, author	28 Hyde Park Gate, SW7
Samuel Clemens (Mark Twain) (1835-1910)	writer	23 Tedworth Sq., SW3
Muzio Clementi (1752-1832)	composer	128 Kensington Church St., W8
Joseph Conrad (1857-1924)	novelist	17 Gillingham St., SW1
Charles Darwin (1809-1882)	naturalist	University College, Science Building, WC1
General Charles de Gaulle (1890-1970)	French president	4 Carlton Gdns., SW1
Charles Dickens (1812-1870)	novelist	48 Doughty St., WC1
Benjamin Disraeli (1804-1881)	prime minister 1868, 1874-80	19 Curzon St., W1
General Dwight D. Eisenhower (1890-1969)	U.S. president	31 St. James's Sq., SW1
T.S. Eliot (1888-1965)	poet and critic	3 Kensington Ct., W8
Mary Ann Evans (George Eliot) (1819-1880)	novelist	4 Cheyne Walk, SW3
Benjamin Franklin (1706-1790)	statesman and inventor	36 Craven St., WC2
Thomas Gainsborough (1727-1788)	portrait artist	82 Pall Mall, SW1
John Galsworthy (1867-1933)	novelist and playwright	1-3 Robert St., WC2
Edward Gibbon (1737-1792)	historian	7 Bentinck St., W1
George Frederick Händel (1685-1759)	composer	25 Brook St., W1
Washington Irving (1783-1859)	author and diplomat	Argyll St., W1
Henry James (1843-1916)	writer	34 De Vere Gdns., W8
Samuel Johnson (1709-1784)	author and lexicographer	17 Gough Sq., EC4(museum)
Rudyard Kipling (1865-1936)	poet and writer	43 Villiers St., WC2
Lillie Langtry (1852-1929)	actress	Pont St., SW1 (Cadogan Hotel)
T.E. Lawrence (1888-1935)	soldier and writer	14 Barton St., SW1
Gugliemo Marconi (1874-1937)	inventor of the wireless,	71 Hereford Rd., W2
Karl Marx (1818-1883)	economist and philosopher	28 Dean St., W1
Somerset Maugham (1874-1965)	novelist and playwright	6 Chesterfield St., W1
Samuel Morse (1791-1872)	inventor and painter	141 Cleveland St., W1
Wolfgang A. Mozart (1756-1791)	composer	180 Ebury St., SW1
Sir Isaac Newton (1642-1727)	physicist and mathematician	87 Jermyn St., SW1
Florence Nightingale (1820-1910)	founder of modern nursing	10 South St., W1
Samuel Pepys (1633-1703)	diarist	14 Buckingham St., WC2
Sir Joshua Reynolds (1723-1792)	portrait painter	Leicester Sq., WC2
Dante Gabriel Rossetti (1828-1882)	poet and painter	16 Cheyne Walk, SW3
George Bernard Shaw (1856-1950)	playwright and critic	29 Fitzroy Sq., W1
Percy Bysshe Shelley	Romantic poet	15 Poland St., W1

(1792-1882)

William Makepeace Thackeray (1811-1863)	novelist	36 Onslow Sq., SW7
Anthony Trollope (1815-1882)	novelist	39 Montagu Sq., W1
Vincent Van Gogh (1853-1890)	impressionist painter	87 Hackford Rd., SW9
R. Vaughn Williams (1872-1925)	composer	10 Hanover Terrace, NW1
James A. McNeil Whistler (1834-1903)	painter and etcher	96 Cheyne Walk, SW10
Oscar Wilde (1854-1900)	wit and dramatist	34 Tite St., SW3.

Getting Around London

London's public transit system, operated by **London Regional Transport,** is comprehensive. The Tube alone is impressive in its coverage, and it is supplemented by LRT buses and **British Rail (BR).** With all of these options, public transport will very often prove quicker and cheaper than a taxi.

London is divided into six concentric transport zones. Central London, including most of the major sights, is covered by Zone 1; Heathrow Airport takes off in Zone 6. Fares depend on the distance of the journey and the number of zones crossed, and are high. Arm yourself with a **Travelcard,** the savior of the budget traveler, which will prove a bargain if you make more than a couple of trips. This pass allows unlimited rides on buses, tube, and British Rail in the relevant zones. It also eliminates the hassle of waiting on long lines in crowded stations or fumbling for change on the top deck of a lurching bus. The one-day Travelcard (£2.30 for zones 1 and 2, £2.70 for zones 1-4, and £3.10 for all zones) is not valid before 9:30am Monday through Friday or for night buses (see Buses below). The seven-day card is available for any combination of zones (from zone 1, £7.80, to all zones, £22.00). Cards are also available for month- or year-long periods, or for custom-designed periods (they pro-rate the weekly rate).

For the seven-day or longer cards, you will need one passport-sized photo. Photo booths are located at major tube stations, including Victoria, Leicester Sq., Earl's Ct., and Oxford Circus.

If you want a Travelcard before 9:30am on a weekday, you can buy an LT card. More expensive than the One-Day Travelcard, the LT card is valid all day, but not on BR trains (£3.50 for zones 1 and 2, £4.50 for zones 1-4, £5.50 for zones 1-6).

Information on both buses and the tube is available 24 hrs. (tel. 222 1234). Pick up free maps and guides at London Transport's information offices (look for the lower-case "i" logo at information windows and on signs). You can find well-staffed booths with free maps and information on buses, Underground trains, and tours at Heathrow Airport, Euston and Victoria rail stations, and six major tube stops: King's Cross (open Sat.-Thurs. 8:15am-6pm, Fri. 8:15am-7:30pm); Piccadilly Circus (open daily 8:15am-6pm); Oxford Circus (open Mon.-Sat. 8:15am-6pm); St. James's Park (open Mon.-Fri. 9am-5:30pm); Liverpool St. (open Mon.-Fri. 9:30am-6:30pm, Sat. 8:30am-6:30pm, Sun. 8:30am-3:30pm); Heathrow Terminals 1, 2, 3 station (open Mon.-Sat. 7:15 am-6:30pm, Sun. 8:15am-6:30pm); Euston BR station (open Mon.-Thurs. 7:15am-6pm, Fri. 7:15am-7:30pm, Sat. 7:15am-6pm, Sun. 8:15 am-6pm); Victoria BR station (open daily 8:15am-9:30pm); Heathrow Terminal 1 arrivals (open Mon.-Fri. 7:15am-10:15pm, Sat. 7:15am-9pm, Sun. 8:15am-10pm); Terminal 2 arrivals (open Mon.-Sat. 7:15am-9pm, Sun. 8:15am-10pm); Terminal 3 arrivals (open Mon.-Sat. 6:30am-1:15pm, Sun. 8:15am-3pm); and Terminal 4 arrivals (open Mon.-Sat. 6:30am-6:30pm, Sun. 8:15am-6:30pm). For information on how the buses and Underground trains are currently running, phone 222 1200 (open 24 hrs.). London Transport's **lost property office** (tel. 486 2496) lies just down the road from Sherlock at 200 Baker St. (Tube: Baker St.; open Mon.-Fri. 9:30am-2pm). Allow two working days for articles lost on buses or the tube to reach the office.

Underground

The color-coded **Underground** railway system, or the **Tube,** is the easiest way to get around London, with 269 stations on 11 lines (Bakerloo, Central, Circle, District, East London, Hammersmith and City, Jubilee, Metropolitan, Northern, Pic-

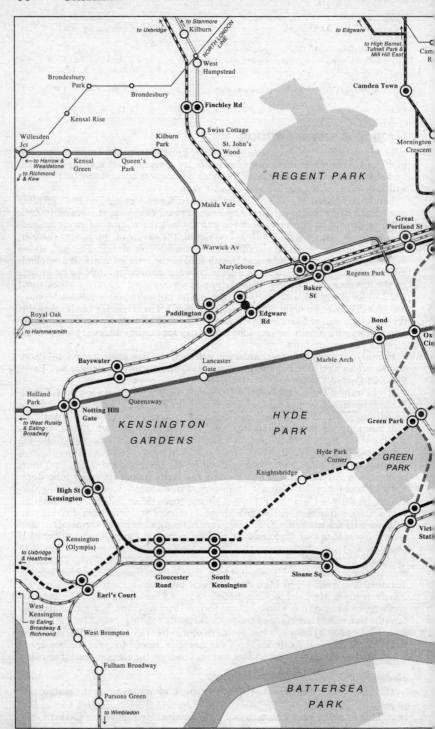

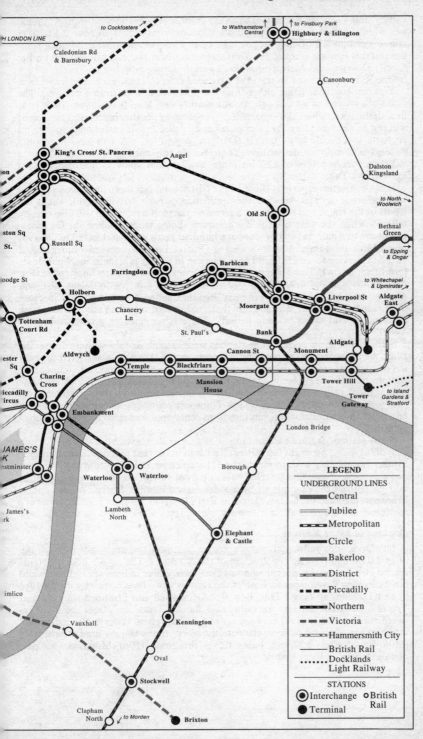

cadilly, and Victoria). **Fares** depend on the number of zones passed through. A journey wholly within central zone 1 costs 80p; one from zone 1 to zone 2 £1.10. A trip to a distant suburb may set you back up to £3.80. On Sundays and Public Holidays, trains run less frequently. All transfers are free. Bicycles are allowed on the Circle, District, and Metropolitan lines except during morning and evening rush hours. Riders under age 16 travel at a reduced fare; children under five travel free.

You can buy your ticket either from the ticket window or from a machine. The ticket allows you to go through the automatic gates; keep it until you reach your final destination, where it will be collected or eaten by another machine. Travelcards will not be swallowed by the gates or taken by collectors. If you change your mind en route and decide to go farther than you've paid for, you will have to pay the "excess fare" at your destination. Those people convicted of traveling without a ticket can receive fines of £200 or more. Similar fines apply to dishonesty about age (on the Tube, that is).

Some platforms, especially those on the District and Northern lines, receive trains with differing destinations. For the destination of each arriving train, watch the fronts of the trains and the electric sign above the platform, which will also usually tell you when the next train is due to arrive. Some stops—Baker St., for example—have two different stations, about a hundred yards apart and linked to different lines. Most tube lines' **last trains** leave Central London between midnight and 12:30am; service resumes around 6am. The gap in service is bridged by Night Buses (see Buses below). The Tube, unremittingly packed during rush hour (Mon.-Fri. roughly 7-10am and 4:30-7:30pm), earns its share of flak due to delays, dirt, and diverted trains; the Northern Line has been nicknamed "the misery line" because of its rush hour bedlam. Bear in mind that some distant suburban tube stations close on Sundays and other off-peak periods. There is no smoking anywhere (on the Tube).

Some of London's deepest tube stations were used as air-raid shelters during the Blitz. At the worst of the bombing, as many as 175,000 people sheltered in them in one night; some were unable or unwilling to leave for days on end. While some stations may still bring bomb shelters to mind (indeed many of them look the same now as then), others are quite jazzy with their intricate, colorful mosaics, often cryptically related to their name. London Transport continues its tradition of stylish poster art by commissioning paintings from contemporary artists for its "By Tube" posters.

Many stations feature endless tunnels and steep staircases, so if you're carrying a lot of luggage, you might fare better on a longer route that requires fewer transfers. Fitness zealots may wish to tackle the 331-step climb at Hampstead station, London's deepest. If you find yourself suffering from vertigo on the endless escalator, take heart from the example set by wooden-legged Bumper Harris. When London Transport installed the first escalators at Earl's Court in 1911, they hired "Bumper" to ascend and descend all day, thereby encouraging weak-kneed passengers.

Docklands Light Railway

The Docklands railway, London's newest transport system, winds through the dilapidation and frenetic construction of the old docks. The semi-automatic trains run on elevated tracks, providing an unusual perspective of both the old slums and the flashy new developments. Both of the railway's two lines connect with the tube in east London, at Tower Hill, Bow Road, Shadwell and Stratford stations, and Travelcards can be used on the railway. Without a Travelcard, fares are £1.10 between zones 1 and 2, £1.40 between zones 1-3. The system is currently undergoing major expansion, and to accommodate the work, trains run on limited schedules (Mon.-Fri. 5:30am-9:30pm); buses travel the route (50p) Mon.-Fri. 9:30pm-midnight, Sun. 7:30am-midnight.

Buses

> The way to see London is from the top of a bus—the
> top of a bus, gentlemen.
> —William Gladstone

London's buses are more complicated to use than the Underground and invariably slower, but often prove more economical. In addition, the tunnels of London are far less attractive than its streets, and being shuttled about underground can hardly match the majesty of rolling along the street enthroned on the front seats of the top of a double-decker. Unfortunately, double-decker **Routemaster** buses, with their conductors and open rear platforms, are being replaced to save money. On modern double-deckers and on single-deck "hoppa" buses, you pay your fare to the driver as you board. On Routemaster buses, take a seat and wait for the conductor, who can tell you the fare and let you know when to get off. Smoking is not permitted on London's buses.

London Transport issues a free bus map for London called, remarkably, the *London Bus Map*, which is available at some tube stations and LRT information offices. The *Central Bus Guide* is a more manageable pamphlet, describing only bus routes in zone 1. Bus stops are marked with route information; at busy intersections or complicated one-way systems, maps tell where to board each bus.

On stops marked "request," buses stop only if you flag them down (to get on) or pull the bell cord (to get off). While waiting, you must form a queue (line up); bus conductors may refuse some passengers at the stop during crowded periods. One stop may be served by a whole selection of buses. Completely ignore any daytime bus timetables you may come across, as the service has a notoriously sporadic nature. Ask Londoners what they'll be doing in the year 2000 and they'll reply, "still waiting for a 214." Within zone 1, fares range from 50-70p. Other journeys cost from 30p-£3. A Travelcard is a worthwhile investment if you plan to make more than a couple of trips. **Bus passes** are valid only on buses and thus are not as versatile as Travelcards. Regular buses run from about 6am to midnight, although they can be impossibly slow during rush hour. **Night buses** (the "N" routes) now run frequently throughout London. All night bus routes run through Trafalgar Sq. (Tube: Charing Cross), so as the time of the last train approaches, head there. Victoria, King's Cross, and Liverpool St. stations are also good spots to catch one. Travelcards are not valid on night buses. London Transport's 24-hr. information line (tel. 222 1234) can tell you about all routes. Alternatively, pick up their free brochure about night buses, which includes times of the last British Rail and Underground trains, from a London Transport information office.

British Rail

Most of London is fully served by buses and the tube. Some districts, however, notably southeast London, are most easily reached by train. Travelcards are valid on Network South East (the portion of the BR system covering London) within the zones. The North London Link, stretching across north London from North Woolwich to Richmond is a handy line seldom used by visitors: trains (every 20 min.) scoot from Hampstead Heath to Kew in 25 minutes. Information on Network South East services is available at all mainline stations. The travel and information center at Waterloo (open Mon.-Sat. 8am-9pm, Sun. 9am-9pm) has full timetables of all services (20p for each section of London). *London Connections,* a map of all tube and Network South East lines, is free and available at any tube station or information office.

Taxicabs

London taxicab drivers must pass a rigorous exam and demonstrate intimate knowledge of the city to earn a license. The route taken by the cabbie is virtually certain to be the shortest and quickest; the massive London cabs are surprisingly maneuverable and dart in and out (mostly out) of traffic jams unperturbed. Most London cabs are black. You are most likely to find cabs at large hotels, or at major intersections (such as Trafalgar Sq., Hyde Park Corner, and Piccadilly Circus), but cabs abound throughout Central London, easy to hail except during rain. A taxi is available if its yellow light is aglow. You can catch a cab yourself or call a radio dispatcher for one (tel. 286 0286, 272 0272, 253 5000, or look in the Yellow Pages under "taxi"). Drivers are required to charge according to the meter for trips under 6 mi., but for longer distances, you must negotiate the price. A 10% tip is expected, with a surplus charge for extra baggage or passengers. For four or more people, a taxi may prove less expensive than the tube. If you believe that you have been overcharged, get the driver's number.

Apart from the licensed cabs, there are countless "minicab" companies, listed in the Yellow Pages. "Ladycabs" (tel. 254 3501) has only female cabbies (Mon.-Thurs. 7:45am-12:30am, Fri. 7:45am-1am, Sat. 9am-2am, Sun. 10am-12:30am). Be sure to ask the price when you order a minicab, and reconfirm it before you start the trip. Reclaim **lost property** (tel. 833 0996) you have left in a taxi at 15 Penton St., Islington, N1 (Tube: Angel; open Mon.-Fri. 9am-4:30pm). If you left something in a minicab, contact the company.

Bicycles

London's roads are in excellent condition, but on weekdays both the volume and temper of its traffic may seem homicidal. However, bicycling has its advantages, and there are few better ways to spend a Sunday than pedaling through the parks of the city. Great deals on secondhand bikes can be found at the General Auction (see below). Also check outdoor markets, classified ads in the local press, *Exchange and Mart,* and the University of London's bulletin board at 1 Malet St. (Tube: Russell Sq.). Bikes are allowed on BR trains; you may take a bike onto the Circle, District, and Metropolitan line Underground trains (Mon.-Fri. 10am-4:30pm and after 7:30pm, Sat.-Sun. all day) but you will be charged a child's fare for it.

General Auctions, 63 Garrat Lane, Wandsworth, SW18 (tel. (081) 874 2955). Tube: Tooting Broadway, then bus #44, 77, 220, or 280. Police auction as many as 100 used bikes here every Mon. at 11am. Prices range from £1 to £250. Examine bikes Sat. 9:30am-3pm, Mon. 10-11am. Examine the £1 ones with particular care.

On Your Bike, 22 Duke St. Hill, SE1 (tel. 357 6958). Tube: London Bridge. Ten-speeds £8 per day, £14 per weekend, £30 per week. £50 check or credit card deposit required. Mountain bikes £15 per day, £20 per weekend, £60 per week, steep £200 deposit. MC and Visa accepted. Open Mon.-Fri. 9am-6pm, Sat. 9:30am-4:30pm.

Mopeds and Motorcycles

Scootabout Ltd., 59 Albert Embankment, SE1 (tel. 582 0055). Tube: Vauxhall. Mopeds from £23.65 per day, £84.75 per week, including helmet, insurance, panniers, and unlimited miles but excluding VAT. Credit card or £100 deposit required. Call ahead. Open Mon.-Fri. 9am-6pm, Sat. 9am-2pm.

Cars

London is not the place to go spinning about in your Mini—parking is next to impossible, traffic is deplorable, and the gear shift (not to mention your car) is on the left. When all's said and done, you could have biked, bused, tubed, walked, or propelled yourself by your lips more quickly and cheaply. National Car Parks (tel. 499 7050) runs expensive **car parks** (garages) throughout Central London, including ones near Tower Hill (Lower Thames St.), Piccadilly Circus (Brewer St.), and Bedfordbury (48 St. Martin's Lane). Charges are around £4 for two hours. Many streets in central London have parking meters. Obscene rates run from £2 to £4 per hour.

Renting a car will not save you time, money, or hassle compared to public transport in London. If you must rent, note that big rental firms like Avis and Hertz may be convenient, but they are quite expensive. Small cheap companies can be dodgy. Drivers must usually be over 21 and under 70. Make sure you understand the insurance agreement before you rent; some agreements require you to pay for damages that you may not have caused. If you are paying by credit card, check to see what kind of insurance your company provides free of charge. Automatics are generally more expensive to rent than manuals. You have been warned.

Boats

London's main artery during the Middle Ages, the **River Thames** no longer commands as much traffic, but if you venture out on to it in a boat you can still sense the pulse of a major lifeline. Boats make the half-hour trip from Westminster Pier (Tube: Westminster) to the Tower of London every 20 minutes from 10:20am to 5pm (tel. 930 4097; £2.60, £3.60 return). Voyages downstream to Greenwich (tel. 930 4097; every ½ hr. from 10:30am-5pm; £3.80, £4.80 return) and the Thames Barrier (tel. 930 3373; daily at 10am, 11:15am, 12:45pm, 1:45pm, and 3:15pm; £3.10, £4.80 return) take in fine industrial dockland scenery. Boats also chug upstream (tel. 930 4721) to Kew Gardens (£4, £6 return), Richmond (£5, £7 return) and Hampton Court (3-4 hr.; £6, £8 return). **The River Bus** (tel. 512 6555) offers speedy transport on the Thames from Charing Cross Embankment to Greenwich (daily, every 20 min. until 8pm; £3.60, £7.20 return).

Regent's Canal, part of the Grand Union Canal, a major industrial passage of the 19th century, runs along the north rim of Regent's Park. **Jason's Trip** opposite 60 Bloomfield Rd., Little Venice, W9 (tel. 286 3428; Tube: Warwick Ave.), runs daily motor barges on the canal through the park to Camden Lock and back (June-Aug. and Easter at 10:30am, 12:30, 2:30, and 4:30pm; otherwise daily at 12:30 and 2:30pm; £2.95, £3.95 return). The **Zoo Waterbus** (tel. 482 2550), also from Little Venice, shuttles passengers to the zoo in Regent's Park, and farther along to Camden Lock (on the hr. 10am-5pm; £2.50, £3.10 return, £6.40 one way including admission to the zoo). The **Jenny Wren,** 250 Camden High St., NW1 (tel. 485 4433; Tube: Camden Town), drifts from Camden Lock to Little Venice and back. (Boats depart weekdays at 11:30am and 2pm; Sat. at 2pm and 3:30pm; Sun. at 11:30am, 2pm, and 3:30pm. 1½ hr. return. £3.20.)

Practical Information

Tourist Offices

LTB Tourist Information Centre: Victoria Station Forecourt, SW1 (tel. 730 3488, phone answered Mon.-Fri. 9am-6pm but difficult to get through). Run by the London Tourist Board; has information on London and England, a well-stocked bookshop, theatre and tour bookings, and an accommodations service (a hefty £5 booking fee, £12 refundable deposit). Expect to take a number and wait at peak hours, around noon. You can book a room by mail if you write to them at least 6 weeks in advance. With a Visa or Mastercard, you can book a room by phone on much shorter notice (tel. 824 8844, answered daily 9am-6pm). Victoria Station center open April-Nov. daily 8am-7pm; Dec.-March Mon.-Sat. 9am-7pm, Sun. 9am-5pm. Bookshop open April-Nov. Mon.-Sat. 8am-6:30pm, Sun. 8am-3:30pm; Dec.-March Mon.-Sat. 9am-6:30pm, Sun. 9am-3:30pm. Additional tourist offices are located at **Heathrow Airport,** (open daily April-Nov. 9am-6pm; Dec.-March 9am-4:30pm), and **Harrods** and **Selfridges** department stores.

British Travel Centre: 12 Regent St., SW1 (tel. 730 3400). Tube: Piccadilly. Down Regent St. from the Lower Regent St. tube exit. Run by the British Tourist Authority and ideal for travelers bound for destinations outside of London. Combines the services of the BTA, British Rail, and American Express with an accommodations service. For the latter, you pay a booking fee (£5) and a deposit (either one night's stay or 10-15% of the total stay depending on the place; does not book for hostels). The office contains very helpful tourist information services of Wales, Ireland, and Northern Ireland (see below for slightly different hours). Also sells maps (an excellent selection), theatre tickets, and books, and can give you every pamphlet known to Englishkind, translated into many languages. Pleasantly relaxed compared to LTB, but the shortage of staff sometimes makes for a long wait. Open May-Oct. Mon.-Fri. 9am-6:30pm, Sat. 9am-5pm, Sun. 10am-4pm; Nov.-April Mon.-Sat. 9am-5pm.

City of London Information Centre: St. Paul's Churchyard, EC4 (tel. 606 3030). Tube: St. Paul's. Specializes in information about the City of London but answers questions on the whole of London. Helpful, knowledgeable staff and mountains of brochures. Open April-Oct. daily 9:30am-5pm., Nov.-March Mon.-Fri. 9:30am-5pm, Sat 9:30am-12:30pm.

London Transport Information Offices: (24-hr information line, tel. 222 1234). At the Heathrow, Victoria, Piccadilly Circus, Oxford Circus, Euston, and King's Cross Tube stops. Officials there answer inquiries regarding Underground and bus travel and push free bus route maps (see Getting Around London).

Irish Tourist Board (Bord Fáilte): 150 New Bond St., W1 (tel. 629 7292). Tube: Bond St. Open Mon.-Thurs. 9:15am-5:15am, Fri. 9:15am-5pm. Also has a combined desk with the Northern Ireland tourist board inside the British Travel Centre on Regent St. (tel. 839 8417), open May-Oct. Mon.-Fri. 9am-6pm, Sat.-Sun. 10am-4pm; Nov.-April Mon.-Sat. 9am-5pm.

Northern Ireland Tourist Board: 12 Regent St., SW1 (tel. 839 8417). Tube: Piccadilly Circus. Inside the British Travel Centre. Open May-Oct. Mon.-Fri. 9am-6pm, Sat.-Sun. 10am-4pm; Nov.-April Mon.-Sat. 9am-5pm.

Wales Tourist Board: 12 Regent St., SW1 (tel. 409 0969). Tube: Piccadilly Circus. Inside the British Travel Centre. Open May-Oct. Mon.-Fri. 9am-6:30pm, Sat. 9am-5pm, Sun. 10am-4pm; Nov.-April Mon.-Sat. 9am-5pm.

Scottish Tourist Board: 19 Cockspur St., SW1 (tel. 930 8661). Tube: Charing Cross. Open May-Sept. Mon.-Fri. 9am-6pm; Oct.-April 9:30am-5:30pm.

Jersey Tourist Information Office: 35 Albemarle St., W1 (tel. 493 5278). Tube: Green Park. Open Mon.-Fri. 9:30am-5pm.

French Tourist Information Office: 178 Piccadilly, W1 (recorded message only, tel. 499 6911). Tube: Piccadilly Circus. Open Mon-Fri. 9am-5:30pm.

Budget Travel Organizations

The organizations listed below specialize in student discounts, youth fares, and other discounts. (See the Getting There section of the General Introduction for more information.) All of them sell ISIC cards at £5 each.

STA Travel: 74 and 86 Old Brompton Rd., SW7 (tel. 937 9921 for European travel, 937 9971 for North American travel, 937 9962 for the rest of the globe). Tube: South Kensington. Cheap flights and tours all over the world. Long lines. Open Mon.-Fri. 9am-6pm, Sat. 10am-4pm.

YHA Travel Office: 14 Southampton St., WC2 (tel. 836 8541). Tube: Covent Garden. Travel services for free-wheeling, independent types, young or old. Bookshop offers a great selection of travel guides to every country under the sun, including *Let's Go.* Can sell you everything you need for your globe-trotting, bike-camping adventure holiday. Information on student discounts and Eurotrain tickets for those under 26. Open Mon.-Wed. and Fri. 10am-6pm, Thurs. 10am-7:30pm, Sat. 9am-6pm. The Kensington Branch is also well-stocked, at 174 Kensington High St., W8 (tel. 938 2948), open Mon.-Wed. and Fri 10am-6:30pm, Thurs. 10am-7:30pm, Sat. 10am-5:30pm.

Council Travel: 28a Poland St., W1 (tel. 437 7767). Tube: Oxford Circus. Affiliated with the pan-U.S. Council Travel group, selling cheap plane, rail, and bus tickets to any chosen destination. Humming with activity. Open Mon.-Fri. 9:30am-6pm.

Trailfinders: 42-48 Earls Court Rd., W8 (tel. 937 5400). Tube: High Street Kensington. Huge and dependable clearing house for cheap airline tickets for Europe and the rest of the world. Information and vaccination section for those using London as a base for long haul flights. Open Mon.-Sat. 9am-6pm; telephone only Sun. 10am-2pm.

Victoria station is a jungle of travel services. Skip the agencies inside the station and cross the street to get to Terminal House, at 52 Grosvenor Gardens, SW1.

London Student Travel: (tel. 730 3402). Tube: Victoria. Competitive rail, coach, and air fares all over the Continent and beyond. No age limit for many of their offers. Come early to avoid long lines. Open June-Oct. Mon.-Fri. 8:30am-6:30pm, Sat. 10am-5pm; Nov.-May Mon.-Fri. 9am-5:30pm, Sat. 10am-5pm.

National Express: (tel. 730 8235). Tube: Victoria. Specializes in coach and train travel in Western Europe. Additional office at Piccadilly (13 Regent St., SW1; tel. 925 0189). Open Mon.-Fri. 9am-5:30pm, Sat. 9am-4pm.

Touropa: (tel. 730 2101). Tube: Victoria. Yet another student travel center. Does most of its business in charter flights to the continent and European rail travel. Not nearly as busy as London Student Travel next door. Open June-Oct. Mon.-Fri. 9am-6pm, Sat. 10am-5pm; Nov-May Mon.-Fri. 9am-5:30pm, Sat. 10am-5pm.

Embassies and High Commissions

All embassies and high commissions close on English national holidays. Check the telephone book for other nationalities, or consult the *London Diplomatic List* for a complete list of embassies (available in the Her Majesty's Stationery Office, 49 High Holborn, WC1; tel. 211 5656; Tube: Holborn).

United States Embassy: 24 Grosvenor Sq., W1 (tel. 499 9000). Tube: Bond St. Someone will always answer the phone, but after 3pm on Sat. almost all counselors will have left. Embassy Travel Services at 22 Sackville St., W1. Tube: Piccadilly Circus. Travel Service office open Mon.-Fri. 10am-4pm.

Australian High Commission: Australia House, The Strand, WC2 (tel. 379 4334; in emergency, tel. 438 8181). Tube: Aldwych or Temple. Visa and passport inquiries tel. 438 8818. Open Mon.-Fri. 10am-4pm.

Canadian High Commission: MacDonald House, 1 Grosvenor Sq., W1 (tel. 629 9492). Tube: Bond St. or Oxford Circus. Visa services open Mon.-Fri. 8:45am-2pm. Information office open Mon.-Fri. 9:30am-5pm.

French Embassy: 58 Knightsbridge, SW1 (tel. 235 8080). Tube: Knightsbridge. For French visas (not necessary for U.S. citizens), contact the **French Consulate,** 6a Cromwell Pl., SW7 (tel. 823 9555). Tube: South Kensington. Open Mon.-Fri. 9-11:30am for applications, 4-4:30pm for collection of passports only.

Irish Embassy: 17 Grosvenor Pl., SW1 (tel. 235 2171). Tube: Hyde Park Corner. Open Mon.-Fri. 9:30am-5pm.

New Zealand High Commission: New Zealand House, 80 Haymarket, SW1 (tel. 930 8422). Tube: Charing Cross. Open Mon.-Fri. 10am-noon and 2-4pm.

Money

The number of travelers who throw money away by using the omnipresent *bureaux de change* is astonishing. The guidelines to spending your money abroad are, in fact, hard and fast. Taking money in traveler's checks is always best. In Britain, however, far fewer establishments than in the US accept traveler's checks as payment.

If you take traveler's checks, get them exchanged at the bank from which you bought them. American Express, Thomas Cook, and Visa checks all have agencies or banks that will change checks with no penalty (Visa and Thomas Cook checks can be exchanged at Barclay's at no cost). If you plan ahead, only in the most life-threatening of circumstances will you be sucked into a *bureau.* Expect banks and American Express offices to be closed or have limited hours on weekends. If you exchange your money in advance, you'll have a worry-free weekend. You should also not lose sleep over the possibility of an unexpected English bank holiday stalling your trip. Since there are at most eight such holidays per year (New Year's, Good Friday, Easter Monday, first Mon. in May, last Mon. in May, last Mon. in Aug., Christmas, and Boxing Day), they can hardly wreck your vacation. But know when they are.

If for some reason you're caught with only foreign currency, shop around at different banks for the best rates. Banks which do not have "window charges" often extort higher commissions. Even better, take your foreign currency into a bank and buy traveler's checks. The usual 1% commission is bound to be better than the usurious *bureau* alternative, and checks are far safer to carry than cash. Don't be lured by *bureaux* that scream "No Charge—No Commission." If it makes you wonder how they make their money, just look at the rates.

American Express: 6 Haymarket, SW1 (tel. 930 4411). Tube: Piccadilly Circus. Message and mail services open Mon.-Fri. 9am-5pm, Sat. 9am-noon. Currency exchange open Mon.-Fri.

9am-5pm, Sat. 9am-6pm, Sun. 10am-6pm. Go to side door Sat.-Sun. Bring ID to pick up mail (60p; free for Amex check or cardholders). Other offices at Victoria Station (147 Victoria St., SW1; tel. 828 7411); Cannon St. (54 Cannon St., EC4; tel. 248 2671); Knightsbridge (78 Brompton Rd., SW3; tel. 584 6182); and at the British Tourist Centre above. Lost or stolen traveler's checks should be reported immediately (tel. 0800 52 1313; 24-hr.).

24-hr. Currency Exchange: If you must, you can find such places at major tube stations. **Thomas Cook,** 15 Shaftesbury Ave. Tube: Piccadilly Circus. **Exchange International** Victoria Station. Tube: Victoria. Expect to pay a hefty fee.

Emergency, Social, and Miscellaneous Services

Emergency medical care, psychological counseling, crash housing, and sympathetic support can often be found in London free of charge.

Britons obtain mainly free health care from the National Health Service (NHS). Foreign visitors do not, of course, get such favorable terms, but are nevertheless eligible for some free treatment, including: outpatient treatment in the Accident and Emergency ward of an NHS hospital; treatment of communicable diseases (such as V.D., typhoid or anthrax); and "compulsory" mental treatment.

Emergency (Medical, Police, and Fire): Dial 999; no coins required.

Hospitals: In an emergency, you can be treated at no charge in the casualty ward of a hospital. You have to pay for routine medical care unless you work legally in Britain, in which case NHS tax will be deducted from your wages and you will not be charged. The advent of socialized medicine has lowered fees here, so you shouldn't ignore any health problem merely because you are low on cash. Try the **Westminster Hospital** at Pimlico (Dean Ryle St., Horseferry Rd., SW1; tel. 828 9811), the **University College Hospital** (Gower St., WC1; tel. 387 9300), the **London Hospital** at Whitechapel (Whitechapel Rd., E1; tel. 377 7000); or the **Royal Free Hospital** at Belsize Park (Pond St., NW3; tel. 794 0500). For others, the phone book has listings at the front, or for a more complete list look under "Hospitals."

Pharmacies: Every police station keeps a list of emergency doctors and chemists in its area. **Bliss Chemists** at Marble Arch (5 Marble Arch, W1; tel. 723 6116) is open daily, including public holidays, 9am-midnight. **Boots Chemists** has branches throughout London. Oxford Circus location (tel. 734 4646) open Mon.-Wed. and Fri.-Sat. 9am-6:30pm, Thurs. 9am-7:30pm. Victoria Station branch (tel. 834 0676) open Mon.-Fri. 7:30am-9pm, Sat. 9am-7pm.

Police: Stations in every district of London, including: Headquarters, New Scotland Yard, Broadway, SW1 (tel. 230 1212). Tube: St. James's Park; West End Central, 27 Savile Row, W1 (tel. 434 5212). Tube: Piccadilly Circus; King's Cross, 76 King's Cross Rd., WC1 (tel. 837 4233). Tube: King's Cross; Kensington, 72-74 Earl's Court Rd., W8 (tel. (081) 741 6212). Tube: Earl's Court.

Samaritans: 46 Marshall St., W1 (tel. 734 2800). Tube: Oxford Circus. Highly respected 24-hr. crisis hotline helps with all sorts of problems, including suicidal depression. A listening rather than advice service.

Rape Crisis Line: London Rape Crisis Centre, P.O. Box 69, WC1 (tel. 837 1600, 24 hr.). Call anytime, emergency or not, to talk to another woman, receive legal or medical information, or obtain referrals. Will send someone to accompany you to the police, doctors, clinics, and courts upon request.

Family Planning Association: 27-35 Mortimer St., W1 (tel. 636 7866). Tube: Oxford Circus. Informational services: contraceptive advice, and pregnancy test and abortion referral. Open Mon.-Thurs. 9am-5pm, Fri. 9am-4:30pm.

Alcoholics Anonymous: Tel. 352 3001. Information on meeting locations and times. Hotline answered daily 10am-10pm; answering machine from 10pm-10am.

Disabled Travelers' Information: Phone the **Disability Advice Service** (tel. (081) 870 7437), **RADAR** (tel. 637 5400), or the **Greater London Association for the Disabled** (tel. 274 0107) for general information. Perhaps the two most useful guides to London for the disabled are Nicholson's *Access in London,* available in any well-stocked travel shop and *Door to Door,* published by Her Majesty's Stationery Office (49 High Holborn, WC1; tel. 211 5656; Tube: Holborn). Disabled persons traveling by Underground should pick up the booklet *Access to the Underground,* available at any Transport Information Center for 70p or by mail for £1 from the Unit for Disabled Passengers (London Regional Transport, 55 Broadway, London SW1H 0BD). London Transport's 24-hr. travel information hotline is also useful for disabled travelers (tel. 222 1234). For transportation by car, call **London Dial-a-Ride Users Associa-**

tion at 482 2325. The "Arts Access" section at the beginning of the new London telephone books details special services available for the disabled at theatres, cinemas, and concert halls around London.

Gay and Lesbian Travelers' Information: London Lesbian and Gay Centre, 67-69 Cowcross St., E1 (tel. 608 1471). Tube: Farringdon. The 5 floors house a bar, café, disco, bookshop, a women-only floor, exhibits, and theatre. Open daily noon-11pm. **London Lesbian and Gay Switchboard** (tel. 837 7324) provides a 24-hr. general advice, information, and support telephone service; mailing address BM Switchboard, Box 1514, London WC1N 3XX. **London Lesbian Line** (tel. 251 6911) operates sporadically in the evenings before 10pm; mailing address LLL, P.O. Box 1514, London WC1N 3XX.

Salvation Army: 101 Queen Victoria St., EC4 (tel. 236 5222). Tube: Mansion House or Blackfriars. Good reputation for advice and emergency short-range shelter.

Legal Trouble: Release, 388 Old St., EC1 (tel. 729 9904; 24-hr. emergency number 603 8654). Tube: Liverpool St. or Old St. Specializes in criminal law and advising those who have been arrested on drug charges. Also psychiatric and abortion referrals. Open Mon.-Fri. 10am-6pm. **Legal Advice Bureau,** 104 Roman Rd., E2 (tel. (081) 980 4205). Tube: Bethnal Green. May provide legal advice and representation for minimal fees.

Discrimination: National Council for Civil Liberties, 21 Tabard St., SE1 (tel. 403 3888). Tube: Borough. Advising and campaigning organization for prevention of all types of discrimination and protection of civil rights. Advice through letters only. Open Mon.-Fri. 10am-1:15pm and 2:15-5:30pm.

Automobile Breakdown: AA Breakdown service, tel. (0800) 887 766; 24-hr. RAC Breakdown service, tel. (0800) 828 282; National Breakdown, tel. (0800) 400 600.

Whole Body Donation: London Anatomy Office, Rockefeller Building, University St., WC1 (tel. 387 7850). In case you've been killed and decide you want something good to come of it. Recorded message advises donors to put cadaver on ice until the morning. Donor cards of any sort can be found at local pharmacies.

Lost Property: If you've lost something on the **Underground** or on a **bus,** go in person to the Lost Property Office, 200 Baker St., W1. Tube: Baker St. Open Mon.-Fri. 9:30am-2pm. For articles lost in a **taxi,** write to the Metropolitan Police Lost Property Office, 15 Penton St., N1. Articles lost on **British Rail** should be reported to the destination station of your train. In all other cases, inquire at the nearest police station.

Baggage Storage: Dozens of cheap storage companies in the London area charge £3-4 per item per week (check the Yellow Pages for one in your area). Lockers in train stations and airports are seldom available because of frequent bomb threats.

The Time: tel. 123

Accommodations

London has not been blessed with large numbers of cheap, decent places to stay. Many budget lodgings make the heart sink, and the rest fill up to the rafters. B&Bs, hostels, and halls of residence all pack them in during the summer; you should plan ahead to nab one of the more desirable rooms.

Be forewarned: your London B&B may disappoint you. Don't look for a welcoming family home or a homemade breakfast. If you expect a small, shabby room with minimal furnishings (bed, light, sink, chair), you may not be disappointed.

Most B&Bs in London cluster around the railway stations. Although abundant and convenient, rooms in these areas can be oppressive. It's well worth scouting out other less obvious but equally accessible areas for more humane surroundings. Hotels also get more crowded in the summertime, and some proprietors often raise prices or try to cram more people into each room.

Before committing yourself to a hotel, see the room and test the bed—its quality may have a huge impact on your stay. Also make sure you understand the rates; quoted fees may conveniently exclude the 17.5% VAT. In winter, ask whether your room will be heated. Some proprietors grant considerable rate reductions to guests who pay by the week; others may impose finicky restrictions and unreasonable check-out times. Some offer a discount for paying in advance, and many reduce their prices between September and May. An "English" breakfast should include eggs, bacon, toast, and tea or coffee, while a "Continental" breakfast means only some form of bread and hot caffeine. Breakfasts vary in quality as much as rooms do, ranging from the stomach-churning to the sublime.

If you don't mind sharing a room with ten other people, London's YHA hostels provide a cheerful alternative, though you should be aware that they, too, will raise their summer rates (by £1). YHA hostels make up in friendliness what they lack in privacy, and can be marvelous places for swapping travel information and finding traveling companions.

Halls of residence of the London colleges and polytechnics offer privacy, but often in the form of small, boxy singles. Some have fantastic locations and beautiful grounds, but rooms generally become brighter and more spacious the farther you move from the center of town. Well-managed and secure, halls are an unadventurous but safe bet.

Making advance reservations (preferably secured with a deposit) seems inconvenient, but ensures that your arrival is as anxiety-free as possible. In the summer months, advance reservations are essential (especially for single rooms), rescuing you from the grungiest of packed railway station B&Bs. Write or phone the hotel to check availability on the date you wish to stay. The proprietor should specify the deposit amount (usually one night's stay, but this varies), which you then send as a signed traveler's check (in pounds if possible). You may be charged for other forms of payment, such as money orders, dollar checks, or credit cards, but the hotel will advise the best way to make the deposit. More and more hotels and most YHA hostels now accept credit card reservations over the phone, so if you don't have the time to make written reservations, it's well worth calling ahead.

The **Tourist Information Centre Accommodations Service,** at Victoria Station (accommodations service tel. 824 8844, answered daily 9am-6pm), bustles during high season. Their least expensive rooms cost about £18 plus an unnerving £5 booking fee. Most rooms cost about £21. Callers carrying a Visa or Mastercard can make bookings by phone. Otherwise bookings can be made in person or by mail at least six weeks in advance. They also sell a booklet, *Where to Stay in London* £2.95, half-geared toward budget travelers.

Youth Hostels

Each of the eight IYHF/YHA hostels in London requires an **International Youth Hostel Federation (IYHF)** or **Youth Hostel Association of England and Wales (YHA) membership card.** Overseas visitors can buy one at YHA London Headquarters and often at the hostels themselves for £9. An **International Guest Pass** (£1.50) permits residents of places other than England and Wales to stay at hostel rates without joining the hostel association. After you purchase six of these Guest Passes, you attain full membership. A membership card for residents of England and Wales costs £8.30 for seniors (ages 21 and over), £4.40 for juniors (16-20) and £1.90 for youths (5-15).

The cheerful staff members, often international travelers themselves, invariably keep London YHA hostels clean and refreshingly well-managed. They can also often provide a range of helpful information on the environs of the hostel. Plan ahead, since London hostels are crowded. During the summer, beds fill up months in advance. In recent years, hostels have not always been able to accommodate every written request for reservations, much less on-the-spot inquiries. But hostels frequently keep some beds free until a few days before—it's always worth checking for vacancies the week before, the day before, or the morning of your intended stay. To secure a place, show up as early as possible and expect to stand in line. With a Visa or Mastercard, you can book in advance by phone. Or you can write to the warden of the individual hostel. Off-season, finding a place will not require such of a strain. But always phone ahead before you schlep across town.

For hostel information, visit the jumbo-market **YHA London Headquarters,** 14 Southampton St., WC2E 7HY (tel. 240 5236; tel. 240 3158 for membership inquiries; Tube: Covent Garden; open Mon.-Wed. and Fri. 10am-6pm, Thurs. 10am-7pm, Sat. 9am-6pm); or the new **YHA Kensington,** 174 Kensington High St., W8 (tel. 938 2948; Tube: High St. Kensington; open Mon.-Wed. and Fri. 10am-6pm, Thurs. 10am-7pm, Sat. 10am-5:30pm).

All permanent hostels listed here are equipped with large lockers that require a padlock. Bring your own or purchase one from the hostel for £2.50.

Prices below are listed by age group: seniors (ages 21 and over); juniors (16-20); and youths (5-15). Prices include rental of a sleeping sack.

Holland House (King George VI Memorial Youth Hostel), Holland Walk, Kensington, W8 (tel. 937 0748), next to Holland Park. Tube: Holland Park or High St. Kensington. The walk from High St. Kensington, while slightly longer, stays better lit at night. Restored Jacobean mansion in a palatial setting on the east side of Holland Park. Londoners play cricket in the park while befuddled squirrels and hostelers look on. Daily pick-up soccer games. Just renovated in 1991: new bathrooms and showers. Bright and clean, including a cafeteria featuring McDonald's chairs. 190 beds. Kitchen facilities and currency exchange available. Reception open 7am-11:30pm. Fills very quickly. No curfew. £14, £12, £10. Breakfast from £2.30. Evening meals from £3.

Oxford Street, 14-18 Noel St., London W1 (tel. 734 1618). Tube: Oxford Circus. Bang in the heart of London. 87 beds in small, plush rooms of 2-4. Microwave available. No laundry. No curfew and 24-hr. security. Currency exchange available. Monitored baggage room during the day. Reception open 7am-10:30pm. Fills up in a flash. Superb location makes up for the expense: £15, £13, and £11. Continental breakfast £1.90. (Walk east on Oxford St. and turn right on Poland St.; the hostel stands next to a rather bleak mural.)

Earl's Court, 38 Bolton Gdns., SW5 (tel. 373 7083). Tube: Earl's Ct. A converted townhouse in a leafy residential neighborhood, peacefully set just off the Earl's Ct. one-way system. 124 beds in rooms of about 10 each. Extensive kitchen amenities. Ongoing modernization should provide expanded shower facilities. Laundry. Currency exchange available. Reception open 7am-midnight in summer, 7am-11pm in winter. No curfew. £12, £11, £9. Breakfast and dinner £2-3; optional vegetarian meals. (Exit from the tube station onto Earl's Court Rd. and turn right; Bolton Gardens is the fifth street on your left.)

Hampstead Heath, 4 Wellgarth Rd., Hampstead, NW11 (tel. (081) 458 9054). Tube: Golders Green, then ½-mi. walk along North End Rd. Serenely positioned at the edge of Hampstead Heath extension and round the corner from The Bull and Bush. Despite its peaceful surroundings, this hostel often falls victim to the school parties that barrage the hostels of Central London. The only wheelchair-accessible hostel in London. 220 beds in surprisingly sumptuous dorms. Cooking and laundry facilities. Currency exchange. Reception open 7am-11pm. No curfew—code-operated doors. £12, £11, £9.

Highgate, 84 Highgate West Hill, N6 6LU (tel. (081) 340 1831). Tube: Archway, then a ¾-mile walk up Highgate Hill and Highgate High St., or take bus #210 or 271 from tube to Highgate Village. Walk down South Grove, which becomes Highgate West Hill. A Georgian house in the middle of historic Highgate village. The walk up the hill can prove strenuous, but you can restore yourself with a pint at The Flask. Out-of-the-way location and pleasant neighborhood make for a homey hostel. 74 beds. Kitchen stocks remarkable crockery. Reception open 7am-10am and 5-11pm. Doors locked 10am-5pm. £9.50, £8, £7.

Wood Green, Wood Green Halls of Residence, Brabant Rd., N22 (tel. (081) 881 4432). Tube: Wood Green, then walk 2 min. west on Station Rd. 157 single rooms in a modern Middlesex Polytechnic building, taken over each summer by the YHA. Laundry and self-catering facilities. No curfew. All-night security guard. £10, regardless of age. Open mid-July to mid-Sept. and 3 weeks at Easter. For advance bookings and enquiries during the closed period, contact the Hampstead Heath hostel.

White Hart Lane, All Saints Halls of Residence, White Hart Lane, N17 8HR (tel. (081) 885 3234). Tube: Seven Sisters, then BR to White Hart Lane, or BR direct from Liverpool St.; or tube to Wood Green, then bus #W3. Travelcard will undoubtedly be the cheapest way here. Women should avoid walking alone to the hostel from the tube at night. More completely unremarkable Middlesex Poly Halls, in a solidly working class district reminiscent of Coketown in *Hard Times.* Two kestrels nest in an adjacent house. 170 beds, mainly in plain, decently sized singles, with wash basins. Bathtubs only. Self-catering and laundry facilities. Reception open 7am-2pm and 5pm-midnight. No curfew. £10, regardless of age. Open mid-July to Aug. 31. Contact Hampstead Heath hostel during closed period.

Epping Forest Youth Hostel, Wellington Hall, High Beach, Loughton, Essex IG10 4AG (tel. (081) 508 5161). Tube: Loughton (zone 6, 45 min. from central London), then a good 2-mi.

walk (have a map handy) through the forest. A taxi from the tube station costs £2.70 for 1 or 2 people—about 60p extra for additional passengers. A marvelous retreat from London havoc and London prices. Set remotely in the heart of 6000 acres of ancient woodland. Simple washing facilities and no laundry, but large and well-equipped kitchen. Cheap and utterly rural. Reception open 7-10am and 5-11pm. £5.50, £4.40, £3.50. Open April-Oct.

Carter Lane, 36 Carter Lane, London EC4V 5AD (tel. 236 4965). Tube: St. Paul's or Blackfriars. Closed for refurbishment and due to reopen in early 1992, but call ahead for up-to-date information.

Private Hostels and Halls of Residence

Private hostels, which do not require an IYHF card, almost always have a youthful clientele and often contain coed dorms. Some have kitchen facilities. There are usually no curfews.

London's university residences often accommodate visitors for limited periods during the long summer break (usually July-Aug.), and often during Christmas and Easter vacations. Many of these halls are not exceptionally pleasant—unless you enjoy tall, barren buildings and box-like rooms. Most charge £10-20, although some have student discounts. Reliable, well-maintained, and well-located, they substitute convenience for character. Write to the bursar of the hall several months before your arrival. (Contact individual halls for London University residences.) These places frequently have short-term openings.

Bloomsbury

Passfield Hall, 1 Endsleigh Place, WC1 (tel. 387 3584 or 387 7743). Tube: Euston Sq. A London School of Economics hall between Gordon and Tavistock Sq. Lots of long-term residents and a boisterous atmosphere. Rooms vary tremendously in size, but all have desks and high ceilings. Laundry and cooking facilities. Singles £16. Doubles £25. Triples £33, breakfast included. Open July-Sept. (rooms scarce July and early Aug.), and for 1 month around Easter.

Carl Saunders Hall, 18-24 Fitzroy St., W1 (tel. 580 6338). Tube: Warren St. A newer LSE building west of Tottenham Court Road. Laundry facilities, TV lounge. 96 single study bedrooms, 12 doubles. Singles £18-34. Doubles £36-68. Breakfast included. Self-catering apartments across the street also available, min. stay 1 week. Weekly: doubles £217, triples £335, quads £434, quints £542, excluding VAT. Open July-Sept.

Rosebery Avenue Hall, 90 Rosebery Ave., EC1 (tel. 278 3251). Tube: Angel, also buses #19 and 38 from Piccadilly. Further out of the way than the other halls, and plainer. Carpeted, compact study bedrooms with sink, desk, wardrobe, and shelves. Bar, game lounge, kitchens, laundry facilities, TV room, and small garden. Singles £16.50-19. Doubles £25. Breakfast included. Discounts for stays over 5 weeks. Open June-Sept., and for 5 weeks around Easter.

John Adams Hall, 15-23 Endsleigh St., WC1 (tel. 387 4086), off Tavistock Sq. Tube: Euston Sq. Elegant London University building. High-ceilinged rooms come in different sizes; some have small balconies overlooking the street. 124 singles, 22 doubles. Laundry facilities, TV lounge, requisite ping-pong table, and quiet reading room. Reception open Mon.-Fri. 8am-1pm and 2-10pm, Sat.-Sun. 9am-1:30pm and 5:30-10pm. Singles £19. Doubles £34. English breakfast included. Weekly: singles £123, doubles £222. Open July-Sept. and at Easter. Book well in advance and confirm in writing; usually no deposit required.

Central Club Hotel, 16-22 Great Russell St., WCI (tel. 636-7512). Tube: Tottenham Court Rd. A stone's throw from the British Museum. Clean, comfortable rooms with firm beds, high ceilings, and minimal decor. Hardwood floors, TV, phones, hotpots in singles and doubles. Breakfast not included, but cheap coffee shop downstairs. Don't expect a lovely view. Laundry facilities (£1 per load) and an excellent basement swimming pool. Ideal for longer stays. Singles £30. Doubles £55. Triples £49. Quads £65.20. Quints £69. Weekly: singles £200, doubles £319. Monthly: singles £675, doubles £1076. Special monthly rate for students (with ID): singles £506, doubles £807.

Central University of Iowa Hostel, 7 Bedford Pl., WC1 (tel. 580 1121). Tube: Holborn or Russell Sq. On a quiet B&B-lined street near the British Museum. Bright, spartan rooms. Laundry facilities, TV room. 2-week max. stay. Reception open May-Aug. 8am-1pm and 3-8pm. Dorm rooms £13.50 per person. Doubles £29. All-you-can-eat continental breakfast included. Write as soon after April 1 as possible.

Museum Inn, 27 Montague St., WC1 (tel. 580 5360), off Bloomsbury Sq. Tube: Holborn, Tottenham Court Rd., or Russell Sq. Great location and young international clientele compensate for the drab dorms. Rock music plays at reception. No curfew. Dorm rooms £9-11 per person. Doubles £29. Triples £35. Quads £45. Continental breakfast included. Weekly rates available Oct.-April.

Helen Graham House (YWCA), 57 Great Russell St., London WC1B (tel. 430 0834). Tube: Holborn or Russell Sq. 289 beds, but only 20 or so for men. TV lounge. Laundry and kitchen facilities. Employment and long-term housing advice given. Both singles and doubles, but singles scarce because women already sharing rooms receive preference over newcomers. Watch out for the 6-month min. stay rule. 6-month waiting list. Weekly: singles £45, doubles £34 per person.

Tonbridge School Clubs, Ltd., (tel. 837 4406). Corner of Judd and Cromer St., 2 blocks south of St. Pancras station. Tube: King's Cross/St. Pancras. The price is right for desperadoes. Iffy neighborhood, but then you won't be around the club in the day—lockout 10am-10pm. Students with non-British passports only. Men sleep in basement gym, women in karate-club hall. Blankets and foam pads provided, hot showers, TV lounge. Storage space for backpacks during the day, but safety is not guaranteed. Student ID required. Arrive 10-11:30pm, leave by 10am. £2.50 per person.

Connaught Hall, 36-45 Tavistock Sq., WC1H 9EB (tel. 387 6181). In a lush square off Upper Woburn Pl. Tube: Euston Sq. London University Hall catering primarily to large, academic groups but private travelers accommodated as availability permits. 200 small, single study bedrooms with wardrobes, desks, basins, and tea-making facilities. Decidedly staid atmosphere. Laundromat, reading rooms, private garden, and TV lounges. Singles £18. Full English breakfast included. Open July-Sept. except for 3 weeks; call or write for dates. Book well in advance.

Hughes Parry Hall, Cartwright Gdns., WC1H 9EF (tel. 387 1477). Tube: Russell Sq. Mammoth modern London University hall with plain, smallish institutional singles. Squash and tennis, laundry facilities, libraries, TV lounge, bar, 24-hr. porter. Students: singles £14, breakfast and dinner included. Non-students: singles £17, breakfast included, £20 with dinner. Open July-Aug.

Canterbury Hall, 12-28 Cartwright Gdns., WC1H 9EB (tel. 387 5526). Tube: Russell Sq. A smaller, older hall sandwiched between Hughes Parry and Commonwealth Halls. Organized groups get the lion's share of accommodations here but some individual rooms free up during the summer. 250 small, single rooms. One bathroom with bathtub for 2 singles. Squash courts, tennis courts, 3 TV lounges, and laundry facilities (£1 per load). No curfew. No student ID required. Singles £19. English breakfast included. Open July-Aug., except 3 weeks in late Aug.-early Sept.

Commonwealth Hall, 1-11 Cartwright Gdns., WC1H 9EB (tel. 387 0311). Tube: Russell Sq. Rooms and facilities similar to those in Canterbury Hall. 408 small singles with institutional decor. Squash and tennis, laundry facilities, ping pong, TV lounges, library, music rooms, and a pleasant bar (pint of beer, £1.20). No curfew. No student ID required. No inquiries before June. Singles £20; students, £14. Breakfast and evening meal included. Open July-Aug.

Paddington and Bayswater

Centre Français, 61 Chepstow Place, Notting Hill Gate, W2 (tel. 221 8134). Tube: Notting Hill Gate or Bayswater. A delightful Gallic atmosphere pervades this immaculate hostel. In a chic residential area—look out for Princess Di delivering her sons to school round the corner. Bilingual staff welcomes a vibrant international clientele, half of whom hail from France. No curfew. 180 beds. All but 2 rooms have washbasins. Free lockers. Singles £21. Doubles £18 per person. Triples/ Quads £15 per person. Off-season prices drop £1-2. Dorm rooms £12 per person. Weekly: singles £126, doubles £110 per person, triples and quads £89 per person, dorm rooms £82 per person. Further reductions after 5 weeks. Breakfast included. Book at least 2 months in advance, if possible—phone reservations by Visa and MC accepted.

Palace Hotel, 31 Palace Ct., W2 (tel. 221 5628). Tube: Notting Hill Gate or Queensway. Young community atmosphere and big bright dorm rooms make this a great deal for hostelers. TV lounge and pool table. 8 beds per room. £8, weekly £ 50.

Quest Hotel, 45 Queensborough Terrace, W2 (tel. 229 7782). Tube: Queensway. A terraced house on an intermittently renovated street. Standard hostel accommodation in rooms of 4-8 beds. Central location. Kitchen facilities, snack bar, and free music videos. No curfew. £8.50-10per person. Key deposit £2.

Talbot Hotel, Talbot Sq., W2 (tel. 402 7202). Tube: Paddington This hotel has now co-opted 4 buildings. Basic but habitable rooms. Rather thin mattresses on bunk beds. You'd be hard pressed to find cheaper central accommodation. TV lounge and kitchen facilities. 24-hr. security. Arrive in the morning to secure a place. Very few singles £10. Twins £20, £120 per week. Bed in rooms of 3-4 £8, £48 per week. Key deposit £5.

Glendale Hotel, 8 Devonshire Terrace, W2 (tel. 262 1770). Tube: Paddington. Management really crams 'em in. Noisy but convivial. Continental breakfast included. Self-catering facilities. Doubles £25. Beds in 4-bunk room £9.50. In 6-bunk room £9.

Lancaster Hall Hotel Youth Annexe (YMCA), 35 Craven Terrace, W2 (tel. 723 9276). Tube: Lancaster Gate. For persons under 25, basic hostel facilities at the German YMCA in London. All rooms have washbasins. Singles £18. Doubles £32. Triples £40. Quads £50.

Kensington, Chelsea and Victoria

King's College, part of the University of London, controls summer bookings for the residence halls listed below. Their locations are often hard to beat. Accommodations include continental breakfast, linen, soap, towel, and cooking and laundry facilities. There are no curfews. To reserve a room from July through September, write before May 1 to Elspeth Young, King's Campus Vacation Bureau, 552 King's Rd., London SW10 0UA (tel. 351 6011). A £5 deposit is required for each week reserved. For last minute arrangements, call the halls directly. Prices vary slightly according to location, but hover at £21-23 per person in single and double rooms. Accommodations are available in 1992 from January 2-7, March 26 to April 26, July 9 to September 30, and December 20-23.

Queen Elizabeth Hall, Campden Hill Rd., W8 (tel. 333 4255). Tube: High St. Kensington. Walk one block west and two north from the Tube. One of the finest of the King's College halls. Set in a picturesque location midway between Holland Park and Kensington Gardens.

Lightfoot Hall, Manresa Rd. at King's Rd., SW3 (tel. 351 2488). Tube: Sloane Sq. or South Kensington. From South Kensington, take bus #49; from Sloane Sq., bus #11. Prime location. Rooms in a modern and institutional tower block.

Ingram Court, 552 King's Rd. (no tel.). Tube: Fulham Broadway, then a 10-min. walk. One of the most popular halls, located on the main campus. Green lawn with romantic duck pond in the middle. No charge for use of the two tennis courts.

Wellington Hall, 71 Vincent Sq., Westminster, SW1 (tel. 834 4740). Tube: Victoria, then walk one long block along Vauxhall Bridge Rd. and turn left on Rochester Row to Vincent Sq. Old brick hall on a pleasant, quiet square where cricket is polished and perfected.

The following cost less than the residence halls listed above (about £16-18 per person), but a lack of convenience accompanies the price difference: **King's College Hall,** Champion Hill, SE5 (tel. 733 2167; BR to Denmark Hill); and **Malcolm Gavin Hall,** Beachcroft Rd., SW17 (tel. (081) 767 3119; Tube: Tooting Bec).

Other private residence halls and hostels include:

Curzon House Hotel, 58 Courtfield Gdns., SW5 (tel. 373 6745). Tube: Gloucester Rd. A *Let's Go* home away from home. Charles, the owner, has a knack for hiring the friendliest of managers and staff. Kitchen facilities, TV lounge, and no curfew. Book at least 1 month in advance. Continental breakfast included. Dorms £13 per person. Singles £26. Doubles £34. Triples £45. Quads £64. Reduced weekly rates in winter.

Queen Alexandra's House, Kensington Gore, SW7 (tel. 589 3635 or 589 4053), by the Albert Hall. Tube: South Kensington. Women only. Ornate Victorian building next to the Proms. Welcoming, with a touch of class. Cozy rooms, window seats. Kitchen and laundry facilities, sitting room, Tyler tiara, and sunny dining hall. All this and an English breakfast too. Rooms available mid-July to mid-Aug.; send written reservations weeks in advance to Mrs. Makey. £20 per person.

Albert Hotel, 191 Queens Gate, SW7 (tel. 584 3019). Tube: South Kensington or Gloucester Rd. Bus #2 from South Kensington. Large, smoke-free, but spartan rooms in an elegant Victorian building. Most rooms have private facilities. Great location, near the Kensington museums and Hyde Park. TV lounge includes pool table. Deposit valuables at reception. 24-hr. reception. Continental breakfast included. No reservations; call when you arrive in London. Dorms £8. Singles £18. Doubles £28. Weekly: bed in four-person dorms £51, in six-person dorms £45; singles £100, doubles £120.

Anne Elizabeth House Hostel, 30 Collingham Pl., SW5 (tel. 370 4821). Tube: Earl's Ct. Caters to the needs of travelers on extended stays: kitchen, laundry, and ironing board. Right around the corner from the biggest supermarket in London. Dorm-style rooms. No curfew. Continental breakfast heaped on. Prices vary depending on the exact dates of stay. Singles £14-17, doubles £23-29, triples £31-39. Larger rooms available. Weekly rates 10% off; longer-term rates 12% off. Reserve 1 month in advance for the summer.

Lee Abbey International Students' Club, 57-67 Lexham Gdns., W8 6JJ (tel. 373 7242). Tube: Earl's Ct. Large, private student accommodations. Student status required for the school year. Write to the warden at least 1 month in advance and include a self-addressed stamped envelope or an international reply coupon. Continental breakfast with the option of purchasing inexpensive weekly meal tickets (£2 for dinner, £11 for a week's ticket). Flat deposit £20. All fees payable upon arrival. Wide range of rooms. Singles £14.60-18.80. Doubles £32-34. Triples £35-45. Weekly: singles £102-131, doubles £222-238, triples £247-308. Fantastic long-term rates after 1 month (singles £91-118 per week, doubles £200-212 per week).

Fieldcourt House, 32 Courtfield Gdns., SW5 (tel. 373 0152). Tube: Gloucester Rd. Dorm rooms large and spare, with astronomically high ceilings. Rickety lockers and a gloomy atmosphere. Small TV and spongy furniture in large lounge. Continental breakfast included. Range of dorms and rooms: quints £9 per person, quads £10, triples £11, doubles £12. Singles £35. Weekly rates £50 per person in a larger dorm, £65 in a triple, £70 in a double, and £85 for a single. Deposit £10.

Maranton House Hostel, 14 Barkston Gdns., SW5 (tel. 373 5782). Tube: Earl's Ct. Newly tiled private bathrooms and a bar downstairs. Watch out for minotaurs in the labyrinthine bathrooms. Dorm rooms shared with only 3 or 4 other people. Continental breakfast. Small dorms £10. Singles £25-26. Doubles £35-45. Kitchen facilities £3 extra. Key deposit £5.

Elizabeth House (YWCA Hostel), 118 Warwick Way, SW1 (tel. 630 0741), at St. George's Dr. Tube: Victoria. Not for women only; young people, students, and families with children over 5 welcome. Large and unsullied rooms. Friendly staff diminishes the slight institutional feel. Both smoking and non-smoking TV lounges. Continental breakfast. Phone booth in lobby looks like some strange brain-sucking device. 24-hour reception service. Reserve 2-3 months in advance. Non-refundable £10 deposit required to secure a reservation. Dorms £13 per person. Singles £20. Doubles £35-36. Weekly rates: singles £130, doubles £220. Larger rooms available.

North London

International Student House, 229 Great Portland St., W1 (tel. 631 3223), at the foot of Regent's Park. Tube: Great Portland St. 60s building lacks architectural merit but compensates with great location. A thriving metropolis with its own films, discos, study-groups, expeditions, parties, and mini-markets. Use of multi-gym costs 60p per hour. Well-stocked information desk. 300 beds in doubles and singles. Well-maintained but uninspiring rooms, although many in the second building at 10 York Terrace East have views of Regent's Park. Lockable cupboards. No curfew. Singles £20. Doubles £17 per person. Triples £14 per person. Quads £10 per person. English breakfast included. Reserve through main office on Great Portland St. at least 1 month ahead, earlier for academic year. Letter of confirmation required.

James Leicester Hall, Market Rd., London N7 9PN (tel. 607 3250 or 607 5417). Tube: Caledonian Rd. A Polytechnic of North London residence hall right around the corner from the tube station. 156 beds. Bright, modern buildings clustered around a courtyard. All rooms have wash basins. Licensed bar. No curfew. Singles only, £16.35. English breakfast included. Advance reservations compulsory—phone at least 5 days in advance and send a letter of confirmation to the Bookings Officer at the above address. Open July-Sept and Easter.

Tufnell Park Hall, Huddleston Rd., Tufnell Park N7 (tel. 607 3250). Tube: Tufnell Park. The second Polytechnic of North London residence hall. A modern tower block set in the residential area of Tufnell Park, reportedly the editorial center of the universe. 207 not unfriendly single rooms. Licensed bar. Prices, opening times, and reservation details same as for James Leicester Hall—all bookings taken through the James Leicester office. (Walk down Tufnell Park Rd., turn left, and go to the end of Huddleston Rd.) Open July 8-Sept. 22.

Bed and Breakfast Hotels

Bloomsbury

Despite its proximity to the West End, Bloomsbury manages to maintain a quiet residential atmosphere. Hotels here cost a pound or two more than those in less gracious areas, but you're paying for location and style. Feel the knowledge from the British Museum diffuse into you as you lie in bed.

Budget hotels cram along Gower St. (Tube: Goodge St.). Singles go for around £25, doubles for £35, including VAT and an English breakfast. The hotels all line one side of the street and have exactly the same layout, which means that all have the same wild variations in room size. Singles tend to be small.

Regency House Hotel, 71 Gower St., WC1 (tel. 637 1804). Clean, fresh, cool blue rooms with TV. Small garden. Book well in advance to be guaranteed a room. Singles £25, with shower £45. Doubles £35, with shower £55. Triples £48. Quads £58. Quints £68. Several pounds cheaper in winter.

Ridgemount Hotel, 65 Gower St., WC1 (tel. 636 1141). Bright, agreeable rooms with flowery wallpaper and firm beds, lovingly maintained by gracious owners. Comfy TV lounge. Doubles £36. Triples £47.25. Quads £60.

Jesmond Hotel, 63 Gower St., WC1 (tel. 636 3199). Cozy and neat, if slightly worn-looking rooms. TV lounge. Electric hot pots with coffee and tea in all rooms. Singles £24. Doubles £37. Triples £57. Private bath £12-15 extra.

Maree Hotel, 25-27 Gower St., WC1 (tel. 636 4868). Spare and spartan, but one of the cheapest on the street. Spacious TV lounge. Continental breakfast. Shades of mustard and beige throughout. Singles £22. Doubles £32. Triples £36. Quads £48. Big winter discount: singles £16; doubles £24.

Garth Hotel, 69 Gower St., WC1 (tel. 636 5761). Some rooms charmingly furnished, others (mostly smaller) more standard. TV lounge, helpful manager. Singles £25. Doubles £35. Triples £45. Quads £56.

The Langland Hotel, 29-31 Gower St., WC1 (tel. 636 5801). The clean, well-appointed rooms offset the uninspiring decor. Generous English breakfast. TV lounge. Singles £28. Doubles £38, with shower £45. Triples £45, with shower £48. Quads £64, with shower £80. Winter discounts average 20-25%. Major credit cards accepted.

The grass grows a little greener and the traffic jams a little less on the other side of the British Museum—but the rates run a little higher. (Tube: Holborn or Russell Sq.) The area around Russell Sq. draws a preponderance of American visitors, much as Earl's Ct. attracts Australians.

Thanet, 8 Bedford Pl., WC1 (tel. 636 2869). Family-run hotel with speckless, spacious rooms. Color TV, radio, and hot pots with tea and coffee in every room. Rooms in the back overlook a peaceful patio. Singles £33. Doubles £45, with private bath £55. Triples £55, with shower £65. Quads £70. Good breakfast menu. To book in advance, send a personal check or your credit card number for the first night.

Repton House, 31 Bedford Pl., WC1 (tel. 636 7045). Cheaper and only slightly less ornate than its neighbors. Back rooms overlook a rose garden. Continental breakfast included. Singles £25. Doubles £35. Triples with private bath £55.

Hotel Crichton, 36 Bedford Pl., WC1 (tel. 637 3955). Has its share of peeling paint, but standard rooms come with TV, phone, tea-making facilities, and private safe. Singles £28. Doubles £45-50. Triples £57. Quads £69. With shower, £2.50 extra. Major credit cards accepted.

Cosmo House Hotel, 27 Bloomsbury Sq., WC1 (tel. 636 4661 or 636 0577), on a tranquil square off Southampton Row. Clean, light, small but comfortable rooms with color TVs and jazzy bedspreads. Rooms in the back overlook a tree-filled garden. Singles £27. Doubles £42. Triples £55.

Celtic Hotel, 62 Guilford St., WC1 (tel. 837 9258), around the corner from the Hotel Russell. Excellent location in the heart of Bloomsbury. More pleasant than it may seem from the outside. Clean, spare rooms and fine facilities. Payment required in advance. Singles £28.50. Doubles £40.

Ruskin Hotel, 23-24 Montague St., WC1 (tel. 636 7388). Scrupulously clean and well-kept modern furnishings, but a little pricier. Back rooms quiet. Singles £32. Doubles £44-48, with private shower £55-60.

An invariably pleasant set of Bloomsbury B&Bs blooms in **Cartwright Gardens** (Tube: Russell Sq. or King's Cross/St. Pancras). Although a bit farther from most sights and somewhat more expensive, they offer plusher rooms and tennis in the gardens. Families will find comfort at all of them. Apart from crucial distinctions in carpet patterns, they are much of a muchness. Most accept MC and Visa.

Jenkins Hotel, 45 Cartwright Gdns., WC1 (tel. 387 2067). Quiet, genteel family-run B&B. Bright, tidy rooms with soft pastel wallpaper, floral prints, phones, teapots, color TV, hairdryers, and mini-refrigerators. Some with charming coal-burning fireplaces. Small singles £30. Doubles £44, with private bath £53. Triples with bath £67.

Euro Hotel and George Hotel, 58-60 and 51-53 Cartwright Gdns., WC1 (tel. 387 1528 or 387 6789). Ornate rooms with TV, radio, and telephone. Reserve well in advance. Children under 13 sharing parents' room £8. Singles £29.50, with shower £35. Doubles £43, with shower £47. Triples £52, with shower £57.

Crescent Hotel, 49-50 Cartwright Gdns., WC1 (tel. 387 1515). Family-run with care; proprietor lives here. Attractive and homey, with full English breakfast and TV lounge. Singles £30, with shower £35. Doubles £44, with shower and toilet £53. Family rooms (for four) £66, with shower and toilet £74.

Grange House Hotel, 5 Endsleigh St., WC1 (tel. 380 0616), off Tavistock Sq. Tube: Euston Sq. Just on the other side of Upper Woburn, this B&B is more expensive but truly pristine. Immaculate, newly-furnished rooms with cool blue interiors. Second-story rooms open onto an ornate wrought-iron balcony. Breakfast served in your room. Singles £29.50. Doubles £47.

Mentone Hotel, 54 Cartwright Gdns., WC1 (tel. 387 3927). Pastel wallpaper, pink and lavender bedspreads in good-sized rooms. Bright neat hallways. All rooms with color TV. Singles £32. Doubles £42, with shower £56. Triples £56-60. Family rooms £68.

Devon Hotel, 56 Cartwright Gdns., WC1 (tel. 387 1719). Not as ornate as some of its neighbors, but just as cozy and comfortable. All rooms with color TV. Singles £30. Doubles £45, with private bath £50.

Bloomsbury's cheapest B&Bs cluster around tiny Argyle Square (Tube: King's Cross/St. Pancras)—a strip of grass enclosed within a run-down neighborhood of varicolored townhouses. Many of the so-called "hotels" in this area are actually guest houses, catering to low-income families whose long-term stays are subsidized by Camden Council. All of the hotels listed below accept tourists; many are cramped and drab, but can offer significant value to the budget traveler.

Hotel Apollo, 43 Argyle St., WC1 (tel. 837 5489). Bright rooms with lacy draperies and color TV. One of the neatest and cleanest on the block. Singles £20. Doubles £30.

Salters Hotel, 3-4 Crestfield St., WC1 (tel. 837 3817). Bright red all over in tidy rooms and halls. TV lounge, bar. Singles £25, with shower £28. Doubles £35, with shower £40.

Riviera Hotel, 14 Argyle Sq., WC1 (tel. 837 7159). Bright red carpets and floral wallpaper. All rooms with color TV. Singles £20, with shower £26. Doubles from £32.

Near Victoria Station

Victoria Station is a traveler's purgatory. In exchange for your penitence in fairly expensive accommodation, you will be rewarded with an ideal location, within walking distance from London's major attractions. To get a room for the summer, make reservations at least two weeks in advance, for some places even earlier. Most B&Bs require a deposit—usually the price of one night's stay—to secure your reservation. Be sure to ask the manager how to send the deposit, as few places accept foreign currency.

Most rooms include a sink, a color TV, and a full English breakfast. Private bathrooms and showers are normally, but not always, available, and cost extra. Also, if you know that you will be arriving after 11pm, let the proprietor know. Banging on the door in the middle of the night is rude and ineffectual.

All of these places charge lower rates in the winter. Furthermore, the competition grows fierce enough around here that many will negotiate a reduced rate for long stays, especially in low season. Show reluctance to take a room, and you may see prices plummet.

On **Belgrave Road** (Tube: Victoria or Pimlico), a noisy thoroughfare south of the station, ask for a back room or one on an upper story; these tend to be quieter.

Luna House Hotel, 47 Belgrave Rd., SW1 (tel. 834 5897). Take bus #24 to the doorstep. Incorporates Simone House next door. Inexpensive and clean. All rooms have private baths and many have firm, new mattresses. Reserve at least 1 month in advance. Singles £20. Doubles £34, with showers and facilities £42. Triples from £51. Winter rates up to 40% lower.

Sidney Hotel, 74-76 Belgrave Rd., SW1 (tel. 834 2738). Newly renovated and very comfortable. All rooms equipped with telephone and tea- and coffee-making facilities. Tasteful decor in sizable rooms. 10% senior citizen discount. Join the nineties and reserve your room by fax (tel. 630 0973). Singles £28-37. Doubles £42-48. Triples £60.

Melbourne House, 79 Belgrave Rd., SW1 (tel. 828 3516). Closer to Pimlico than Victoria. Large, immaculate rooms in this, the health food of B&Bs. No private facilities, but pristine common baths and showers. Owned and operated for the past 20 years by a genial Maltese family. Pleasant tiled courtyard in back. Singles £24. Doubles £34.

Belgrave House Hotel, 30-32 Belgrave Rd., SW1 (tel. 834 8620). Large, spotless, and recently renovated rooms, with double glazing on the street side. Red leather furniture and chandelier in lobby give the place the air of a hotel rather than of a homelike B&B. Singles £25-30. Doubles £35-40. Prepare to bargain. Extra bed £12.

Easton Hotel, 38 Belgrave Rd., SW1 (tel. 834 5938). Large, basic, and tidy rooms, some with TV. Lounge with bar downstairs. Kind and efficient management. Singles £28-38. Doubles £38-48. Triples £48.

Marne and Alexander Hotels, 34 Belgrave Rd., SW1 (tel. 834 5195), just past Eccleston Square, close to the station. Run by the same family for 25 years and the wear really shows. Spacious, high-ceilinged rooms. Some mattresses past their prime. Management arranges home stays for students in association with Homestay U.K. Write 6 months in advance. Singles £25-30. Doubles £35-40. Triples from £50. Larger rooms available.

Dover Hotel, 44 Belgrave Rd., SW1 (tel. 821 9085). Most rooms include the full suite of extras: private facilities, telephone, hair dryer, and a tea and coffee bar. Rooms and bathrooms clean but oddly decorated, with some unfortunate color combinations. Singles from £35. Doubles from £45. Triples from £60.

Calvados Hotel, 42 Belgrave Rd., SW1 (tel. 834 6425). Some rooms have very plush beds and bathrooms, although most of the place is worn. Singles £32-34. Doubles £40-44.

St. George's Drive (Tube: Victoria or Pimlico), parallel to Belgrave Rd. and one block south, proves quieter and generally less worn. **Warwick Way,** which crosses both near Victoria Station, resembles the other two.

Olympic Hotel, 115 Warwick Way, SW1 (tel. 828 0757). A solid choice. All rooms sport TVs, clocks, and cushy beds; some balconies. Breakfast here celebrated as a social event. Rooms sometimes available on short notice. Singles £25-35. Doubles £35-40.

Georgian House Hotel, 35 St. George's Dr. (tel. 834 1438). Soft beds, newly and well furnished rooms make this hotel very comfortable. Firendly management. Singles £26-28. Doubles £45 and up.

Arden House Hotel, 10-12 St. George's Dr., SW1 (tel. 834 2988). Victoria Station uncomfortably close; light sleepers should bring earplugs. Soft mattresses and large, spartan rooms. Some rooms come with baths instead of showers. Rooms sometimes available on short notice. Singles £25-28. Doubles £35-45. Triples £48 and up. Larger rooms available.

Greystones Hotel, 73 Warwick Way, SW1 (tel. 834 0470). Smallish rooms without bathrooms, and claustrophobic corridors, but clean and respectable. Upstanding proprietor. Singles £23. Doubles £27.

Colliers Hotel, 97 Warwick Way, SW1 (tel. 834 6931). Smallish rooms, with tea and coffee facilities. Closets deceptively small, mattresses uncomfortably soft. Large common bathrooms. Tacky carpet in some rooms. 8% discount for senior citizens. Reserve 1 week in advance. Singles from £24. Doubles from £32. Triples £42.

For a hotel off the main thoroughfares, but still within easy walking distance of Victoria Station, try one of these:

Oxford House, 92-94 Cambridge St., SW1 (tel. 834 6467). A fortuitous combination of kindness, aesthetic logic, a quiet location, and good cooking. Run by a hospitable family and their 2 corpulent pets, China the Cat and Hannibal the Rabbit. Large rooms and firm beds ensure a good night's sleep. Reserve 3-4 weeks in advance, but give them a try even if you've just arrived. Singles £26. Doubles £36. Triples £45. Quads £44-54.

Windsor Guest House, 36 Alderney St., SW1 (tel. 828 7922), off Warwick Way 1 block south of Cambridge St. Clean and simple B&B at an unbeatable price. Breakfast room features a Trinitron and solid wooden tables. Spacious rooms with a safe, homey feel. Kind manager prefers not to accept reservations far in advance. Singles £20. Doubles £26-30. Triples £36.

Melita House Hotel, 33-35 Charlwood St., SW1 (tel. 828 0471). Turn right near the end of Belgrave Rd. Family-run and clean, with small, dull rooms. Eclectic decor and furnishings. Geriatric mattresses on some beds. Talkative manager and well-perfumed bathrooms. Reserve 1 month in advance. Singles £30. Doubles £42. Triples from £51.

Historic **Ebury Street** lies west of Victoria station in the heart of Belgravia. The B&Bs along this route get quieter, less worn, and more expensive. Those who can afford to stay here will enjoy a peaceful respite, away from the bustle of the station, but still close to London's major sights. Many B&Bs along Ebury St. cater to regular clients and consequently have a less-than-usual tolerance for loud, obnoxious guests. Music fans should mosey down the street to see the house where Mozart composed his first symphony (180 Ebury St.).

Ebury House Hotel, 102 Ebury St., SW1 (tel. 730 1350). Well-decorated, well-scented, and spotless rooms. Comforters on all beds. No private facilities. Electric fireplace in family rooms. Energetic housekeeper serves breakfast-'til-you-drop. Experienced management gives sight-seeing advice. Reserve 3 weeks in advance. Singles £36. Doubles £48-60. Triples £60 and up.

Eaton House Hotel, 125 Ebury St., SW1 (tel. 730 8781). A small, homey B&B, family-run for over 20 years. All 10 rooms have new beds, but none have private facilities. Soap, towels, TV, and hair dryer provided. Reserve at least 1 month in advance. Woody the family cat really swings. Singles from £28. Doubles £40. Triples £54.

Westminster House, 96 Ebury St. (tel. 730 4302). Another slightly expensive and modestly luxurious B&B on Ebury St. No private facilities, but large common baths available. In addition to the normal amenities, all rooms have tea- and coffee-making facilities. Watch Casper the fish topple the statue in his tank at breakfast. Try to reserve 3-4 weeks in advance. Singles £28. Doubles £38-44. Triples from £56.

Pyms Hotel, 118 Ebury St., SW1 (tel. 730 4986). Spiffy decor and a kind management present a warm welcome. Perhaps the only B&B brave enough to have white carpet, walls, and bed-covers—it's gotta be clean. Small breakfast room decorated with fresh flowers. Reserve 1 month in advance. Worth the expense if you can afford it. Singles £40 and up. Doubles £55 and up. Larger rooms available.

Paddington and Bayswater

A humble village in 1820, Paddington became a major railway terminus of the Industrial Revolution only three decades later. It soon became a suburb, and as the 19th century wore on, part of London proper. Today, the rows of terraces and trees lining the wide avenues don't do much to cheer up depressing accommodations. Undistinguished hotels abound—expect nothing more than a plain, characterless room. Slightly decrepit B&Bs cluster around Norfolk Sq. and Sussex Gdns. As you travel west, the hotels become vaguely less anonymous. (Tube: Paddington, unless noted otherwise.)

Garden Court Hotel, 30-31 Kensington Gardens Sq., W2 (tel. 229 2553). Tube: Bayswater. Clean rooms with telephones. Aspires to acceptance into a higher class of hotel. Singles £25, with shower £27. Doubles £37, with shower £49. Triples £49, with shower £55.

Ruddimans Hotel, 160 Sussex Gdns., W2 (tel. 723-1026). Unfinished wood paneling gives these bright rooms a strange cabin-like feel. Very clean, with washbasin and TV in room. Singles £25, with shower and toilet £28. Doubles £34, with shower and toilet £38.

Hyde Park Rooms Hotel, 137 Sussex Gdns., W2 2RX (tel. 723 0225 or 723 0965). Cheery proprietor will not hard sell her trim, decent rooms. All come with TV and washbasin. Enticing, spotless bathtubs. Singles £20. Doubles £30.

Belvedere Hotel, 52 Norfolk Sq., W2 (tel. 723 8848). Well-maintained. Color TV and radio in every room. Singles £20, with shower £24. Doubles £32, with shower £40. Triples £42

Berry House Hotel, 12 Sussex Pl., W2 (tel. 723 7340). Amenable manager receives diverse international clientele. Bright rooms with TVs and kettles, and some with desks. Wow! Singles £25. Doubles £38, with shower £46.50. Triples £53.

Linden House Hotel, 4 Sussex Pl., W2 (tel. 723 9853). Trim, comfortable rooms. Lots of tasteful pink. TV and washbasin in each room. Singles £25.75. Doubles £37. Triples £49. Decently sized quads £60. Bathroom in suite £10-16 extra. 10% discount for a week stay.

Balmoral Hotel, 156 Sussex Gdns., W2 (tel. 723 7445). Neat and trim rooms. Satellite TV. Singles £25. Doubles £36. Triples £48.

Gower and Hopkins Hotel, 129 Sussex Gdns., W2 (tel. 262 2262). A touch more style than some of its neighbors. Pleasant, uncrowded rooms with showers. Singles £32. Doubles £42. Triples £57.

Westpoint Hotel, 170-172 Sussex Gdns., W2 (tel. 402 0281). Friendly staff, anonymous rooms. Mix 'n' match decor. Large couples may find the double beds a bit cramped. Singles from £22. Doubles £28, with shower £40. Triples £32.

Lords Hotel, 20-22 Leinster Sq., W2 (tel. 229 8877). Tube: Bayswater. Halls have high ceilings; basic rooms are clean, some have balconies. Tired wallpaper. Frequented by German students. Continental breakfast included. Singles £21.50, with shower £27.50. Doubles £32, with shower £38. Triples £42, with shower £47. Quads £50, with shower £55. £2-6 higher in summer.

Kensington and Chelsea

Times have certainly changed since Gilbert and Sullivan's day, when one of their characters had a nightmare that a swarm of relations who "all had got on at Sloane Square and South Kensington stations" invaded his coach. These days, the Royal Borough of Kensington and Chelsea is much more posh, and the few hotels here tend to the luxurious.

Vicarage Hotel, 10 Vicarage Gate, W8 (tel. 229 4030). Tube: High St. Kensington. Just like home—if you happen to live in a palace. Fabulous value. Dignified, friendly, newly renovated, and very clean. A cozy TV lounge, with cushions and old photos. Around the corner from Kensington Palace and Millionaires' Row. Singles £26. Doubles £48. Triples £57. Quads £62. Book 3 months ahead in the summer.

Abbey House Hotel, 11 Vicarage Gate, W8 (tel. 727 2594). Tube: High St. Kensington. Guests return year after year, drawn by charming owners, a superb location, and an English breakfast *par excellence.* Recently renovated rooms, each with color TV. Magnificent entrance hall does good impression of a palm house. All rooms have color TV. Singles £38. Doubles £48. Triples £58. Quads £68.

Ravna Gora, 29 Holland Park Ave., W11 (tel. 727 7725). Tube: Holland Park. Set back from a busy thoroughfare in a green yard. Quiet and family-run, with room for 50 guests. Spacious but styleless rooms. Free parking. Singles £23. Doubles £36, with shower £48. Triples £45-57. Quads £56-68.

More House, 53 Cromwell Rd., SW7 (tel. 589 6754 or 589 8433). Tube: South Kensington. Unmarked Victorian building across the street from the National History Museum. In between the Yemeni Embassy and the Brunei High Commission. Attractive old wooden furniture. New shower units. Relaxed student atmosphere. Cheap laundry and a small library. Open July-Aug. Singles £20. Doubles £35. Triples £45. £5 supplement for one night stands, 10% weekly discount.

Still farther south you can stay in **Chelsea,** home of the trendy-chic, but you'll have trouble finding moderately priced hotels south of the King's Rd. To get to Oakley St., sandwiched neatly between the river and King's Rd., take the tube to Sloane Sq., then bus #11, 19, or 22; or the tube to South Kensington, then bus #49.

Oakley Hotel, 73 Oakley St., SW3 (tel. 352 5599). Comfortable, youthful, and friendly. Cheerful Australasian staff. Cooking facilities; tea and coffee readily available. Videos, games, and travel magazines in lounge. Singles £19, £100 per week. Doubles £34. Triples £42. Beds in quads £9.50, £59 per week. Book in advance.

Earl's Court

A slightly tawdry bargain basement of accommodations spreads east of the monstrous Earl's Court Exhibition Building. The area feeds on the budget tourist trade, overdosing on travel agencies, souvenir shops, take-away eateries, and the vile *bureaux de change*. The accents of tireless, globe-trotting Australians dominate the neighborhood, sometimes known as "Kangaroo Court." Try to avoid late-night solo strolls in the area. (Tube: Earl's Ct.)

Philbeach Gardens, a quiet, tree-lined crescent north of the exhibition hall, offers the best B&B accommodations in the area, including two gay B&Bs. Reserve rooms here in advance. Leave Earl's Ct. station at the exhibition hall's west exit.

York House Hotel, 28 Philbeach Gdns., SW5 (tel. 373 7519). Helpful, experienced manager. Clean and spacious rooms with tasteful wallpaper. Sinks, radios, and intercoms in all rooms; TV lounge. Full English breakfast. Breakfast room juxtaposes miniature Dutch paintings and red-checkered tablecloths; ideal for longer stays. Reception open 7am-11pm. Singles £21-31. Doubles £34-37. Triples £42-48. Weekly rates at least 25% less, but with continental breakfast only.

The Beaver Hotel, 57-59 Philbeach Gdns., SW5 (tel. 373 4553). Congenial managers. Well-furnished rooms with various degrees of space include direct-dial phones, color TV, radio, and English breakfast. Pool table and elegant TV lounge in basement. Some first floor rooms have balconies. All rooms with bath have hairdryers. Well-trained pets allowed. An added nicety: bedspreads match the decor. The Cleavers would approve. Singles £28-42. Doubles £37-50. Triples with bath £64. 10% discount for longer stays.

Philbeach Hotel, 30-31 Philbeach Gdns., SW5 (tel. 373 1244). The largest gay B&B in England. Popular with both gay men and women. Bar (open to guests and their visitors) and a superb Thai restaurant (open to the public 7-11pm) downstairs. Helpful, knowledgeable manager presides over affable staff. Sunbathing encouraged in backyard garden. Full English breakfast. North Americans galore. Reserve a few weeks in advance. Singles £33-38. Doubles £47-55. Will arrange weekly rates in advance if asked.

Hotel Halifax, 65 Philbeach Gdns., SW5 (tel. 373 4153). Another gay B&B, but smaller, more down at heel, and not as popular as the Philbeach Hotel above. Kind management. Color TV, radio, and basins in large, well-decorated rooms with firm mattresses. Continental breakfast plus cereal and a boiled egg. Full payment upon arrival. Singles £26-36. Doubles £38-44.

Guest houses and B&Bs dot all of the avenues branching off Earl's Court Rd. Most survive on the sheer volume of tourist traffic rather than on the quality of their services. Shop selectively and ask to see a room before you plunk down your money.

The Henley House Hotel, 30 Barkston Gdns., SW5 (tel. 370 4111). Slightly expensive but comparatively luxurious B&B frequented by an older, sedate clientele. Recently remodeled but smallish rooms. Price includes continental breakfast, color TV, telephone, and tea- and coffee-making facilities. Singles £34-43. Doubles £53. Triples £58.

Merlyn Court Hotel, 2 Barkston Gdns., SW5 (tel. 370 1640). Clean but aged B&B. Overlooks a quiet garden. Squeaky beds. No rooms with private facilities. Exemplary bathrooms. Full English breakfast. Singles £27-30. Doubles £34-45.

Half Moon Hotel, 10 Earl's Court Sq., SW5 (tel. 373 9956). Clean, modest accommodation includes color TV and continental breakfast. Large breakfast room holds a small fish tank. 24-hr. reception. Singles £22, with shower £27. Doubles £32, with shower £42. Triples £40, with shower £46.

Mayflower Hotel, 26-28 Trebovir Rd., SW5 (tel. 370 0991). Spacious and dreamy lavender rooms have color TVs and direct-dial phones. Rooms come with bath or shower. 24-hr. reception behind smoked marble. 10% weekly discount. Uncontinental breakfast includes cereal and orange juice. Singles £35. Doubles £45. Triples £55. Quads £60.

Oxford Hotel, 24 Penywern Rd., SW5 (tel. 370 5162). Rooms with color TVs and furniture that's seen better days. Clean bathrooms. Vegetation out back. Continental breakfast. Singles £20-32. Doubles £28-40. Triples £35-45.

Mowbray Court Hotel, 28-32 Penywern Rd., SW5 (tel. 373 8285). Look for the ostentatious display of flags out front; easy to mistake for your favorite embassy. Color TV and phone in well-furnished pinstriped rooms. Bar and TV lounge. Continental breakfast. Deductible service charge included in the price. Singles £28-34. Doubles £38-44. Triples £48-54. Larger rooms available.

Hotel Flora, 11-13 Penywern Rd., SW5 (tel. 373 6514). Limited choice of clean, well-maintained rooms with all the fixin's: private facilities, color TV, hair dryer, phone, radio, and coffee-tea bar. Bar downstairs. Continental breakfast. 24-hr. reception. Singles £25. Doubles £35. Triples £55.

Windsor House Hotel, 12 Penywern Rd., SW5 (tel. 373 9087). Tolerable rooms and use of kitchen facilities at rock-bottom rates. 24-hr. reception. TV room. Singles £17-22. Doubles £22-28.

Lord Jim Hotel, 23-25 Penywern Rd., SW5 (tel. 370 6071). An odd hotel named in honor of Joseph Conrad by the idiosyncratic Polish owners. TV lounge with ugly brown furniture. Decent rooms with sinks and soft beds. Clean bathrooms. Continental breakfast includes cereal. Singles £17-22. Doubles £25-35.

White House Hotel, 12 Earl's Court Sq., SW5 (tel. 373 5903). Bare Victorian sprawl and a grandiose breakfast room compensate for simple quarters. Continental breakfast. Laundry facilities. No curfew. Doubles only, £25-35.

Hotel Earl's Court, 28 Warwick Rd., SW5 (tel. 373 0302). Back to basics. Old rooms and worn showers. Darkish toilets. Small, surprisingly clean breakfast room. Adjacent TV room closes at midnight. Continental breakfast. Singles £16-20. Doubles £26-30. Triples £11 per person.

Chelsea Hotel, 33-41 Earl's Court Sq., SW5 (tel. 244 6892). Huge labyrinthine clearinghouse with 112 dorm beds for budgeteers with a mass mentality. Security at a loss with such a big, rambling building, and comfort well down there. Noisy and basic: restaurant and bar open late. Dorm beds £8. Doubles £26.

Somewhat distanced from the tourist trade of Earl's Court, the area around **Gloucester Road** proves quieter, more expensive, and comparably convenient to the Kensington museums, Kensington Gardens, and all of Chelsea.

Abcone Hotel, 10 Ashburn Gdns., SW7 (tel. 370 3383). Tube: Gloucester Rd. Close to the station. Plush hotel facilities: photocopying and wordprocessing facilities, in-house movies, and bright pink toilet paper. Continental breakfast. Singles £35-49. Doubles £48-59. Triples £64-78.

Queensbury Court Hotel, 7-11 Queensbury Pl., SW7 (tel. 589 3693). Tube: South Kensington. Cheap, well-used rooms. Clean bathrooms. In the center of the museum area, and right across from the College for Psychic Studies. TV lounge, prominent pool table. Singles £25-30. Doubles £36-42. Triples £48-52, with facilities £55.

North London

Dillons Hotel, 21 Belsize Park, Hampstead, NW3 (tel. 794 3360). Tube: Belsize Park or Swiss Cottage. Lovely, spacious B&B run by a kind Irish woman. Continental breakfast. Singles £20. Doubles £28, with shower £33.

Frank and Betty Merchant, 562 Caledonian Rd., N7 (tel. 607 0930). Tube: Caledonian Rd., then 8-min. walk. Small bungalow with no sign but a lovely garden out front. Friendly proprietors. Room for 5 people only. Call in advance. £12 per person.

Camping

Camping in London is not the most convenient of options. For one thing, you probably won't be in London. Even with a travelcard, the cost of shuttling in and out might better be spent on a cheap (and rain-proof) hostel. In summer months, even the few campsites near London fill up. You'll have to make reservations one to two weeks in advance. And it helps to own a tent. If you decide to buy outdoor equipment, try **Blacks Camping & Leisure,** 53 Rathbone Place, W1 (tel. 636 6645), or the **Youth Hostel Association,** 14 Southampton St., WC2 (tel. 836 8541).

Hackney Camping, Millfields Rd., Hackney Marshes, E5 (tel. (081) 985 7656). Bus #38 or 55 from Victoria via Piccadilly Circus, or bus #22a from Piccadilly Circus. An expanse of flat green lawn in the midst of London's ethnic East End. Free hot showers, baggage storage, snack bar, and laundry facilities. No caravans. Open June-Aug. daily 8am-11:45pm. £2.50 per person, children under 12 £1.50.

Tent City, Old Oak Common, East Acton, W3 (tel. (081) 743 5708). Tube: East Acton. Your tent is already set up and waiting for you here. Extremely friendly campsite, full of backpackers. Deservedly popular. Open April-Sept., £4 per person.

Lee Valley Park, Picketts Lock Centre, Picketts Lock Lane, N9 (tel. (081) 803 4756). From Trafalgar Sq. take eastbound bus #6 to Hackney, then #333 to Picketts Lock Centre. Large; no need to book ahead. Laundry facilities and showers available. Open year-round. Electrical hook-up £1.50. £3.60 per person, children £1.60.

Crystal Palace Camp Site, Crystal Palace Parade, SE19 (tel. (081) 778 7155). Take BR from London Bridge to Crystal Palace (about 20 min.). Wonderfully close to the healthful activities at the Crystal Palace National Sports Centre. Showers and laundry facilities. One-week max. stay in summer, 2 weeks in winter. Open year-round. £6.25 per person.

The Housing Crunch

Don't head blithely into the Great Outdoors; sleeping in parks is unsafe and illegal. Impromptu campers are usually asked, urged, or forced to move along. If you are absolutely desperate, call the **Housing Advice Switchboard** (tel. 434 2522; Mon.-Fri. 10am-6pm, emergencies at any time). Solitary travelers who are really absolutely desperate might also want to call the **Alone in London Service** (tel. 278 4224; Mon.-Tues. and Thurs.-Fri. 9am-4pm, Wed. 9am-12:30pm), or the **Salvation Army** (tel. 236 5222; usually open Mon.-Fri. 9am-4pm).

Food

One of the few victors in the struggle for world empire was undoubtedly the English palate. While British cooking still persists in all its boiled glory, ethnic cuisines from around the world have breathed new life into English kitchens. London has few rivals in its range of foreign food—Lebanese, Greek, Indian, Chinese, Thai, Italian, Cypriot, African, and West Indian. But variety costs. In too many places, you pay a premium price for a minimum of atmosphere and service. Watch the fine print: perfectly innocent entrees that appear inexpensive on the menu often end up supplemented with side dishes, shamefully priced drinks, VAT, minimum per-person charges, and an occasional (and outrageous) £1-2 cover charge. You don't have to tip in those restaurants that include service charge (10-12½%) on the bill. And if the service has disappointed you, you can complain to the manager and then legally subtract part or all of the service charge. You may run into a puzzling sign saying something like, "Service included but individual gratuities are discretionary"—but don't be misled.

If you eat only one ethnic meal while in London, make it Indian. The Indian restaurants in London nearly outnumber the pubs. Most are quiet and candle-lit (except for the ever-popular Khan's, listed below), if a little on the garish side. In general, Indian restaurants are cheaper around Westbourne Grove (Tube: Bayswater) than in Piccadilly and Covent Garden.

For a cheaper alternative to restaurant dining, try a meal in a **café** (often pronounced and occasionally spelled "caff")—something akin to a U.S. diner. Caffs serve an odd mix of inexpensive English and Italian specialties (£4-5 for a full meal). Interiors range from the serviceable to the dingy, and tables may be shared, but the food is often very good. The owner is usually called Mick. Recently, diners actively styled to look and feel American have grown popular (most conspicuously Ed's Easy Diner). These sparkling formica hotspots breed a semi-surreal atmosphere: English youth crowd the booths and counters, downing English-brewed Budweiser and English-bottled Coke and eating cholesterol-laden U.S. favorites.

London's wealth of foreign restaurants shouldn't deter you from sampling Britain's own famous (or infamous) cuisine. While there are some dedicatedly British restaurants, like Porter's (listed below), **pubs** are your best bet for cheap, filling English fare. Those who object to meat pastries and potatoes can take refuge in the salads and sandwiches available in most pubs. The farther you get from central London, the greater your chances of encountering such authentic cockney favorites as jellied eels, cockles, mussels, smoked mackerel, and Scottish Arbroath smokies. Pubs are best for lunch. The **fish-and-chip shops** on nearly every street vary little in price but lie oceans apart in quality. Look for queues out the door and hop in line.

Not surprisingly, groceries cost less in supermarkets than in charming little corner shops. **Tesco** has branches at Goodge St., Portobello Rd. (Tube: Notting Hill Gate), and near Paddington and Victoria stations. **Safeway** stores squat on King's Rd., High St. Kensington, Edgware Rd. (not too far from Paddington), in the Barbican CEntre, and in the Brunswick Shopping Centre (Tube: Russell Sq.; open daily until 8pm). Beneficent **Sainsbury** has branches on Victoria Rd., not far from Victoria Station, on Cromwell Rd. (Tube: Gloucester Rd.), and on Camden Rd. (Tube: Camden Town), as well as an immense "SavaCentre" Hypermarket in Merton (Tube: Collier's Wood). **Marks & Spencer** (the department store) sells reliable produce for a bit more than Sainsbury; they have two branches on Oxford St. (one near Marble Arch, one on Poland St.) and others all over the city. Both Sainsbury and "Marks and Sparks" sell satisfying prepared dishes (Sainsbury chicken pasty 65p, quiche lorraine £2.10 per lb, chicken tandoori £1.50). Fine fresh produce and excellent deli and bakery goods make Sainsbury and M&S your best bet for picnics and kitchen meals. Avoid supermarkets from 6-8pm and on Saturdays when the lines grow prohibitively long. The ubiquitous **Europa** groceries charge more but stay open until 11pm (look for the yellow sign). The enormous, regal foodhalls of **Harrods,** on Brompton Rd., offer almost everything under the sun at out-of-the-budget-world prices; visit if only to gawk. For the thrill of shopping outdoors, try **open-air markets** (see Shopping below). **Berwick Market,** near Piccadilly, sells cheap fruits and vegetables. Fruit markets pop up all over central London, offering fresh and healthy snacks at reasonable prices. The numerous small **grocery shops** stay open two or three hours later than supermarkets and also stay open on Sunday.

All these alternatives should make it easy to avoid the Anglicized versions of U.S. steak houses and the numerous fast-food chains (the mildly sinister Wimpy Bars, for example) that infest areas such as Piccadilly and Leicester Sq. For more advice or help finding little-known ethnic restaurants, contact the free **Restaurant Switchboard** (tel. (081) 888 8080, Mon.-Sat. 9am-8pm).

The West End

Soho, Piccadilly and Covent Garden offer an inexhaustible jumble of food. Prices in the West End are high; you may want to order your food to take away. Free seating reposes at Leicester Square (halfway between the Leicester Sq. and Piccadilly Circus Tube stops), under the Eros fountain at Piccadilly Circus, or by the lions in Trafalgar Sq. Don't overlook **Berwick Market** on Berwick St. for fresh fruit during the day. Piccadilly Circus, Leicester Sq., Covent Garden, and Charing Cross Tube stations are all within easy walking distance of most of the West End. Oxford Circus station is only a 10-min. walk north from Piccadilly. Tottenham Court Rd. station requires a similar stroll from Leicester Sq.

Soho and Piccadilly Circus

Pollo, 20 Old Compton St., W1 (tel. 734 5917). Tube: Leicester Sq. or Tottenham Court Rd. Popular and inexpensive Italian cuisine. Squeeze in early for dinner. Spaghetti from £2.20. *Chicken cacciatore* and 2 vegetables £4. *Tortellini carbonara* £2.90. Open Mon.-Sat. noon-11:30pm.

Gaby's, 30 Charing Cross Rd., WC2 (tel. 826 4233). Tube: Leicester Sq. Low on atmosphere but up there on great Middle Eastern and vegetarian food. Don't be put off by the steaming food photos out front. Large *latkes* £1. Smoked salmon sandwich £2.60. Large spinach egg rolls £1.50. Salads to go. Open Mon.-Sat. 9am-midnight, Sun. 11am-10pm.

Rabin's Nosh Bar, 39 Great Windmill St., W1 (tel. 434 9913). Tube: Piccadilly Circus. Small restaurant serving fresh, delicious food. Kosher dishes. Hot salt beef sandwich £2.60. Roast turkey bagel £1.85. Boiled or fried *gefilte* fish £1.80. Walls covered with photos of British and U.S. boxing legends. Open Mon.-Sat. 11am-8pm, occasionally later.

The Wren of St. James's, 35 Jermyn St., SW1 (tel. 437 9419). Tube: Piccadilly Circus or Green Park. When will you have another chance to eat turkey and ham pie (£1.95) in the courtyard of a church designed by Sir Christopher Wren? *Carpe diem.* Casserole of the day with roll and butter £3. Quiche from £1.85. Open Mon.-Sat. 8am-7pm, Sun. 10am-4pm.

Alpha One Fish Bar, 43 Old Compton St., W1 (tel. 437 7344). Tube: Piccadilly Circus. Look for the green neon sign. No drunken trout, just good, greasy fun. Big fish and great chips. Large cod only £2.40. Chips 65-85p. Large shish kebab and salad £2.50. Tartar sauce extra. Open Mon.-Thurs. 11:30am-1am, Fri.-Sat. 11:30am-2am, Sun. 11:30am-midnight.

Passage to India, 5 Old Compton St., W1. Tube: Leicester Sq. Serene, low-priced, but cramped Indian restaurant. Half a *tandoori* chicken £4. Vegetable dishes in the orbit of £3. Service charge 10%. Open Mon.-Thurs. noon-midnight, Fri.-Sat. noon-1am.

Almalfi Ristorante, 31 Old Compton St., W1 (tel. 437 7284). Tube: Piccadilly Circus. Upscale Italian cuisine in the heart of Soho. Pasta & pizza from £5 (including salad and garlic bread). Succulent *pulcino alla rosmarino* £6.25. Scrumptious desserts from £2.45. Service charge 10%. Open "daily all day:" from 9am for pastries, from noon for lunch, closes at 11:15pm.

Rasa Sayang, 10 Frith St., W1 (tel. 734 8720). Tube: Leicester Sq. Extremely popular Indonesian restaurant with a cool, tasteful interior. Try the coconut-based chicken soup, *satay* (skewered meat), or spicy Singapore *laksa. Nasi goreng* (fried rice, eggs, shrimp, chicken, and peas) £4. Open Mon.-Thurs. noon-2:45pm and 6-11:30pm, Fri. noon-2:45pm and 6-11:45pm, Sat. 6-11:30pm, Sun. 1-10pm.

Prima Pasta, 1 Cranbourn St., WC2 (tel. 836 0484). Tube: Leicester Sq. Succulent pasta dishes served in a trendy, neo-Tuscan interior. *Penne al pollo* £5. £1.25 extra for huge portions. Open Mon.-Sat. noon-midnight, Sun. noon-11:30pm.

The Dugout Café, 12a Irving St., WC2 (tel. 925 0547), off Charing Cross Rd. Tube: Leicester Sq. A must for homesick Yankee fans or anyone else craving a first-rate cheese steak. Tex-Mex and other regional American specialties served up in a lively, photo-studded shrine to baseball heroes and other sporting gods. Mexican tortilla stack £5. Open Mon.-Sat. 11:30am-11pm, Sun. noon-11pm.

The Stockpot, 40 Panton St., SW1 (tel 839 5142), by the Cannon cinema. Tube: Piccadilly Circus. Packed, woodsy atmosphere, and big plates. Breakfast from £1.95, English entrees £2-4. Open Mon.-Sat. 8am-11:30pm, Sun. noon-10pm.

Pizza Express, 10 Dean St. (tel. 437 9595). Tube: Tottenham Court Rd. Good, varied pizza for around £3-4. Live jazz Mon.-Sat. from 9:30pm. Admission £4-7. Open daily noon-midnight. Also 30 Coptic St. Tube: Tottenham Court Rd. or Holborn, near the British Museum. Open daily noon-midnight.

Chinatown

London's Chinatown (Tube:Leicester Sq.) may disappoint those familiar with the splendors of the Chinese districts of New York, San Francisco or Vancouver. Nevertheless the few blocks north of Leicester Sq. remain a fine place to eat. Because of the Hong Kong connection, Cantonese cooking dominates here, but Chinese food from every region can be found. Despite the Chinese tradition of eating *dim sum* only on Sundays, most Cantonese restaurants serve it every afternoon. A piece of fruit and a pork bun (70p) or a curry beef bun (60p) from a Chinese bakery makes a delicious and inexpensive lunch. The meat is a flavoring, not a filling. Try the **Garden Restaurant** (51 Charing Cross Rd., W1; open Mon.-Sat. 10am-11:30pm. Sun. 10am-11pm) or the olfactorily sensational **SuperCake Shop** (21 Wardour St., W1; open Mon.-Sat. 11am-8pm.).

Wong Kei, 41-43 Wardour St., W1 (tel. 437 8408). Three stories of the rudest waiters and the best value Chinese food in Soho. Roasted duck and chicken rice £2.40. Singapore fried noodles £2.20. Soup but no appetizers. Set dinner for £6. Open daily noon-11:30pm.

Chuen Cheng Ku, 17 Wardour St., W1 (tel. 437 3433). Some consider it one of the planet's best restaurants. Certainly one of the largest menus. Look out for the dragon. *Dim sum* dishes £1.50. Try the dried and fried *Ho-Fun* noodles with beef £4. Open daily 11am-midnight.

The Dragon Inn, 12 Gerrard St., W1 (tel. 287 2206). Restaurant buzzes until late. Yummy *dim sum* served daily noon-4:45pm. Stuffed crab's claws £5.30. Open daily noon-11:45pm.

Young Cheng, 76 Shaftesbury Ave., W1. Small, crowded, hip Chinese joint. A wild variety of tantalizing dishes. Grilled pork chops prepared with fresh orange juice £7. Watch the food cook as you wait for a table. Set dishes are bargains at £7 per person. Decent wine list. Open daily noon-11:30pm.

Lee Ho Fook, 15-16 Gerrard St., W1 (tel. 439 0422). A perennially popular and inexpensive *dim sum* restaurant; slightly greasy *dim sum* dishes £1.20. Malayan-style rice sticks £2.90. Open daily 11:30-midnight.

Yung's Restaurant, 23 Wardour St., W1 (tel. 437 4986). Late-night Chinatown cuisine. Rice sticks from £3.80. Cold roast Bartle £5. Fried beef in oyster sauce £5.80. Set lunches from £5.80. Spanking new decor. Service charge 10%. Open daily noon-4:30am.

Covent Garden

Covent Garden offers an enticing—but often expensive—array of eateries to playgoers in the heart of London's theatre district. Tube: Covent Garden.

Palms, 39 King St., WC2 (tel. 240 2939). A smaller and less crowded branch of the Italian restaurant on High St. Kensington. A lively mix of scrumptious Italian dishes and loudish pop music. Pastas £3-5, service included. Open daily noon-midnight.

Food for Thought, 31 Neal St., WC2 (tel. 836 0239). Expect a line at noon. Generous servings of delicious vegetarian food straight from the pot in a tiny downstairs restaurant packed with plants. Daily specials £3, flapjacks and granola 60p, cake £1. Take-away after 3pm. Open Mon.-Sat. 9am-7pm.

Calabash Restaurant, 38 King St., WC2 (tel. 836 1976). In the basement of the Africa Centre. Authentic African restaurant serving dishes from all over the continent. Entrees £4.10-7.50. *Doro Wat* (chicken stew served with eggs and rice or ingera) £6.50. Open Mon.-Fri. 12:30-3pm and 6-11:30pm, Sat. 6-11:30pm.

Café Casbar, 52 Earlham St., WC2 (tel. 379 7768). You pay a wee bit more for the trendiness here. Munch a hot french bread sandwich for £3 beneath changing art exhibits. Open Mon.-Sat. 10:15am-8pm, Sun. 10:15am-6pm.

Porter's, 17 Henrietta St., WC2 (tel. 836 6466). It's delightful, it's delicious, it's Dickensian, it destroys your budget. But worth the price to learn how fine British food can be. Huge assortment of hot pies with traditional crust (turkey-chestnut, steak-mushroom, lamb-apricot, fish) and vegetables or salad £7.10. Sausage and mash £6.40. Minimum charge £4. Open Mon.-Sat. noon-3pm and 5-11:30pm, Sun. 5:30-10:30pm.

Bhatti, 37 Great Queen St., WC2 (tel. 831 0817). Award-winning Indian cuisine served in the center of theatreland. *Tandoor bater* (quail) £4.75. Very inexpensive vegetable dishes. Three-course pre-theatre set menu £9 per person (served 6-7:15pm). Make reservations. Service charge 15%. Open daily noon-2:45pm and 5:45-11:30pm.

Poons of Covent Garden, 41 King St., WC2 (tel. 240 1743). Excellent Cantonese restaurant owned and operated by a chef descended from a long line of Chinese sausage makers. Perfect pre-theatre dinner (£6.90; served 5-7:30pm) includes chicken and sweetcorn soup, rice, and a choice of entree. Cover charge £1. Reservations suggested. Open daily noon-midnight.

Café Pasta, 2-4 Garrick St., WC2 (tel. 497 2779). A pleasant Italian café with a cozy downstairs bar and sidewalk seating. Pasta dishes £4. Open Mon.-Sat. 9:30am-11:30pm, Sun. 9:30am-11pm. Also at 184 Shaftesbury Ave., WC2 (tel. 379 0198).

Piazza, corner of Cecil Court and St. Martins Lane, WC2 (tel. 623 6296). A bright, spacious café with lavender ceilings and marble tabletops. Excellent salad bar, health food counter, and selection of homemade pastas. Open daily 8am-midnight.

Grunt's Chicago Pizza Company, 12 Maiden Lane, WC2 (tel. 379 7722). Lots of greenery and a 34-ft. mural of the Windy City. Big screen TV. Chicago-style pizza £5.45 for 2 people. Open Mon.-Sat. noon-11:30pm, Sun. noon-9pm.

Frank's Café, 52 Neal St., WC2 (tel. 836 6345). Somewhat spare. Homestyle pasta about a pound cheaper than anyplace else. Open Mon.-Sat. 8am-8pm.

Scott's, corner of Bedfordbury St. and New Row, WC2 (tel. 240 0340). Office workers queue up on the sidewalk at lunchtime to get into this delicious *patisserie* and sandwich shop. Rustic tables and chairs counterpoint a cool ceramic interior. Smoked salmon platter £4.50. Open daily 8am-11:30pm.

Roberto, 2 Mays Ct., WC2 (tel. 836 9180). A dark, rustic pasta bar bustling with business from the local Italian community. Fresh pastas from £4. Open daily noon-3pm and 5:30-11:30pm.

Diana's Diner, 39 Endell St., WC2. Generous servings of food in a warm, homemade café. Steak and kidney pie £4.50, sandwiches £2-3. Outdoor seating in summer. Open Mon.-Sat. 7am-7pm, Sun. 9am-5pm.

Sammy's Coffee Bar, 37 Bedford St., WC2. Cheap and delicious sandwiches from £1. Spiffier surroundings than most nearby shops. Egg, bacon, and sausage breakfast £1.80. Try to avoid the luncheon rush. Open Mon.-Fri. 8am-4:30pm.

Coliseum Dairy, 7 New Row, WC2. Humble dairy and deli counter with makeshift sidewalk seating serves the cheapest meals in Covent Garden. Assorted sandwiches from 90p. Quarter-pound beefburger 65p. Open daily 6am-6pm.

Farmer Brown Café, 4 New Row, WC2 (tel. 240 0230). Quaint, country kitchen-style restaurant dishing out tried and true barnyard favorites. Roast turkey sandwiches £2.30, tuna salad £4.20. Open daily 7:30am-6pm.

La Toscana Trattoria, 33 Southampton St., WC2. Superior Italian food served in an elegant setting. Ask to be seated upstairs if you relish recordings of Pavarotti. *Penne al Salmone* £4.85. Open Mon.-Fri. 7:30am-3pm, 5:30-11:15pm, Sat. noon-11:15pm.

Taste of India, 25 Catherine St., WC2 (tel. 836 2538). Directly across from Theatre Royal Drury Lane. An intimate Indian dining experience. Four-course pre-theatre menu (served 5:30-7:30pm) from £9. Minimum £6.50 for dinner. Service charge 12.5%. Open daily noon-2:30pm and 5:30pm-midnight.

Bloomsbury and Euston

Superb Italian and Middle Eastern restaurants line **Goodge Street** and **Charlotte Street,** and the vegetarian restaurants in the area offer some of the best values around. Intriguing, authentic Indian food can be had farther north, in the area near Euston Rd. (Drummond St., for example). Near the University of London, cushy outdoor cafés and colorful pubs clutter the secluded pedestrian pathways of **Cosmo Place,** off Queen Sq., and **Woburn Walk.** The cheapest food cooks at the student refectories of the University of London. Officially, you need a Union Card to eat there.

Near Euston

Diwana Bhel Poori House, 121 Drummond St. NW1 (tel. 387 5556). Tube: Warren St. Quick and tasty Indian vegetarian food in a clean and airy restaurant worth the wait. Try *samosas* or *thali* (an assortment of vegetables, rices, sauces, breads, and desserts meant to be shared). Meals £1.50-5. BYOB. Open daily noon-midnight. Another branch at 50 Westbourne Grove (Tube: Bayswater). **Gupta Sweet Centre,** across the street at 100 Drummond St., has excellent Indian take-away sweets and savories at half the sit-down price. Try their delicious *chum-chum,* a moist orange pastry sweetened with honey. Open daily Mon.-Thurs. 11am-7pm, Fri.-Sat. 10am-7pm, Sun. noon-7pm.

Rhavi Shankar Bhel Poori House, 133-135 Drummond St. (tel. 338 6488). Tube: Euston Sq. An inconspicuous Indian-vegetarian restaurant renowned as one of London's finest. Most entrees £2.50-3. *Paper Dose* (paper-thin, crispy rice pancake served with rich vegetable filling, spicy-sweet *sambhar* sauce, and coconut chutney) £3.25. Open daily noon-11pm.

Great Nepalese Restaurant, 48 Eversholt St., NW1 (tel. 338 5935). Tube: Euston. Great indeed. Huge lunch of tandoori chicken, vegetable curry, rice, nan bread, papedam and drink £5.50. Good vegetarian dishes under £3. Minimum charge £5. Open Mon.-Sat. noon-2:45pm and 6-11:45pm.

Chive's, 1 Woburn Walk, WC1 (tel. 388 3479). Tube: Euston. In a quiet, tree-filled alley between Upper Woburn Pl. and Duke's Rd. A traditional café serving fresh pastries, jacket potatoes, and highly original sandwiches (such as cream cheese and pineapple, £1.20). A favorite of area dance students; at noon, look down to see silken ballet slippers everywhere. Open Mon.-Fri. 7am-5:30pm.

Anwar's, 64 Grafton Way, W1 (tel. 387 6664). Tube: Warren St. Atmosphere created by the fluorescent lights at the counter. Solid Indian food at a good price. Vegetable curries £1.60-1.90. Meat curries £2.60-2.70. Open daily 10am-10pm.

Chutney's, 124 Drummond St., NW1 (tel. 338 0604). Tube: Warren St. A light, cheerful Indian vegetarian café with a 12-dish, all-you-can-eat lunch buffet, £3.95. Open daily noon-2.45pm, 6-11:30pm.

Wot The Dickens, 3 Woburn Walk WC1. Tube: Euston. Trendier than its neighbors, this slick, chic joint draws huge crowds at lunchtime. Good espresso and sandwiches. Shady sidewalk seating. Smoked scotch salmon plate £1.70. Open Mon.-Fri. 7am-6:15pm, Sat. 9am-4pm.

Sorrento Snack Bar, 8 Woburn Walk WC1 (tel. 388 3554). Tube: Euston. A cheap no-nonsense cafe with excellent breakfast specials and assorted pizzas. Green-tiled interior. Bacon, egg, beans, and sausage £2.30. Pizzas from £1.90. Open Mon.-Fri. 7am-6pm.

Near Goodge Street.

Cranks Health Food, 9-11 Tottenham St, W1 (tel. 631 3912). Tube: Goodge St. Large portions of vegetarian food served in cheerful surroundings. Delicious carrot cake £1.05. Many selections £1.50-2.25, large salad £3.25. Open Mon.-Fri. 8am-8pm, Sat. 9am-6pm.

Greenhouse Vegetarian Restaurant, basement of 16 Chenies St., WC1 (tel. 637 0838). Tube: Goodge St. Very fresh food that you choose by sight. Main courses £3.40, salad 85p, thick pizza £1.85, desserts 75p-£1.25. BYOB. Open Tues.-Fri. noon-9pm, Mon. and Sat. noon-8pm.

Spaghetti House Ristorante, 15-17 Goodge St. W1 (tel. 636 6582). Tube: Goodge St. A well-established pasta restaurant with pretty, oaken booths and sidewalk seating. *Linguine al funghetto* (pasta ribbons with wild mushrooms and white wine sauce) £4.50. Open Mon.-Sat. noon-11pm, Sun. 5:30-10.30pm.

NatRaj, 93 Charlotte St., W1 (tel. 637 0050). Tube: Goodge St. Quiet, modestly decorated tandoori restaurant. Cheap curries £3-4. 4-course set menu for 2, £13. *Shak Suka* (minced lamb cooked in a mild cream sauce with eggs) £4. Minimum charge £4.50. Open daily noon-3pm and 6pm-midnight.

Cosma's Taverna, 29 Goodge St., W1 (tel. 636 1877). Tube: Goodge St. Tasty lamb kebab £6. Ouzo £1.60. Crazy atmosphere downstairs features late-night belly dancing and plate smashing. Former presidential hopeful Michael Dukakis once entered the fray here. Open Mon.-Sat. noon-3pm and 5:30pm-midnight. Basement taverna open Tues.-Sat. 5:30pm-2am.

Shuler's Sandwiches, 35 Goodge St., W1 (tel. 636 4409). Tube: Goodge St. Perfect fixings for a picnic lunch. Incredibly cheap sandwiches and baked goods. Sandwich with any filling £1. Huge French loaves 70p. May run out of food early on Fri. Open Mon.-Fri. 8am-4pm.

Champagne, 16 Percy St., W1 (tel. 636 4409), off Tottenham Court Rd. Tube: Goodge St. Popular Chinese restaurant with candles and wax roses at every table. Filling 3-course lunch special (soup, entree, fried rice, and sherbet) £4.50. Open daily noon-midnight.

Trattoria Mondello, 36 Goodge St., W1 (tel. 637 9037). Tube: Goodge St. An array of zesty pasta dishes served in a rustic dining room with open-beam ceilings and hanging ferns. *Lasagna Pasticciata* £3.80. 50 p cover. Open Mon.-Wed. noon-3pm and 5:30-11:30pm, Thurs.-Fri. noon-3pm and 5:30-midnight, Sat. noon-midnight.

Around Russell Square

Wooley's Wholefood and Take-Away, 33 Theobald's Rd., WC1 (tel. 405 3028). Tube: Holborn. Good place for healthy and delicious picnic fare. Interesting sandwiches (apple and brie £1.85), provocative salads. Also a wide selection of breakfast snacks. Outdoor seating. Open Mon.-Fri. 7am-3:30pm.

The Fryers Delight, 19 Theobald's Rd., WC1. Tube: Holborn. One of the best chippies around, always crowded with Londoners. Fish or chicken with chips £2-3. You pay for the food, not the decor. Popular with British Library scholars. Open Mon.-Sat. noon-11pm.

British Museum Café, in the British Museum on Great Russell St., WC1 (tel. 636 1555). Tube: Holborn, Russell Sq., or Tottenham Court Rd. Lunches and dinners in a classical setting: draping vines and a replica of the Parthenon's western frieze. Tempting, exotic salad bar £4. Sandwich platters £2.65. Open Mon.-Sat. 10:30am-4:15pm, Sun. 2-5pm.

My Old Dutch Pancake House, 131-32 High Holborn, WC1 (tel. 242 5200). Tube: Holborn. 107 varieties of giant Dutch pancake, thin and 18 in. in diameter. Popular toppings include ham, chicken, salami, chili, and curry. Vegetarian pancakes also available. All from £2.90. May be crowded. Open daily noon-midnight.

Queen Charlotte's Restaurant, 1 Queen Sq., WC1 (tel. 837 5627), opposite St. George the Martyr . Tube: Russell Sq. Queen Charlotte used the cellar of this building in 1710 to store sweetmeats and special delicacies for her husband, George III, while he was taking treatment in Queen Sq. for a brief episode of insanity. Today the restaurant, named in Charlotte's honor, dishes up hearty servings of traditional English fare. Harvest vegetable pie £5. Excellent luncheon special £4. Daily vegetarian dish. Open Mon.-Fri. noon-2:30pm and 6:30-9:30pm, Sat. 6:30-9:30pm, Sun. 7-9:30pm.

Café Dot, 42 Queen Sq., WC1, on the ground floor of the Mary Ward Center (tel. 831 7711). Tube: Russell Sq. No sign on the street. Look for the 18th-century townhouse next to the Italian Hospital. Barely visible behind the window, a life-size, papier-mâché dowager leans eternally over her bowl of soup. Good, hot food at rock-bottom prices. Scampi and chips £2. Assorted jacket potatoes with cheese and beans £1.20. Sandwiches £1. Open Mon.-Fri. 11am-3pm and 4-9pm, Sat. 11:30am-5pm.

Cagney's Restaurant, 13 Cosmo Pl., WC1 (tel. 278 8498), off Queen Sq. Tube: Russell Sq. An upbeat Irish-American bistro and shrine to the late film star, James Cagney. Movie stills of the latter grinning, glowering, and crooning cover the walls. Superior seafood, ribs, and exotic burgers. "Sinner's Holiday" burger £3.40. Open Sun.-Fri. 11:30am-3pm, Sat. 5-11.30pm.

Cosmoba, 9 Cosmo Pl., WC1, off Queen Sq. (tel. 837 0904). Tube: Russell Sq. Exceptional Italian restaurant serving an array of pastas (£3.50-4) and superior veal platters £5. Empty wine bottles dangle precariously from the rafters. Minimum charge £4.50. Open daily 11:30am-3pm and 5:30-11pm.

North Sea Fish House, 7-8 Leigh St. WC1, off Cartwright Gardens (tel. 387 5892). Tube: Russell Sq. Popular seafood restaurant with an adjacent fish and chips shop the locals swear by. Fish and chips £1.05-2.95. Open daily noon-2:30pm and 5:30-11:30pm.

Leigh St. Café, 16 Leigh St., WC1. Tube: Russell Sq. A bright, giddy, student-filled café serving creative sandwiches and pastries. Sandwiches with salad £1.25-2.40. Excellent smoked salmon and avocado sandwich on whole wheat £2.40. Garden seating out back. Open Mon.-Fri. 7am-5pm, Sat. 9:30am-3:30pm.

Conduit Coffee House, 61 Lamb's Conduit St., WC1 (tel. 242 8707). Tube: Russell Sq. Six-table coffee house with outdoor seating. Good café for breakfast or cheap take-away sandwiches (80p-£1.50). Breakfast £1.40-2.50, lunch £2.50-4. Open Mon.-Fri. 7am-5:30pm.

Gombarti, 38 Lamb's Conduit St., WC1 (tel. 405 7950). Tube: Russell Sq. Fresh, green café serves English breakfast for £2.25, plus sandwiches for 80p and delicious pastries. Open Mon.-Fri. 7am-5pm.

Palms Restaurant, at the University of London Union, 1 Malet St., WC1. 4th floor. Tube: Russell Sq. Slip past the reception desk and take the elevator. Snacks, sandwiches, and a salad bar. Open Sept.-July Mon.-Fri. 9:30am-5pm. Wine bar 6-11pm.

Victoria, Kensington, and Chelsea

Victoria

Victoria Station languishes amid a wasteland of eating options. Those determined to avoid mediocre sandwich shops and chain restaurants will have to venture far from the station to encounter anything not prepared with a tourist in mind. The avenues radiating north and east from the station (Buckingham Palace Rd., Victoria Rd., and Vauxhall Bridge Rd.) bristle with such eateries.

Grandma's Kitchen, 22 Terminus Pl., SW1 (tel. 834 7602). Grandma might chuckle at the absurdity of the idea. Nonetheless a good place to put down your bags and grab a bite to eat. Plentiful seating upstairs. Eggs, bacon, and toast £1.40. Take-away sandwiches from 85p. A bevy of baked potato choices from £1.20. Open daily 7am-8pm.

Capri Sandwich Bar, 16 Belgrave Rd., SW1 (tel. 834 1989). Ideal for hungry B&B hunters. Stop in for a coffee or sandwich to discuss your options. An assembly line of workers serves up well-presented sandwiches from £1-2.50. Open Mon.-Wed. and Fri. 8am-3:30pm, Thurs. 8am-3pm.

Giulio's Snack Bar, 4 Palace St., W1. Across the road from the Royal Mews. The cheapest sandwich take-away in the area; sandwiches from 60p. Open Mon.-Fri. 7am-5pm.

Knightsbridge and Hyde Park Corner

Growling stomachs fed up with window shopping may groan with disappoint-ment at the dearth of eateries near Knightsbridge. Knightsbridge Green, northwest of Harrods off Brompton Rd., hides several sandwich shops (**Mima's Café** open Mon.-Sat. 6:30am-6pm and the **Knightsbridge Express** open Mon.-Sat. 7am-5:30pm). Coffee shops and expensive bistros also lurk between the antique boutiques along Beauchamp Place, southwest of Harrods.

The Stockpot, 6 Basil St., SW3 (tel. 589 8627). Tube: Knightsbridge. One of 3 branches of this restaurant serving palatable and inexpensive English cuisine. Salads from £2.10. Tasty escaloped chicken or steak and mushroom pie, £2-3. Handsome English breakfast (£2.10) served until 11am. Quick service may make you feel rushed. £1.70 minimum charge. 10% service charge. Open Mon.-Sat. 8am-11:30pm, Sun. noon-10:30pm. Other branches at Sloane Sq. (273 King's Rd., SW3) and Piccadilly (40 Panton St., SW1).

Borshtch n' Tears, 46 Beauchamp Pl., SW3 (tel. 589 5003). Tube: Knightsbridge. Boisterous manager makes you feel welcome, as if among good and drunk friends. Dining here can prove an evening's entertainment. Blinis & smoked salmon £4.95. Entrees (both Russian and conti-nental) £6-9. *Pirozhki* from £2.15. Live music nightly. Last orders at 1am. Service charge 10%. Open daily 6pm-2am.

Hard Rock Café, 150 Old Park Lane, W1 (tel. 629 0382). Tube: Hyde Park Corner. Hype! The *Financial Times* reports rumors that areas of the Café are closed off to ensure lines of people on the street on slow afternoons. But behind the PR you'll find a damn good ham-burger (from £5-7). Wide selection of American beers. Jimi Hendrix's guitar dangles over the bar. Arrive before 5pm to avoid the long "wait." Paraphernalia sold to queues of patient tourists up the street. Restaurant open Sun.-Thurs. 11:30am-12.30am, Fri.-Sat. 11:30am-1am.

South Kensington

Old Brompton Rd. and **Fulham Rd.** are the main thoroughfares in this graceful area of London. South Kensington tube station lies closest, but some of the restau-rants below require a substantial hike from there. Old Brompton Rd. is served by bus #30; Fulham Road by bus #14 or #45.

Up-All-Night, 325 Fulham Rd., SW10 (tel. 352 1996). Ferns, art-deco fans, and Swedish sauna-style wooden booths—stop in after a late-night double bill at the Paris Pullman cinema. ¼-lb. burgers with fries, salad garnish from £3.40. Banana splits £2.65. Service charge 10%. Open daily noon-5:30am.

Johnny Rocket's, 140 Fulham Rd., SW10. Zippy new burger joint American-chrome-style, with limited counter seating. Burgers from £3.50. Great shakes and fries (£1). Open daily 11:30am-midnight.

Bar Escoba, 102 Old Brompton Rd., SW7. Lively Spanish restaurant and bar, a bit further out from the tube station. Sit outside and watch the cars go by on a sunny afternoon. Biggish entrees from £6.50-9. Open Mon.-Sat. 11am-11pm, Sun. 11am-10:30pm.

Caffé Nero, 66 Old Brompton Rd., SW7. Polished chrome and a plethora of choices on big blackboards. Stand-up joint; best for a cappuccino (80p) on the run. Double espresso to go £1.10. Superb ricotta cheesecake from £1.30 per slice. Fudge brownies (90p) remarkably simi-lar to solid blocks of chocolate. Open Mon.-Sat. 7:30am-8pm, Sun. 10am-7pm.

La Cascina, 17a Harrington Rd., SW7. Tube: South Kensington. An unremarkable but af-fordable Anglo-Italian restaurant. Pasta from £2.95. Bountiful salads from £3. Pizzas (from £2.95) made to your specifications. Open daily 11:30am-midnight.

Tandoori of Chelsea, 153 Fulham Rd., SW3 (tel. 589 7617). Set off from the other restaurants on Fulham Rd. and a short walk from the South Kensington Tube station, between dressmak-er's and antique shops. Inviting northwestern Indian cuisine. Entrees £5-7. Vegetarian dishes £3.50-4. Cover charge £1. Service charge 15%. Open Mon.-Sat. 12:30-3pm and 6:30pm-midnight, Sun. 12:30-11:30pm.

Il Falconiere, 84 Old Brompton Rd., SW7 (tel. 589 2401). A bit of Italy, strangely enough, on Old Brompton Rd.—complete with sidewalk tables, pink tablecloths, and Italian menus. Pasta from £3.50. *Scaloppa di pollo valdostana* (chicken with ham and cheese) £5.50. Open Mon.-Sat. noon-2:45am and 6-11:45pm.

Star of India, 154 Old Brompton Rd., SW5 (tel. 373 2901). Unusual decor, chairs draped in fabric. Slightly expensive but superior Indian cuisine. Entrees £5-8. Cover charge 75p. Open daily noon-3:30pm and 6-11:30pm.

Prima Pasta Bar, 313 Fulham Rd, SW10. Generous portions of pasta (£4-5) in a café atmosphere. Even larger portions only £1.25 extra. 10% service charge. Open Mon.-Sat. 11am-midnight, Sun. 11am-11pm. Another branch at 390 King's Rd.

Nizam, 152 Old Brompton Rd., SW5 (tel. 835 1850). Similar fare to adjacent Star of India, and featuring an excellent all-you-can-eat Sunday buffet for £6.50 (noon-5:30pm). Entrees from £4.50. Open daily noon-2:30pm and 6-11:45pm.

High St. Kensington

Inexpensive meals won't come running to greet you at High St. Kensington. Shoppers looking for a coffee break should stop at the **Café Gstaad** in the Kensington Arcade (sandwiches under £1.70; lunchtime £1.50 minimum; open Mon.-Sat. 7am-6:15pm). If coffee and a sandwich won't cut it, head to Henry's (see Wine Bars) or a wine bar on Kensington Church St.

Stick and Bowl, 31 High St. Kensington, W8 (tel. 937 2778). Cheap Chinese cuisine; seating scarce. Crispy beef £3.40. Try a special mixed dish for £4 (includes spring roll, sweet and sour pork, fried rice and vegetables, and 1 exploding prawn). Special dishes made upon request. £2 minimum. Open daily 11:40am-11:15pm.

Palms Pasta on the Hill, 17 Campden Hill Rd., W8. Café-style Italian restaurant popular with trendies young and very young. Spaghetti *carbonara* £4.60. *Fettucine con funghi e prosciutto* £4.65. Italian newspapers bedeck the ceiling. Happy Hour 5:30-7pm. Service charge 12.5%. Open daily noon-11:30pm. Another branch at Covent Garden (39 King St., WC2).

Phoenecia, 11-13 Abingdon Rd., W8 (tel. 937 0120). Take westbound bus #31 along Kensington High St., alighting between Allen and Abingdon St. Highly regarded Lebanese cuisine in a peaceful setting. Lebanese *kalta* (lamb cooked on skewers with onions, parsley, spices) £6. All-you-can-eat luncheon buffet (£8) served 12:15-2:30pm. Cover charge £1.40. Service charge 15%. Open Mon.-Sat. noon-midnight.

Chelsea

King's Road, a private thoroughfare until the middle of the 19th century, extends leisurely through Chelsea. Bus #11 runs the length of the road from the Sloane Sq. Tube station. Almost every destination along King's Rd. requires a bus ride or a considerable walk.

Chelsea Kitchen, 98 King's Rd., SW3 (tel. 589 1330). A 5-10 min. walk from the tube station. Locals rave about this place and its cheap, filling English and continental food: gazpacho, curried eggs, steak and kidney pie, and shish kebab. Head downstairs and acquire a booth for a cozier atmosphere. Expect to wait at meal times. Lunch £3-4, dinner £4-5. Breakfast served 8-11:25am. Open Mon.-Sat. 8am-11:30pm, Sun. noon-11:30pm.

Chelsea Pot, 356 King's Rd., SW3 (tel. 351 3605). Another Anglo-Italian adventure. Generous helpings. Lasagna £3.50. Omelettes from £2.40. Open Mon.-Fri. noon-3pm and 6-11:30pm, Sat.-Sun. noon-11:30pm.

Bamboo Kitchen, 305 King's Rd., SW3 (tel. 352 9281), at Beaufort St. Cheap Chinese takeaway; no seating. The ultimate in chintz: bring your own utensils. Chopsticks cost 40p, spoons and forks 5p. Sweet and sour pork or Singapore-style chow mein £2.50. Call ahead for convenience. Open Mon.-Sat. noon-midnight, Sun. 5pm-midnight.

La Bersagliera, 372 King's Rd., SW3. Some of the best homemade pizza and pasta in London (both £4-5). Cozy atmosphere. Very Italian clientele. Friendly owner. Open Mon.-Sat. 12:30-3pm and 7pm-midnight.

Earl's Court

Earl's Court and **Gloucester Road** eateries generously cater to their tourist traffic. Earl's Court, a take-away carnival, revolves around cheap, ethnic, and palatable food. Groceries in this area charge reasonable prices; shops stay open late at night and on Sunday. The closer you get to the highrise hotels around Gloucester Station, the more expensive restaurants become. Look for the scores of coffee shops and Indian restaurants on Gloucester Rd. north of Cromwell Rd. (especially around Elvaston Place).

Benjy's, 157 Earl's Court Rd., SW7. Tube: Earl's Ct. Like the menu and the foil walls say, this is not the Ritz. Filling "Builder Breakfast" (bacon, egg, chips, beans, toast, 2 sausages, and all the coffee or tea you can drink) £2.80. Oodles of burly Australian types mirror the huge plates. Expect to share a table during mealtimes. Open daily 7am-9:30pm.

Vecchiomondo Ristorante Italiano, 118 Cromwell Rd., SW7. Tube: Gloucester Rd. Comfy Italian restaurant with wine flasks hanging from the ceiling and profuse greenery. Spaghetti *carbonara* £3. Pizza from £2. Open daily 10am-3pm and 5pm-1am.

Green Village Chinese Restaurant, 15 Kenway Rd., SW5. Tube: Earl's Ct. Tidy and tranquil Chinese restaurant, away from the roar of the tourist traffic. Set menu for 2 means tons of food (£10 per person). Fried rice £2-2.80. Open Mon.-Fri. and Sun. noon-2:30pm and 6-11:30pm, Sat. 6-11:30pm.

The Delhi Brasserie, 134 Cromwell Rd., SW5. Tube: Gloucester Rd. Alluring and acclaimed Indian cuisine, pricier and spicier than the norm, served in a quiet, comfortable setting. *Chana masala* £2.15. *Saag* chicken £5. £8 minimum. Service charge 10%. Open daily noon-2:30pm and 6-11:30pm.

Notting Hill and Bayswater

This area is chock-full of high-quality, reasonably-priced restaurants, especially around Notting Hill Gate. Head to Westbourne Grove (Tube: Bayswater or Royal Oak) for large concentrations of decent, if rather unremarkable, Indian and Pakistani places.

Khan's, 13-15 Westbourne Grove, W2 (tel. 727 5240). Tube: Bayswater. Unlike many other Indian restaurants in London, Khan's is noisy and bustling. Excellent for a party. Great *tandoori* £4-5. Good-sized meals £4-6. Minimum order £4.50. Open daily noon-3pm and 6pm-midnight. Take-away available. 10% service charge.

Geale's, 2 Farmer St., W8 (tel. 727 7969). Tube: Notting Hill Gate. Efficient service. Consummately crisp fish and chips (from £3.50). Order the homemade fish soup instead of the canned crab soup. Three-course set lunch £5.50. Often a wait—sit it out in the bar upstairs. Take-away available. Overwhelming 15p cover charge. Open Tues.-Sat. noon-3pm and 6-11pm.

Panzer's Pasta and Pizza, 14 Notting Hill Gate, W11, opposite the fortress of the Czech embassy. Tube: Notting Hill Gate. Alliterative, comfortable family restaurant. Various pizzas £3.50-4. Open daily noon-11:30pm. For cheap sandwiches (65p-£2.20), try Panzer Café at No. 24.

Tootsie's, 115 Notting Hill Gate, W8 (tel. 727 6562). Tube: Notting Hill Gate. Quintessential, cheap American burger place, complete with Cadillac hubcaps. Sashay on over after the show at the Gate Cinema. Burgers £ 3-5, fries 85p. Shakes £1.70. Open Mon.-Sat. noon-midnight, Sun. noon-11:30pm. 12½% service charge.

Malabar, 27 Uxbridge St., W8, (tel. 727 8800). Tube: Notting Hill Gate. Crowded, with wide ranging Indian cuisine. *Murg Dansak* £4.35. Open Mon.-Sat. noon-2:45 pm and 6:30-11:30pm, Sun. buffet lunch 1-2:45pm, dinner 6:30-11pm.

El Greco, 15 Hereford Rd., W2, at Leinster Sq. (tel. 229 3101). Tube: Bayswater. Greek/Cypriot food. *Kalamarakia* (lightly fried squid in red wine) £3.50, *Dolmadia* (stuffed vine leaves) £5, *moussaka* £6.50. Open Mon.-Sat. 6:30pm-12:30am.

Costas Fish Restaurant, 18 Hillgate St., W8 (tel. 727 4310). Tube: Notting Hill Gate. Round the corner from Geale's on restaurant row. Fish and chips £3.50, take-away £2.80. Open Tues.-Sat. noon-2:30pm and 5:30-10:30pm.

Himalaya, 107 Westbourne Grove, W2. Tube: Bayswater or Notting Hill Gate. One of the cheapest Tandoori restaurants in town. *Tikka masala* (boneless lamb) £4, curries £2-3. Don't let the manager talk you into ordering too much. Colorful Malaysian umbrellas hang from the ceiling. Open daily noon-3pm and 6pm-midnight.

Manzara, 24 Pembridge Rd., W11 (tel. 727 3062). Tube: Notting Hill Gate. Good Turkish food. Unusual appetizers £3. *Incik* (lamb knuckle on the bone) for £5.65. Turkish wine available, but expensive. Open Mon.-Sat. 11am-3pm and 6:30-11:30pm.

The City of London

This area is splendid for lunch (when food is fresh for the options traders) and disastrous for dinner (when the commuters go home and the food goes stale). The City overflows with pubs, wine bars, sandwich bars, and the odd trendy vegetarian place, filled each lunchtime with brogues and ties.

The Place Below, in St. Mary-le-Bow Church crypt, Cheapside, EC2 (tel. 329 0789). Tube: St. Paul's. Attractive and generous vegetarian dishes served to the hippest of City folks in a unique location. Quite super. Quiche and salad £4.45. Meals about £1 cheaper take-away. Open Mon.-Fri. 7:30am-3pm, plus Thurs. evenings 6-10:30pm.

Ye Olde Cheshire Cheese, 145 Fleet St., EC4 (tel. 353 6170 or 353 4388). Tube: Blackfriars. Closed for refurbishment, due to reopen in summer of 1992. Samuel Johnson's old watering hole, just 100 steps from his home. Famous for solid English cooking such as steak and kidney pie.

The City, 1 Seething Lane, EC3 (tel. 488 4224). Tube: Tower Hill. This seething pub-restaurant-wine-bar-nightclub is perfect after a day at the Tower. Hefty sausage with vegetables, £3.60. Open Mon., Wed. 11:30am-9pm; Tue, Thurs. 11:30am-10:30pm; Fri. 11:30am-11pm. Dinner Mon.-Thurs. only, until 8:30pm.

The East-West Restaurant, 188 Old St., EC1 (tel. 608 0300). Tube: Old St. Sublime macrobiotic cooking. Buy a small loaf of bread next door to go with the extra-large portions of hummus. Meals £4-5, side dishes £1 each. Tofu cheesecake £1.50. Open Mon.-Fri. 11am-8:30pm, Sat.-Sun. 11am-3pm.

Futures, 8 Botolph Alley, EC3 (tel. 623 4529). Tube: Monument. Fresh take-away vegetarian breakfast and lunch from a sleek little kitchen. Daily main dishes £3. Open Mon.-Fri. 7:30-10am, 11:30am-3pm.

Leadenhall Tapas Bar, 27 Leadenhall Market, EC3. Tube: Bank. A singular setting; note the marked contrast between the restored Victorian marketplace and the revolutionary Lloyd's building. Try to grab the table by the marvelous oval window overlooking the marketplace. Attractive, unusual Spanish buffet; dishes £2-5. Open Mon.-Fri. 11:30am-8:30pm.

Sir Christopher Wren, 17 Paternoster Sq., EC4 (tel. 248 1708). Tube: St. Paul's. Tremendous smoked glass windows bestow instant atmosphere upon this restaurant/pub. Watched over by Wren's masterpiece. Bar meals £3-5. Open Mon.-Fri. 11am-10pm, Sat. 11am-2:30pm.

The Nosherie, 12 Greville St., EC1 (tel. 242 1591). Tube: Chancery Lane. Inset among the jewellers of Hatton Garden. As close as you'll get in London to a New York-style deli. The nosh ain't cheap, but try the salt beef sandwiches (around £2.50). Open Mon.-Fri. 7:30am-4pm.

Ludgate, 9-11 New Bridge St., EC4 (tel. 583 0670). Tube: Blackfriars. Friendly, unpretentious diner serving good, cheap dishes, mostly Italian. Veal *milanese* with vegetable £3.90. Open Mon.-Fri. 6am-6pm, Sat. 7am-12:30pm.

The East End

Bloom's, 90 Whitechapel High St., E1 (tel. 247 6001). Tube: Aldgate East. London's finest kosher restaurant, with good salt (corned) beef and chopped liver sandwiches under £2.60. No seating for sandwich orders. Popular on Sun. Open Sun.-Thurs. 11am-10pm, Fri. 11am-3pm.

The Cherry Orchard, 241 Globe Rd., E2 (tel. 980 6678). Tube: Bethnal Green. A lovely un-Chekhovian restaurant run by Buddhists, with some of London's cheapest vegetarian cuisine. Entrees £2-3, salads £1. Open Tues.-Fri. noon-3pm and 6:30-10:30pm, Sat. noon-10:30pm.

Shampan, 79 Brick Lane, E1 (tel. 375 0475). Tube: Aldgate East. A tad more expensive than its neighbors, but still very reasonable, and a plusher atmosphere. *Nawab lamb biryani* £3.95. Open daily noon-3pm and 6pm-midnight.

Bengal Cuisine, 12 Brick Lane, E1 (tel. 377 8405). Tube: Aldgate East. Also above average on elegance, and competitive prices. Curry dishes from £2.85. Open daily noon-3pm and 6pm-midnight.

Nazrul, 130 Brick Lane, E1 (tel. 247 2505). Tube: Aldgate East. One of the most original names on the street. Dead cheap, with most dishes £2.50-4. Open Mon.-Sat. noon-3pm and 5:30-midnight, Sun. noon-midnight.

Islington

You can choose from a variety of good value meals in Islington. Stylish, down-to-earth restaurants cluster around Upper Street. Be careful when seeking specific addresses, though, since Upper Street numbers ascend on one side of the street and descend on the other. (Tube: Angel).

Indian Veg Bhelpoori House, 92 Chapel Market, N1. An unmistakable bargain—all-you-can-eat lunch buffet (noon-3pm) of Indian vegetarian food for a startling £3.25. Cheap evening meals (around £4) 6-11pm.

Café Pasta, 8 Theberton St., N1. A comfortable restaurant with a dash of elegance, for those seeking romance at a discount. Don't sit too near the door in windy weather. *Fusilli* with ham and leeks £4.50, side salads £1.55. (for each salad purchased, 10p is donated to Friends of the Earth). Open Mon.-Sat. 9:30am-11:30pm, Sun. 9:30am-11pm.

Upper St. Fish Shop, 324 Upper St., N1. A well-known chippy offering daily specials varied according to the catch. Take-away substantially cheaper than eat-in—cod and chips £3, mushy peas 40p. Open Mon. 5:30-10pm, Tues.-Fri. 11:30am-2pm and 5:30-10pm, Sat. 11:30am-3pm and 5:30-10pm.

Café Olé, 118 Upper St., N1. Endless breakfast: egg, bacon, sausage, tomato, mushroom, black pudding, bubble and squeak, toast and coffee £3.50. Open Mon.-Fri.. 7am-7pm., Sat. 7am-6pm.

Camden Town and Hampstead

Fine, cheap eateries are scattered throughout the borough of Camden, from the trendy cafés of Camden Town to the très chic Crepe Van in Hampstead.

Marine Ices, 8 Haverstock Hill, NW3 (tel. 485 3132). Tube: Chalk Farm. The savior of ice cream devotees. Superb Italian ice cream (40p per scoop) and sundaes—the top of the range. *Vesuvius* (£4.20) can defeat even the most Herculean appetite. Start off with a subtly flavored pizza (*quatro stagioni* £4). Massively popular with the north London *cognoscenti.* Ice cream counter open Mon.-Sat. 10:30am-10:45pm, Sun. noon-8pm. Restaurant open Mon.-Fri. noon-2:45pm and 6-10pm, Sat. noon-10:15pm.

Chequers, 18 Chalk Farm Rd., NW1. Tube: Chalk Farm or Camden Town. Close to Camden Lock. Unusual Egyptian vegetarian food (dishes £3-4). Sweet, addictive Egyptian doughnuts 30-80p. Open daily 10am-midnight.

Café Delancey, 3 Delancey St., NW1 (tel. 387 1985). Tube: Camden Town or Mornington Crescent. Classic coffee-shop atmosphere somewhat reminiscent of Greenwich Village (see *Let's Go New York City*). Award-winning brunch. Open daily 8am-midnight.

Ruby in the Dust, 102 Camden High St., NW1 (tel. 485 2744). Tube: Camden Town or Mornington Crescent. Young crowd drawn by playful setting and cheap prices. Burgers, wings, skins (£5-7). Open Mon.-Sat. 10:30am-11:30pm, Sun. 10:30am-11pm.

Nontas, 16 Camden High St., NW1. Tube: Mornington Crescent or Camden Town. One of the best Greek restaurants in the area. The famed, incomparable *Meze* (£8.75) offers an apparently unending selection of dips, meats, and cheeses, all well worth the expense. Other Greek fare £4-6. Open Mon.-Sat. noon-3pm and 6:30pm-midnight.

Kohinoor, 23 Camden High St. (tel. 388 4553). Tube: Mornington Crescent or Camden Town. Indian meat and vegetarian dishes. All-you-can-eat Sunday buffet good value at £5.75.

Camden's Friend Restaurant, 51A Camden High St. (tel. 387 2835). Tube: Mornington Crescent or Camden Town. Vital Chinese food accompanied by lethal cocktails. Entrees £3-6.

Bar Gansa, 2 Inverness St., NW1 (tel. 267 8909). Tube: Camden Town. Just around the corner from the station. Award-winning Tapas £3. Open Mon. noon-11:30pm, Tues-Sat. 10:30am-11:30pm, Sun. 10:30am-10:30pm.

Le Petit Prince, 5 Holmes Rd., NW5 (tel. 267 0752). Tube: Kentish Town. Tucked away in a side street off Kentish Town Rd. Left out of station, then first right onto Holmes past McDonalds. Loyal following swears by the *couscous.* French/North African flavored food and decor. Vegetable *couscous* £4.50, with chicken £6.50. Open daily noon-3pm, 7-11:30pm.

Mange Too, 244 Kentish Town Rd., NW5. Tube: Kentish Town. Serves heaping sandwiches, including "American Clubs" (£2.55-3). Great salad bar (tons o' ingredients) £4. Open Mon.-Fri. 10am-6pm, Sat. 10am-5pm.

Crepe Van, outside the King William IV pub, 77 Hampstead High St., NW3. Tube: Hampstead. A Hampstead institution. Paper-thin Brittany crepes made in front of your eyes in the tiniest van imaginable. Sweet fillings (including banana and Grand Marnier) £1.50-2.50, savory £1.45-2.60. Open Mon.-Sat. 1-11pm, Sun. 1:30-11pm.

Pubs

> *Would I were in an alehouse in London!*
> *I would give all my fame for a pot of*
> *ale, and safety.*
> *—Shakespeare, Henry V*

> *There is nothing that has yet been contrived by man,*
> *by which so much happiness is produced as by a good*
> *tavern or inn...*
> *—Samuel Johnson*

"As much of the history of England has been brought about in public houses as in the House of Commons," said Sir William Harcourt. Even if you don't happen to witness history in the making, you can certainly absorb the spirit of this major social institution. As you down a pint or two, drink in the ancient velvet and mahogany of your surroundings. Many pubs are centuries old, and each has its distinctive history, ambience, and regulars. London's 7000 pubs are as colorful and historic as their counterparts throughout England, with clientele varying considerably from one neighborhood to the next. Pubs in the City pack in tourists and pin-stripes at lunch. The taverns up in Bloomsbury tend to draw a mix of tourists and students, while those in Kensington and Hampstead cater to the trendy element. Around the wholesale markets, tradesmen grab early morning pints. Pub crawling, the English equivalent of bar hopping, can easily be done on all fours given the concentration of alehouses in London. Taverns and inns no longer play the role of staging post for coach and horses; but pubs remain meeting-places, signposts ("turn left at The Porcupine"), bus stops, and bastions of Brittania.

Beer is the standard pub drink. You may be surprised by the number of brews on tap in London pubs. Some stock as many as a dozen ales and two ciders. Pubs owned by one of the giant breweries, e.g. Courage, Ind Coope, or Taylor Walker, are compelled to sell only that brewery's ales. Independents, called "Free Houses," can sell a wider range of beers. **Bitter** is the staple of English beer, named for the sharp hoppy aftertaste. Young's, Fuller's, Ruddle's, Tetley's, John Smith, Courage Director's, and Samuel Smith are all superb ales. "Real ale," naturally carbonated and drawn from a barrel, retains its full flavor. Brown, mild, pale, and India pale ales—less common varieties—all have a relatively heavy flavor with noticeable hop. **Stout** is rich, dark, and creamy. **Guinness,** the national drink of Ireland, is the quintessential Stout beer—try standing a match on the amazing head of silky foam. All draught ales and stouts are served "warm"—at room temperature—and by the pint or half-pint. If you can't stand the heat, try a **lager,** the European equivalent of American beer. Budweiser and Miller, where available, cost at least 30% more than German and British brews. **Cider,** an alcoholic apple drink, can prove as potent as the ales; a few pints of it will make you Brahms and Liszt, as cockneys say. Those who don't drink alcohol should savor the pub experience all the same; fruit juices and colas are served (but tend to get expensive), and low-alcohol beers have become more widely available. Buy all drinks at the bar—bartenders are not usually tipped. While the last pint for less than a pound in London has probably been poured a long time ago, prices vary greatly with area and even clientele. Generally, a pint will set you back £1.30-1.55, but in the very center of London this could rise to as much as £1.70. Along with food and drink, pubs often host traditional games, including darts, pool, and bar billiards, an ingenious derivative of billiards played from only one end of the table. More recently, a brash and bewildering array of video games, trivia quiz machines, and fruit (slot) machines has invaded many pubs. CD jukeboxes extort music lovers at 50p a play.

In general, avoid pubs within a half-mile radius of an inner-city train station (Paddington, Euston, King's Cross/St. Pancras, and Victoria). They prey upon tourists by charging 20-40p extra per pint. For the best pub prices, head to the East End. Stylish, lively pubs cluster around the fringes of the West End. Many historic alehouses lend an ancient air to areas swallowed up by the urban sprawl, such as Highgate and Hampstead. Some pubs have serious theatre groups performing upstairs, while others are meeting places for community groups, readings, and other entertainment.

In June 1987, Parliament voted to scrap a 1915 liquor law that required English pubs to close in the afternoon from 3-6pm. Now, publicans have the option of keeping their establishments open throughout the day (Mon.-Sat. 11am-11pm and Sun noon-10:30pm), but most still close from 3-7pm on Sundays. A bell 10 minutes before closing time signifies "last orders." A second bell and the publican's hallowed cry, "Time, gentlemen, PLEASE" right at closing time give patrons 10 minutes to finish their beers. Most pubs are fairly relaxed about the drinking-up time but there are those that will kick you out at 11:10pm on the dot (10:40pm on Sun.).

Look before you buy pub food. Quality and prices vary greatly with virtually no relation between the two, although enough places serve good food that you need not make a martyr of yourself. **Steak and kidney pie** or **pudding** is a mixture of steak and kidney, mushrooms, and pastry or pudding crust. A **cornish pasty** is filled with potato, onion, and meat. **Cottage pie** is minced meat with onion, saddled with mashed potatoes, and baked. **Shepherd's pie,** found nearly everywhere, is like cottage pie, but made with beef or lamb. A **ploughman's lunch** encompasses bread, cheese, and pickled onions. The very lucky may even find the early-childhood favorites, **bangers and mash** (sausages and mashed potatoes) or **bubble and squeak** (cabbage and mashed potatoes). All of the the above are best accompanied with much ale.

The West End

Lamb and Flag, 33 Rose St., WC2. Tube: Covent Garden or Leceister Sq. A formerly obstreperous pub where a mob of angry readers seized Augustan poet John Dryden and nearly beat him to death—just one of the events that earned it the name "Bucket of Blood." Today a more docile crowd poised on window seats drinks in Regency calm.

Maple Leaf, 41 Maiden Lane, WC2. Tube: Covent Garden. London's only Canadian pub, ay, and a good place to satisfy that late-night urge, eh, for a pint of Molson (£1.50), ay, after an evening at the theatre, eh.

Globe, 37 Bow St., WC2. Tube: Covent Garden. Right by the Royal Opera House—ideal for killing the ringing in your ears, along with orchestra members. Depicted in Hitchcock's *Frenzy.*

Round House, New Row at Bedford St., WC2. Tube: Covent Garden. *Let's Go* researchers and editors are believed to have been meeting here since Saxon times. The scarcity of seats forces patrons to drink and mingle with the hurly-burly post-5pm office-worker crowd.

The Chandos, 29 St. Martin's Lane, WC2. Tube: Charing Cross. A warm place to quaff tea after the National Gallery or the English National Opera; tiled interior and semi-enclosed alcove booths.

The Salisbury, 90 St. Martin's Lane, WC2. Tube: Leicester Sq. Extravagantly ornate glass and gilt become increasingly bewildering as the beers slip down—it's almost possible to get lost in here.

Nag's Head, 10 James St., WC2 (tel. 836 4678). Tube: Covent Garden. Not a tacky North Carolinian beach resort, but a favorite of London's theatre elite. The round, light beige "booths" recall airport seating.

The French House, 49 Dean St., W1. Tube: Piccadilly. Diminutive pub with grand liaisons, an unofficial H.Q. for the Free French forces during World War II. Decent French fare served in lieu of the usual English pub goodies: better wine selection than beer. Charles de Gaulle and Dylan Thomas both downed a few here.

The Porcupine, Great Newport St. at Charing Cross, WC2. Tube: Leicester Sq. The West End's most schizophrenic pub: young folks on the first floor generate smoke and noise, while a sedate older crowd (perhaps their parents) pecks at tasty pub meals (£4-5) upstairs before the theatre.

Sherlock Holmes, 10 Northumberland St. WC2. Tube: Charing Cross. Upstairs room a replica of Holmes' den at 221B Baker St. A host of relics to thrill the Holmes trivia fiend—the tobacco in the slipper, correspondence affixed to the mantlepiece with a dagger, and the head of the Hound of the Baskervilles. Many older American tourists and a devoted local crowd.

Grenadier, 18 Wilton Row, SW1. Tube: Hyde Park Corner. Wellington's Grenadier Guards, the heroes of Waterloo, lived and did most of their drinking here. Look for the bright red doors and guard post outside (just tall enough for a beaverskin).

The Albert, 52 Victoria St., SW1. Tube: Victoria. A 10-min. walk east along Victoria St. from the station. Award-winning pub with terrific service and mouth-watering, costly food. Come early or late to miss the tourist dinner deluge. Last orders for food at 9:30pm.

Kensington and Chelsea

Admiral Codrington, 17 Mossop St., SW3. Tube: South Kensington. From the station head east on Pelham St. and then on Draycott Ave., and turn left on Mossop St. This old, handsome pub with a peaceful patio off the back is a favorite watering hole for young Sloane Rangers. No silver bullets served here. Over 100 different kinds of whiskey.

Shuckburg Arms, 47 Denyer St., SW3. Tube: Sloane Sq. A beacon at the end of the road. Surprisingly successful mix of sloane, transatlantic, and transpacific types. Try not to buy Simon Boudard a pint.

The Australian, 29 Milner St., SW3. Tube: Sloane Sq. Not as Antipodean as it sounds. Everybody and everything tend to overflow into the street towards closing time.

Moore Arms, corner of Moore and Cadogan St., SW3. Tube: Sloane Sq. Relaxed and private atmosphere despite occasional invasions by people called Arabella.

The Antelope, 22 Eaton Terrace, SW1. Tube: Sloane Sq. A quiet, friendly pub that retains a provincial 17th-century ambience.

Duke of Wellington, 63 Eaton Terrace, SW1. Tube: Sloane Sq. East of the station. Popular bar frequented by King's Rd. shoppers and Chelsea locals. Drink a toast to one of the many pictures of the Duke (easier to do once you've already had a few).

Cadogan Arms, King's Rd. near Old Church St., SW3. Invigorating and jovial. Try to ignore the farm implements hanging from the rafters above your head. A good stopping place before a movie at the Cannon Chelsea across the street.

The Goat in Boots, 333 Fulham Rd., SW10. Tube: South Kensington. Perenially popular sloanepoint, with a wide range of beers. No one knows about the name.

The Gloucester, 187 Sloane Ave., SW1. Tube: Knightsbridge. One of the few places in London where you can actually order bangers and mash (£4). Look carefully: the wallpaper could have come from your house. Frequented by locals and shoppers.

Royal Court Tavern, Sloane Sq., SW1. Tube: Sloane Sq. The ideal place to banter about the coy state of French cinema. Patronized, appropriately, by a proto-intellectual sloany crowd. Food served daily noon-2:30pm and 6-10:15pm.

The Surprise, Christ Church St. at Christ Church Terrace, SW3. Tube: Sloane Sq. Take bus #39 from the station, get off at Tite St., walk north and turn left at Christ Church St. Relaxing Chelsea pub virtually fenced in by local BMWs. Surprise: nary a tourist to be seen.

The King's Head and Eight Bells, 50 Cheyne Walk, SW3. Take bus #11 down King's Rd., get off at Oakley St., walk toward the river and turn right on Cheyne Walk. Over the years this richly-textured 16th-century pub has been favored by Whistler, Graves, and Carlyle (whose pad lies just up the block). One of Dylan Thomas' favorites too, though he wasn't particularly choosy. Live music Sunday afternoon and evening.

The Zetland Arms, 2 Bute St., SW7. Tube: South Kensington. Were it not for its food, the Zetland Arms would be just another pub. Popular for its delicious shepherd's pie £2.30 and inexpensive, traditional pub grub. Ploughman's lunch £2.60. Food served all day.

The Windsor Castle, 144 Campden Hill Rd., W8. Tube: Notting Hill Gate. Rumor has it that you could once see the Castle from here, before the advent of industrial haze. Satisfy your appetite at three separate bars or in the packed garden out back.

Earl's Court

The Scarsdale, 23 Pembroke Sq., W8. Tube: Earl's Ct. Walk up Earl's Court Rd. 3 blocks past Cromwell Rd., and turn left at Pembroke Sq. More like a private party than a pub: jovial, stylish, and inexpensive. Unfettered by slot machines and pop music, this place leaves you only one option: to chat over a few delightful pints at vine-covered tables out front.

The King's Head, Hogarth Pl., SW5. Tube: Earl's Ct. From Earl's Court Rd., head west on Childs Way or Hogarth Pl. A quality pub in a quiet location, fireplace included. If you don't feel like ale, order champagne or hot chocolate.

The Prince of Teck, 161 Earl's Court Rd., SW5. Tube: Earl's Ct. Look for the crowd spilling out onto the street. An atmosphere like Venus—some love it, some hate it, either way it's hot and oppressive. Aussie headquarters. Welcoming sign says it all: "G'day and welcome to the land of Oz.'

Bloomsbury

Princess Louise, 208 High Holborn, WC1. Tube: Holborn. This big pub isn't big enough to contain the huge, jovial crowd that assembles after office hours. The Victorian men's room possesses its own preservation order.

The Lamb, 94 Lamb's Conduit St., WC1. Tube: Russell Sq. E.M. Forster and other Blooms-bury luminaries used to do much of their tippling here. Discreet, stained-glass "snob screens"—holdovers from Victorian times—render this pub ideal for nose-picking or danger-ous liaisons.

The Sun, 63 Lamb's Conduit St., WC1. Tube: Holborn. One of London's largest selections of real ales. A bright, busy pub in a hushed neighborhood of hospitals. Lovely cast-iron fire-places and hardwood floors.

Museum Tavern, 49 Great Russell St., WC1. Tube: Tottenham Court Rd. Karl Marx sipped ale here after banging out his *Das Kapital* across the street in the British Museum reading room. The Star Tavern, which formerly occupied this site, was one of Casanova's rendezvous spots. Thirteen beers on tap.

Queen's Larder, 1 Queen Sq., opposite St. George the Martyr, WC1. Tube: Russell Sq. or Holborn. A pleasant pub with coffered ceilings, dark mahogany paneling, and a fine restau-rant upstairs. Queen Charlotte used the cellar of this building to store sweetmeats for her ailing (read: insane) husband, George III.

Rugby Tavern, corner of Rugby St. and Great St. James, WC1. Tube: Holborn. A light, quiet, elegant pub with a rare, working fireplace. Just off the bustling shopping strip of Lamb's Con-duit St., an oasis of local good cheer.

The Water Rats, 328 Grays Inn Rd., WC1. Tube: King's Cross/St. Pancras. Ordinary appear-ance belies radical historical connections. A favorite haunt of Marx and Engels. Drinkers of the world, unite.

Grafton Arms, 72 Grafton Way, W1. Tube: Warren St. Off the tourist trail, near Regent's Park, and one of the best central London pubs for a relaxed pint. Caters to a London Univer-sity student crowd. Wine bar on roof-top patio.

The City

Ye Olde Cheshire Cheese, Wine Office Court, 145 Fleet St., EC4. Tube: Blackfriars or St. Paul's. An authentic 17th-century pub with sawdust on the floors and Yorkshire beers flowing from the tap. Famous as Dr. Johnson's hangout, and home of a blue parrot whose death (of a cold) was reported worldwide by the BBC. Closed for renovation until summer 1992.

Black Friar, 174 Queen Victoria St., EC4. Tube: Blackfriars. Witty art nouveau monument in marble and bronze to the medieval monks, including a back room called "the Side Chapel."

Dirty Dick's, 202-204 Bishopgate, EC2. Tube: Liverpool St. Named after Nat Bentley from the old English folk ballad. Pub "decorated" with a pair of stuffed felines and cobwebs.

Cartoonist, 76 Shoe Lane, EC4. Tube: Chancery Lane. Headquarters for the Cartoonist Club of Great Britain; decorated with appropriate hilarity.

The Ship and Blue Ball, 13 Boundary St., E2. Tube: Old St. A snug, convivial pub with a prime selection of beers and ales from the Pitfield Brewery, including the organic "Dark Star."

The East End and the River

George Inn, 77 Borough High St., SE1. Tube: London Bridge. A fine 17th-century galleried inn; the older equivalent of Victoria coach station, at the first stop on the old road out of London. Yes, a Dickens connection too (*Little Dorrit* this time).

The Blind Beggar, 337 Whitechapel Rd., E1. Tube: Whitechapel. Sip nervously as you wonder if you're sitting where George Cornell was when he was gunned down by rival Bethnal Green gangster Ronnie Kray in 1966. Spacious pub, and conservatory and garden.

Mayflower, 117 Rotherhithe St., SE16. Tube: Rotherhithe. Named in honor of the Pilgrims who embarked for the New World from this tavern in 1606. Cozy, nautical interior with wood paneling and views of the Thames from the second story.

The Angel, 101 Bermondsey Wall, SE16. Tube: Rotherhithe. A 16th-century pub with an undescribed view of the river to the Tower Bridge and the City. Intriguing trap doors (for smugglers) and a balcony in the back.

Prospect of Whitby, 57 Wapping Wall E1, London Docks. Tube: Wapping. 600-year-old watering hole of the diarist Samuel Pepys. Open ceilings and a rustic flagstone bar.

Town of Ramsgate, 62 Wapping High St., E1. Tube: Wapping. A mere 300 years old. Some convicts were imprisoned in the cellar on the way to Australia; others were chained to the bank to succumb to the tide, just beneath the pleasant garden.

Hampstead and Highgate

The Flask Tavern, 77 Highgate West Hill, N6, near the youth hostel. Tube: Archway. Enormously popular on summer evenings and at Sun. noon. Standing on the terrace outside, you can drink a toast to Karl Marx, Yehudi Menuhin, or any other Highgate luminary whose name flits through your giddy brain.

Spaniards Inn, Spaniards End, NW3, on the north edge of Hampstead Heath. Tube: Hampstead, then bus #210 along Spaniards Rd. Pub has provided garden in summer and fire in winter since 1585. The inn and outhouse prevent any road widening; traffic must crawl past the pub. Highwayman Dick Turpin and Dickens were patrons.

The Holly Bush, 22 Holly Mount, NW3. Tube: Hampstead. The quintessential Hampstead pub in a quaint cul-de-sac. Maze of glass and wood makes this place ideal for an illicit rendezvous.

The Bull and Bush, North End Way, NW3. Tube: Golders Green. Immortalized in the classic music hall song "Down at the old Bull and Bush," though the spiffy young gentlemen who crowd the bar seem unlikely to break into chorus. A fine watering hole for Hampstead hostelers.

Jack Straw's Castle, North End Way, NW3, by Whitestone Pond. Tube: Hampstead, then walk up Heath St. Massive timberclad block, frequented by Dickens (is there any pub Dickens did *not* frequent?) and a few German bombs. Vintage 60s exterior.

Camden Town and Islington

Slug and Lettuce, 1 Islington Green, N1. Tube: Angel. Patrons of the Screen on the Green conduct earnest discussions of *Casablanca* in huge, revealing windows. Good observation post for spotting Islington trendies. Try upstairs for a comfy, cosy setting.

Minogues, 80 Liverpool Rd., N1. Tube: Angel. Touted as one of London's few Irish pubs, complete with live music. Noticeable for its faux blue marble exterior. Just down the street from Café Pasta.

Edinburgh Castle, 57 Mornington Terrace, NW1. Tube: Camden Town. Deflated or elated sports teams from Regent's Park crowd the large terrace on summer evenings, oblivious to the main-line tracks in the cutting over the wall. Outdoor barbecue in summer.

Hammersmith and Putney

Half Moon, 93 Lower Richmond Rd., SW15. Tube: Putney Bridge. A no-nonsense pub known for live music in the room at the back, every night of the week. Check *Time Out* for gig details.

Star and Garter, 4 Lower Richmond Rd., SW15. Tube: Putney Bridge. A veritable monument of a riverside pub, with a roomy lounge.

The Dove, 19 Upper Mall, SW6. Tube: Hammersmith. Fantastic view of the river and the pinnacles of Hammersmith Bridge, taken in along with delicious lunches.

Tea

English "tea" refers to both a drink and a social ritual. Tea the drink is the preferred remedy for exhaustion, ennui, a row with one's partner, a rainy morning, or a slow afternoon. English tea is served strong and milky; if you want it any other way, say so. Tea anywhere—in plush hotels or railway cars—tastes more or less the same until you graduate into the higher echelons of Jackson's or Fortnum & Mason's teas.

Tea the social ritual centers around a meal. Afternoon high tea includes cooked meats, salad, sandwiches, and pastries. "Tea" in the north of England refers to the evening meal, often served with a huge pot of tea. Cream tea, a specialty of Cornwall and Devon, includes toast, shortbread, crumpets, scones, and jam, accompanied by delicious clotted cream (a cross between whipped cream and butter). Most Brits take short tea breaks each day, mornings ("elevenses") and afternoons (around 4pm). Sunday takes the cake for best tea day; the indulgent can while away a couple of hours over a pot of Earl Grey, a pile of buttered scones, and the Sunday supplements.

London hotels serve afternoon teas, often hybrids of the clotted and high variety, which are expensive and sometimes disappointing. A full set meal may induce the same after-effects as three bags of M & M's. But the food is terribly British and often delicious. You might order single items from the menu instead of the full set. Most upscale hotels and department stores have some kind of afternoon tea.

Terrace Bar, Harrods, Knightsbridge (tel. 730 1234). Tube: Knightsbridge. Revel in bourgeois satisfaction as you demurely enjoy your expensive set tea inside or out on the terrace (£9). Tea served daily 3-5:30pm.

Julie's Bar, 137 Portland Rd. (tel. 727 7985). Tube: Holland Park. Design your own afternoon tea from a mass of *à la carte* elements. Huge slab of flan for £1.50. Open for tea Mon.-Fri. 4-6pm, Sat.-Sun. 4:30-6pm.

The Orangery Tea Room, Kensington Palace, Kensington Gardens, W8. Light meals and tea served in the marvelously airy Orangery built for Queen Anne in 1705; architecture by Wren and Hawksmoor. Two fruit scones with clotted cream and jam £3. Pot of tea £1.25. Trundle through the gardens afterward, smacking your lips. Morning pastries served 9:30-11:30am, lunch 11:30am-2pm, tea 3-5pm.

Wine Bars

Although traditionalists frown upon "trendy" wine bars, some establishments have pedigrees nearly as distinguished as the most celebrated pubs. Most wine bars serve interesting, if expensive, continental food. The typical menu includes pâtés, cheeses, salmon, quiche, salads, cold meats, and soups. Consume wine by the glass or bottle, but watch out for places with skimpy glasses—unfortunately a common ailment. Wine bars tend to be less rambunctious than pubs and dominated by pinstripes.

Betjeman's, 44 Cloth Fair, EC1 (tel. 796 4981). Tube: Barbican. Market opening hours mean you can enjoy a very Continental breakfast at this refined wine bar and restaurant. Stick to the bar food to save your budget. House wine £1.50 per glass. Open Mon.-Fri. 7:30am-11pm.

Brahms and Liszt, 19 Russell St., WC2 (tel. 240 3661). Tube: Covent Garden. Rhyming slang for the reason to come to the popular bars above and below the ground floor restaurant. Open daily 11am-3:30pm and 5:30-11pm.

Balls Brothers, 2 Old Change Ct., St. Paul's Churchyard, EC4 (tel. 236 9921). Tube: St. Paul's. London's oldest wine bar chain supplies convincing atmosphere and dependability to bankers and tourists. Glasses of wine from £1.50. Also at Cheapside (Tube: St.Paul's), Threadneedle St. (Tube: Bank), Liverpool St., St. Mary's at Hill (Tube: Monument) and Hay's Galleria, Tooley St., Southwark (Tube: London Bridge). Open Mon.-Fri. 11am-10:30pm.

Downs Wine Bar, Arch 166, Bohemia Pl., E8 (tel. (081) 986 4325). Bus #22 or 38 to Hackney Central BR station. Way out in the East End, but worth the trip to a relaxed bar frequented by casual locals. Built underneath the railway arches (trains occasionally rumble overhead), but cozy and tasteful. Good French food and sublime house wine (£2.50). Open Mon.-Sat. 10:30am-11pm, Sun. noon-10:30pm.

Simpson's, 38½ Cornhill, EC3 (tel. 626 9985). Tube: Bank. Glistens with loads of shiny brass and with shiny wooden benches polished by countless besuited bottoms. Steak and kidney pie £3.50, spotted dick (steamed sponge pudding with raisins) £1.25. Wine from £1.50 per glass. Open Mon.-Fri. 11:30am-3pm.

The City Flogger, 120 Fenchurch St., EC3 (tel. 623 3251). Tube: Monument or Tower Hill. Annoyingly empty champagne bottles line the stairs. Wine £1.50-4 per glass, Château Petrus 1955 £425 per bottle. Open Mon.-Fri. 11:30am-4pm and 5:30-9pm.

Solange's Brasserie, 11 St. Martin's Ct., WC2. Tube: Leicester Sq. Right outside of the Hippodrome Leicester Sq. Tube exit. Baroque music, French menu and conversation, and outdoor tables in an L-shaped alleyway. Desserts £3-3.50. Watch out for the 12½% service charge. Open Mon.-Fri. noon-3pm and 5:30pm-midnight, Sat. 5:30pm-midnight.

Basil's, 8 Basil St., SW1. Tube: Knightsbridge. Good food and wine in a relaxed setting. Lends itself to dull write-ups. Live jazz Wed. and Fri. 7-11pm. Open Mon.-Fri. noon-3pm and 5:30-10pm, Sat. noon-3pm.

Dome, 30 Wellington St., WC2. Tube: Covent Garden. A trendy Paris café, mysteriously transported to London. Wine served only during licensed hours. *Baguette fromage* £2.30, *brie amandine* £3.50. Cappuccino from £1. No subtitles. Open daily 8am-11pm. Another branch at 354 King's Rd., SW3.

Henry's, 9 Young St., W8. Tube: High St. Kensington. Part of Henry's nightclub and Henry's Thai restaurant. Ideal for soothing the ol' nerves after shopping manically in the nearby stores. Soon to have Karoake...Open daily 11am-11pm.

Le Café Des Amis, Hanover Pl., WC2, northeast of Covent Garden. Tube: Covent Garden. Gourmet food and drink served in a cozy brick alleyway. Immense selection of cheeses, many pungent enough to drive away any number of friends. Desserts £3-3.50. Entrees £7-10. Open Mon.-Sat. noon-4pm and 6-11:30pm.

Sights

> *The vast mass of London itself, fought street by street, could easily*
> *devour an entire hostile army.*
> —*Sir Winston Spencer Churchill, radio broadcast, 1940*

Most Londoners shun the major sights of their hometown, possibly fearing some dread encounter with the camera-toting masses. True travelers, however, are made of sturdier stuff, and realize that sight-seeing in a tourist Mecca such as London can yield a two-fold fascination: that of the sights themselves and that of looking at the tourists looking. To enlightened eyes, the contrast between the superhuman scale of London's celebrated palaces, parks, churches, and tombs and the stream of humanity shuffling through them is striking.

The landmarks of London that attract those on foot and in ever-lengthening coaches face an onslaught of up to five million visitors a year. These stampedes tend to concentrate from the late morning onwards, so try to down your bangers and mash as early as possible. London's most famous sights are those intimately connected with the royal family in all of its guises: while the Tower is no longer any use in defense of the royals, they are still baptised and buried in Westminster Abbey, reside in the Palace, are married in St. Paul's, and preside over the opening of Parliament every year. Pacing any assault on these particular sights will allow a much more thorough exploration of the various districts that make up the city. Hidden in and around the main sights can be found a serene chapel or an immense carnival, a museum of clocks, a deer park, an Indian film festival, or an exhibition of Masai arms. Modern day tourists are only the latest in a long line of arrivals to try to find out how the city fits together, and where they fit into the puzzle.

Westminster Abbey

> *This is the repository of the British kings and nobility, and very fine monuments are here seen over the graves of our ancient monarchs; the particulars are too long to enter into here, and are so many times described by several authors, that it would be a vain repetition to enter upon it here; besides, we have by no means any room for it.*
>
> *—Daniel Defoe*

That Westminster Abbey has become the city's most prized sight indicates just how heavily the weight of the past bears on London. Plaques honoring the most prominent of England's dead line the grey walls of the Abbey, an extraordinary arsenal of English history. Neither a cathedral nor a parish church, the abbey is a "royal peculiar," controlled directly by the crown and outside the jurisdiction of the Church of England. Death doesn't get any better than this; burial in the abbey is the greatest and rarest honor the British Crown can bestow. Byron was refused burial here because of his unconventional morals (though a plaque now honors him). Over the last 200 years, space has become so limited that many coffins stand upright under the pavement. The late Laurence Olivier is due to be honored in Poet's Corner in the next year or so, when the approval process is finally completed.

The Abbey was consecrated on the 28th of December 1065, although Edward the Confessor was on his deathbed and unable to attend the service. Henry III erected most of the present structure as a Benedictine monastery to honor Edward. Before he died in 1271, Henry built the the high and solid Norman nave in the fashion of the great French cathedrals. You can still see the steps used by the monks along the south and southeastern walls. Most of the visible stone in the abbey is actually refacing from the 18th century onward. Sir Christopher Wren and his Baroque pupil, Hawksmoor, built the two touted towers of the west wing, now blackened by the cars whizzing around Parliament Square.

Just inside the abbey, in the **nave**, rests a memorial to Churchill, a piece of green marble engraved with the immortal words "Remember Winston Churchill." Parliament placed it here 25 years after the Battle of Britain, perhaps prompted by pangs of regret that Churchill's body lay buried in Bladon and not in the Abbey's hall of fame. The grave of the Unknown Warrior, a few paces beyond, commemorates the anonymous legions of WWI war dead. The tomb contains the body of a nameless British soldier transported from Flanders in 1920 and buried "among the kings because he had done good toward God and toward his home." At the foot of the Organ Loft, a memorial to Sir Isaac Newton sits next to the grave of temperate physicist Lord Kelvin. Franklin Roosevelt, David Lloyd George, Lord and Lady Baden-Powell of Boy Scout fame, and the presumptuous David Livingstone number among

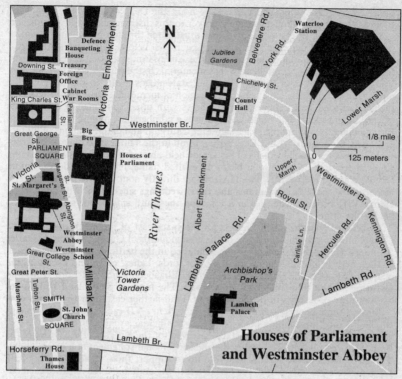

Houses of Parliament and Westminster Abbey

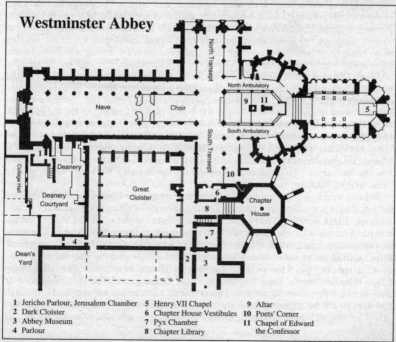

Westminster Abbey

1 Jericho Parlour, Jerusalem Chamber
2 Dark Cloister
3 Abbey Museum
4 Parlour
5 Henry VII Chapel
6 Chapter House Vestibules
7 Pyx Chamber
8 Chapter Library
9 Altar
10 Poets' Corner
11 Chapel of Edward the Confessor

the elect remembered in the nave. On the hour, the Dean of the Abbey climbs the stairs of the pulpit and offers a timely prayer to this distinguished captive audience.

To see the rest of the Abbey, visitors must enter through a gate at the end of the north aisle of the nave and pay admission (see below). **Musician's Aisle,** just beyond this gate, contains the graves of the Abbey's most accomplished organists, John Blow and Henry Purcell, as well as memorials to the composers Elgar, Britten, Vaughan Williams, and William Walton. **Statesman's Aisle,** in the early Gothic north transept, has the most eclectic collection of memorials. Prime Ministers Disraeli, Gladstone, and Palmerston rub elbows with other statesmen in monuments of varying grandeur. The north wall features a cumbersome monument to William Pitt, confidently waving the peace sign that Churchill and, later, millions of hippies emulated. Sir Francis Vere's Elizabethan tomb in the southeast corner of the transept features the cracked shells of his armor held above his body. A strange paving stone in front of the memorial bears no exalted name, only the cold inscription, "Stone coffin underneath." The **High Altar,** directly south of the north transept, has been the scene of coronations and royal weddings since 1066. Anne of Cleves, Henry VIII's fourth wife, lies in a tomb on the south side of the sanctuary, just before the altar.

A series of crowded choir chapels fill the space east of the north transept. The Chapel of Islip contains the grave of the co-conqueror of Quebec, Admiral Charles Saunders. His cohort, General Wolfe, who died in the battle, is memorialized back in the north transept. Among the tombs of lords, ladies, earls, and abbots in the chapel of St. John the Baptist lies the ornate Elizabethan tomb of Lord Hunsdon, featuring a palm tree, and shells by a beach. The tomb of Sir Roland Hill, father of the penny post, rests in the chapel of St. Paul farther east, near the chapel exit.

Beyond these chapels stands the Chapel of Henry VII (added in 1503), perhaps England's most upstanding piece of late-perpendicular architecture. Every one of its magnificently carved wooden stalls, reserved for the Knights of the Order of the Bath, features a headpiece bearing the chosen personal statement of a given knight. The lower sides of the seats, which fold up to support those standing during long services, were the only part of the design left to the craftsmen; they feature cartoon-like images of wives beating up their husbands and other more pagan stories. Lord Nelson's stall was #20, on the south side. Latter-day members of the order include Ronald Reagan and Norman Schwarzkopf. Look for anomalies in the carvings of the 95 saints gazing down upon the stalls (one female saint sports a beard, another saint peers from behind spectacles). The chapel's elaborate ceiling was hand carved after it had been erected. Henry VII and his wife Elizabeth, the least legitimate couple ever to ascend to England's throne, lie at the very end of the chapel. Charles II dug up Oliver Cromwell's body from this part of the Abbey in 1661 and had it hanged; a gleeful crowd of onlookers tore it to pieces. Today only a simple memorial to Cromwell remains. The Royal Air Force (RAF) Chapel, at the far east end, commemorates the Battle of Britain. A hole in the wall in the northeast corner of the Air Force memorial, damage from a German bomb, was deliberately (and somewhat heavy-handedly) left unrepaired. Buried on opposite sides of the Henry VII Chapel lie Protestant Queen Elizabeth I (in the north aisle) and the Catholic cousin she had beheaded, Mary Queen of Scots (in the south aisle). Both, the verger insists, "put Britain back on its feet again."

Behind the High Altar, in the **Chapel of St. Edward the Confessor,** rests the Coronation Chair, on which all but two English monarchs since 1308 (Edward V and Edward VIII) have been crowned. The chair rests on the ancient Stone of Scone, not to be confused with scones of stone served by teashops everywhere. The stone has been kidnapped twice—first by James I of England, who snatched it from Scotland, and again by anti-royalist students in the 1950s. During the Second World War, it was hidden from possible capture by Hitler, and rumor has it that only Churchill, Roosevelt, the Prime Minister of Canada, and the two workers who moved the stone knew of its whereabouts. For coronation convenience, the chair sits next to the seven-foot long State Sword and the handy-dandy shield of Edward III. The chapel contains a hodgepodge of kings and queens, from Henry III (d.

1272), to George II (d. 1760). Sick persons hoping to be cured would spend nights at the base of the Shrine of St. Edward the Confessor, at the center of the chapel. The king purportedly wielded healing powers during his life, and used to dispense free medical care to hundreds with the laying on of his hands. Tiny spiral staircases within small towers at the entrance to the shrine lead up to a higher chapel where Henry V's wife lies.

Visitors befuddled by the graves of obscure English monarchs will be relieved to find recognizable names on the graves and plaques located in **Poet's Corner.** This little shrine celebrates everyone dead, canonized, and anthologized in the annals of English lit. It begins early, with the short Gothic tomb of Geoffrey Chaucer, placed on the east wall of the transept 150 years after his death. Floor panels commemorate Alfred Lord Tennyson, T.S. Eliot, Dylan Thomas, Henry James, Robert Browning, Lewis Carroll, racy Lord Byron, and poets of World War I, all at the foot of Chaucer's tomb. Each one bears an appropriate description or image for puzzle solvers: D.H. Lawrence's publishing mark (a phoenix) or T.S. Eliot's symbol of death ("the fire and the rose are one"). The south wall bears a misspelled medallion of rare Ben Jonson as well as memorials to Edmund Spenser and John Milton. A partition wall divides the south transept, its east side graced with the graves of Samuel Johnson and actor David Garrick, its west side with memorials to an ever-pensive William Wordsworth, Samuel Taylor Coleridge, a tiny Jane Austen, and the granddaddy of them all, William Shakespeare. Plaques mounted just above the Shakespeare memorial romanticize Keats and Shelley, though both poets already had excessively romantic burials in Rome. Memorials to Robert Burns and the Brontë sisters cover the south walls. Handel's massive memorial, on the west wall of the transept, looms over his grave next to the resting place of prolific Charles Dickens. On this side of the wall, you'll also find the grave of Rudyard Kipling and a memorial to that morbid Dorset farm boy, Thomas Hardy.

The abbey's **cloister** rests in a special peace of its own. The entrance in the northeast corner dates from the 13th century, the rest of it from the 14th. The **Chapter House,** east down a passageway off the cloister, has one of the best-preserved medieval tile floors in Europe. The round, spacious room offers some relief from the hectic Abbey: you may find someone reading a novel on the side benches. The windows in the ceiling depict scenes from the abbey's history. The king's council used the room as its chamber in 1257, and the House of Commons used it as a meeting place in the 16th century. Even today, it is the government and not the abbey that administers the Chapter House and the adjacent Pyx Chamber, once the Royal Treasury and now a plate museum.

Royal effigies (used instead of actual corpses for lying-in-state ceremonies) live in the **Westminster Abbey Treasure Museum.** The oldest, that of Edward III, has a lip permanently warped by the stroke that killed him. Those who knew Admiral Nelson found his effigy almost supernaturally accurate—perhaps because his mistress arranged his hair. The museum also includes an exhibit on the history of the abbey as well as some historical oddities, including a Middle English lease to Chaucer and the much-abused sword of Henry V. (Chapter House, Pyx Chamber, and museum open daily 10:30am-6pm. Combined admission £1.60, students £80p, children 40p.) Enter through Dean's Yard and the cloisters on Great College St. to visit the 900-year-old **College Garden,** the oldest in England. (Open April-Sept. Thurs. 10am-6pm, Oct.-March Thurs. 10am-4pm; band concerts Aug.-Sept. Thurs. 12:30-2pm.)

Those who enjoy amazingly informative discussions about architecture or a little fun gossip about the dead should take the excellent all-inclusive Abbey Guided Super Tour, lasting 1¼ hour and costing £6. (Tours depart from the Enquiry Desk in the nave Mon.-Fri. at 10am, 10:30am, 11am, 2pm, 2:30pm, and 3pm; Sat. at 10am, 11am, and 12:30pm.) To book one, inquire at the abbey desk, call 222 7110, or write to Super Tours, 20 Dean's Yard, London SW1P 3PA. Photography is permitted only on Wednesday from 6-7:45pm. (Westminster Abbey open Thurs.-Tues. 8am-6pm, Wed. 8am-7:45pm; free. Chapels and transepts open Mon.-Tues. and Thurs.-Fri. 9am-4:45pm, Wed. 9am-4:45pm and 6-7:45pm, Sat. 9am-2:45pm and

3:45-5:45pm; admission £2.60, students £1.30, children 60p. All parts of abbey free Wed. 6-7:45pm.)

Westminster

In the environs of Westminster Abbey, **St. Margaret's,** the parish church of the House of Commons, provides shelter from the storm. John Milton and Winston Churchill were married here (at different times to different people). The stained glass window to the north of the entrance depicts a blind Milton dictating *Paradise Lost* to one of his daughters. Some scenes from *Paradise Regained* surround the window. The John Piper windows on the south side of the Church, built after the war, are entitled "Spring in London." The stunning east window, made in Holland in 1501, honors the marriage of Catherine of Aragon to Prince Arthur. Beneath the high altar lies the headless body of Sir Walter Raleigh, who was executed across the road in 1618. The inscription on his memorial calls upon readers respectfully not to "reflect on his errors." (Open daily 9:30am-4:30pm.)

On the south side of the abbey group the buildings of the **Westminster School,** founded as a part of the Abbey. References to the school date as far back as the 14th century, but Queen Elizabeth officially refounded the school in 1560. The arch in Dean's Yard is pitted with the carved initials of generations of England's most privileged schoolboys. Alums include Ben Jonson, John Dryden, John Locke, Christopher Wren, Edward Gibbon, and A.A. Milne.

The 14th-century **Jewel Tower,** a surviving tower of Westminster Palace, stands by the southeastern end of the Abbey, across from the Houses of Parliament. Ground floor exhibits reconstruct the tower's past; curious classicists can read a list of palace construction expenses in Latin (the tower held Edward III's personal booty). The museum on the upper floors displays a selection of medieval capitals as well as a Norman sword dredged from the nearby moat. (Tower open Tues.-Sat. 10am-1pm and 2-6pm; Oct.-March Tues.-Sun. 10am-1pm and 2-4pm. Admission 65p, students and seniors 50p, children 35p.) The **Victoria Tower Gardens,** immediately south of the Houses of Parliament, offer a secluded view of the Thames. A bronze replica of Rodin's sculpture *Six Burghers of Calais* depicts the men who surrendered themselves to Edward III during the Hundred Years War so that their city might be spared destruction. Emmeline Pankhurst and her daughter are memorialized in the northwest corner of the gardens for their leadership in the women's suffrage movement, and a stringed-out Giacometti, *Järvenpää Residing,* adorns the Parliament Gate. The "lovingly donated" riverside benches make perfect lunchtime perches.

Four assertive corner towers distinguish **St. John's Church,,** a chamber-music concert hall in nearby Smith Sq. Queen Anne, whose imagination was strained by the effort of telling architects how to build the 50 new churches she had founded by an act of Parliament, supposedly upended a footstool and told Thomas Archer to build the church in its image. Dickens likened Archer's effort to a "petrified monster." Still, Monday lunchtime recitals (£3.50) tend to not to be stony. (Box office tel. 222 1061.) Any flurry of activity around the square is likely to be connected with no. 31, where the Central Office of the Conservative Party lurks, ready to swing into action down the road.

A few blocks down Victoria Street from Westminster proper is **Westminster Cathedral.** Not to be confused with the Anglican Abbey, the Cathedral is the headquarters of the Roman Catholic church in Britain. Finished in 1903, the cathedral is a mix of banded brick, swirling marble, and a starker ceiling, and features a startling rocketlike tower. A lift inside takes visitors up for an unadorned view of the Houses of Parliament, the river, and Kensington (lift open daily 9:30am-5pm, 70p; cathedral open 7am-8pm.)

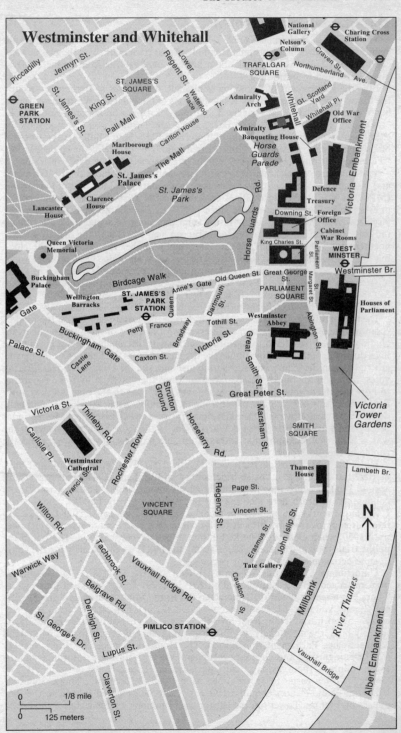

Westminster and Whitehall

Piccadilly

Jermyn St.

St. James's St.

King St.

Pall Mall

St. JAMES'S SQUARE

Regent St.

Lower Regent St.

Waterloo Place

Carlton House Tr.

GREEN PARK STATION

Marlborough House

The Mall

St. James's Palace

Clarence House

Lancaster House

St. James's Park

Queen Victoria Memorial

Buckingham Palace

Gate

Wellington Barracks

Birdcage Walk

ST. JAMES'S PARK STATION

Anne's Gate

Old Queen St.

Queen

Dartmouth St.

Broadway

Petty France

Tothill St.

Victoria St.

Caxton St.

Palace St.

Castle Lane

Buckingham Gate

Victoria St.

Thirleby Rd.

Carlisle Pl.

Westminster Cathedral

Francis St.

Rochester Row

Strutton Ground

Horseferry Rd.

Great Peter St.

Great Smith St.

Marsham St.

SMITH SQUARE

VINCENT SQUARE

Regency St.

Page St.

Vincent St.

Wilton Rd.

Warwick Way

Tachbrook St.

Belgrave Rd.

Denbigh St.

St. George's Dr.

Lupus St.

Vauxhall Bridge Rd.

Erasmus St.

Causton St.

John Islip St.

PIMLICO STATION

Claverton St.

Vauxhall Bridge

National Gallery

Nelson's Column

TRAFALGAR SQUARE

Northumberland Ave.

Craven St.

Charing Cross Station

Admiralty Arch

Whitehall

Gt. Scotland Yard

Whitehall Pl.

Old War Office

Admiralty

Banqueting House

Horse Guards Parade

Victoria Embankment

Defence

Treasury

Downing St.

Foreign Office

King Charles St.

Horse Guards Rd.

Cabinet War Rooms

Parliament St.

Margaret St.

WEST-MINSTER

Westminster Br.

Great George St.

PARLIAMENT SQUARE

Westminster Abbey

Abingdon St.

Houses of Parliament

Victoria Tower Gardens

Lambeth Br.

Thames House

Tate Gallery

Millbank

River Thames

Albert Embankment

N

0   1/8 mile

0   125 meters

The Houses of Parliament

The Houses of Parliament (Tube: Westminster), oft imagined in foggy silhouette against the Thames, have become London's visual trademark. For the classic view captured by Claude Monet, walk about halfway over Westminster Bridge, preferably at dusk and in purple fog.

Like the government offices along Whitehall, the Houses of Parliament occupy the former site of a royal palace. A few portions of the Palace of Westminster (notably Westminster Hall) have survived, but most of it went up in picturesque smoke on October 16, 1834. Sir Charles Barry and A.W.N. Pugin won a competition for the design of the new houses. From 1840 to 1888, Barry built a hulking, symmetrical block that Pugin ornamented with tortured imitations of late medieval decoration. "Tudor details on a classic body," Pugin later sneered, before dying of insanity.

The immense complex blankets eight acres and includes more than 1100 rooms and 100 staircases. Space is nevertheless so inadequate that Members of Parliament (MPs) can not have private offices or staff, and the archives—the original copies of every Act of Parliament passed since 1497—are stuffed into Victoria Tower, the large tower to the south. A flag flown from the tower (a signal light after dusk) indicates that Parliament is in session. You can hear **Big Ben** in the slightly smaller northern tower but you can't see it; it's actually neither the tower nor the clock but the 15-ton bell that tolls the hours. The immortal nickname has a prosaic origin; the bell was cast while a robustly proportioned Sir Benjamin Hall served as Commissioner of Works. Each of the Roman numerals on the clock face measures two feet in length; the "big hand," 14 feet. Over the years Big Ben (the bell) has developed a crack. The mechanism moving the hands is still wound manually.

Destroyed during the Blitz and rebuilt during the austere late 1940s, the modest room now housing the Commons preserves most features of the Old Chamber, including thin red lines fixed two sword-lengths apart. Members may not cross these lines during debates. The government of the day occupies the benches to the Speaker's right, with the Prime Minister sitting just opposite the Despatch Boxes. During votes, members file out of the chamber and into the "division lobbies" according to how they have voted: ayes into west lobby, and nays to the east. As they enter the Commons, members must pass through **Churchill's Arch,** the chipped and half-destroyed stone doorway that the statesman insisted be left untouched as a reminder of England's losses during World War II. One of the most haunting images of the war is a hurried snapshot that shows Churchill standing, head bowed, amid the rubble of the old House.

Until 1825, high treason trials were conducted in **Westminster Hall,** first built in 1097 but derided as a "mere bedchamber" by William II. The hall was rebuilt around 1400, at which time the hammerbeam roof was added. The long list of those condemned to death here includes Sir Thomas More, Guy Fawkes, and Charles I. A plaque marks the spot where Charles sat during his trial. After Charles' ill-fated attempt to arrest five MPs in 1641, no monarch even tried to enter the chamber until 1950, when George VI peeked in on the hall's reconstruction. The last of the public trials took place here in 1806. Today the hall is used primarily for the lying-in-state ceremonies of prominent personages.

Unfortunately, access to Westminster Hall and the Houses of Parliament has been restricted since a bomb killed an MP in 1979. To get a guided tour (Mon.-Thurs.) or a seat at Question Time when the Prime Minister attends (Mon.-Thurs. at 2:30pm), you need to obtain tickets—available on a limited basis from your embassy—or an introduction from an MP. Because demand for these tickets is extremely high, the most likely way of getting into the building is to queue to attend a debate when Parliament is in session. The House of Commons Visitors' Gallery (for "Distinguished and Ordinary Strangers") is open during extraordinary hours (Mon.-Thurs. 4-10pm, Friday 10am-3pm). The more staid House of Lords Visitors' Gallery is often easier to access (open Mon.-Wed. 2:30pm-late, Thurs. 3pm-late, Fri. 11am-late). Visitors should arrive early, and be prepared to wait in the long queues by Victoria Tower (on the left for the Commons, on the right for the Lords.

Free.) Those willing to sacrifice the roar of the debate for smaller, more focused business can attend meetings of any of the various Committees when they are in session by jumping the queue and going straight up to the entrance. For times of committee meetings each week, call the House of Commons Information Office (tel. 219 4272).

The Old Palace Yard, the inner courtyard of the original palace, nestles south of Westminster Hall. Sir Walter Raleigh and Guy Fawkes of the Gunpowder Plot both met their untimely demises here. The New Palace Yard is a good place to espy your favorite MPs as they enter the complex just north of Westminster Hall. West of Big Ben, in Parliament Square, stands a bear-like statue of Winston Churchill (head electrified to ward off pigeons). Metal likenesses of Benjamin Disraeli, Abraham Lincoln, and Lord Palmerston keep Churchill company nearby.

Whitehall

In 1698, Henry VIII's Palace of Whitehall, "the biggest and most hideous place in all Europe," burned to the ground. England's royalty then began the roaming that took successive royal families to the palaces of Kensington and St. James's and finally to Buckingham Palace. Meanwhile, Whitehall (Tube: Westminster or Charing Cross), stretching from Parliament Street to Trafalgar Square, became the center of civil administration.

The **Banqueting House** (corner of Horse Guards Ave. and Whitehall), built in 1625, one of the few intact masterpieces of Inigo Jones, was the first true Renaissance building in England, and the only part of Whitehall to survive the fire that consumed the palace. This Palladian hall achieved notoriety on January 27, 1649 when King Charles I, draped in black velvet, was led out its doorway and beheaded. The allegorical paintings on the 60-ft.-high ceiling (ironically the story of the happy monarchy of James I and Charles I) are the handiwork of Rubens. A cautious James II supposedly placed the weather vane on top of the building to see if a favorable wind was blowing for William of Orange. From 1724 to 1890, the Banqueting House served as a Chapel Royal. These days the hall sees no executions, just some harmless state dinners (behind bulletproof glass) and the occasional concert. (Open Mon.-Sat. 10am-5pm, admission £2, students £1.50, children £1.35.)

Henry VIII's wine cellar was one of the few parts of the palace spared in the fire of 1698. In 1953, the government erected the massive Ministry of Defence Building, just south of the Banqueting House, over Henry's cache. The cellar had to be relocated deeper into the ground to accommodate the new structure. Technically, visitors may view the cellar, but permission is dauntingly difficult to obtain (apply in writing to the Department of the Environment or the Ministry of Defence with a compelling story). Near the statue of General Gordon in the gardens behind the Ministry of Defence Building, you'll find the remnants of Queen Mary's terrace, built for Queen Mary II. The bottom of the steps leading from the terrace mark the 17th-century water level.

Some of Whitehall's major attractions stand off the main street. **Scotland Yard** will probably fall short of crime-hounds' expectations. The home of so many correct but unimaginative detectives humbled by Sherlock Holmes and Hercule Poirot is nothing more than one large and one small building connected by an arch at 6 Derby Gate. The old buildings now contain government offices. The official residence of the British Prime Minister, **10 Downing Street** boasts the most recognizable door in England. Margaret Thatcher's contribution to the local architecture takes the form of large iron gates that now protect the street from terrorists and tourists alike; even the motorcycle messengers have to hand their papers through the gates. Behind the famous exterior of No. 10 beyond the security spreads an extensive political network, one of the centers of British government. The Chancellor of the Exchequer resides at No. 11 Downing St., the Chief Whip of the House of Commons at No. 12. Together, these three houses contain more than 200 rooms. Recently, the Cabinet room overlooking the back garden of No. 10 survived an IRA mortar attack launched from a nearby parked van with its roof cut out. In the middle of Whitehall as it turns into Parliament St. stands the rigorously formal **Cenotaph** honoring the war dead, usually decked with crested wreaths.

On the west side of Whitehall north of Downing St. stand the **Horse Guards,** where two photogenic mounted soldiers keep watch daily from 10am to 4pm. At Whitehall's changing of the guard, as opposed to Buckingham Palace's, you can witness the pageantry without a large crowd in tow. (The head guard meticulously inspects the troops Mon.-Sat. at 11am, Sun. at 10am. The guard dismounts, with some fanfare, daily at 4pm.) Through the gates lies Horse Guards Parade, a large court (opening onto St. James's Park) from which the bureaucratic array of different styles of architecture that make up Whitehall can be seen. In early June, the Beating Retreat that takes place here is a must for lovers of pomp and circumstance (for information on tickets, call 218 3955).

Charing Cross and Trafalgar Square

The original **Charing Cross,** last of 13 crosses set up to mark the stages of Queen Eleanor's royal funeral procession in 1291 ("charing" comes from "beloved queen" in French), was once the center of Trafalgar Square. It has since been moved to the front of Charing Cross railway station. This spot used to be the true focus of London life as well as the geographical center of the city. "Why, Sir, Fleet Street has a very animated appearance," Samuel Johnson once remarked, "but I think the full tide of human existence is at Charing Cross." Now the full tide of traffic engulfs the place, and the bronze statue of King Charles drowns in the ebb and flow of automobiles.

Unlike many squares in London, **Trafalgar Square,** sloping down from the National Gallery to Charing Cross, has been public land ever since the razing of several hundred houses made way for its construction in the 1830s. **Nelson's Column,** a fluted granite pillar, commands the square, with four majestic, beloved lions guarding the base, and troops of pigeons everywhere. The monument and square commemorate brilliant Admiral Nelson, killed during his greatest victory off Trafalgar in Spain. Floodlights bathe the square after dark. Every year, Norway donates a giant Christmas tree for the square in thanks for Britain's help during World War II; in 1990, it and two policemen were nearly cut down by a man armed with a chainsaw protesting strict Norwegian drugs laws. Enthusiastic, even rambunctious New Year's celebrations take place here, including universal indiscriminate kissing.

At the head of the square squats the ordering façade of the National Gallery, Britain's collection of the Old Masters (see Museums below). A competition to design a new extension to the gallery ended in Prince Charles' denouncement of the winning entry as a "monstrous carbuncle" on the face of London, and the subsequent selection of a new architect. Robert Venturi's wing to the west of the main building has just been opened; the mock columns and pillars that echo the old building and even Nelson's Column are much discussed and generally liked.

The church of **St. Martin-in-the-Fields,** on the northeastern corner of the square opposite the National Gallery, dates from the 1720s. Designer James Gibbs topped its templar classicism with a Gothic steeple. St. Martin, which has its own world-renowned chamber orchestra, sponsors lunchtime and evening concerts, as well as a summer festival in mid-July. (Box office in the bookshop open Mon.-Sat. 11:30am-7:30pm, Sun. 11am-6pm; telephone bookings open 12:30pm-2:30pm and 4:30-6:30pm; tel. 702 1377; tickets £4-12.50.) At the **Brass Rubbing Centre** in the church, you can replicate images of England's past from brass tablets. (Prices from £1. Open Mon.-Sat. 10am-6pm, Sun. noon-6pm.) The suitably dark, atmospheric café in the Crypt serves cappuccino with a Baroque flair (open daily 10am-8:30pm; church open daily 7:30am-7:30pm).

The Mall

Lacking a royal processional avenue befitting a world power of its stature, Britain hurried up and built one in 1906, in honor of the late great Queen Victoria. Lined with double rows of plane trees, **the Mall** grandly traverses the space from Trafalgar Square to Buckingham Palace. Two monuments to Queen Victoria contribute to the Mall's grandeur: the golden horses of the **Queen Victoria Memorial,** near Buckingham Palace, and the massive **Admiralty Arch** opening onto Trafalgar Square (most striking when floodlit on summer nights). From Trafalgar Sq., the arch leads to the Admiralty building on the south side, where naval officers confer under strangely configured and conspicuous radio aerials. The building was built to be bombproof in 1940. The large lawn on the roof is no doubt part of the shock absorption system.

St. James's Park borders the Mall to the South. Henry VIII declared St. James's London's first royal park in 1532. Ever since, the park has been one of London's favorite places for a stroll. Kings and queens have been known to fritter away their time here wandering about and feeding the birds. These days the aviary aspect of St. James's has become quite serious. The fenced-off peninsula at the west end of the park's pond, Duck Island, is the mating ground for thousands of waterfowl. Near the bridge spanning the pond, plaques describe the flocks of rare ducks, geese, and other flying things who call St. James's "nest." Listen for the peculiar call of the Fulvous Whistling Duck. The funny-looking duck with the white forehead and semi-webbed feet is called a Coot. Birds here are so diverse, in fact, that it's hard to spot a regular Joe Duck—blue beaks, red feathers, and yellow eyes prevail. St. James's is also a good place to discover that lawn chairs in England are not free (rental 50p). Don't blame the prices on Thatcherism—chairs have been hired out here since the 18th century. For a good view of the guards who change at Buckingham Palace, wait between the Victoria Memorial and St. James's Palace from about 10:40 to 11:25am. You might miss the band (it usually travels down Birdcage walk from Wellington Barracks), but you will also avoid the locust swarm of tourists.

Along the north side of the Mall from Traflagar Sq. lie the imposing façades of grand houses, starting with **Carlton House Terrace,** demolished, rebuilt, and remodeled since it went up along the Mall as part of the 18th-century Regent's Park route by Nash. The building became the office of the Free French Forces from 1940 to 1945 under the leadership of General Charles de Gaulle. It now contains the Royal Society of Distinguished Scientists and the avant-garde **Institute of Contemporary Arts** (see Museums and Theatre below).

Further down on the Mall is **Marlborough House,** built by Wren in 1710, but much altered. The former residence of Queen Mary and Edward VII, it is now a centre for administration of the Commonwealth, and guest quarters for Commonwealth dignitaries visiting London. On the other side of St. James's Palace (see St. James's below) from Marlborough House at Stable Yard Rd. is **Clarence House,** the official residence of the much-loved Queen Mother, acknowledged as the coolest member of the Royal family. Behind Clarence House at Cleveland Row is **Lancaster House,** a splendid and extremely solid residence built for the Duke of York in 1841, which now hosts government and royal receptions.

St. James's

> She shall have all that's fine and fair,
> And ride in a coach to take the air,
> And have a house in St. James's Square.
> —*Unknown*

Just north of Buckingham Palace and the Mall, up Stable Yard or Marlborough Rd., stands **St. James's Palace,** the residence of the monarchy from 1660 to 1668 and again from 1715 to 1837. King Charles I passed his last night in the palace's guardroom before crossing St. James's Park to be executed at the Banqueting House in 1649. History does not record whether he slept soundly. Only Henry VIII's gateway and clock tower and a pair of parading guards at the foot of St. James's St.

still hark back to the Tudor palace. You can visit Inigo Jones' fine **Queen's Chapel,** built in 1626, by attending Sunday services at 8:30 and 11:15am (Oct.-July).

The fashionable area around the palace has also come to be called St. James's. Bordered by St. James's Park and Green Park to the south and Piccadilly to the north, it begins at an equestrian statue of George III on Cockspur Street off Trafalgar Sq. **St. James's Street,** next to St. James's Palace, runs into **Pall Mall**—the name derives from "pail-mail," a predecessor of the 17th-century noble game of croquet. Many of the storefronts along the two streets have remained relatively unchanged since the 18th century, among them wine merchants Berry Bros. & Rudd and Lock & Co. (with rotting hats in the window), both on St. James's St. They rub storefront elbows with a number of famous London coffeehouses-turned-clubs. The chief Tory club, the Carlton, at 69 St. James's St., was recently bombed by the IRA. The chief Liberal club, the Reform at 104 Pall Mall, served as a social center of Parliamentary power. In 1823, a Prime Minister and the presidents of the Royal Academy and the Royal Society founded the Athenaeum, on Waterloo Place, for scientific, literary, and artistic men. Gibbon, Hume, Burke, and Garrick belonged to the Whig Brooks, founded in 1764 (60 St. James's St.). The offices of *The Economist* loom on St. James's St. in a modern highrise, though not as modern as the brand new office block (nicknamed the blackbird after a military jet) at no. 66.

Off Pall Mall, a statue of "The Grand Old Duke of York" perches on a tall column in Waterloo Place. In nearby St. James's Square, a statue of William III stands surrounded by a beautiful (and unapproachable) lawn. At the northeast corner of the square a memorial marks the spot where a policewoman was shot dead in 1984 by a submachine-gun-wielding diplomat in the adjacent Libyan embassy.

Around the corner from St. James's Palace stand royal coin collectors Spink's, and Christie, Manson, and Wodds Fine Art Auctioneers—better known as **Christie's,** 8 King St. (tel. 839 9060; Tube: Green Park). The pamphlet describing the jewelry, furniture, historical documents, and artworks being auctioned is scintillating, but costs £10. Auctions, open to the public, are held most weekdays at 10:30am. **Sotheby's** also holds fine arts auctions, at 34 Bond St. (tel. 493 8080; Tube: Bond St. or Oxford Circus). Amuse yourself on a rainy afternoon by watching the dealers do their bidding.

Between fashionable Jermyn St. and Piccadilly, you can enter **St. James's Church,** a post-war reconstruction of what Wren considered his best parish church. Blake was baptized here amidst the typical Wren single room interior, with galleries around the main space. The rector of the parish encourages "Protest through Prayer," and the church community sponsors encounter groups, musical recitals, and films on South Africa. (Tube: Green Park or Piccadilly Circus. Open Mon.-Sat. 10am-6pm, Sun. noon-6pm.)

Buckingham Palace

When a freshly-crowned Victoria moved from Kensington Palace in 1837, Buckingham Palace, built in 1825 by John Nash, had faulty drains and a host of other leaky difficulties. When the flag is flying, the Queen is at home, but don't plan on paying her a visit; no part of Buckingham Palace ever opens to the public. The Palace's best side, the garden front, is seldom seen by ordinary visitors as it is protected by the 40-acre spread where the Queen holds her garden parties. Nasty-looking spikes appeared four years ago on top of the wall surrounding the area; recently barbed wire was added, in an effort to stop occasional forays by admirers who managed to reach the Queen's bedroom and ask for a cigarette.

The oft-photographed **Changing of the Guard** takes place daily from April to July, and on alternate days from August to March. The "Old Guard" marches from St. James's Palace down the Mall to Buckingham Palace, leaving at approximately 11:10am. The "New Guard" begins marching as early as 10:20am. When they meet at the central gates of the palace, the officers of the regiments then touch hands, symbolically exchanging keys, et voilà—the guard is changed. The soldiers gradually split up to relieve the guards currently protecting the palace. The ceremony moves to the beat of royal band music and the menacing clicks of thousands of cameras. In wet weather or on pressing state holidays, the Changing of the Guard does not occur. To witness the spectacle, show up well before 11:30am and stand directly in front of the palace. You can also watch along the routes of the troops prior to their arrival at the palace (from 10:40-11:25am) between the Victoria Memorial and St. James's Palace or along Birdcage walk. Throughout the day, a couple of guards pace back and forth methodically in front of the palace.

Once prime viewing ground for the the Changing of the Guard, the **Victoria Memorial** has recently been restricted as a vantage point. Executed in 1911 by Sir Thomas Brock, the memorial was designed by Sir Aston Webb. Allegorical Truth, Motherhood, and Justice share the center column with the Queen, while the figures of Peace and Progress, Science and Art, Manufactures and Agriculture, and Naval and Military Powers pose at cardinal directions on the monument's outer rim. A recent repair job on Queen Victoria's nose, however, reveals poor workmanship. If you look closely you can see that the new nose looks discolored and has disproportionately large nostrils.

In the extravagant **"Trooping the Colour"** ceremony, held on the Queen's official birthday, a Saturday in early June, the colors of a chosen regiment are paraded ceremonially before the royals. The parade in honor of the Queen brings out luminaries mounted on horses while somewhat less influential types putter about in limousines with little golden crowns on top. The best view of all this is on TV, but you might catch a glimpse of the Queen in person as she rides down the Mall. Tickets for the event must be obtained in advance through the mail. Write to the Household Division HQ, Horse Guards, SW1 before March 1. If you don't get a ticket for the event, you may receive one for one of the rehearsals on the two preceding Saturdays. Since the Queen does not need to rehearse, these tend to be noticeably less crowded.

Down the left side of the Palace, off Buckingham Gate, an enclosed passageway leads to the **Queen's Gallery** (tel. 930 4832). Selected treasures from the royal collection fill the rooms of this modern suite. The exhibition changes every few months, but you can usually catch a few of Charles I's Italian masters, George IV's Dutch still-lifes, Prince Albert's primitives, and occasionally some of the Leonardo da Vinci drawings from Windsor. (Open Tues.-Sat. 10am-5pm, Sun. 2-5pm. Admission £2, students £1.50, children £1. Take the Tube to Victoria and walk up Buckingham Palace Rd.; Green Park and St. James's Park Tube stops are also convenient.) Nearby, you can drop in on the **Guards Museum** at Wellington Barracks on Birdcage Walk, off Buckingham Gate. (Open Mon.-Thurs., Sat.-Sun. 10am-4pm. Admission £2, students and children £1.) The courtyard outside Wellington Barracks is probably the only place where you'll ever see the Guards at relative ease. Also off Buckingham Gate stands the curious **Royal Mews Museum,** which houses the royal coaches and other historic royal riding implements. (Open July-Sept. Wed.-Fri. noon-4pm, Oct.-Apr. Wed. noon-4pm. Admission £1.30, students £1, children 70p.)

Piccadilly

All of the West End's major arteries—Piccadilly, Regent Street, Shaftesbury Avenue, The Haymarket—merge and swirl around Piccadilly Circus, one of the world's great meeting places and the bright, giddy hub of Nash's 19th-century London. Today the circus earns its place on postcards with towering bluffs of neon, circular traffic congestion, and an absurd statue everyone calls "Eros," though it was intended to be the Angel of Christian Charity in memory of the reformer, Lord Shaftesbury. Despite the misleading romantic title of the statue, don't try to meet your lover here—you'll only lose each other in the crowds.

The circus became a center of popular entertainment during Victoria's reign, and while the old stages no longer stand, the façades of the great music halls remain, propped up against contemporary tourist traps and commercial ventures. Statues of Michael Jackson, Madonna, and Tina Turner wave to passersby from the balcony of the **London Pavillion,** 1 Piccadilly Circus, a historic theatre recently converted to house the Tussaud Group's latest enterprise, **Rock Circus,** (tel. 734 8025; Tube: Piccadilly Circus), an impressive wax-work museum and revolving theatre dedicated to the history of rock-and-roll. Elvis, the Beatles, David Bowie, the Stones, Sid Vicious, and Sting stand among the 50 rock and pop artists eerily re-created as life-like wax effigies and androids. Infrared headsets trigger a CD soundtrack for each display as you wander through the exhibits. Unfortunately there is also commentary, haughtily informing us that Sting wrote "perceptive lyrics about real life and real love." It's pretty high-tech, though, and a *Let's Go* researcher fave. (Open July-Sept. Wed.-Mon. 10am-10pm, Tues. noon-10pm; Oct-June Wed.-Mon. 11am-9pm, Tues. noon-9pm. Admission £5.95, students and seniors £4.95, children £3.95.) Rainy afternoons can be whiled away in the glitzy galleries, shops, arcades and eating emporia of the adjacent **Trocadero Centre,** (entrance on Coventry St.), an oh-so-trendy mall and entertainment complex housed within a giant, triple-tiered atrium. On the third floor of the much-hyped centre you can find a campy, multimedia shrine to the *Guinness Book of World Records'* wide range of superlative accomplishments and aberrations. (Tel. 439 7331; open daily 10am-10pm. Admission £4.50, seniors and students £3.60, children £2.85.)

Aristocratic mansions once lined Piccadilly, a broad mile-long avenue stretching from Regent St. in the east to Hyde Park Corner in the west. The name derives from Piccadilly Hall, the 17th-century home of Robert Baker, an affluent tailor who did brisk business in the sale of "pickadills," frilly, lace collars that were much in fashion in his day. The only remnant of Piccadilly's stately past is the formidable **Burlington House,** built in 1665 for the Earls of Burlington and redesigned in the 18th century by Colin Campbell to accommodate the burgeoning **Royal Academy of Arts** (tel. 439 7438; Tube: Piccadilly or Green Park). Founded in 1768, the Academy consists of 40 academicians and 30 associates who administer the exhibition galleries and maintain a free school of art (see Museums). Reynolds, Gainsborough, Constable, and Turner are a few of the many eminent names associated with the academy, while Romney, Blake, and Rossetti head up an equally impressive list of English artists whom the academy overlooked. The annual summer exhibition is an always noteworthy and often controversial mix of established masters and newer artists, hoping for recognition. The ambitious **Museum of Mankind** backs onto Burlington House behind the Royal Academy (see Museums).

A quiet courtyard just east of the Academy opens onto **Albany,** an 18th-century apartment block widely renowned as one of London's most prestigious addresses. Built by William Chambers in 1771 and remodeled in 1812 to serve as "residential chambers for bachelor gentlemen," Albany has evolved into an exclusive enclave of literary excellence. Swinger-soldier Lord Byron wrote his epic "Childe Harold" here. Other eminent men of letters associated with Albany include Macaulay, Gladstone, Canning, "Monk" Lewis, J.B. Priestley and Graham Greene.

Piccadilly continues south and west, running past imperious Bond Street, past the Ritz Hotel with its distinctive arcade and cluster of bright lights, and past a string of fashionable men's clubs on the rim of Green Park. At the gateway of the Wellington Museum in **Apsley House,** described by its first owner as "No. 1, London," the avenue merges into the impenetrable Hyde Park corner. Apsley House was built by Robert Adam in the 1780s as a residence commemorating Wellington's victory at Waterloo.

Running north from Piccadilly Circus are the grand façades of **Regent Street,** leading to Oxford Circus. The buildings and street were built by John Nash in the early 19th century as part of a processional route for the Prince Regent to follow from St. James' Park north through Oxford Circus to his house in Regent's Park. The façades have changed since Nash's time, and today the street is known for the crisp cuts of Burberry raincoats and Aquascutum suits as well as Hamley's, the giant warehouse of Santa's goodies.

Photo taken in Grindelwald, Switzerland, by Doris Muir, Shrewsbury, Pa.

No print film gives you truer, more accurate color. Why trust your memories to anything less?

Kodak
Official Film
of the 1992
Olympic Games

Kodak FILM
Gold

Show Your True Colors.™

When all you've got is one week, even a morning of diarrhea is too much.

Bad weather isn't the only thing that can spoil a vacation. That's why you want the most effective diarrhea medicine you can buy — Imodium® A-D. It can stop diarrhea with just one dose, instead of dose after dose of the other leading brand.

Take it along in convenient caplets. And enjoy every moment of your next vacation.

Imodium. A-D. It can stop diarrhea with just one dose.

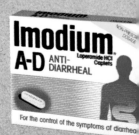

Soho and Leicester Square

For centuries, Soho was to sex what the Houses of Parliament are to affairs of state. It has, however, undergone a well-funded renaissance, and the few porn shops that remain merely add an illicit edge to the newly recovered area. Many of London's most fashionable clubs, restaurants, and shops now occupy buildings that once housed massage parlors. As a result of strict vice laws, prostitutes can only sell their wares from upper-story windows, leaving the sidewalks free for more subtle forms of seduction. The area is loosely bounded by Oxford Street in the north, Piccadilly and Coventry St. in the south, Charing Cross Road in the east, and Regent Street in the west.

Soho's cosmopolitan atmosphere stems in part from a long history of immigration. The district was first settled by French Huguenots fleeing religious persecution after the Revocation of The Edict of Nantes in 1685. In more recent years, an influx of settlers from the New Territories of Hong Kong have forged London's Chinatown in the neighborhoods south of Shaftesbury Avenue. A strong Mediterranean influence can be discerned in the aromas of espresso, garlic, and sizzling meats mixing all along the mellow shopfronts of **Old Compton Street,** an avenue of bistros and intimate Italian eateries. Bring your cravings for fresh Italian pasta, frogs' legs, and imported French produce.

Wardour Street runs north through the offices of Britain's film industry from the eerie ruins of **St. Anne's Soho.** German bombers leveled most of this church in 1940; only Wren's anomalous tower of 1685 and the ungainly, green, bottle-shaped steeple added by Cockerell in 1803 emerged unscathed. William Hazlitt (who died two blocks away at no. 6 Frith St.) lies buried somewhere in the old churchyard; his memorial rests below the tower wall. A quiet garden spreads around the base of St. Anne's. Its park benches and surrounding lawns fill up with vagrants and rapacious pigeons.

Just to the north, a blue plaque above Leoni's Quo Vadis restaurant at **28 Dean Street** locates the austere, two-room flat where the impoverished Karl Marx lived with his wife, maid, and five children while writing *Das Kapital.* Running parallel to Dean St., Frith and Greek St. end at **Soho Square.** A breeding ground for mansions in the 17th century, the square has become a center of the film industry. Blurred by rough weather and cracked with age, an ancient statue of Charles II (1681) presides over the **Soho Village Green.** The ill-fated Duke of Monmouth once commissioned a palatial house on this site; according to local legend, the district's current name comes from his rallying cry at the battle of Sedgemoor, *"Soe-hoe."*

A shadow of Soho's former grandeur can be glimpsed at the southeastern corner of the square in the **House of St. Barnabas-in-Soho.** Built for the Bedford family in 1746, and presently endowed as a home for the destitute, the mansion encloses an exquisite rococo interior and a curious chapel dating from 1862. Dickens used the rear courtyard as the setting for Dr. Manette's encounter with Sidney Carton in *A Tale of Two Cities.* (Open Wed. 2:30-4:15pm and Thurs. 11am-12:30pm. Small donation encouraged.) The area has a rich literary past: Thomas de Quincey quaffed strange substances in his houses on Greek and Tavistock St., and earlier John Dryden lived at no. 43 Gerrard St.

On weekdays, the fruit and vegetable market on **Berwick Street** rumbles with trade and far-flung Cockney accents. Brewer Street and Greek Street to the southeast retain the most seedy trappings of Soho's recent past. Near Regent Street, the neighborhood calms down, and **Meard Street** yields an impression of Soho in its earlier, more residential days. **Carnaby Street,** a notorious hotbed of 60s sex and sedition, has since lapsed into a lurid tourist trap crammed with stalls of junky gimmicks and souvenirs.

Leicester Square, just south of Shaftesbury Ave. (and Chinatown) between Piccadilly Circus and Charing Cross Rd., is an entertainment nexus, framed by the giant billboards of grand, expensive first run cinemas. The square is a pedestrian area, once called "Leicester Fields" and owned by descendants of the flashy Renaissance poet, Sir Philip Sidney. Current park remodelling is due to be completed in late

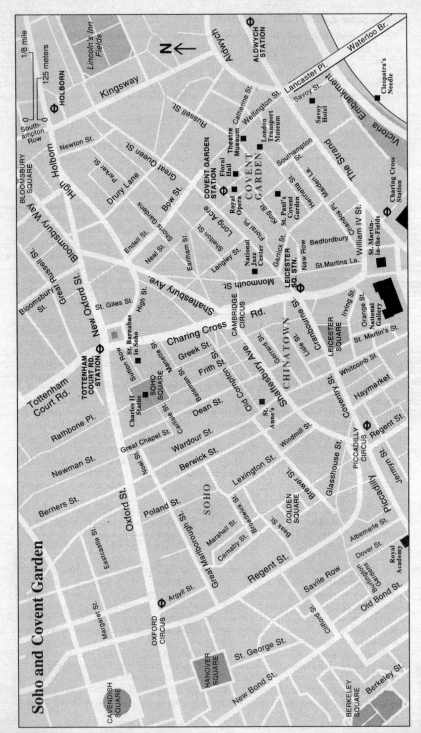

Soho and Covent Garden

1992. A plaque on the west side of the square marks where Royal Academician Joshua Reynolds lived and died. On the north side, on Leicester Place, the French presence in Soho manifests itself in **Notre-Dame de France.** This church may not be anything to exclaim over architecturally, but it rewards visitors who go inside with an exquisite Aubusson tapestry lining the inner walls. And don't miss the tiny chapel built into the western wall, which features an arresting, cartoon-like mural by Jean Cocteau (note Judas's uncanny resemblance to the Creature From the Black Lagoon).

Mayfair

The center of London's glamorous *beau monde* was named for the 17th-century May Fair (held on the site of Shepherd's Market), a notorious haunt of prostitutes. Modern Mayfair, especially on Hill St. and Chesterfield Hill and among the shop windows on Bond St., Burlington Arcade and Jermyn St., has a distinctly patrician atmosphere; it is the most expensive property in the London version of *Monopoly.* Mayfair is bordered by Oxford St. to the north, Piccadilly to the south, Park Lane to the west and Regent St. to the east. Tube: Green Park, Bond St., or Piccadilly Circus.

Park Lane, the western border of Mayfair at Hyde Park, is famous for the astronomically priced and overwhelmingly tasteful hotels which grace its length, running north from Wellington's Apsley House and the newer Hard Rock Café. The Hilton, Grosvenor House Hotel, and the Dorchester can be found here, while Claridges is hidden further inside Mayfair on Brook St.

Grosvenor Square, between Brook and Grosvenor St., is the largest of its breed in central London. Developed by Sir Richard Grosvenor in 1725, the central garden spreads across the site of Oliver's Mount, a makeshift barricade erected by the people of London in 1643 to repel the invading armies of Charles I. Once a fashionable residential area and home to Shelley, the square has gradually evolved into an American military and political enclave. Future President John Adams lived at no. 9 while serving as the first American ambassador to England in 1785. Almost two centuries later, General Eisenhower established his wartime headquarters here at no. 20, and memory of his stay persists in the area's postwar nickname, "Eisenhowerplatz." A statue of Franklin Roosevelt—freed from his wheelchair by the sculptor, Reid Dick—towers above a white pedestal on the north side of the green. From here you can see the streamlined **U.S. Embassy** rising in the west, where protesters occasionally assemble to denounce the latest American indiscretion.

Shepherd's Market, the tiny village-like area just above Piccadilly, has become expensive and respectable since the 60s. Its web of little streets teems with inviting restaurants and pubs. P.G. Wodehouse's fictional aristocrat Bertie Wooster and insightful butler Jeeves lived in foreboding **Half Moon Street.** Blake saw mystical visions for 17 years on South Molton Street, Händel wrote the *Messiah* on busy Brook Street, and the reigning queen was born in a house (recently demolished) at no. 17 Bruton Street. Laurence Sterne ended his life and adventures in poverty on haughty Bond Street (no. 39).

The connoisseur will be drawn to the storefronts of **Bond Street** by the discreet promise of luxury: *haute couture* and handmade shotguns, emerald tiaras and platinum swizzle sticks, antique furniture and objets d'art. An array of art dealers and auctioneers with public galleries frequently offer special shows of exceptional quality. Try Marlborough (entrance by Albemarle Street) for the biggest contemporary names, Agnews (no. 43), or Colnaghi's (no. 14). For the Old Masters and even some nouveau excitement visit **Sotheby's** at no. 34: wander through art works on exhibit before auction, or desperately try not to sneeze during an auction (open Mon.-Fri. 9am-4:30pm). Modern art aficionados should also note the rugged Henry Moore frieze high up on the crest of the **Time/Life Building** (corner of Bruton St.), and duck inside for a glance at the splendid mural by Ben Nicholson.

Hanover Square, smaller than Grosvenor or the equally impressive **Berkeley Square,** provides a quaint residential setting for **St. George's Hanover Church,** an

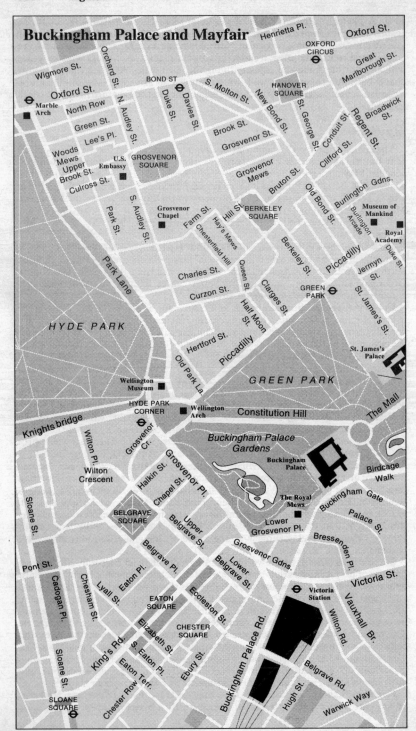

Buckingham Palace and Mayfair

institution renowned for society weddings. Built by John James in 1724, the church's huge, somber exterior, with wide Corinthian columns and a heavy, soot-stained pediment, belies a surprisingly light and intimate interior. Here to be married beneath the radiant barrel vault, with Händel's organ playing at their backs, came Percy Bysshe Shelley, George Eliot, Benjamin Disraeli, and the whispering Teddy Roosevelt. Just to the west of Regent St., **Savile Row** has become synonymous with the elegant and excessively priced tailoring that has prospered there for centuries. The playwright Sheridan, who lived at no. 14, was no doubt always immaculately turned out.

Hyde Park and Kensington Gardens

Totalling 630 acres, **Hyde Park** and the contiguous **Kensington Gardens** constitute the largest open area in the center of the city, earning their reputation as the "lungs of London." Environmentally unsound Henry VIII used to hunt deer here. At the far west of the Gardens, you can drop your calling card at **Kensington Palace** (tel. 937 9561), originally the residence of King William III and Queen Mary II and recently of Princess Margaret. Currently, the Prince and Princess of Wales, the little Princes, and other stray members of the Royal Family live in the palace. A museum of uninhabited royal rooms and regal memorabilia includes a Court dress collection, with Di's wedding gown prominently displayed. Although Queen Victoria was born here, with characteristic propriety she left few traces of herself, aside from a nondescript statue outside the palace grounds. The palace gift shop appears to be the happening place to purchase Beatrix Potter memorabilia. (Palace open Mon.-Sat. 9am-5:30pm, Sun. 11am-5:30pm. Admission £3.75, students and OAPs £2.80, children £2.50.) A walk west of the palace along Kensington Palace Gardens, one of London's most opulent thoroughfare, reveals the homes of a crew of millionaires and embassies.

Remind yourself that parks were meant for children by walking north or east of the palace. The Round Pond east of the palace plays the ocean for a fleet of toy sailboats on weekends. In the playground north of the palace, younger children frolic around a fairy tree adorned with elves. Roughly at the center of the gardens, G.F. Watts' 1904 Physical Energy statue, a muscle-bound man, rides an equally muscular steed off into the sunset. The ramshackle Italian Gardens, farther north, is a hotspot for sunbathers and derelict waterfowl.

The Serpentine, a lake carved in 1730, runs from these fountains in the north, near Bayswater Rd., south to Knightsbridge. From the number of people who pay the £2 (children £1) to sunbathe at the fenced-off Serpentine beach (the Lido), one would think the sun shone more brightly there than anywhere else in London. Harriet Westbrook (P.B. Shelley's first wife) numbers proudly among the famous people who have drowned in this man-made "pond." The **Serpentine Gallery** (tel. 402 6075), in Kensington Gardens, often hosts interesting exhibitions of contemporary works, as well as art workshops. (Gallery open daily 10am-6pm. Parks open Mon.-Fri. 10am-6pm, Sat.-Sun. 10am-7pm; off-season Mon.-Fri. 10am-dusk, Sat.-Sun. 10am-4pm. Free.) On the southern edge of Kensington Gardens, the Lord Mayor had the **Albert Memorial** built to honor Victoria's beloved husband, whose death Victoria mourned for nearly 40 years. Considered a great artistic achievement when first unveiled in 1869, the extravagant monument now seems an embarrassing piece of imperial Victorian excess. Unfortunately, you will be unable to judge for yourself since the Albert Memorial will be under designer scaffolding for another six years as it undergoes restoration. The **Albert Hall,** with its ornate oval dome, hosts the Promenade Concerts (Proms) in summer (see Entertainment below; no tours). Also built to honor the Prince Consort, the hall is simpler than the memorial, and features a frieze of the "Triumph of the Arts and Sciences" around its circumference. Avoid the east-west path through southern Hyde Park at night. Called Rotten Row, from a corruption of *Route du Roi* (King's Rd.), the walk can be dangerous.

Speakers' Corner, in the northeast corner of Hyde Park (Tube: Marble Arch, not Hyde Park Corner), is the finest example of free speech in action anywhere in

Hyde Park, Belgravia, and Chelsea

Bayswater Rd.

N. Carriage Dr.

GROSVENOR SQUARE

Grosvenor St.

BERKELEY SQUARE

0   1/4 mile
0   250 meters

HYDE PARK

Park Lane

S. Audley St.

Curzon St.

N

Serpentine Rd.

The Serpentine

Piccadilly

Green Park

Rotten Row

S. Carriage Dr.

HYDE PARK CORNER

Constitution Hill

Knightsbridge

Kensington Rd.

KNIGHTSBRIDGE

Wilton Pl.

Grosvenor Pl.

LOWNDES SQUARE

Sloane St.

BELGRAVE SQUARE

Upper Belgrave St.

Lower Belgrave St.

Harrod's

Hans Rd.

Beauchamp Pl.

Pont St.

Pavilion Rd.

Pont St.

Belgrave Pl.

Eccleston St.

Brompton Rd.

Yeoman's Row

Cadogan Pl.

Eaton Pl.

EATON SQUARE

Egerton Ter.

Walton St.

CADOGAN SQUARE

Milner St.

Cadogan St.

SLOANE SQUARE

Eaton Pl.

Ebury St.

Buckingham Palace Rd.

Draycott Ave.

SLOANE SQUARE

Eaton Ter.

Fulham Rd.

Ixworth Pl.

Sloane Ave.

Bourne St.

Pimlico Rd.

Cale St.

Elystan Pl.

Ebury Bridge Rd.

Sydney St.

King's Rd.

Smith St.

St. Leonard's Ter.

Royal Hospital Rd.

Chelsea Br. Rd.

Ranelagh Gardens

Redesdale St.

Christchurch St.

Royal Hospital Chelsea

Chelsea Br.

Chelsea Manor St.

Flood St.

Oakley St.

National Army Museum

Tite St.

Chelsea Embankment

the world. On Sundays from late morning to dusk, and on summer evenings, soap-box revolutionaries, haranguers, madmen and visionaries scream about anything from Kierkegaard to socialism to knitting. Test your patience and your vocal chords and go heckle with the best of them. At the southern end of Hyde Park cluster a group of statues: a Diana fountain, the "family of man," a likeness of Lord Byron, and London's first nude statue (1822), an Achilles molded from cannonballs. Royal park band performances take place in the bandstand 200 yards from Hyde Park Corner, in the direction of the Serpentine (June-Aug. every Sun. at 3 and 6pm).

Kensington, Knightsbridge and Belgravia

Kensington, a gracious and sheltered residential area, reposes between multi-ethnic Notting Hill to the north and trendy Chelsea to the south. Kensington High Street, which pierces the area, has become a shopping and scoping epicenter. Antique and obscure specialty shops fill the area along Kensington Church Street in the north, Victorian-era museums and colleges dominate South Kensington, while the area around Earl's Court has mutated into something of a tourist colony.

Take the Tube to High St. Kensington to reach **Holland Park,** a rabbit-ridden, peacock-peppered garden. Beyond the cricket pitches and tennis courts (open to the public), a block west of the park's southern entrance on the High St., stands the curious **Leighton House,** 12 Holland Park Rd. (tel. 602 3316). Devised by the imaginative Lord Leighton in the 19th century, the house is a bold and amusing pastiche. The Arab Hall, with inlaid tiles, a pool, and a dome, is a stunning mixture of English imagination and burglary of the Middle East. Now a center for the arts, Leighton House features concerts, receptions, and other events in the evenings, as well as frequent contemporary art exhibitions. Lord L. himself was quite a dabhand with the oils. An excellent taped commentary helps you find your way around. (House open Mon.-Sat. 11am-5pm, until 6pm for some exhibitions. Free.)

The large flag-ridden modern building between Holland Park and Leighton House is the **Commonwealth Institute,** (tel. 603 4535) built to honor the continuing links between parts of the former British Empire. Beneath the roof of Zambian copper, the Institute has permanent and temporary exhibits of life and art in various parts of the world, as well as evening performances (open Mon.-Sat. 10am-5pm, Sun 2-5pm).

To reach the grandiose South Kensington museums, take the Tube or the #49 bus from Kensington High St. The Great Exhibition of 1851 funded many of these buildings built between 1867 and 1935. North of Cromwell Rd., the various royal institutions of learning and culture include the Imperial College of Science, the Royal College of Music, the Royal College of Art, the Albert Hall, the august Royal School of Needlepoint, and **Royal Geographic Society.** Inside the Geographic Society, just east of the Albert Hall, can be seen 800,000 maps, and the explorer Stanley's boots (open Mon.-Fri. 10am-1pm and 2-5pm. Free). Museums cluster between and around these institutions, bringing younger folk into the area to dilute the high concentration of professors and graduate students. The massive Museum of Natural History cathedral, the more modern Science Museum, and the eminently Victorian Victoria and Albert Museum all exhibit themselves at Cromwell and Exhibition Rd. (See Museums below.) **Brompton Oratory,** just east of the V&A museum, is a showpiece of Italian art and architecture. H. Gribble built the aggressively Roman Baroque edifice in 1884 and cluttered its interior with Italian statues; the enormous Renaissance altar in the Lady Chapel came from Brescia (Oratory open 6:30am-8pm).

While **Knightsbridge** may be wealthy and stylish, its snooty reputation rests more on tradition than on practice. Knightsbridge is defined most of all by London's premier department store, **Harrods.** Founded in 1849 as a grocery store, by 1880 Harrods employed over 100 workers. In 1905 the store moved to its current location; today it requires 5000 employees to handle its vast array of products and services. Besides an encyclopaedic inventory, Harrods also has a pub, several restaurants,

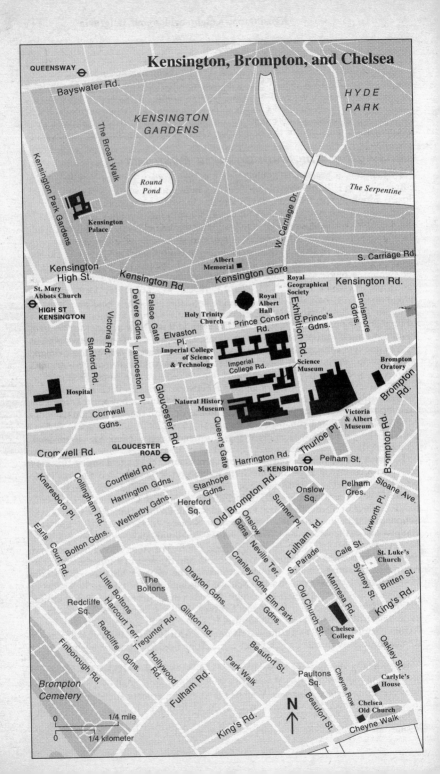

Kensington, Brompton, and Chelsea

QUEENSWAY ⊖

Bayswater Rd.

HYDE PARK

KENSINGTON GARDENS

The Broad Walk

Kensington Park Gardens

Round Pond

The Serpentine

W. Carriage Dr.

S. Carriage Rd.

Kensington Palace

Kensington High St.

Kensington Rd.

Kensington Gore

Kensington Rd.

Albert Memorial

St. Mary Abbots Church

HIGH ST KENSINGTON ⊖

DeVere Gdns.

Palace Gate

Victoria Rd.

Stanford Rd.

Launceston Pl.

Royal Geographical Society

Exhibition Rd.

Ennismore Gdns.

Royal Albert Hall

Holy Trinity Church

Prince Consort Rd.

Prince's Gdns.

Elvaston Pl.

Imperial College of Science & Technology

Imperial College Rd.

Science Museum

Brompton Oratory

Hospital

Gloucester Rd.

Natural History Museum

Victoria & Albert Museum

Brompton Rd.

Cornwall Gdns.

Queen's Gate

Thurloe Pl.

Cromwell Rd.

GLOUCESTER ROAD ⊖

Harrington Rd.

Pelham St. ⊖

Knaresboro Pl.

Collingham Rd.

Courtfield Rd.

Stanhope Gdns.

Old Brompton Rd.

S. KENSINGTON ⊖

Pelham Cres.

Sloane Ave.

Harrington Gdns.

Hereford Sq.

Onslow Sq.

Ixworth Pl.

Earls Court Rd.

Wetherby Gdns.

Bolton Gdns.

Onslow Gdns.

Neville Ter.

Sumner Pl.

S. Parade

Fulham Rd.

Cale St.

St. Luke's Church

Little Boltons

The Boltons

Drayton Gdns.

Cranley Gdns.

Elm Park Gdns.

Old Church St.

Sydney St.

Manresa Rd.

Britten St.

King's Rd.

Redcliffe Sq.

Harcourt Terr.

Tregunter Rd.

Gilston Rd.

Redcliffe Gdns.

Finborough Rd.

Hollywood Rd.

Fulham Rd.

Park Walk

Beaufort St.

Chelsea College

Paultons Sq.

Cheyne Row

Oakley St.

Carlyle's House

Brompton Cemetery

King's Rd.

Beaufort St.

Chelsea Old Church

Cheyne Walk

N ↑

0 _____ 1/4 mile
0 _____ 1/4 kilometer

and naturally, a tourist information center. (Open Mon.-Tue. and Thurs.-Sat. 9am-6pm, Wed. 9am-8pm. See Shopping below.)

Belgravia was first constructed as an area to billet servants after the building of Buckingham Palace in the 1820s, but soon became the stately bastion of wealth and privilege it is today. Belgravia lies south of Hyde Park, ringed by fashionable Sloane St. to the west, Victoria station to the south, and Buckingham Palace Gardens to the east. The spacious avenues and crescents of the district center on Belgrave Square, 10 acres of park surrounded by late Georgian buildings that became the setting for *My Fair Lady*. Nearby **Eaton Square** was one of Henry James' London favorites. Belgravia presents a quieter, more dignified façade than busier Knightsbridge or Mayfair. Money has refined and dehumanized the area, as embassies and big corporations take over imposing buildings, and apartments become the *pied-á-terres* of wealthy businesspeople.

Chelsea

From Thomas More to Oscar Wilde to Johnny Rotten and the Sex Pistols, Chelsea has a checkered past and remains the flashiest district in London. Few streets in London scream louder for a visit than the **King's Road.** Mohawked UB40s and silk-scarved or pearl-necklaced Sloane Rangers (awfully loosely the English equivalent of preppies) gaze at trendy window displays, probably looking no further than the glass. Optimal viewing time is Saturday afternoon. The tube is practically non-existent around here, so you'll have to rely on buses (like #11 or #22—or better yet, your feet—along King's Rd. and Fulham Rd.

Any proper exploration of Chelsea begins at **Sloane Square.** The square takes its name from Sir Hans Sloane (1660-1753), one of three collectors whose artifacts made up the original collections of the British Museum. The nearby Royal Court Theatre debuted many of George Bernard Shaw's plays. Until 1829, King's Rd., stretching southwest from Sloane Square, served as a private royal thoroughfare from Hampton Court to St. James's. Hidden among the trendy boutiques lurk cheap restaurants, historic pubs, and the **Chelsea Antique Market** (where one can purchase first editions of Gibbon's *Decline and Fall*).

Off King's Rd., things become more peaceful. Hardly touched by the Underground, Georgian Chelsea remains a world apart from the rest of London. By the river stands Wren's **Royal Hospital,** of 1691, founded by Charles II for retired soldiers and still inhabited by 400 army pensioners. Ex-soldiers welcome visitors to the spacious grounds, dressed in uniform adapted only slightly to the present day. (Open Mon.-Sat. 10am-noon and 2-4pm, Sun. 2-4pm. Free.) East of the Hospital lie the **Ranelagh Gardens** (usually open until dusk). The **Chelsea Flower Show** blooms here in mid-May (in 1992, May 19-22), but even members of the Royal Horticultural Society have trouble procuring tickets for the first two days. The **National Army Museum** stands directly west of the hospital, along Royal Hospital Rd (see Museums below).

Across Chelsea Bridge from the Royal Hospital and Ranelagh Gardens loom the four towers of the derelict **Battersea Power Station,** which once belched out tons of coal smoke over the city. Recent plans for the satanically huge industrial plant, the largest brick building in Europe and one often likened to an upside-down dead pig, included building an amusement park within its shell, complete with roller coaster rides, but this idea has been abandoned, along with the building.

Cheyne Walk, Cheyne Row, and Tite Street formed the heart of Chelsea's artist colony at the turn of the century. Watch for the blue plaques on the houses. J.M.W. Turner moved into a house in Cheyne Walk, and Edgar Allan Poe lived nearby. Mary Ann Evans (a.k.a. George Eliot) moved into #4 just before her death. Dante Gabriel Rossetti kept his highly disreputable *ménage* in #16, where he doused himself with chloral hydrate and hammered the image of the artist as nonconformist into the public mind. Mick Jagger searched for satisfaction on the Walk in the 60s. The area's most notorious resident, Oscar Wilde, lived at 16 Tite St. and was arrested for homosexual behavior at Chelsea's best-known hotel, the Cadogan. John

Singer Sargent, James MacNeill Whistler, Augustus John, and Bertrand Russell also lived on Tite Street. Today, fashionable artists' and designers' homes line the street.

At the west end of Cheyne Walk lies the **Chelsea Old Church,** restored after bombing in 1941. Sir Thomas More designed part of the church in the 1530s, and the south chapel is dedicated to the Man for All Seasons. The friendly verger will point out **Crosby Hall** down the street, a 15th-century hall that was More's residence in Bishopsgate before it was moved, stone by stone, to its present position. The hall now serves as part of a student center hosting long-term students from abroad. (Church open daily 10am-6pm; Crosby Hall open Mon.-Sat. 10am-noon and 2:15-5pm. Free.)

Chelsea's most famous resident, Thomas Carlyle, churned out his magnificent prose on Cheyne Row. On this miraculously quiet street colored by flowers and tidy houses, **Carlyle's House,** 24 Cheyne Row (Tube: Sloane Sq.), has remained virtually unchanged since the Sage of Chelsea expired in his armchair. Glass cases shield his books and manuscripts; family portraits and sketches ornament the walls. In his attic study Carlyle wrote and rewrote *The French Revolution* after John Stuart Mill's chambermaid accidently burned Carlyle's first finished draft. The hat of this extraordinary man hangs on the peg of the garden door, and the water pitcher still stands ready for his cold morning showers. (Open Apr.-Oct. Wed.-Sun. 11am-5:30pm. Admission £2.30, children £1.15.)

Camden Town and Regent's Park

In the 19th century Camden Town was a solid working-class district, spliced with railways and covered in soot. It was here that Charles Dickens spent his childhood, crowded in a four room tenement with his extended family at no.16 (now 141) Bayham St. The experience served as the model for the Cratchit family in *A Christmas Carol.*

Waves of Irish, Cypriot and Portuguese immigrants brought a diversity to the area that remains today. Trends are instigated and terminated at **Camden Lock market,** now London's fourth largest tourist attraction, which draws 200,000 funky visitors each weekend. Opened in 1974 with only four stall holders, the market now crams in 400 bohemian vendors. Still, Camden Town remains very much down-to-earth, as the dilapidated warehouses along Regent's Canal testify. And just around the corner from the tube station stands Arlington House, the largest doss-house in Europe.

Just south of Camden Town lies the 500-acre **Regent's Park.** Larger than either Hyde Park or Kensington Gardens, and full of gardens, lakes, promenades, and Dakotan open spaces, the park has become a popular spot for family cricket matches and the scene of many tribulations of two-year-old future football champs. On summer evenings, American expatriates, enthusiastic British architects, and civil servants slug away at softball. On Sunday from June through August, you can hear tubas and trumpets entertain at the bandstand or see performances in the **Open Air Theatre** near Queen Mary's Gardens (see Entertainment). If you're feeling energetic or romantic, rent a boat on the park's lake (£5 an hour, open daily 10am-dusk).

Laid out in 1812 by John "Buckingham Palace" Nash for the Prince Regent (the future George IV), the park is edged on three sides by majestic Nash terraces. The recently restored "Regency" terraces present a magnificent façade. The smart, cream-colored, porticoed and pillared buildings have been home to the likes of H.G. Wells (17 Hanover Terrace) and Mrs. Simpson (7 Hanover Terrace). Regent's Park Canal, part of the Grand Union Canal, dips around the unprotected north side of the park and into neighboring Paddington. From "Little Venice" you can take a leisurely trip down the canal (see Boats under Getting Around).

The park's most popular attraction, the privately owned **London Zoo** (tel. 722 3333), commands a high admission price and large crowds, but can charm you nonetheless. Although low on funds, the zoo expects to remain open, possibly in a scaled-down form. The menagerie has an endless playlist of stars, including the ever-

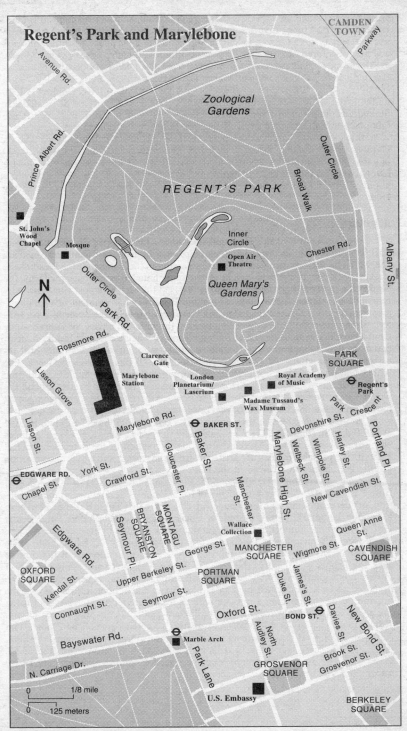

Regent's Park and Marylebone

CAMDEN TOWN
Parkway

Avenue Rd.

Zoological
Gardens

Prince Albert Rd.

Outer Circle

Broad Walk

REGENT'S PARK

St. John's
Wood
Chapel

Mosque

Inner
Circle

Open Air
Theatre

Chester Rd.

Albany St.

N

Outer Circle

Park Rd.

Queen Mary's
Gardens

Rossmore Rd.

Lisson Grove

Clarence
Gate

PARK
SQUARE

Marylebone
Station

London
Planetarium/
Laserium

Royal Academy
of Music

Regent's
Park

Park Crescent

Lisson St.

Marylebone Rd.

BAKER ST.

Madame Tussaud's
Wax Museum

Devonshire St.

Harley St.

Portland Pl.

EDGWARE RD.

York St.

Crawford St.

Gloucester Pl.

Baker St.

Manchester St.

Marylebone High St.

Welbeck St.

Winpole St.

New Cavendish St.

Chapel St.

Edgware Rd.

BRYANSTON
SQUARE

MONTAGU
SQUARE

Seymour Pl.

Wallace
Collection

George St.

MANCHESTER
SQUARE

Wigmore St.

Queen Anne
St.

CAVENDISH
SQUARE

OXFORD
SQUARE

Kendal St.

Upper Berkeley St.

PORTMAN
SQUARE

Duke St.

James's St.

Connaught St.

Seymour St.

Oxford St.

BOND ST.

North Audley St.

Davies St.

New Bond St.

Bayswater Rd.

Marble Arch

Park Lane

GROSVENOR
SQUARE

Brook St.

Grosvenor St.

N. Carriage Dr.

0   1/8 mile

0   125 meters

U.S. Embassy

BERKELEY
SQUARE

popular sweet-smelling elephants. Allow a good four hours to really do this place justice. The zoo's innovative design makes the animals feel right at home—the Mappin Terraces of 1913 (currently being rebuilt) offer a most natural habitat for bears and hogs. Children can ride camels, ponies, or llamas for 60p. The Snowdon Aviary, looking somewhat like an early-warning radar station, allows wonderfully close contact with its inhabitants. (Open March-Oct. Mon-Sat. 9am-6pm, Sun. 9am-7pm; Nov.-Feb. daily 10am-dusk. Admission £5.30, students £4.40, children £3.30, under 4 free.) Tube: Camden Town. Regent's Park, Great Portland St., and Baker St. stations are all on the south edge of the park—walk north through to the zoo (about 20 min.). Bus #74 brings you from Baker St. Station to the door.

Within the Inner Circle at the heart of the park, the delightful **Queen Mary's Gardens** erupt in color in early summer. The rose garden dazzles with 20,000 blooms. (Open until dusk.) North of Regent's Park stands **Primrose Hill,** long a favorite spot for picnics and kite-flying, and location of an epic scene from the once-popular British TV show *Minder.* On a clear day you can see as far as the Surrey Downs.

Marylebone

Located between Regent's Park and Oxford St., the grid-like district of Marylebone is dotted with decorous late-Georgian town houses. The name derives from "St. Mary-by-the-bourne," the "bourne" referring to the Tyburn or the Westbourne stream, both now underground. The eternally dammed Westbourne now forms the Serpentine in Hyde Park. Wimpole Street housed the reclusive poet Elizabeth Barrett until she eloped with Robert Browning. Britain's most eminent private physicians have Harley Street addresses. 19 York Street has been the home of John Milton, John Stuart Mill, and William Hazlitt (at different times, of course—they would have made an unfortunate rooming group). The area's most fondly remembered resident is undoubtedly Sherlock Holmes who, although fictitious, still receives about 50 letters per week addressed to his 221B Baker Street residence. The Abbey National Building Society currently occupies the site and employs a full-time secretary to answer requests for Holmes' assistance in solving mysteries around the world. One imagines the appeal for help from the American embassy in Beijing must have been tongue-in-cheek. The official line is that Holmes has retired from detective work and is keeping bees in the country. The **Sherlock Holmes Museum,** located at 239 Baker St. (marked "221b") is singularly steep at £5 (children £3) but Holmes enthusiasts will be thrilled by the meticulous re-creation of the detective's rooms. Upstairs is a passable display of "artifacts" from the stories, and a hilarious selection of letters Holmes has received in the last few years.

Ever since the redoubtable **Madame Tussaud,** one of Louis XVI's tutors, jetsetted from Paris in 1802 carrying wax effigies of French nobles decapitated in the Revolution, her eerie museum on Marylebone Rd. (tel. 935 6861; Tube: Baker St.) has been a London landmark. Nelson Mandela, Cher, Archbishop Desmond Tutu, Benny Hill, and Voltaire number among the luminaries re-created in life-size wax models. Most seem disconcertingly life-like, a few disappointingly uncharacteristic. The Chamber of Horrors downstairs shows grisly scenes of London from the time of Jack the Ripper and features the heads of Marie Antoinette and company; Adolf Hitler stands guard. You may enjoy a stroll among the famous personages, but be prepared to be accompanied by hordes of tourists and schoolchildren. Avoid the horrific queues by forming a minyan with at least nine fellow sufferers and using the group entrance. (Open June-Sept. daily 9am-5:30pm; Oct.-May 10am-5:30pm. Admission £5.95, under 16 £3.95.) The distinctive green dome of the **Planetarium** (tel. 486 2242), next door, encloses a mini-universe. (Planetarium open June-Sept. daily 10:20am-5pm; Oct.-May 12:20-5pm. Shows every 40 min. Admission £3.60, under 16 £2.30. Joint admission to Madame Tussaud's and the Planetarium £7.75, under 16 £5.10.)

Bloomsbury

Today, very little of the famed intellectual gossip, literary argot, and modernist snobbery still emanates from 51 Gordon Square, where Virginia Woolf lived with her husband Leonard. Leonard always insisted that the brilliant novelist he married maintained a strong presence, stronger than her image "as a frail invalidated lady living in an ivory tower in Bloomsbury and worshipped by a little clique of aesthetes." The clique in question, the overrated Bloomsbury Group, included biographer Lytton Strachey, novelist E.M. Forster, economist John Maynard Keynes, art critic Roger Fry, painter Vanessa Bell (sister of Virginia Woolf) and, on the fringe, T.S. Eliot, the eminent British poet from St. Louis.

The **British Museum** makes an appropriate Bloomsbury centerpiece; forbidding on the outside but quirky and amazing within, the collection contains a near-complete account of Western civilization (see Museums below). Nearby, close to the former houses of Strachey and Keynes stands the **Percival-David Foundation of Chinese Art,** 53 Gordon Sq. (tel. 387 3909; Tube: Russell Sq. or Goodge St.), a connoisseur's hoard of fabulously rare ceramics presented in 1950 to the University of London. You may dally before pots depicting "a scholar standing on the head of a dragon fish," but do save time for the illuminating Ming Gallery on the top floor. Waft by the intricate fan given in 1930 by the last emperor of China to his English tutor, Sir Reginald Johnston. (Open Mon.-Fri. 10:30am-5pm. Free.)

Buildings of the **University of London** pepper this area. Excluded from the Anglican-dominated universities at Oxford and Cambridge, Jeremy Bentham and a group of radical dissenters founded **University College,** Gower St., in 1827. They modeled the curriculum after those of German research universities, banned the teaching of theology, and admitted Catholics, Jews, and, later, women. Rumor has it that an embalmed Bentham resides in a closet there and is rolled out for meetings of the trustees. University College was chartered, along with King's College in the Strand, as the University of London in 1836, making London the last major European capital to acquire a university. London University grew up with Victoria, and its rather defiant utilitarianism has altered the character of the area. University buildings line Malet St., dominated by the tower of the Senate House, directly behind the British Museum.

To the south of the museum looms the massive, shrapnel-scarred Corinthian portico of Hawksmoor's 18th-century church, **St. George's Bloomsbury** in Bloomsbury Way. A contemporary statue of George I crowns the heavy steeple. Inside, novelist Anthony Trollope was baptized before the magnificent, gilded mahogany altar, where Dickens set his "Bloomsbury Christening" in *Sketches by Boz.* (Open sporadically: "We try to keep the church open all day, but we can't leave it unattended.") **St. Giles in the Fields,** a modest rectangular church surmounted by a beautiful Flitcroft tower (1731), rises above a 1687 Resurrection relief over a lush churchyard on St. Giles High St. John Wesley and his brother Charles preached from the pulpit here between 1743 and 1791. George Chapman, the celebrated translator of Homer and inspirer of Keats, lies buried beneath a heroic tomb attributed to Inigo Jones in the north aisle. The children of numerous London literati came here to be baptized-including Milton's daughter (and patient reader) Mary, Byron's daughter Allegra, and William and Clara Shelley, Percy and Mary's kids. (Open Mon.-Fri. 9am-4pm.)

Russell Square squares off as central London's second-largest, after Lincoln's Inn Fields. T.S. Eliot, the "Pope of Russell Square," often hid from his emotionally ailing first wife at number 24 while he worked as an editor and later a director of Faber and Faber.

Charles Dickens lived at 48 Doughty St. from 1837 to 1839, scribbling parts of *The Pickwick Papers, Nicholas Nickleby, Barnaby Rudge,* and *Oliver Twist.* Now a museum and library of Dickensia, the **Dickens House** (tel. 405 2127; Tube: Russell Sq. or Chancery Lane.) contains an array of prints, photographs, manuscripts, letters, and personal effects. The handsome drawing room has recently been restored to its original appearance. The rusty iron grill mounted on a basement wall was

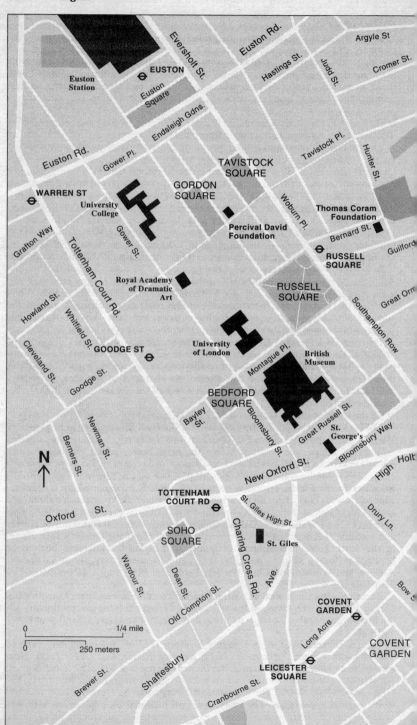

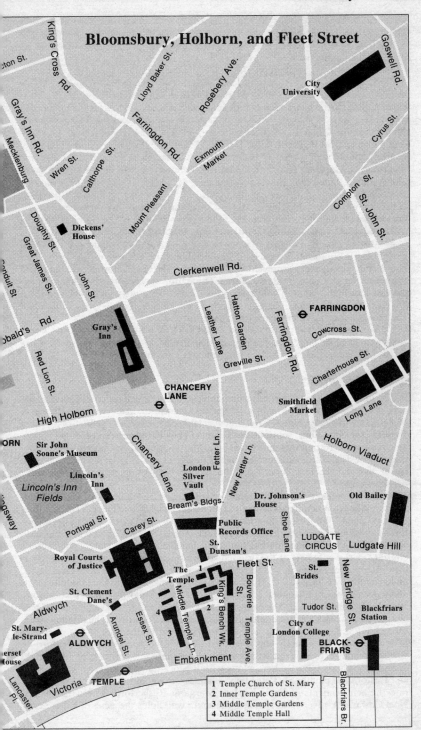

Bloomsbury, Holborn, and Fleet Street

King's Cross Rd.

Gray's Inn Rd.

Mecklenburg

...ton St.

Lloyd Baker St.

Rosebery Ave.

City University

Goswell Rd.

Farringdon Rd.

Cyrus St.

Wren St.

Calthorpe St.

Exmouth Market

Compton St.

St. John St.

Mount Pleasant

Doughty St.

Great James St.

Dickens' House

John St.

Clerkenwell Rd.

FARRINGDON

...obald's Rd.

Conduit St.

Red Lion St.

Gray's Inn

Leather Lane

Hatton Garden

Greville St.

Farringdon Rd.

Cowcross St.

Charterhouse St.

High Holborn

CHANCERY LANE

Smithfield Market

Long Lane

...ORN

Sir John Soane's Museum

Chancery Lane

Fetter Ln.

New Fetter Ln.

Holborn Viaduct

Lincoln's Inn

Lincoln's Inn Fields

London Silver Vault

Dr. Johnson's House

Old Bailey

Bream's Bldgs.

Shoe Lane

...gsway

Portugal St.

Carey St.

Public Records Office

LUDGATE CIRCUS

Ludgate Hill

Royal Courts of Justice

St. Dunstan's

Fleet St.

St. Brides

New Bridge St.

St. Clement Dane's

The Temple

1

Middle Temple Ln.

King's Bench Wk.

Bouverie St.

Temple Ave.

Tudor St.

Blackfriars Station

Aldwych

Arundel St.

Essex St.

4

2

3

City of London College

BLACK-FRIARS

St. Mary-le-Strand

ALDWYCH

Embankment

Blackfriars Br.

...erset ...ouse

Lancaster Pl.

Victoria

TEMPLE

1 Temple Church of St. Mary
2 Inner Temple Gardens
3 Middle Temple Gardens
4 Middle Temple Hall

salvaged by the author from the Marshalsea Jail, a notorious debtor's prison where Dickens' father did time for three months in 1824, while his young son labored in a shoe-black factory. (Open Mon.-Sat. 10am-5pm. Admission £2, students £1.50, children £1, family £4.)

While serving as governor of the nearby Thomas Coram Foundling Hospital, William Hogarth solicited paintings and other artwork from his friends and fellow artists to publicize the condition of abandoned children and elicit funds for their care. Although the hospital was torn down in 1926, its art treasures remain, displayed in a suite of splendidly restored 18th-century rooms in the **Thomas Coram Foundation for Children**, 40 Brunswick Sq. (tel. 278 2424; Tube: Russell Sq.) Several canvasses by Hogarth (look for his "March to Fincheley" and portrait of Coram) mingle with works by Gainsborough, Benjamin West, and Roubiliac and a cartoon by Raphael. Händel donated the diminutive organ on the second floor, along with a signed manuscript copy of the "Messiah." The adjacent Governor's Court Room, with its ornate ceilings and rococo plaster work, houses a poignant collection of tokens and trinkets (bits of yellowing ribbon, tiny tarnished crosses, crushed silver thimbles) left with the foundlings admitted to the hospital between 1741 and 1760. (Open Mon.-Fri. 10am-4pm. Admission 50p, children 25p.)

Further north, **St. Pancras Station** (Tube: King's Cross/St.Pancras) rises as a monument to Victorian prosperity over a neighborhood of present-day decay. This neo-gothic fantasy was completed in 1867, and is due to be refurbished along with the whole King's Cross/St. Pancras area. The station may become the Channel Tunnel rail terminal; planning continues ad nauseam. Next door, in stylistic contrast but in harmonious brick, the new British Library nears completion, amidst royal controversy over insufficient reading space.

Up St. Pancras Road, past the station's red brick effluvia, **St.Pancras Old Church** sits serenely in its large and leafy garden, where Mary Godwin first met Shelley in 1813. Parts of the church date from the 11th century.

Covent Garden

The beguilingly chic Covent Garden of today seems much different from the unruly marketplace where Fielding, Hogarth, Goldsmith, and even the Prince of Wales met with their cronies. Fruit and vegetable carts have left the **Central Market Building** for Nine Elms, south of the Thames. They have been replaced by fashionable, expensive restaurants and shops in a tourist-oriented but tasteful redevelopment. Crowds and street performers offer a modern version of the jostling conviviality of the 18th century: watch for the rubbish-bin drummers and cobble-stone breakdancers.

The area's name recalls the ancient convent garden tended by the monks of Westminster Abbey. When he abolished the monasteries in 1536, Henry VIII bestowed this land upon John Russell, first Earl of Bedford. The Earl's descendants developed it into a fashionable *piazza* (designed by Inigo Jones) in the 17th century; the sixth earl had the Market Building built in 1830. Jones' **St. Paul's Church**, the "actor's church," is the only part of the original square to survive and testifies to the poor-little-rich-boy minimalism of the Bedford dynasty. Gouged by heavy taxes levied on his family by Charles I, the Duke of Bedford warned Jones to keep building costs down even if the church ended up looking like a barn. Following these instructions, Jones built what he called "the handsomest barn in England," his version of a Greek temple, free of classical ornamentation. Although a fire destroyed the original structure in 1795, the replacement was reconstructed faithfully, true to the character of Jones' work. The church can be entered through the heavy gates on Bedford St. Several famous artists lie entombed in the austere interior. Restoration playwright William Wycherly is buried here, along with Restoration sculptor Grinling Gibbons and Restoration painter Sir Peter Lely. Plaques throughout the church commemorate the achievements of Boris Karloff, Margaret Rutherford, Vivien Leigh, and Noel Coward. A silver casket set into the south wall holds the ashes of Ellen Terry.

An inscription on the portico marks the first known performance of a Punch and Judy puppet show, recorded by Samuel Pepys in 1662. (Open Mon.-Fri. 9am-4pm.)

In the 18th century, Covent Garden began to fill the void left by the suppression of entertainments in Southwark. King George granted the first theatre charter in 1728, and for over a century the royal playhouses in Covent Garden and on adjacent Drury Lane held a virtual monopoly over theatre in London. The present buildings of the **Theatre Royal** and **Royal Opera House** both date from the 19th century. The present Theatre Royal replaced a 1674 Wren building, the site of attempted assassinations of Kings George II and III. As it burned in 1809, playwright Sheridan drank and watched, commenting, "Surely a man may take a glass of wine by his own fireside." (See Entertainment.)

Right across the street from the Royal Opera House stands **Bow Street Magistrates' Court,** the oldest of London's 12 magistrates' courts and the home of the Bow Street Runners, predecessors of the city's present-day police. In the courthouse, novelist Henry Fielding and his brother Sir John Fielding presided over a bench famed for its compassion. Nearby, a blue plaque at 8 Russell St. marks the site of the booksellers' home where Boswell first met Dr. Johnson in 1763.

The **London Transport Museum** and the **Theatre Museum** (see Museums) bloom in the old Flower Market building in the southeast corner of the *piazza*.

At the **Cabaret Mechanical Theatre,** 33-34 The Market, Covent Garden (enter via Punch and Judy's or the nearby stairways leading to the basement level; tel. 379 7961), you can watch miniature wooden machines perform amusing actions when you insert a coin—a whimsical way to rid yourself of all that heavy British change rattling around in your pockets. (Admission £1.75, students and children £1. Open Mon. noon-6:30pm, Tues.-Sat. 10am-6:30pm, Sun. 11am-6:30pm.)

Even outside the renovated area, Covent Garden hums with activity. Curious stage-design shops cluster near the Opera House, and the surrounding streets are studded with moss-covered artisans' studios and an odd assortment of businesses connected with the theatre. Rose Street leads to the notorious **Lamb and Flag,** a lively pub where Dryden was attacked and nearly murdered by an angry mob opposed to his writings.

Holborn and the Inns of Court

The historical center of English law lies in a small area straddling the precincts of Westminster and The City and surrounding long and litigious High Holborn, Chancery Lane, and Fleet Street. The Strand and Fleet St. converge on the **Royal Courts of Justice** (tel. 936 6000), a formidable Gothic structure designed in 1874 by architect G.E. Street for the Supreme Court of Judicature. The cavernous central hall with fine mosaic floors outshines the tiny display of legal costume that makes financial law seem interesting by comparison. (Courts and galleries open to the public Mon.-Fri. 10:30am-4:30pm.)

Barristers in The City are affiliated with one of the famous **Inns of Court** (Lincoln's Inn, Middle Temple, Inner Temple, and Gray's Inn), four ancient legal institutions which provide lectures and apprenticeships for law students and regulate admission to the bar. The tiny gates and narrow alleyways that lead to the inns are invisible to most passersby. Inside, the Inns are organized like colleges at Oxford, each with its own gardens, chapel, library, dining hall, common rooms, and chambers. Most were founded in the 13th century when a royal decree barred the clergy from the courts of justice, giving rise to a new class of professional legal advocates. Today, students may seek their legal training outside of the Inns, but to be considered for membership they must "keep term" by dining regularly in one of the halls.

Named after Henri de Lacy (Earl of Lincoln), an advisor to Edward I and an early champion of legal studies, **Lincoln's Inn** (Tube: Holborn) was the only Inn to emerge unscathed from the Blitz. New Square and its cloistered churchyard (to the right as you enter from Lincoln's Inn Fields) appear today much as they did in the 1680s. The **Old Hall,** east of New Square, dates from 1492; here the Lord

High Chancellor presided over the High Court of Chancery from 1733 to 1873. The most well-known chancery case is that of Jarndyce and Jarndyce, whose life-sapping machinations are played out in the pages of *Bleak House.* Dickens knew well the world he described, having worked as a lawyer's clerk in New Court just across the yard. To the west, **New Hall,** an impressive, Tudor-style building, houses a fine 19th-century mural by G.F. Watts and a lugubrious collection of legal por-traits. Built in 1497, the adjacent library—London's oldest—holds over 70,000 vol-umes in its stacks. John Donne, William Pitt, Horace Walpole, and Benjamin Dis-raeli number among the many luminaries associated with Lincoln's Inn. (See the porter at 11A Lincoln's Inn Fields for admission to the halls. Whimsical opening policies.) On the north side of Lincoln's Inn Fields smugly sits **Sir John Soane's Museum;** it's the house bedecked with sculpture amidst a row of plain buildings (see Museums).

   Gray's Inn (Tube: Chancery Lane), dubbed "that stronghold of melancholy" by Dickens, stands at the northern end of Fulwood Pl., off High Holborn. Reduced to ashes by German bombers in 1941, Gray's Inn was restored to much of its former splendor during the 1950s. The Hall, to your right as you pass through the archway, retains its original stained glass (1580) and most of its ornate screen. The first per-formance of Shakespeare's *Comedy of Errors* took place here in 1594. Francis Bacon maintained chambers here from 1577 until his death in 1626. Bacon supposedly designed the magnificent gardens, the most extensive of any Inn north of Field Court.

   Of the nine Inns of Chancery, only **Staple Inn's** building survives (located where Gray's Inn Road meets Holborn) (Tube: Chancery Lane). The half-timbered Eliza-bethan front dates from 1586. Devoted son Samuel Johnson wrote "Rasselas" here in one week to pay for a funeral for his mother.

   But none of these Inns can compare with the **Temple** (Tube: Yes, Temple). South of Fleet St., it houses both the Middle and Inner Temples, the other two Inns of Court. Its name derives from the crusading order of Knights Templar who em-braced this site as their English seat during the 12th century. The bellicose order dissolved in 1312, and this property, then forfeited to the crown, was eventually passed on to the Knights Hospitallers of St. John, who leased it to a community of common law scholars in 1338. Virtually leveled by enemy action in the early 1940s, only the church, crypt, and buttery of the Inner Temple survive intact from the Middle Ages.

   Held in common by both the Middle and Inner Temples, the **Temple Church,** also known as the Church of St. Mary the Virgin, should appear near the top of every list of sights in London. The finest of the few round churches left in England, it contains a handsome 12th-century Norman doorway, an altar screen by Wren (1682), and nine arresting, armor-clad effigies of Knights Templar dating from the 12th and 13th centuries. Author Oliver Goldsmith, whose late-night revelry at the Temple often irritated his staid neighbor, Blackstone, lies buried in the yard behind the choir. (Open Oct.-July Mon.-Sat. 10am-4pm, Sun. 2-4pm.) According to Shake-speare (*Henry VI*), the red and white roses that served as emblems throughout the War of the Roses were plucked from the Middle Temple Garden. On Ground Hog day in 1601, Shakespeare himself supposedly appeared in a performance of *Twelfth Night* in **Middle Temple Hall,** a grand Elizabethan dining room now open to the public whenever it's not serving as a student refectory. (Usually open Mon.-Fri. 10am-noon.) **Fountain Court,** just north of Middle Temple Hall, was the setting of Ruth Pinch's incestuous liaison with her brother Tom in Dickens' novel, *Martin Chuzzlewit.* Nearby, a handful of London's last functioning gaslamps line Middle Temple Lane.

   North of the Temple and east of Lincoln's Inn stands the **Public Records Office** and its adjoining museum on Chancery Lane, where William the Conqueror's *Domesday Book,* a statistical survey of England written on animal skins, outclasses the rest of the exhibits. Still, in the museum's lone room you can skim some amusing scraps of British parchment salvaged from the confetti mills of time; the exhibits are rotated regularly from the office's vast collection. (Museum open Mon.-Fri. 10am-5pm; tel. 876 3444.)

Holborn continues east towards the City, crossing the "Hole-bourne" on the **Holborn Viaduct,** one of only two road-over-road bridges in central London. Archway is the other.

The Strand and Fleet Street

Hugging the ancient embankment of the River Thames, **The Strand** (Tube: Charing Cross, Temple, or Aldwych—rush hours only) has not fared well through London's growth. Once lined with fine Tudor houses, this major thoroughfare now pierces a jumbled assortment of lame commercial buildings and suffers from incessant traffic jams. **Somerset House,** a magnificent Palladian structure built by Sir William Chambers in 1776, stands on the site of the 16th-century palace where Elizabeth I resided during the brief reign of her sister Mary. Formerly the administrative center of the Royal Navy, the building now houses the exquisite **Courtauld Collection** (see Museums) and the less exquisite offices of the Inland Revenue.

Farther east, the impeccable **St. Mary le Strand,** with its slender steeple and elegant Ionic portico, rises above an island of decaying steps in the middle of the modern roadway. Designed by James Gibbs and consecrated in 1724, the church overlooks the site of the original Maypole, where London's first hackney cabs assembled in 1634. Inside, the baroque complexities of the barrel vault and ornamental altar walls reflect Gibb's architectural training in Rome. The intricate floral moldings were crafted by two brothers, John and Chrysostom Wilkins, who received a mere 45p for each elaborate bloom. Isaac Newton was an early parishioner, and Dickens' parents got married here in 1809. (Open Mon.-Fri. 11am-3:30pm.) Across the north side of The Strand, cultured newsreaders pompously intone "This is London" every hour from Bush House, the nerve center of the worldwide radio services of the BBC.

To the east stands **St. Clement Danes** whose melodious bells get their 15 seconds of fame in the nursery rhyme "Oranges and lemons, say the bells of St. Clement's." Designed by Wren in 1682, the church was built over the ruins of an older Norman structure reputed to be the tomb of Harold Harefoot, leader of a colony of Danes who settled the area in the 9th century. In 1720, Gibb replaced Wren's original truncated tower with a slimmer spire. Although German firebombs gutted the church in 1941, the white stucco and gilt interior has been restored to its former splendor by the Royal Air Force (RAF), which adopted St. Clement's as its official church after World War II. RAF commemorations strafe the reconstructed church. Note the marble floors inlaid with brass squadron medallions. A quiet crypt-*cum*-prayer-chapel houses an eerie collection of 17th-century funereal monuments. Samuel Johnson worshipped here, and a paunchy bronze statue of the great Doctor (sculpted in 1910 by Fitzgerald) stands outside the east apse of the church. (Open daily 8am-5pm.) The nearby Gothic giant houses the Royal Courts of Justice (see Holborn and Inns of Court section above). **Twining's Teas** (tel. 353 3511) brews at 216 The Strand. It is both the oldest business in Britain still operating on original premises and the narrowest shop in London. The building dates from 1787. Just east stands the only Strand building to survive the Great Fire: the **Wig and Pen Club,** 229-230 The Strand, constructed over Roman ruins in 1625. Frequented by the best-known barristers and journalists in London, the Wig and Pen is, in the sage words of the *Baltimore Sun,* "a window through which you can see Fleet Street in all its aspects." The club is open to members only, though a passport-toting overseas traveler can apply for free and immediate temporary membership. Walk up the ancient, crooked staircase—the only remnant of the original 17th-century house. Backpackers beware: the doorman will haughtily reject denim-bedecked budget travelers. The **Temple Bar Monument** stands in the middle of the street where the Strand meets Fleet Street, marking the boundary between Westminster and the City. The Sovereign must still obtain ceremonial permission from the Lord Mayor to pass the bar and enter the City here.

Fleet Street, named for the one-time river (now a sewer) that flows from Hampstead to the Thames near Blackfriar's Bridge, was until recently the hub of British journalism. Before the late 1980s, all of London's major papers had their offices on the "Street of Shame," lampooned by Evelyn Waugh through the *Daily Beast* in his 1938 novel *Scoop.* All have left, led by the *Times,* which moved to cheaper land at Tobacco Dock, Docklands, in 1986. The *Daily Telegraph* vacated its startling Greek and Egyptian revival building, moving to Marsh Wall in 1987. The *Daily Express,* once the occupant of an art deco monster of chrome and black glass on Fleet Street, now headlines in Blackfriars.

A handsome half-timbered house dating from 1610 remains intact at No. 17 Fleet St., just above the gateway to the **Temple Church** (see Holborn and Inns of Court above). On the first floor, **Prince Henry's Room,** with its ornate 17th-century ceiling (arguably London's finest example of Jacobean plaster-work), richly carved mahogany paneling, and Samuel Pepys memorabilia is well worth investigating. (Open Mon.-Fri. 1:45-4:45pm. Free.) Farther north stands the octagonal, neo-Gothic **St. Dunstan in the West,** crowned with a magnificent lantern tower and a curious 17th-century clock—its chimes are sounded on the quarter hour by a pair of hammer-wielding, mechanical giants. A rare statue of Elizabeth I (one of the few contemporary likenesses of the Queen) rises above the vestry door. The three 16th-century effigies leaning against the porch may represent King Lud, the mythical founder of London, and his sons. In the central archway, you can see a rough carving of poet-priest John Donne. Both the lascivious Donne and his biographer, fellow Elizabethan Izaak Walton, maintained close ties with St. Dunstan.

Both Johnson and Bolt Courts lead north to Gough Square, and **Samuel Johnson's House** at No. 17 (tel. 353 3745). Remarkably enough, this is where Dr. Johnson lived, from 1749 to 1758. Follow the signs carefully; Carlyle got lost on his way here in 1832. Here Johnson completed his *Dictionary,* the first definitive English lexicon, even though rumor insists that he omitted "sausage." (His closest predecessor, Nathaniel Bailey, defined the heart as "a most noble part of the body" in 1717.) Johnson scholars will not find many original documents here but may be touched by the sparseness of the decor, a reminder of the poverty in which Johnson lived. Tours are self-guided, but the curator, a knowledgeable and charming woman, will supplement your visit with anecdotes about the Great Cham and his hyperbolic biographer, James Boswell. (Open May-Sept. Mon.-Sat. 11am-5:30pm; Oct.-April Mon.-Sat. 11am-5pm. Admission £2, students, children, and senior citizens £1.50.)

The spire of Wren's **St. Bride's** (1675), south of Fleet St. near Ludgate Circus, became the inspiration for countless English wedding cakes, via a copy-cat local baker. Excavations of the ancient crypt beneath the church (called the "printer's church"), have revealed traces of a late Saxon cemetery, the foundation of a 6th-century Roman structure, and the ruins of several earlier churches. A gentle, intriguing museum, housing a musty collection of relics and rocks, has been improvised in the lower chambers, alongside an exhibit detailing the evolution of printing in Fleet Street and an interesting array of manuscripts and literary memorabilia. (Open daily 8:15am-4:45pm.)

To the south, the **Embankment** runs along the Thames, parallel to The Strand. Between the Hungerford and Waterloo Bridges stands London's oldest landmark, **Cleopatra's Needle,** an Egyptian obelisk from 1450 BC presented by the Viceroy of Egypt in 1878. A sister stone stands in Central Park in New York.

The City of London

Once enclosed by Roman walls, the one-square-mile City of London is the financial center of Europe. Each weekday 350,000 people surge in at 9am and out again unfailingly at 5pm, leaving behind a resident population of only 6000. At the center of the City, the massive Bank of England controls the nation's finances, and the Stock Exchange makes the nation's fortune. At the heart of the area is Cheapside; "cheap" derives from the Old English for "purchase," and many street names here pay homage to commerce: Bread Street, Milk Street, Poultry Street, and Thread-

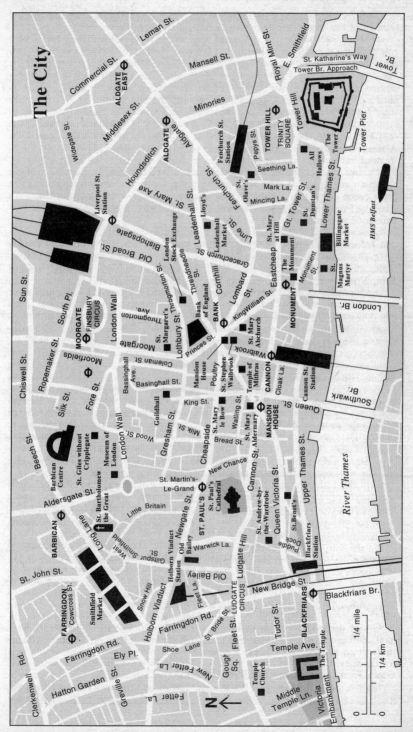

needle Street. Proliferating cranes, office building sites, and rising share indices bear witness to the British economic resurgence of the late 80s.

The City owes much of its graceful appearance to Sir Christopher Wren, who was the chief architect working in the City after the fire of 1666 almost completely razed it. In his *Diary*, Samuel Pepys gives a most moving first-hand account of the fire that started in a baker's shop in Pudding Lane and leapt between the o'erhanging houses to sweep the City with destruction. Afterwards, Charles II issued a proclamation that City buildings should be rebuilt in brick and stone, rather than highly flammable wood and thatch. Wren's studio designed 51 churches to replace the 89 destroyed in the fire, and the surviving 24 churches are some of the only buildings in the City from the period immediately following the Great Fire. A host of variations on a theme, they gave Wren a valuable chance to work out, in stone rather than on paper, problems of design that came up as he rebuilt St. Paul's. Inside his churches, light plaster, dark carved oak, and an abundance of gilt create an airy elegance. The original effect of a forest of steeples surrounding the great dome of St. Paul's must be reckoned his greatest contribution to London's cityscape; unfortunately, the modern skyscrapers so energetically condemned by Prince Charles now obscure the effect.

Many of the churches have irregular or random opening times. The **City of London Information Center,** St. Paul's Churchyard (tel. 606 3030); Tube: St. Paul's) can give you up-to-date details on all of the City's attractions, and sells John Betjeman's guide, *City of London Churches,* for £1.75. (Open May-Oct. daily 9:30am-5pm; Nov.-April Mon.-Fri. 9:30am-5pm, Sat. 9:30am-12:30pm.)

The buildings of the Livery Companies represent perhaps the most important secular structures of the City. Originally organizations with a broad range of social and political obligations, the guilds also played a role in fixing trade standards; now many contribute to charity and education. Wealthier guilds such as the Haberdashers and the Merchant Taylors maintain schools. The twelve "great companies" are the Mercers (textile dealers, chartered in 1393), Grocers (1345), Drapers (1364), Fishmongers (1364), Goldsmiths (1327), Skinners (1327), Merchant Taylors (1326), Haberdashers (1448), Salters (1558), Ironmongers (1454), Vintners (1436), and Clothworkers (1528). The phrase "at sixes and sevens" arose from an argument between the Skinners and the Merchant Taylors as to who should march in sixth place in City processions. The 84 **livery halls,** many distinguished, are scattered around the square mile. Most halls do not open to the public; those that do require tickets. The City of London Information office (see above) receives a batch of tickets in March, but they disappear rapidly. Inquire there for the current opening situation. Some halls sponsor spring celebrations, and a few hold fascinating exhibits—for example, of the finest products of London's goldsmiths.

Until the 18th century, the City of London *was* London; all the other boroughs and neighborhoods now swallowed up by "London"—even Westminster—were neighboring towns or outlying villages. Enclosed by Roman and medieval walls, the City had six gates, whose names survive: Aldersgate, Aldgate. Bishopsgate, Cripplegate, Newgate, and Ludgate. The **London Wall Walk** runs along the course of the old wall from the Museum of London to the Tower, passing a few exposed remains. Start just outside the Tower Hill tube station and follow the signs and historical panels. Today's City hums with activity during the work week, is dead on Saturdays, and ghostly on Sundays. To catch the flavor of the City, visit on a weekday. Everyone you see will either be in a suit and working in a bank, or in a hard hat and building a bank. Endless blocks of mediocre modern architecture are lent life by these nine-to-five crowds; the city turns eerie when the workers go home. However, the area's museums and some of the Wren churches remain open Sundays, and you can contemplate the good and the evil of City architecture without being crushed by umbrellas and briefcases.

From Bank to Ludgate—the Western Section

The few remaining stones of the Roman **Temple of Mithras,** Queen Victoria St., dwell incongruously in the shadows of banal modern structures. Discovered during construction work and shifted a few yards from its original location, the temple still retains a recognizable outline. Down the road, **St. Mary Aldermary** (so called because it is older than any other St. Mary's church in the City), towers over its surroundings. (Open Tues.-Fri. 11am-3pm.) A rare Gothic Wren, it is especially notable for its delicate fan-vaulting. The bells that recalled Dick Whittington to London rang out from the church of St. Marie de Arcubus, replaced by Wren's **St. Mary-le-Bow,** Cheapside, in 1683. The range of the Bow bells' toll is supposed to define the extent of true-blue Cockney London. Being a Bow bell has never been easy—the first lot were annihilated by the Great Fire, the second destroyed by the Blitz. (Open Mon.-Fri. 8:15am-5:45pm.) Up Aldermanbury huddles the **Guildhall,** a cavernous space where dignitaries were once tried for treason. The building now accommodates the town clerk, a library, offices, and the clock museum (see Museums). The Great Hall houses excessive monuments to Nelson, Wellington, Pitt, and others. (Open Mon.-Sat. 10am-5pm; May-Sept. daily 10am-5pm.) The **Public Library,** founded in 1420, opens to the public on weekdays from 9:30am to 5pm.

St. Paul's dominates the cathedral scene in the western end of the City (see St. Paul's below), but Wren groupies should check out three fine churches in the environs. **St. James Garlickhythe** gets its name from the garlic sold nearby. Its modest but pleasing Hawksmoor steeple is dwarfed by the huge Vintners Place development across the street. West on Upper Thames St. stands a rare red brick Wren church, **St. Benet's,** with an elegant cupola. The burial place of Inigo Jones and site of one of Henry Fielding's marriages, **Benet's** survived an arson attempt in 1971.

Just to the north the **College of Arms** rests on its heraldic authority behind ornate gates. The College regulates the granting and recognition of coats of arms, and is directed by the Earl Marshal, the Duke of Norfolk. The officer-in-waiting at the Earl Marshal's stately paneled Court Room can address your claim to the throne. (Open Mon.-Fri. 10am-4pm.)

St. Andrew-by-the-Wardrobe was originally built next to Edward III's impressive closet. Now the church cowers beneath the Faraday building, the first building allowed to exceed the City's strict height limit.

Queen Victoria's Street meets New Bridge Street in the area known as Blackfriars, in reference to the darkly-clad Dominican brothers who built a medieval monastery here. Shakespeare acted in James Burbage's theatre here in the late 1500s. Ludgate Circus, to the north, is now the noisy site of a major redevelopment. A peaceful haven is offered by **St. Martin-within-Ludgate,** a Wren church untouched by the Blitz. The square interior boasts some fine Grinling Gibbons woodwork, and the slim spire still pierces the dome of St. Paul's when seen from Ludgate Circus, just as Wren intended. (Open Mon.-Fri. 10am-4pm.) Around the corner, the **Old Bailey** (tel. 248 3277), technically the Central Criminal Courts, crouches under a copper dome and a wide-eyed figure of justice on the corner of Old Bailey and Newgate St.—infamous as the site of Britain's grimmest prison. Trial-watching persists as a favorite occupation, and the Old Bailey fills up whenever a gruesome or scandalous case is in progress. You can enter the public Visitors' Gallery and watch bewigged barristers at work (Mon.-Fri. 10am-1pm and 2-4pm); it can be a touch depressing. When court is not in session (from the last week in July to Sept. 15), the building opens from 11am to 3pm. The Chief Post Office building, off Newgate to the north, envelops the stunning, nay mind-blowing, **National Postal Museum** (see Museums).

The Barbican and the Northern Section.

The **Barbican Centre,** covering 60 acres and opened in 1982, stands as one of the most impressive and controversial post-Blitz rebuilding projects. Widely considered a symbol of the brutalism of the postwar landscape, the Barbican is also universally acknowledged as a vital cultural centre. A city unto itself, the complex of apartments and offices houses the **Royal Shakespeare Company,** the **London Symphony Orchestra,** and the **Museum of London** (see Museums). (For information on the Festival of the City of London, see Music below.)

St. Bartholomew The Great, off Smithfield, one of London's oldest churches, is reached through a delightfully narrow Tudor house. Parts of the church date from

1123, although 800 years of alteration have much embellished it. (Open Mon.-Thurs. 8am-4:30pm, Fri. 10:45am-4:30pm, Sun. 8am-8pm.) For an early pint, try one of the pubs around **Smithfield**, a meat and poultry wholesale market. (Market open daily 5am-noon; some surrounding pubs open 6:30am.) Smithfield's associations with butchery go back further than the meat market. Scotsman William Wallace and rebel Wat Tyler rank among those executed here in the Middle Ages. Smithfield was a favorite site for burning Protestants under Queen Mary I. **Charterhouse** (tel. 253 9503.), a peculiar institution first established as a priory and converted in 1611 to a school and hospital for poor gentlemen, stands on the edge of Charterhouse Square. The school has moved to Surrey, but the fine collection of 15th- to 17th-century buildings still houses around 40 brethren. Residents must be over 60 and either bachelors or widowers. A jolly time is had by all. (Tours April-July Wed. at 2:15pm. Nominal charge for charity.)

Just north of the square, now in Islington, stands **St. John's Gate**, St. John's St. On the ground floor, a museum commemorates the volunteer St. John Ambulance Brigade, the savior of thousands of people who have fainted at Rolling Stones concerts, among others. (Open Mon.-Fri. 10am-4:30pm, Sat. 10am-4pm.) The **Clerkenwell Centre** (tel. 250 1039), at St. John's St. and Clerkenwell Rd., can give you further information about this area. (Open Mon.-Fri. 10am-6pm.)

From Bank to the Tower—the Eastern Section

The massive windowless walls and foreboding doors of the Bank of England enclose four full acres. The present building dates from 1925, but the eight-foot thick outer wall is the same one built by eccentric architect Sir John Soame in 1788. The only part open to the public is the plush **Bank of England Museum** (see Museums). The **Stock Exchange** next door is no more welcoming. Struck by an IRA bomb in 1990, the Visitors' Gallery is no longer open. **St. Margaret Lothbury** (down Throgmorton St.), Wren's last church apart from St. Paul's, contains a sumptuous carved wood screen (1689). Most of the church's furnishings come from other City churches which have been demolished. A couple of blocks north, the **National Westminster Tower** hovers at over 600 ft. The City is getting a run for its money from the Docklands, and in the latest encroachment the Canary Wharf tower surpassed NatWest's as Britain's tallest. Back through the land of threading needles and throgging mortons, behind the imposing, tautological Mansion House, home of the Lord Mayor, stands **St. Stephen Walbrook.** Arguably Wren's finest, and allegedly his personal favorite, the church combines four major styles: the old-fashioned English church characterized by nave and chancel; the Puritan hall church, which lacks any separation between priest and congregation; the Greek-cross-plan church; and the domed church, a study for St. Paul's. The Samaritans, a social service group that advises the suicidal and severely depressed, was founded here in 1953. The mysterious cheese-like object in the center is actually the altar, sculpted by Henry Moore, and is as controversial as you think. Unfortunately, St. Stephen's is completely surrounded by six-story buildings. (Open Mon.-Fri. 9am-4pm.) The church of **St. Mary Woolnoth**, at King William and Lombard St., may look odd without a spire, but the interior proportions and the black and gilt reredos confirm the talents of Wren's pupil Nicholas Hawksmoor. The only City church untouched by the Blitz, it "kept the hours" in Eliot's *The Waste Land.***Mary Abchurch,** off Abchurch Lane, provides a neat domed comparison to St. Stephen's, its mellow, dark wood and baroque paintings contrasting with St. Stephen's bright airy interior. (Opening times vary. Usually open Thurs. 10am-4pm.)

Before even the most basic rebuilding of the city, Wren designed a tall Doric pillar, completed in 1671 and named simply the **Monument,** at the bottom of King William St. Supposedly, the 202-ft. pillar stands exactly that many feet from where the Great Fire broke out in Pudding Lane on September 2, 1666 and "rushed devastating through every quarter with astonishing swiftness and worse." High on Fish Street Hill, the column offers an expansive view of London. Bring stern resolution and £1 to climb its 311 steps. (Tube: Monument. Open April-Sept. Mon.-Fri. 9am-6pm, Sat.-Sun. 2-6pm; Oct.-March Mon.-Sat. 9am-4pm.)

The current **London Bridge** succeeds a slew of ancestors. The famed version crowded with houses stood from 1176 until it burned in 1758. The most recent predecessor didn't fall down as the nursery rhyme prophesied; worse, it was sold to an American millionaire for £1.03 million and shipped, block by block, to Lake Havasu City, Arizona. **St. Magnus Martyr,** on Lower Thames St., stands next to the path to the somewhat older 12th-century London Bridge, and proudly displays a chunk of wood from a Roman jetty. According to T.S. Eliot, the walls of the church "hold inexplicable splendor of Ionian white and gold," a soothing contrast to the forlorn Billingsgate fish market next door. The deserted trading floors there pine for the bustle and carp transported to the new Billingsgate in Docklands. (St. Magnus Martyr open Tues.-Fri. 9am-4pm, Sat.-Sun. 9:30am-1pm.)

St. Mary at Hill, Lovat Lane, is a typical Wren church with a surprisingly convincing reworking of the old Wren interior by early Victorian craftsmen, and an even more convincing contemporary reconstruction project. **St. Dunstan-in-the-East,** St. Dunstan's Hill, suffered severe damage in the Blitz; only Wren's amazing spire remains. The ruins have been converted into a gorgeous little garden that makes a lovely picnic spot, popular with stockbrokers trying to commune with nature.

Pepys witnessed the movement of the Great Fire from the tower of **All Hallows by the Tower.** Just inside the south entrance is an arch from the 7th-century Saxon church, discovered in 1960. To the left, the baptistery contains a striking wood font cover by Grinling Gibbons. William Penn was baptized, and John Quincy Adams married, in All Hallows. Another victim of the bombing, **St. Olave's** in Hart St., underwent restoration after the war. It was one of the few City churches to survive the fire of 1666. An annual memorial service is held for Pepys, who is buried here with his wife. (Open Mon.-Fri. 8am-3:30pm.) Don't be frightened by the name of Seething Gardens across the street; the lush spot is perfect for a take-away lunch.

The 1986 **Lloyd's** building and **Leadenhall Market,** off Leadenhall St., supply the most startling architectural clash in the City. The ducts, lifts, and chutes of Lloyd's would not look out of place on the *Brazil* set; one almost expects racing air-conditioning repairmen rather than stockbrokers to emerge from its doors. The futuristic setting houses the **Lutine Bell,** which is still occasionally rung—once for bad insurance news, twice for good. (Viewing gallery open Mon.-Fri. 10am-12:30pm.) Across a narrow alley, one looks for Jack the Ripper to emerge from the ornate cream and maroon of Victorian Leadenhall Market. A market has stood here since the middle ages.

St. Paul's Cathedral

Sir Christopher Wren's domed masterpiece dominates its surroundings even as modern usurpers sneak up around it. The third cathedral to stand on the site, St. Paul's has become a grand and moving monument, at once a physical and spiritual symbol of London. The first cathedral was founded in 604; fire destroyed it in 1089. The second and most massive cathedral was a medieval structure, one of the largest in Europe, topped by a spire ascending 489 feet. Falling into almost complete neglect in the 16th century, the cathedral became more of a marketplace than a church, and plans for its reconstruction were in the works well before the Great Fire. Wren had already started drawing up his grand scheme in 1666 when the conflagration demolished the cathedral, along with most of London, and gave him the great opportunity to build from scratch. Like his Renaissance predecessors, Wren preferred the equal-armed Greek cross plan, while ecclesiastical authorities insisted upon a traditional medieval design with a long nave and choir for services. Wren's final design compromised by translating a Gothic cathedral into baroque and classical terms: a Latin Cross floor plan with baroque detailing. The huge classical dome, second in size only to St. Peter's in Rome, towers at 365 feet.

Both the design and the building of the cathedral were dogged by controversy. Wren's second model received the king's warrant of approval (and is thus known as the "Warrant Model") but still differed from today's St. Paul's. The shrewd archi-

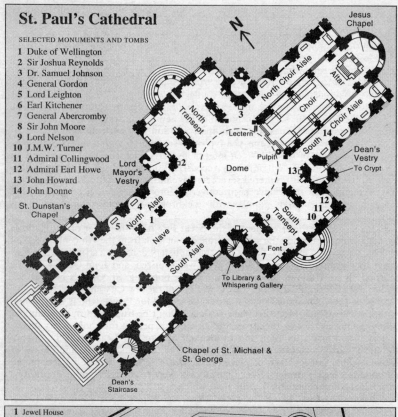

St. Paul's Cathedral

SELECTED MONUMENTS AND TOMBS

1 Duke of Wellington
2 Sir Joshua Reynolds
3 Dr. Samuel Johnson
4 General Gordon
5 Lord Leighton
6 Earl Kitchener
7 General Abercromby
8 Sir John Moore
9 Lord Nelson
10 J.M.W. Turner
11 Admiral Collingwood
12 Admiral Earl Howe
13 John Howard
14 John Donne

Jesus Chapel

North Choir Aisle
Choir
Altar
South Choir Aisle
North Transept
Lectern
Pulpit
Dome
Dean's Vestry
To Crypt
Lord Mayor's Vestry
St. Dunstan's Chapel
North Aisle
Nave
South Aisle
South Transept
Font
To Library & Whispering Gallery
Chapel of St. Michael & St. George
Dean's Staircase

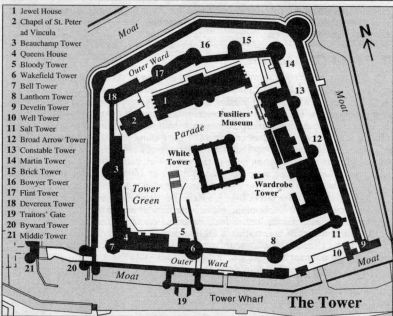

1 Jewel House
2 Chapel of St. Peter ad Vincula
3 Beauchamp Tower
4 Queens House
5 Bloody Tower
6 Wakefield Tower
7 Bell Tower
8 Lanthorn Tower
9 Develin Tower
10 Well Tower
11 Salt Tower
12 Broad Arrow Tower
13 Constable Tower
14 Martin Tower
15 Brick Tower
16 Bowyer Tower
17 Flint Tower
18 Devereux Tower
19 Traitors' Gate
20 Byward Tower
21 Middle Tower

Moat
Outer Ward
Parade
Fusiliers' Museum
White Tower
Wardrobe Tower
Tower Green
Moat
Outer Ward
Moat
Tower Wharf

The Tower

tect won permission to make necessary alterations as building proceeded and, behind the scaffolding, Wren had his way with it.

In December 1940, London burned once again. On the night of the 29th, at the height of the Blitz, St. Paul's stood in a sea of fire. This time it survived. Fifty-one firebombs landed on the cathedral, all swiftly put out by the heroic volunteer St. Paul's Fire Watch. Two of the four high-explosive bombs that landed did explode, wrecking the north transept; the clear glass there bears silent testimony. A small monument in the floor at the end of the Nave honors the Firewatch. St. Paul's is a majestic and durable place, saturated with tough British pride and crowded with monuments of imposing generals affectedly dressed as Roman senators. The cathedral held the wedding of Prince Charles and Lady Diana, who chose St. Paul's for its spaciousness and excellent acoustics, breaking the 200-year tradition of holding royal weddings in Westminster Abbey.

Dotted with sculptures, bronzes and mosaics, St. Paul's makes a rewarding place for a wander. Above the choir, three Byzantine glass mosaics by William Richmond, done in 1904, tell the story of creation. The third ("the birds") was struck by a bomb in the Blitz. A trial mosaic adorns the east wall of **St. Dunstan's Chapel,** on the left by the entrance. On the other side of the nave in the **Chapel of St. Michael and St. George** sits a richly carved throne by Grinling Gibbons, made for the coronation of William and Mary in 1710. Along the south aisle hangs Holman Hunt's third version of *The Light of the World,* allegedly the most well-traveled picture in the world. Showing remarkable royal talent, Queen Victoria's daughter, Princess Louise, personally produced the fine bronze on the south wall of the south transept. Monuments to the mighty abound—Wellington, Nelson, Kitchener, and Samuel Johnson are all remembered here. The inscription beneath Cornwallis opposite Nelson in the south transept singularly omits mention of his defeats in the American War of Independence.

The stalls in the **Choir,** carved by Grinling Gibbons, narrowly escaped a bomb, but the old altar did not. It was replaced with the current marble "High Altar," covered by a St. Peter's-like *baldacchino* of oak, splendidly gilded. Above looms the crowning glory, the ceiling mosaic of Christ Seated in Majesty.

The **ambulatory** contains a shrouded statue of poet John Donne (Dean of the cathedral from 1621-1631), one of the few monuments to survive from old St. Paul's. Amble through the ambulatory to see Henry Moore's *Mother and Child* and the American Memorial Chapel (formerly Jesus Chapel), restored after the Blitz, and dedicated to U.S. servicemen based in Britain who died during World War II. Note the graceful and intricate choir gates, executed by Jean Tijou early in the 18th century.

The **Crypt,** stuffed with tombs and monuments, forms a catalogue of Britain's great figures from the last couple of centuries. (A few remnants made it through the Great Fire, including a memorial to Francis Bacon's father Nicolas.) The massive tombs of Wellington and Nelson command attention; Nelson's coffin, placed directly beneath the dome, was originally intended for Cardinal Wolsey. A bust of George Washington stands opposite a memorial to the ultimate romantic hero, Lawrence of Arabia. Around the corner lounges Rodin's fine bust of Henley. **Painter's Corner** holds the tombs of Sir Joshua Reynolds, absurd romantic Sir Lawrence Alma-Tadema, and J.M.W. Turner, along with memorials to John Constable and William Blake. Nearby, a black slab in the floor marks Wren's grave, with his son's famous epitaph close by: *Lector, si monumentum requiris circumspice.* This instruction to seek Wren's memorial in the glory of his creation was bombed through to the Crypt from the north transept. The display of **models** of St. Paul's details the history of the cathedral in all of its incarnations. Creating the star exhibit, the great model of 1674, cost as much as constructing a small house. In these models you can see how the upper parts of the exterior walls are mere façades, concealing the flying butresses which support the nave roof. Audio-visual presentations are shown every ½ hr. from 10:30am to 3pm.

Going up St. Paul's proves more challenging than going down: 259 steps lead to the suicidal, vertiginous **Whispering Gallery,** on the inside base of the dome.

Words whispered against the wall whizz round the sides. Take in the overwhelming prospects up into the dome and down into the church. A further 118 steps up, the first external view glitters from the **Stone Gallery,** only to be eclipsed by the uninterrupted and incomparable panorama from the **Golden Gallery,** 153 steps higher at the top of the dome. Wren's church spires fight with building cranes for supremacy over the City; the monolithic Bankside power station dominates the South Bank; and the Gothic extravaganza of St. Pancras station struts to the north, laced with the greenery of Hampstead Heath. Before descending, take a peek down into the cathedral through the small glass peephole in the floor; Nelson lies over 400 feet directly below. (Open Mon.-Sat. 9am-4:15pm; ambulatory open Mon.-Sat. 9:30am-4:15pm; crypt open Mon.-Fri. 9:30am-4:15pm, Sat. 11am-4:15pm; galleries open Mon.-Sat. 9:45am-4:15pm. Admission to cathedral, ambulatory, and crypt £2, students £1.50, children and seniors £1; galleries £2, students £1.50, children and seniors £1. Comprehensive 1½-hr. guided tours include the crypt and some sections not open to the public: Mon.-Sat. at 11am, 11:30am, 2pm, and 2:30pm; £4, students, children, and seniors £2.)

St. Paul's Churchyard, a fine picnic spot popular since Shakespeare's day, is surrounded by railings of oft-unappreciated interest; they were one of the first uses of cast iron. The modern St. Paul's Cross marks the spot where the papal pronouncement condemning Martin Luther was read to the public.

The Tower of London

The Tower of London, the largest fortress in medieval Europe and the palace and prison of English monarchs for over 500 years, is soaked in blood and history. Its intriguing past and striking buildings attract over two million visitors per year. The oldest continuously occupied fortified building in Europe, "The Tower" was founded by William the Conqueror in 1066 in order to protect—and command—his subjects. Not one, but 20 towers stand behind its walls, though many associate the image of the **White Tower,** the oldest one, with the Tower of London. Completed in 1097, the White Tower overpowers all the fortifications that were built around it in the following centuries. Originally a royal residence-*cum*-fortress, it was last lived in by James I, and subsequently served as wardrobe, stonehouse, public records office, armory, and prison.

Although more famous for the prisoners who languished and died here, the Tower has seen a handful of spectacular escapes. The Bishop of Durham escaped from Henry I out a window and down a rope. But the unfortunate Welsh Prince Gruffyd ap Llewelyn, prisoner of Henry III in 1244, apparently had not learned his knots properly—his rope of knotted sheets broke and he fell to his death. The prisoners may be gone (except for a few hapless tourists locked in after hours), but the weapons and armor remain. An expansive display from the **Royal Armouries,** testifying to Henry VIII's fondness for well-melded metal suits, takes up three floors. Both brutal and ornate, the collection mirrors its surroundings. Notice the early examples of firework launchers. To find a serious glut of arms and weaponry, also visit the **Oriental Armoury** in the Waterloo barracks, north of the White Tower, or the **New Armouries** to the east. The former features a full suit of elephant armor, captured by Clive at the Battle of Plassey in 1757. On the first floor of the White Tower nests the **Chapel of St. John,** dating from 1080, the finest Norman chapel in London. Stark and pristine, it is the only chapel in the world with an "aisled nave and encircling ambulatory", whatever that means. Beneath this chapel Guy Fawkes of the Gunpowder Plot was tortured.

The towers connect by massive walls and gateways, forming fortifications disheartening to visitors even today. Richard I, the Lionheart, began the construction of defenses around the White Tower in 1189. Subsequent work by Henry III (1216-72) and Edward I (1272-1307) brought the Tower close to its present condition.

Two rings of defenses surround the White Tower. On the **Inner Ward,** the **Bell Tower** squats on the southwest corner. Since the 1190s, this tower has sounded the curfew bell each night. Sir Thomas More spent some time here, courtesy of his former friend Henry VIII, before that same former friend had him executed in the Tower Green.

Along the curtain wall hovers the **Bloody Tower,** arguably the most famous, and certainly the most infamous, part of the fortress. Once pleasantly named the Garden Tower, due to the officers' garden nearby, the Bloody Tower supposedly saw the murder of the Little Princes, the uncrowned King Edward V and his brother (aged 13 and 10), by agents of Richard III. The murder remains one of history's great mysteries; some believe that Richard was innocent and that the future Henry VII arranged the murders to ease his own ascent. Two children's remains found in the grounds in 1674 (and buried now in Westminster Abbey) have never been conclusively identified as those of the Princes. Sir Walter Raleigh did some time in the prison here off and on for 15 years and occupied himself by writing a voluminous *History of the World Part I.* Before he got around to writing Part II, James I had him beheaded. Henry III lived in the adjacent **Wakefield Tower,** largest after the White Tower. The crown kept its public records and its jewels here until 1856 and 1967 respectively, although unsuprisingly, the Wakefield Tower also has a gruesome past. Lancastrian Henry VI was imprisoned by Yorkist Edward IV during the Wars of the Roses and was murdered while praying here. Students from Eton and Cambridge's King's College, founded by Henry, annually place lilies on the spot of the murder. Counter-clockwise around the inner **Wall Walk** come the **Lanthorn, Salt, Broad Arrow, Constable, and Martin** towers, the last scene of the inimitable self-styled "Colonel" Thomas Blood's bold attempt in 1671 at stealing the Crown Jewels. Martin's lower level now houses a small, boring exhibit of **Instruments of Torture.** The inner ring comes full circle, completed by the **Brick, Bowyer** (where, according to Shakespeare's constantly accurate *Richard III,* the Duke of Clarence died after being drowned in Malmsey wine), **Flint, Devereux,** and **Beauchamp** towers.

Within the inner ring adjoining the Bell Tower lurks the Tudor **Queen's House** (which will become the King's House when Prince Charles ascends to the throne). The house has served time as a prison for some of the Tower's most illustrious guests: both Anne Boleyn and Catherine Howard were incarcerated here by charming hubby Henry VIII; Guy Fawkes was interrogated in the Council Chamber on the upper floor; and in 1941, Hitler's Deputy Führer Rudolf Hess (or, as some believe, an imposter) was brought here after parachuting into Scotland. The only prisoners remaining today are the clipped ravens hopping around on the grass outside the White Tower; tradition has it that without the ravens the Tower would crumble and the British Empire disintegrate. Charles II hoped to banish the pests, but superstitions are superstitions and under pressure from advisers he granted them Royal protection. Unfortunately ravens mate only in flight, so new recruits have to be imported each time an old stager dies (a separate item in the national budget wisely provides for their upkeep and replacement). The ravens even have a tomb and gravestone of their own in the grassy moat near the ticket office.

Prisoners of the highest rank sometimes received the honor of a private execution rather than one before the spectators' benches of Tower Hill, just east of the present tube station. A block on the Tower Green, inside the Inner Ward, marks the spot where the axe fell on Queen Catherine Howard, Lady Jane Grey, and the Earl of Essex, Queen Elizabeth's rejected suitor. Fearing long wooden handles, Anne Boleyn chose to die by French sword instead. Sir Thomas More, "the king's good servant but God's first," was beheaded in public. The nearby **Chapel of St. Peter ad Vincula** (St. Peter in Chains) was once called "the saddest place on earth" by Lord Macaulay; the remains of prisoners were transported here after their executions. The decapitated bodies of Henry VIII's two executed queens lie beneath the altar and in the crypt. (Entrance to the chapel by Yeoman tour only. See below.)

Visitors enter the Tower through the **Byward Tower** on the southwest of the **Outer Ward,** which sports a precariously hung portcullis. The password, required for entry here after hours, has been changed every day since 1327, so bring your dictionary. German spies were executed in the Outer Ward during World War II. Along the outer wall, **St. Thomas's Tower** (after Thomas à Becket) tops the evocative **Traitors' Gate,** through which boats once brought new captives. The low gateway still has a dispiriting atmosphere.

The whole castle used to be surrounded by a broad **moat** dug by Edward I. Cholera epidemics forced the Duke of Wellington to drain it in 1843. The filled land became a vegetable garden during World War II but has since sprouted a tennis court and bowling green for inhabitants of the Tower.

The prize possessions of the Tower and of England, the **Crown Jewels,** pull in the crowds. Oliver Cromwell melted down much of the existing royal loot; most of the collection dates from after Charles II's Restoration in 1660. You may have seen thousands of pictures of the crowns and scepters before, but no camera can capture the dazzle. The **Imperial State Crown** and the **Sceptre with the Cross** feature the Stars of Africa, cut from the Cullinan Diamond. Scotland Yard mailed the precious stone third class from the Transvaal to London in an unmarked brown paper package, a scheme they believed was the safest way of getting it to England. **St. Edward's Crown,** made for Charles II in 1661, is only worn by the monarch during coronation.

The Tower is still guarded by the Yeoman Warders and the Yeomen of the Guard, *Beefeaters.* (The name does actually derive from "eaters of beef"—well-nourished domestic servants.) To be eligible to become a Beefeater, a candidate must have at least 22 years honorable service in the armed forces. Free, entertaining tours of about 45 minutes, given every half hour by Yeomen, start outside Byward Tower. (Tower of London open March-Oct. Mon.-Sat. 9:30am-5pm, Sun. 2-5pm; Nov.-Feb. Mon.-Sat. 9:30am-4pm. Admission £6, students £4.50, under 15 £3.70) Try to avoid the phenomenal Sunday crowd—queues start around noon. The best times to visit are Mondays and Tuesdays. Once inside, expect to queue for 20 to 30 minutes for entry to the Crown Jewels. For tickets to the **Ceremony of the Keys,** the nightly ritual locking of the gates, write in advance to Resident Governor, Tower of London, EC3 (Enquiries, tel. 709 0765).

Tower Bridge, a granite and steel structure reminiscent of a castle with a drawbridge, is a familiar sight. To walk across the upper level of the bridge costs a steep £2.50 (under 16 £1) but affords a spectacular view of the dirty Thames, the cluttered skyline, and the latest London Bridge. The roadway is occasionally raised (in less than 90 seconds) to allow taller ships to pass. (Open April-Oct. daily 10am-5:45pm; Nov.-March 10am-4pm.)

Southwark

> . . . but now wee see the thing in worse case than ever . . .
> wherein are builded many houses, some of them like Midsommer
> pageantes, all for shewe and pleasure.
>
> —*John Stow*

Across London Bridge from the City lies Southwark, a distinctive area with a lively history of its own. The neighborhood has strong historical associations with entertainment, from Elizabethan bear-baiting to the even more vicious pleasures of Defoe's Moll Flanders. But the greatest "vice" of Southwark was theater. Shakespeare's and Marlowe's plays were performed at the **Rose Theatre,** built in 1587 and rediscovered during construction in 1989. The remnants are to be preserved and displayed underneath a new office block at Park St. and Rose Alley. Shakespeare's **Globe Theatre** lay nearby; a project is underway to build a new Globe on the riverbank. The **Shakespeare Globe Museum,** 1 Bear Gardens Alley (tel. 928 6342), a gallery devoted to Southwark history, concentrates on the Globe and less respectable neighborhood entertainments. (Open Mon.-Sat. 10am-5pm, Sun. 2-5:30pm. Admission £2, students £1.)

Near the bridge rises the tower of **Southwark Cathedral** (tel. 407 2939), probably the best Gothic church in the city after Westminster Abbey. Mostly rebuilt in the 1890s, the original 1207 choir and retro-choir survive. The glorious altar screen is

Tudor, with 20th century statues. The church is dotted with interesting stone and wood effigies, with explanatory notes. Medieval poet John Gower is buried here in a colorful tomb, as is a pillmaker named John Lockayer, he of the humorous epitaph. This was the parish church of the Harvard family, and a chapel was dedicated to the memory of John Harvard in 1907. For reasons which remain unclear, the Harvard chapel also contains a memorial to lyricist Oscar Hammerstein.

Just a couple of blocks southeast, your hair will rise and your spine will chill at **St. Thomas's Old Operating Theatre** (tel. 955 5000), a carefully preserved 19th-century surgical hospital. (Open Mon., Wed., Fri. 12:30-4pm. Admission £1, concessions 60p.) If your appetite for destruction is stronger, the **London Dungeon** awaits at 28 Tooley St. Not for the squeamish, this museum recreates horrifying historical scenarios of execution, torture, and plague. Deadpan historical comments accompany the scenes of hanging, drawing and quartering, as if to justify and apologize for the stomach-churning reconstructions. (Tube: London Bridge. Open daily April-Sept. 10am-5:30pm, Oct.-March 10am-4:30pm. Admission £5, under 14 £3.)

Moored on the south bank of the Thames just upstream from Tower Bridge, the World War II warship **HMS Belfast** (tel. 407 6434) led the bombardment of the French coast during D-Day landings. The labyrinth of the engine house and the whopping great guns make it a fun place to play sailor. Mind your head. You can take the ferry that runs from Tower Pier on the north bank to the Belfast whenever the ship is open, or take the tube to London Bridge. (Open daily April-Oct. 10am-5:20pm, Nov.-March 10am-4pm. Admission £3.60, seniors, students, and children £1.80. Admission and ferry £4.40, seniors, students, and children £2.40.) East of Tower Bridge, the bleached Bauhaus box of the **Design Museum** perches on the Thames (see Museums).

The South Bank

A hulk of worn concrete and futuristic slate, the South Bank gestures defiantly at the center of London from across the Thames. The massive **South Bank Arts Complex** is the modern, more respectable descendant of the brothels and theatres that flourished in medieval Southwark. Until the English Civil Wars, most of this area fell under the legal jurisdiction of the Bishop of Winchester, and was thus protected from London censors. The region stayed almost entirely rural until the 18th-century Westminster and Blackfriars bridges were built. The current development began in 1951 during the Festival of Britain, the centenary celebration of the Great Exhibition of 1851. Current plans that call for a demolition and replacement of the Queen Elizabeth Hall and the Hayward Gallery have prompted many to reveal their fondness for the complex. The concrete blocks of the Royal Festival and Queen Elizabeth Halls, the Hayward Gallery, the National Film Theatre, and the National Theatre dominate the riverbank. The 3000-seat **Royal Festival Hall** is home to the Philharmonia and London Philharmonic Orchestras and host to countless others. The **National Theatre,** Waterloo Rd. (tel. 633 0880; Tube: Waterloo), opened by Lord Olivier in 1978, has become London's liveliest cultural center. The complex promotes "art for the people" through convivial platform performances, foyer concerts, lectures, and workshops. Excellent backstage tours are given regularly. (1¼-hr. tours Mon.-Sat. at 10:15am, 12:30pm, 12:45pm, 5:30pm, and 6pm. Admission £2.50, students £2.25. Book in advance.) The **Hayward Gallery** on Belvedere Rd. (tel. 928 3144; Tube: Waterloo) houses imaginative exhibitions primarily devoted to 20th-century artists. (Open during exhibits Thurs.-Mon. 10am-6pm, Tues.-Weds. 10am-8pm. Admission £4, students and seniors £2; £2 for all Mondays.) Multicolored posters displaying Russian titles and Asian warriors distinguish the entrance to the **National Film Theatre** (tel. 928 3232; Tube: Waterloo), directly on the South Bank. This cinema shows 2000 films per year and hosts most of the **London Film Festival** every November. (Films at festival £4. £10.25 annual membership required for advance priority bookings. See Entertainment for more details.) The Film Theatre also operates the innovative **Museum of the Moving Image** (see Museums).

The jumbled stalls of the **Cut Street Market** sprawl around the entrances to Waterloo station, London's busiest railway terminal. The station is at the end of "the drain," a BR line that shuttles commuters directly to and from the City. The market's old character has waned as ambitious development projects consume more of the area's residential neighborhoods. But prices have stayed low, and used-book sellers and curiosity stands have maintained the district's flavor. Farther along Waterloo Road, the magnificently restored **Old Vic** (tel. 928 7616), former home of Olivier's National Repertory Theatre, now hosts popular seasons of lesser-known classics and worthy revivals. (Box office open Mon.-Sat. 10am-8pm. Tickets £10-30.)

Emblazoned with the Stars and Stripes in memory of President Lincoln, the **Christ Church Tower** of 1876 rises above a mundane block of office buildings at the corner of Kennington Rd. Farther north, the refreshing **Jubilee Gardens,** planted for the Queen's Silver Jubilee in 1977, stretch along the Embankment to **County Hall,** a formidable Renaissance pile with a massive riverfront façade. The Hall was headquarters of the London County Council from 1913 until 1965, and of the Greater London Council, until it was controversially abolished in 1986. The building that once housed "Red" Ken Livingstone may be redeveloped into a hotel.

Lambeth Palace (Tube: Lambeth North), on the Embankment opposite the Lambeth Bridge, has been the Archbishop of Canterbury's London residence for seven centuries. Although Archbishop Langton founded it in the early 13th century, most of the palace dates from the 1800s. The palace's notable exterior features include the entrance at the 15th-century brick Morton's Tower, and Lollard's Tower, where John Wyclif's followers were thought to be imprisoned. (Open by prior arrangement only. Enquire to Lambeth Palace, Lambeth Palace Road, SE1.) West on Lambeth Road is the **Imperial War Museum** (see Museums).

Greater London

Greater London goes on...and on...and on. London has tended to expand horizontally rather than vertically; sheets of unremarkable commuter housing stretch in all directions. Far-flung villages, swallowed up by this sprawl, resolutely maintain their own identities amidst anonymous "dormitory" suburbs. London Regional Transport and British Rail cover Greater London thoroughly; most areas are easily accessible without a car.

Hampstead and Highgate

The urban villages of Hampstead and Highgate, poised on hills north of Regent's Park, seem entirely detached from central London. The very air is different, and the fragrance of roses steals over the red brick walls that line the streets. Hampstead, 1004 years old, has traditionally been a refuge for artists. Although the area is rapidly becoming a less eccentric suburb for the rich, Hampstead still seems like a charmed country retreat. Former Labor Party leader Michael Foot and authors John Le Carré, G.G. Franey, and Margaret Drabble live here, as does rock star and "perceptive" lyricist Sting. Escape from the city and come here for a leisurely pub crawl, a cream tea, or a stroll past the displays of local artists' work near Whitestone Pond in summer.

Nestled in the midst of Hampstead, the **Keats House,** Keats Grove, is one of London's finest literary shrines. To get there, take the Underground to Hampstead, turn left down High St., and follow the signs. Before dashing off to Italy to breathe his last consumptive breath and die in true Romantic poet style, John Keats spent the last years of his life in Hampstead, pining for his fiancée, Fanny Brawne, who lived next door with her widowed mother. He allegedly composed "Ode to a Nightingale" under a plum tree here—the distant ancestor of the one growing in the garden today. The house is furnished as it was during Keats's life, complete with his manuscripts and letters. (Open April-Oct. Mon.-Fri. 2-6pm, Sat. 10am-1pm and 2-5pm, Sun.

2-5pm; Nov.-March Mon.-Fri. 1-5pm, Sat. 10am-1pm and 2-5pm, Sun. 2-5pm. Free.) The **Keats Memorial Library** next door contains a unique collection of books on the poet's life, family, and friends. (Open by appointment only. Tel. 435 2062.)

Now a National Trust property open to the public, **Fenton House,** Windmill Hill (tel. 435 3471) conserves a marvelous collection of 18th-century porcelain and of early keyboard instruments still used for occasional concerts. (For permission to play them, apply in writing to the Warden, Windmill Hill, London NW3 6RT.) You can see the walled garden and orchard free of charge. (House open April-Oct. Sat.-Wed. 11am-6pm; March Sat.-Sun. 2-6pm. Admission £2.) Round the corner, the **Admiral's House,** Admiral's Walk, tries to look like a ship, but doesn't quite cut it. **Church Row,** off Heath St., vehemently retains its 18th-century style; horseless carriages look out of place in front of its dignified terraces. The painter John Constable lies buried in St. John's churchyard down the row. At the bottom of Flask Walk, another cozy lane incongruously crammed with cars, **Burgh House** contains the interesting little exhibitions of the Hampstead Museum. Stop for lunch or a genteel cup of tea at The Buttery in the basement. (House open Wed.-Sun. noon-5pm. Buttery open Wed.-Sun. 11am-5:30pm.)

Hampstead Heath separates the two villages from the rest of London. Once a hangout for outlaws, it now attracts harmless picnickers and somewhat more dangerous kite flyers. You can get lost here; the heath remains the wildest patch of turf in London. On a hot day, take a dip in **Kenwood Ladies' Pond, Highgate Men's Pond,** or the outlandish **Mixed Bathing Pond.**

Presiding over the heath stands **Kenwood House,** Hampstead Lane, a picture-perfect example of an 18th-century country estate. This airy mansion now houses the **Iveagh Bequest,** an outstanding collection of 18th-century British portraiture and furniture, with a few fine works by Dutch masters, including Vermeer's *Guitar Player* and the last of Rembrandt's self-portraits. The original owner of Kenwood, influential chief justice Lord Mansfield, decreed the end to slavery on English soil. Mansfield's progressive policies did not win him universal popularity and, after destroying his abandoned townhouse in Bloomsbury, the Gordon Rioters pursued him north to Hampstead. Luckily for him (and for Kenwood House), his pursuers stopped for a drink at the **Spaniard's Inn** on Spaniards Rd., and a considerate publican made sure they got too drunk to continue. In summer, Kenwood hosts a hugely popular series of **outdoor concerts** (see Entertainment below) in which top-flight orchestras play from a bandshell across the lake. (Tube: Archway or Golders Green, then bus #210 to Kenwood. Kenwood open mid-April to Sept. daily 10am-6pm, Oct. to mid-April daily 10am-4pm. Free.)

Parliament Hill, on the southeastern tip of the heath, marks the southern boundary between Hampstead and Highgate and commands a Laurieresque view of London, sweeping from the docklands to the Houses of Parliament. The height of the hill, some say, owes much to the piles of corpses left here during the Plague. The bones of Queen Boudicca also reputedly lie here. It was toward this hill that Guy Fawkes' accomplices fled after depositing explosives under the House of Commons in 1605 to watch the big bang. (The explosives were discovered and the men captured, much to the disappointment of pyromaniacs everywhere. Britons commiserate on November 5 of every year by shooting fireworks at each other and burning effigies of Fawkes.)

To get from Hampstead to Highgate, walk across the heath or up Hampstead Lane. **Highgate Cemetery,** Swains Lane, is a remarkable monument to the Victorian fascination with death. Its most famous resident, rather inaptly, is Karl Marx, buried in the eastern section in 1883. An unmistakably Stalinist bust, four times life size, was placed above his grave in 1956 and attracts pilgrims from everywhere. Death makes for strange bedfellows; novelist George Eliot lies buried nearby. The magically spooky, and far wilder, western section contains some of the finest tombs. The zealously conscientious staff of the Friends of Highgate Cemetery (FOHC) provide a slice of Highgate life in themselves. (Tel. (081) 340 1834 or (081) 348 0808. Eastern Cemetery open April-Oct. daily 10am-5pm; Nov.-March 10am-4pm. Admission £1. Western Cemetery access by guided tour only in summer Mon.-Fri.

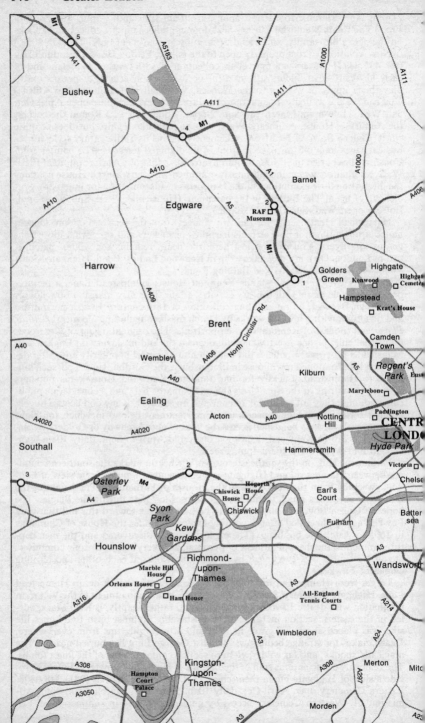

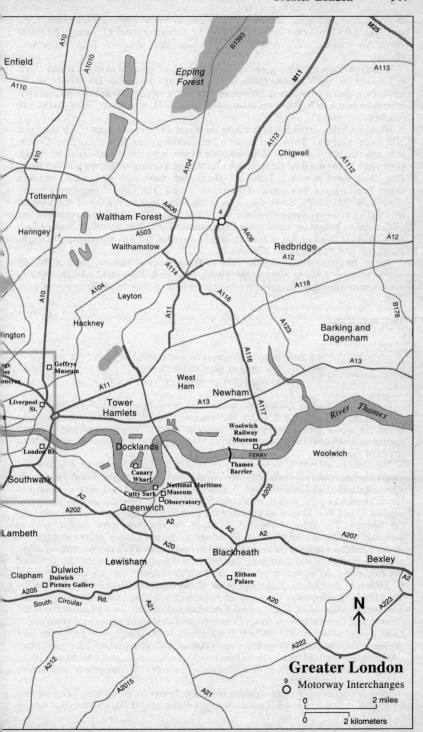

Greater London

9 ⊕ Motorway Interchanges

0   2 miles

0   2 kilometers

at noon, 2pm, and 4pm, Sat.-Sun. 11am-4pm; in winter Mon.-Fri. at 11am, 2pm, and 3pm, Sat.-Sun. 11am-3pm. Admission £2. Camera permit £1, valid in both sections. No tripods, video cameras, or machine guns allowed. Times subject to change.)

Waterlow Park affords a gorgeous setting in which you can shed the urban grime of London and the Victorian gloom of the graveyard next door. The sociable ducks never turn down a good feed. By the eastern entrance, **Lauderdale House,** supposedly once home to Nell Gwyn, mistress of Charles II, now serves light snacks and lunches.

Highgate Village stands 424 ft. above the River Thames. You can climb Highgate Hill from Archway Tube station for a breathtaking view across London. On the way up, you will pass **Dick Whittington's Stone,** where 600 years ago the young, poor Dick heard the Bow Bells calling him back to London—"Turn again Whittington, thrice Lord Mayor of London." He turned, went back to London, and was thrice Lord Mayor. His petrified cat stands guard. The base of Highgate's parish church, **St. Michael's,** South Grove, is at the same level as the top of the cross on St. Paul's Cathedral dome. Opposite the church hides The Grove, an avenue of late 17th-century houses secluded behind magnificent elms. Poet and critic Samuel Taylor Coleridge lived at No. 3 for the last 18 years of his life, entertaining Carlyle, Emerson, and sundry other visitors.

To get to Hampstead, take the tube to Hampstead or Belsize Park, or the BR North London Line to Hampstead Heath. To reach Highgate, take the tube to Archway or Highgate. Either trip takes about half an hour from the center of London.

Docklands

> *We have many developments, but nothing on anything like the scale of the London Docklands.*
> *—Ed Koch, former mayor of New York City*

London Docklands, the largest commercial development in Europe, has utterly changed the east of London within the space of 10 years. Developers plan to make these old docks into a heavyweight financial center. Massive building sites are springing up all over the deserted dockyards as successful regeneration attracts hundreds of businesses.

Londinium, already a prominent port in Roman times, sprouted wharves and quays that spread east from the City during the Middle Ages; Royal Dockyards were established at Deptford and Woolwich in 1515. As London grew in importance, the docks grew with it, streching miles down the Thames, until by the beginning of World War II they had become the powerful trading center of the vast British Empire. The Blitz obliterated much of the dockland area, whilst the war seriously diminished Britain's world influence. As the sun set on the empire, the docks continued to do good business until the early 60s. Then roll-on, roll-off ships, the advent of container transport, and modern shipping methods rapidly rendered the Leviathan docks redundant—by 1982 all had closed, leaving sweeping tracts of desperate dereliction. Redevelopment of the area, spearheaded by the London Docklands Development Corporation formed in 1981, has since kicked into gear. The building has taken place, as Ed Koch has recognized, on a phenomenal scale. Cranes and dumptrucks swarm, offices rise, and businesses move in. Construction races over desolation. But while redevelopment is bringing a new prosperity to a region in decline, many locals feel that it comes at their expense. Old communities are being steamrolled into cute, yuppie condo blocks, and slums continue to decay as money is funneled into office complexes. There is real resentment, as a glance at local graffiti will show.

Docklands covers a huge expanse, from the Tower to Woolwich. The best way to see the region is via the Docklands Light Railway (DLR), a swish (but not yet entirely bug-free) semi-automatic railway opened in 1987. (Connect with the tube at Tower Hill, Shadwell, Bow Rd., or Stratford. Due to extension of the track, the railway closes on weekends and after 9:30pm on weekdays.) Getting off at Shadwell Station, you'll see the old dock community: traditional brick housing, dusty streets, old-fashioned pubs and pie-and-mash shops. Southwest of the station, on The Highway, is the turreted **St. George in the East,** a church by Wren student Nicholas Hawksmoor. Bombed in the war, the 1724 exterior was restored with a modern interior in 1964. Across The Highway, the new face of Docklands appears in the form of **Tobacco Dock,** a gimmicky new shopping mall, complete with replica "pirate ships." On Wapping Wall, a 16th century pub, Prospect of Whitby, looks over the river.

From the next stop, Limehouse, walk east on Commercial Rd. to another Hawksmoor church, **St. Anne's,** presiding over a leafy churchyard. (Open to visitors Sun. 3-4:30pm only.) The legacy of Limehouse's's 19th-century Chinese community can be seen in the Chinese restaurants along West India Dock Rd.

The most exciting building is taking place on the **Isle of Dogs** (a peninsula named after the hounds of Edward III which once resided here), notably the enormous and highly prominent Canary Wharf. The section of the DLR from West India Quay to Island Gardens resembles a Disneyland ride, as the train glides through building sites and high over water, past brand new shopping malls and over barren wasteground. The enthusiastic staff at **Docklands Visitor Centre,** (tel. 512 3000, DLR: Crossharbour) is happy to expound on the virtues of the area. (Open Mon.-Fri. 9am-6pm.) Crossharbour also harbors the **London Arena,** a fledgling 12,000-seat concert and sports venue.

If all the concrete and steel gets you down, you can lose yourself (nearly) in the pastoral expanses of **Mudchute Park,** acres of grassy hill and a small farm (DLR: Mudchute). **Island Gardens,** at the end of the line, offers a sweeping view of Greenwich across the river. You can walk through the smelly foot tunnel (the steps at either end are quicker than waiting for the lift) and take in some of the sights. (See Greenwich and Blackheath below.)

A **Museum of Docklands** has an official but not a physical existence; call 515 1162 for an update. The Docklands Development Corporation offers a free coach tour every Thursday morning. For information and required advance booking call 512 3000, ext. 3510 or 3513.

Greenwich and Blackheath

Greenwich means time. Charles II authorized the establishment of a small observatory here in 1675 "for perfecting navigation and astronomy." Successive royal astronomers perfected their craft to such a degree that they were blessed with the prime meridian in 1884. The Royal Naval College, which moved here from Portsmouth in 1873, enhanced Greenwich's strong maritime character. In a nation with a livelihood dependent on the waves, the village became hallowed ground.

Only select parts of the **Old Royal Observatory** (tel. (081) 858 4422; BR: Greenwich), designed by Sir Christopher Wren, remain open to the public. The well-proportioned Flamsteed House houses an excellent collection of early astronomical instruments—astrolabes, celestial globes, and orreries—displayed with almost comprehensible explanations. The **prime meridian** is marked by a brass strip in the observatory courtyard. Have fun jumping from one hemisphere into the next. Our researcher did. Greenwich Mean Time, still the standard for international communications and navigation, is displayed on a 120 year old clock. The red time ball, once used to indicate time to ships on the Thames, drops daily at 1pm. In 1894, an anarchist blew himself up while trying to destroy the observatory. Polish sailor Joseph Conrad used this bizarre event as the seed for his novel *The Secret Agent.* (Open Mon.-Sat. 10am-6pm, Sun. 2-6pm; winter hours until 5pm. Planetarium shows on Sat. at 2:30 and 3:30pm. Admission £3.25, children £2.25.)

At the foot of the hill is the **National Maritime Museum** (see Museums). The museum forms the west addition to **Queen's House,** the 17th-century home built for Charles I's wife Henrietta Maria. Designed by the age's master architect, Inigo Jones, it is England's first Palladian villa. The house has been renovated and now exhibits sumptuous 17th-century furnishings and rich silk hangings. (Open Mon.-Sat. 10am-6pm, Sun. 2-6pm; in winter until 5pm. Admission £3.25, children £2.25.)

Charles II also commissioned Wren to tear down an old Tudor palace and to construct the building opposite the Queen's House, now the **Royal Naval College.** Stop in to see James Thornhill's frescoed optical illusions in the painted hall. In the chapel hangs Benjamin West's painting of a shipwrecked St. Paul. (Open Fri.-Wed. 2:30-5pm. Free. Services Sun. at 11am.) By the River Thames in Greenwich, the *Cutty Sark,* one of the last great tea clippers on the route from China to Britain, anchors in dry dock. The ship (whose name, meaning "short shift," comes from Burns's poem "Tom O'Shanter") brought 1.3 million pounds of tea on each 120-day trip. Now it is filled with Long John Silver's collection of ships' figureheads but no whiskey. (Open Mon.-Sat. 10am-6pm, Sun. noon-6pm; winter hours until 5pm. Admission £2.50, children £1.25.) The *Gypsy Moth IV,* in which Sir Francis Chichester sailed around the globe all by his lonesome, rests nearby. Chichester, 65 at the time, was knighted for the accomplishment. (Open April-Sept. Mon.-Sat. 10am-6pm, Sun. noon-6pm; Oct. daily 10am-5pm. Last admission ½ hr. before closing. Admission 50p, children 30p.)

Genteel terraces now encircle **Greenwich Park,** used as a burial ground during the 1353 plague. The shriveled trunk of an oak tree on the east side of the park (now fenced off and covered in ivy) marks the spot where Henry VIII frolicked with an unsuspecting Anne Boleyn. The garden in the southeast corner of the park combines English garden and fairy tale, with a wild deer park thrown in for good measure. Just outside the observatory, you can share a splendid view of the Thames with a statue of General Wolfe (conqueror of French Canada) kindly donated by the Canadian government. The nearby Tea House serves a decent lunch (sandwiches from £1.30, scones 40p). In the southwest corner of the park, **Ranger's House** (circa 1700), one of Greenwich's few free attractions, contains the Suffolk Collection of Jacobean portraits and the fascinating Dolmetsch Collection of antique musical instruments. (Open April-Sept. daily 10am-6pm; Oct.-March 10am-4pm.)

In summer, bands perform at Greenwich Park as a part of the Royal Park Band performance series. Shows begin at 3 and 6pm (every Sun. June-Aug. 1½ hr.) and take place in the bandstand north of the gardens. From the last week of July to the middle of August, the young and the young at heart can watch puppet shows in the playground at the northeast corner of the park (Mon.-Sat. at 11:30am and 2:30pm). The Children's Boating Pool next to the playground (open daily 10am-dusk) gives kids a chance to unleash pent-up seafaring energy accumulated in the nearby museums. A show at the **Greenwich Theatre** (Croom's Hill, SE18) can be a relaxing conclusion to a day spent traipsing about galleries. The season runs from April to August. (Box office tel. (081) 858 7755 from 10am-8:30pm. Performances Mon.-Fri. at 7:45pm, Sat. at 2:30 and 7:45pm. Tickets £6-10, £4 for students and seniors.)

The most picturesque (and appropriate) passage to Greenwich is by boat. Cruises to Greenwich pier depart from the Westminster, Charing Cross, or Tower piers (every ½ hr. 10:30am-4pm, 1 hr., £3.80, £5 return). The crew provides commentary on the major sights along the voyage. Trains leave from Charing Cross, Cannon St., and Waterloo (East) for Greenwich (25 min., £1.50 day return). The Docklands Light Railway whizzes from Tower Gateway to Island Gardens (16 min.). From there Greenwich is just a 10-minute walk through the foot tunnel. Bus #188 runs between Euston and Greenwich stopping at Kingsway, Aldwych, and Waterloo. One-day passport admission to the Observatory, Museum, Queen's House, and the Cutty Sark costs £6 (seniors and students £3.95, families £12). The **Greenwich Tourist Office,** 46 Greenwich Church St., SE10 (tel. (081) 858 6376; open daily 10am-6pm) conducts a variety of afternoon tours (£2.50-3, 1-1½ hr.).

Just on the south side of Greenwich Park lies **Blackheath,** a large sloping field where Wat Tyler and his fellow peasants revolting over the Poll Tax congregated in 1381. **The Royal Blackheath Golf Club,** constituted in 1766 and founded on the common much earlier, is the world's oldest; James I was known to take an occasional bash here with his three wood. Standard highwayman problems once plagued Blackheath, but the fine houses near the common have since made it one of the more fashionable addresses in South London. A traditional site for royal celebrations, Blackheath still holds fairs on Bank Holidays, and is the start point every spring for the London Marathon, the largest 26-miler in the world.

A bit farther down the river, the newly steel and concrete **Thames Barrier,** the world's largest movable flood barrier, is the reason that London no longer enjoys the exciting high tides of yesteryear (tel. (081) 854 1373; open Mon.-Fri. 10:30am-5pm, Sat.-Sun. 10:30am-5:30pm; admission £2.20, seniors and children £1.35). From Charing Cross take BR to Charlton Station; from there it's a 15-min. walk. Alternatively take the boat from Greenwich pier (25 min.; 75 min. from Westminster pier). Call 930 3373 for details of Westminster service; (081) 305 0300 for Greenwich.

Dulwich

In the middle of London's southern suburbs, Dulwich retains the rural character of a small village, with beautiful Georgian houses set back among spacious greens (take British Rail to North or West Dulwich). Walk along Dulwich Village Rd. and College Rd., which pass between sports ground, parkland, and playing fields, running south towards Crystal Palace. East of College Rd. is **Dulwich Park,** the village's old common, which centers around a pond usually filled with toy boats. In late spring, the park is overwhelmed by blooming rhododendrons and azaleas. Opposite the park entrance on College Rd. is the **Dulwich Picture Gallery,** picturesquely designed by Sir John Soane in 1814. The building is the oldest public art gallery in England, and contains not only works by Rubens, Rembrandt, Reynolds, and Gainsborough, but also a mausoleum for the collection's benefactors. The paintings were moved here from central London because it was thought that they would survive better in the less foggy conditions (see Museums). The same trust that runs the Picture Gallery administers **Dulwich College,** founded as a public (meaning private) school for boys by Edward Alleyn, a Shakespearean actor, in the 17th century. More recent graduates include that arbiter of social manners, P.G. Wodehouse. The College's red buildings and severe chapel stand out among the green of the surrounding fields, south of the junction of College Rd. and Dulwich Common. Further south from the college stands the last remaining toll house in London, still inhabited but long since defunct.

Chiswick

Six miles west of central London, the riverside village of Chiswick was long ago engulfed by London's suburban sprawl. Two houses of great historical and artistic interest are situated here. The Palladian style of **Chiswick House** (BR: Chiswick) took English society by storm when it was built by Lord Burlington and William Kent in 1729. Lord Harvey sneered, "You call it a house? Why? It is too small to live in, and too large to hang from one's watch." But most of the day's notables were more than happy to see and be seen when Burlington entertained at Chiswick.

The striking exterior with its magnificent staircases is best viewed from the Burlington Road entrance. Inside, the most notable rooms are on the first floor, including the Dome Saloon, still crowded with works of art collected by Burlington. Elaborate ceilings top the Red, Green, and especially the Blue Velvet rooms. The gardens, laid out by William Kent, mix traditional ordered and manicured horticulture with wild spontaneity. (House open April-Sept. daily 10am-6pm; Oct.-March daily 10am-4pm. Admission £1.90, students and seniors £1.50, children 95p.

Just northeast of the Chiswick House grounds, on Hogarth Lane, artist and social critic William Hogarth lived in a more modest abode. **Hogarth's House** (tel. (081) 994 6757), called by its owner his "country box by the Thames," has been refurbished after decades of neglect, and now makes a proper home to some of his best paintings and engravings. Follow down the path of ruin in *A Harlot's Progress* or *Marriage à la Mode,* and turn from the degradation of *Gin Lane* to the prosperity of *Beer Street.* (Open April-Sept. Mon., Wed.-Sat. 11am-6pm, Sun. 2-6pm; Oct.-March Mon., Wed.-Sat. 11am-4pm, Sun 2-4pm. Free.)

Richmond

Ever since Henry I came up the Thames in the 12th century, Richmond has preened its royal pedigree. Richmond Palace was demolished during the shocking Commonwealth, yet the town has not lost its dignified sheen. The 18th century houses around **Richmond Green** make it possibly the most serene in or around London. The **Richmond Tourist Information Centre,** in the old Town Hall on Whittaker Ave., has complete information on Richmond and surrounding areas (tel. (081) 940 9125; open Mon.-Fri. 10am-6pm, Sat. 10am-5pm, Sun. 10:15am-4:15pm; BR or Tube: Richmond).

Most of Richmond's sights are scattered around the actual village. **Richmond Park,** atop Richmond Hill, is Europe's largest city park. Its 2500 acres were once a royal hunting ground, and still are home to several hundred nervous deer. Intrigue surrounds the Isabella Plantation woodland garden, deep inside the park.

Across Richmond Bridge, on Richmond Road, the gleaming cube of **Marble Hill House** perches on the Thames, amid vast trimmed lawns. Like its contemporary Chiswick House, it is a villa inspired by both Palladio and Inigo Jones. The Great Room, on the first floor, is lavishly decorated with gilt and carvings by James Richards and the original Panini paintings of ancient Rome. During the summer, a series of outdoor concerts are held on the grounds (see Entertainment). (Tel. (081) 892 5115; house open April-Sept. daily 10am-6pm; Oct.-March daily 10am-4pm. Admission free).

Just next door, the remains of the 18th-century **Orleans House** (tel. (081) 892 0221) hold a gallery of art and artifacts of local history. Only the Octagon Room survives from the original house, which put up with the Duc D'Orleans (the future King Louis Philippe) for three years in the 19th century. (Open April-Sept. Tues.-Sat. 1-5:30pm, Sun. 2-5:30pm; Oct.-March Tues.-Sat. 1-4:30pm, Sun. 2-4:30pm. Admission free.) A ferry crosses the river here to **Ham House,** a restored 17th-century mansion, closed in 1992 for refurbishment.

Kew Gardens

Yet another example of the encyclopedic collecting frenzy of the Empire, the **Royal Botanic Gardens** at Kew display thousands of flowers, plants, bushes, fruits, trees, and vegetables from all over the world, spread over 300 perfectly maintained acres. Founded in 1759 by Princess Augusta, Kew gradually grew in size until it became a royal park in 1841. Inside, not far from the main gate stands **Kew Palace.** Built in 1631 but leased as a royal residence since 1730, this inconspicuous summer residence of King George III and Queen Charlotte has evolved into a small museum depicting the vagaries of late 18th-century monarchical life. You can spend hours with the extensive royal toy collection inside or the well-documented herb garden out back. (Open daily 11am-5:30pm. Admission £1, students and seniors 75p.)

Kew's glasshouses, just a stone's throw away from the palace, may make you wonder why you didn't pursue gardening more seriously. A brutal storm in 1987 ravaged the gardens, but provided an opportunity for new landscaping and renovations of the greenhouses, and today Kew is better than ever. The **Princess of Wales Conservatory** allows you to browse through tropical climates among your favorite plants; it's just a few steps from a rainforest to an arid desert. The award-winning pyramidal design not only allows the building to rise from the hedges without disruption, it conserves energy remarkably well, too. Don't miss the spectacular giant waterlilies or the amiable pineapple family. The muggy **Palm House** will stun you with the revelation that bananas are in fact giant herbs. Climb the white spiral stairs to the upper gallery for the toucan's-eye view. The 1848 house is Kew's most graceful, but is dwarfed by its younger Victorian sibling, the **Temperate House,** which calmly nurtures 3,000 species in its 50,000 square feet. As an English Garden, Kew would not be complete without its unusual **pagoda** (in the southeast corner of the park) or the simulated ruins of a Roman gate. The southwest corner of the park rambles on in a controlled but highly scenic state of wilderness. Just when you're convinced you've escaped into the wilds you'll come across an ice-cream stand or a tourist admiring a squirrel.

The best way to reach Kew is by boat from Westminster pier (every 30 min. 10:30am-3:30pm, 1½ hr., £6, £8 return) and the cheapest way is by tube or BR North London line (Kew Gardens station, 50 min.). Ample parking space is available outside the gardens should you choose to drive. (Tel. (081) 940 1171. Gardens open Oct.-Jan. daily 9:30am-4pm; Feb.-Sept. Mon.-Sat. 9:30am-6:30pm, Sun. 9:30am-8pm. Glasshouses open daily 10am-4:30pm. Call to confirm closing times. Admission £3, students and seniors £1.50, children £1.)

Across the river at Kew Bridge, the **Kew Bridge Steam Museum** once was the proud water pumping station for West London. The engines still pump it up for ecstatic steam enthusiasts on weekends and Bank Holidays. (Tel. (081) 568 4757. Open daily 11am-5pm. Admission £1.50, children and seniors 75p.)

Syon Park

Syon Park, just across the Thames from Kew in Brentford (walk across Kew Bridge and left along London Rd.), harbors stately **Syon House.** The castellated exterior of the house is Tudor, built to incorporate the buildings of a monastery where Queen Catherine Howard was imprisoned before her execution in 1542. In 1553 the ownership of the house passed to the Duke of Northumberland, who offered the crown to his daughter-in-law Lady Jane Grey here. Not a week later, Mary Tudor took back the house, and the Duke's head.

After changing hands several more times, the house reverted to the Northumberlands in the 18th century, and the perfect interior was created by Robert Adam in 1766. The Anteroom, a green marble and gilt extravaganza, is dazzling; the Long Gallery has a more balanced elegance.

In the grounds you'll find a six-acre rose garden and the largest collection of historic British cars in the world (open March-Oct. 10am-5:30pm; Nov.-Feb. 10am-4pm. Admission £2). The **London Butterfly House** has over 1,000 live butterflies flying "free", as well as some less pleasant insects (open Apr.-Oct. 10am-5pm; Nov.-March 10am-3pm. Admission £2). (Tel. 560 0881. Syon House open Easter-Sept. Sun.-Thurs. noon-5pm; Oct. Sun. noon-5pm. Last admission 4:15pm. Admission £2.50; children, students, and seniors £1.75. Gardens open daily 10am-6pm or dusk. Admission £1.50; children, students, and seniors £1. Admission to house and gardens £3.75, children, students, and seniors £2.50.)

Osterley Park

Hidden between the motorways and industrial warehouses of western London is the refined classicism of **Osterley Park,** a mansion rebuilt by Robert Adam between 1760 and 1780. The Palladian sharpness of the temple-like portico seems awkward between the towers of the more medieval keep. Inside, there is a noticeable difference between the neo-classsical rooms designed by Adam, such as the entrance hall, with its Roman coffering, crisp lines, and friezes, and those designed by Sir William Chambers, who affected a more simple elegance. Built on the shell of an Elizabethan house, Osterley Park is not nearly as precisely classical as nearby Chiswick House, but seems more comfortable. The most fascinating rooms, the servants' quarters and kitchen with huge copper sinks and large chopping tables, are below the two main floors. (House open April-Oct. Wed.-Fri. 1-5pm, Sat.-Sun. 11am-5pm. Tel. (081) 560 3918. Admission £2.50. Tube: Osterley.)

Chambers, of Kew Gardens fame, also designed the park (look for models of the Kew Chinese pagoda in the drawing room). The spacious grounds are a sanctuary from the haze of London. The Tudor stable right next to the main house seems less refined than, but perhaps just as beautiful as Adam's mixed façade. (Park open daily 9am-dusk. Free.)

Hampton Court

What the public can see of Buckingham Palace is drab; Hampton Court seems fit for royalty. Cardinal Wolsey built it in 1519, showing Henry VIII by his example how to act the part of a splendid and all-powerful ruler. Henry learned the lesson too well and confiscated Hampton Court in 1529, when Wolsey fell out of favor. Today, the palace stands in three parts. The first and most endearing, designed by Wolsey, adapted the Renaissance style with a free hand. The windows wander over the wine-dark brick, disdaining formal symmetry. The more proper colonnade on the south side was a later modification by Sir Christopher Wren. When working properly, the clock indicates the hour, day, month, phase of the moon, and approximate time for high tide at London Bridge. The sun revolves around the earth.

Henry VIII, upon seizing the palace, resolved to leave his mark on it. By 1535, the king had converted to Anglicanism and become an English chauvinist, and Wolsey's Renaissance designs seemed tainted with Catholicism. Henry's great hall is monumental but empty, a set piece turned back to the Middle Ages. When William and Mary ascended the throne in 1689, they commissioned Wren to demolish the entire building and build a highly symmetrical, more spacious palace that would rival Versailles. Luckily, Wren ran out of money. Hence the uniqueness of Hampton Court—its harmonious blend of 16th-century motifs and 18th-century classicism.

Hampton Court looks best on the outside. Inside, you can see two curiosities of Renaissance art: the tapestries woven from the Raphael cartoons in the Victoria and Albert Museum, and a roomful of grisaille work originally by Mantegna but poorly repainted in the 18th century. You'll also find a selection of paintings from the royal collection. Note the intriguing ceilings, woodwork, and ornaments, especially in the downstairs kitchen and cellars.

The grounds of Hampton Court contain some highly celebrated amusements: the famous maze (open March-Oct.), first planted in 1714, a hedgerow labyrinth that served as the prototype for such later structures as Stanley Kubrick's Overlook Hotel; the great vine planted in 1796 that still produces grapes but now encloses a whole room with its foliage; and Henry VIII's tennis court (built in 1529), still used by "real tennis" purists. Henry's is one of only four courts left in England designed for this early brand of tennis, which looks much like squash. Also note the exhibit of Tijou's ironwork gates, left freestanding for the most part, and admirable from all sides. (Hampton Court open mid-March to mid-Oct. daily 9:30am-6pm; mid-Oct. to mid-March daily 9:30am-4:30pm. Tel. 977 8441. Admission £4.50, under 16 £2.90. Entry to the maze included in admission price.) BR runs trains from Waterloo to Hampton Court every half hour (35 min., £3.10 day return). Green Line coach #718 makes the journey from Eccleston Bridge behind Victoria daily every hour from 9:40am (40 min., £2.70) whilst #715 leaves Oxford circus and then Marble Arch for the Palace (Mon.-Sat. every hr. from 10am, Sun. every 2 hrs., 55 min.). A boat runs from Westminster Pier to Hampton Court from June to September 4 times every morning (3-4 hr. one way, £6 single, £8 return).

Windsor and Eton

Royalty is an English national obsession, and **Windsor Castle,** (tel. (0753) 868 286)—where virtually everyone royal has been born, married, or imprisoned—has become one of its most visible symbols. The castle dominates this river town of cobbled lanes, small antique stores, and quaint tea shops surrounded by walking country in the 4800-acre Great Park. Built by William the Conqueror as a fortress rather than as a residence, the castle is now hospitable but guarded, lazily stretching its limbs over and around one extended hill. You can saunter blithely in and out of its labyrinthine terraces, and enjoy beautiful views of the Thames Valley. As you enter the castle, **St. George's Chapel** rises across the courtyard. The chapel is a sumptuous 15th-century building with delicate fan vaulting and stained glass, dedicated to the Order of the Garter (open Mon.-Sat. 10:45am-4pm, Sun. 2-4pm, £2, children £1). Here Henry VIII rests in a surprisingly modest tomb near George V, Edward IV, Charles I, and Henry VI. A ceremonial procession of the Knights of the Garter takes place here every year; look for the crest on one of the houses opposite the chapel. As you walk up by the Round Tower, whose foundations have recently been shifting, keep an eye out for the stone hippo in the moat garden. Past the gargoyles of the (not really) Norman Gate, built by Edward III, at the top end of the castle, you can visit the elegantly furnished **state apartments** (£2.90, child £1.25), and **Queen Mary's giant dolls' house** (£1.45, child 60p). Windsor's impressive changing of the guard takes place at 11am. (Grounds open April-Sept. daily 10:15am-6:15pm, Oct.-March daily 10:15am-4:15pm. Free. State apartments and dolls' house open April-Sept. Mon.-Sat. 10:30am-5pm, Sun. 12:30-5pm; Oct.-March Mon.-Sat. 10:30am-4pm, Sun. 12:30-4pm.)

Windsor's old town is directly across the road from the castle gate (look for the house leaning at an obtuse angle). Follow the road that bears left around royal grounds to come to the entrance to **Windsor Great Park,** a huge expanse of parkland where deer graze and the royals ride. The Long Walk leads from the castle towards the Copper Horse. At the other end of the park lie the Savill Garden (a delight for those with green thumbs) and the Smith's Lawn polo fields, where accident-prone Prince Charles used to play.

About 15 minutes down Thames St. and across the river is **Eton College,** a preeminent public (that is, private) school founded by Henry VI in 1440. Eton boys still wear tailcoats to every class, and solemnly raise one finger in greeting to any teacher on the street. Wellington claimed that the Battle of Waterloo was "won on the playing fields of Eton": catch a glimpse of the unique and brutal "Wall Game" and see why. Eton has molded some notable dissidents and revolutionaries—Percy Bysshe Shelley, Aldous Huxley, George Orwell, and even former Liberal Party leader Jeremy Thorpe. John Le Carré taught here, and Denys Finch-Hatton, who was portrayed as the fated flyer in *Out of Africa* by Robert Redford, is memorialized in the bridge by the cricket pitches. The Queen is the only female honorary Old Etonian.

Wander around the schoolyard, a central quadrangle featuring a statue of Henry VI, and the chapel, an unfinished cathedral. This route leads to the dreamy **cloisters** beyond, and an intriguing museum explaining some of the antiquated traditions that obscure the completely modern educational task of the school. (Yard, cloisters, and museum open April and July-Sept. 10:30am-4:30pm, May-June and Oct.-March daily 2-4:30pm. Admission £2.20, children £1.40.) Invest one or two more pounds on a tour to see more of the school. **Lower school,** one of the oldest classrooms currently in use in the world, dates from 1443. Students still hold Latin prayers here every Sunday night. Above, mischeveous students still face the Head Master in a room whose walls are carved with the names of scholars and *Let's Go: London* researchers.

The railway serves Windsor and Eton Central station and Windsor and Eton Riverside station). Trains leave from Paddington via Slough or directly from Waterloo (every 30 min., £4 cheap day return). Green Line coaches #700, 701, 702, and 718 also make the trip from Victoria Station (£3.80 day return). The tourist office (tel. (0753) 852 010) is in the Central station.

Ethnic London

Most visitors to London are drawn by the city's status as a capital of Western culture. But London's position at the hub of the once-great Great British empire has made the city remarkably diverse. A liberal Commonwealth immigration policy in the fifties and sixties attracted large Asian, West Indian, and African communities. Cypriots fled to London in the 1960s during fighting between Turkish and

Greek factions in Cyprus. London's Jewish community, traditionally based around the East End, dates back to the Conquest. Escape from England in England's capital.

The East End

Today's East End—relatively poor, but enlivened by ethnic diversity—is on a trajectory begun in the 19th century. A large working-class population moved into the district during the Industrial Revolution, followed by a wave of Jewish immigrants fleeing persecution in Eastern Europe, who settled around **Whitechapel.** Most of the Jewish community has moved on to suburbs in the north and west, like Stamford Hill and Golders Green (see below), but notable remnants include the renowned kosher restaurant **Bloom's** (see Food) and the city's oldest standing synagogue, **Bevis Marks Synagogue** (Bevis Marks, EC3; Tube: Liverpool St.), built in 1701. **Cable Street,** to the south, saw anti-Semitic violence by British Fascists in the 1930s.

Many South Asians, especially Muslim Bangladeshis, settled in the East End during the period of large-scale Commonwealth immigration. At the heart of this community is **Brick Lane** (Tube: Aldgate East), a street lined with Indian and Bangladeshi restaurants, colorful textile shops, and grocers stocking exotic foods. On Sundays, vibrant market stalls flank the street. At Fournier Street, a former church now holds a mosque; on Friday afternoons after prayer the street fills with chatter. The **East London Mosque,** 84-86 Whitechapel Road (Tube: Aldgate East), was London's first to have its own building.

An over-dramatized aspect of the East End's history is its association with London's more famous criminals. Jack the Ripper's six murders took place in Whitechapel; more recently, Cockney Capone twins Ron and Reggie Kray ruled the 60s underworld from their mum's terraced house in Bethnal Green. Ron wiped out an ale-sipping rival in broad daylight in 1966 at the **Blind Beggar** pub at Whitechapel Rd. and Cambridge Heath Rd.

Golders Green

North of Hampstead, Golders Green is a small and quiet residential area that has become the center of London's Jewish community. An estimated 80% of Britain's Jews live in the capital; while Stamford Hill, to the east of Golders Green, is a core of the orthodox community, it is in Golders Green that Jewish culture seems to pervade the streets. While there is no formal center to the diverse sects that make up the population, and while Golders Green at first appears to have the same shopping streets that can be found all over the country, the area is different. Alongside the typical chain stores on Golders Green Rd. and Finchley Rd., north and south of Golders Green Tube station, are kosher butchers and banks with Hebrew advertisements. Two Jewish social service centres are being built towards the expanse of Golders Hill Park, and synagogues lie behind the busy high streets. Followers of fame and notoriety might want to check out **Golders Green Crematorium,** on Hoop Lane Rd., NW11 (tel. (081) 455 2374; open daily 9am-5pm), where Sigmund Freud's ashes can be found, along with memorials to Lord Sieff, founder of Mark's and Spencer's, rocker Marc Bolan, and *Dracula* creator Bram Stoker.

At 146a Golders Green Rd., NW11, **Jerusalem the Golden** is a hodgepodge of Jewish children's books and arts and crafts (tel. (081) 455 4960; open Mon.-Sat. 9:30am-6pm). The shops around it sell kosher food, as does the ever-busy **Bloom's** restaurant and takeaway, a branch of the famous restuarant at Whitechapel, at no. 130 (tel. (081) 455 1338; open Sun.-Fri. 10am-11pm). At no. 111a, try a delicious pancake (£1) or a pita (£2) in **Yossi's Nosh,** (tel. (081) 455 6777; open Sun.-Thurs. noon-midnight, Fri. noon-5pm). The **Jewish Vegetarian Society** at 855 Finchley Rd., NW11 (tel. (081) 455 0692) offers lunch and dinner for about £5 (open Sun.-Thurs. noon-3pm and 6-10pm). The *Jewish Chronicle* provides information on Jewish events around London (tel. 405 9252).

Southall

London's largest South Asian community congregates in Southall, about 10 miles west of central London (BR: Southall). Don't expect a garish Little India theme-park; the streets here are lined with the same charmingly gabled and gardened Victorian homes found in many other suburbs. But South Road and Broadway are also filled with Asian restaurants, grocers, and sweet shops. Video stores burst with the latest classics from the prolific Indian film industry, and every other window displays mannequins modeling dazzling saris.

While the East End is home to many Muslims, Sikhs concentrate in Southall. Many worship at the **Guru Granth Gurdwara** temple on Villiers Road, in a former church. Colored light bulbs festoon façade of the Hindu Vishwa Temple, 2 Lady Margaret Rd.

Brixton

The genteel Victorian shopping and residential district of SW9 has become the focus of the **Afro-Carribean** community since World War II, following large scale Commonwealth immigration in the 1950s and 1960s. The neighborhood has revived since its days of riots in 1981—as the firms "Backing Brixton" on the railway bridge testified—but radicalism still thrives here; outside the station revolutionaries hawk a hundred different militant left-wing newspapers. (Tube: Brixton.)

The **Black Cultural Archives,** at Coldharbour Lane and Atlantic Rd., displays small but informative exhibits on Black history and local issues. Next door, the Timbuktu Bookshop sells books of African cultural and political interest, as well as clothes, art, and crafts.

Much of excitement of Brixton is in its market (see Street Markets), sprawling around the Brixton station. Shoppers from all over London mix with local crowds among vendors of food, clothing (both wild and wan) and junk, surrounded by street preachers and performers and waves of music from record stalls and shops. For the best selection of African, hip-hop, and other groovy tunes, try Red Records at 500 Brixton Rd.

Notting Hill

Notting Hill is an area with a chequered past, famous for the race riots of the 50s and 60s (the dynamic gang fights of the film *Absolute Beginners* were set here). Lying between Holland Park Ave. to the south and the Westway to the north, Notting Hill is most vivacious along Portobello Rd. and in the area around Ladbroke Grove Tube station, along Ladbroke Grove and Westbourne Park Rd. Here, the crescents that emulate quiet and refined Kensington (and which were originally built this shape as a racecourse in the 1830s) give way to the real Notting Hill: a completely eccentric mix of different ethnic communities, now also coming to grips with yuppification.

Trendy places to eat and desigher shops trade among dilapidated cheapo stores, wafts of incense, and Bob Marley posters. Here, the Body Shop is right across the street from a tattoo parlor and the Anglo-Yugoslavian Butcher. This mix can be seen on Saturdays in Portobello Market: the antique stores and thriving art galleries on the south end of Portobello Rd. give way to racks and racks of tatty but busy secondhand clothes stalls. If you're looking for secondhand vinyl in the form of records, check out the strip around the corner of Portobello Rd. and Lancaster Rd.

Notting Hill seems to celebrate its vital existence more than other areas of London. On a far greater scale than Portobello Market, the area becomes one giant party in late August during the **Notting Hill Carnival,** Europe's biggest outdoor festival. Every type of Afro-Carribean music reverberates through the streets packed with colorful floats, crucial, skanking followers, and dancing policemen. Although recently plagued by security problems, the carnival has considerably cleaned up its act (Carnival in 1992: 25-26 Aug.) The more highbrow Portobello Festival in early June celebrates film, theatre, art and music across the area (tel. 229 7981 for details).

Grab a delectable sandwich at **Mr. Christian's,** 11 Elgin Crescent: pure hedonism (£1-2). Vegetarians should look into **Ceres,** at 269a Portobello Rd., selling salads, pies, cakes, and other goodies: you may have to queue. To head up into the young yuppie market, schmooze in the **Market Bar,** at 240a, always packed on the weekends. If "the last word in funky world food and modern rococo deco" is your thing, get down to the **First Floor Restaurant,** at 186 Portobello Rd.

Chinatown

Cantonese immigrants first arrived in Britain as cooks on British ships, and London's first Chinese community formed around the docks near the Isle of Dogs. Now, however, Leicester Square (Tube: Leicester Sq.) holds the heart of London's Chinatown. The new Chinatown swelled with arrivals from Hong Kong in the 50s, and 50,000 more immigrants to Britain are expected as 1997, the date for Hong Kong's transfer to China, approaches. Between the theatres of Shaftesbury Avenue and the cinemas of Leicester Square, the atmosphere of the West End dissolves as street signs in Cantonese spring up, and even the staid British telephone booths become capped with pagodas. **Gerrard Street,** Chinatown's main thoroughfare, runs closest to the Leicester Sq. Tube station; the street where poet John Dryden once lived is now a pedestrian avenue framed by scrollworked dragon gates.

Chinatown is most vibrant during the year's two major festivals: the Mid-Autumn Festival, at the end of September, and the **Chinese New Year Festival,** around the beginning of February (Feb. 9, 1992; Jan. 25, 1993). Long dragons stalk down streets while performers strut their stuff in Leicester Square. In 1992, the celebration ushers in the Year of the Monkey. For further information on festivals or on Chinatown call the **Chinese Community Centre** at Newport Pl. and Gerrard St. (tel. 439 3822). Those thirsty for information in the form of eastern newspapers (in English or Chinese) should check out the bustling bookshop **Guang Ho,** at 7 Newport Pl. (tel. 437 3737; open daily 10:30am-7pm). Every type of literature abounds here, from the extremely learned to the utterly garish. The latest big-screen exploits of Jackie Chang and his cinematic fellows can be seen on Sunday nights at the Odeon Leicester Square (tel. 930 6111), which shows double bills starting around 11pm. The otherwise classical church of St. Martin-in-the-Fields in Trafalgar Sq. also switches to Chinese every Sunday afternoon.

Museums

Rainy days, although quite numerous here, will not suffice for London's museums. You may find yourself indoors in the best of weather. London has more than its fair share of world-class institutions of art, archaeology, and science, and a host of smaller, more specialized collections.

Weekday mornings tend to be the most peaceful. Admission is usually free, but many museums, no longer heavily subsidized by the government, now charge or request a £1-2 donation. Most charge for special exhibits and offer student and senior citizen discounts. Many museums sponsor free films and lectures. A number have recently begun scrambling to modernize, with an eye toward attracting tourists.

British Museum

The British Museum is a stunningly comprehensive tribute to the succession of Western civilizations and, implicitly, to the British Empire. It was the political, military, and economic scope of the Empire that allowed such a collection to be amassed. The museum was founded in 1753, and the present building was created to house the overflowing contents in 1852. The national archaeological collections represent the glory days of Egypt, western Asia, Greece, Rome, and medieval Europe. The museum also houses temporary exhibitions of its coin and medal, and print and drawing collections. The **British Library's** galleries share the building now, but its cases of canonical manuscripts are due to move with the rest of the library to a new building in St. Pancras, beginning in 1993. Wandering randomly can be rewarding, if you've got about a month to spare. To catch the main attractions, buy the £2 short guide; for a more in-depth look, guides to each collection are available for about £5. Guided tours (£5) cover the highlights.

To your right as you enter are the **British Library** galleries. The **Manuscript Saloon** contains the English Literature displays, including manuscripts of *Beowulf* (c. 1000) and the *Canterbury Tales* (1410), and scrawlings form nearly every figure in English Literature up to Philip Larkin. Biblical displays include some of the oldest surviving fragments (the *Codex Sinaiticus* and the *Codex Alexandrinus*), third-century Greek gospels, and the Celtic *Lindisfarne Gospels*. Händel, Beethoven, and Stravinsky are represented in the music cases. You can read Henry VIII's complaint to Cardinal Wolsey that he found writing "sumwhat tedius and payneful," but probably not as much as did his predecessor King John, when assenting to the *Magna Carta,* of which the library has two copies. The highlight of the printed books in the **King's Library** is the Gutenberg Bible. The circular reading room, where Marx wrote *Das Kapital,* is open to visitors only on tours, Mon.-Sat. every hour on the hour from 11am to 4pm.

The ancient **Egypt** collection, housed on both floors of the museum, is outstanding. Entering the ground floor gallery, one is greeted by two of the many imposing statues of Amenophis III. To the left rests the **Rosetta Stone,** discovered in 1799 by French soldiers. Its Greek text enabled Champollion to finally crack the hieroglyphic code. Among the sculptures, the sublime, unidentified royal head in green schist (1490 BC) and the colossus of megalomaniac pharaoh Ramses II stand out. In the side gallery 25a, don't miss three of the finest and best known Theban tomb paintings, including *Nobleman hunting in the marshes.*

The upstairs Egyptian gallery contains brilliant sarcophagi and grisly mummies, and an ancient body "dessicated by the dry, hot sand." Delicate papyri include the famous *Book of the Dead of Ani.*

The **Greek antiquities** are rightly dominated by the white pieces of the Parthenon that reside in the spacious Duveen Gallery. In 1810, Lord Elgin, an enterprising British ambassador to Constantinople, procured the statues and pieces of the Parthenon frieze from the Sultan of Turkey. Later, for reasons of financial necessity, he sold them to Britain for £35,000 (they had cost him £75,000). Every so often, the Greeks renew their efforts to convince the British government to return the **Elgin Marbles.** The marbles, carved under the direction of ancient Greece's greatest sculptor, Phidias, comprise three main groups: the frieze, which portrays the most important Athenian civic festivals; the metopes, which depict incidents from the battle of the Lapiths and Centaurs (symbolizing the triumph of civilization over barbarism); and the remains of large statues that stood in the east and west pediments of the building. Keats, Byron, and Shelley all wrote a few stanzas to these inspiring stones.

Other Greek highlights include the complete Ionic façade of the Nereid Monument, one of the female caryatid columns from the Acropolis, and two of the Seven Wonders of the Ancient World: fragments of the **Mausoleum and Halicarnassus** and the Ephesian **Temple of Artemis.**

Among the many sculptures of the **Roman antiquities,** the dark blue glass of the **Portland Vase** stands out. The vase, which was the inspiration for ceramic designer Josiah Wedgwood, was shattered by a drunken museum-goer in 1845, but has been twice beautifully restored. A crisp second-century mosaic from France is outdone only by the Roman Christian mosaic upstairs found by a Dorset farmer in 1963. Nearby crouches **Lindow Man,** an Iron Age Celt killed in a ritual, and preserved by peat-bog.

In the **Roman Britain** section, the Mindenhall Treasure is a magnificent collection of fourth-century silver (the true story behind this find inspired Roald Dahl's story of the same name). The **Sutton Hoo Ship Burial,** an Anglo-Saxon ship buried (and subsequently dug up) in Suffolk complete with an unknown king, is the centerpiece of the **Middle Ages** galleries.

The museum is located at Great Russell St., WC1 (tel. 636 1555; Tube: Tottenham Court Rd. or Holborn). Open Mon.-Sat. 10am-5pm, Sun. 2:30-6pm.

National Gallery

The National Gallery maintains one of the finest collections of European painting in the world, especially well-known for works by Rembrandt, Rubens, and 15th- and 16th-century Italian painters. The Berggruen collection of works from the turn of the 20th century, including many Impressionist masterpieces and a large selection of Picassos, has recently been loaned to the National for five years. The Tate Gallery has joint custody of the British collection.

The National Gallery's collection is undergoing a complete renovation and rehanging, which will probably be finished sometime in spring 1992. Until then, you may have to check with the information desk to the right of the entrance to find your favorite paintings. You can spend days in this maze of galleries.

The National's collection is now split into four color-coded sections, and paintings within these sections are arranged by school. The collection starts in the new Sainsbury wing, to the west of the main building, designed by postmodernist Robert Venturi. Amid much-discussed fake ceiling supports and false perspectives hang works painted from 1260 to 1510. Early Italian paintings such as Paulo Uccello's grand fluorescent battle scene, *The Battle of San Romano,* Botticelli's *Venus and Mars,* Raphael's *Crucifixion,* and Leonardo da Vinci's famous *Virgin of the Rocks* are framed by the arches and columns of the new building.

Paintings from 1510 to 1600 are exhibited in the West Wing, to the left of the main entrance on Trafalgar Sq. These include paintings by late Renaissance masters such as Michelangelo, Venetians Titian (such as the beautiful *Bacchus and Ariadne*) and Tintoretto, and stormy pastels by El Greco. In the North Wing, further back behind the West Wing, are works of the 17th century. Rembrandt's gripping *Belshazzar's Feast* and graceful *Woman Bathing* are here, near a sprinkling of Vermeer and Hals. Serene Claude and Poussin landscapes are routed by the startling chiaroscuro of Caravaggio's *Supper at Eumaeus,* and the romanticism of Velàzquez's *Toilet of Venus.*

The East Wing of the National Gallery, to the right of the main entrance, is devoted to painting from 1700 to 1920, including the recent arrivals from the Berggruen collection. The natural lighting provides the perfect setting for viewing the paintings; many, such as Turner's *Rain, Steam, and Speed* (note the tiny jackrabbit running alongside the train), seem to acquire a special luminosity. Gainsborough's tight *Mr. and Mrs. Andrews,* and Gerard Honthorst's compelling *Christ before the High Priest* whet the appetite before the Impressionists clamor for attention. Impressionist works include a number of Monet's most lavender and poignant waterlilies, Cézanne's *Les Grandes Baigneuses,* and Rousseau's rainswept *Tropical Storm with a Tiger.* Picasso's *Fruit Dish, Bottle, and Violin* (1914) represents the National Gallery's first foray into the abstract, complemented by a roomful of Picassos recently added to the collection.

The National Gallery holds frequent special exhibitions in the basement galleries of the new Sainsbury Wing. A large Rembrandt exhibition is planned for March-May 1992. Free hour-long guided tours of the collection start at 11am, 1pm, and 3pm Monday through Saturday. The National shows free films every Monday at 1pm in the lower-floor theatre, and lectures take place in the afternoons (Tues.-Fri. at 1pm, Sat. at noon). Each summer Wednesday the Gallery offers "Picture Promenade" lecture tours (July-Aug.; start at 6:30pm, 45 min.). Call for information regarding topics and times of lectures or films. The Gallery Shop sells detailed books and reproductions of many works in sizes ranging from postcard to poster.

The gallery is located at Trafalgar Sq. WC2 (tel. 839 3321, recorded information 839 3526; Tube: Charing Cross or Leicester Sq). Disabled access at Orange St. entrance. Open July-Aug. Mon.-Sat. 10am-8pm, Sun. 2-6pm. Sept.-June Mon.-Sat. 10am-6pm, Sun. 2-6pm. Free.

National Portrait Gallery

This unofficial *Who's Who in Britain* began in 1856 as "the fulfillment of a patriotic and moral ideal"—namely to showcase Britain's most noteworthy citizens. Alternatively you can think of the NPG as a response by the artistic community to Madame Tussaud's. The museum's declared principle of looking "to the celebrity of the person represented, rather than to the merit of the artist" does not seem to have affected the quality of the works displayed—many are by such top portraitists as Reynolds, Lawrence, Holbein, and Sargent. The 9000 paintings have been arranged more or less chronologically, though the order gets garbled on the lower floors. The earliest portraits hang in the top story—maligned Richard III, venerated Elizabeth I, and canny Henry VII. Charles II is here, surrounded by his wife and mistresses (Nell Gwyn is the one with the lamb).

Follow the flow of British history through the galleries: from the War of the Roses (Yorks and Lancasters), to the Civil War (portraits of Cromwell and his buddies), to the American Revolution (George Washington), to imperial days (Florence Nightingale), and on to modern times (Margaret Thatcher). On the first floor the emphasis shifts from crowned to creative heads: the Brontë sisters, painted by their brother Branwell, and William Blake. Famous geologists, politicians, reformers, and eccentric fops populate the Victorian section, along with literary figures including Tennyson, Thackeray, and Dickens. Portraits of Queen Elizabeth II and the present Royal Family are displayed on the mezzanine. (The likeness is better here than at Madame Tussaud's.) The basement shelters relatively modern portraits, including a sketch of W.H. Auden and a bust of Sir Alec Guinness. The annual British Portrait Award brings out a selection of works from England's most promising artists (on display June-Sept.). Visit the gift shop and buy classy postcards of your favorite personalities to send home to your friends or worship on your walls. Informative lectures transpire at 2:10pm Tuesday through Friday, at 5pm on Saturday. Check the monthly schedule for locations.

The gallery portrays at St. Martin's Pl., WC2 (tel. 306 0055; Tube: Charing Cross or Leicester Sq.). Museum open Mon.-Fri. 10am-5pm, Sat. 10am-6pm, Sun. 2-6pm. Free, except for some temporary exhibits £1-3.

Tate Gallery

The Tate Gallery opened in 1897 expressly to display modern British art. Since then, the gallery has widened its scope, obtaining a superb collection of British works from the 16th century to the present and a distinguished ensemble of international modern art. Like the National Gallery, the Tate has recently been completely reorganized; work should be completed by early 1992. The new captions and introductory notes in each gallery are particularly helpful.

The Tate's British collection is organized chronologically into schools, starting with a room at the far end of the gallery devoted to the Age of Hogarth. The parade of Constables includes the famous views of Salisbury Cathedral, and a bunch of Hampstead scenes, many dotted with the requisite red saddle splashes. George Stubbs' landscape and sporting portraits are enlivening, and lead up to Gainsborough's landscapes and Sir Joshua Reynolds' portraits. The haunting and visionary works of poet, philosopher, and painter William Blake are not to be missed, especially his marvelous illustrations of the Bible and of Dante's *Divine Comedy*. The psychological state of man is terrifyingly portrayed in his crawling *Nebuchadnezzar*.

The Tate's outstanding modern collection confronts you in the central halls with sculptures by Henry Moore, Epstein, Eric Gill, and Barbara Hepworth. The paintings include works of Monet, Degas, Van Gogh, Beardsley, Matisse, and the Camden Town Group (Sickert, Bevan), to the left of the entrance. The Bloomsbury Group, Francis Bacon, and the styles that have dominated since the 1950s (constructivism, minimalism, pop, super-realism, and process art) lie to the right of the main halls. Visit the extraordinary room of Rothko's studies in maroon and black.

The Tate's J.M.W. Turner collection has been moved to the **Clore Gallery,** an extension of the main building designed by the noted architect James Stirling. This vast display of 300 oil paintings and selected drawings and watercolors ranges from the early dreamy landscapes, such as *Chevening Park,* to the late visionary works, in which the subject gets lost in a sublime array of light and color. The natural light from above, cleverly allowed to filter through by the architect, illuminates scenes from the serene *Peace—Burial at Sea* to the furious depictions and raging paint of rain and snowstorms on the ocean.

Tours run Monday through Friday at 11am for the British collection, noon for Impressionism to expressionism, 2pm for expressionism to the present day, 3pm for the Turner collection. Lectures are given Mon.-Sat. at 1pm, Sun. at 2:30pm. The Tate puts on some of the most important special exhibitions in the world, both in the main building and in the Clore Gallery (admission usually £4-5, half price for students and children). Exhibitions scheduled for 1992 include the works of Otto Dix (March-May), pop artist Richard Hamilton (June.-Aug.) and English portraiture from Van Dyck to Augustus John (Oct.-Jan. 1993).

The Tate is located at Millbank, SW1 (tel. 821 1313; Tube: Pimlico). Open Mon.-Sat. 10am-5:50pm, Sun. 2-5:50pm. Free.

Victoria and Albert Museum

Housing the best collection of Italian Renaissance sculpture outside Italy, the greatest collection of Indian art outside India, and the world center for John Constable studies, the mind-boggling V&A specializes in fine and applied arts from every epoch and region of the world. Take an eight mile trek through art history in its 12 acres of galleries, divided among Art and Design galleries, Special Collections, and Materials and Techniques Collections.

The stars of the Renaissance art collection are the famed *Raphael Cartoons*—seven of the 10 large, full-color sketches (scenes from the Acts of the Apostles) done by Raphael and his apprentices as tapestry patterns for the Sistine Chapel. The endless galleries of Italian sculpture include Donatello's *Ascension* and *Madonna and Child.* The Medieval Treasury, in the center of the ground floor, features well-displayed vestments, plate, stained glass, and illuminations. The most spectacular treasure is the domed Eltenburg Reliquary. Plaster cast reproductions of European sculpture and architecture (the 80-ft.-tall Column of Trajan from Rome; the façade of the Santiago Cathedral in Spain; Michelangelo's *Moses, Dying Slave, Rebellious Slave,* and *David*) occupy rooms 46A-B on the ground floor. Next door, test the knowledge you've gained here to tell imposters from the real things in the Fakes and Forgeries gallery. Don't feel bad if you're fooled—in many cases, the V&A was too. The Dress Collection, also on the ground floor, traces popular clothing fashions from 17th-century shoes to the latest Armanis.

The first floor holds the large collection of British art and design. Shakespeare immortalized the immense Great Bed of Ware (room 54) in *Twelfth Night.* Cool, dim room 74, "1900-1960," exhibits the best in modern British design, including works by Wyndham Lewis, Charles Rennie Mackintosh, and Eric Gill. International design classics—mostly chairs—grace "Twentieth Century Design." The jewelry collection (rooms 91-93), so unwieldy that it has been annotated in bound catalogues instead of posted descriptions, includes pieces dating from 2000 BC. The National Art Library, located on the first floor, houses numerous Beatrix Potter originals as well as first editions of Pooh Bear adventures.

The V&A's formidable Asian collections have recently been beefed up by the new Nehru Gallery of Indian Art and the T.T. Tsui Gallery of Chinese Art. The Nehru Gallery contains splendid examples of textiles, painting, Mughal jewelry and decor, and enlightening displays about Europeans and Indians. You can see Tippoo's Tiger, a life-sized wooden model in the act of consuming a European gentleman, alluded to by consumption-obsessed John Keats in his poem *The Cap and Bells.*

The Tsui Gallery divides its 5000-year span of Chinese art into six areas of life—Eating and Drinking, Living, Worship, Ruling, Collecting, and Burial. Treasures include the Sakyamuni Buddha and an Imperial Throne. The Toshiba Gallery of Japanese Art has a prime collection of lacquer art, as well as traditional armor and intriguing contemporary sculpture. The V&A also has fine displays of Islamic art, particularly in the carpet department.

John Constable's prodigious collection of weather studies resides on the sixth floor of the Henry Cole Wing. For those whose tastes run smaller, room 406 showcases English and Continental portrait miniatures (including Holbein's *Anne of Cleves* and *Elizabeth I*).

The V&A offers scores of special events. Introductory tours of the museum start Mon.-Sat. at 11am, noon, 2pm, or 3pm; Sun. at 3pm. Theme tours begin Mon.-Sat. at 11:30am, 1:30pm, and 2:30pm. Both last approximately one hour. Individual lectures of V&A summer courses can be attended for partial tuition: contact the Education Services Department (tel. 938 8638). Numerous free lectures throughout the summer cover anything from Impressionism to Japanese quilt technique. The V&A society hosts members' evenings on summer Wednesdays. Membership costs £25 (three-month membership £12); nonmembers may attend meetings for £2. Bookings can be made with the Box Office (tel. 938 8407), Victoria & Albert Museum, South Kensington, London SW7 2RL.

The V&A is located at Cromwell Rd., SW7 (tel. 938 8500; Tube: South Kensington). Open Mon.-Sat. 10am-5:50pm, Sun. 2:30-5:50pm. Donation £2, seniors and students 50p.

Other Major Collections

Bank of England Museum, Threadneedle St., EC2 (tel. 601 5792). Tube: Bank. Entrance on Bartholomew Lane. A cultured history of banknotes and check-writing features a topical review of five-pound notes. Absorbing forgery exhibits. Worth a 30-min. browse, although the fake gold bullion waxes tacky. Open Easter-Sept. Mon.-Fri. 10am-5pm, Sun. 11am-5pm; Oct.-Easter Mon.-Fri. 10am-5pm. Free.

Bethnal Green Museum of Childhood, Cambridge Heath Rd., E2 (tel. (081) 980 3204). Tube: Bethnal Green. Those seeking serious fun will only find the seriousness. As the sign says inside, it's "primarily a place for looking, not for doing." Still, the doll houses provide a surprisingly interesting architectural and social history. Open Mon.-Thurs. and Sat. 10am-6pm, Sun. 2:30-6pm.

Cabinet War Rooms, Clive Steps, King Charles St. (tel. 930 6961 or 735 8922). Tube: Westminster. Churchill's secret underground headquarters during the Blitz present a fascinating glimpse into a world at war. The entrance is hidden; look for the queue. See the room where Churchill made his famous wartime broadcasts and listen to cuts of some of his speeches. Spot the 20-ton transatlantic hotline disguised as a loo. Free cassette guides available in English, French, German, Italian, Japanese, and Spanish. The 21-room narrated exhibit lasts about an hour. Open daily 10am-6pm. Last entrance 5:15pm. Admission £3.60; students, seniors, and under 16 £2.70, children £1.80. Additional discounts for groups of 10 or more.

Commonwealth Institute, (tel. 603 4535). Tube: High St. Kensington. Exhibitions and events celebrating the far-flung elements of the British Commonwealth cluster under a roof made, suitably, of Zambian copper. Call ahead for details of frequent art exhibits in the main hall, and dance and music performances in the evenings (often free). Exhibits open Mon.-Sat. 10am-5pm, Sun. 2-5pm.

The Courtauld Institute, Somerset House, The Strand (tel. 873 2526). Tube: Charing Cross or Aldwych (rush hour only). An intimate, intense, 11-room gallery with an extensive gathering of Impressionist and post-Impressionist masterpieces. The collection features works of Cézanne, Degas, Gauguin, and Renoir and includes Van Gogh's *Portrait of the Artist with a Bandaged Ear,* and Manet's wonderful *Bar aux Folies Bergère.* The Institute's other collections include early Italian religious works (both paintings and sculpture) and key works by Botticelli, Rubens, Breugel, and Cranach, plus Oskar Kokoschka's stunning *Prometheus Triptych.* Open Mon.-Sat. 10am-6pm, Sun. 2-6pm. Admission £2.50; students, seniors, and children £1.

The Design Museum, Butlers Wharf, Shad Thames, SE1 (tel. 403 6933). Tube: Tower Hill, then river shuttle from Tower Pier. In an appropriately Bauhausy box on the river, this museum is dedicated to mass-produced classics of culture and industry, such as the automotive bombshell dropped by the Citroen DS in the 1950s. Happily, you *can* sit in some of the century's most influential chairs. Open Tues.-Sun. 11:30am-6:30pm. Admission £3, students and children £2.

Dulwich Picture Gallery, College Rd., SE21 (tel. (081) 693 5254), next to the Dulwich college administration building. England's first public art gallery and well worth the BR ride from Blackfriars to West Dulwich. French art dealer Noel Desenfans assembled the gallery's original collection of Dutch masters. Desenfans' collection passed to Sir Francis Bourgeois, who expanded it and later bequeathed the paintings to the college. Sir John Soane, who worked out the design in 1811, included a mausoleum for the gallery's founders (you can visit Bourgeois and Mme. Desenfans in the center of room 6). Notable works include Van Dyck's *Madonna and Child* and *Lady Digby,* Murillo's *Flower Girl,* and Gainsborough's portraits of the Linley family. Much Rubens, Rembrandt, Cuyp, Van Dyck. Art connoisseurs fancied Rembrandt's *Jacob III de Gheyn* so much that a few of them stole it in 1983 (it has since been recovered). Stop across the street at the park for brilliant azaleas when you tire of handmade beauty. Guided tours Sat.-Sun. at 3pm. Open Tues.-Fri. 10am-1pm and 2-5pm, Sat. 11am-5pm, Sun. 2-5pm. Admission £1.50, students 50p, children free.

Geffrye Museum, Kingsland Road, E2 (tel 739 9893). Tube: Liverpool St., then bus 22A or 22B. This humble but absorbing little museum meticulously chronicles the English home interior, beginning in Elizabethan times and culminating at the height of the Linoleum Age in the Fifties. Open Tues.-Sat. 10am-5pm, Sun. 2-5pm.

Guildhall Clock Museum, Guildhall, Aldermanbury, EC2 (tel. 606 3030). Tube: Bank, St. Paul's, or Moorgate. About as exciting as watching second hands tick. Most of the watches (from 1620) are stationary, anyway. Open Mon.-Fri. 9:30am-4:45pm. Free.

Imperial War Museum, Lambeth Rd., SE1 (tel. 416 5000), on the South Bank of the Thames in Lambeth. Tube: Lambeth North. Do not be misled by the jingoistic resonance of the name; this museum is above all a moving reminder of the human cost of war. The atrium is filled with a striking collection of tanks and planes, but the real treasure is downstairs. Gripping exhibits illuminate every aspect of two world wars, in every medium possible. The Blitz and Trench Experiences recreate every sad detail (even smells); veterans and victims speak through telephone handsets. The powerful Belsen exhibit documents the horrors of the concentration camp and the fascinating story of the rescue and rehabilitation of survivors. Unmissable documents include the "peace in our time" agreement that Neville Chamberlain triumphantly brought back from Munich in 1938, and Adolf Hitler's "political testament," dictated in the chancellery bunker and witnessed by Joseph Goebbels and Martin Bormann. Upstairs, the art galleries keep fine examples of war painting, such as Sargent's *Gassed, 1918.* Open daily 10am-6pm. Admission £3, students and children £1.50. Free on Fri..

Institute of Contemporary Arts, the Mall, SW1 (tel. 930 3647). Tube: Piccadilly Circus or Charing Cross. Institutional outpost of the avant-garde in visual and performance art. Three galleries, a cinema featuring first-run independent films (£5), experimental space for film and video, theatre (from £5.50), seminars and lectures (£3), video library, and poetry readings (call for schedule). Day membership £1.50, students £1 (included in other ticket prices). Student art pass (£10) gets ½-price on any ticket for a year; normal membership £20. Galleries open daily noon-11pm.

The London Toy and Model Museum, 21/23 Craven Hill, W2 (tel. 262 7905.) Tube: Paddington or Queensway. On Sundays, the mini railway in the garden gives rides to small children (and, presumably, small adults). Inside, legions of dolls and cars inhabit cabinets. Open Tues.-Sat. 10am-5:30pm, Sun. 11am-5:30pm. Admission £2.70, students £1.70, children £1.20, families £6.

London Transport Museum, 39 Wellington St., WC2 (tel. 379 6344), on the east side of the Covent Garden flower market. Tube: Covent Garden. Traces the history of London transport from horse-drawn carriage to double-decker to Tube. Even non train- or bus-spotters will be impressed by the collection of old vehicles. Absorbing details on how London and its transport system grew up around each other. First-class museum shop sells stylish old (and new) London Transport posters and postcards at low prices. Museum open daily 10am-6pm, last admission 5:15pm. Admission £3, students, seniors, and children £1.50, families £7. Shop open daily 10am-5:45pm.

Museum of London, 150 London Wall, EC2 (tel. 600 3699). Tube: St. Paul's or Barbican. Located amongst old Roman walls and chaotic building sites, exhibits in themselves. The museum traces the metropolis from its beginnings as Londinium to the present. The flashiest new acquisition, the Lord Mayor's 1757 coach, steals the show from the prehistoric artifacts and the Great Fire animation. Cross-sectional models of Victorian sewers and Roman floors beneath a modern basement can mesmerize even the most blasé of tourists. Historical lectures given Wed.-Fri. at 1:10pm. Open Tues.-Sat. 10am-6pm, Sun. 2-6pm. Open Bank Holiday Mon. 10am-6pm. Free.

Museum of Mankind, 6 Burlington Gdns., W1 (tel. 437 2224). Tube: Green Park or Piccadilly Circus. Behind the Royal Academy. The ethnography collection of the British Museum, it includes a mass of engrossing artifacts, primarily from nonwestern cultures. Changing exhibits re-create the lifestyles of ancient and modern tribes, featuring everything from everyday tools to ritual objects. Useful introductory gallery gives a cross-section of the permanent collection, which includes Mexican turquoise mosaics, African pipes, British Columbian stone carvings, and Sioux war bonnets. Many exhibits appear sinister to Western eyes. Take a look at the amazing feathered image, found by Captain Cook, representing a Hawaiian god with a mohawk. Films Tues.-Fri. at 1:30pm and 3pm. Open Mon.-Sat. 10am-5pm, Sun. 2:30-6pm. Free.

Museum of the Moving Image (MOMI), South Bank Centre, SE1 (tel. 928 3232). Tube: Embankment or Waterloo. An outgrowth of the adjoining National Film Theatre, this entertaining museum charts the development of image-making with light, from 2000-year-old Chinese shadow puppets to present-day film and telly. Costumed actor-guides lead you through interactive exhibits—act out your favorite western, or read the TV news. The camera-shy will equally enjoy countless clips and famous props, from the gaudy days of the silents to the gaudy days of "Dr. Who." Open June-Sept. daily 10am-8pm, Oct.-May Tues.-Sat. 10am-8pm, Sun. 10am-6pm. Last admission 1 hr. before closing. Admission £4; students, seniors, and children £2.75.

National Army Museum, Royal Hospital Rd., SW3 (tel. 730 0717). Tube: Sloane Sq. Established by royal charter in 1960, this museum chronicles the history of the British Army from 1458 to the present. An upstanding collection of uniforms and weapons, and exhibits on past battles: children can follow the engaging "Museum Curiousities Trail." Note the skeleton of Marengo, the horse Napoleon rode at Waterloo. Open daily 10am-5:30pm.

Natural History Museum, Cromwell Rd., SW7 (tel. 938 9123). Tube: South Kensington. The original collection, 1 of 3 founding collections of the British Museum, was purchased from Sir Hans Sloane in 1753 for the nominal fee of £20,000. Today the museum's personality is split between a glorious but ultimately dull Victorian past (the encyclopedic frenzy only slightly subsided) and a modern, technological present (buttons, levers, and microscopes galore). In the "Life Galleries," the dinosaur exhibit mixes the best of new and old with its fierce robotic reconstructions and huge plaster skeletons. Other notable exhibits include Human Biology (useful for parents wondering how much their children really know), and Discovering Mammals (learn the truth behind "Superhog, could it really happen?"). The Geological Museum has recently become the "Earth Galleries" section. Shake and quake in the Earthquake room, and follow the Story of the Earth's interactive exhibits. Lectures and films presented summer Wed. and Sat. at 1 or 2pm; check at the information desk as you enter. Open Mon.-Sat. 10am-6pm, Sun. 11am-6pm. Admission £3.50, students and senior citizens £2, children £1.75, families (up to 2 adults and 4 children) £8. Free Mon.-Fri. 4:30-6pm, Sat.-Sun. 5-6pm.

National Maritime Museum, Romney Road, Greenwich, SE10 (tel. (081) 858 4422). Set picturesquely in Greenwich, the Maritime Museum documents the history of British sea power—which is, in effect, the history of British power up to the World War I. Its origins are well captured in the new exhibition, "Discovery and Sea Power 1450-1700." The lower floors display great underwater discoveries, the tugboat *Reliant,* and the coat in which Nelson was struck down by a French sniper. Open Mon.-Sat. 10am-6pm, Sun. noon-6pm; winter Mon.-Sat. 10am-5pm, Sun. noon-5pm. Admission £3.25; students, seniors, and children £2.25.

National Postal Museum, King Edward Building, King Edward St., EC1 (tel. 239 5420). Tube: St. Paul's. Ardent philatelists will have a field day here, wandering through the claustral galleries and stooping down to inspect drawer after dreary drawer of ancient stamps. Those who prefer to lick 'em and leave 'em will be bored. Insanely, you must make a special appointment to see the collection of postal boxes. Open Mon.-Thurs. 9:30am-4:30pm, Fri. 9:30am-4pm.

North Woolwich Old Station Museum, Pier Road, North Woolwich, E16 (tel. 474 7244). BR: North Woolwich. Beneath walls crowded with colorful railway signs, ads, and signals, exhibits recall the glory that once was the British railway. An engine at back is occasionally steaming. Open Mon.-Wed., Sat. 10am-5pm; Sun. 2-5pm.

Pollock's Toy Museum, 1 Scala St., W1 (tel. 636 3452). Tube: Goodge St. Housed above a modern toy-shop in a maze of tiny, 18th-century rooms congested with antique puppets, dolls, teddy bears, lead soldiers, and playthings of every size and description. The exhibits appeal more to the nostalgia of adults than to the interests of children. Open Mon.-Sat. 10am-5pm. Admission £1, students and children 50p.

Royal Academy, Piccadilly, W1 (tel. 439 7438). Tube: Green Park or Piccadilly Circus. The academy frequently hosts traveling exhibits of the highest order: exhibition space has recently been enlarged by high-tech architect Norman Foster. The annual summer exhibition is a British institution where the works of contemporary artists are reviewed at the uncompromising rate of 10 per minute. Open daily 10am-6pm. Admission usually £3-5, students about £2, children £1. Summer exhibition admission: £3.60, students £2.10, under 18 £1.50. Advance tickets are occasionally necessary for popular exhibitions.

Royal Air Force Museum, Hendon, NW9 (tel. (081) 205 2266). Tube: Colindale. 8-min. walk from the station. A sensational assortment of aircraft, way out in an unlikely suburb of north London. The main hall houses the backbone of the display, planes ranging from the Blenot X1 and Sopwith Camel to the Lightning and Harrier jump jet. £1.25 will take you on a simulator ride—far more scary from the outside than from within. The 1918 dogfight is quite spiffing. In the awe-inspiring adjacent Bomber Command Hall, a Wellington, Lancaster, and a Vulcan V-bomber fight for attention; the memorial to the U.S. Air Force nestles by a Flying Fortress. The eerie remains of a Halifax rescued almost complete from the bottom of a Norwegian lake lie unrestored on a plinth of gravel. Around the huge halls, galleries display dioramas, models, videos, and widgets of every conceivable nature concerning the RAF's history, intended more for those with their heads truly in the clouds. For more Spitfires and Messerschmitts, peel across the car park to the Battle of Britain Hall. Open daily 10am-5:30pm. Admission £4.10, seniors and students £2.05. Ticket includes free return visit within 6 months.

Science Museum, Exhibition Rd., SW7 (tel. 938 8000). Tube: South Kensington. The Science Museum can enlighten you on subjects ranging from the exploration of space to papermaking to basic topology. The museum's introductory exhibit romps through a "synopsis" of science since 6000 BC. Well-executed exhibits; the hands-on Flight Lab is interactive heaven for kids. Launch Pad, a special hall of child-run experiments on the first floor, is irresistible to kids of all ages: toddlers and *Let's Go* researchers alike. The Science Museum has recently absorbed the gloomy Wellcome Museum of the History of Medicine (on the 4th and 5th floors). Spock would no doubt find the museum's "Glimpses of Medical History" unbearably fascinating. Open Mon.-Sat. 10am-6pm, Sun. 11am-6pm. Admission £3.50, seniors £2, students and children £1.75.

Sir John Soane's Museum, 13 Lincoln's Inn Fields, WC2 (tel. 405 2107). Tube: Holborn. Soane was an architect's architect, but the home he designed for himself will intrigue even philistines. The anonymous façade hides an interior of funny angles and weird distortions. The famous breakfast room and the "Monk's Parlor" downstairs typify the house's individuality. The columns in the "Colonnade" room are actually supporting a room-within-a-room above. Important artifacts include Hogarth paintings and the massive sarcophagus of Seti I, which Soane put here after the British Museum inexplicably rebuffed his offer to donate it. Those who enjoy Soane's architectural imagination can glimpse his unexecuted designs in the drawings room. Open Tues.-Sat. 10am-5pm; lecture tour Sat. at 2:30pm.

Theatre Museum, 1E Tavistock St., WC2, public entrance on Russell St. (tel. 836 7891). Tube: Covent Garden. Britain's richest holding of theatrical memorabilia, such as the golden angel or "Spirit of Gaiety" rescued from the apex of Gaiety Theatre in Aldwych. See numerous 19th-century Shakespearean daggers before you. Evocative photograph collection and eccentric temporary exhibits. Box office just inside the door sells tickets to London plays, musicals, and concerts. Box office open Tues.-Sat. 11am-8pm, Sun. 11am-7pm. Museum open Tues.-Sun. 11am-7pm. Museum admission £2.50; students, seniors, and under 14 £1.50.

The Wallace Collection, Hertford House, Manchester Sq., W1M (tel. 935 0687). Tube: Bond St. Formed by various Marquises of Hertford and the illegitimate son of the fourth Marquis, Sir Richard Wallace, the collection exudes opulence. A strong selection of fine 18th-century paintings is somewhat overshadowed by *The Laughing Cavalier* (1624), by Frank Hals. A stunning collection of armor, swords, and guns dazzles. Guided lectures Tues.-Sat. 11:30am and 1pm. Call ahead for a schedule. Open Mon.-Sat. 10am-5pm, Sun 2-5pm. Free.

Wellington Museum, Apsley House, on the north side of Hyde Park Corner, W1 (tel. 499 5676). Tube: Hyde Park Corner. Ardent followers of the first Duke of Wellington and his campaigns will be captivated; everyone else will be mildly bemused. Come admire numerous paintings and busts of Arthur Wellesley (the Duke's real name), super-swanky plate and china gifts given to the Duke by grateful governments, the Duke's painting collection, and an extraordinary 15-ft. nude sculpture of Napoleon. Open Tues.-Sun. 11am-4:30pm. Admission £2.50.

Whitechapel Art Gallery, Whitechapel High St., E1 (tel. 377 0107). Tube: Aldgate East. The sunny galleries of the Whitechapel contain no permanent collection, but host some of Britain's and Europe's most daring exhibitions of contemporary art, as well as shows flowing from the gallery's interaction with its East London community. Open Tues., Thurs.-Sun. 11am-5pm, Wed. 11am-8pm.

Entertainment

> When a man is tired of London, he is tired of life;
> for there is in London all that life can afford.
> —*Samuel Johnson, 1777*

On any given day or night, Londoners and visitors can choose from the widest range of entertainment a city can offer. Broadway bluff aside, the West End is still the world's theatre capital, supplemented by an unpredictable "fringe." Music scenes range from the black ties of the Royal Opera House to Wembley mobs and nightclub throbs. Rep and new films, dance, comedy, sports, and countless unclassifiable happenings can leave you poring in bewilderment over the listings in *Time Out* (£1.30), *City Limits* (£1), and *What's On* (70p). **Kidsline** (tel. 222 8070) answers queries on children's events. **Artsline** (tel. (081) 388 2227) provides information about disabled access at entertainment venues across London.

Theatre

The focus of a national dramatic tradition dating from Shakespeare's day, London maintains lofty theatrical standards. London has respect for acting, and most of its actors have studied their craft seriously in some intensive drama program or other. Go to a show, or two, or a dozen, to experience the range of crisp witty comedies, class-conscious political dramas, or large-scale musicals; to watch well-directed Shakespearean swordplay and wordplay in action; or to see British actors pull off a French farce or even American accents. You can visit any one of a charming slew of velvety playhouses with baroque balconies and see some of the world's best-trained actors joust or emote. Thanks to government subsidies, tickets are relatively inexpensive; the cheapest seats in most theatres cost about £5, progressing upward to £25 for orchestra seats. British theatres are small so you can see and hear well from almost anywhere. Previews and matinees offer even less expensive tickets, and many theatres (indicated by the letter "S" or some abbreviation of the word "concessions" in the *Evening Standard, Time Out,* and *City Limits*) offer rush tickets or student discounts on evening performances (tickets about £5 shortly before the performance—students must show ID); come to the theatre two hours ahead of curtain time to be certain of a seat. Most theatres also offer senior citizen discounts, especially on weekday matinees. For information on discounts offered by the Society of West End Theatres, call 836 0971. For the latest information on student standbys, listen to Capital Radio (95.8 FM) Mon.-Fri. at 6pm.

The **Leicester Square Ticket Booth** sells tickets at half-price (plus £1 booking fee, £1.25 for tickets over £5) on the day of the performance, but carries only expensive tickets, for selected plays. (Open for matinees Mon.-Sat. noon-2pm, for evening performances 2:30-6:30pm. Cash only.) If you schlep to the box office in person, you can select your seats from the theatre seating plan. (Box offices are usually open 10am-8pm.) Seats may also be reserved by phone by calling the box office directly and paying by post or in person within three days. Credit card-holders can charge the tickets over the phone but should be prepared to produce the card when picking up the tickets. Patronize ticket agencies only if you're desperate—they charge up to 20% commission. Not all plays start at 8pm—some curtains go up at 7:30 or 7:45pm.

Theatre schedules are published in *Time Out* and *City Limits.* You can obtain a fortnightly *London Theatre Guide* free from information centers and ubiquitous leaflet racks. Avoid the package-deal specials cooked up for tourists, and be aware that many of the shows around Piccadilly are tawdry farces and sex shows. For big-name shows, try to get tickets months in advance. Write or call first to the theatre box office; failing this, try **Keith Prowse** (tel. 793 1000), London's largest ticket agency (which also has an office at 234 W. 44th St., New York, NY 10036; tel. 1-800-669-7469), **Ticketmaster** (tel. 379 4444), or other agencies advertising in the

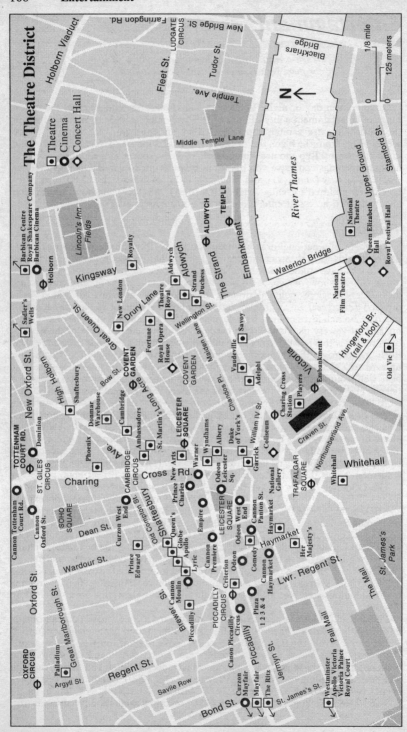

The Theatre District

- ■ Theatre
- ● Cinema
- ◆ Concert Hall

SWET *London Theatre Guide.* These agencies charge a standard fee. Beware of other agencies you see congregating around Piccadilly and tube stations—they can, and will, charge whatever they like. If you have to buy a ticket from an agent, make sure you ascertain the exact face value and fee.

Aside from what's going on inside them, many West End theatres themselves form part of the city's fabric. A restored Victorian music hall, the **Old Vic** currently houses an excellent repertory company. The **Theatre Royal Drury Lane** dates from 1812 and even has a ghost. The **Theatre Trust** has protected many historic theatres from demolition; noteworthy landmark theatres include the Theatre Royal, Haymarket, the Albery, the Palace, the Criterion, the Duke of York, Her Majesty's, the Shaftesbury, the Savoy, and the Palladium.

National Theatre: Tel. 928 2252 for box office and information on standby tickets. Tube: Waterloo or Embankment. Excellent summer standby scheme. All unsold seats in the **Olivier, Lyttleton,** and **Cottesloe** theatres reduce to £9-12.50 at 10am on the day of performance; 40 seats in the first two rows are also sold at that time, to ensure that the most enthusiastic patrons occupy these seats. General standby seats sold from 2 hr. before performance at £8.50; student standby 45 min. before show, £5. Senior citizen Sat. matinees £8. The brilliant repertory companies in the Olivier and Lyttleton theatres generally put up classics from Shakespeare to Ibsen as well as mainstream contemporary drama. The Cottesloe plays with more experimental works. Platform performances (lectures or selections from plays) presented as pre-play appetizers (£2). The complex features live music, exhibitions, and other free activities. Tours offered Mon.-Sat. at 10:15am, 12:30pm, 12:45pm, 5:30pm and 6pm (£2.50; booking tel. 633 0880).

Barbican Theatre: Tel. 628 2295 for information; tel. 638 8891 for reservations. Tube: Moorgate or Barbican. London home of the Royal Shakespeare Company. Tickets £5-15; standby seats available from 90 min. before curtain at £10, £5 for students and seniors. Fascinating futuristic building; patrons enter their rows in the large auditorium through a side door (there are no aisles), and the forward-leaning balconies guarantee that no one sits farther than 65 ft. from center stage. Some of the funkiest productions take place in the smaller space, **The Pit** (matinees £10, evenings £12, senior citizen matinees £8, student standbys £5 from ½ hr. before performance). Try to leave time after the show to look around the complex, which some observers berate as a glorified airport lounge and others laud for its innovative use of space. Box office on Level 7 of the Centre open daily 9am-8pm.

Open Air Theatre: Regent's Park (tel. 486 2431 or 486 1933 for credit card bookings). Tube: Baker St. Mostly Shakespeare; you have to sit close to catch every word. Bring a blanket and a bottle of wine. Open in summer only; tickets £6-13.50, student tickets 1 hr. before performance (£5). Call to check on availability.

West End Theatres

Adelphi Theatre, The Strand, WC2 (tel. 836 7611). Tube: Charing Cross.

Albery Theatre, St. Martin's Lane, WC2 (tel. 867 1115). Tube: Leicester Sq.

Aldwych Theatre, Aldwych, WC2 (tel. 836 6404). Tube: Covent Garden.

Ambassadors Theatre, West St., WC2 (tel. 836 2132). Tube: Leicester Sq.

Apollo Shaftesbury Theatre, Shaftesbury Ave., W1 (tel. 437 2663). Tube: Piccadilly Circus.

Apollo Victoria Theatre, Wilton Rd., SW1 (tel. 828 8665). Tube: Victoria.

Cambridge Theatre, Earlham St., WC2 (tel. 379 5299). Tube: Covent Garden.

Comedy Theatre, Panton St., SW1 (tel. 867 1045). Tube: Piccadilly Circus.

Criterion Theatre, Piccadilly Circus, W1 (tel. 930 3216). Tube: Piccadilly Circus.

Donmar Warehouse, 41 Earlham St., WC2 (tel. 836 3028). Tube: Covent Garden.

Drury Lane Theatre Royal, Catherine St., WC2 (tel. 836 8108). Tube: Covent Garden.

Duchess Theatre, Catherine St., WC2 (tel. 836 8243). Tube: Covent Garden.

Duke of York's Theatre, St. Martin's Lane, WC2 (tel. 836 5122). Tube: Leicester Sq.

Fortune Theatre, Russell St., WC2 (tel. 836 2238). Tube: Covent Garden.

Garrick Theatre, Charing Cross Rd., WC2 (tel. 379 6107). Tube: Leicester Sq.

Globe Theatre, Shaftesbury Ave., W1 (tel. 437 3667). Tube: Piccadilly Circus.

Haymarket, Theatre Royal, Haymarket, SW1 (tel. 930 8800). Tube: Piccadilly Circus.

Her Majesty's Theatre, Haymarket, SW1 (tel. 494 5001). Tube: Piccadilly Circus.

London Palladium Theatre, Argyll St., W1 (tel. 437 7373). Tube: Oxford Circus.

Lyric Theatre, Shaftesbury Ave., W1 (tel. 437 3686). Tube: Piccadilly Circus.

Mermaid Theatre, Puddle Dock, Blackfriars, EC4 (tel. 410 0000). Tube: Blackfriars.

New London Theatre, Drury Lane, WC2 (tel. 405 0072). Tube: Covent Garden.

Palace Theatre, Shaftesbury Ave., W1 (tel. 434 0909). Tube: Leicester Sq.

Phoenix Theatre, Charing Cross Rd., WC2 (tel. 867 1044). Tube: Tottenham Court Rd.

Piccadilly Theatre, Denman St., W1 (tel. 867 1118). Tube: Piccadilly Circus.

Players Theatre, The Arches, Villiers St., WC2 (tel. 839 1134). Tube: Charing Cross.

Playhouse Theatre, Northumberland Ave., WC2 (tel. 839 4401). Tube: Embankment.

Prince Edward Theatre, Old Compton St., W1 (tel. 437 6877). Tube: Leicester Sq.

Prince of Wales Theatre, Coventry St., W1 (tel. 839 5972). Tube: Piccadilly Circus.

Queen's Theatre, Shaftesbury Ave., W1 (tel. 494 5040). Tube: Piccadilly Circus.

Royal Court Theatre, Sloane Sq., SW1 (tel. 730 1745). Tube: Sloane Sq.

Sadler's Wells Theatre, Roseberry Ave., EC1 (tel. 278 8916). Tube: Angel.

St. Martin's Theatre, West St., WC2 (tel. 836 1443). Tube: Leicester Sq.

Savoy Theatre, The Strand, WC2 (tel. 836 8888). Tube: Charing Cross.

Shaftesbury Theatre, Shaftesbury Ave., WC2 (tel. 379 5399). Tube: Tottenham Court Rd.

Strand Theatre, Aldwych, WC2 (tel. 836 2660). Tube: Covent Garden.

The Old Vic, Waterloo Rd., SE1 (tel. 928 7616). Tube: Waterloo.

Vaudeville Theatre, The Strand, WC2 (tel. 836 9987). Tube: Charing Cross.

Victoria Palace Theatre, Victoria St., SW1 (tel. 834 1317). Tube: Victoria.

Wyndham's Theatre, Charing Cross Rd., WC2 (tel. 867 1116). Tube: Leicester Sq.

Fringe

London's fringe, born in the late 1960s, mixes the intimate with the avante-garde. The renaissance of experimental drama abides in London's **fringe theatres,** presenting low-priced, high-quality drama. Check the fringe listings in *Time Out* or *City Limits,* and phone the theatre in advance for details. Listed below are a few of the more prominent theatres, some of which require a nominal membership fee. Most tickets run £3.50-10; all have student discounts. Some may require that you buy membership 48 hours in advance. One of the newest theatre companies, **Arts Threshold,** won first place in the fringe competition at the Edinburgh theatre festival, and has since toured Poland, Romania, Hong Kong, and Singapore. (Call (081) 994 4681 for information on their current London shows; tickets £4-5.)

Almeida Theatre, 1A-1B Almeida St., N1 (tel. 359 4404). Tube: Angel or Highbury and Islington. Doubles as an avant-garde music showcase. The same managers run the excellent wine bar next door.

Battersea Arts Centre, Old Town Hall, Lavender HIll, SW11 (tel. 223 2223). BR: Battersea Park or Clapham Junction. Main and studio stages with mainstream and experimental works, plus improv in the Arts Café.

Bloomsbury Theatre, Gordon St., WC1 (tel. 387 9629). Tube: Euston Sq. Classics and new works in the heart of literary land.

Bush Theatre, Bush Hotel, Shepherd's Bush Green, W12 (tel. (081) 743 3388). Tube: Goldhawk Rd. Above a busy Irish pub. Plays usually Mon.-Sat. at 8pm.

Drill Hall Arts Centre, 16 Chenies St., WC1 (tel. 637 8270). Tube: Goodge St. Politically active productions, including many adaptations from other media.

Hampstead Theatre, Avenue Rd., Swiss Cottage Centre, NW3 (tel. 722 9301). Tube: Swiss Cottage. One of London's oldest small theatres: many notable alumni/ae. Shows begin at 8pm.

Holland Park Theatre, Holland Park, W14 (tel. 602 7856). Tube: Holland Park. Mainstream shows share the open-air stage with opera and ballet in the summer.

Institute of Contemporary Arts (ICA) Theatre, Nash House, The Mall, W1 (tel. 930 3647). Tube: Charing Cross. One of the least conventional: some plays without dialogue, some based on political themes or dreams.

King's Head, 115 Upper St., N1 (tel. 226 1916). Tube: Highbury and Islington or Angel. The slightly ramshackle atmosphere of this pub theatre is well-known among dedicated London theatre-goers.

Lyric Hammersmith, King St., W6 (tel. (081) 741 2311 or (081) 741 8701.) Tube: Hammersmith. High-quality repertory in the Main House, more far-out doings in the Studio.

New End Theatre, 27 New End, NW3 (tel. 794 0022). Tube: Hampstead. Reputable new works presented by various local companies.

Shakespeare Globe Site, Bankside, SE1 (tel. 620 0202). Tube: London Bridge. Entrance on Emerson St. Shakespeare plays, often with members of Britain's most prestigious companies, are presented with proceeds towards completely rebuilding Shakespeare's Globe.

Soho Poly, 16 Riding House St., W1 (tel. 636 9050). Tube: Oxford Circus. Reputation for bizarre yet realistic drama. Fosters many young and aspiring writers.

Theatre Royal Stratford East, Gerry Raffles Sq., E15 (tel. (081) 534 0310). Tube: Stratford. Acclaimed and popular new drama attracts audiences from all over London.

Theatre Upstairs, Royal Court, SW1 (tel. 730 2554). Tube: Sloane Sq. Highly experimental theatre barely surviving the late 80s but home to consistently good plays and performances.

Tricycle Theatre, 269 Kilburn High Rd., NW6 (tel. 328 1000). Tube: Kilburn. A favorite among locals—some good avant-garde performances. Occasionally dance or music on Sun. Call for ticket prices.

Young Vic, 66 The Cut, SE1 (tel. 928 6363). Tube: Waterloo. Besides giving new talent a chance at the classics, they sponsor a community-oriented summer festival—everything from masked Balinese dancers to school kids doing Chekhov.

Lunchtime theatre productions are generally less serious than evening performances, but at £1.50-3 they're a great way to start the afternoon. (Most productions start around 1:15pm.) The **Kings Head** (see above) is probably the most successful theatre in this group. For courtyard performances of Shakespeare in June and July, check **The George Inn,** 77 Borough High St. (tel. 609 1198; Tube: London Bridge). **St. Paul's Church,** at the central marketplace in Covent Garden, often has lunchtime theatre on its steps. In the summer, call **Alternative Arts** for information on their street theatre around the city; recent shows include a performance of *War and Peace* entirely inside a motorcycle sidecar. If you can scrape together a group of 12-17 on a weekday evening, you can try London's largest theatre—the Underground. Follow a **Tube Theatre** comic posing as a bumbling commuter onto the trains and watch the real-life reactions. (Tel. 586 6828; tickets £11 per person.)

A world of fringe comes to London every two years (next in 1993) in the **London International Festival of Theatre (LIFT).** For four weeks in June and July, theatres all over the city host the best mainstream and avant-garde productions from all over the world, from Shakespeare in Romanian to speechless performance works (information tel. 379 0653).

Film

Hollywood blockbusters can be seen at the many multi-screen, chain cinemas throughout the West End and Central London. The degenerate heart of the celluloid monster and the place to see 100-foot images of Stallone and Schwarzenegger battling for the audiences is Leicester Square. The most recent hits premiere here a day before hitting the chains around the city: they are expensive, however. West End screens for first-run hits include the Odeon West End, Leicester Sq. (tel. 930 5252; Tube: Leicester Sq.), the Warner West End (tel. 439 0791; Tube: Leicester Sq.), the Cannon Haymarket (tel. 839 1527; Tube: Piccadilly Circus), and the Cannon Oxford St. (tel. 636 0310; Tube: Tottenham Court Rd.). All have recorded messages detailing times and prices.

Other cinemas around London tend to have one screen only, and you may find youself inside a converted theatre, complete with gilt boxes for the audience. The film on the Nepalese fashion industry you have always wanted to see will probably be on soon: thousands of films pass through the capital every year, old and new. Newspapers have listings, while *Time Out* and *City Limits* include unbeatable guides both to expensive, commercial films and to the vast range of cheaper, more varied alternatives— including late-night films, free films, "serious" films, and repertory cinema clubs. Cinema clubs charge a small membership fee (usually 30p-£1.50), which entitles cardholders and one guest to reduced admission; some cards can be used at more than one theatre. For evening performances it's wise to buy your ticket early, or book in advance, especially on weekends. Most London moviehouses charge £5-6, but many charge only £3 all day Monday and for matinees Tuesday through Friday.

Repertory theatres include:

National Film Theatre, part of the South Bank Arts Complex, SE1 (tel. 928 3232). Tube: Waterloo or Embankment. Open to members only; yearly membership £10.25, £7.50 for students (of British schools only). Monthly membership £4. Daily 40p. Encyclopedic schedule (up to 6 films daily) with first runs, topical and directors' series, and special events. Hosts the London Film Festival in November. Best restaurant on the South Bank, too. Tickets £4.95, students £3.50.

London Film-maker's Co-op Cinema, 42 Gloucester Ave., NW1 (tel. 586 8516). Tube: Camden Town or Chalk Farm. Devoted to avant-garde and British films. Some double bills. Membership £3.50 per year, 30p per day; tickets £3, students £2.20.

The Institute of Contemporary Art (ICA) Cinémathique, Nash House, The Mall, W1 (tel. 930 3647). Tube: Piccadilly or Charing Cross. First-run films and esoteric *cinématique* offerings at £3. Day membership £1.50.

Scala Cinema Club, 275-277 Pentonville Rd., N1 (tel. 278 8052). Tube: King's Cross/St. Pancras. Great European double features, but in a sleazy neighborhood. Membership 50p per year; tickets £4, students £2.50 before 4:30pm.

Renoir, Brunswick Centre, Brunswick Sq., WC1 (tel. 837 8402). Tube: Russell Sq. British bohemian and popular foreign-language films (subtitled). Tickets £5, students £2.30 for first showing.

Phoenix, 52 High Rd., N2 (tel. (081) 883-2233). Tube: East Finchley. Double bills mix and match European, American, and Asian mainstream hits and classics. Cozy auditorium. Children's cinema club on Sat. mornings. Tickets £4, students £2.80 (except on weekends), children and seniors £1.70.

Minema, 45 Knightsbridge, W1 (tel. 235 4225). Tube: Hyde Park Corner. Small screen behind a tiny door, showing reborn art classics and popular foreign films. Tickets £6.25, students £3.50.

Electric Cinema, 191 Portobello Rd., W11 (tel. 792 2020). Tube: Ladbroke Grove or Notting Hill Gate. Great classics in a fantastic theatre. Tickets £4.50, students £3 before 4:30.

Screen on Baker St., 96 Baker St., NW1 (tel. 935 2772). Tube: Baker St. Mainstream if slightly strange European films, tickets £4.75.

Screen on the Green, Islington Green, N1 (tel. 226 3520). Tube: Angel. Revived and topical foreign classics. Trendy north London clientele. Tickets £4.75, £3 on Mondays.

Première, Swiss Centre, Leicester Sq. (tel. 439 4470). Tube: Leicester Sq. or Piccadilly Circus. New French films with subtitles for the needy. Hidden around the left-hand side of the centre. Tickets £5.80.

Gate Cinema, Notting Hill Gate, W11 (tel. 727 4043). Tube: Notting Hill Gate. Recent foreign language and art films. Tickets £5.50, students £3 before 6pm.

Lumière, St. Martin's Lane, WC2 (tel. 836 0691). Tube: Leicester Sq. Slightly offbeat Spanish and French films. Tickets £6.

Ritzy Cinema Club, Brixton Rd., SW2 (tel. 737 2121). Tube: Brixton. Good all-night triple features. Bring beer, sandwiches and a toothbrush. Membership 50p; tickets £4, students with ID £2.80, children £1.70.

Everyman Cinema, Hollybush Vale, Hampstead, NW3 (tel. 435 1525). Tube: Hampstead. Double and triple bills based on either a theme or an obscure celluloid figure. Special seasonal runs; membership 60p per year. Tickets £4.20, students £3.20 Mon.-Sat. before 4:30pm. Children £2.20.

Riverside Studios, Crisp Rd., W6 (tel. (081) 748 3354). Tube: Hammersmith. A bold mix of British prestige work, hard-hitting documentaries, and Fellini. Housed in a remodeled film studio. Tickets £3.60, students £2.50.

Goethe Institute, 50 Princes Gate, Exhibition Rd., SW7 (tel. 581 3344). Tube: South Kensington. Old German classics (generally without subtitles) and a sprinkling of U.S. favorites. Tickets £1.50.

French Institute, 17 Queensbury Pl., SW7 (tel. 589 6211). Tube: South Kensington. Excellent series of French masterpieces, usually subtitled. Tickets £3.50, students £2.50.

Music

Everyone from punk-rocker to opera-head can exploit the richness of the London music scene. Unparalleled classical resources include five world-class orchestras, two opera houses, two huge arts centers, and countless concert halls. The rock scene, home of the London Underground of the late 60s, birthplace of the Sex Pistols and punk in the 70s, and lately blessed with Billy Bragg and Soul II Soul, has taken its most recent step ahead (and to the side of) the world with a strange lurching dance from Camden Town.

Summer is the best time for festivals and outdoor concerts, but the entire year offers enough music to satisfy and deafen you. Check the listings in *Time Out* or *City Limits.* Keep your eyes open for special festivals or gigs posted on most of the city's surfaces, and for discounts posted on student union bulletin boards.

Classical

London's five world-class orchestras make the city unique even among musical meccas. Yet they provide only a fraction of the notes that fill London's major music centres, and those are only a fraction of the concert venues of the city.

London has been the professional home of some of the greatest conductors of the century—Sir Thomas Beecham, Otto Klemperer, and Andre Previn, as well as fertile ground for Britain's greatest composers (who are well represented on London playlists). The venerable **London Symphony Orchestra,** led by Michael Tilson Thomas, inhabits **Barbican Hall** in the **Barbican Centre.** (Tube: Moorgate or Barbican; tel. 638 4141 for information. Box office open daily 9am-8pm, tel. 638 8891. Tickets £5-25; student standbys, when available, sold shortly before the performance at reduced prices.)

Klaus Tennstedt's **London Philharmonic** and Giuseppe Sinopoli's **Philharmonia Orchestra** play in the vast **Royal Festival Hall** in the grim labyrinth of the **South Bank Centre.** (Tube: Waterloo, or Embankment and walk across Hungerford Bridge; information tel. 928 3002, box office tel. 928 8800; open daily 10am-9pm. Tickets £3-25; student standbys, when available, sold 2 hr. before performance at lowest ticket price.) Vladimir Ashkenazy's **Royal Philharmonic Orchestra** performs at both the Barbican and the South Bank, and the **BBC Symphony Orchestra** pops up around town as well. These two main venues, as well as the South Bank's smaller halls, the **Queen Elizabeth** and the **Purcell Room** (both slated for demolition and replacement), play host to a superb line-up of other groups, including the Academy of St. Martin-in-the-Fields, the London Festival Orchestra, the London Chamber Orchestra, the London Soloists Chamber Orchestra, the London Classical Players, and the London Mozart Players, in addition to diverse national and international orchestras. Although the regular season ends in mid-July, a series of festivals on the South Bank in July and August take up the slack admirably, offering traditional orchestral music along with more exotic tidbits (tickets £3-20).

Exuberant and skilled, the **Proms (BBC Henry Wood Promenade Concerts)** never fail to enliven London summers. For eight weeks from July to September, an impressive roster of musicians performs in the **Royal Albert Hall** with routinely outstanding programs of established works and annually commissioned new ones. A special atmosphere of camaraderie and craziness develops in the long lines for standing room outside Albert Hall. (Gallery £2, arena £2.50—join the queue around 6pm; tickets £4-10.) The last night of the Proms traditionally steals the show, with the massed singing of *Land of Hope and Glory,* and closing with a rousing chorus of *Jerusalem.* Don't expect to show up at the last minute and get in; a lottery of thousands determines who will be admitted and allowed to dress up in Union Jack T-shirts and "air-conduct" along with the music. (Box office tel. 823 9998; open daily 9am-9pm; or try Ticketmaster at 379 4444. Tube: South Kensington.)

Small, elegant, and Victorian, **Wigmore Hall,** 36 Wigmore St. (tel. 935 2141; Tube: Bond St. or Oxford Circus), sponsors a summer festival in addition to its master concerts and chamber music series. (Tickets £5-15; 1 hr. standbys at lowest price.) In summer, Sunday morning coffee concerts greet enthusiasts at 11:30am. (Tickets £5, coffee free.) Many young artists make their debut at Wigmore, which lines its fine bar with photographs of modern European composers and performers. **St. John's Smith Square,** a converted church just off Millbank, presents a similar schedule, weighted toward chamber groups and soloists. (Tickets £3-15, usually reduced for students and seniors. Box office tel. 222 1061. Tube: Westminster.)

During the first three weeks or so of July, the **Festival of the City of London** explodes in activities around the city's grandest monuments: music in the livery halls, singing in churches, plays at various venues, grand opera, art exhibitions, and a trail of dance winding among the monuments. (Contact the Box Office, St. Paul's Churchyard, London EC4; tel. 248 4260; open Mon.-Fri. 9:30am-5:30pm. Many events free, other tickets £2-25. Information from early May at box office. Tube: St. Paul's.)

In June, the early moderns swoop down on the city in a German airliner, in the **Lufthansa Baroque Festival.** The main site is **St. James's Church, Piccadilly** (tel. 734 4511, tickets £6-12). Also in June, the **Greenwich Festival** stages performances all over the Greenwich area; admission ranges from nothing to £10 (tel. (081) 854 0055).

One of the Greenwich Festival sites, **Blackheath Concert Halls,** attracts top performers east year-round (23 Lee Road, Blackheath, SE3. Tube: Blackheath. Tel. 318 9758. Tickets £3.50-20; reductions for students and seniors.)

Medieval and Renaissance music still commands a following in England; many, many London churches—especially in the city—offer performances of both liturgical and concert music, often at lunchtime. Premier among them are St. James's Piccadilly (tel. 734 4511; Tube: Piccadilly Circus); St. Bartholomew-the-Great, Smithfield (tel. 601 5171; Tube: Barbican); St. Bride's, Fleet St. (tel. 353 1301; Tube: Blackfriars); and St. Martin-in-the-Fields, Trafalgar Sq. (tel. 930 0089; Tube: Charing Cross). Concerts are usually free, but a donation is customary. Check daily papers for full listings of church concerts. Also watch for the **Academy of Ancient Music,** the **Early Music Consort of London,** and the **Praetorius Ensemble.**

Artists from the **Royal College of Music** (Prince Consort Rd., SW7; tel. 589 3643) and the **Royal Academy of Music** (Marylebone Rd., NW1; tel. 935 5461) play at their home institutions and at the main city halls. Concerts at these schools are often free—call for details. Check with the **University of London Union** (1 Malet St., WC1; tel. 580 9551) for on-campus music there (Tube: Goodge St.).

Outdoor concerts in summer are phenomenally popular and relatively cheap. The **Kenwood Lakeside Concerts** at Kenwood, on Hampstead Heath present top-class orchestras, often graced by firework displays. (Tube: Golders Green or Archway, then bus #210; for information tel. 973 3427, for booking tel. Ticketmaster, 379 4444—no booking fee.) On Saturdays at 7:30pm, music floats to the audience from a performance shell across the lake. (Reserved deck chairs £7-9, students and seniors £3.50-4.50. Grass admission £4.50-6, students and seniors £3.50-4.) If the "outdoor" part is more important to you than the "concert," you can watch from afar for free. The grounds of stately **Marble Hill House** also host concerts, on summer Sundays at 7:30pm. (Tube/BR: Richmond, then bus #33, 90, 290, H22 or R70; information tel. 973 3427, booking tel. Ticketmaster, 379 4444—no fee.) Bring a blanket and picnic. Members of the audience eat anything from cheese sandwiches in Tupperware to salmon on alabaster.

Opera and Ballet

London's major opera companies have limited runs in summer. The **Royal Opera**, Box St. (tel. 240 1911 or 240 1066; Tube: Covent Garden), performs in the grand old Royal Opera House at Covent Garden. (Tickets run as high as £90; standbys—"amphitheatre" seats in back with a decent view—£7.50-12 from 10am on the day of the performance; when available, student standbys about £10 1 hr. before performance; tel. 836 6903 for recorded standby information; upper slips—on uncomfortable benches with a view of about half the stage—from £1.50.) Covent Garden has taken up the practice of "surtitling" all non-English works in the repertoire, which means subtitling, with a twist. (Box office 48 Floral St.; open Mon.-Sat. 10am-8pm.) For all its populism, the **English National Opera** commands no less respect. The repertoire leans more towards the contemporary, and all works are sung in English. Seats in the Opera's London Coliseum on St. Martin's Lane (tel. 836 6161; Tube: Charing Cross or Leicester Sq.) range from £4 to £40; standby tickets £10-15 available from 10am on day of performance. (Box office open Mon.-Sat. 10am-8pm.)

The ENO was founded as the Sadler's Wells Opera, and the current **Sadler's Wells Theatre** (Rosebery Ave, EC1; tel. 278 8916) presents a spring series called **"Opera 80."** (Tickets £5-20; 40 standby stalls seats available at £5 from 10:30am on performance day. Tube: Angel.) The **Holland Park Theatre** (Holland Park; Tube: Holland Park) presents open-air productions from a number of companies in June and July, in both English and the original languages. (Box office in the Visitor Centre, tel. 602 7856. Tickets £7.50-12, concessions £4-6.) On the cutting edge, the Royal Opera's **Garden Venture** stages new chamber opera at Riverside Studios in Hammersmith, from the end of May. (Crisp Rd., W6; tel. (081) 748 3354. Tickets £10, concessions £5.50. Tube: Hammersmith.)

The **Royal Ballet** performs at the Royal Opera House in Covent Garden. The box office stands around the corner at 48 Floral St. (tel. 240 1066 or 240 1911; open Mon.-Sat. 10am-8pm). Tickets cost £1.50-50. At 10am on the day of the show, 65 amphitheatre seats go on sale (strictly 1 per person; lines often long; £6-8.50). When available, standbys for students and senior citizens are sold from one hour before curtain; call 836 6903 for information. In the summer, when the English National Opera is off, the **English National Ballet** and visiting ballet companies perform in the London Coliseum, St. Martin's Lane, WC2 (tel. 836 3161; Tube: Leicester Sq.; tickets £5-55. Student and senior citizen discounts available by advance booking only). Visiting companies also grace the stage of the **Royal Festival Hall** in the South Bank Centre year-round (tel. 928 3002).

Sadler's Wells Theatre serves as the principal stage for visiting troupes ranging from Twyla Tharp to national folk companies. Tickets cost £4-20; student discounts are available. In summer, you can see dance outdoors at the Holland Park Theatre (tel. 602 7856; tickets £7.50-8.50, concessions £4-4.50).

For two weeks in July, the **Dance Days** festival puts on a diverse and energetic show of contemporary and folk dance; call the Battersea Arts Centre (tel. 223 2223) for details. London borough festivals also sponsor dance programs—most are widely publicized on tube station posters and at tourist offices. Fringe and experimental work is the focus of **The Place,** 17 Duke's Rd., WC1 (tel. 387 0031; Tube: Euston), and the **Institute of Contemporary Art,** Carlton House Terrace, SW1 (tel. 930 3647; Tube: Charing Cross; see Museums above). Some of the best fringe works make their way to the **Royal Court Theatre** in Sloane Square (tel. 730 1745. Tickets £5-12, standby £4. Tube: Sloane Sq.).

Jazz, Rock, Pop, Reggae, Folk, and Indie

London generates and attracts almost every type of performer under the sun: while the charts may be filled with the kind of wax performance idolized in the Rock Circus, the clubs and pubs of the capital offer a wider, stranger, and more satisfying variety of musical entertainment. Often, thrash metallists play the same venue as Gaelic folk singers: check weekly listings carefully to find the right stuff.

Time Out, What's On, and *City Limits* have extensive listings and information about bookings and festivals. You can make credit card reservations for major events by calling **Ticketmaster** (tel. 379 4444).

Rock and Pop

Major venues for rock concerts include the indoor **Wembley Arena** and the huge outdoor **Wembley Stadium** (Tube: Wembley Park or Wembley Central; tel. 902 1234 for both), the **Marquee,** and the **Town and Country Club** (see below). In the summer, many outdoor arenas such as **Finsbury Park** become the venues for major concerts and festivals. (For more rock listings, see Dance Clubs.)

Town and Country Club, 9-17 Highgate Rd., NW5 (tel. 284 0303). Tube: Kentish Town. Hot, hard-rocking bands, wild dancers, cheap drinks, and great sound make this club ideal for late-night weekend blow-outs. Big-name acts use this stage to tune up before nationwide tours. Admission £7-10. Open Mon.-Thurs. 8-11pm, Fri.-Sat. 7:30pm-2am.

The Marquee, 105 Charing Cross Rd., WC2 (tel. 437 6603). Tube: Leicester Sq. A loud, busy showcase for the latest bands: hundreds churn through each month. Admission £5-6:50. Open daily 7pm-midnight.

Powerhaus, 1 Liverpool Rd., N16 (tel. 837 3218). Tube: Angel. Quirky mix of live rock and folk music in a converted pub. Admission £4-6. Open Mon.-Sat. 8pm-3am, Sun. 7-10:30pm.

Borderline, Orange Yard, Manette St., WC2 (tel. 497 2261). Tube: Leicester Sq. or Tottenham Court Rd. British record companies use this basement club to test new rock and pop talent. Admission £5. Open Mon.-Sat. 8pm-3am.

Academy Brixton, 211 Stockwell Rd., SW9 (tel. 326 1022). Tube: Brixton. Time-honored and rowdy venue for the harder end of popular rock. Admission (advance tickets) £9-12. Open daily 7-11pm.

Rock Garden, the Piazza, Covent Garden, WC2 (tel. 240 3901). Tube: Covent Garden. Great new bands play nightly—send them your demo tape. Admission £8. Open Mon.-Sat. 7:30pm-3am, Sun. 7:30pm-midnight.

Odeon Hammersmith, Queen Caroline St., W6 (tel. (081) 748 4081). Tube: Hammersmith. Large theatre featuring starry rock and pop acts. Admission (advance tickets) £9-15.

Le Palais, 242 Shepherds Bush Rd., W6 (tel. (081) 748 2812). Tube: Hammersmith. Large venue for rock and pop, with dance floor. Admission (advance tickets) £6-12.

New Pegasus, 109 Green Lanes, N16 (tel. 226 5930). Tube: Manor House. A colorful, crowded pub with a provocative nightly mix of indie, ska, and goth. Membership £1, admission £1.50-3. Music nightly 8:30-midnight.

Mean Fiddler, 24-28 Harlesden High St., NW10 (tel. (081) 961 5490). Tube: Willesden Junction. Formerly renowned as London's premiere spot for country western and folk, the Fiddler now specializes in indie rock. Cavernous club with high balconies and good bars. Admission £4-6. Open Mon.-Sat. 8pm-2am, Sun. 8pm-1am. Music nightly 10pm-closing.

Half Moon, 93 Lower Richmond Rd. (tel. 788 2387). Tube: Putney Bridge. Rocking pub with a mix of rock, jazz, and folk. Admission £3-5. Open daily from 8:30pm.

T&C2, 20-22 Highbury Corner, N1 (tel. 700 5716). Tube: Highbury & Islington. Rawish acts in a happy atmosphere. Open daily from 7:30pm.

Fairfield Halls, Croydon, Surrey (tel. (081) 688 9291). Take BR to East Croydon. Large venue for festivals and concerts. Admission £5-11.

Jazz

Jazz clubs tend to open and close down very quickly in London, apart from a few honored favorites. In the summer, hundreds of jazz festivals appear in the city and its outskirts, including the heavy-hitting Capital Radio Jazz Parade (July; tel. 379 1066), the North London Festival (June-July; tel. (081) 449 0048), and the City of London Festival (July; tel. 248 4260).

Ronnie Scott's, Frith St., W1 (tel. 439 0747). Tube: Leicester Sq. or Piccadilly Circus. The most famous jazz club in London. Expensive food and great music. Rock/soul/world music on Sun. Admission £12, students £6. Book ahead or arrive by 9:30pm. Open Mon.-Sat. 8:30am-3am.

Bass Clef, 35 Coronet St., N1 (tel. 729 2476), off Hoxton Sq. Tube: Old St. Hosts British jazz and Latin performers, as does its sister venue, Tenor Clef. Call for a reservation or arrive early. Admission £4.50-7. Open daily 7:30pm-midnight.

University College School, Frognal, NW3 (tel. 435 2215). Tube: Hampstead. Jazz in the most unlikely of venues—the school theatre of UCS. In between instructing students not to begin sentences with "also," English teacher David Lund assembles a quite exceptional line up of performers. (Also, prepositions are something he will not put up with.) The 1991 program included Art Farmer, Ronnie Scott, and Elaine Delmar. Concerts Thurs. during term time. Tickets £4, £5 at the door. All proceeds to charity.

Jazz Café, 5 Parkway, NW1 (tel. 284 4358). Tube: Camden Town. Top new venue in a converted bank. Classic and experimental jazz; groups sometimes last all week. Admission £7-10. Open daily from 8:30pm.

Jazz at Pizza Express, 10 Dean St., W1 (tel. 439 8722). Tube: Tottenham Court Rd. Packed, dark club hiding behind a pizzeria. Fantastic groups, and occasional greats; get there early. Admission £6-8. Music 9:30pm-1am.

Pizza on the Park, 11 Knightsbridge, SW1 (tel. 235 5273). Tube: Knightsbridge. Another smoky basement hideaway beneath another restaurant in the chain. Often sold out. Admission £5-8. Music 9:15pm-1am.

100 Club, 100 Oxford St., W1 (tel. 636 0933). Tube: Tottenham Court Rd. Strange mix of traditional modern jazz, swing, and rockabilly. Admission £5-8. Open Mon.-Sat. 7:30pm-1am, Sun. 7:45-11:30pm.

Palookaville, 13a St. James St., WC2 (tel. 240 5857). Tube: Covent Garden. Relaxed restaurant and wine bar with cool live jazz ensembles and an intimate dance floor. Admission free. Music nightly 8:45pm-1:30am.

Bull's Head, Barnes Bridge, SW13 (tel. (081) 876 5241). Tube: Hammersmith, then bus #9. A waterside pub renowned for good food and fine, traditional jazz. Admission £3-6. Open Mon.-Sat. 11am-11pm, Sun. noon-3pm and 7-10:30pm. Music starts at 8:30pm, and at lunchtime on Sun.

Africa Centre, 38 King St., WC2 (tel. 836 1973). Tube: Covent Garden. The centre of the world. Music and dance from Africa, including jazz and world music. Admission £7. Open Mon.-Sat. 8:30pm-3am.

Folk

To a large extent, folk music in London means Irish music. But there is some variation on the Celtic theme: folk rock, English ballads, and even English country-and-western. Many pub events are ephemeral: check weekly listings. Some of the best are free, but welcome donations or consumption.

Archway Tavern, Archway Roundabout, N19 (tel. 272 2840). Tube: Archway. Sponsors a mix of groups with a Gaelic accent (but rock only Mon.-Tues.). Admission from £2.50. Open Mon.-Sat. from 9:30pm.

Bunjie's, 27 Litchfield St., WC2 (tel. 240 1796). Tube: Covent Garden. Packed, with lively, dancing audience. Admission £2-2.50. Open Mon.-Sat. from 8:30-11pm.

Sir George Robey, 240 Seven Sisters Rd., N4 (tel. 263 4581). Tube: Finsbury Park. Varied schedule with Celtic rock and country rock, as well as traditional English and Irish folk. Occasional all-day festivals. Admission £2-3. Open daily from 7:30pm.

Cecil Sharp House, 2 Regent's Park Rd. (tel. 485 2206). Tube: Camden Town. Traditional dancing as well as raucous folk. Admission £2-5. Music Sat. 7:30-11pm.

Dance Clubs

London happens to dance to anything. Clubs in the capital pound to Unbelievable 100% groovy Liverpool tunes, ecstatic Manchester rave, hometown soul and house, and imported U.S. rap and funk. Check out the 12" bins at record stores for the obscure Dub mixes that dominate the playlists. Fashion evolves and revolves: acid-hoods and sneakers are giving way to flares and platforms.

Many clubs host a variety of provocative one-nighters (theme parties, like "Leather and Old Spice Night") throughout the week. Call ahead and ask about the club's dress code, since your gold-sequined transparent catsuit may not be adequately appreciated. When you pay the cover, you are buying a one-night "membership" (subject to the club's approval). Remember that the Tube shuts down two or three hours before most clubs and that taxis can be hard to find in the wee hours of the morning. Arrange transportation in advance; otherwise you can try your luck with an unlicensed mini-cab or acquaint yourself with London Regional Transport's extensive network of night buses (for information call 222 1234). As always, check the listings in *Time Out, What's On,* and *City Limits.*

Subterania, 12 Acklam Rd., W10 (tel. 081 960 4590) Tube: Westbourne Park. This is where it's at—directly beneath the Westway flyover. Relaxed, multi-ethnic crowd comes to dance, not to pull, to wicked house-thump. Crucial on Fri. and Sat., from midnight onwards. Admission £6-7. Open daily 10pm-3am. Casual dress.

The Fridge, Town Hall Parade, Brixton Hill (tel. 326 5100). Tube: Brixton. A serious dance dive with a multi-ethnic crowd, abandoned home of Jazzie B from Soul II Soul. Dress for heat and come prepared to move to house funk. Dress code: wear anything. Telly psychedelia. Admission £5-7. Lively mixed-gay night on Tues. and some Thurs. Open Mon.-Thurs. 10pm-3am, Fri.-Sat. 10pm-4am.

Africa Centre, 38 King St., WC2 (tel. 836 1973). Tube: Covent Garden. On weekends, "Club Limpopo" features DJ Wala's African grooves and a live set. Admission £6-7. Open 9pm-3am.

Camden Palais, 1a Camden High St. NW1 (tel. 387 0428). Tube: Mornington Crescent on weekdays, or Camden Town on weekends. Enormously popular with tourists and Brits alike, especially on Wednesdays, when "Twist and Shout," and 50s-60s music predominates. Gothic night on Tuesdays. Get hold of discount tickets handed out around the tube station and High St. Admission variable: Wed. £4, Thurs. free for women. Fri and Sat. £6. Go early.

The Electric Ballroom, 184 Camden High St. (tel. 485 9006). Tube: Camden Town. Cheap and fun; catch Gothic tunes on Fri., or funk and hip hop on Sat. Admission £5.

Gossips, 69 Dean St., W1 (tel. 434 4480). Tube: Leicester Sq. or Tottenham Court Rd. A dark basement club renowned for hosting a wide range of great one-nighters. Anything goes here, from heavy metal to ska to psychedelia to reggae. Call ahead for details; music and crowd changes on a nightly basis. **Hard Club 92** (Wed.) claims to be the place for "Euros and trendy wierdos," while the notorious **Gaz's Rockin' Blues** (now in its 11th year) on Thurs. is highly recommended for its ska, blues, and soul. Open Mon.-Sat. 10pm-3:30am. Admission £4-6.

Crazy Larry's, 533 King's Rd., SW10 (tel. 376 5555). Tube: Fulham Broadway or Sloane Sq. A posh, civilized club with a fine restaurant and good sound. Popular feeding and breeding ground for Sloane Rangers and Mayfair trendies. Admission £5-7. Open Mon.-Wed. 9pm-1am, Fri.-Sat. 9pm-2:30am, Sun. 6pm-midnight.

Legends, 29 Old Burlington St., W1 (tel. 437 9933). Tube: Green Park or Piccadilly Circus. Smart, chic club. Hosts excellent one-nighters: Wed. is swingbeat night, Thurs. is student "Troubled House" night. Dress up. Admission £6-9. Open Mon.-Thurs. 10:30pm-3:30am, Fri.-Sat. 9:30pm-4am.

Samantha's, 2 New Burlington St. (tel. 734 6249). Tube: Piccadilly Circus or Oxford Circus. Crowded double dance floors. DJs mix hip-hop, house, and the latest combination thereof for a well-dressed group. Admission £5-7. Open Mon.-Sat. 9pm-3:30am.

The Tattershall Castle, Victoria Embankment, King St., SW1 (tel. 839 6548). Tube: Embankment. A high-charged dance mix of mainstream rock and pop blasted on a riverboat-*cum*-disco. Admission £2.50 Mon., £6 Fri.-Sat. Open Mon. 8:30pm-2am, Fri.-Sat. 9pm-3am.

Town and Country Club, 9-17 Highgate Rd. NW5 (tel. 284 0303). Tube: Kentish Town. Primarily a top rock spot, but also stages unpretentious dancing to Wendy May's Locomotion on Fri. at 11pm (60s and 70s soul and R&B). Popular with Dartmouth Park trendsetters. Admission £5.50.

T&C2, 20-22 Highbury Corner, N5 (tel. 700 5716). Tube: Highbury and Islington. Mixed, student-based crowd gets down to Motown and 70s R&B late, after the tables from the comedy show have been cleared away. Admission to comedy show and dance, £6-7 (doors open 7:30pm); dance £5-6.

Brain Club, 11 Wardour St., W1 (tel. 437 7301). Tube: Leicester Sq. Live music on Wed. Comes complete with stage sets to dance on. Admission £5. Open daily 10pm-3am.

Prohibition, 9 Hanover St., W1 (tel. 493 0689). Tube: Oxford Circus. Variety of rockish bands play to a jammed bar room. Friday can be dance fever night—watch out. Admission £2-5. Open daily 10pm-3am.

Limelight, 136 Shaftesbury Ave., WC2 (tel. 434 0572). Tube: Piccadilly Circus. Big, roomy club with all the trimmings. Latin rhythms on Wed. Gay night on Mon. Admission £7. Open daily 10pm-3am.

The Wag Club, 35 Wardour St. (tel. 437 5534). Tube: Piccadilly Circus. Hosts one-nighters so popular that you may have to spiff up to be admitted. Funkadelic night on Thurs. Admission £5-9 (bring student ID). Open Mon.-Thurs. 10:30pm-3:30am, Fri.-Sat. 10:30pm-6am.

Busby's, 157 Charing Cross Rd. (tel. 734 6963). Tube: Tottenham Court Rd. Has assorted one-nighters. Heavy metal "LA Rock" on Wed., gay nights Mon. and Sat. ("Bang"), and Thurs. ("Propaganda"). Admission £4. Open 10pm-3am.

Hippodrome, Charing Cross Rd. (tel. 437 4311). Tube: Leicester Sq. Infamously enormous, expensive, loud, and tourist-ridden. Admission £6-12 for the spectacle; leave your blue jeans and trainers behind. Witching-hour laser shows. Open Mon.-Sat. 9pm-3:30am.

Gay and Lesbian Nightlife

London's gay scene ranges from the flamboyant to the outrageous to the cruisy to the mainstream. The 24-hr. **Lesbian and Gay Switchboard** (tel. 837 7324) is an excellent source of information. Bars particularly popular among gay men are **Brief Encounter,** 42 St. Martin's Lane, WC2, and **Comptons of Soho,** 53 Old Compton St., W1; both are fairly touristy (Tube: Leicester Sq.). The wilder **London Apprentice,** 333 Old St. EC1 (Tube: Old St.) has a macho male crowd (leather nights Fri.-Sun.; £2.50 after 11pm). Women-only nights can be found at **Heds,** at HQ, Camden Lock, NW1, on Sundays from 9pm to 3am (Tube: Camden Town). Both *Time Out* and *City Limits* (the "Out" section) have a plethora of detail on bars, nightclubs, and special events.

Heaven, Villiers St., W2 (tel. 839 3852), underneath The Arches. Tube: Embankment. One of the coolest places to dance: gay/straight club with capacity of nearly 4000. Large dance floors, high-tech lighting, pool tables, and bars. Men only on Wed. ("Pyramid") and Sat. nights. Mixed/straight nights Fri. ("Garage"). Admission £4-6. Open Tues.-Wed. 10:30pm-3am, Fri.-Sat. 9:30pm-3am.

The City Apprentice, 126 York Way, N1 (tel. 278 8318). Tube: King's Cross. Adventurous, mainly male disco with amateur strippers on Mon., mud wrestling on Tues., and male strippers on Fri.

Black Cap, 171 Camden High St., NW1. Tube: Camden Town. Oldest gay bar in London, with a mixed male/female crowd and an olde worlde atmosphere. Admission £2-3 (Mon. free). Open Mon.-Sat. 3pm-2am, Sun. noon-3pm and 7pm-midnight.

Madame Jo-Jo, 8-10 Brewer St., W1 (tel. 734 2473). Tube: Piccadilly Circus. A fun, flamboyant cabaret club featuring raucous drag reviews. Small, crowded dance floor. Reserve tables well in advance. Admission £8-10. Open Mon.-Sat. 10pm-3am.

Club Copa, 180 Earl's Court Rd., SW5 (tel. 373 3407). Tube: Earl's Ct. Amiable and relaxed, this popular gay club is a good place to wind down after an evening out in Earl's Court. Men only. Admission £2.50-4.50. Open Mon.-Sat. 10:30pm-2am.

Comedy Clubs

Ten years after the "alternative" scene hit town, the London comedy circuit remains vibrant and original. These clubs tend to be informal, good for a great laugh or at least a fine night out. After seeing a few shows, though, you may find the alternatives wearing a little thin, and the gut-wrenching bouts of guffaws becoming less frequent. Comedy listings appear under "Cabaret" in *Time Out* and *City Limits.*

Comedy Store, 28a Leicester Sq., WC2 (tel. 839 6665). Tube: Leicester Sq. The most famous comedy venture in London, and birthplace of the alternative comedy revolution. The Comedy Store Players appear on Wed. and Sun., top guests on other nights. Shows at 8pm, plus midnight on Fri.-Sat. Arrive early. Admission £7.

Jongleurs, The Cornet, 49 Lavender Gardens, SW11 (tel. 924 2766). BR: Clapham Junction. Lively melange of mime, clowning, and humor; renowned for audience food-throwing. Shows Fri.-Sat. Admission £8, concessions £6.

Banana Cabaret, The Bedford, Bedford Hill, SW12 (tel. 081) 673 8904). Renowned stand-up and musical comedy in both the domed cabaret room downstairs and the cozy space upstairs. Admission £4, concessions £3.

Chuckle Club, Fri. at the Marquis of Cornwallis, 31 Marchmont St., WC1 (tel. 476 1672; Tube: Russell Sq.); Sat. at the Shakespeare's Head, Carnaby St., W1 (tel. 476 1672; Tube: Oxford Circus). Boisterous atmosphere makes for a great group night out. Compere is Eugene Cheese—what more can be said? Shows Fri.-Sat. at 8:30pm. Admission £4, concessions £3.

Comedy Café, 66 Rivington St., EC2 (tel. 739 5706). Tube: Old St. Open Spot nights on Wed.—less risky comedy and magic the rest of the week. Admission £2-4.

Red Rose Cabaret, Red Rose Club, 129 Seven Sisters Rd., N7. (tel. 281 3051). Tube: Finsbury Park. The cream of the London circuit, hosted by Ivor Dembina. Shows Fri.-Sat. at 9:30pm. Admission £4.75, concessions £3.50, occasional discounts with a copy of *Time Out.*

Screaming Blue Murder, Rose and Crown, 61 High St., Hampton Wick (tel. (081) 398 0298). BR: Hampton Wick. Breeding ground for new talent. Sweaty and friendly. Shows at 8:30pm. Admission £3.50, concessions £3.

Air Raid Shelter, The Hemingford Arms, 158 Hemingford Rd., N1 (tel. 607 2681). Tube: Caledonian Rd., N1. Wide variety of stand-ups and improv teams in an atmosphere more relaxed than frenzied. Membership £1, admission £4, £3 concessions.

Downstairs at the King's Head, 2 Crouch End Hill, N8 (tel. (081) 340 1028). Tube: Finsbury Park, then bus #W7. Brilliant, accessible Sun. night shows featuring class British acts. Tuesday night is Club Submarine, a hot comedy/dance music combo. Admission £4, concessions £3, plus 50p membership.

Coconuts Comedy Club, Larry's Bar, 20 Mercer St., W2 (tel. 836 0572). Tube: Covent Garden. Homesick Yanks can cheer up to the accents of American comics. Shows Wed., Thurs., Sat., and Sun. Admission £6, concessions £3.

T&C2, 20-22 Highbury Corner, N5 (tel. 700 5716). Tube: Highbury and Islington. Relaxed atmosphere, with dancing after the shows (see Dance Clubs). Fri.-Sat. nights, £7.

Offbeat Entertainment

> *London, that great sea, whose ebb and flow*
> *At once is deaf and loud, and on the shore*
> *Vomits its wrecks, and still howls on for more.*
> *—Percy Bysshe Shelley*

5am on a dirty morning. . .the smell of stale perfume. . .the howl of a stray dog . . .the distant sirens. . .the glare of the red street light. . .the shudder of the night-train. . .that's entertainment.

The College of Psychic Studies, 16 Queensberry Place, SW7 (tel. 589 3292). Tube: South Kensington. Eager for you to become their newest subject. Unlock your true self through graphoanalysis, harness universal wisdom and release life blocks (karmic or otherwise) with regression therapy, or achieve that eternally-sought-after harmony between body and spirit through aromatherapy. Open Mon.-Thurs. 10am-7:30pm, Fri. 10am-4:30pm, closed most of August.

London Skydiving Centre, Cranfield Airport, Cranfield, Bedfordshire, MK43 (tel. (0234) 751 866). Two-day static-line training courses with jump for £95, plus £17 per each additional dive. Open Tues.-Sun. 9am-dusk.

Porchester Baths, Queensway, W2 (tel. 798 3689). Tube: Bayswater. A Turkish bath with steam and dry heat rooms and a swimming pool. Built in 1929, the baths charge high rates (£11.35 for 3 hr.), but devoted fans keep taking the plunge. Open daily 7am-8pm. Men only Mon., Wed., and Sat.; women only Tues., Thurs., and Fri.; Sun. mixed (couples only).

Vidal Sassoon School of Hairdressing, 56 Davies Mews, W1 (tel. 629 4635). Tube: Bond St. Become your own offbeat entertainment. Cuts, perms, and color at the hand of a Sassoony. Cut and blow dry £6.50, with student ID £3. All-over tint £9.25. Call ahead for an appointment.

Tube Theatre, (tel. 586 6828). Follow a comedian acting as a bumbling commuter onto the Underground, and keep a poker face as you savor the hilarious situations. Group bookings (12-17) only. £11.

Conway Hall, Red Lion Sq., WC1 (tel. 242 8032). Tube: Holborn. Atheist lectures Sun. morning, chamber music Sun. evening.

Speaker's Corner, in the northeast corner of Hyde Park. Tube: Marble Arch. Crackpots, eccentrics, political activists, and more crackpots speak their minds and compete for the largest audience every Sun. 11am-dusk. (See Hyde Park under Sights.)

Crafts Council, 12 Waterloo Place, Lower Regent St., SW1 (tel. 930 4811). Tube: Piccadilly Circus. Amiable, hospitable. Exhibitions, advice, conversation, and more. Books and slides on crafts, too. Open Tues.-Sat. 10am-5pm, Sun. 2-5pm.

Design Council, 28 Haymarket, SW1 (tel. 839 8000). Tube: Piccadilly Circus. Free exhibitions and information on the best and brightest of British design of absolutely everything. Open Mon.-Sat. 10am-6pm, Sun. 1-6pm.

Victorian Society, 1 Priory Gdns., W4 (tel. (081) 994 1019). Tube: Turnham Green. Genial company, historical knowledge, lectures, and guided walks through London. Membership £15, but the sneaky can probably join a walk without paying. Open Mon.-Fri. 9am-5:30pm.

Daily Mail and *Evening Standard.* Northcliffe House, 2 Derry St., W8 (tel. 938 6000). Tube: High St. Kensington. See an issue of one of these aspiring tabloids in production. For information write to the Personnel Administrator, Hammondsworth Quays Ltd., Surrey Quays Rd., SE16 1PJ.

Radio and Television Shows. Become part of a live studio audience. Get free tickets for the endless variations on "Master Mind." Write to the **BBC Ticket Unit,** Broadcasting House, Portland Pl., W1; **Thames TV Ticket Unit,** 306 Euston Rd., NW1; or **London Weekend Television,** Kent House, Upper Ground, SE1.

City Farms. Designed to bring the sights and smells of country life to the asphalt dwellers, city farms happily are growing in number. Goats, ducks, rabbits, sheep, poultry, and sometimes cattle, horses, and donkeys bleat, quack, baa, moo, and whatever for you at **Kentish Town,** Grafton Rd., NW5 (tel. 482 2681; open daily 9:30am-5:30pm; Tube: Kentish Town);

Freight Liners, Sheringham Rd., N7 (tel. 609 0467; open Tues.-Sun. 11am-5pm; Tube: Highbury and Islington); **Hackney,** 1a Goldsmith's Row, E2 (tel. 729 6381; open Tues.-Sun. 10am-4:30pm; Tube: Shoreditch, then bus #6, 48, or 55); **Stepping Stones,** Stepney Way, E1 (tel. 790 8204; open Tues.-Sun. 9:30am-6pm; Tube: Whitechapel); and **Surrey Docks,** Rotherhithe St., SE16 (tel. 231 1010; open Tues.-Sun. 10am-5pm; Tube: Surrey Quays). All are free.

Literary Life

National Poetry Centre, 21 Earl's Court Sq., SW5 (tel. 373 7861). Tube: Earl's Ct. Vibrant center for information on poetry and the arts in London. Compelling poetry readings, often preceded by lavish cocktail parties open to the audience. Readings Sept.-July, usually at 7:30pm. Admission £3-4.50, students £2-3.50. "Poetry Round" is a forum for all to read or discuss their poetry, (Mondays at 8pm £2.50, students £1.50).

The Voice Box, Level 5, Red Side, Royal Festival Hall, SE1 (tel. 921 0906). Tube: Waterloo. Readings of international prose and poetry at an Orwellian address. £2.50, students £1.50.

Blue Nose Poetry, at the Market Tavern, 2 Essex Rd., Islington, N1. Tube: Angel. Readings often by highly respected poets from around the world. Opportunities to present your own work if you arrive early. Every other Tuesday at 7:45pm; £3, students £2.

Hard Edge Club, upstairs at the Red Lion, 20 Great Windmill St., W1. Tube: Leicester Sq. Holds provocative poetry readings. Different line-up of poets every week. Open Mon. at 8:30pm. Admission £3, students £1.50.

Basement Writers, at Harkness House, Christian St., E1 (tel. 791 2970). Tube: Shadwell. Welcomes newcomers to weekly meetings for discussion and readings of members' poetry, short fiction, and drama. Meetings Tues. 8-10pm. Free. Call for 1992 schedule.

Islington Poetry Workshop, at the Gatehouse, Finsbury Park Education Centre, Prah Rd., N4 (tel. 281 2369). Tube: Finsbury Park. Warm and supportive group of writers who encourage newcomers to bring along their poetry for reading and discussion. Meetings Wed. 7-9pm. Donations accepted but not required.

Greenwich Writers Group, Bar du Musée (basement), Nelson Rd., SE10 (tel. (081) 293 4982). Very informal weekly discussions of poetry and prose. All welcome. Participants tend to get happily plastered by the end of the evening. Meetings Tues. 7-11pm. Free.

First Quarter, upstairs at the Marquis of Granby, Rathbone Pl., W1 (tel. (081) 669 9337). Tube: Tottenham Court Rd. "Adventurous" poets present their work, Wed. 8-10pm. £1.

Spectator Sports

Leg-stump yorkers, up-and-unders, in-swinging corners: they're all here. London remains the place to see the whole range of British sports.

Association Football

> Many evils may arise which God forbid.
> —King Edward II, banning football in London,
> 1314

> It's a game of two halves, Brian.
> —anon.

Football (soccer) has stirred passion and controversy for centuries. In its modern form, it draws huge crowds—over half a million people attend professional matches in Britain every Saturday. Each club's fans dress with fierce loyalty in team colors and make themselves heard with remarkable ritual songs and chants. At games, you can hear the uncanny synchronized singing of such simple but tuneful classics as "Ere we go" or "There's only one Michael Thomas."

Football hooliganism—mass violence and vandalism at stadiums—has dogged the game for years. 38 spectators died at the Liverpool-Juventus match in Brussels in 1986 after a wall collapsed during fighting. 95 people were crushed to death in Sheffield in 1989 after a surge of fans tried to push their way into the ground. A period of rehabilitation has greatly improved matters—as the large numbers safely watching the games week by week testify. Still, visitors may feel more comfortable buying a seat rather than standing on "the terraces."

The season runs from August to April. Most games take place on Saturday, kicking off at 3pm. Allow time to wander through the crowds milling around the stadium. London has been blessed with 13 of the 92 professional teams in England. The big two are the League champions **Arsenal,** Highbury, Avenell Rd., N5 (tel. 359 0131; Tube: Arsenal) and the F.A. Cup holders **Tottenham Hotspur,** White Hart Lane (tel. (081) 808 1020; BR: White Hart Lane). The others are **Chelsea,** Stamford Bridge, Fulham Rd., SW6 (tel. 381 6221; Tube: Fulham Broadway); **Crystal Palace,** Selhurst Park, Whitehouse Lane, SE25 (tel. (081) 653 4462; BR: Selhurst or Norwood Junction); **Queen's Park Rangers,** Loftus Rd., South Africa Rd., W12 (tel. (081) 749 5744; Tube: Shepherd's Bush); **West Ham United,** Upton Park, Green St., E13 (tel. (081) 470 1325; Tube: Upton Park); **Charlton Athletic,** also at Selhurst Park (tel. (081) 771 6321); **Millwall,** The Den, Cold Blow Lane, E14 (tel. 639 3143; Tube: New Cross Gate); **Fulham,** Craven Cottage, Stevenage Rd., SW6 (tel. 736 6561; Tube: Putney Bridge); **Leyton Orient,** Brisbane Rd., E10 (tel. (081) 539 2223; Tube: Leyton); **Brentford,** Griffin Park, Braemar Rd., Brentford (tel. (081) 560 2021; BR: Brentford Central); **Wimbledon,** (tel. (081) 946 6311; Tube:Wimbledon Park); and **Barnet,** Barnet Rd., Barnet, Herts. (tel. (081) 441 6932; Tube: High Barnet). Tickets are available in advance from each club's box office; many now have a credit card telephone booking system. Seats cost £5-20. England plays occasional international matches at Wembley Stadium, usually on Wednesday evenings (tel. (081) 902 8833); Tube: Wembley Park).

Rugby

Played between September and April (preferably on a winter day when the ground has turned to slush), this bastard child of soccer operates on two principles, both of which bear some resemblance to those of American football. That is, players throw and kick the ball, or their opponents. **Rugby League,** a professional sport played by teams of 13, has traditionally been a northern game. The only London side is **Fulham,** Crystal Palace National Sports Centre, SE19 (tel. (081) 517 2778). Wembley stadium (tel. (081) 862 0202) stages some of the championship matches in May. **Rugby Union,** far more popular in the south, matches two teams of 15 amateur, hearty young men. A random *mêlée* of blood, mud, and drinking songs, "rugger" can be incomprehensible to the outsider, yet aesthetically exciting nonetheless. The season runs from September to April, encompassing many perfect (read: bitter, wet) rugby days. The most significant contests, including the Oxford vs. Cambridge varsity match in December and games of the five nations championship (featuring England, Scotland, Wales, Ireland, and France) are played at **Twickenham** (tel. (081) 892 8161; BR: Twickenham). First-rate games can be seen in relaxed surroundings at one of London's premiere clubs such as **Saracens,** Green Rd., N14 (tel. (081) 449 3770); **Rosslyn Park,** Priory Lane, Upper Richmond Rd., SW15 (tel. (081) 876 1879); or **Blackheath,** Rectory Field, SE3 (tel. (081) 858 1578).

Cricket

Cricket, which Robin Williams has likened to "baseball on valium," remains a confusing spectacle to most North Americans. The impossibility of explaining its rules to an American has virtually become a national in-joke in England. A game of great subtlety, cricket fuses Caribbean calypso with Old-World decorum. Once a synonym for civility, cricket's image has been dulled by time-wasting, intimidating bowling, and arguments with umpires. The much-used phrase "It's just not cricket" has recently taken on an ironic edge.

While purists disdain one-day matches, novices find these the most exciting. "First class" matches amble on rather ambiguously for days, often ending in "draws." Excitement mounts in summer at International Test Matches, which last for five days, and at comparatively boisterous one-day internationals pitting England against former members of its empire.

London's two grounds stage both county and international matches. **Lord's,** St. John's Wood Rd., NW8 (tel. 289 1615; Tube: St. John's Wood), is *the* cricket ground, home turf of the Marylebone Cricket Club, the established governing body of cricket. An archaic stuffiness pervades the MCC; women have yet to see the inside of its pavilion. **Middlesex** plays its games here (tickets £5-6). Tickets to international matches cost £12-34. The club grounds and the **MCC Museum** can be seen only on a guided tour; on display, you can see a sparrow killed in mid-air by a ball in 1937 and an urn containing the ashes of a wicket (the three uprights). It is for these ashes that Test Matches between England and Australia are played, though they never leave their hallowed resting place at Lord's. (Call ahead; Tickets £3.50, students and children £2.) The **Oval,** Kensington, SE11 (tel. 582 6660; Tube: Oval), home to **Surrey** cricket club (tickets £5), also fields Test Matches. (Tickets for internationals £14-25.)

Rowing

The **Henley Royal Regatta,** the most famous annual crew race in the world, behaves both as a proper hobnob social affair (like Ascot) and as a popular corporate social event (like Wimbledon). The rowing is graceful, though laypeople are often unable to figure out what on earth is going on. The event transpires for five days in late June or early July (July 1-5 in 1992). Saturday is the most popular and busy day, although some of the best races are the finals on Sunday. Public enclosure tickets (£4 for the first two days, £5 for the last three) are usually available by the river (the side opposite the station) or write to the Secretary's Office, Regatta Headquarters, Henley-on-Thames, Oxfordshire, England RG9 2LY (tel. (0491) 572 153). Take BR from Paddington to Henley, or a National Express coach from Victoria.

The **Boat Race,** between eights from Oxford and Cambridge Universities, runs from Putney to Mortlake on a Saturday in late March or early April. Bumptious crowds line the Thames and fill the pubs. (Tube: Putney Bridge or Hammersmith. BR: Barnes Bridge or Mortlake.) Cambridge has won only once in the last 15 years.

Tennis

For two weeks in late June and early July, tennis buffs all over the world focus their attention on **Wimbledon.** The English take pride in their Wimbledon and keep everything about it highly polished. Most Brittanically, the grass-court tennis is unsurpassed and the traditional snack is strawberries and cream. If you want to get in, arrive early—9am the first week, 6am the second; the gate opens at 10:30am (get off the tube at Southfields, before Wimbledon proper). Check the weather report before you go: only show court tickets (i.e. not ground passes) are refunded and even then you must be around for next year's Wimbledon to take advantage of your ticket. Entrance to the grounds (including lesser matches) costs £6, less after 5pm. If you arrived in the queue early enough, you will be able to buy one of the few show court tickets that were not sold months before. Depending on the day, center court tickets cost £10-30, court 1 tickets £9-24. Other show courts (courts #2, 3, 13, 14), where top players play their early rounds, cost anywhere from £6-16. Other courts have first come, first served seats. Get a copy of the order of play on each court, printed in most newpapers. If you fail to get center and court 1 tickets in the morning, try to find the resale booth (usually in Aorangi Park), which sells tickets handed in by those who leave early (open from 2:30pm; tickets £2). On the last two days, the Band of the Royal Corps of Signals performs in Aorangi Park between 11:30am and 12:30pm.

For details of the 1992 championships call the All England Club (tel. (081) 946 2244) or send a self-addressed stamped envelope between Aug. 1 and Dec. 31 to The All England Lawn Tennis and Croquet Club, P.O. Box 98, Church Rd., Wimbledon SW19 5AE. Topspin lob fans mustn't miss the **Wimbledon Lawn Tennis Museum** (tel. (081) 946 6131), located right on the grounds. (Open Tues.-Sat. 11am-5pm, Sun. 2-5pm; call ahead to check near tournament time.)

You can buy food at Wimbledon at fairly reasonable prices (fish and chips £2.50); nonetheless, tradition mandates a picnic. Those who forget their belongings at home, or just like to travel light, can hire anything from a cushion to binoculars. Don't let the crowds get you down; the BBC offers commercial-free live coverage of center court and court 1 matches, and rebroadcasts highlights in the evenings.

Many top tournament players spend mid-June preparing for Wimbledon at the **Stella Artois Grass Court Championships,** Queen's Club, Palliser Rd. (tel. (081) 741 8999; Tube: Baron's Court). You'll have an easier time obtaining seats here. Book by phone. If the national tennis mania has got you aching to volley a few, see the listings in Participatory Sports below. Buy balls at Lillywhites (see Shopping, Specialty Stores) or Astral Sports, House of Fraser, 318 Oxford St., W1 (Tube: Bond St. or Oxford Circus). The **Racquet Shop,** 22 Norland Rd. W11; (tel. (081) 603 0013; Tube: Holland Park), does excellent stringing jobs.

Horses

The **Royal Gold Cup Meeting** at **Ascot** takes place each summer in mid-June; for most, the event provides an excuse to gawk at whatever haberdashery Princess Di has seen fit to perch on her head. The Queen takes up residence at Windsor Castle in order to lavish her full attentions on this social-political vaudeville act. The enclosure is open only by invitation; grandstand tickets £8:50-20, Silver Ring £3; tel. (0344) 222 11). In July, the popular George VI and Queen Elizabeth Diamond Stakes are run here, and during the winter Ascot hosts excellent steeplechase meetings. (BR from Waterloo to Ascot.) Top hats, gypsies, and fairs also distinguish the **Derby** (pronounced darby), run in early June at **Epsom** Racecourse, Epsom, Surrey (tel. (03727) 263 11; grandstand tickets £7-20). More accessible, less expensive summer evening races run at **Windsor,** the racecourse, Berkshire (tel. (07538) 652 34; BR: Windsor Riverside; admission to tattersalls and paddock £5), and **Kempton Park** Racecourse, Sunbury-on-Thames (tel. (0932) 782 292; BR: Kempton Park; admission to grandstand £6, Silver Ring £4).

Those interested in **show jumping** should contact the British Show Jumping Association, Equestrian Centre, Stoneleigh, Kenilworth, Warwickshire CV8 2LR (tel. (0203) 696 516), for a list of 1991 meetings. The enormously popular **Royal International Horse Show** takes place in October at Wembley Arena (tel. (081) 862 0202); take the train to Wembley Park; tickets £7.50-24). In late June, **polo** aficionados flock to the Royal Windsor Cup, The Guards Polo Club, Smiths Lawn, Windsor Great Park (tel. (0784) 434 212; BR: Windsor & Eton Central; admission £4, £10 per car). You can stand on the "wrong" side of the field for free.

Motor Sport

The name **Brands Hatch** sends tingles up the stickshift of all MG and Jaguar drivers. Britain's most famous racing circuit, it must now fight to stage the British Grand Prix; but less major track races are held there on Sundays throughout the year (Brands Hatch, Fawkham, Dartford, Kent; tel. (0474) 872 331; tickets £4-7). Take British Rail to Swanley; then taxi to Brands Hatch, approx. £3.60.

Speedway racing involves overpowered, brakeless motorbikes powersliding around tight dirt tracks. A season of short, chaotically exciting races runs from mid-March through October. Races are held in London on Friday evenings at **Hackney Stadium,** Waterden Rd., E15 (tel. (081) 986 3511; BR: Hackney Wick; tickets £5) and on Wednesday evenings at **Wimbledon Stadium,** Plough Lane, SW17 (tel. (081) 946 5361; Tube: Wimbledon Park; tickets £5.50).

Greyhound Racing

Greyhound racing—a.k.a. "the dogs"—is the second most popular spectator sport in Britain, after football. Races are held year-round at Hackney and Wimbledon Stadiums (see Motor Sport), Catford (tel. (081) 690 2261), Walthamstow (tel. (081) 531 4255), Haringey (tel. (081) 800 3474), and Wembley (tel. (081) 902 8833). In late June, Wimbledon hosts the Greyhound Derby, nephew to its horseracing uncle (tel. (081) 946 5361).

American Football

For better or worse, American football has slowly but surely gained a foothold in the UK over the last several years. And now, British fans can do more than swig Budweiser in front of the TV at 2am on Super Bowl Monday. The World League's **London Monarchs** play European and American teams at Wembley Stadium (tel.

(081) 862 0202) in the spring (tickets £10-45). In the **American Bowl** at the end of July, two American NFL teams face off, also at Wembley (tickets £15-35). To check the progress of the game at grass-roots level, check *Time Out*'s Sport section for local games in the Coca-Cola league on Sundays.

Participatory Sports

If you fancy something a little more adventurous than a kickaround in the park or kite flying on Parliament Hill, then just do it. London provides a satisfyingly wide variety of sporting opportunities. *Time Out's Guide to Sport, Health, & Fitness* (£5) can give you more complete information on the sports listed below and many others. For general fitness during your visit, **London Central YMCA,** 112 Great Russell St. (tel. 637 8131; Tube: Tottenham Court Rd.), has a pool, gym, weights, and offers weekly membership for £25.50, off-peak weekly membership (use after 4pm prohibited) £17. (Open Mon.-Fri. 8am-10pm, Sat.-Sun. 10am-10pm.) The Sportsline answers queries on a vast range of clubs and locations (tel. 222 8000; Mon.-Fri. 10am-6pm).

Swimming

Swimming in London has become an increasingly sophisticated enterprise, as more and more neighborhood pools and placid ponds have given way to glitzy fitness centers and gadget-ridden leisure complexes. Today, those looking for a quick, refreshing dip may find themselves awash in a world of winding chutes, floating dragons, and ominous wave-making machines. Or they may fall afoul of a canoeing course, a synchronized swim club, or an underwater birthing class. It pays to call ahead and ask about a particular pool's daily programs.

Dive into the **Britannia Leisure Centre,** 40 Hyde Rd., N1 (tel. 729 4485; Tube: Old Street), an unashamedly sensational aquatic playground replete with a towering flume, fountains, and monstrous inflatables (open Mon.-Fri. 9am-10pm, Sat.-Sun. 9am-6pm; admission 50p). Outdoor bathers may prefer the popular **Serpentine Lido,** a chlorinated lake in Hyde Park with surprisingly luxurious changing rooms and a kiddie pool and sandpit for children (tel. 262 5484; Tube: Knightsbridge; open May-Sept. daily 10am-5pm; admission £2, children £1. Deck chairs 50p.) Indoorsy types might want to try the beautiful Edwardian pool in the **Chelsea Sports Centre,** Chelsea Manor St., SW3 (tel. 352 6985; Tube: Sloane Sq.) or lounge in their adjacent solarium. (Open Mon.-Fri. 8am-10pm, Sat. 8am-5pm and 6-10pm, Sun. 8am-6:30pm; admission £1.50, children 50p.) At no cost, you can try **Highgate Pond,** N6 (tel. (081) 340 4044; Tube: Highgate) for men only (open daily 7am-dusk). The pool at the **University of London Union,** 1 Malet St., WC1, is closer to the center of town; you don't usually need a ULU ID. (Open during term-time Mon.-Fri. 9:30am-6:30pm, Sat. 11am-4pm; admission 70p.) As centrally located as your nose, **The Oasis Baths,** 32 Endell St., WC2 (tel. 831 1804; Tube: Covent Garden or Holborn), possess an outdoor pool as well as an indoor pool that churns to the beat of nightly aqua aerobics classes (admission £1.80, children 50p). **The Crystal Palace National Sport Centre,** Upper Norwood, SE26 (tel. (081) 778 0131; BR to Crystal Palace), a hotspot for competitive diving and water polo, offers an array of classes for swimmers of every level in their excellent Olympic-sized pool. Call ahead for pool times which vary weekly. (Centre open Mon.-Sat. 9:30am-10pm; admission £1.80, children £1.10.)

Riding

Even in the middle of town, you can get out of your horseless carriage and onto the back of the real thing. In **Hyde Park,** Richard Briggs Riding Stables, 63 Bathurst Mews, W2 (tel. 723 2813), sends rides out about every hour Tuesday through Sunday (£21 per hr., including hat and boots). Nye Ross Stables, at 8 Bathurst Mews, W2 (tel. 262 3791), will let you out into the park Tuesday through Sunday for £16 an hour, but is closed for a month at Easter, and for July and August. You may have to compete with the deer in **Richmond Park,** where Roehampton Gate

Riding Stables, Priory Lane, SW15 (tel. (081) 876 7089), will saddle you up for £16 per hour.

Badminton

It isn't just for breakfast anymore. Badminton in England has moved out of the back yard and into the serious fray. The fierce All England Championships take place at Wembley Stadium in March (tel. (081) 903 4864), the Junior championships at Waterford, Herts. The Badminton Association of England (National Badminton Centre, Bradwell Rd., Loughton Lodge, Milton Keynes, Bucks; tel. (0908) 568 822) promotes national and local events and can direct you to a local club. Most shops that sell tennis equipment (for example, the second floor of Harrods) also sell badminton equipment.

Squash

While London is honeycombed with squash courts, the vast majority reside within private health and racquet clubs that charge £200-400 for an annual membership plus steep hourly court fees. Visitors and casual players can, however, use the courts maintained by the city's numerous sports centers on a "pay as you play" basis; most charge around £6 per hr. plus around 70p for equipment rental. The **Chelsea Sports Centre** (tel. 352 6985), the **Queen Mother Sports Centre** (tel. 798 2125), the **Sobell Sports Centre** (tel. 609 2166), and the **Saddlers Sports Centre** (tel. 253 9285) are all reasonably priced, centrally located, and open to the public. (For details see Health and Fitness Centres below.)

Tennis

If you weren't wild-carded for Wimbledon, London does have alternatives. Private tennis clubs serve the plushest facilities, but are expensive and often require you to be the guest of a member. **Public courts** vary in quality; all cost about £3 per hour. You'll need to call ahead and book three days in advance. Courts include **Battersea Park** (tel. (081) 871 7542; BR: Battersea Park); **Holland Park** (tel. 262 5484; Tube: South Kensington); **Lincoln's Inn Fields** (tel. 405 5194; Tube: Holborn); **Parliament Hill**, Hampstead Heath (tel. 485 4491; BR: Gospel Oak); and **Regent's Park** (tel. 935 5729; Tube: Regent's Park). All are hard.

Real Tennis

Real Brits still play a version of tennis that dates from the time of Henry VIII—referred to as "real tennis." Most real tennis goings-on occur at Queen's Club (address above; Real Tennis office tel. 381 3301). For information on the sport that questions reality as we know it, write to the Tennis & Rackets Association, c/o Queen's Club, Palliser Rd.

Basketball

Basketball in England remains a very American game. Competition takes place only at a club level. Playoffs take place at the Crystal Palace National Sports Centre (tel. (081) 778 0131). The **English Basketball Association** (Calomax House, Lupton Ave., Leeds, W. Yorks; tel. (0532) 496 044) can direct you to the club in your area or tell you where to find a court. If you forgot to pack your basketball and absolutely need to play, buy one at Slick Willies, 41 Kensington High St., W8 (tel. 937 3824; Tube: High St. Kensington). At this bastion of American sports in London, you may even be able to round up enough players for a pick-up game.

Cycling

Traffic and pollution interfere with the art of cycling during the day. Setting out for a late-night ride is probably your best bet for a jaunt within the city. The Mall makes a great late-night criterion track, though be careful not to disturb the Queen. Cycling on Sundays can be more tolerable (especially in the weekend wasteland of the City), but still requires a good deal of care and skill. The **British Cycling Federation**, 16 Woburn Pl., WC1 (tel. 387 9320), divulges information on upcoming races and can give advice on where to ride outside the city. Also try the Cyclists Touring Club, 69 Meadrow, Godalming, Surrey, GU7 3HS, for advice (tel. (04868) 7217).

On Your Bike, 22 Duke St. Hill, SE1, rents 10-speeds and mountain bikes by the day, weekend, or week (see Getting Around London). **Condor Cycles,** 144-148 Gray's Inn Rd., WC1 (tel. 837 7641; Tube: Chancery Lane), a cycle-shop strictly for pros, sells custom frames and high quality racing components. If you just want to get a cheap bike fixed, go to **Bike Peddlers,** 50 Clathorpe St., WC1, for friendly service and an inexpensive repair (tel. 278 0551; Tube: Russell Sq.).

Ice Skating

Budding Torvills and Deans can do their Bolero thing at the **Sobell Sports Center,** Hornsey Rd., N7 (tel. 609 2166; Tube: Holloway Rd. or Finsbury Park; open Mon. and Sat. 10am-noon and 2-4pm, Wed.-Thurs. 7:30-9:30pm, Fri. 2-4pm and 7:30-9:30pm, Sun. 10am-noon and 2:30-4:30pm; some sessions restricted to family groups; £1.70 including skate hire). Or try the **Queens Ice Skating Club,** Queensway, W2 (tel. 229 0172; Tube: Bayswater or Queensway; open Mon.-Fri. 11am-4:30pm and 7:30-10pm, Sat. 10am-noon, 2-5pm and 7:30-10:30pm, Sun. 10am-12:30pm, 2:30-5pm, and 7-10pm; £2.30-5, hire £1.20.)

Alpine Sports

No one has ever accused London of being a world skiing center—virtually devoid of hills and snow, it seems divinely intended for almost anything but. Miraculously, however, you can ski in London—on the dry slope at Alexandra Palace ("Ally Pally"), N22 (tel. (081) 888 2284, closed in summer). On the rare days that it does snow, take your toboggan or plank or tray to Parliament Hill or Primrose Hill and crash into everybody else on the slopes.

Fishing

If you have the time and the patience, London, believe it or not, has the fish—but don't expect to win any awards for the world's largest catch. Even fanatics who vacation with their fishing tackle will still need a license. The **London Anglers' Association,** Forest Road Hall, Hervey Park Rd. E17 (tel. (081) 520 7477), can tell you where the fish are biting and where you need apply for your license. In the London area perch, roach, and tench are the most common varieties of fish, though carp, rainbow trout, and even eels are not unknown in nearby waters. Fishing gear can be purchased at the enormous Lillywhites (see Shopping, Specialty Stores).

Golf

Municipal golf courses, where you don't have to be a member, near London include: **Picketts Lock Centre,** Picketts Lock Lane, N9 (tel. (081) 803 4756), a nine-hole course close to central London, and **Hainault Forest,** Chigwell Row, Hainault, Essex (tel. (081) 500 2470), with two 18-hole courses. Call the English Golf Union (tel. (0533) 553 042) for further information or for other courses around London. Members of foreign golf clubs yearning to play at a private club in England can usually have guest privileges extended to them by presenting club identification. If you need to buy or repair clubs, try Lillywhites (see Shopping, Specialty Stores), Astral Sports and Leisures (see Tennis), or Golf City, 13 New Bridge St. EC4 (tel. 353 9872; Tube: Blackfriars). The *Daily Telegraph Golf Course Guide* (available in bookstores), prints a wealth of details about all the courses in England.

Health and Fitness Centers

London is blessed with over 200 public sports and fitness centers. The few listed below are some of the most central and comprehensive in the city. Consult the yellow pages for more exhaustive listings, or call the local borough council for a list of centers near you.

Jubilee Hall Recreation Centre, Tavistock St., WC2 (tel. 836 4835), on the south side of Covent Garden. Tube: Covent Garden. Regular classes and activities include weight-lifting, yoga, martial arts, gymnastics, dance, badminton, and aerobics. Special facilities include a sauna, solarium, and an alternative sports medicine clinic. Crowded with West End office workers at lunchtime. Annual membership £45. Admission free to members; £1 for nonmembers plus £2-3 for activities. Open Mon.-Fri, 7:30am-10pm, Sat.-Sun. 10am-5pm.

Queen Mother Sports Centre, 223 Vauxhall Bridge Rd., SW1 (tel. 798 2125). Tube: Victoria. Activities: aerobics, badminton, basketball, bowls, canoeing, diving, gymnastics, judo, martial arts, indoor skiing, squash, swimming, trampolining, volleyball, and weight-lifting. Special facilities: solarium, café, and bar. Equipment rental. Activities £2-5 per hour. Open Mon.-Fri. 7:30am-10pm, Sat. 8am-6pm, Sun. 9am-6pm.

Chelsea Sports Centre, Chelsea Manor St., SW3 (tel. 352 6985). Tube: Sloane Sq. or South Kensington. Activities: aerobics, badminton, basketball, bowls, canoeing, dance, football, lacrosse, martial arts, racquetball, roller skating, squash, swimming, tennis volleyball, weight training, yoga, zzz. Special facilities: sauna, solarium, and spa baths. No membership or admission charge. Activities 75p-£3. Open Mon.-Fri. 7:30am-10pm, Sat. 8am-10pm, Sun. 8am-6:30pm.

Saddlers Sports Centre, Goswell Rd., EC1 (tel. 253 9285). Tube: Barbican. Activities: aerobics, badminton, basketball, canoeing, climbing, cricket, fencing, gymnastics, racquetball, squash, tennis, volleyball, weight training, yoga. Special facilities: sauna and solarium. Young, casual clientele. No membership or admission charge. Activities £1-2.50. Open Mon.-Tues. and Fri. 9am-9:30pm, Wed. 7:30am-9:30pm, Thurs. 9:30am-9:30pm, Sat. 9:30am-2pm.

Sobell Sports Centre, Hornsey Rd., N7 (tel. 609 2166). Tube: Holloway Rd. or Finsbury Park. Aerobics, squash, gymnastics, weight training, ice skating, and swimming; £1-3 per activity. Open Mon.-Sat. 9am-10:30pm.

Shopping

London does sell more than royal commemorative mugs and plastic police helmets. However, many visitors to London do not buy anything but royal commemorative mugs and plastic police helmets. First-time shoppers may be disappointed by the amount of junk thrown at them; but dodge the barrage and you'll be able to satisfy any purchasing urge, be it for shortbread or howitzers.

For department stores and fashion outlets, try Oxford St., Knightsbridge, and Kensington; for expensive designer goods, Sloane St., Bond St., and Piccadilly; for hip young clothes, Soho, Kensington, Chelsea, and Camden; for specialty stores, Bloomsbury and Covent Garden. London Transport's handy *Shoppers' Bus Wheel* instructs bus-loving shoppers on the routes between shopping areas (available free from any London Transport Information Office). *Nicholson's Shopping Guide and Streetfinder* (£2.50) should suit bargain hunters seeking further guidance. Serious shoppers should read *Time Out's* massive *Directory to London's Shops and Services* (£6) cover to cover.

Prices descend during sale seasons in July and January. Tourists who have purchased anything expensive should ask about getting a refund on the 17.5% VAT. But most shops have a VAT minimum; Harrods, for instance, requires you to spend £150 before refunding VAT. Many shops stay open late on Thursday; almost all close on Sunday.

Department Stores

Occupying an entire turreted, terracotta block, **Harrods** (tel. 730 1234) remains the ultimate department store. They can do everything from finding you a live rhinoceros to arranging your funeral. They stock more than 450 kinds of cheese. Harrods also pours a rather elegant afternoon tea (see Teas, under Food). (Open Mon. and Thurs.-Sat. 9am-6pm, Tues. 9:30am-6pm, Wed. 9am-8pm.)

Except during sales, comprehensive department stores tend not to be the cheapest places to shop. The ubiquitous **Marks and Spencer** (tel. 935 7954), also known as Marks and Sparks, sells its own British staples in a classy but value-conscious manner. The clothes err on the side of frump; Margaret Thatcher buys her underwear here. (Branches near Bond St., Marble Arch, and Kensington High St. Tube stations. Open Mon.-Wed. and Fri. 9am-7pm, Thurs. 9am-8pm, Sat. 9am-6pm.) Also near the Bond St. Tube station on Oxford St. is **Selfridges** (tel. 629 1234), an enormous pseudo-Renaissance building with a vast array of fashions, homewares, and foods. (Open Mon.-Tues. and Fri.-Sat. 9am-7pm, Wed.-Thurs. 9am-8pm.) **Debenham's** (tel. 580 3000) at 334 Oxford St. (Tube: Oxford Circus) is a bit staider but cheap (open Mon.-Tues. 9am-6pm, Wed.-Fri. 9am-8pm, Sat. 9am-7pm). **John Lewis** has a giant emporium off Oxford Circus worth visiting (tel. 629 7711; open Mon.-Sat. 9:30am-5:30pm, Thurs. until 8pm). Its sister shop, **Peter Jones** on Sloane Sq. (tel. 730 3434; Tube: Sloane Sq.; open same hours) is equally wide-ranging. If you can find the same goods cheaper elsewhere, John Lewis will refund the difference. **Fenwick's** at 63 New Bond St. (tel. 629 9161; Tube: Bond St.) is slightly more upmarket (open Mon.-Sat. 9am-6:30, Thurs. until 7pm).

South of Oxford Circus on Regent St. stands **Liberty and Co.** (tel. 734 1234; Tube: Oxford Circus). A prime exponent of the 19th-century arts and crafts movement, Liberty peddles silk scarves, fine cotton fabrics, elegant fashions, and furnishings in unusual Renaissance and Tudor buildings. Bargain hunters can get their Victorian wares on sale at the beginning of July and after Christmas. (Open Mon.-Wed. and Fri.-Sat. 9:30am-6pm, Thurs. 9:30am-7:30pm.)

At the renowned **Fortnum & Mason,** 181 Piccadilly (tel. 734 8040; Tube: Green Park or Piccadilly Circus), liveried clerks serve expensive foods in red-carpeted and chandeliered halls. Queen Victoria naturally turned to Fortnum & Mason when she wanted to send Florence Nightingale 250 lbs. of beef tea for the Crimean field hospitals. Visit the costly but satisfying tea shop, or splurge on an ice cream sundae in the fountain room. (Open Mon.-Sat. 9:30am-6pm.)

Clothing

Those who'd rather not swap a cherished limb for some new clothes should explore some of London's second-hand clothing stores. **The Frock Exchange,** 450 Fulham Rd., SW6 (tel. 381 2937; Tube: Fulham Broadway) sells second-hand designer items in excellent condition and at low prices. (Open Mon.-Sat. 10am-5:30pm.) The rage for second-hand American fashions has produced a number of cheap clothing outlets: **American Classics,** 400-404 King's Rd., SW10 (tel. 351 5229; Tube: Sloane Sq., then bus #11; open Mon.-Sat. 10am-6:30pm); **Flip,** 125 Long Acre, WC2 (tel. 836 7044; Tube: Covent Garden; open Mon.-Wed. and Fri.-Sat. 10am-7pm, Thurs. 10am-8pm, Sun. noon-7pm); and **High Society,** 46 Cross St., N1 (tel. 226 6863; Tube: Angel; open Mon.-Sat. 10:30am-6:30pm). **Kensington Market,** (49-53 Kensington High St., W8), has some better bargains (including second-hand clothes) and even wilder stalls, including a tattoo parlor. (Open Mon.-Sat. 10am-6pm.) Along the same lines, try **Camden Lock** market (see Street Markets), or the **Garage,** 350 King's Rd., SW3 (tel. 351 3505); Tube: Sloane Sq., then bus #11; open Mon.-Fri. 10am-6pm, Sat. 10am-7pm). Small secondhand shops of the same ilk dot the King's Rd. between Sloane Sq. and the Chelsea Town Hall.

For the traditional and more expensive British look—grey and brown tweeds, woollens, raincoats, etc.—try the shops along Regent St., New Bond St., and Savile Row: **Aquascutum,** 100 Regent St., W1 (Tube: Oxford Circus; tel. 734 6090; open Mon.-Wed. and Fri. 9:30am-6pm, Thurs. 9:30am-7pm, Sat. 9:30am-6:30pm); **Burberrys,** 18 Haymarket, SW1 (Tube: Piccadilly Circus; tel. 930 3343; open Mon.-Sat. 9am-5:30pm, Thurs. until 7pm); or **Jaeger,** 204 Regent St., W1 (tel. 734 8211; Tube: Piccadilly Circus; open Mon.-Sat. 9am-6pm, Thurs. until 7pm). **Laura Ashley,** at 256 Regent St., W1 (tel. 437 9760; Tube: Oxford Circus) and many other locations, peddles pretty pastel pastoral prints—cheaper than at their shops abroad. (Open Mon.-Wed. and Fri. 9:30am-6pm, Thurs. 9am-8pm, Sat. 9am-6pm.) For less tweed and more neon, try **Hyper-Hyper,** 26-40 Kensington High St., W8 (tel. 938 4343; Tube: Kensington High St.). A former antique market, it now hawks British street fashions by more than 70 young designers. (Open Mon.-Sat. 10am-6pm, Thurs. until 7pm.)

Interesting young fashions go for reasonable prices countless chain stores such as **Warehouse** or **Next.** Even cheaper **Top-Shop/Top Man** has an awe-inspiring megastore at Oxford Circus (tel. 636 7700). You need not worry about their clothes wearing out—they'll be embarrassingly out of fashion long before then. (Open Mon.-Sat. 10am-6:30pm, Thurs. until 8pm.)

For hats, try **Herbert Johnson,** 30 New Bond St., W1 (Tube: Bond St.). From top hat to solar topee, this shop has had it all since 1889; prices range from £15-400. (Open Mon.-Fri. 9:45am-6pm, Sat. 10am-5pm.)

For the latest in beat-tapping inexpensive shoes, try **Shelly's Shoes,** 159 Oxford St. (tel. 437 5842; open Mon.-Sat. 9:30am-6:30pm, Thurs. until 8pm; branches throughout London), the spiritual home of Doc Marten. **Russell and Bromley, Saxone** and **Dolcis** have shops across the capital.

Bookstores

In London, even the chain bookstores are wonders. Mammoth independents and countless specialized gems make up the capital's catalogue. An exhaustive selection of bookshops lines Charing Cross Road between Tottenham Court Rd. and Leicester Sq. and many vend second-hand paperbacks. Shops along Great Russell Street stock esoteric and specialized books on any subject from Adorno to Zemlinsky. The best place to look for maps is **Stanford's,** 12 Long Acre (open Mon. and Sat. 10am-6pm, Tue.-Wed. and Fri. 9am-6pm, Thurs. 9am-7pm; Tube: Covent Garden); also try Harrods and the YHA shop (see Specialty Shops below).

Hatchards, 187 Piccadilly, W1 (tel. 437 3924). Tube: Green Park. Oldest and most comprehensive of London's bookstores, undergoing expansion in 1991. Tremendous selection of travel narratives. Also at 150 King's Rd. (tel. 351 7649); 390 The Strand (tel. 379 6264); 63 Kensington High St., (tel. 937 0858); and Harvey Nichols in Knightsbridge (tel. 235 5000). Open Mon.-Fri. 9am-6pm, Sat. 9am-5pm.

Foyles, 119 Charing Cross Rd., WC1 (tel. 437 5660). Tube: Tottenham Court Rd. or Leicester Sq. The largest bookstore in London, stockpiling over 6 million books. Come roam through this amazing colossus, but don't expect too much guidance from the staff. Open Mon.-Sat. 9am-6pm, Thurs. 9am-7pm.

Dillons, 82 Gower St., WC1 (tel. 636 1577), near University of London. Tube: Goodge St. The most graceful bookstore in London. Easier to navigate and almost as complete as Foyles, though with a more academic focus, particularly on history and politics. Fair selection of reduced-price and second-hand books, plus classical CDs and tapes. Open Mon.-Fri. 9:30am-7pm, Sat. 9:30am-6pm.

Waterstones, 121-125 Charing Cross Rd. WC1 (tel. 434 4291), next door to Foyles. Tube: Leicester Sq. An extensive and well-ordered selection of paperbacks; calmer and friendlier than its neighbor though also a little cramped. They mail books to the US. Also at 193 Kensington High St. (tel. 937 8432); 99 Old Brompton Rd. (tel. 581 8523); 68-69 Hampstead High St. (tel. 794 1098). Open Mon., Wed.-Sat. 9:30am-8pm; Tue. 10am-8pm, Sun. 11am-6pm. Kensington High St. open until 10pm Mon.-Fri.

Skoob Books, 15 Sicilian Ave., Southampton Row and Vernon Pl., WC1 (tel. 404 3063). Tube: Holborn. The best used bookstore in Bloomsbury; academic and general interest. Students receive a 10% discount. Also at 19 Bury Pl. (tel. 405 0030). Open Mon.-Sat. 10:30am-6:30pm.

Maggs Brothers Ltd., 50 Berkeley Sq., W1 (tel. 493 7160). Tube: Green Park. A bibliophile's paradise housed in a haunted (so stories run) 18th-century mansion. Tremendous selection of 19th-century travel narratives, illuminated manuscripts, militaria, orientalia, maps, and autographs. Formal but engaging staff. Open Mon.-Fri. 10am-5:30pm.

Southeran's of Sackville Street, 2-5 Sackville St., W1 (tel. 439 6151). Tube: Piccadilly Circus. Founded in 1815, Southeran's has established itself as an institution of literary London. Dickens frequented these unnervingly silent stacks, and the firm handled the sale of his library after his death in 1870. Today, strong antiquarian collections of English literature, ornithology, and natural science are complemented by a department specializing in maps, drawings, and military prints. Open Mon.-Fri. 9:30am-6pm, Sat. 10am-4pm.

Compendium, 234 Camden High St., NW1 (tel. 485 8944). Tube: Camden Town. A good general selection, but specializing in postmodern literature, occult, and the all-around avant-garde. Open Mon.-Sat. 10am-6pm, Sun. noon-6pm.

Pleasures of Past Times, 11 Cecil Ct., WC2 (tel. 836 1142). Tube: Leicester Sq. A friendly, fascinating shop specializing in the stuff of youthful enchantment: early children's books with exquisite color plates and engravings, adventure stories, fairy tales, antique postcards, Victorian valentines, and other vintage juvenilia. Open Mon.-Fri. 11am-2:30pm and 3:30-5:45pm.

Bernard Stone, 42 Lamb's Conduit St., WC1 (tel. 405 6058). Tube: Russell Sq. An inviting little shop specializing in poetry, children's literature, and detective fiction. Good selection of both new and used books. Look for the wax-work gentleman dressed in tweeds gazing out the window. Open Mon.-Sat. 9:30am-5pm.

Bell, Book and Radmall, 4 Cecil Ct., WC2 (tel. 240 2161). Tube: Leicester Sq. A small antiquarian bookstore with a zippy staff, an exceptional selection of American and British first editions, and an impressive supply of sci-fi and detective novels. Fascinating original illustrations line the staircase (for sale; but forget it). Open Mon.-Fri. 10am-5:30pm.

Art bookstores splatter the streets around the British Museum (Tube: Holborn or Tottenham Court Rd.) and Christie's (Tube: Green Park or Piccadilly Circus). Close to Christie's, **Thomas Heneage & Co.,** 42 Duke St. St. James's (Tube: Green Park), houses a truly outstanding collection of art books (tel. 930 9223; open Mon.-Fri. 10am-6pm). Art books also adorn **Zwemmers,** 80 Charing Cross Rd. (tel. 379 7886; open Mon.-Fri. 9:30am-6pm, Sat. 10am-6pm), while 50s magazines and film posters clutter **Vintage Magazine Market,** on the corner of Brewer and Great Windmill St. near Piccadilly Circus (tel. 439 8525; open Mon.-Sat. 10am-7pm; Sun. noon-7pm). For theatre and opera books, try **Samuel French's,** 52 Fitzroy St. (tel. 387 9373; open Mon.-Fri. 9:30am-5:30pm). Parents should stop in at the **Children's Book Centre,** 229 Kensington High St. (tel. 937 7497; open Mon.-Sat. 9:30am-6pm), or the **Puffin Bookshop,** The Market, Covent Garden (tel. 379 6465; open Mon.-Sat. 10am-8pm).

You'll find several alternative bookshops scattered around the city. The **Kilburn Book Shop,** 8 Kilburn Bridge, Kilburn High Rd., NW6 (Tube: Kilburn; tel. 328 7071) features politically correct reading material, as does **Sister Write,** 190 Upper St., NW1 (Tube: Islington; tel. 226 9782), the first radical feminist bookshop in Britain. (Open Mon.-Sat. 10am-6pm, Thurs. until 7pm.) **Silver Moon,** at 68 Charing Cross Rd., WC2, is more central and less radical (Tube: Charing Cross; tel. 836 7906; open Mon.-Fri. 10:30am-6:30pm). **Central Books,** 37 Gray's Inn Rd. (tel. 242 6166), mixes feminist fiction with left-wing politics. (Tube: Chancery Lane; open Sun.-Fri. 10am-6pm, Sat. 10am-5pm). **Collet's International Bookshop,** 129 Charing Cross Rd., complements leftist social and cultural studies with London's most comprehensive Soviet and Eastern European department (Tube: Leicester Sq.; open Mon.-Sat. 10am-6pm).

Record Stores

If a record can't be found in London, it's probably not worth your listening time. London, for years the hub of the English music scene, has a record collection to match. The Big Three, **HMV, Virgin,** and **Tower Records,** fall over each other in claiming to be the world's largest record store. Crammed with records, tapes, CDs, videos, T-shirts, and intimidating security apparatuses, they all offer a broad and comprehensive selection from rock, soul, and reggae, to jazz and classical. Don't expect any bargains or rarities, and remember that when it comes to records, "import" means "rip-off." For rarities, second-hand, and specialist records, try the wealth of diverse shops scattered throughout the West End and the suburbs. At **Camden Town, Brixton,** or **Ladbroke Grove/Notting Hill,** you can have a good afternoon's browse in search of an obscure *Blyth Power* 12-inch or some Ska standards.

Virgin Megastore, 14-30 Oxford St., W1 (tel. 580 5822). Tube: Tottenham Court Rd. Part of Richard Branson's empire. Open Mon.-Sat. 9am-8pm, Sun. noon-7pm.

HMV, 150 Oxford St., W1 (tel. 631 3423). Tube: Oxford Circus or Tottenham Court Rd. The ageless dog by the old gramophone still listens to His Master's Voice. Open Mon.-Sat. 9:30am-7pm, Thurs. until 8pm. Branches at 363 Oxford St., 142 Wardour St., and the Trocadero.

Tower Records, 1 Piccadilly Circus, W1 (tel. 439 2500). Tube: Piccadilly Circus. Open daily 9am-midnight. Also at 62 Kensington High St., W8.

Record and Tape Exchange, 229 Camden High St., NW1 (tel. 267 1898). Tube: Camden Town. Dirt-cheap 70s stuff in the basement. Fewer modern bargains. Open daily 10am-8pm. Branches at 38 Notting Hill Gate, W11, and 90 Goldhawk Rd., W12.

Rough Trade, 130 Talbot Rd., W11 (tel. 229 8541). Tube: Ladbroke Grove. Independent of the legendary record label. Broad indie selection. Open Mon.-Sat. 10am-6:30pm.

Vinyl Solution, 231 Portobello Rd., W11 (tel. 229 8010). Tube: Ladbroke Grove. Hard-core and indie. Open Mon.-Sat. 10:30am-6:30pm.

Rhythm Records, 281 Camden High St., NW1 (tel. 267 0123). Tube: Camden Town. Second-hand reggae and ska. Open daily 10:30am-6:30pm.

Cheapo Cheapo Records, 53 Rupert St., W12 (tel. 437 8272). Tube: Piccadilly Circus. A rabbit warren of 70s and early 80s records at rock bottom prices. Open Mon.-Sat. 11am-10pm.

Plastic Passion, 2 Blenheim Crescent, W11 (tel. 229 5424). Tube: Notting Hill Gate. New Wave and punkish. Small but extremely dedicated collectors. Open Fri.-Sat. 10am-6:30pm.

Specialty Shops

From tennis rackets to cricket wickets, **Lillywhites,** 24-36 Regent St., SW1 (tel. 930 3181; Tube: Piccadilly Circus), caters to the needs of British sports fanatics. (Open Mon., Wed., and Fri.-Sat. 9:30am-6pm, Tues. 9:45am-6pm, Thurs. 9:30am-7pm.) London's largest toy shop, **Hamley's,** 188-196 Regent St., W1 (tel. 734 3161; Tube: Oxford Circus), offers six floors of every conceivable toy and game. Bring a leash for the kids. (Open Mon.-Sat. 10am-6pm, Thurs. until 8pm.) Appropriately enough, **Just Games,** 71 Brewer St., W1 (tel. 734 6124; Tube: Piccadilly Circus) is London's oldest shop devoted only to games. (Open Mon.-Sat. 10am-6pm.) Miniature planes, trains, and automobiles can be purchased from **Beatties,** 202 High Holborn, WC1 (tel. 405 6285; Tube: Holborn; open Mon. 10am-6pm, Tues.-Sat. 9am-6pm). **The Museum Store,** 37 The Market, WC2 (tel. 240 5760; Tube: Covent Garden) collects and sells items found in museum stores from around the world—everything from teddy bears to astronaut ice cream. (Open Mon.-Sat. 10:30am-6:30pm, Sun. 11am-5pm.)

Southpaws will be delighted to find **Anything Left-Handed,** 65 Beak St., W1 (tel. 437 3910; Tube: Piccadilly Circus; open Mon.-Fri. 10am-5pm, Sat. 10am-1pm). Stamp collectors should explore the many shops along the Strand—start at **Stanley Gibbons,** 399 Strand, WC2 (tel. 836 8444; Tube: Charing Cross) a funhouse of postal history books, collector phone cards, and stamps of every persuasion. They take a licking and keep on ticking. (Open Mon. 9:30am-5:30pm, Tues.-Fri. 8:30am-5:30pm, Sat. 10am-4pm.) Tobacco enthusiasts will revel in the scent of the 122 years of tobacco history at **Smith and Sons Snuff Shop,** 74 Charing Cross Rd., WC2 (Tube: Leicester Sq.; open Mon.-Fri. 9am-6pm).

Hope and Glory, 131A Kensington Church St., W8 (tel. 727 8424; Tube: Notting Hill Gate) sells a unique collection of antique royal commemorative china. (Open Tues.-Fri. 10am-5pm, Sat. 10am-2pm.) If you think you'll miss English tea when you leave, take some home from **The Tea House,** 15a Neal St., WC2 (tel. 240 7539; Tube: Covent Garden; open Mon.-Sat. 10am-7pm). An outgrowth of Britain's Green movement, **Lynx,** 79 Long Acre, WC2 (tel. 836 9702; Tube: Covent Garden), sells T-shirts, boxers, and other items emblazoned with environmentally conscious slogans. (Open Mon.-Wed. and Sat. 10am-6pm, Thurs.-Fri. 10am-8pm.)

Markets

Street Markets

Many street markets sell modern junk or ordinary produce at non-bargain prices; an exceptional handful push offbeat styles and unique trinkets. Entertaining salespeople and an informal atmosphere make the markets livelier and more invigorating than shopping malls. With some luck and ingenuity, you may find cheap, unusual goods—come prepared to haggle and to participate in some cheerful, often incomprehensible, banter.

194 **Shopping**

London has over 70 street markets, the majority of them unremarkable local shopping centers. Listed below is the more entertaining minority. Opening times vary considerably—Saturday is usually the busiest and best day.

Camden Lock, NW1, by Regent's Canal and along Camden High St. Tube: Camden Town. One of the funkiest, trendiest places to tap those Doc Marten soles. Plastic Pollock ties, wicked leather gear, crafts, grub, and seas of music. Camden Town Bootleggers do a roaring trade—check the quality of the tapes before buying. Open Sat.-Sun. 9am-6pm.

Brixton Market, Electric Ave., Brixton Station Rd. and Popes Rd., SW2. Tube: Brixton. Covered market halls and outdoor stalls sprawl out from the station. The wide selection of African and West Indian fruit, vegetables, fabrics, and records make Brixton one of the swingingest markets. Open Mon.-Sat. 8am-5:30pm; closed Wed. afternoons.

Portobello Road, W11. Tube: Notting Hill Gate or Ladbroke Grove. High-quality antiques at high prices. Some Londoners call this "a place to visit your stolen silver;" others consider it nothing more than a tourist trap. Immortalized by Paddington Bear. Watch out for pickpockets. Over 2000 dealers; prices from £10-10,000. To the north, tourists thin out as antiques give way to produce and general secondhand. Antique market Sat. 7am-5pm.

Greenwich Market, College Approach, SE10, near the Cutty Sark. BR: Greenwich. A popular crafts market frequented by London lawyers on daytrips down the river. Open Sat. 9am-5pm; also in summer Sun. 9am-5pm.

Petticoat Lane, E1. Tube: Liverpool St., Aldgate, or Aldgate East. A London institution—street after street of stalls, mostly cheap clothing and household appliances. The real action begins at about 9:30am. The street called Petticoat Lane (Middlesex St. on some maps) proves the least interesting part of the market; for better buys and second-hand stuff, head north toward Brick Lane. Open Sun. 9am-2pm; starts shutting down around noon.

Camden Passage, Islington High St., N1. Tube: Angel. Turn right as you come out of the Underground, then bear right on Islington High St. One of the biggest antique markets, plus prints and drawings on Thurs. and some cheaper junk. Open Wed.-Thurs. 7am-4pm, Sat. 8am-5pm.

Merton Abbey Mills, Meranton Way, SW19. Tube: Colliers Wood or South Wimbledon. An excellent, earthy crafts and clothes market on the river Wandle: brown rice yogurt, and Chinese food galore. Morden Hall Park (National Trust) just along the river. Open Sat.-Sun. 10am-5pm.

Chapel Market, N1. Tube: Angel. Turn left off Liverpool Rd. Emphasis on produce, but also household goods, those dubious electronics, and clothes, spiced with nuts and African music. Open Tues.-Wed. and Fri.-Sat. 8am-6:30pm, Thurs. and Sun. 8am-12:30pm.

Earl's Court, at Earl's Court Exhibition Centre. Tube: Earl's Ct. Take exhibition exit, then a short walk to entrance on Lillie Rd. Sells everything from electrical adaptors to leather coats to felafel. Clothing leans towards Bart Simpson counterfeits. Open Sun. 10am-3pm.

Trade Markets

London's fresh produce comes in through the massive wholesale markets. They don't exactly roll out red carpet for visitors, but they have wall-to-wall atmosphere. You won't find a more fascinating place to have a pint at 6am than near the trading. The new **Billingsgate** market (DLR: West India Quay or Poplar; open Tues.-Sat. 5:30-9am) decently removed its lovely fishy smells from the old site by St. Magnus Martyr in the City. **Smithfield,** Charterhouse St., EC1 (Tube: Farringdon or Barbican; open Mon.-Fri. 5am-noon), allegedly the largest meat market in the world, sells wholesale only. It's entertaining, in a ghoulish way. The **New Covent Garden Market,** Nine Elms Lane, SW8 (Tube: Vauxhall), handles London's fruit, vegetables, and flowers; traders only. **Borough Market,** Southwark St., SE1 (Tube: London Bridge; open Mon.-Sat. 2:30-11am), also barters in fruit and vegetables and allows casual visitors to look around.

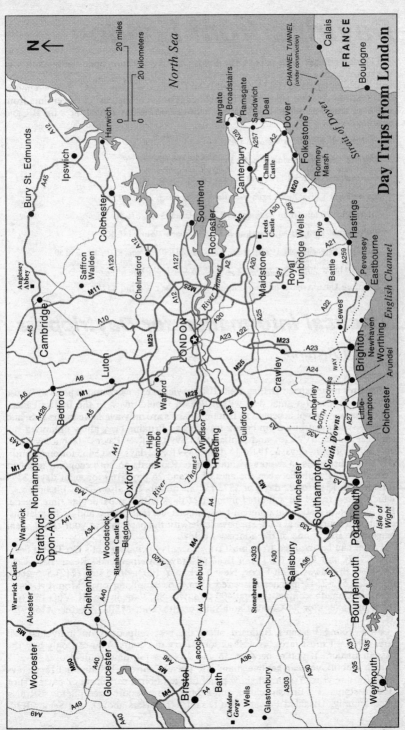

Day Trips from London

Daytrips from London

The daytrip has been part of the British holiday culture since the invention of the steam engine. Many cities in central England, East Anglia, the West Country, and southern England can be reached from London by train in less than two hours. (See Getting Around below). Listed below, in order of increasing travel time from London, are some suggested daytrips; listings include day return fares for BR and coaches.

Brighton: 50 min. from Victoria, £9.50; by coach 2 hr., £8.75.

Oxford: 1 hr. from Paddington, £9.50; by coach 1½ hr., £4.50.

Cambridge: 1 hr. from Liverpool St., £10.60; by coach 2 hr., £8.

Canterbury: 1 hr. 20 min. from Victoria, £10; by coach 2 hr., £7.75.

Bath: 1 hr. 20 min. from Paddington, £23; by coach 3 hr., £16.50.

Portsmouth: 1½hr. from Waterloo, £13.20; by coach 2½hr., £10.50

Salisbury (Stonehenge): 1½ hr. from Waterloo, £13.90; by coach 2½ hr., £10.50.

Dover: 1½ hr. from Charing Cross, £13.40; by coach 2½ hr., £10.25.

Stratford Upon Avon: 2 hr. from Euston, £27; by coach 3½ hr., £12.75.

Practical Information for Daytrippers

Getting Around

Trains

Britain's nationalized **British Rail (BR)** service is extensive and expensive. Those who plan to travel a great deal within Britain should invest in the **BritRail Pass.** (Eurailpasses are not accepted in Britain.) Passes are only available in the U.S. and Canada; you must buy them before traveling to Britain. They allow unlimited rail travel in England, Wales, and Scotland. In 1990, "Silver Passes" (economy class) cost $209 for eight days, $319 for 15 days, $399 for 22 days, and $465 for one month. BR offers discounts to seniors without Senior Railcards on both economy and first class tickets. People between the ages of 16 and 25 pay $169 for eight days, $255 for 15 days, $319 for 22 days, or $375 for one month. BR also offers "Flexipasses," which allow travel on a limited number of days within a particular time period. For more information on different pass options, current prices, and additional discounts (on tours, rental cars, etc.) available with the pass, talk to your travel agent or contact BR at one of the addresses below.

Passes can be acquired from most travel agents (including Let's Go Travel Services, CIEE, and Travel CUTS) or BritRail Travel International's Reservation Centre, 1500 Broadway, 10th Floor, New York, NY 10036-4015 (tel. (212) 575-2667, fax (212) 575-2542; phones answered Mon.-Fri. 9am-8pm; open Mon.-Fri. 9am-5pm). In Canada, contact them at 409 Granville St., Vancouver, BC V6C 1T2 (tel. (604) 683-6896), or 94 Cumberland St., Toronto, Ont. M5R 1A3 (tel. (416) 929-3334).

BR's **Young Person's Railcard** offers the best reductions on individual rail fares—1/3 off most fares, as well as some ferry discounts. You can only buy the pass in Britain. If you're between 16 and 23 (or a full-time student over 23 at a British school), you can get one at any BR Travel Centre in Britain for £16; it stays valid for one year. You must show proof of age (a birth certificate or passport) or student status at a British school, and submit two passport-sized photos. BR also offers Family, Disabled Persons (see Disabled Travelers above), and Senior Railcards (for those over 60): purchase these in Britain. A careful check of prices can often save you money. Day returns often cost little more than a single ticket and returns can save you a substantial amount of the cost of two single tickets.

Coaches and Buses

Once upon a time, in 1986, bus travel in Britain was straightforward. Then came denationalization, followed closely by chaos, followed by a modicum of order. **National Express** is the principal operator of long-distance bus (coach) services and has offices in all major cities in the south. Each county or region has its own company for rural service. In towns where two or three inter-city rural-services companies link up (such as Glastonbury), the confusion can be immense; head for the local tourist office or bus station for help. *Let's Go* lists both for each town. Don't give up, because beneath the confusion lurks a wonderfully inexpensive long-distance bus system.

The British distinguish between **buses**, which cover short local, rural, and city routes, and **coaches**, which cover long distances with few stops. **Excursion coaches** go to special places of interest, and some conduct regimented and expensive tours. Most coaches, however, are merely means of public transportation. **Express coaches** offer some of the lowest fares on long-distance travel within Britain. Although they may take up to twice as long to reach their destination as trains, coaches can cost as little as a third as much. Some require advance reservation. **Student Coach Cards** (£5) are valid on National Express, reducing standard fares by 30%.

Some local bus companies offer their own travel passes. The **Explorer** ticket (£4.40), which can be purchased from any local ticket office or on the bus, allows one day's unlimited travel on virtually all bus routes in East Kent, Maidstone and District, Hastings and District, Southdown, and eastern Hampshire regions. **Busrangers** offer seven-day travel in the same districts (£18).

Cars and Caravans

The advantages of car travel speak for themselves. Disadvantages include high gasoline prices and the unfamiliar laws and habits associated with driving in foreign lands on the wrong side of the road. Since drivers in Britain sit on the right-hand side of the car and drive on the left-hand side of the road (so that right-handed drivers can joust with oncoming traffic), traffic patterns are particularly difficult to assimilate. The British, however, manage without undue fuss. Be particularly cautious at roundabouts (rotary interchanges): give way to traffic from the right. British law requires drivers and front-seat passengers to wear seat belts; a 1991 law now mandates that rear-seat passengers wear belts whenever fitted. Britain's speed limits are 60mph on single carriageways (non-divided highways), 70mph on motorways (highways) and dual carriageways (divided highways), and usually 30mph in town. (Speed limits are always marked at the beginning of town areas; upon leaving, you'll see a circular sign with a slash through it, signalling the end of the speed restriction.) Speed limits aren't rabidly enforced. Remember, though, that many British roads are curvy and single-track; drivers should, remarkably, use common sense. A few major bridges and tunnels require tolls.

England is covered by a skeletal but adequate system of limited-access expressways ("M-roads" or "motorways"), mainly radiating from London. The M-roads are supplemented by a tight web of "A-roads" and "B-roads" that covers every pocket of the United Kingdom. Labelling of the "A" and "B" roads follows a clock pattern: road buffs can roughly locate themselves just by knowing they are on the A13.

Hiring (renting) an automobile is the least expensive autokinetic option if you plan to drive for a month or less. For more extended travel, you might consider **leasing** instead. Major rental companies with agencies almost everywhere in Britain include **Avis, Budget Rent-A-Car, Geoffrey Davis Europcar, Hertz, Kenning,** and **Swan National.** Prices range from £150 to £300 per week with unlimited mileage, plus VAT; for insurance reasons, the minimum age for renting in Britain is almost always 21. **Europe by Car** (see listing below) will rent to younger people if someone hustles through the paperwork in advance, in the States. All plans require sizable deposits unless you're paying by credit card. Several U.S. firms offer rental and leasing plans in Britain and Ireland; for starters, try **Kemwel Group**, 106 Calvert St., Harrison, NY 10528-3199 (tel. (800) 678-0678 or (914) 835-5454); **Auto-Europe**, P.O. Box 1097, Sharp's Wharf, Camden, ME 04843 (tel. (800) 223-5555); or **Europe by Car**, 1 Rockefeller Plaza, New York, NY 10020 (tel. (800) 223-1516 or (212) 581-3040, 5% student and faculty discounts). CIEE and Let's Go Travel Services have discount rental and leasing plans for students and faculty members.

Purchasing a car in Britain may in the end save you money if you travel for extended periods. The car must conform to safety and emission standards should you bring it back to the U.S.; write or call the wonderful and unique U.S. Environmental Protection Agency, Public Information Center (tel. (202) 382-2080), 401 M St. SW, Washington, DC 20460, for *Automotive Imports—Fact Sheet.* Crankshaft collecters should consider buying a used car or van and selling it before leaving. *Europe by Van,* available for $8.50 from David Guterson, 13024 Venice Loop, Bainbridge Island, WA 98110, explains the intricacies of buying and selling a van in London. David Shore and Patty Campbell's *Europe Free!: The Car, Van, & RV Travel Guide,* offers advice. Write to 1842 Santa Margarita Dr., Fallbrook, CA 92028.

Bicycles

For information about routes, independent cyclists can consult tourist offices or any of the numerous books on cycling in Britain. Rodale Press, 33 E. Minor St., Emmaus, PA 18908 (tel. (800)-441-7761; (800) 441-7768 in PA) offers a wide range of books on biking. *Bike Touring* (Sierra Club, 730 Polk St., San Francisco, CA 94109; tel. (415) 923-5600; $8.95 plus $3 shipping) offers general advice on planning for a bike excursion. The **Cyclists' Touring Club,** Cotterell House, 69 Meadrow, Godalming, Surrey, England GU7 3HS (tel. (0483) 417 217; fax (0483) 426 994), provides information, maps, and a list of bike rental firms in Britain. Annual membership costs £20, under 21 £10, and family £34. The club's bi-monthly magazine, *Cycletouring and Campaigning,* is a valuable resource. A pamphlet on bike/train travel can be procured from BR and at most stations; the maze of regulations and restrictions will scare you at first, but in the end many of these are not enforced.

Riding a bike with a heavy pack on your back is about as safe as rollerskating blindfolded on ice. Be sure to purchase adequate **touring equipment:** a good **helmet,** a selection of tools, a repair book, skin-tight fluorescent turbo-nutter shorts, and pairs of back and front panniers (saddlebags) with proper connecting attachments for the frame. To secure your bike, invest in a U-shaped **lock** made by Nashbar or Kryptonite ($25-40). British law states that at night your bike must show a white light at the front of the cycle and a red light (as well as a red reflector) on the back. Police enforce this rule with remarkable assiduity. Adequate maps are also a necessity; Ordnance Survey maps (1 in. to 1 mi.) or Bartholomew maps (½ in. to 1 mi.) are available in most bookstores.

Most of your bicycle needs will be answered by wondrous **Bike Nashbar,** 4111 Simon Rd., Youngstown, OH 44512 (tel. (800) 627-4227). If you can find a nationally advertised lower price, they will beat it by 5¢. Call their toll-free number (open 24 hr.) and the order should be on its way the same day. They regularly ship anywhere in the U.S. and Canada and will also ship overseas.

Renting a bike is preferable to bringing your own if your touring will be confined to one or two regions. A three-speed will cost anywhere from £8-20 per week, a mountain bike up to £30.

Feet

If you plan to make any serious hikes, bring adequate maps. Explorers will enjoy the Ordnance Survey 1:25,000 Second Series maps, which mark almost every house, barn, standing stone, graveyard, and pub. Less ambitious walkers will probably be satisfied with the 1:50,000 scale maps. Other essentials include a waterproof jacket, compass, sturdy shoes, thick woolen socks, a first-aid kit, a flashlight, and, for long distance hikers, a whistle. The **Ramblers' Association,** 1-5 Wandsworth Rd., London SW8 2XX (tel. (071) 582 6878), and the **Backpackers' Club,** P.O. Box 381, 7-10 Friar St., Reading, Berkshire, England RG3 4RL (24-hr. tel. (04917) 739), give written information on both feet. For more information on national trails and recreational paths, contact the **Countryside Commission,** John Dower House, Crescent Place, Cheltenham, Gloucestershire, England GL50 3RA (tel. (0242) 521 381) or at 71 Kingsway, London WC2 (tel. (071) 831 3510). They publish *Walking in Britain, Out in the Country,* and *Heritage Coasts of England and Wales,*.

Thumb

Adventurous daytrippers often hitchhike in parts of Britain outside of London. A wait of more than an hour is rare on major roads in summer. *Let's Go* does not recommend hitching. Consider all of the risks before you take a ride. A woman alone especially should not take the chance. Never accept a ride in the back of a two-door car. In an emergency, open the door; this usually surprises the driver enough to make him or her slow down. If you feel uneasy about the ride for any reason, get out at the first opportunity.

Hitch-Hikers' Manual: Britain (£3.95) contains practical information on the laws concerning hitching, tips on techniques, and advice about the best places to hitch in 200 British towns. For a copy, contact Vacation Work, 9 Park End St., Oxford, England OX1 1HJ. *A Hitch-hiker's Manual to Great Britain* is also an excellent guide (Penguin, $7.50). You might also try the Britain section of Ken Welsh's *Hitchhiker's Guide to Europe.*

Accommodations Outside London

That swift jaunt from the capital can easily turn into an extended tour of southern England. It may simply prove more convenient not to return to London after each foray. A night by the sea rapidly dissolves much accumulated London grime. Tourist information centers outside London provide invaluable aid in the search for accommodations. These offices often have free or inexpensive lists of accommodations available in town, which they will post on their doors after hours. For about £1, most offices will book you a place to stay. Most also offer a "book-a-bed-ahead" service; for a fee of about £2, they will reserve you a room in the next town on your itinerary.

Hostels

IYHF-affiliated hostels pepper all major British cities and towns. To stay in one, you must be a member of the International Youth Hostel Federation or pay extra for a guest pass. Regional directories of British hostels are available from YHA headquarters in London and most hostels. (See London Youth Hostels above).

Some hostels are strikingly beautiful, others little more than barracks. Hostels and their grounds usually close from 10am to 5pm, and evening curfews (usually about 11pm) plague all but a few hostels. Many hostels have laundry facilities, ranging from washing machines to troughs in the backyard. Most large hostels offer hot evening meals, and almost all provide kitchen facilities and utensils at no extra charge. Some house small stores, where canned goods and campers' food are sold. Hostel rates vary with the traveler's age and the hostel's grade.

Independent hostels crop up throughout Britain. These lodgings cost roughly the same as IYHF hostels, yet can be less rule-ridden and afflicted with curfews.

Bed and Breakfasts

The hospitality of British B&B establishments is celebrated the world over—with good reason. Those accustomed to the impersonal management of budget motel chains will often thrill to the geniality of B&B proprietors. B&Bs outside the capital can charm the most cynical revolutionary, showing the cozy side of the capitalist system.

Cheap hotels, often called guest houses, can sometimes offer as good bargains as B&Bs. But the quality of these establishments varies from delightful to dismal.

Small-hotel proprietors are often brusque; very few are as funny as John Cleese's Basil Fawlty in the raucous BBC comedy *Fawlty Towers*. For those on the run, hotels offer fewer restrictions and more flexible arrangements than B&Bs. Check at the tourist offices for listings.

Camping

Camping can provide either the best or worst of overnight accommodations. Some nights you will pitch your tent against an ancient standing stone and fade into sleep under the infinite violet sky, amid the watchful silence of nature. Other nights you will be surrounded by gas-belching RVs, obnoxious children, pot-bellied families beating their domestic animals, and the ethereal blue haze of portable televisions. Most campsites stay open from April through October, and some remain open year-round. A few youth hostels have camping facilities (usually at half the hostel charge; hostel card required). But most campsites are privately owned and were designed for people with RVs rather than tent-dwellers. You can legally set up camp only in specifically marked areas unless you receive permission from a private landowner. It is legal to cross private land by **public rights of way;** any other use of private land without permission is considered trespassing. Farmers may allow you to camp on their land. Never camp without permission, and always leave the site cleaner than you found it. For more information about camping in Britain, send for the British Tourist Authority's free brochure *Caravan and Camping Parks* (see Useful Addresses above).

University Accommodations

Most British universities open their dormitories to groups and individuals during the long school vacations (mainly July-Sept., some available mid-March to mid-April). Accommodations usually consist of single study bedrooms. B&B or full board is sometimes available for short stays. Occasionally minimum stays may be imposed. Dorms are usually convenient if not charming. Write well in advance to the British Universities Accommodation Consortium (BUAC), P.O.Box 544, University Park, Nottingham, England NG7 2RD (tel. (0602) 504 571).

Oxford

Shrouded in 800 years of tradition, Oxford's forty colleges and halls are a soft sheltered world. A measure of mayhem, squealing coach brakes, foreign language students, and rattling bicycle chains have, however, forced directors of BBC dramas to shoot Oxford's "dreaming spires" from very select camera angles. Oxford enjoys the attention but wishes seats on the buses were easier to find.

Orientation and Practical Information

From London, trains run from Paddington (every hr., 1 hr., £9.50 not-so-cheap day return, £17 period return). The **Oxford Tube** (every 20 min., 1¼ hr., £4.50 day return, £6.50 period return) and **Oxford CityLink** (3 per hr., 1½ hr., £4.50 day return, £6.50 period return) provide competing coach services between Oxford's bus station and London's Victoria coach station.

Queen, High, St. Aldates, and Cornmarket St. intersect at right angles in **Carfax,** the town center. The colleges surround Carfax; the bus and train stations lie to the west. Past the east end of High St. over Magdalen Bridge, the neighborhoods of **East Oxford** stretch along **Cowley Road** (marked "To Cowley" on the map) and **Iffley Road** (marked "To Reading"). To the north along **Woodstock** and **Banbury Roads,** leafier residential areas roll on for miles.

Getting Around

The **Oxford Bus Company** (tel. 711 312) operates the red double-deckers and the lime-green "City Nipper" minibuses, as well as the CityLink service to London;

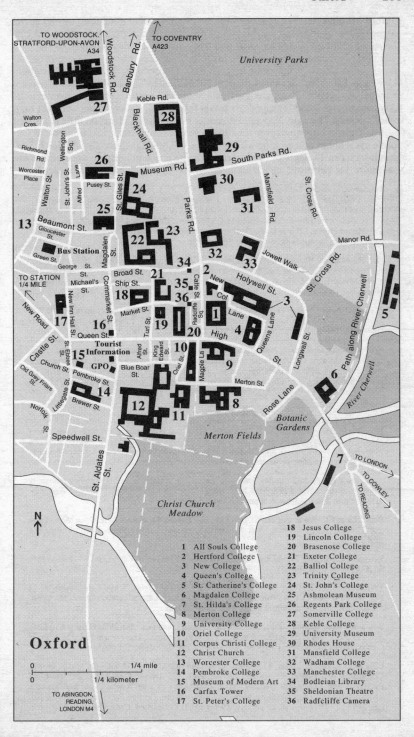

TO WOODSTOCK,
STRATFORD-UPON-AVON
A34

TO COVENTRY
A423

Woodstock Rd.

Banbury Rd.

University Parks

Walton
Cres.

Keble Rd.

27

28

Richmond
Rd.

Wellington
Sq.

Blackhall Rd.

Museum Rd.

South Parks Rd.

29

Worcester
Place

St. John's St.

Alfred
Lane

Pusey St.

26

30

Mansfield Rd.

St. Cross Rd.

Walton
St.

31

Beaumont St.

St. Giles St.

24

Parks Rd.

13

Gloucester
St.

25

Green St.

Bus Station

22

23

32

Jowett Walk

Manor Rd.

George St.

Magdalen St.

33

Path along River Cherwell

TO STATION
1/4 MILE

Michael's
St.

St.

34

21

Broad St.

2

Holywell St.

St. Cross Rd.

3

Longwall St.

5

New Rd.

New Inn Hall St.

Cornmarket St.

Ship St.

35

Catte St.

New
Col
Lane

18

36

1

New Road

17

16

Queen St.

Market St.

Turl St.

19

20

4

Queens Lane

Path along River Cherwell

River Cherwell

Castle St.

**Tourist
Information**

St. Ebbes St.

15

Alfred
St.

King
Edward
St.

10

High

9

Church St.

GPO

Blue Boar
St.

Oriel St.

Magpie La.

6

Old Grey Friars
St.

Pembroke St.

14

Merton St.

Norfolk
St.

Littlegate St.

Brewer St.

12

11

8

Rose Lane

*Botanic
Gardens*

Speedwell St.

St. Aldates St.

Merton Fields

7

TO LONDON

TO COWLEY

TO READING

*Christ Church
Meadow*

N

Oxford

0   1/4 mile
0   1/4 kilometer

TO ABINGDON,
READING,
LONDON M4

1 All Souls College	18 Jesus College
2 Hertford College	19 Lincoln College
3 New College	20 Brasenose College
4 Queen's College	21 Exeter College
5 St. Catherine's College	22 Balliol College
6 Magdalen College	23 Trinity College
7 St. Hilda's College	24 St. John's College
8 Merton College	25 Ashmolean Museum
9 University College	26 Regents Park College
10 Oriel College	27 Somerville College
11 Corpus Christi College	28 Keble College
12 Christ Church	29 University Museum
13 Worcester College	30 Rhodes House
14 Pembroke College	31 Mansfield College
15 Museum of Modern Art	32 Wadham College
16 Carfax Tower	33 Manchester College
17 St. Peter's College	34 Bodleian Library
	35 Sheldonian Theatre
	36 Radcliffe Camera

Oxford Minibus (tel. 771 876) operates the checkered-flag minibuses, as well as the Oxford Tube London service. Masses of minibuses scoot around Oxford, and cut-throat competition makes for swift and frequent service. **South Midlands** (tel. 262 368) also runs some Oxford services. Most local services board on the streets immediately adjacent to Carfax; some longer-distance buses depart from the bus station. Abingdon Rd. buses are often marked "Red Bridge;" some Iffley Rd. buses are marked "Rose Hill." Fares are low (most about 80p return). Some companies issue Compass tickets, good for one day's travel (about £4), but companies disdain each other's tickets. The signs all over town reading "No Cycles Here" do little to prevent cyclists from riding whereever they like, even in heavy traffic. Stop in one of Oxford's cycle shops and pick up a copy of the free 45-page guide *Cycling in Oxford*, which includes 17 pages of cycling maps of the city and outlying areas. Bikes are especially not permitted on Cornmarket St. or in college parklands or quads.

Tourist Information Centre: St. Aldates St. (tel. 726 871), just south of Carfax. Their *Welcome to Oxford* guide (50p) is a valuable resource. If you're staying for the day, just pick up a map (20p). Local accommodations service £2.30. Accommodations list 35p. Open Mon.-Sat. 9:30am-5pm, Sun. 10:30am-1pm and 1:30-3:30pm. **Thames and Chilterns Tourist Board,** The Mount House, Church Green, Whitney (tel. (0993) 778 800). Covers surrounding countryside. Open Mon.-Sat. 9am-5:30pm, Sun. 1-4pm.

Accommodations Bureau: Bravalta House, 242 Iffley Rd. (tel. 241 326 or 250 511). When the tourist office is closed, call Mrs. Downes, the city's Secretary of Accommodations and a B&B owner herself. Phone before 10pm. No fee. Or check in the window of the tourist office.

Discount Student Travel: Campus Travel, 13 High St. (tel. 242 067). Eurotrain tickets, ISICs, railcards, discount airfare, coaches, insurance. Open Mon.-Fri. 9:30am-5:30pm, Sat. 10am-5pm. **STA Travel,** 19 High St. (tel. 240 547). Open Mon.-Fri. 9am-5:30pm, Sat. 10am-4pm.

Guided Walks: Good daily tourist office walking tours (11-11:30am and 2-3pm every ½ hr.; tickets £3, children £1.50). Alternatively you could support student life and take a tour from one of the many student groups that offer them (£2.50, students £2). Some students will regale you with stories you won't hear on the official tours and will give your money back if you're dissatisfied. Others won't. Often the more reliable student guides hang out right near the tourist office.

Currency Exchange: Try one of the many banks near Carfax: **Barclay's,** Cornmarket St. (open Mon.-Fri. 9:30am-4:30pm, Sat. 9:30am-noon); **National Westminster,** Cornmarket St. (open Mon.-Fri. 9:30am-4:30pm, Sat. 9:30am-3:30pm); **Lloyd's,** in Selfridge's, Queen St. (open Mon.-Sat. 9:30am-4:30pm); and **Thomas Cook,** at 5 Queen St. (open Mon.-Sat. 9am-5:30pm) and at the train station (open daily 9am-5pm).

American Express: Keith Bailey Travel Agency, 98 St. Aldates St. (tel. 790 099), a few doors down from the tourist office. Mail held; postal code OX1 1BT. Open Mon. and Wed.-Fri. 9am-5:30pm, Tues. 9:30am-5:30pm, Sat. 9am-5pm.

Post Office: 102/104 St. Aldates St. (tel. 814 783). **Bureau de change** inside. Open Mon.-Tues. and Thurs.-Fri. 9am-5:30pm, Wed. 9:30am-5:30pm, Sat. 9am-12:30pm. **Postal Code:** OX1 1ZZ.

Telephones: Banks of Phonecard and intercontinental phones at Carfax and on Cornmarket St. **Telephone Code:** (0865).

Train Station: Botley Rd. (tel. 722 333 or 249 055), west of Carfax. Travel Centre open Mon.-Fri. 8am-7:45pm, Sat. 8:30am-5:30pm, Sun. 11:15am-6:45pm. Station open Mon.-Fri. 5:50am-8:15pm, Sat. 6:30am-7:50pm, Sun. 7am-8:30pm.

Bus and Coach Station: Gloucester Green. **Oxford Tube** (tel. 772 250); **Oxford CityLink** (tel. 711 312); and **National Express** (tel. 791 579). **National Travelworld** (tel. 726 172), at Carfax, books for National Express. Open Mon.-Fri. 9am-5pm, Sat. 9am-1pm.

Bike Rental: Thakes Cycles, 55 Walton St., Jericho (tel. 516 122), about 1 mi. north of town. Cheapest 3- or 10-speeds £5 per day, £10 per week; £25 deposit. Open Mon.-Sat. 9am-6pm. **Pennyfarthing,** 5 George St. (tel. 249 368). Closest to town center. Rental £5 per day; 3-speeds £10 per week; £20 deposit. Open Mon.-Sat. 8am-5:30pm. **Beeline Bicycles,** 33 Cowley Rd. (tel. 246 615). Three-speeds £5 per day, £9 per week; £25 deposit. Open Mon.-Sat. 9am-6pm.

Boat Rental: Hubbock's Boat Hire, Folly Bridge (tel. 244 235), south of Carfax, along St. Aldates St. Punts £5.50 per hr.; £20 deposit. Open June-Sept. daily 10am-7pm. **C. Howard & Son,** Magdalen Bridge, east of Carfax at end of High St. Punts £6 per hr.; £15 deposit. Open daily 10am-dusk. Arrive early, especially on sunny days, to avoid a long, long wait. **Salter Brothers,** Folly Bridge (tel. 243 421). Runs cruises to Abingdon (at 2:30pm, 1 hr., £7.15 return, children £5), Rose Island (2 per day, 90 min., £3.50 return, children £2.50), and Iffley (5 per day, 20 min., £2.75 return, children £1.65). Open May-Sept. Mon.-Sat. 9am-6pm, Sun. 9am-4pm.

Camping and Hiking Supplies: YHA Shop, on Magdalen Bridge roundabout (tel. 247 948). Youth hostel membership available. Open Mon. and Wed.-Fri. 10am-6pm, Tues. 10am-7pm, Sat. 9am-5:30pm.

Bookstores: Blackwell's, 48-51 Broad St. (see Sights below). Oxford's largest. Open Mon.-Sat. 9am-6pm, Sun. noon-5pm. **Music department,** 38 Holywell St. Open Mon.-Sat. 9am-6pm, Sun. noon-5pm. **Dillon's,** William Baker House, Broad St. Blackwell's competition. Open Mon.-Fri. 9am-8pm, Sat. 9am-6pm, Sun. 10am-5pm. **Thornton's,** Broad St. Used student books. Open Mon.-Thurs. 9am-6pm, Fri.-Sat. 9am-4pm. **EOA Books,** 34 Cowley Rd. Good selection of alternative and radical titles. Open Mon.-Sat. 10am-5:30pm.

Public Library: Westgate Shopping Centre (tel. 815 509). Fine local history collection. Open Mon.-Tues. and Thurs.-Fri. 9:15am-7pm, Wed. and Sat. 9:15am-5pm.

Ticket Office: Tickets-in-Oxford, tourist office (tel. 727 855). Tickets for local events and the Royal Shakespeare Company in Stratford. Open Mon.-Sat. 9:30am-5pm.

Laundromats: Clean-o-Fine, 66 Abingdon Rd., South Oxford. Open daily 8am-9:30pm. **Valuematic,** 184 Cowley Rd., across Magdalen Bridge. Open Sun.-Fri. 8am-9pm, Sat. 8am-5pm.

Crisis: Samaritans, 123 Iffley Rd. (tel. 722 122). Phone 24 hrs.; drop in 8am-10pm. **Drug and Alcohol Hotline,** tel. 244 447 or 248 591. 24-hr. answer phone.

Rape Crisis: The Women's Line, tel. 726 295. Open Mon.-Tues. 7-9pm, Wed. 2-10pm, Thurs.-Fri. 2-4pm; answering machine other times; in emergency call London Rape Crisis Center at (071) 837 1600.

Women's Center: 35 Cowley Rd. (tel. 245 923). Phone answered Mon.-Sat. noon-4pm.

Gay and Lesbian Switchboard: Tel. 726 893. Phone answered Tues.-Wed. and Fri. 7-9pm.

Pharmacy: Boots, Cornmarket St. Open Mon. and Fri.-Sat. 8:45am-6pm, Tues.-Wed. 9am-5:30pm, Thurs. 8:45am-8pm.

Hospital: John Radcliffe Hospital, tel. 647 11. Take bus #10.

Police: St. Aldates and Speedwell St. (tel. 249 881).

Emergency: Dial 999; no coins required.

Accommodations and Camping

Book at least a week ahead, especially for singles, and expect to mail in a deposit. B&Bs line the main roads out of town, all of them a vigorous walk from Carfax. The No. 300s on **Banbury Road,** fern-laced and domestic, stand miles north of the center (catch a Banbury bus on St. Giles St.). You'll find cheaper B&Bs in the 200s and 300s on Iffley Rd. and from No. 250-350 on Cowley Rd., both served by frequent buses from Carfax. **Abingdon Road,** in South Oxford, is about the same price and distance, though less colorful. Wherever you go, expect to pay at least £15-18 per person.

IYHF Youth Hostel, Jack Straw's Lane (tel. 629 97). Catch any minibus departing from the job center south of Carfax (every 15 min., last bus 10:30pm). Remote but well-equipped, with showers, kitchen, and food shop. Lockout 10am-1pm. Curfew 11pm. £6.30, ages 16-20 £5.10. Breakfast £2.30. Sleepsack rental 80p. Open March-Oct. daily; Nov. and Jan.-Feb. Mon.-Sat.

YWCA, Alexandra Residential Club, 133 Woodstock Rd. (tel. 520 21), quite a walk up Cornmarket St. and down Woodstock Rd., or bus #60 or 60A. Women over 16 only. Bunk rooms, TV lounge, kitchen and laundry facilities. Limited accommodations in summer; fills up with students during term. Reserve about 2 weeks in advance for summer. Office open Mon.-Fri. 8:30am-1pm and 2:30-7:30pm, Sat. 10am-noon and 4-5pm, Sun. 11am-noon. Curfew: Sun.-Thurs. 2am, Fri.-Sat. 2:30am. Three-night max. stay. £6; 2 nights £11; 3 nights £15.

Tara, 10 Holywell St. (tel. 244 786 or 248 270). The best B&B in town, situated among the colleges. Kind hearing-impaired proprietors, Mr. and Mrs. Godwin, lip-read and speak clearly—no communication problems. Desks, basins, TVs, and refrigerators in every room; kitchenette on the 2nd floor. Breakfast room a virtual museum of academic regalia, college coats-of-arms, and other Oxford paraphernalia. Open July-Sept.; the rest of the year it fills up with students, but check anyway. Reserve at least 2 weeks in advance. Singles £18. Doubles £30. Triples £36.

White House View, 9 White House Rd. (tel. 721 626), off Abingdon Rd. Good-sized rooms only 10 min. from Carfax. Solicitous proprietors and excellent breakfasts. £14 per person.

Micklewood, 331 Cowley Rd. (tel. 247 328). Enchanting proprietor will shelter you in rooms decorated with excruciating detail. Comfort and cleanliness abound. Singles £16. Doubles £27.

Newton Guest House, 82-84 Abingdon Rd. (tel. 240 561), about ½ mile from town center; take any Abingdon bus across Folly Bridge. Antique enthusiasts will be taken with the monolithic wooden wardrobes in every room. Affable proprietor. No singles. Doubles £30, with bath £40.

King's Guest House, 363 Iffley Rd. (tel. 241 363). Spacious doubles in a modern, comfortable home. Helpful proprietors. No singles. Rooms £30, with bath £35.

Gables' Guest House, 6 Cumnor Hill (tel. 862 153). Oxford's finest pink B&B. One mile from train station, 2 mi. from city center. Best for motorists: lots of parking and close to the ring road. Gargantuan bathroom on first floor. Full English breakfast. Reserve ahead with 1 night's deposit. Comfortable rooms. £17 per person, £20 with facilities.

Camping: Oxford Camping International, 426 Abingdon Rd. (tel. 246 551), behind the Texaco Station. 129 nondescript sites on a manicured lawn. Laundry and warm showers. Open year-round. £6 for 2 people and tent. **Cassington Mill Caravan Site,** Eynsham Rd., Cassington (tel. 881 081), about 4 mi. northwest on the A40. Take bus #90 from the bus station. 83 pitches. £5.50 for 2 people and tent. Hot showers included. Neither of these places rents tents.

Food

Oxford brandishes innumerable restaurants and cheap cafés to distract students from disagreeable college food; expect an upbeat atmosphere at most places. During the summer, walk a few blocks away from the four major streets to escape coach tourists and generic food. For fresh produce and deli goods, visit the **Covered Market** between Market St. and Carfax. (Open Mon.-Sat. 8am-5:30pm.) For dried fruit, whole grains, and the like, head for **Holland & Barrett,** King Edward St. (Open Mon.-Sat. 9am-5:30pm.) Eat and run at one of the better take-aways: **Bret's Burgers,** Park End St., near the train station, with delectable burgers and chips from £2 (open Sun.-Thurs. noon-11:30pm, Fri.-Sat. noon-midnight); or **Parmenters,** High St., near Longwall St., the trendiest take-away in town (date flapjacks 60p, enormous slices of carrot cake £1.10; open Mon.-Fri. 8:30am-6:30pm, Sat. 9am-6pm, Sun. 9:30am-5pm).

Munchy Munchy, 6 Park End St., on the way into town from the rail station. Stark wooden decor and absurd name somehow redeemed by spirited cooking and an energetic proprietor. Different dishes daily, all Indonesian or Malaysian, at least 1 vegetarian (£5-8). BYOB but 50p corkage per person. Open Tues.-Sat. noon-2pm and 5:30-10pm.

Brown's Restaurant and Wine Bar, 5-9 Woodstock Rd. Renovation has somehow both diminished the chic atmosphere and improved the English cuisine. Large helpings of spaghetti, burgers, vegetable salad all under £6. Open Mon.-Sat. 11am-11:30pm, Sun. noon-11:30pm.

Poor Student Restaurant, Ship St., off Cornmarket St. Well, not utterly destitute. Student-style English food served in a bright, ritzy interior with art deco lamps. Pasta £5-5.35. Open daily noon-10pm.

Cherwell Boathouse, Bardwell Rd. (tel. 527 46), off Banbury Rd., 1 mi. north of town. Romantically perched on the bank of the Cherwell and run by amiable young proprietors. A good place to propose. Menu offers a choice of 3-course meals—1 vegetarian, both unorthodox. Well-loved wine list. Expect to spend the entire evening; book well in advance. Dinner usually under £20, and worth every penny. When you're finished, rent a punt next door (£5) and drift off into the watery evening. Open Mon. and Wed.-Sat. 7:30-10pm, Sun. 12:30-2pm.

The Nosebag, 6-8 Michael's St. Vegetarian and wholefood meals served in sauna-like sur-roundings for under £5. Open Mon. 9:30am-5:30pm, Tues.-Thurs. 9:30am-5:30pm and 6:30-10pm, Fri. 9:30am-5:30pm and 6:30-10:30pm, Sat. 9:30am-10:30pm, Sun. 9:30am-6pm.

Pastificio, George St. near Cornmarket St. and the Apollo Theatre. Deep-dish pizza (£3.75-4.75) and fresh pasta (£4.35-5.35) served in clean modern surroundings. Open daily noon-midnight.

Polash Tandoori Restaurant, 25 Park End St. Inexpensive and delicious Indian cuisine served in a quiet setting near the train station. Chicken curry £4.15. Vegetable dishes under £2.15. Lunch buffet £7.50 per person. Open Mon.-Thurs. noon-2:30pm and 6-11:30pm, Fri.-Sat. noon-2:30pm and 6pm-midnight, Sun. noon-11:30pm.

Pubs

The Perch, Binsey. From Walton St. in Jericho, walk down Walton Well Rd. and over Port Meadow, cross Rainbow Bridge, head north and follow the trail west. This pub will make your whole vacation worthwhile. Definitely worth the trouble of finding. The lovely garden makes an ideal place for Sunday lunch or twilight drinks. Lunch served noon-2pm, cold buffet Mon.-Fri. 6:30-8:30pm. Occasional do-it-yourself barbecues.

The Turf Tavern, 4 Bath Pl., off Holywell St. A rambling, 13th-century building, intimate and relaxed. Good selection of drinks: beers, punches, ciders, and country wines—mead, el-derberry, apple, and red-and-white currant. Wine about £1. Great salad buffet and hot meals noon-2pm.

The Bear, Alfred St. and Bear Lane. Christ Church's local: a dyed-in-the-wool Oxford land-mark since 1242. Wouldn't be the same without the collection of ties, some of them snipped from England's best, brightest, and most boastful. Lunch served 12:30-2:15pm, dinner 7-10:30pm.

Victoria Arms, Marston Rd., by the river. A student favorite. The Happy Mondays did not play here on their recent tour.

The King's Arms, Holywell St. at Parks Rd. The university's unofficial student union and center for saturnalia studies. Punks, drunks, and a few scholars. Crowded and charmless, but keen with students.

The Head of the River, Folly Bridge. Immense river pub popular with the young and avail-able. Large patio and multitudinous tables provide a great variety of settings in which to enjoy your ale.

The Bakery and Brewhouse, Gloucester St., just down from the bus station. Fast and lively crowd. Jazz on Wed. evenings and Sun. afternoons. Lunch served noon-2:15pm, dinner 5:30-8:30pm. Try their home-brewed ale and home-baked bread.

The Blue Boar, Blue Boar St. The quintessential English pub—starting with the name. Excel-lent ale, and no piped-in music.

The Eagle and Child, 49 Giles St. An inn since the 17th century, popular with the likes of J.R.R. Tolkien and C.S. Lewis. The owner has adorned the walls with photos and newspaper clippings from his days as a stunt double for Peter Ustinov. Popular with tourists.

Sights

Oxford University, England's first, was founded in 1167 by Henry II. Until then, Englishmen had traveled to Paris to study, a fact that never sat well with the fran-cophobic English king. After his tiff with Thomas à Becket, Archbishop of Canter-bury, Henry ordered the return of English students studying in Paris, so that "there may never be wanting a succession of persons duly qualified for the service of God in church and state." Over 800 years, the university has flourished into an interna-tional center of learning. In the ever-fierce competition with that other university on the Cam, Oxford boasts among its graduates Sir Christopher Wren, Oscar Wilde, Indira Gandhi, 13 prime ministers, and Dudley Moore.

Oxford has no official "campus." The university's 40 independent colleges, where students live and learn, are scattered throughout the city; central libraries, laborato-ries, and faculties are established and maintained by the university. At the end of their last academic year, students from all the colleges come together for their "degree examinations," a grueling three-week process that takes place in the Examination Schools on High St. Each year, university authorities unsuccessfully undertake to prohibit the vigorous post-examination celebrations in the street. The tourist office guide *Welcome to Oxford* (50p) and the tourist office map (20p) list colleges' public visiting hours (often curtailed with neither prior notice nor explanation). Christ Church, Magdalen, and New College charge admission.

Before tackling the university on your own, you may or may not want to visit **The Oxford Story,** Broad St. This museum of sorts (visitors are hauled around roller-coaster style in medieval "desks") recreates various scenes of Oxford's history. Guide yourself through the exhibits by cassette (narrated by Sir Alec Guinness) and participate in the St. Scholastica's Day Riot in 1355 or the development of Boyle's Law. (Open July-Aug. 9:30am-7pm; April-June and Sept.-Oct. 9:30am-5pm; Nov.-March daily 10am-4pm. Admission £3.75, students and seniors £3, children £2.25.)

Start your walking tour at Carfax, the center of activity, with a hike up the 97 spiral stairs of **Carfax Tower** for an overview of the city. Before hitting the heights, get a map of the rooftops from the attendant at the bottom. (Open March-Oct. Mon.-Sat. 10am-6pm, Sun. 2-6pm. Admission 80p, children 40p.) Then head down St. Aldates Street to the **Museum of Oxford** (across from the tourist office at the corner of Blue Boar St.), probably the most comprehensive and complete local-history collection in Britain. The seemingly endless but nevertheless entertaining walk-through displays outline Oxford's growth from a Roman and Saxon river-crossing for oxen to a famed intellectual watering hole. (Open Tues.-Sat. 10am-5pm. Free.)

Just down St. Aldates St. stands **Christ Church,** an intimidating mass of sandy stone that dwarfs the other colleges. "The House" has Oxford's grandest quad and its most socially distinguished, obnoxious students. (Open Mon.-Sat. 9:30am-6pm, Sun. 12:45-5:30pm. Admission £1, seniors, students, and children 40p.) Christ Church's chapel is also Oxford's **cathedral,** the smallest in England. In the year 730, St. Frideswide, Oxford's patron saint, built a nunnery on this site, in thanks for two miracles she had prayed for: the blinding of an annoying suitor, and his recovery. In the **hall,** college students and faculty take their meals on long wooden tables in a solemn setting. The cathedral's right transept contains a stained glass window (c. 1320) depicting Thomas à Becket kneeling in supplication, just before being put to death in Canterbury Cathedral. The 20-minute film shown continuously in the vestry (free) gives a concise history of the college and cathedral.

The Reverend Charles Dodgson (who wrote under the name Lewis Carroll) was friendly with Dean Liddell of Christ Church—and friendlier with his daughter Alice—and used to visit them in the gardens of the Dean's house at the eastern end of the cathedral. From the largest tree in his garden, the Cheshire Cat first grinned and vanished. Dodgson, who also taught mathematics at Oxford, used to come here to photograph and chat with Alice and her sisters. Among the nonsensical in-jokes that populate his Wonderland (on subjects ranging from Disraeli to religious reform to the early tweedles) Dodgson inserted several subtle references complaining about dining hall food at Oxford.

Curiouser and curiouser, the adjoining **Tom Quad** sometimes becomes the site of undergraduate lily pond-dunking. The quad takes its name from **Tom Tower,** which looms over the gate and in turn takes its name from **Great Tom,** the seventon bell it houses, which has faithfully rung 101 strokes (the original number of students) at 9:05pm (the original undergraduate curfew) every evening since 1682. Sixty coats of arms preside over the ceiling under the tower. Nearby, the fan-vaulted college hall bears imposing portraits of some of Christ Church's most famous alumni—Charles Dodgson, Sir Philip Sidney, W.H. Auden, John Ruskin, and John Locke. Other stately faces peer down in stone from the trim of the building's exterior. If you can, visit the kitchens and see the spits used for roasting oxen.

Through an archway (to your left as you face the cathedral) lies **Peckwater Quad,** encircled by the most elegant Palladian building in Oxford. Look here for faded rowing standings chalked on the walls and for Christ Church's library, closed to visitors. The adjoining **Canterbury Quad** houses the **Christ Church Picture Gallery,** a fine collection of Italian primitives and Dutch and Flemish paintings. (Open Mon.-Sat. 10:30am-1pm and 2-5:30pm, Sun. 2-5:30pm. Admission 50p. Visitors to gallery only should enter through Canterbury Gate off Oriel St.) Spreading east and south from the college's main entrance, **Christ Church Meadow** helps compensate for Oxford's lack of "backs" (riverside gardens in Cambridge).

Across St. Aldates at 30 Pembroke St., the **Museum of Modern Art** exhibits works ranging from anti-war sculptures to a photographic history of Israel. (Open Tues.-Wed. 10am-6pm, Thurs. 10am-9pm, Fri.-Sat. 10am-6pm, and Sun. 2-6pm. Admission £2.50, children £1.50.)

Across the street from the entrance to Christ Church lives neurophysiology professor Roger Bannister, the master of **Pembroke College** and the first human to break the 4-minute mile. Less speedy Samuel Johnson graduated from Pembroke, and his teapot and portrait still reside in its Senior Common room. Visitors must apply at the lodge to see the College.

Oriel College (real name "The House of the Blessed Mary the Virgin in Oxford") is wedged between High and Merton St. Oriel became a hotbed of the "Tractarian Movement" in the 1830s, when college clergy such as Keble and Newman tried to push the Anglican church back toward Rome. (Open daily 2-5pm.) Behind Oriel, **Corpus Christi College** surrounds a quad with an elaborate sundial in the center, crowned by a golden pelican. (Open daily 1:30-4:30pm.) Next door, **Merton College,** off Merton St., features a fine garden; the college's 14th-century library holds the first printed Welsh Bible. The college is also home to the **Mob Quad,** Oxford's oldest, dating from the 14th century. (College open April-Sept. Mon.-Fri. 2-5pm, Sat.-Sun. 10am-5pm; Oct.-March until 4pm.) A peaceful stroll down Merton Grove leads to **Merton Fields,** a quiet dab of green adjoining Christ Church Meadow.

University College, obviously up Logic Lane from Merton St., dates from 1249 and vies with Merton for the title of oldest college, claiming Alfred the Great as its founder. (Open afternoons when conferences are not in residence.) Percy Bysshe Shelley was expelled from University for writing the pamphlet *The Necessity of Atheism,* but has since been immortalized in a prominent Godless monument inside the college (to the right as you enter from High St.). Farther down High St. on the right lies the **Botanic Garden,** a sumptuous array of plants that has flourished for three centuries. (Open daily 9am-5pm; in winter daily 9am-4:30pm. Glasshouses open daily 2-4pm. Free.) For an esoteric escape from the weight of Oxford's tradition, visit **Oxford Holographics,** 71 High St., an exhibition hall of over 65 holograms. (Open daily 9:30am-6:30pm. Admission 50p, children 35p.)

With flowers lining the quads, a deer park on its grounds, the river flanking its side, and Addison's Walk (a verdant circular path) framing a meadow at one edge, **Magdalen College** has traditionally been considered Oxford's handsomest. Its spiritual patron is probably alumnus Oscar Wilde—the place has always walked on the flamboyant side. Edward Gibbon declared the 14 months he spent here "the most idle and unprofitable of my whole career." Every May Day, the college choir climbs up Magdalen's open-air stone pulpit and the bell tower to serenade the crowd below. (Open daily 2-6:15pm. Admission 75p.) Just up High St. toward Carfax, a statue of Queen Caroline (wife of George II) crowns the front gate of **Queen's College.** Wren and Hawksmoor went to the trouble of rebuilding Queen's in the 17th and 18th centuries, with a distinctive Queen Anne style in glorious orange, white, and gold. With its neat lawns and military flowerbeds, the college approaches Magdalen's beauty. A trumpet call summons students to dinner; a boar's head graces the Christmas table. The latter tradition supposedly commemorates an early student of the college who, attacked by a boar on the outskirts of Oxford, choked his assailant to death with a volume of Aristotle. (Open daily 2-5pm.) Next to Queen's stands **All Souls,** a graduate college with a prodigious endowment. Candidates who survive the terribly difficult pre-admission exams get invited out to dinner, where it is ensured that they are "well-born, well-bred and only moderately learned." (Open daily 2-5pm.)

Turn up Catte St. to the **Bodleian Library,** Oxford University's principal reading and research library with over six million books and 50,000 manuscripts. Sir Thomas Bodley endowed the library's first wing in 1602 on a site that had housed university libraries since 1489; the institution has since grown to fill the immense **Old Library** complex, the round **Radcliffe Camera** next door, and two newer buildings on Broad St. As a copyright library, the Bodleian receives a copy of every book printed in Great Britain—gratis. Admission to the reading rooms is by ticket only (if you can prove you're a scholar and present 2 passport photos, the Admissions Office will issue a 2-day pass for £2). No one has ever been permitted to take out a book, not even Cromwell. Well, especially not Cromwell. The library's unusual and entertaining exhibition includes Shelley's guitar, a lock of his hair, the only folio copy of Shakespeare's *Venus and Adonis,* a manuscript of a Haydn sonata, and an illuminated Aztec scroll. (Library open Mon.-Fri. 9am-5pm, Sat. 9am-12:30pm.) Across Broad St. from the Bodleian you can browse at **Blackwell's,** the famous bookstore with a seemingly erudite clientele. Blackwell's extends to a vast music department on Holywell St., an art shop next door, and a paperback shop and children's bookshop across the street (see Practical Information above).

The **Sheldonian Theatre,** set beside the Bodleian, is a Roman-style jewel of an auditorium built by Wren as a university theatre and home of the University Press. Graduation ceremonies, which are conducted in Latin, take place in the Sheldonian and can be witnessed with permission from one of the "bulldogs" (bowler-hatted university officers on duty). At the *Encaenia* in June, a vast procession of robed academics and luminaries winds with great pomp through the streets toward the Sheldonian. The cupola of the theatre affords an inspiring view of the spires of Oxford. (Open Mon.-Sat. 10am-12:45pm and 2-4:45pm; Nov.-Feb. until 3:45pm. Admission 50p, children 25p.) The **Museum of the History of Science,** next to the Sheldonian, houses a bewildering miscellany of arcania; including antique microscopes, charming astrolabes, and a blackboard touched by Einstein. (Open Mon.-Fri. 10:30am-1pm and 2:30-4pm. Free.)

The gates of **Balliol College,** across Broad St. (open daily 10am-6pm), still bear scorch marks from the immolations of 16th-century Protestant martyrs (the pyres were built a few yards from the college). The martyrs' monument is sometimes identified to gullible tourists as Oxford's "famous sunken cathedral." Housed in flamboyant neo-gothic buildings, Balliol is a mellow place that recently had a Marxist master. Swinburne went here. Balliol students preserve some semblance of tradition by routinely hurling bricks over the wall at their arch-rival, conservative **Trinity College,** on Broad St. (open daily 2-5pm). Trinity, founded in 1555, has a perfectly baroque chapel, with a limewood altarpiece, cedar lattices, and angel-capped pediments. Trinity's series of eccentric presidents includes Ralph Kettell, who used to come to dinner with a pair of scissors and chop away at members' hair that he deemed too long.

Across Catte St. from the Bodleian, New College Lane leads to **New College.** So named because of its relative anonymity at the time of its founding by William of Wykeham in 1379, New College has become one of Oxford's most prestigious colleges. The accreted layers of the front quad—compare the different stones of the first and second stories—reveal the continuous architectural history of the college. The chapel contains Jacob Epstein's sculpture *Lazarus,* an El Greco painting, and some fine stained glass. Look for the exquisitely detailed misericords, carved by sympathetic carpenters into the pews to support the monks' bottoms. A peaceful eastern garden is encircled by part of the **old city wall,** and every few years the mayor of the City of Oxford visits the college for a ceremonial inspection to ascertain the wall's good repair. One of the more notable members of the college was Warden Spooner, former head and originator of the "spoonerism." This stern but befuddled Oxford academic would raise a toast to "our queer old dean," or rebuke a student who had allegedly "hissed all the mystery lectures" and "tasted the whole worm." (Open daily 11am-5pm; off-season 2-5pm. Admission 50p.)

LET'S G🖐® Travel

1992 Catalog

The One-Stop Travel Store

For over 30 years, our travel agents have worked to help the budget traveler find the most convenient and affordable way to travel--offering travel gear, discount airfares, Eurail passes, and more.

Take a look inside to see the 42 ways we can make your trip easier.

LET'S PACK IT UP

Let's Go® Backpack/Suitcases
Innovative hideaway suspension with internal frame turns backpack into carry-on suitcase. Detachable daypack makes it 3 bags in 1. Water-proof Cordura® nylon. Lifetime Guarantee. 3750 cu. in. Navy, teal or black. **Supreme** adds lumbar support pad, torso and waist adjustment, two daypack pockets, leather trim, and *FREE shoulder strap.*

A1.	Supreme	$154.95
A2.	Backpack/Suitcase	114.95
A3.	Shoulder Strap	4.50

A1

A2

B. Chateau
Top-opening rucksack pack. Drawstr closure. 3 compartments. Taped insea Lifetime Guarantee. 1310 cu. in. Black.
$34.

C. Undercover Neck/Waist Pouch
Secure & comfortable. Ripstop nylon w soft Cambrelle® back. 2 pockets. 6 ½ x Lifetime Guarantee. Black or tan.
$7.

D. Passport/Money Case
Waterproof nylon with zippered pouch. 7 ½ x 4 ½" Navy or gray.
$6

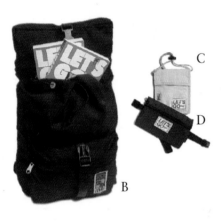

C

D

B

Duffles
Tough, capable, and appealing. 11 oz. waterproof Cordura-Plus® with 3" nylon web. Lifetime Guarantee. Red, black, purple, or blue.

E1.	XL–36 x 15 x 15"	$69.95
E2.	L–30 x 15 x 15"	59.95

H. Travel Case
Perfect carry-on luggage. Large compartment with 2 side pouches. Mesh pocket. No-sag bar and shoulder strap. Lifetime Guarantee. 20 x 16 x 9" Black or blue.
$94.95

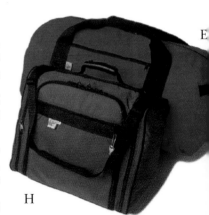

E

H

Call 1-800-5LETS GO for flight reservations.

LET'S SEE SOME I.D.

1992 International ID Cards
Provides discounts on accommodations, cultural events, airfares and accident/medical insurance. Valid 9-1-91 to 12-31-92.

T1.	Teacher (ITIC)	$15
T2.	Student (ISIC)	14
T3.	Youth International Exchange Card (YIEE)	14

FREE "International Student Travel Guide."

J1

T1   T2

T'S GO HOSTELING

-93 Youth Hostel Card (AYH)
lired by most international hostels.
t be U.S. resident.

Adult (ages 18-55)		$25
Youth (under 18)		10

leepsack
lired at all hostels. Washable durable
/cotton. 18" pillow pocket. Folds to
·h size.   **$13.95**

1992-93 International Youth Hostel
le (IYHG)
ntial information about 3900 hostels
lrope and Mediterranean.   **$10.95**

FREE map of hostels worldwide.

LET'S GO BY TRAIN

Eurail Passes
Convenient way to travel Europe. Save up to 70% over cost of individual tickets. Call for national passes.

First Class

V1.	15 days	$430
V2.	21 days	550
V3.	1 month	680
V4.	2 months	920

First Class Flexipass

V5.	5 days in 15 days	$280
V6.	9 days in 21 days	450
V7.	14 days in 1 month	610

Youth Pass (Under 26)

V8.	1 month	$470
V9.	2 months	640
V10.	15 days in 2 months	420

FREE Eurail Map, Timetable, & Travelers' Guide with passes.

s Go® Travel Guides
ppe; USA; Britain/Ireland; France; Italy;
·l/Egypt; Mexico; California/Hawaii;
n/Portugal; Pacific Northwest/Alaska;
·ce/Turkey; Germany/Austria/Switz-
·d; NYC; London; Washington D.C.

USA or Europe	$14.95
Country Guide (specify)	13.95
City Guide (specify)	9.95

$1.00 off the cover price.

LET'S GET STARTED

PLEASE PRINT OR TYPE. Incomplete applications will be returned.

International Student/Teacher Identity Card (ISIC/ITIC) (ages 12 & up) enclose:
1. Letter from registrar or administration, transcript, or proof of tuition payment. FULL-TIME only.
2. One picture (1 1/2 x 2") signed on the reverse side.

Youth International Exchange Card (YIEE) (ages 12-25) enclose:
1. Proof of birthdate (copy of passport or birth certificate).
2. One picture (1 1/2 x 2") signed on the reverse side.
3. Passport Number _____   4. Sex: M   F

_____ / ____ / ____
Last Name   First Name   Date of Birth

_____
Street   We do not ship to P.O. Boxes. U.S. addresses only.

_____
City   State   Zip Code

(____) _____
Phone   Citizenship

_____ / ____ / ____
School/College   Date Trip Begins

Item Code	Description, Size & Color	Quantity	Unit Price	Total Price

Shipping & Handling		Total Merchandise Price	
If order totals: Add		Shipping & Handling (See box at left)	
Up to $30.00 $4.00			
30.01-100.00 6.00	For Rush Handling Add	**$8 for Continental U.S.** **$10 for AK & HI**	
Over 100.00 7.00	MA Residents (Add 5% sales tax on gear & books)		
		Total	

ENCLOSE CHECK OR MONEY
ORDER PAYABLE TO:
HARVARD STUDENT AGENCIES, INC.

Allow 2-3 weeks for delivery.
Rush orders delivered within one
week of our receipt.

LET'S G🖐 Travel

Harvard Student Agencies, Inc., Harvard University, Thayer B, Cambridge, MA 02138

(617) 495-9649   1-800-5LETSGO (Credit Card Orders Only)

Prices subject to chan

The bridge over New College Lane reveals the obsession of British architects with replicating the *Bridge of Sighs* in Venice. Cambridge has a replica too, theirs more appropriately straddling a river.

Turn left at the end of Holywell St. and then bear right on Manor Rd. to see **St. Catherine's,** one of the most striking of the colleges. Built between 1960 and 1964 by the Danish architect Arne Jacobsen, "Catz" has no chapel, and its dining hall was funded by that curmudgeonly eccentric, Esso Petroleum. (Open daily 9am-5pm.) At the corner of St. Cross and South Parks Rd., the **Zoology and Psychology Building** looms like a great concrete ocean liner. Many colleges hold sporting matches nearby on the **University Parks,** a refreshing expanse of green.

If, for some reason, you want to see over 1000 bees within an inch of your nose, visit the **University Museum,** Parks Rd. (Open Mon.-Sat. noon-5pm. Free.) Walk through to the **Pitt Rivers Museum** and examine a wonderfully eclectic ethnography and natural history collection that includes shrunken heads and rare butterflies. (Open Mon.-Sat. 1-4:30pm. Free.) Just up Banbury Rd. on the right, the **Balfour Buildings** house 1400 musical instruments from all over the world. (Open Mon.-Sat. 1-4:30pm. Free.)

Keble College, across from the University Museum, was designed by architect William Butterfield to stand out from the sandstone background; the intricate and multi-patterned red brick, known as "The Fair Isle Sweater," was deemed "actively ugly" by Sir Nikolaus Pevsner. (Open daily 10am-dusk.) Through a passageway to the left, the **Hayward** and **deBreyne Buildings** squat on the tarmac like a black plexiglass spaceship ready for takeoff.

The imposing **Ashmolean Museum,** Beaumont St., was Britain's first public museum when it opened in 1683. Its outstanding collection includes drawings and prints by Leonardo da Vinci, Raphael, and Michelangelo; copious French impressionist and Italian works; and Rembrandts, Constables, and assorted Pre-Raphaelites. The Ashmolean also houses mummies, a Stradivarius violin, and the lantern carried by Guy Fawkes as he tangoed through the cellars of Parliament. (Open Tues.-Sat. 10am-4pm, Sun. 2-4pm. Free.) Ashmolean's **Cast Gallery,** behind the museum, stores over 250 casts of Greek sculptures. (Open Tues.-Fri. 10am-4pm, Sat. 10am-1pm. Free.)

A few blocks up St. Giles, as it becomes Woodstock Rd., stands **Somerville College,** Oxford's most famous women's college. (The oldest is Lady Margaret Hall.) Somerville's alumnae include Dorothy Sayers, Indira Gandhi, Margaret Thatcher, Ena Franey, and Shirley Williams. Women were not granted degrees until 1920—Cambridge held out until 1948. Today, women comprise 38% of the student body.

At the remote end of Beaumont St., you'll reach **Worcester College.** Derisively called Botany Bay, the college has attracted some of Oxford's more swashbuckling students, including essay fiend and opium addict Thomas De Quincey and handsome poet Richard Lovelace. Worcester enjoys a large and dreamy garden and a lake shore that stages summertime plays. (Open daily 2-6pm; also 9am-noon during vacations.) At the very end of Beaumont St., on the north side, look for a stone tablet on the wall marking the birthplace of King Richard I in 1157.

By far the most self-indulgent of Oxford's neighborhoods is the five blocks of **Cowley Road** nearest the Magdalen Bridge roundabout. The area is a living version of the *Whole Earth Handbook,* a fascinating clutter of alternative lifestyles, Marxist bookstores, jumble shops, and scruffy wholefood and ethnic restaurants. Check out **Rainbow's End,** a comic-book shop at 78 Cowley Rd. (tel. 251 140; open Mon.-Thurs. and Sat. 10am-12:45pm and 1:30-6pm, Fri. 10am-12:45pm and 1:30-5:30pm), and **Jeremy's,** a stamp-collector's, used-paperback and postcard shop at 98 Cowley Rd. (tel. 241 011; open Mon.-Fri. 10am-12:30pm and 2-5pm). The **women's center** is nearby (see Practical Information above). To the north of Worcester College along Walton St., past the palatial **Oxford University Press** complex, lies the neighborhood of **Jericho.** A working-class suburb in the 19th century, the area has been redeveloped and today houses a varied ethnic population.

Entertainment

No teeming student carnival, the town closes down fairly early. Posters plastered around advertising upcoming events make the best entertainment guide. Check the bulletin boards at the tourist office or pick up a free copy of *This Month in Oxford.* Keep in mind that public transport peters out by 11pm.

The university itself offers marvelous entertainment. Throughout the summer, college theatre groups stage productions in gardens or in cloisters. Music at Oxford is a particularly cherished art; try to attend a concert or an evensong service at one of the colleges, or a performance at the **Holywell Music Rooms,** the oldest in the country. **City of Oxford Orchestra,** the city's professional symphony orchestra (tel. 240 358), plays a subscription series ("Beautiful Music in Beautiful Places") in the Sheldonian Theatre and college chapels throughout the summer. (Shows at 8pm. Tickets £3.50-9, students £2.50-8.) The year-long **Music at Oxford** series plays in halls throughout the city; for information, call 864 056 or write to 6a Cumnor Hill, Oxford OX2 9HA. The annual **Dorchester Abbey Festival** (music, drama, and poetry readings) runs for two weeks beginning in late June in Dorchester-on-Thames, nine miles south of Oxford. Coach transportation is available from Oxford. Call 240 358 or write to Dorchester Abbey Festival, Oxford OX1 2BR. The **Apollo Theatre,** George St. (tel. 244 544), presents a wide range of performances, including comedy, drama, rock, jazz, and the Royal Ballet. (Tickets from £6, student and senior discounts.) The **Oxford Union,** St. Michael's St., hosts modern productions performed by the small, avante-garde Mayfly theatre company in July and August. Tickets are available from Tickets-in-Oxford (tel. 727 855). Ask at the tourist office about student and community theatre productions in Oxford and environs.

The best cinema in Oxford is the **Penultimate Picture Palace,** better known as the **PPP,** Jeune St. (tel. 723 837), off Cowley Rd. Different double features play every day (one show £2.75). **The Phoenix,** Walton St. (tel. 549 09), shows mostly serious (read: foreign) films. (Tickets £2.75.) *What's On In Oxford* lists the clubs and pubs that play music. The less student-oriented **Jericho Tavern,** at the corner of Walton and Jericho St. (tel. 545 02), features local rock and jazz bands. (Open Mon.-Sat. until 2:30am, Sun. noon-2pm and 7-10:30pm.)

A favorite pastime in Oxford is **punting** on the River Thames (known in Oxford as the Isis) or on the River Cherwell. (See Boat Rental under Practical Information above.) Punters receive a long pole and a small oar, and are advised not to fall into the river. The flat-bottomed boat is propelled by pressing the pole against the river floor. It is very easy to end up in the river; if you're afraid to punt yourself, at least take a seat on the deck of the Head of the River pub at Folly Bridge and watch braver souls go by. Also, don't be surprised if you suddenly come upon **Parson's Pleasure,** a small riverside area where men sometimes sunbathe nude. Female passersby are expected to open their parasols and tip them at a discreet angle to obscure the view.

The university celebrates **Eights Week** at the end of May, when all the colleges enter crews in the bumping races, and beautiful people gather on the banks to sip strawberries and nibble champagne. In early September, **St. Giles Fair** invades one of Oxford's main streets with an old-fashioned carnival, complete with Victorian roundabout and whirligigs. Daybreak on **May 1** brings one of Oxford's loveliest moments: the Magdalen College Choir greets the summer by singing madrigals from the top of the tower to a crowd below, and the town submits to morris dancing, beating the bounds, and other age-old rituals of merrymaking—pubs open at 7am.

Near Oxford

The largest private home in England and birthplace of Winston Churchill, **Blenheim Palace** was built to reward the Duke of Marlborough for defeating Louis XIV's armies at the Battle of Blenheim in 1704, and in appreciation of his wife Sarah's friendship with Queen Anne. The palace's rent is currently one French franc, payable each year to the Crown. Sir John Vanbrugh's design is at once immense and coherent. Blenheim has wonderful rambling grounds designed by Capability Brown, as well as a lake and a fantastic garden center. Whilst attending a party here, Churchill's mother gave birth to the future cigar smoker and Prime Minister; the historic event transpired in a closet. (Palace open mid-March to Oct. daily 10:30am-5:30pm, last entrance 4:45pm. Grounds open daily 9am-5pm. Admission £4.50, children £2.20) Blenheim sprawls in Woodstock, eight miles north of Oxford on the A34; South Midlands (tel. (0993) 776 679) runs an express coach from Oxford's Gloucester Green (3 per day, 20 min., £1, children 50p). Woodstock, a tidy little village, chirps and hops with shops and pubs. Geoffrey Chaucer once lived here, and Winston Churchill is buried in the nearby village churchyard of Bladon.

Stratford-upon-Avon

> *It is something, I thought, to have seen the dust of Shakespeare.*
>
> *—Washington Irving*

In 1930, the owners of the Great Texas Fair cabled Stratford-upon-Avon: "Please send earth Shakespeare's garden water River Avon for dedication Shakespeare Theater Dallas Texas July 1," revealing a classic case of obsession with Shakespeare's hometown. The soil of Stratford has been a totem of literary ritual ever since David Garrick's 1769 Stratford jubilee. England and this town have made an industry of the bard, emblazoning him on £20 notes and casting him and all of his long-lost twin brothers in beer advertisements. Yet this rich and strange form of relic-worship has more to it than another ill-begotten encounter with Polonius in polyester. Mary Arden's house, described as the home of Shakespeare's mother, may be a complete fiction, but despite—or perhaps because of—its unverifiable or imagined associations, Stratford keeps itself in the tourist limelight. There's no business like Bard business, and this helluva town may even upstage London as the center of England's cultural consciousness.

Orientation and Practical Information

Stratford performs 2¼ hours from London by rail or by the coach/rail "Shakespeare Connection." (Departs London Euston Mon.-Sat. 4 per day, Sun. 2 per day, 2 hr., £24.50, £27 return. Only the Shakespeare Connection operates at night after plays.) Several coach services run to and from London and Oxford. The closest thing Stratford has to a bus or coach station is the Travel Shop office (tel. 204 181; open daily 9am-5pm), at the corner of Warwick Rd. and Guild St. Here most National Express and Midland Red South buses and coaches arrive and depart. You can purchase tickets for coaches run by both of these companies at the Travel Shop office. Coaches run to and from London's Victoria Station (8 per day, 2¾ hr., £12.75 single or day return, £15.50 period return); local Midland buses head to Warwick and Coventry (every 15 min., explorer ticket £3.50) and to Birmingham (every hr., 1 hr., £2.20). Tickets can be bought on buses.

Tourist Information Centre: Bridgefoot (tel. 293 127). Local accommodations service 10% of first night's stay (deducted from final bill). Open Mon.-Sat. 9am-5:30pm, Sun. 2-5pm; Nov.-March Mon.-Sat. 10:30am-4:30pm.

Royal Shakespeare Theatre Box Office: Tel. 295 623. Standby tickets may be available immediately before the show at the RST and the Swan for students and seniors (£6-12). Open Mon.-Sat. 9am-8pm. 24-hr. ticket information: tel. 691 91.

American Express: Bridgefoot CV37 6GW (tel. 415 784), in the tourist information center.

Post Office: 24 Bridge St. Open Mon.-Fri. 9:30am-5:30pm, Sat. 9am-12:30pm. **Postal Code:** CV37 6AA.

Telephone Code: (0789).

Train Station: Alcester Rd. (tel. 204 444). To London Paddington, change at Reading and Leamington Spa (every 1½ hr., 2¼ hr., £15, £15 return). To Oxford (every 1½ hr., £7.90, £7.90 return). To Warwick (12 per day, £2.60 return).

Bus and coach: Corner of Warwick Rd. and Guild St. **National Express** to London (£12.75), to Oxford (£5.75). **Midland Red** (tel. 204 181) Explorer ticket (£3.50).

Shakespeare Connection: Train leaves London Euston (Mon.-Sat. 4 per day, Sun. 2 per day), coach connections at Coventry (2¼ hr., £24.50, £27 return). Inform Guide Friday Ltd. (tel. 294 466) in advance if you plan to travel on late-night Shakespeare Connection. Discount rail fares can be had by purchasing both rail and theatre tickets from Theatre and Concert Travel (tel. (0727) 411 15).

Bike Rental: Clarke's Gas Station, Guild St. at Union St. (tel. 205 057). Look for the Esso sign. £5.50 per day, £25 per week; £50 deposit. Open daily 7am-9pm. **Rent-a-Bike,** Guild St. (tel. 292 603). Free delivery of bike to wherever you need it. £5 per day. £50 deposit. Open Mon.-Sat. 9am-6pm.

Boat Rentals: Stratford Marina, Clapton Bridge (tel. 696 69). £5 per hour. Across from the Dirty Duck pub. At the same dock you can chug across the Avon on the last of England's chain ferries (20p).

Laundromat: Fountain Cleaners, 18 Greenhill St. wash £1.20; dry £1. Senior discount days on Wed. and Thurs. Open Mon.-Fri. 8am-9pm, Sat. 8am-6pm, Sun. 9am-2pm.

Market Day: Fri., at the intersection of Greenhill, Windsor, Rother, and Wood St.

Police Station: Rother St. (tel. 414 111), up Greenhill St. from American Fountain, turn left.

Emergency: Dial 999; no coins required.

Accommodations and Camping

To B&B or not to B&B? This hamlet has tons of them, but singles are hard to find. Finding doubles involves less toil and trouble. In summer, 'tis nobler to make advance reservations by phone. Guesthouses (£14-18) line **Grove Road, Evesham Place,** and **Evesham Road.** (From the train station, walk down Alcester Rd., take a right on Grove Rd., and continue to Evesham Place, which becomes Evesham Rd.) If these fail, try **Shipston Road** across the river. The tourist office describes local farms that take paying guests (£12.50-16).

IYHF Youth Hostel, Hemmingford House, Wellesbourne Rd., Alverton (tel. 297 093), 2 mi. from Stratford. Follow the B4086; take bus #518 from the Travel Shop (every hr.), or walk. Large, attractive 200-year-old building; recently renovated bath facilities. Kitchen facilities available. Curfew 11pm (11:30pm after a show). Lockout 10am-1pm. £3.90-5.60. Very crowded; call ahead. Open March-Dec.

The Hollies, 16 Evesham Pl. (tel. 668 57). Exceptionally warm and attentive proprietors, for whom the guest house is a labor of love. Green prevails. TV and tea-making facilities in every room. Spacious doubles; no singles. £15-18 per person.

The Glenavon, 6 Chestnut Walk (tel. 292 588), off the end of Evesham Place. Prime location and comfortable rooms. English breakfast. Singles and doubles £14 per person.

Nando's, 18 Evesham Pl. (tel. 204 907) Delightful owners, homey rooms. £14.50-16 per person.

Strathcona, 47 Evesham Rd. (Tel. 292 101). Lovely gardens, caring owners. £13 per person with full English breakfast.

Carlton Guesthouse, 22 Evesham Pl. (tel. 293 548). Elegant proprietor serves original English breakfasts in an antique-laden breakfast room. TV in every marvelous room. Come just to meet Saba, the gentle "bacon hound." Singles and doubles £16-19 per person.

Greensleeves, 46 Alcester Rd. (tel. 292 131). On the way to the train station. Mrs. Graham will dote on you in her cheerful home. £14 per person with breakfast.

Bradbourne Guest House, 44 Shipston Rd. (tel. 204 178). Easygoing proprietors. Charming rooms in a quiet location only ¾ mi. from the center of town. Doubles £14 per person.

Compton House, 22 Shipston Rd. (tel. 205 646). Small comfortable house run by the ever-helpful Mrs. Bealing. £14.50-17.50 per person.

Camping: Elms, Tiddington Rd. (tel. 292 312), 1 mi. northeast of Stratford on the B4056. Open April-Oct. Tent and 1 person £2.50, each additional person £1.50. **Dodwell Park,** Evesham Rd. (tel. 204 957), 2 mi. from Stratford on the A439. Open year-round. Tent and 1 person £4.50, each additional person £1.50. Both have showers available.

Food

Imitation-Tudor fast food places mock the Bard's hometown. Check out the half-timbered Pizza Hut with extra cheese. Supermarkets are on Greenhill St.

Kingfisher, 13 Ely St. A take-away that serves chips with everything (fish, chicken, eggs). Cheap, greasy, and very popular; lines form outside. Meals £1-3.10. Open Mon. 11:30am-2pm and 5-9:30pm, Tues.-Thurs. 11:30am-2pm and 5-11pm, Fri.-Sat. 11:30am-2pm and 5-11:30pm.

Café Natural Wholefood Vegetarian Restaurant, Greenhill St. Lurking behind a health food store, this highly acclaimed café serves elaborate vegetarian foods. 10% discount on Tues. for students and seniors. Entrees £1.25-3.25. Open Mon.-Thurs. and Sat. 9am-5:30pm, Fri. 9am-7:30pm.

Hussain's Indian Cuisine, 6a Chapel St. Probably Stratford's best Indian cuisine; a slew of tandoori specialties. A favorite of Ben Kingsley. Chicken tikka £6.75.

Elizabeth the Chef, Henley St., opposite the Birthplace. Cafeteria-style lunch (£1.55-3.25) in a setting reminiscent of Holly Hobby. Open daily 10am-6pm.

Vintner Bistro and Cafe Bar, Sheep St. Satisfying ham, beef, and turkey salads (£4.25-4.75). Dinner about £4.75. Desserts may render you suddenly sockless. Open daily 10:30am-11pm.

Dirty Duck Pub, Southern Lane. Soothing river view. Indulge. Pub lunch £1-4.25. Fancy dinners more expensive. Chicken *Provençale* £8.95. Photos of actors adorn the walls.

Sights

Stratford's sights are most pleasant before 11am (when the herds of daytrippers have not yet arrived) or after 4pm (when most have left). Bardolatry peaks at 2pm. A ticket to all five **Shakespeare properties** costs £6, a savings of £2.50 if you manage to make it to every shrine. They are: Shakespeare's Birthplace and BBC Costume Exhibition, Anne Hathaway's cottage, the fictitious Mary Arden's House and Countryside Museum, Hall's Croft, and New Place or Nash House. You might not want to visit them all—dark timbered roof beams and floors begin to look the same no matter who lived between them. (Skip the "World of Shakespeare.")

The least crowded way to pay homage to the institution himself is to visit his grave in **Holy Trinity Church,** Trinity St., although the little arched door funnels massive tour groups at peak hours. (Admission 40p, students 20p.) In town, start your walking tour at **Shakespeare's Birthplace** on Henley St. (Enter through the adjoining museum.) The Birthplace, half period recreation and half Shakespeare life-and-work exhibition, includes an admonishment to Will's father for putting his rubbish in the street. Amazingly, half a million visitors shuffle each year through these narrow corridors and twisting staircases. The adjacent **BBC Costume Exhibition** features costumes used in the BBC productions of the Shakespeare plays, complete with photo stills. Avoid this exhibition if the idea of a Disney plastic show turns your stomach; one half expects the mannequin cast of Hamlet to launch into a chorus of "Zip-a-Dee-Do-Dah." (Birthplace and BBC exhibition both open Mon.-Sat. 9am-6pm, Sun. 10am-6pm; Nov.-March Mon.-Sat. 9am-4:30pm, Sun. 1:30-4:30pm. Admission £2.20, children 90p.) On High St., you can see another example of humble Elizabethan lodgings in the **Harvard House** (so called because Katherine Rogers, John Harvard's mom, grew up here). Period pieces sparsely punctuate this authentic Tudor building. The caretaker can tell you many truths about how the Rogers family passed the time in the 16th century. (Open Mon.-Sat. 9am-1pm and 2-6pm, Sun. 2-6pm. Admission £1.25, students 75p.) **New Place,** Chapel St., was

Stratford's hippest home when Shakespeare bought it back in 1597. Also visit the **Great Garden** at the back. (Open Mon.-Sat. 9am-6pm, Sun. 10am-6pm; Nov.-March Mon.-Sat. 9am-4:30pm. House admission £1.50, children 60p. Garden free.)

Shakespeare learned his "small Latin and less Greek" at the **Grammar School,** on Church St. To visit, write in advance to the headmaster, N.W.R. Mellon, King Edward VI School, Church St., Stratford-upon-Avon, England CV37 6HB (tel. (0789) 293 351). The **guild chapel,** next door, is open daily. Shakespeare's eldest daughter once lived in **Hall's Croft,** Old Town Rd., an impressive building with a beautiful garden in tow. (Open Mon.-Sat. 9am-6pm, Sun. 10am-6pm; Nov.-March Mon.-Sat. 9am-4:30pm. Admission £1.50, children 60p.)

Head down Southern Lane and stroll through the **theatre gardens** of the Royal Shakespeare Theatre. You can fiddle with RSC props and costumes at their **gallery museum.** (Gallery open Mon.-Sat. 9:15am-8pm, Sun. noon-5pm. Admission £1.50, students and seniors £1.) The shed in the gardens houses a **brass-rubbing studio,** an alternative to plastic Shakespeare memorabilia. (Admission free, but materials cost 60p-£6.)

The modern, well-respected **Shakespeare Centre,** Henley St., has a library and a bookshop (across the street) and archives open to students and scholars. The center exhibits 16th-century books, holds madrigal concerts, and hosts a fine poetry festival in July and August. (Concerts £1-£1.50. Festival tel. 204 016. Poetry readings Sun. at 8pm; tickets £3.50-5.50.)

Anne Hathaway's Cottage, the birthplace of Shakespeare's wife, lies about a mile from Stratford in Shottery; take the footpath north from Evesham Place or the bus from Bridge St. The cottage exhibits portray the swinging Tudor rural lifestyle. (Open Mon.-Sat. 9am-6pm, Sun. 10am-6pm; Nov.-March Mon.-Sat. 9am-4:30pm, Sun. 1:30-4:30pm. Admission £1.80, children 80p.) **Mary Arden's House,** the lettice 'n' lovage style farmhouse home that a 19th-century entrepreneur determined to be that of Shakespeare's mother, stands four miles from Stratford in Wilmcote; a footpath economically connects it to Anne Hathaway's Cottage. (Open April-Oct. Mon.-Sat. 9am-6pm, Sun. 10am-6pm; Nov.-March Mon.-Sat. 9am-4:30pm. Admission £2.50, children £1.)

Entertainment

RSC spells relief. After enduring the cultural commodity-fetishism of the tourist hot spots, seek solace in a performance by the skillful and often sublime **Royal Shakespeare Company.** To reserve seats (£5-28), call the box office (tel. 295 623; 24-hr. recorded information tel. 691 91); they hold tickets for three days only. The box office opens at 9:30am. Good matinee seats are often available after 10:30am on the morning of a performance, and some customer returns and standing-room tickets may be available on the day of an evening performance (queue up 1-2 hr. before curtain). Student standbys for £6-12 just before curtain exist, but are rare. The company does not perform in Stratford in February or the first half of March. You can take a 45-minute **backstage tour** at 1:30 and 5:30pm and after performances, Monday through Saturday (except matinee days) or Sunday at 12:30, 2:15, 3:15, and 4:15pm (tours £3.50, students and seniors £2.50).

The new **Swan Theatre** has been specially designed for RSC productions of plays written by Shakespeare's contemporaries. The theatre is located down Waterside, in back of the Royal Shakespeare Theatre, on the grounds of the old Memorial Theatre. (Tickets £8-19, standing room £3.) It's smaller and often more crowded than the RST; line up early for tickets.

The **Stratford Festival** (July 13-Aug. 4) refreshingly celebrates artistic achievement other than Shakespeare's. The festival typically features world-class artists from all aspects of performance art (the likes of Simon Rattle to the anachronistic theatrical troupe Regia Anglorum). Tickets (when required) can be purchased from the Stratford Festival box office (2 Chestnut Walk, tel. 679 69). The theme for 1992 is Europe.

Near Stratford

Within an hour's drive of Stratford cluster dozens of stately homes and castles, testimony to England's "teeming womb of royal kings." Assorted historians, architects, and ad copy writers regard **Warwick Castle,** between Stratford and Coventry, as England's finest medieval castle. Its magnificent battlements loom over gracious, meandering grounds. A collection of wax models by Madame Tussaud occupies the castle's private apartments; the dungeon and torture chamber feature gruesomely detailed exhibits. (Castle and grounds open daily 10am-5:30pm; Nov.-Feb. 10am-4:30pm. Admission £5.75, children £3.50.) A Midland Red bus journeys from Stratford to Warwick every hour (#18 or X16, 15-20 min.), and trains make the trip frequently (£2.60).

Ragley Hall, eight miles west of Stratford, a Palladian mansion, is home to the Marquis and Marchioness of Hertford. The estate boasts a fine collection of paintings, including Graham Rust's modern mural, "The Temptation," which took 15 years to paint. The 400-acre park includes a captivating maze. (Open in summer Tues.-Thurs. noon-5pm, Sat.-Sun. 1:30-5:30pm.) Take a bus (Mon.-Sat. 5 per day) from Stratford to Alcester, then walk one mile to the gates of Ragley Hall and then another ½ mile up the drive. (Admission £4, children £3.)

Cambridge

Cambridge the town has been dominated by Cambridge the university for 700 years. Each term, battalions of bicycle-riding students invade this quintessential university town. Competing in everything with Oxford, Cambridge loses in age and boat races but wins on charm and spectacle; the terribly beautiful Backs, along the River Cam, imbue both Cantabrigians and visitors with an understandable sense of self-indulgence. Cambridge has ceased to be the exclusive preserve of upper-class sons, although roughly half of its students still come from independent schools, and only 35% are women. Most of the students are refreshingly down-to-earth; only a few, bedecked with brogue, cravat, and cane, strive to preserve the old image.

Cambridge University itself exists mostly as a bureaucracy that handles the formalities of lectures, degrees, and real estate. The individual colleges within the university provide the small tutorials and seminars that form the crux of a Cambridge education. Third-year finals alone determine the academic future of many students; during the official "quiet periods" of May and early June, students disengage themselves from the social mêlée, and most colleges close to visitors. At the end of exams, the University explodes with gleeful gin-soaked revelry. Mayweek—logically enough, a week in mid-June—ushers in a dizzying schedule of cocktail parties and mirth, starting with a health-threatening number on aptly named Suicide Sunday.

Orientation and Practical Information

Cambridge (pop. 102,000) is about 60 miles north of London. Trains to Cambridge run frequently, from both London's King's Cross and Liverpool Street stations (every ½ hr., 1 hr., £10.60 day return, £9.50 period return with railcard). From the train station, you can take a Cityrail Link bus to Market Sq. in the city center (Mon.-Sat. daytime every 8 min., Sun. and evenings every 15 min., 50p); or walk down Hills Road (20 min.). National Express coaches travel hourly between London's Victoria Station and Drummer St. Station in Cambridge (2 hr., £8 single or day return). Buses travel between Oxford and Cambridge every two hours from 8:40am to 4:40pm (3 hr., £11.75 single or day return). **Cambus,** the town's bus service, also runs numerous local and regional routes from Drummer St.

Cambridge has two main avenues. The main shopping street starts at Magdalene Bridge and becomes Bridge Street, Sidney Street, St. Andrew's Street, Regent Street, and finally Hills Road. The other—St. John's Street, Trinity Street, King's Parade, Trumpington Street, and Trumpington Road—is the academic thoroughfare, with several colleges lying between it and the River Cam.

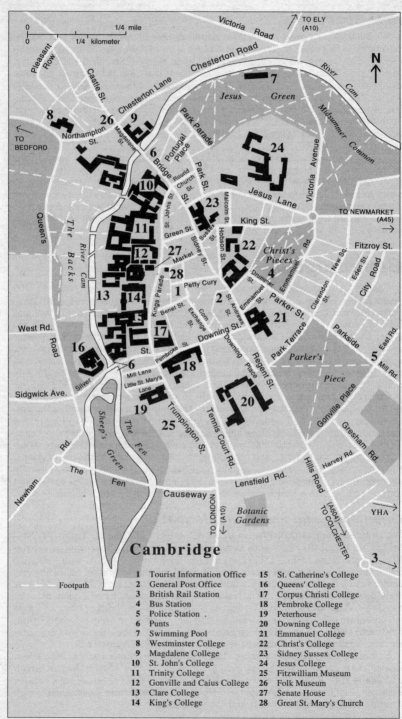

Cambridge

1   Tourist Information Office
2   General Post Office
3   British Rail Station
4   Bus Station
5   Police Station
6   Punts
7   Swimming Pool
8   Westminster College
9   Magdalene College
10 St. John's College
11 Trinity College
12 Gonville and Caius College
13 Clare College
14 King's College
15 St. Catherine's College
16 Queens' College
17 Corpus Christi College
18 Pembroke College
19 Peterhouse
20 Downing College
21 Emmanuel College
22 Christ's College
23 Sidney Sussex College
24 Jesus College
25 Fitzwilliam Museum
26 Folk Museum
27 Senate House
28 Great St. Mary's Church

Tourist Information Centre: Wheeler St., Cambridge CB2 3QB (tel. 322 640), 1 block south of the marketplace. Railway and coach schedules available. Accommodations service £1.25. Accommodations list (40p) posted. Mini-guide 30p. Maps of the town 10p. Open July-Aug. Mon.-Tues. and Thurs.-Fri. 9am-7pm, Wed. 9:30am-7pm, Sat. 9am-5pm; March-June and Sept.-Oct. Mon.-Tues. and Thurs.-Fri. 9am-6pm, Wed. 9:30am-6pm, Sat. 9am-5pm; Nov.-Feb. Mon.-Tues. and Thurs.-Fri. 9am-5:30pm, Wed. 9:30am-5:30pm, Sat. 9am-5pm. Also open Easter-Sept. Sun. 10:30am-3:30pm. Information on Cambridge events also available at Corn Exchange box office (tel. 357 851), Corn Exchange St., opposite the tourist office.

Tours: Unbeatable 2-hr. walking tours of the city and some colleges leave the main tourist office daily. April-June at 11am and 2pm; July-Aug. every hr. 11am-3pm and at 6:30pm; Sept. every hr. 11am-3pm. Tours less frequent during the rest of the year. Sun. and bank holidays, first tour at 11:15am. £2.85. 1½-hr. tours focusing on the town rather than the university leave the tourist office July-Aug. daily at 6:30pm. £2.85.

Student Travel Offices: STA Travel, 38 Sydney St. (tel 669 66). Open Mon.-Fri. 9am-6pm, Sat. 10am-4pm. **Campus Travel,** 5 Emmanuel St. (tel. 324 283). Open Mon.-Sat. 9am-5:30pm.

Currency Exchange: Most banks open Mon.-Fri. 9:30am-3:30pm; some stay open until 4:30 or 5pm. **Barclay's,** Market Sq., also open Sat. 9am-noon. **Thomas Cook,** 5 Market Hill, open Mon.-Fri. 9am-5:30pm, Sat. 9am-5pm. No exchange facilities open Sun.

American Express: Abbot Travel, 25 Sydney St. CB2 3MP (tel. 351 636). Open Mon. and Wed.-Fri. 9am-5pm, Tues. 9:30am-5pm, Sat. 9am-4pm.

Post Office: 9-11 St. Andrew's St. (tel. 351 212). Open Mon.-Tues. and Thurs.-Fri. 9am-5:30pm, Wed. 9:30am-5:30pm, Sat. 9am-12:30pm. **Postal Code:** CB1 1AA.

Telephone Code: (0223).

Train Station: Station Rd. (tel. 311 999; recorded London timetable Mon.-Fri. 359 602, Sat. 467 098, Sun. 353 465). Trains to Ely (every hr., 20 min., £2.90 day return) and King's Lynn (every 2 hr., 1 hr., £10.50 day return). Travel Centre open Mon.-Sat. 5am-11pm, Sun. 6:30am-11pm. Free timetables.

Bus and Coach Station: Drummer St. Station. **National Express** (tel. 460 711). **Cambus** (tel. 423 554) handles city and area service (fare 50p-£1). Some local routes serviced by **Miller's** or **Premier** coaches. **Whippet Coaches** run daytrips from Cambridge. Travel Centre open Mon.-Sat. 8:15am-5:30pm.

Taxis: Camtax (tel. 313 131). Open 24 hrs. Ranks overrun St. Andrew's St. and Market Sq.

Bike Rental: University Cycle, 9 Victoria Ave. (tel. 355 517). £4 per day, £10 per week; £25 cash deposit. Repairs. Open Mon.-Fri. 9am-6pm, Sat. 9am-5pm. **Geoff's Bike Hire,** 65 Devonshire Rd. (tel. 656 29). £5 per day, £12 per week; £20 deposit. Open daily 9am-5:30pm. **C. Frost,** 188 New Market Rd. (tel. 356 464). £4 per day, £12 per week; £20 deposit. Open Mon.-Fri. 9am-1pm and 2-6pm, Sat. 9am-1pm and 2-5pm. Most bike rental firms cater to block bookings of more than 2 weeks from groups of language students.

Bookstores: Heffers. Main branch at 20 Trinity St. (tel. 358 51), maps at 19 Sidney St. (tel. 358 241), and paperbacks at 31 St. Andrew's St. (tel. 354 778). Assorted other branches. Most open Mon.-Sat. 9am-5:30pm. **Sherratt and Hughes,** 1 Trinity St. (tel. 355 488). Site of a bookshop since 1581. Open Mon.-Sat. 9am-5:30pm, Sun. 11am-6pm. **Galloway and Porter,** 30 Sydney St. (tel. 678 76). Cheap second-hand books in great condition upstairs. Open Mon.-Fri. 8:30am-5:30pm, Sat. 9am-5:15pm. Second-hand bookstalls cluster around St. Edward's passage and the marketplace.

Public Library: 7 Lion Yard (tel. 652 52). Reference library with helpful information desk on 2nd floor sells comprehensive *Citizen's Guide* (23p). Open Mon.-Fri. 9:30am-7pm, Sat. 9:30am-5pm.

Laundromat: Coin-Op Laundry, 28 King St. Wash £1.20, dry 20p. Open daily 7am-10pm. One closer to the hostel can be found underneath the painted bull at 44 Hills Rd. Wash £1.20, 7-min. dry 10p. Open daily 9am-9pm.

Rape Crisis Group: Tel. 358 314. Open Mon. 7-9pm, Wed. 6pm-midnight, Sat. 11am-5pm.

AIDS Helpline: Tel. 697 65. Open Tues.-Wed. 7:30-10pm.

Hospital: Addenbrookes, Hills Rd. (tel. 245 151). 1½ mi. southeast of the train station; follow Station Rd. to Hills Rd. and turn left.

Police Station: Parkside (tel. 358 966). From the train station, follow Hills Rd. to Gonville Place. Turn right onto Gonville and then left onto Parkside. The station will be on your right.

Emergency: Dial 999; no coins required.

Accommodations and Camping

Cambridge has no shortage of rooms for visitors, but it's advisable to book ahead during high season. Many of the cheap B&Bs around Jesus Lane convert into student housing during the academic year and only open to visitors during the summer. If one house is full, ask for other accommodations in the neighborhood (B&Bs are often not labeled as such). Check the comprehensive list in the window of the tourist office.

IYHF Youth Hostel, 97 Tenison Rd. (tel. 354 601), entrance on Devonshire Rd. Extremely close to the train station; walk straight ahead and then right on Tenison Rd. Relaxed, welcoming atmosphere; boppy music in reception, well-equipped kitchen, laundry room, TV lounge, game room, and store. 125 bunks in 5-bed rooms, a few doubles. Couples may share a room, space permitting. Three-night max. stay when busy. Lockout 10am-1pm, but early arrivals can leave their bags in the morning. Curfew 11:30pm. £8.30, ages 16-20 £7. £1 surcharge June-Aug. Sleepsack rental 80p. English breakfast £2.30, packed lunch £2.50, evening meal £3. Open all year and crowded March-Oct.; call a few days in advance and arrive by 6pm.

Mrs. Connolly, 67 Jesus Lane (tel. 617 53). A recently refurbished house decorated in sunny shades. Open year-round. £12.50 per person.

Mrs. Bennett, 70 Jesus Lane (tel. 654 97). Visitors can reap the benefits of extensive renovations carved out by Christ's College. 2 doubles, 2 twins, 2 singles. Open June-Sept., Easter, and Christmas. £12 per person.

Mrs. French, 42 Lyndewode (tel. 316 615), off Tenison Rd. One of the best buys near the train station. £10 per person.

Mrs. Fesenko, 15 Mill Rd. (tel. 329 435). Decent rooms with schizophrenic wallpaper. Charming proprietor natters away in a bewildering *mischung von Englisch and German*. A good buy. £10 per person.

Mrs. West, 2 Malcolm St. (tel. 359 814). Cheerful rooms cared for by maternal owner. Open June-Sept. £12.50 per person.

Tenison Towers, Mrs. J. Tombo, 148 Tenison Rd. (tel. 639 24). A touch of the Mediterranean near the train station. Clean and comfy. Singles £15. Doubles £24.

Camping

Highfield Farm Camping Site, Long Rd., Comberton (tel. 262 308). Head west on A603 for 3 mi. then left on B1046 for another mile. Or take Cambus #118 from the Drummer St. bus station (every 45 min.). Flush toilets, showers, and a washing machine. Open April-Oct. £6 per tent. Call ahead.

Camping and Caravaning Club Ltd., 212a Cambridge Rd., Great Shelford (tel. 841 185), 3 mi. south on A10, then left onto A1301 for ¾ mi., or take Cambus #103. Flush toilets, showers, washing machine, and facilities for the disabled. No unaccompanied children under 16. Open April 12-Oct. 30. £3.50, children £1.50; off-season £3, children £1.25. Call ahead.

The tourist office also has a list of 16 other camping sites in the Cambridge vicinity (25p).

Food

Market Square has bright pyramids of fruit and vegetables for the hungry budgetarian. (Open Mon.-Sat. approximately 8am-5pm.) For vegetarian and wholefood groceries, try **Arjuna,** 12 Mill Rd. (Open Mon.-Wed. and Fri. 9:30am-6pm, Thurs. 9:30am-2pm, Sat. 9am-5:30pm.) The local branch of the **Holland and Barrett** wholefood chain, in Bradwell's Court off St. Andrew's St., carries a more extensive but more expensive selection. (Open Mon.-Tues. and Thurs.-Sat. 9am-5:30pm, Wed. 9:30am-5:30pm.) Students buy their gin and cornflakes at **Sainsbury's,** 44 Sydney St., the only grocery store in the middle of town. (Open Mon.-Tues. 8:30am-7pm,

Wed.-Fri. 8:30am-8pm, Sat. 8am-6pm.) The food section in **Marks and Spencer,** 8 Sydney St., includes some high-class picnic items. (Open Mon. 9:15am-5:30pm, Tues. 9:30am-5:30pm, Wed. 9am-8pm, Thurs. 9am-6pm, Fri.-Sat. 8:30am-6pm.) On Sundays, pick up groceries at the **Nip-In General Store,** 30 Mill Rd. (open daily 8am-10pm); **H.T. Cox,** 67 Regent St. (open daily 8am-9pm); or **Spenser's,** 33 Hill Rd. (open daily 8am-11:45pm).

Cambridge turns up its nose at most restaurant chains—though pizza parlors grace almost every block, hamburger take-aways are limited to **Burger King.** Cambridge has some fantastic ethnic food, including a wealth of satisfying curry restaurants (before ordering, make sure that Christ's College football club has not arrived on their ritual curry night out). Both Hills Rd. and Mill Rd., south of town, brim with good, cheap restaurants just becoming trendy with student crowds.

Nadia's, 11 St. John's St. The best bakery in town, and one of the cheapest. Wonderful filled rolls and quiches 70p-£1.30. Stuff your face for £2. Take-away only. Open Mon.-Fri. 7am-5:30pm, Sat. 8am-5:30pm, Sun. 8am-5pm.

Nettles, 5 St. Edward's Passage, off King's Parade. A tiny place with seating for 10 tiny people. Delicious wholefood dishes, dirt cheap. Hot casseroles £1.75-2.30. Large sandwiches 80p. Take-away even cheaper. Open Mon.-Sat. 9am-8pm.

Rajbelash, 36-38 Hills Rd. A bewildering array of curries, *tandooris,* and *biryanis* £2.60-6.40. Give your mouth some relief with a chewy unleavened *naan* bread (£1.10). Take-away available. Open daily noon-2:30pm and 6pm-midnight.

Corner House Restaurant, 9 King's St. Generous portions and low prices make up for the vinyl-fluorescent atmosphere. Spaghetti and chips £3.25. Open Mon.-Fri. 11:30am-2:30pm and 5-9:30pm, Sat.-Sun. 11:30am-9:30pm.

Clown's, 52 King St. A meeting place for foreigners, bozos, and beautiful people. Affable, entertaining proprietor. Practice your Esperanto over cappuccino (90p), quiche (£1.25), or cake (£1.15). Open daily 9:30am-10pm.

Hobbs' Pavillion, Parker's Piece, off Park Terrace. Renowned for imaginative, overpowering pancakes. (Note that the English like their pancakes thin, like French crepes.) Bacon, eggs, and maple syrup pancake £3.90. Mars Bar and cream pancake £3.50—expect not to feel like eating again for 2 weeks. Open Tues.-Wed. and Fri.-Sat. noon-2:30pm and 7-10pm, Thurs. noon-2:30pm and 8:30-10pm.

King's Pantry, 9 King's Parade. A vegetarian restaurant popular with the 90s-alternative crowd. Concerned allergics can examine a list of ingredients for each dish. Deep south pecan pie £4. Open Mon.-Sat. 8am-5:30pm. Dinner served Wed.-Sat. 7-9:30pm.

The Little Tea Room, 1 All Saints' Passage, off St. John's St. Not as hopelessly generic as it sounds; tip-top teas served in a fun basement room. Scone, jam, and cream with a pot of tea £2.20. Open Mon.-Sat. 9:30am-5:30pm.

Auntie's Tea Shop, 1 St. Mary's Passage, off King's Parade. Lace tablecloths, clinking china, and triangular sandwiches. Egg-and-cress sandwich £1.05, carrot cake £1.25. £1.50 min. after noon. Don't expect to see many students. Open Mon.-Fri.. 9am-6:30pm, Sat. 9:30am-6:30pm, Sun. noon-5:30pm.

Mr. Chips, 78 King St. Fish-and-chip connoisseurs may sneer at the polystyrene trays that pathetically substitute for classic greaseproof bags and newspapers, but the product is as satisfying as ever. Cod and chips £2.40. Battered sausage 50p. Open Mon.-Thurs. 11:30am-midnight, Fri.-Sat. 11:30am-12:30am, Sun. 5:30pm-midnight.

Pubs

Cantabrigian hangouts offer good pub-crawling year-round, though they lose some of their character and their best customers in summer. Most pubs stay open from 11am to 11pm, noon to 10:30pm on Sundays. A few close from 3 to 7pm, especially on Sundays. The local brewery, Greene King, supplies many of the pubs with the popular bitters IPA (India Pale Ale) and Abbott. Along the river, try the **Anchor,** Silver St., or **The Mill,** Mill Lane, off Silver St. Bridge. Their tranquil river views contrast sharply with the bustle inside. The **King Street Run,** King St., a down-to-earth towny pub, is named after a historic pub crawl. Two stops on "the run" along King St. are the **Cambridge Arms,** a large renovated brewery, and the **Champion of the Thames,** a miniscule, charming closet of a pub—groups of more than five might not even fit. (King St. gets a bit dicey around closing time on Sat. nights.) A favorite with Magdalene men and women from Cambridge secretarial colleges, the **Pickerel** on Bridge St. is Cambridge's oldest pub. Down the road, the lively town pub **Baron of Beef,** 19 Bridge St., has resisted the onset of flashy décor. **The Maypole,** Park St., sports one of the few bar-billards tables in the center of town. Locals and Christ's College crew members pack the **Free Press,** Prospect St.; tourists might not feel comfortable walking in alone. The **Sir Isaac Newton,** Cattle St., is one of the few pubs in town with facilities for the disabled.

Sights

Cambridge is an architect's dream, packing some of the finest examples of English architecture over the last 700 years into less than one square mile. You should see the world-famous King's College Chapel—but if you explore some of the more obscure courts (quads), you'll discover gems unseen by the majority of visitors.

If you are pressed for time, visit at least one chapel (preferably at King's College), one garden (try Christ's), one library (Trinity's is the most interesting), and one dining hall (difficult without befriending a Cambridge undergrad, although no one will prevent you from taking a surreptitious peek). Most of the historic university buildings line the east side of the River Cam between Magdalene Bridge and Silver St. On both sides of the river, the gardens, meadows, and cows of the **Backs** lend Cambridge a pastoral air. If you have time for only a few colleges, **King's, Trinity, Queens', Christ's, St. John's,** and **Jesus** should top your list, though the whistle-stop traveler could manage 12 or 14 colleges in a few hours. The pamphlet *Cambridge, a Brief Guide for Visitors* (available at the tourist office) includes a street plan and basic information about the colleges and museums.

Cambridge University has three eight-week terms: Michaelmas (Oct. 9-Dec. 7), Lent (Jan. 15-March 15), and Easter (April 23-June 14). Most of the colleges are open daily from 9am to 5:30pm, though most close to visitors during the Easter term, and virtually all are closed during exam period (mid-May to mid-June). Unlike many U.S. campuses, Cambridge has no armed University police. Security is maintained by plump ex-servicemen called Porters, who wear bowler hats. Look and act like a student (i.e. wear no backpack, no camera and, for heaven's sake, no Cambridge University sweatshirt) and you should be able to wander freely through most college grounds—but not on the preciously tended lawns. In the summer, a few undergrads stay to work or study, but most abandon the town to the mercies of mobs of teenage language students. Some university buildings shut down over vacations.

King's College, on King's Parade, is the proud possessor of the university's most famous chapel, a spectacular Gothic monument. In 1441, Henry VI cleared away most of the center of medieval Cambridge for the foundation of King's College, and he intended its chapel to be England's finest. Although Hank wanted the inside of the chapel to remain unadorned, his successors ignored his wishes and spent nearly £5000 and three years carving an elaborate interior. If you stand at the southwest corner of the courtyard, you can see where Henry VI's master mason John Wastell (who also worked on the cathedrals of Peterborough and Canterbury) left off and where later work under the Tudors began—the earlier stone is off-white, the later, dark. The interior of the chapel consists of one huge room cleft by a carved wooden choir screen, one of the purest examples of the early Renaissance style in England.

Wordsworth described the fan-vault ceiling as a "branching roof self-poised, and scooped into ten thousand cells where light and shade repose." Stained glass windows depicting the life of Jesus were preserved from the iconoclasm of the English Civil War, allegedly because John Milton, then Cromwell's secretary, groveled on their behalf. On the walls, alternating Tudor rose and portcullis pendants symbolize Henry VI's reign (look for the grinning pendant on the left). Behind the altar hangs

Ruben's magnificent *Adoration of the Magi* (1639), protected by an electronic alarm since a crazed would-be stonemason attacked it with a chisel several years ago. (Chapel open during the term Mon.-Sat. 9am-3:45pm, Sun. 2-3pm and 4:30-5:45pm; during vacation Mon.-Sat. 9am-5pm, Sun. 10:30am-5pm. Free. Chapel exhibition open during the term Mon.-Sat. 9:30am-3:30pm; during vacations Mon.-Sat. 9:30am-5pm, Sun. 11am-5pm. Admission £1, students 60p.) Take in the classic view of the chapel and of the adjacent **Gibbs Building** from the river.

In early June, in the Georgian **Senate House** opposite the chapel, the university posts the names and final grades of every student; about a week later, degree ceremonies are held here. Cambridge graduates are eligible for the most readily available master's degrees in the world; after spending three and a third years out in the world, a graduate sends £15 to the university to receive one without further ado, provided that said graduate is not in the custody of Her Majesty's Prison Service.

Trinity College, on Trinity St., is Cambridge's largest and wealthiest. Founded in 1546, Trinity used to specialize in literature (alums include George Herbert, John Dryden, Lord Byron, and Lord Tennyson), but in this century has instead spat forth scientists and philosophers (Ernest Rutherford, Ludwig Wittgenstein, G.E. Moore, and Bertrand Russell). The heir apparent, Prince Charles, was an average student in anthropology. The **Great Court** is the largest yard in Cambridge, so huge that its utter lack of straight lines and symmetry is hardly noticeable. Inside the courtyard, in a florid fountain built in 1602, Byron used to bathe nude. The eccentric young poet who lived in Nevile's Court also shared his rooms with a pet bear, which he claimed would take his fellowship exams for him. Although the movie was filmed at Eton College, the story behind *Chariots of Fire* took place here. What William Wordsworth called the "loquacious clock that speaks with male and female voice" still strikes 24 times each noon. Sir Isaac Newton, who lived on the first floor of E-entry for 30 years, first measured the speed of sound by stamping his foot in the cloister along the north side of the court. Underneath the courtyards lie the well-hidden, well-stocked Trinity wine cellars. Recently the college purchased over £20,000 worth of port that won't be drinkable until 2020. The college's wealth is legendary—myth-mongers hold that it was once possible to walk from Cambridge to Oxford without stepping off Trinity land.

Walk through the college toward the river to reach the reddish stone walls of the stunning **Wren Library.** Notable treasures in this naturally lit building include A.A. Milne's handwritten manuscript of *Winnie-the-Pooh* and less momentous works such as John Milton's *Lycidas.* The collection also contains works by Byron, Tennyson, and Thackeray. German-speakers should look for Wittgenstein's journals. His phenomenal *Philosophical Investigations* was conceived here during years of intense discussion with G.E. Moore and students in his K-entry rooms on the top floor. (Library open year-round Mon.-Fri. noon-2pm; also Sat. 10am-2pm during the term. Free. Trinity's courtyards close at 6pm. Closed during exams.)

Established in 1511 by Lady Margaret Beaufort, mother of Henry VIII, **St. John's College,** is one of seven Cambridge colleges founded by women. The striking brick and stone gatehouse bears Lady Margaret's heraldic emblem. The college's two best buildings stand across the river. A copy of Venice's Bridge of Sighs connects the older part of the college to the towering neo-Gothic extravagance of New Court, likened by philistines to a wedding cake in silhouette. Next door, you can see more adventurous college architecture, the modern **Cripps Building,** with clever bends that create three distinct courts under the shade of a noble willow. The **School of Pythagoras,** a 12th-century pile of wood and stone rumored to be the oldest complete building in Cambridge, hides in St. John's Gardens. (Courtyard and some buildings open until 6pm. Closed during exams.)

Queens' College, founded in 1448 by two queens, Margaret of Anjou and Elizabeth Woodville, has few rivals in the "cute" department. It possesses the only unaltered Tudor courtyard in Cambridge, containing the half-timbered President's Gallery. The **Mathematical Bridge,** just past Cloister Court, was built in 1749 without a single bolt or nail, relying only on mathematical principle. A meddling Victorian took the bridge apart to see how it worked and the inevitable occurred—he couldn't put it back together without using a steel rivet every two inches. (College open daily 1:45-4:30pm; during summer vacation also 10:15am-12:45pm. Closed during exams.)

Clare College, founded in 1338 by the thrice-widowed, 29-year-old Lady Elizabeth de Clare, has preserved an appropriate coat of arms: a shield with golden teardrops on a black border. Across Clare Bridge (the most elegant on the river) lie the **Clare Gardens.** (Open Mon.-Fri. 2-4:45pm.) Walk through Clare's Court (open during exams to groups of less than three) for a view of the University Library, where 82 miles of shelves hold books arranged according to size rather than subject. George V called it "the greatest erection in Cambridge;" more recently it appeared in the cinematic masterpiece *Brazil.*

Christ's College, founded in 1505, has won fame for its gardens (open Mon.-Fri. 2-4pm) and its connection with John Milton—a mulberry tree reputedly planted by the "Lady of Christ's" still thrives here. The gardens are also home to Blyth's Footprint, planted some 350 years later. To reach the gardens, walk under the lovely neoclassical Fellows Building dubiously accredited to Inigo Jones. New Court, on King St., is one of the most impressive, horrible modern structures in Cambridge; its strikingly symmetrical white stone walls and black-curtained windows look like the cross-bred offspring of an Egyptian pyramid, a Polaroid camera, and a typewriter. Charles Darwin survived among the fittest at Christ's, taking his undergraduate degree. His rooms (closed to visitors, and unmarked) were on G staircase in First Court. The entire college closes during exams, except for access to the chapel during services and concerts. (Inquire at the porter's desk.)

Built on a more secluded site than most back in 1496, **Jesus College** has preserved an enormous amount of unaltered medieval work. Beyond the long, high-walled walk called the "Chimny" lies a three-sided court fringed with colorful gardens. Through the archway on the right lie the remains of a gloomy medieval nunnery. The Pre-Raphaelite stained glass of Burne-Jones and ceiling decorations by William "Wallpaper" Morris festoon the chapel. (Courtyard open until 6pm. Closed during exams.)

Magdalene College (MAUD-lin), founded in 1524, has acquired an unsavory, aristocratic reputation. The **Pepys Library,** in the second court, displays the noted statesman and prolific diarist's collection in the original cases. You can see the dining hall on the left as you walk to the second court. (Library open Mon.-Sat. 2:30-3:30pm; also Easter-Aug. 11:30am-12:30pm. Free. Courtyards closed during exams.)

In **Peterhouse** (1284), the oldest college, Thomas Gray wrote his *Elegy in a Country Churchyard.* The newest of Cambridge's colleges is **Robinson College,** on Grange Rd. Founded in 1977, this mod-medieval brick pastiche sits just behind the university library. Bronze plants writhe about the door of the college chapel, which features some interesting stained glass. James Stirling's **History Faculty building,** between West Rd. and Sidgwick Ave., once provoked much debate about its aesthetic merits; of its leaky roof, there were never any doubts.

Corpus Christi College, founded in 1372, contains a dreary but extremely old courtyard forthrightly called Old Court, unaltered since its 1352 enclosure by town merchants. The library maintains the snazziest collection of Anglo-Saxon manuscripts in England, including the Parker Manuscript of the *Anglo-Saxon Chronicle.* The 1347 **Pembroke College** next door harbors the earliest architectural effort of Sir Christopher Wren. (Courtyards open until 6pm. Closed during exams.)

A chapel designed by Wren dominates the front court of **Emmanuel College.** Emmanuel, founded in 1584, on St. Andrew's St. at Downing St., and **Downing College,** founded in 1807, just to the south along Regent St., are both pleasantly isolated. (Courtyards open until 6pm. Chapel open when not in use.) Downing's austere neoclassical buildings open onto an immense lawn. (Open daily until 6pm. Dining hall open when not in use. Closed during exams.)

The **Round Church,** Bridge St., one of five round churches surviving in England, was built in 1130 (and later rebuilt) on the pattern of the Church of the Holy Sepulchre in Jerusalem. The pattern deserves comparison with **St. Benet's Church,** a rough Saxon church on Benet St. The tower of St. Benet's, built in 1050, is the oldest structure in Cambridge.

You can easily get caught up in the splendor of the colleges, but try to take the time to explore a few museums. The **Fitzwilliam Museum,** Trumpington Rd. (tel. 332 900), a 10-minute walk down the road from King's College, dwells within an immense Roman-style building. Inside, a cavernous marble foyer leads to a collection that includes paintings by Leonardo da Vinci, Michelangelo, Dürer, Corot, Monet, and Seurat. A mixture of Egyptian, Chinese, and Greek antiquities bides its time downstairs, coupled with an extensive collection of 16th-century German armor. Check out the interesting illuminated manuscripts under their protective cloths. The drawing room displays William "Barmy" Blake's books and woodcuts. (Open Tues.-Sat. ground floor 10am-2pm, upper floor 2-5pm, Sun. both floors 2:15-5pm. Free. Call to inquire about lunchtime and evening concerts. Guided tours Sat.-Sun. at 2:30pm, £1.50.) The **Museum of Zoology** (tel. 336 650), off Downing St., houses a fine collection of dead wildlife specimens in a modern, well-lit building. (Open Mon.-Fri. 2:15-4:45pm. Free.) Across the road, opposite Corn Exchange St., the **Museum of Archeology and Anthropology,** Downing St. (tel. 333 516), contains an excellent collection of prehistoric artifacts from American, African, Pacific, and Asian cultures, as well as exhibits from Cambridge through the ages. (Open Mon.-Fri. 2-4pm, Sat. 10am-12:30pm. Free.) If you're near Magdalene College, stop by the **Folk Museum,** 2 Castle St. (tel. 355 159), at Northampton St., an appealing junk heap. (Open Mon.-Sat. 10:30am-5pm, Sun. 2-5pm. Admission £1, children 50p.) **Kettle's Yard,** at the corner of Castle and Northampton St., houses a collection of early 20th-century art. (Open Tues.-Sat. 12:30-5pm, Sun. 2-5:30pm. Free.) The **Scott Polar Research Institute,** Lensfield Rd. (tel. 336 540), commemorates icy expeditions with photographic and artistic accounts, equipment, and memorabilia. (Open Mon.-Sat. 2:30-4pm. Free.)

The **Botanic Gardens** (tel. 336 265; enter from Hill Rd., Trumpington Rd., or Bateman St.) are a xerox copy of Eden. The gardens were ingeniously laid out by Henslow, Sir Joseph Hooker's father-in-law, in 1856. When the wind gets friendly, the scented garden turns into an olfactory factory. The adders (poisonous snakes) in the gardens have yet to bother visitors; keep to the path nevertheless. (Open Mon.-Sat. 8am-6pm, Sun. 10am-6pm. Admission £1 on Sun., free Mon.-Sat.)

Entertainment

On a sunny afternoon, bodies sprawl on the lush banks of the River Cam. The Cam is almost always stocked with narrow, flat-bottomed **punts,** England's retort to the gondola. Punting is the sometimes stately, sometimes soggy pastime of propelling a flat little boat (a punt) by pushing a long pole into the river bottom. If your pole gets stuck, leave it in the mud instead of taking a plunge. Punters can take two routes—one from Magdalene Bridge to Silver St., and the other from Silver St. along the River Granta (the name given to the Cam as it passes out of town) to Grantchester. On the first route—the shorter, busier, and more interesting one—you'll pass the colleges and the Backs. The art of punt-bombing, in which students jump from bridges into the river right next to a punt, thereby tipping its occupants into the Cam, has been largely discontinued since the advent of increased river policing a few years ago. You can rent a punt from **Scudamore's Boatyards,** at Magdalene Bridge or Silver St. (tel. 359 750); hourly rates are £6 for punts, rowboats, and canoes, plus a £30 cash deposit. (Open daily 9am-6pm.) Upstart **Tyrell's,** Magdalene Bridge (tel. 352 847), has punts and rowboats for £5.20 per hour, plus a £25 deposit. Tyrell's offers chauffered rides (45 min.) for £15 per group.

You can expect long lines for punts on weekends, particularly on Sunday—rowboats and canoes are easier to come by. To avoid bumper-punting, go late in the afternoon when the river traffic dwindles, but remember that boats must be returned by 6pm. Guided tours, punted by students, offer a cop-out option to those unwilling to risk a plunge. Inquire at the tourist office.

During the first two weeks of June, students celebrate the end of the term with **May Week** (this is, perhaps, a May of the mind), crammed with concerts, plays, and elaborate balls which feature anything from hot air balloon rides to lying utterly drunk face down in the street to breakfast on the Seine. Along the Cam, the college boat clubs compete in an eyebrow-raising series of races known as the **bumps.** Crews line up along the river rather than across it, and attempt to ram the boat in front before being bumped from behind. May Week's artistic repertoire stars the famous **Footlights Revue,** a collection of comedy skits; its performers have gone on to join such troupes as Beyond the Fringe and Monty Python. John Cleese, Eric Idle, and Graham Chapman graduated from the Revue. (At the Arts Theatre box office, tel. 352 000.)

During the rest of the summer, entertainment is geared more toward tourists than students, but the **Cambridge Festival,** a series of concerts and special exhibits culminating in a huge **folk festival,** brightens the last two weeks of July. (The 1992 festival is scheduled for July 10-26.) Tickets for the weekend (around £32) include camping on the grounds. (For the main festival, call the Corn Exchange box office, tel. 357 851; for the folk festival, tel. 463 359.)

During the third week of June the **Midsummer Fair,** which dates from the early 16th century, appropriates Midsummer Common for about five days. The **Strawberry Fayre,** Cambridge's answer to Glastonbury, takes place the first Saturday in June. (Address all festival inquiries to the tourist office.)

John Maynard Keynes, the resident economic voodoo-master of Cambridge during the first half of this century, took time off from his dubious science to found the **Arts Theatre Club** (box office tel. 352 000; open Mon.-Sat. 10am-8pm), which sponsors drama, film, and dance. The theatre is located at 6 St. Edward's Passage. Students pay £5.50 for advance tickets and £4.50 for any ticket still unsold an hour before the show starts. Tickets usually cost £8-12.50. The **Arts Cinema,** Market Passage (tel. 352 001), screens comedy classics and undubbed foreign films and holds a film festival during the Cambridge Festival. (Tickets £2.50-3.50. Box office open Mon.-Fri. 1-9:15pm, Sat. 11am-9:15pm, Sun. 1:30-9:15pm.) During the term and the Cambridge Festival, the **ADC Theatre** (Amateur Dramatic Club), Park St., offers lively entertainment, including student-produced plays (£2.50-6) and movies (£3). Call the box office (tel. 359 547) for the latest schedule. The best source of information on student activities is the *Varsity,* free to undergrads, 25p in a news shop; or enquire at the tourist office.

You can get an earful of concerts at the **Cambridge Corn Exchange,** at the corner of Wheeler St. and Corn Exchange, a venue for band, jazz, and classical concerts. (Box office tel. 357 851; tickets £5.50-12.50, 50% off for student standby 30 min. before performances. Box office open Mon.-Sat. 10am-6pm.) The **Cambridge Union,** a private debating club, sponsors social activities during the summer (officially only for people enrolled in language courses, but check anyway). The clubhouse orates on Round Church St., off Sydney St. Students pack the **Anchor,** Silver St. (tel. 353 554), on Tuesday and Thursday nights, when live bands play hot jazz. **Flambard's Wine Bar,** Rose Crescent, has jazz on Friday nights. To the east, **The Geldart,** 1 Ainsworth St. (tel. 355 983), features Irish folk music on Tuesday and Sundays. **Route 66,** Benet St., draws a house crowd on Wednesdays and motor traffic on bank holiday weekends.

The Junction, Clifton Rd., off Cherry Hinton Rd. south of the town, proves a popular alternative dance venue on Friday nights, and hosts top local bands such as *The First Five Minutes of Betty Blue.* **Cinderellas Rockefellers,** Lion Yard, right in the center draws a gay crowd from throughout East Anglia on Sunday nights. Popular night spots change constantly; students, bartenders, and the latest issue of *Varsity* will be your best sources of information.

Canterbury

In the Middle Ages, England's most heavily traveled road was the one from London to Canterbury, lined with pilgrims striding to the shrine of Thomas à Becket. Becket clashed with Henry II over the clergy's freedom from state jurisdiction. Henry cried in exasperation, "Who will deliver me from this turbulent priest?" In December 1170 four loyal knights answered their king's query and murdered Becket in the cathedral. A shrine was born. Becket became a martyr and a saint; Henry died a mere mortal.

Chaucer's blockbuster exposé of materialism on the pilgrimage trail has proved strangely prescient. While Canterbury Cathedral, parts of which date to the 11th century, is awe-inspiring, most of this town is now geared toward raking in money from visitors dressed in high-tops and mirrored sunglasses.

Orientation and Practical Information

Trains run hourly from London's Victoria Station to **Canterbury East Station,** the stop nearest the youth hostel, and from London's Charing Cross and Waterloo stations to **Canterbury West Station** (1¼ hr., £9.70, £10.50 day return). **Buses** to Canterbury leave London's Victoria Coach Station twice daily (2 hr., £8.25 day return). Canterbury is as easy to reach from the Continent as from the rest of Anglelonde, since it's on the rail and bus lines from the Dover, Folkestone, and Ramsgate hovercraft terminals.

Canterbury is roughly circular, enclosed by a ring road around a city wall that has been slowly disappearing over the centuries. The circle is crossed from west to east by an unbroken street that is named, in different sections, **St. Peter's Street, High Street,** and **St. George's Street.** The cathedral kneels in the northeast quadrant. To reach the tourist office from East Station, cross the footbridge, take a left down the hill, and turn right onto Castle St., which becomes St. Margaret's St. From West Station, walk up Station Rd. West, turn left onto St. Dunstan's St., and walk through Westgate tower onto St. Peter's St. (which becomes High St.) and then right onto St. Margaret's.

Tourist Information Centre: 34 St. Margaret's St. CT1 1AA (tel. (0227) 766 567). Accommodations service for a 10% deposit, list free. Book a bed ahead for £2.15. Those who won't call it quits after a look around the cathedral should buy the invaluable *Canterbury, the Pilgim's Guide* (£2). Ambitious sightseers can also procure a wide range of maps and guides for Canterbury and the rest of Kent. Open Apr.-Oct. daily 9:30am-5:30pm; Nov.-March 9:30am-5pm.

Tours: Guided tours of the city depart from the tourist center on St. Margaret's St. May-Sept. Mon.-Sat. at 11am and 2pm, Sun. at 2pm; generally only one tour per day in winter, depending on the weather (consult the tourist office). Tour £2.20, students £1.50.

Student Travel Office: Kent Union Travel, Student Union at the University of Kent (tel. 674 36). Sells bus tickets and offers a wide range of student tours. Open Mon.-Fri. 10am-5:30pm. **Pickford's Travel,** St. Margaret's St., offers Eurotrain services and cheap rates to the Continent. Open Mon.-Fri. 9am-5:30pm.

Currency Exchange: Several major banks on High St. Banks close at 3:30pm.

Post Office: 26 High St., across from Best Lane. Open Mon.-Fri. 9am-5:30pm, Sat. 9am-12:30pm. **Postal Code:** CT1 1AA.

Telephones: The city's phone numbers have been standardized at 6 digits. Old 5 digit numbers may remain. If a 5 digit number beings with a 5, add a 4; with a 6, add a 7. **Telephone Code:** (0227).

Train Station: East Station, Station Rd. East, off Castle St., southeast of town. **West Station,** Station Rd. West, off St. Dunstan's St. (tel. 455 511 for both).

Bus Station: St. George's Lane (tel. 634 82), off St. George's St. Extensive local and long-distance services. Frequent buses to Deal, Sandwich, and Dover; coaches run every 1½ hr.

to London Victoria (2 hr., £8.25 single or day return). Also daily excursions in summer; check the list outside the ticket office.

Bike Rental: Canterbury Cycle Mart, 33 Lower Bridge Rd. (tel. 761 488). Three-speeds £6 per 24 hrs., £25 per week; £40 deposit. Open Mon.-Fri. 9am-5:30pm, Sat. 9am-5pm.

Laundromat: 36 St. Peter's St., near Westgate Towers. Open Mon.-Fri. 8:30am-5pm. Also at 20 Dover St., near the youth hostel. Open Mon.-Fri. 8:30am-5pm.

Market Day: Wed. 9am-1:30pm. Fruits, vegetables, clothing, assorted signifiers. ¼ mi. north of town along Northgate St., at Kingsmead Rd.

Disabled Travelers: DIAL (Disabled Informations Advice Line), 7 Victoria Rd. (tel 450 001 or 462 125).

East Kent Gay Switchboard: Tel. (0843) 588 762. Open Tues. 7:30-10pm.

Crisis: Samaritans (tel. 457 777), on the corner of Love and Ivy Lanes.

Early Closing Day: Thurs., small shops only.

Hospital: Kent and Canterbury Hospital (tel. 766 877), off Ethelbert Rd.

Police: Old Dover Rd. (tel. 762 055), outside the eastern city wall.

Emergency: Dial 999; no coins required.

Accommodations and Camping

Rooms fill up quickly from June through September; try to book at least three days in advance, or at the very least arrive by midday. B&Bs bunch near both train stations and on London and Whitstable Rd., just beyond West Station. If you're desperate, head out for the more expensive B&Bs along New Dover Rd., a ½-mi. walk from East Station, near the youth hostel. Singles are scarce.

IYHF Youth Hostel, 54 New Dover Rd. (tel. 462 911), ¾ mile from East Station. Turn right as you leave the station and continue up the main artery; at the second rotary, turn right onto St. George's Pl., which becomes New Dover Rd. 56 beds. Victorian villa with good facilities, washing machines, and hot showers. Doors open 8-10am and 5-11pm. £7, ages 16-20 £5.90. Book a week in advance in July and Aug. Open March-Oct. daily. Call for off-season openings.

Mrs. Pigden, 37 Orchard St. (tel. 765 981), near West Station. Look carefully—there is no sign on the door. Location seems arbitrary. Simple but comfortable rooms £10 per person with English breakfast. If full, cheerful Mrs. Pigden will refer you elsewhere.

London Guest House, 14 London Rd. (tel. 765 860). Run by Shirley and Peter Harris, their mutt Shane, and their nameless ginger kitten. Spacious Victorian house in immaculate condition. £15 per person with breakfast.

The Tudor House, 6 Best Lane (tel. 765 650), off High St. Clean, bright rooms with TV. Agreeable owners and a central location. Canoes and boats for hire to guests. £15 per person.

Alexandra House, 1 Roper Rd. (tel. 767 011), a short walk from West Station. TV in all rooms. Upbeat new carpets and quilts. Singles £15. Doubles £29, wth shower £32. Families £12-14 per person.

Milton House, 9 South Canterbury Rd. (tel. 765 531). Tidy rooms and a warm welcome on a quiet street. Doubles £25.

York House, 22 Old Dover Rd. (tel. 765 743), close to East Station, just outside the city wall. Large, spacious B&B, all rooms with TV. One shower for every 3 rooms. £14 per person. English breakfast included.

Camping: St. Martin's Touring Caravan and Camping Site, Bekesbourne Lane (tel. 463 216), off A257 (Sandwich Rd.), 1½ mi. east of city center. Take Longport Rd. from the city wall. Good facilities. 60 pitches for tents. Open April-Sept. Tent sites £3.75, with vehicle £6.25.

Food

The streets around the cathedral seethe with bakeries and sweet shops; **Ward's,** Mercery Lane, is especially popular. For pub lunches, try the **Cherry Tree,** White-horse Lane, or the **Black Griffin,** High St. The **Sweet Heart Patisserie,** in the Weaver's House, St. Peter's St., has light lunches, ice cream, and *wunderbar* German pastries. Fresh fruits and vegetables await you at **Gambell's Farmshop,** Castle St., and **Bodsham's,** 44 High St.

> **Caesar's Restaurant,** 46 St. Peter's St. Hefty portions at decent prices. Appetizers a meal unto themselves. ½-lb. burger and a mountain of fries £4.60, vege-burger £3.75. Open daily 11:30am-10:30pm.

> **Alberry's,** 38 St. Margaret's St. Pasta, pizza, and vegetarian dishes from £4. Serve yourself and sit by the bar. Open Mon.-Sat. noon-2:30pm and 6:30pm-midnight.

> **The White Hart,** Worthgate Pl., close to East Station on a small street within the city walls. Congenial pub with homemade luncheon specials (£3-6). Live a little and ask to eat in the rose garden. Open for lunch Mon.-Sat. noon-2:30pm.

> **The Three Tuns,** Watling St. Just down the street from tourist information. A pub with traditional English fare. Four daily specials at £3.95, various salads £3.90. Lunch daily 11am-3:30pm, dinner 6-9pm.

> **Tea Pot,** 34 St. Peter's St. A warm, woodsy tea shop and vegetarian restaurant with 182 varieties of tea. Cream tea £3.60. Open Mon.-Sat. 10am-9pm, Sun. 11am-9pm.

> **Marlowe's,** 59 St. Peter's St. Extremely friendly place with theatrical decor and an eclectic mix of vegetarian and beefy English, American, and Mexican food. Seven kinds of 6-oz. burger £5.75, burritos £6.45. Open daily 11am-11pm.

Sights

For the most famous view of **Canterbury Cathedral,** England's most historically potent shrine, stare from tiny Mercery Lane just past Christchurch Gate. To observe every detail of this soaring 537-ft. building, walk through the grounds of King's School off Palace St. As you enter **Trinity Chapel** behind the altar, you can study the architectural plan to the right. Above the high altar, by Becket's Shrine, 12 windows patiently narrate his life and miracles. In the north aisle, a recently uncovered 17th-century mural tells the legend of St. Eustace, a 2nd-century martyr. Below you lies the vast Norman **crypt,** the oldest part of the cathedral. Immerse yourself in nine centuries of ritual and history by attending a choral evensong (45 min., Mon.-Fri. at 5:30pm, Sat.-Sun. at 3:15pm). (Cathedral open Easter-Sept. Mon.-Sat. 8:45am-7pm, Oct.-Easter 8:45am-5pm; Sun. year-round 12:30-2:30pm and 4:30-5:30pm. Tours Mon.-Fri. at 11:30am, 12:30pm, 2:30pm, and 3:30pm; tickets £2, students £1, available at south exit in the nave. Thirty min. walkman tour £1.)

The remainder of medieval Canterbury crowds around the branches of the River Stour on the way to the **Westgate,** the only one of the city's seven medieval gates to survive the wartime blitz. A small museum in Westgate tower houses collections of old armor and prison relics. (Open April-Sept. Mon.-Fri. 10am-1pm and 2-5pm; Oct.-March Mon.-Fri. 2-4pm. Admission 50p.)

The majority of Canterbury's other sights cluster on High and St. Peter's St., between Westgate and the cathedral. The **Royal Museum and Art Gallery** sponsors the work of local artists and also houses the Gallery of the "Buffs," one of the oldest regiments in the British army. (Open Mon.-Sat. 10am-5pm. Free.) Several rickety monastic houses perch precariously along the banks of the River Stour. For a quiet break, walk over to Stour St. and visit the riverside gardens of the **Greyfriars,** the first Franciscan friary in England, built over the river in 1267. The Franciscan friars arrived in England in 1224, two years before Francis died. A small museum and a chapel can be found inside the simple building. (Open in summer Mon.-Fri. 2-4pm. Free.) The lovely medieval **Poor Priests' Hospital,** also on Stour St., now houses the **Museum of Canterbury Heritage,** an unprecedented "time-walk through

Canterbury's past." (Open June.-Oct. Mon.-Sat. 10:30am-4pm, Sun. 1:30-4pm. Admission £1.20, students 60p.)

On St. Peter's Street, across from Stour St., stand the famous **weaver's houses,** where Huguenots lived during the 16th century. Walk through the gift shop and into the garden to see an authentic **ducking stool** (a medieval test for those suspected of witchcraft) still swinging over the river. Half-hour river tours leave from here every half hour. (£2.25). You can also rent a rowboat for a 40-minute trip along the Stour (£2.25, deposit £5. Open Easter-Oct. daily 11am-dusk, river and weather permitting.)

Chaucer would have been enthralled by **Canterbury Tales,** St. Margaret's St. (tel. 454 888), a new exhibit that brings the *Canterbury Tales* to life. Deploying wax figures, slides, moving sets, and costumed personnel, this museum attempts to recreate the telling of the tales with intelligence and wit and without unrecognizable dipthongs; it's better than the Rock Circus. (Open daily 9am-6:30pm. Admission £3.75.) Under the Longmarket, an **underground museum** displays romantic Roman mosaic pavement. (Open April-Sept. Mon.-Sat. 10am-1pm and 2-5pm; Oct.-March Mon.-Sat. 2-4pm. Admission 50p.)

Near the medieval city wall across from East Station, lie the **Dane John Mound and Gardens** and the massive, solemn remains of the Norman **Canterbury Castle.** If you fail to encounter the ghost of Canterbury's own Christopher Marlowe "rolling down the streets a-singing" (as one local historian put it) you can at least find a statue of his muse in the garden. Not much remains of St. **Augustine's Abbey** (598 AD), but older Roman ruins and the site of St. Augustine's first tomb (605 AD) can be viewed outside the city wall near the cathedral. (Open Mon.-Sat. 9:30am-6pm, Sun. 2-6pm; off-season Mon.-Sat. 9:30am-4pm. Admission 95p, students 75p.) Just around the corner from St. Augustine's on North Holmes St. stands the **Church of St. Martin,** the oldest parish church in England. Inside pagan King Ethelbert was married to the French Christian Princess Bertha in 562. Outside lie the remains of multilingual Polish writer Joseph Conrad.

Entertainment

Pubs keep Canterbury awake through dusk. The **Miller's Arms,** Mill Lane off Radigund St., offers six draught beers. **Alberry's,** 38 St. Margaret's St., the most stylish wine bar in the area, has live music Thursday nights from 9:30 to 11:30pm. Pick up a copy of the brochure *Around Canterbury* at the tourist office for an up-to-date listing of events, or call 767 744 for a recorded announcement. The **Gulbenkian Theatre,** at the University of Kent, University Rd. (tel. 769 075), west of town out St. Dunstan's St., past St. Thomas' Hill, stages a series of amateur and professional productions in summer. (Box office open from April daily 2-5:30pm. Tickets £3-6; ask for student discounts. You can also purchase tickets from Pickford's Travel Service, St. Margaret's St.) The new **Marlowe Theatre** (tel. 767 246) stages London productions and variety shows. (Tickets £4.50-7.) Professional actors perform medieval mystery plays in the Cathedral from mid-July to mid-August. (Tickets £6.50, student £5.) Contact Forward Bookings (tel. (0227) 455 600), 37 Palace St., Canterbury, Kent CT1 2D2.

For 10 days at the end of June, the **Stour Music Festival,** a celebration of Renaissance, baroque, and classical music, takes place in beautiful All Saint's Boughton Aluph Church, near Ashford, 5 miles southwest of Canterbury on the A28 or by rail from West Station. Tickets start at £4; reserve at least a month in advance. Ashford's **Tourist Information Centre,** Lower High St. (tel. (0233) 373 11), provides details, or you can call Forward Bookings (see above). For information on summer arts events and the **Canterbury Festival**—three weeks of concerts, drama, opera, cabaret, chamber music, dance, and exhibitions inspired by the French culture—call 452 853 or write to Canterbury Festival, P.O. Box 83, Canterbury, Kent CT1 3YU.

Near Canterbury

Leeds Castle, 23 miles southwest of Canterbury on the A20 London-Folkestone road, near Maidstone, was named after the fun-loving chief minister of Ethelbert IV. Henry VIII transformed it into a lavish dwelling. The surrounding 500 acres of woodlands and gardens host some of the world's most unusual waterfowl, including black swans; the castle itself houses a faintly alarming collection of dog collars from the Middle Ages. From Canterbury, take the train from West Station and change at Ashford. (Open March-Oct. daily 11am-6pm; Nov.-Feb. Sat.-Sun. 11am-5pm. Admission to castle and grounds a hefty £5.60, students £3.90.) For information call (0622) 765 400.

Chilham Castle stands six miles southwest of Canterbury along the A28. Only the octagonal keep survives from the 12th-century fortress that was pulled down to supply building stone. The replacement modern castle represents the pinnacle of large-scale 17th-century architecture. Displays of jousting transpire here on Sundays, and tournaments of knights on Sundays, Mondays, and bank holidays. The castle falconer gives daily demonstrations. For general inquiries, call 730 319. (Open March-Oct. daily 11am-5pm. Admission £2.50, children £1.25.)

Deal

In 55 BC, Julius Caesar invaded Britain along Deal's shoreline and was confronted by a swarm of fierce Britons in primitive galoshes wading into the sea to do battle. The town's maritime identity was reinforced during the next few centuries, as ships waiting to cross the English Channel would shelter off Deal and use the town's services. Deal no longer rules the waves, but its quiet seaside charm continues to attract visitors from London.

Orientation and Practical Information

Deal lies 8 miles north of Dover and 12 miles southeast of Canterbury; hourly trains and frequent buses stop in Deal on their way to these better-known cities. The town extends from north to south along the coast. Beach St., High St., and West St.—the major arteries—parallel the coast. The train station stands just west of town off Queen St., which becomes Broad St. as it runs toward the sea. To reach the center, turn left onto Queen St. and follow it until you reach the pedestrian precinct of High St. The bus station idles on South St., which runs between High St. and Beach St., one block south of Broad St. Incomprehensible? Well, it'll make more sense when you get there.

Tourist Information Centre: Town Hall, High St. (tel. 369 576). Turn left off Queen St. onto High St. Accommodation service free (deposit 10% of first night). Open June-Aug. Mon.-Fri. 9am-6pm, Sat. 10am-4pm, Sun. 10am-2pm; Sept.-May Mon.-Fri. 9am-5pm.

Currency Exchange: Several banks grace High St.

Post Office: Stanhope Rd., a left turn off High St. and Victoria St. Open Mon.-Tues. and Thurs.-Fri. 9am-5:30pm, Wed. 9:30am-5:30pm, Sat. 9am-12:30pm. **Postal Code:** CT14 6AA.

Telephone Code: (0304).

Train Station: Queen St. Every half hour service to London (£13.40 return) via Dover (£2.20 return), and to Sandwich (£1.50 return).

Bus and Coach Station: South St. Turn right on to Victoria; take second left. Office open Mon.-Fri. 8am-5:15pm, Sat. 9am-3:45pm. Frequent service to Sandwich, Dover, and Folkestone. For information, call (0843) 581 333.

Bike Rental: Park Cycles, 23 Queen St. (tel. 366 080). From £7.50 per day, £29.50 per week; £30 deposit. Repairs. Open Mon.-Sat. 8:30am-6pm, Sun. 10am-4pm.

Laundromat: 5 Queen St. Open Mon.-Fri. 8am-8pm, Sat.-Sun. 8am-6pm; last wash 1 hr. before closing.

Market Day: Sat. 9am-4pm, Union Rd. Car Park, 1 block north of Town Hall off High St. Also a small **indoor market** on Oak St. Open Tues. and Fri.-Sat. 9am-4pm.

Early Closing Day: Thurs., smaller shops only (usually 1pm).

Emergency: Dial 999; no coins required.

Accommodations, Camping, and Food

Guesthouses are pricey, and the nearest youth hostels are in Dover and Canterbury. Call in advance on weekends.

Goodwin House, 38 Victoria Rd. (tel. 365 468). From Queen St. turn right on to High St.; it becomes Victoria Rd. Just 50 yards from the castle. Central location, friendly owner. Singles £13. Doubles £26.

Cannongate, 26 Gilford Rd. (tel. 375 238). From the station turn right down Blenheim Rd.; Gilford Rd. is 10 min. down on the left. Hefty house on a placid street. Singles and doubles £12 per person.

Alma Tavern, 126 West St. (tel. 360 244). Turn left onto West St. from the train station. Rooms above a pub. Tidy family-run establishment. Doubles £20, with breakfast £25.

The **Peking and Canton** on Broad St. has full lunches for dealers for under £5. Dinner is a bit steeper with a £6.50 minimum, takeaway half price. (Open Wed.-Mon. noon-2:30pm and 6pm-midnight.) **Dunkerley's,** around the corner on Beach St. facing the coast, has an elegant 2-course lunch deal for £3.75. (Open Mon.-Fri. 11:30am-3pm and 6-10pm, Sat. 11:30am-3pm and 6-11pm, Sun. noon-10pm.) **Middle St. Fish Bar** deals dealfish and chips (£1-2) on Middle St. (Open Mon.-Sat. noon-2pm, 5:30-10pm.) You will probably never find a tea shop more beautifully furnished than **Ronnie's,** just off High St. on Stanhope Rd., with cream tea for £2. Grocery stores deal in the center of town.

Sights

To ward off Catholic invaders from the Continent, Henry VIII zealously built fortifications along the coast of Deal. All were built in the "Tudor Rose" style: Deal Castle's ornamentation boasts six petals while that on Walmer Castle has but four. **Deal Castle,** the largest of the network, is a castle in the early sense of the word: a stern and impenetrable fort rather than an elegant home. Lose yourself in the dark, dank tunnels of the keep, or wander around the battlements. Inside, a display describes the strategy behind Henry VIII's castles and their importance in defending English coasts from the snail-eating French. (Open April-Sept. daily 10am-6pm; Oct.-March Tues.-Sun. 10am-4pm. Admission £1.60, students £1.20, children 80p.) **Walmer Castle** is the best preserved and most elegant, having been softened by formal gardens and gradually transformed into a country estate. Since the 18th century, it has been the official residence of the Lords Warden of the Cinque Ports, a defensive system of coastal towns with origins in the reign of Edward the Confessor. Notable Lords Warden include William Pitt, the Duke of Wellington (who died here in 1852), and Winston Churchill. The post is currently filled by the Queen Mother. (Open April-Sept. daily 10am-4pm; Oct.-March Tues.-Sun. 10am-4pm. Admission £2.20, students £1.60, children £1.10.)

If you walk along the Coast to Dover Castle, you'll pass the **Timeball Tower,** a fascinating contraption connected by electric current to Greenwich Observatory. When ships used the Downs as a makeshift port before crossing the Channel, the ball on top of the tower was lowered at precisely 1pm each day to indicate the time to the isolated sailors. Today, you can still see the ball drop every hour on the hour, but a simple quartz mechanism now keeps the correct time. Climb to the top to see the panorama of town and sea. (Open late spring to Sept. Tues.-Sun. 10am-5pm. Admission 80p.) The **Museum of Maritime and Local History,** 22 St. George's Rd., right behind the tourist office, contains unusual displays of relics from old seafaring vessels. (Open May-Sept. daily 2-5pm. Admission 40p, students 30p.)

If you're in Deal in late July-early August, the **Deal Festival** offers an array of music concerts (pastoral 16th-century, classical, Victorian, as well as modern). Call the box office at the Astor Theatre for details (366 077, tickets £5-10).

Dover

> The sea is calm tonight.
> The tide is full, the moon lies fair
> Upon the straits;—on the French coast the light
> Gleams and is gone; the cliffs of England stand
> Glimmering and vast, out in the tranquil bay.
> —Matthew Arnold, "Dover Beach"

Matthew Arnold inaugurated the modernist movement in poetry with these lines. The "melancholy, long, withdrawing roar" of the English Channel has since been drowned out by the puttering of ferries, the hum of hovercraft, and the incomprehensible squabbling of French families *en vacances.* But Dover has retained its sense of identity despite the grating roar of tourist traffic. The white chalk cliffs tower staunchly above the beach, and Dover's fortress has withstood the potent threats of Napoleon and Hitler. While the town remains quite ordinary, the dramatic coast, with its darkling plain of lighthouses and Norman ruins, is a stirring reminder of England's history.

Orientation and Practical Information

Trains for Dover's Priory Station leave from London's Victoria, Waterloo, and Charing Cross stations every 45 min. (2 hr., £13.40). Beware when you board at London as many trains branch off en route. From Victoria, express lines continue to the Western Docks Station. There is also regular **coach service** (2 per hr.) from London's Victoria Coach Station; coaches continue to the Eastern Docks after stopping at the bus station on Pencester Rd. (tel. (0403) 206 813; 2 hr. 45 min., £8.25). Make an advance reservation. On Sundays, trains provide much better service between Dover and London than do coaches.

The main part of the town stretches up from the coast in a north/south strip, bordered on the east by York St., which becomes High St., and then London Rd., home to the hostel. The west side of town is enclosed by a very steep hill (the one with Dover Castle on top).

Tourist Information Centre: Townwall St. (tel. 205 108), 1 block from the shore. Once you leave the station parking lot, turn left onto Folkestone Rd. and right onto York St. at the rotary—Townwall St. is at the next rotary on the left. Keep walking along on York St. (even though you probably suspect, at this point, that you're lost). Accommodations service free, book-a-bed-ahead £3. Even if you arrive late, they can usually find you a room, and after hours they post a list of available accommodations. Ferry tickets, hoverport tickets, and rental cars available. Open June-Aug. daily 7:45am-10pm; off-season daily 9am-6pm.

Travel Office: Pickfords, 10 Worthington St. (tel. 206 273). Eurotrain services. Open Mon.-Sat. 9am-5:30pm.

Currency Exchange: Five major banks at Market Sq. roundabout. Try **Midland** or **Barclay's** for the best rates. After-hours *bureau de change* next to the tourist office open daily 8am-10pm; in winter 8am-8pm. **Natwest Bank,** at the Eastern Docks (tel. 201 474). Open July 7-Sept. 9, 24 hrs.; Sept. 10-Oct. 13 daily 7am-9pm; Oct. 14-Dec. 31 8am-5pm.

Post Office: 65 Biggin St. Currency exchange available. Open Mon.-Fri. 9am-5:30pm, Sat. 9am-12:30pm. **Postal Code:** CT16 1AA.

Telephone Code: (0304).

Train Station: Priory Station (tel. (0227) 454 411), off Folkestone Rd. To: Canterbury East Station (2 per hr., ½ hr., £3.20); Deal (1 per hr., 15 min., £2.20); Sandwich (1 per hr., 25 min., £2.90). Service to London 5am-10pm.

Bus Station: Pencester Rd., which runs between York St. and Maison Dieu Rd. (tel. 240 024). Hourly service to Canterbury (£2.80), Deal (£2), and Sandwich (£2.50). To Folkestone (every 2hr., £1.70). Purchase tickets on the bus or in the ticket office. Open Mon.-Fri. 8:30am-5:30pm, Sat. 8:30am-4pm.

Taxi: Dover Taxis, Market Sq. or train station (tel. 201 915).

Hitching: To London, take the A2 straight from the docks. For areas along the southeastern coast, try the A20 west, but prepare for a long wait. The A258 east toward Deal might be a better idea.

Crisis: Samaritans, Folkestone (tel. (0303) 550 06). Open daily 24 hrs.

Hospital: Buckland Hospital (tel. 201 624), on Coomb Valley Rd. northwest of town. Take local bus D9 or D5 from outside the post office.

Police: Ladywell St., right off High St. (tel. 240 055).

Emergency: Dial 999; no coins required.

Ferries

Dover is England's busiest passenger port. Major ferry companies operate ships from Dover to the ports of Calais (1½ hr.), Oostende (4 hr.), Zeebrugge (4¼ hr.), and Boulogne (1¾ hr.). **Sealink** (tel. 240 280) has service from Dover Eastern Docks (and, less frequently, from the Western Docks) to Calais (£19, students £17). A 60-hr. return costs the same as a single. Five-day returns run £31, student £25. Ferries leave at least every 2 hr., more frequently in summer. **P&O European Ferries** (tel. 203 388) charges the same prices for foot passengers, and also has 60-hr. returns and 5-day returns. The ferries depart about as often as Sealink, but only from the Eastern Docks terminal (accessible by P&O bus from the Dover Priory train station).

Hovercrafts to the Continent leave from the Hoverport (tel. 208 013; reservations 240 241), down the Prince of Wales Pier (bus from Priory Station), to Calais or Boulogne (35 min.). Book a few days in advance (£23 single, 60-hr. return £23, 5-day return £35.

Free bus service leaves the Priory Station for the docks and the Hoverport one hour before sailing time. Several offices, including the Dover tourist office, can book both Hovercraft and ferry crossings at last-minute notice. Only the Eastern Docks have facilities for the disabled, but all locations can provide wheelchairs if notified beforehand.

Accommodations and Camping

Accommodations can be hard to find at the height of the tourist season; the ferry terminal often becomes a rudimentary campground. Several of the hundreds of B&Bs on **Folkestone Road** (by the train station) stay open all night; if the lights are on, ring the bell. For daytime arrival, also try the B&Bs near the center of town on **Castle Street.**

Charlton House Youth Hostel (IYHF), 306 London Rd. (tel. 201 314), a ½-mi. walk from the train station. Turn left onto Folkestone Rd., left onto Effingham St., past the gas station onto Saxon St., and left at the bottom of the street onto High St., which becomes London Rd. Recently-refurbished. Kitchen facilities, lukewarm showers, and a lounge area with billiards. Strictly enforced lockout 10am-5pm, curfew 11pm. £7, ages 16-20 £5.90. No phone bookings July-Aug. Cheaper overflow hostel at **14 Goodwyne Rd.** has no showers.

Gordon Guest House, 23 Castle St. (tel. 201 894). Management very friendly. B&B in top condition. All rooms with color TV and kettles. Doubles £28, with shower £30.

Mrs. Hackney, Church Villas, 6 Harold St. (tel. 203 684). Turn right from the bus station and cross Maison Dieu Rd.; walk 1 block up Taswell St. to Harold St. Clean, well-kept, and cozy rooms £9 per person.

Amanda Guesthouse, 4 Harold St. (tel. 201 711). Next door to Mrs. Hackney. Victorian house with bright sunny rooms. Doubles £26.

Camping: Harthorn Farm, at Martin Mill Station off the A258 between Dover and Deal (tel. 852 658). Large site in a gorgeous rural setting, but a little too close to the railway. 200 pitches. July-Sept. £2.55 per person, off season £2.30 per person, £1.25 electricity hook-up.

Food

Despite the proximity of the Continent, Dover's cuisine remains loyally English. Inexpensive food fries from dawn to dusk in the fish-and-chip shops and grocery stores on London Rd. and Biggin St., and a decent pub lunch can be had almost anywhere in the city center.

Chaplin's, 2 Church St. A popular cheap restaurant in the center of town. Runs the gamut for lunch from sandwiches (£1.50) to chicken burgers with fries (£3.10). Open Mon.-Sat. 8:30am-8pm.

Jermain's Café, Leighton St., on a quiet street off London Rd., just past the hostel; turn onto Beaconsfield Rd. Roast beef, potatoes, and vegetable £2.50. Open Mon.-Sat. 11:30am-2:30pm, Sun. 11:30am-2pm.

Moonflower, 32-34 High St. (tel. 212 198). A wide variety of Chinese and English dishes in a newly and tastefully decorated café. Take-away too. Chinese dishes £4-5, chicken and chips £4.70. Open Mon.-Sat. noon-2:30pm and 5pm-midnight, Sun. 5pm-midnight.

Dino's, 58 Castle St. Italian food served by a gaggle of friendly young waiters. For lunch, pasta dishes £5, veal dishes £6. Dinner upwards of £10. Open Tues.-Sun. noon-2pm and 6-10:30pm.

Sights

The view from Castle Hill Rd., on the east side of town, reveals why **Dover Castle** is famed both for its magnificent setting and for its impregnability. (Take bus #90 bound for Deal from the bus depot on Pencester Rd.) Many have launched assaults by land, sea, and air on the castle: the French tried in 1216; the English during the English Civil Wars in the mid-17th century; and the Germans in World Wars I and II. All failed. The exhibits in the keep encompass an odd assortment of trivia and relics from the 12th century to the present; climb to the top for an arresting view of the battlements and countryside. Notice the graffiti from French, Dutch, and Spanish prisoners. (Open Easter-Sept. daily 10am-6pm; Oct.-Good Friday 10am-4pm. Admission £3, students £2, children £1.50.) On a clear day, Boulogne can (barely) be seen 22 miles away across the water; it was from that coast that the Germans launched V-1 and V-2 rocket bombs in World War II. These "doodle-bugs" destroyed the **Church of St. James,** the ruins of which crumble at the base of Castle Hill.

The empty **Pharos,** built in 43 BC sits alongside **St. Mary's,** the Saxon church. Once a beacon for Caesar's galleys, it is the only Roman lighthouse still in existence and quite possibly the only complete Roman building in Britain. For £1.50 (£1 students and seniors) take a fascinating guided tour of **Hell Fire Corner,** a labyrinth of "secret" tunnels only recently declassified. The tunnels, originally built in the late-18th century to defend Britain from attack by Napoleon, were the strategic base for the evacuation of Allied troops from Dunkirk in World War II. Now they're filled with well-informed guides and historical newsreels. Tours leave every 20-30 min. and last 55 min.

Recent excavation has unearthed a remarkably well-preserved **Roman painted house,** New St., off Cannon St. near Market Sq., the oldest Roman house in Britain complete with wall paintings and under-floor central heating system. The house was dug out from 20 feet of soil and centuries of Roman, Saxon, medieval, and Victorian relics, some of which are on display. An accompanying exhibit reveals the fascinating work of the Kent Archaeological Rescue Unit. (Open April-Oct. Tues.-Sun. 10am-5pm. Admission £1, children 50p.)

A few miles west of Dover (25 min. by foot along Snargate St.) sprawls the whitest, steepest, most famous, and most unaccommodating of the white cliffs. Known as **Shakespeare Cliff** (look for the signs), it is traditionally identified with the cliff scene in *King Lear.* Closer to town on Snargate St. is the **Grand Shaft,** a 140-ft. triple spiral staircase shot through the rock in Napoleonic times to link the army stationed on the Western Heights and the city center. The first stairwell was for "officers and their ladies", the second for "sergeants and their wives", the last for "soldiers and their women".(You can ascend and descend May-Sept. Wed.-Sun. 2-5pm for a mere pittance of 80p, children 40p.) The **Dover Museum,** at the corner of Ladywell and High St. (tel. 201 066), has a permanent collection including curious bits of Victoriana, ship models, and clocks. (Open Mon.-Tues. and Thurs.-Sat. 10am-4:45pm.) The **White Cliffs Experience,** Market Sq., the newest tourist attraction in town, chronicles Dover's history from Roman Britain to the present day. Not as good as the Rock Circus. (Open April-July 7 daily 10am-6:30pm; July 8-Sept. daily 10am-7:30pm. £3.95, seniors £3, children £2.50.)

Rye

Settled before the Roman invasion, Rye's port flourished until the waterways choked with silt. Until the 19th century, Rye was best known for its gangs of smugglers, who darted past royal authorities to stash contraband in an elaborate network of massive cellars, secret passageways, and adjoining attics.

Orientation and Practical Information

Rye (pop. 4440), a tiny town surrounded on three sides by waterways, stands at the mouth of the Rother River. Rye makes a good base for other excursions in the area. Trains leave from London's Charing Cross and Cannon St. stations (change at Ashford; 1½hr., 35 min., £11.90 cheap day return). You can also go via Tunbridge Wells, changing at Hastings. As you leave the train station or dismount from a bus, Cinque Port St. is in front of you; about 50 yards down turn left for the tourist office. It's about five minutes away; look for signs. To reach the oldest and prettiest part of town, go from Cinque Port St. up Market Rd. to High St., Lion St., and Mermaid St.

Tourist Information Centre: 48 Cinque Port St., Rye, East Sussex TN31 7AN (tel. 222 293), ½ block from the train station. Free accommodations list. Open daily 9am-6pm. Get *Adam's Guide to Rye Royal,* (£1.50) a good walking guide on Rye.

Currency Exchange: The 4 banks in town cluster at the corner of High and West St., 1 block south of Cinque Port St. Also at the post office.

Post Office: Cinque Port St. Open Mon. 9:30am-5:30pm, Tues.-Fri. 9am-5:30pm, Sat. 9am-12:30pm. **Postal Code:** TN31 7AA.

Telephones: Outside the post office. **Telephone Code:** (0797).

Train Station: Off Cinque Port St. For information call Hastings (0424) 429 325. Most destinations require changes at Hastings (for Brighton £8, and Eastbourne £4.60) or Ashford (for London £11.90, and Dover £6.80). Trains run every hr. to both stations; either trip takes 25 min.

Bus Station: Coaches stop in front of the train station. Regular service to points beyond Rye and Hastings and further destinations; schedules posted on signs in the parking lot. For information, call 223 343.

Market Day: Thurs. 8:30am-3pm, fresh fruit and used books beside the train station.

Early Closing Day: Tues., small shops only (most at 1pm).

Police Station: Cinque Port St. (tel. 222 112).

Emergency: Dial 999; no coins required.

Accommodations and Camping

IYHF Youth Hostel, Guestling, Rye Rd., Hastings (tel. (0424) 812 373), 5 mi. down the A259 past Winchelsea. Take bus #11 or 12 from Rye to the White Hart in Guestling (roughly every hr. Mon.-Sat., every 2 hr. on Sun., £1.60, last bus around 5pm). You can also take the train to Three Oaks (£1.90) and walk 1¼ miles. £5.50, ages 16-20 £4.40. Open July-Aug. daily; Sept. and April-June Tues.-Sun.; Oct.-Dec. and Feb. Wed.-Sun.; March Tues.-Sat.

Mrs. Jones, 2 The Grove (tel. 223 447), a 5-min. walk from the train station. Turn left onto Cinque Port St. and left again onto Rope Walk, which becomes The Grove just after the train tracks. Best B&B in town. Pleasant proprietors. Clean and attractive rooms, all with color TV and books. £11-12.50 per person.

Mrs. Hollands, 13 Winchelsea Rd. (tel. 223 000). Turn right onto Cinque Port St., which becomes Wish St. and then Winchelsea Rd. Run by a kind woman who enjoys her job. Good value at £12.50 per person. If she's booked, try her daughter-in-law at **Riverhaven Guest House,** 60 New Winchelsea Rd. (tel. 223 267; £12.50).

Mrs. Ross, 37 Winchelsea Rd. (tel. 224 656). Right next to Mrs. Hollands' place. Peaceful and tidy. £11 per person.

Jeakes House, Mermaid St. (tel. 222 828), in a handsome 17th-century house down the street from the Mermaid Pub. Easily among the most dramatic and delightful B&Bs in Britain. Large, lovely rooms with low ceilings, exposed timbers, antique furniture, and ancient, leaded-glass windows opening onto a quiet, cobbled street. All rooms with private bath, color TV, telephones and tea-making facilities. U.S. poet Conrad Aiken lived here for 23 years and T.S. Eliot was a frequent guest. Reserve well in advance (at least 3 weeks during the summer). £18.50-24.50 per person.

Camping: Silver Sands Caravan Park, Lydd Rd. (tel. 225 282), 3 mi. east of Rye in Camber, 100 yd. from the beach. Take bus #11, 12, or 799 to Camber Silver Sands. £5.50 for a 2-person tent. **Old Coghurst Farm,** Three Oaks (tel. (0424) 753 622), near Guestling and the youth hostel. Take same buses as above. £4 per tent or caravan, £1 per adult.

Food

Rye is riddled with full-service eateries, fast food joints, and teashops. **Tuckers of Rye** sells pizza, burgers, and salads (£2.50-4). The Fish and Chip Shop, next door on Mint St., fries a popular and cheap alternative. For a special pub experience, buy a drink at the **Mermaid Inn** and sit on top of old smuggling tunnels.

Fletcher's House, Lion St., in front of the church. Dramatist John Fletcher was born here in 1579. Open for morning coffee, lunch, and tea. After a meal, wander upstairs to the 15th-century oak room filled with antiques. Filling lunches £4-6; cream tea £2.80. Open daily 10am-5:15pm.

The Peacock, Lion St. Friendly service and romantic setting. Good dinners £5-7. Try their country *pâté* (£3.50) and a pint of Master Brew XX (£1.65). Open Mon.-Sat. noon-2pm and 7-9pm.

Toff's, 36-38 Cinque Port St. Best for lunch, dinners more expensive. Char-grilled meats, deep pan pizza (£4.25), and pasta (£3.50). Open Tues.-Sun. noon-3pm, 6pm-midnight.

Swan Cottage Tea Rooms, 41, The Mint (tel. 222 423). Delicious cream teas (from £1.50) and suprisingly hearty meals served in an old half-timbered house with rustic fireplaces and stained-glass windows. Roast beef with horseradish sauce £2.75. Excellent homemade quiche £2. Open Mon.-Sat. 10:30am-5pm.

Sights

Rye is extraordinarily well-preserved. A walk down Mermaid Street will bring you to the famed Mermaid Inn, where smugglers once cavorted until dawn. At the end of the cobbled street stands **Lamb House,** where novelist Henry James lived and wrote the most insufferable of his later novels, including *The Wings of the Dove* and *The Golden Bowl.* (Open mid-April to Oct. Wed. and Sat. 2-5:30pm. Admission £1.40.) **St. Mary's,** the huge medieval parish church at the top of Lion St., houses one of the oldest functioning clocks in the country. The clock's gold-plated "quarter boys,"—so named because they toll every quarter hour—might ring a bell. The original quarter boys, forced into early retirement years ago by upstart fiberglass models, now rest in a dignified position on the window sill. You can climb up the tower steps (£1) to see the inner-workings of the clock. Down the road stands 13th-century **Ypres Tower,** a castle that houses the **Rye Museum.** Formerly a town jail, the museum now contains a haphazard display on reform politics, military paraphernalia, domestic life, and Rye pottery. (Open Easter-Oct.15 Mon.-Sat. 10:30am-1pm and 2:15-5:30pm, Sun. 11:30am-1pm and 2:15-5:30pm. Admission £1, students 75p.) Rye holds a week-long **festival** in early September, with poetry, music, and theater. (Tickets £2-5.)

Near Rye: Battle, Pevensey, Bodiam

Appropriately named after the decisive fight between William of Normandy and King Harold of England in 1066, **Battle** makes a fine expedition from Rye. To commemorate his victory, William the Conqueror had **Battle Abbey** built in 1094, meanly positioning its high altar upon the very spot where Harold died. The abbey town grew prosperous enough to survive Henry VIII's closing the abbey in 1538. Now little remains apart from the gate and a handsome series of 13th-century common quarters. (Open daily 10am-4pm. Admission £1.90, students £1.50.) The battlefield itself, where William's outnumbered band rushed uphill to fight Harold's astonished troops, is now a pasture trampled only by demented sheep. In summer, you can take a tour of the abbey and walk the **battlefield trail,** a one-mile jaunt up and down the green hillside. **Buckley's Shop Museum,** 90 High St., re-creates the "corner shops" one might have encountered in England in the early 1900s (admission £1).

Battle railway station is a half-hour from Hastings on the mainline hourly service from London to Hastings. (For information call (0424) 429 325.) Buses run frequently from Rye in summer, but check the timetables on High St. or call (0424) 431 770 for information. Buses stop on the abbey green. Battle's **telephone code** is (0424).

Rooms in Battle cost around £12.50 per person and can be booked by the **tourist office** at Abbey Green Corner, 88 High St. (tel. 3721; open May-Sept. daily 10am-1pm and 2-5:30pm; Oct.-April Mon.-Fri. 10am-1pm and 2-5:30pm). When that's closed, call the office in the quiet coastal resort of **Bexhill-on-Sea** (tel. (0424) 212 023) for accommodations.

William the Conqueror began his march to Battle from the Roman fortress **Anderita.** He gave the castle to his brother, who added a Norman keep; around this castle grew **Pevensey,** one of the more delightful towns of the southern coast. (Castle open April-Sept. daily 10am-6pm; Oct.-March Tues.-Sun. 10am-4pm. Admission £1.30, students £95p, children 65p.) **St. Mary's,** in Westham, claims to be the first church built by the Normans after their conquest of England.

The best part of Pevensey owes its origins to commerce rather than conquest. The **Mint House,** High St., began as a mint under the Normans; Henry VIII's physician, Dr. Andrew Borde, transformed it into a country retreat; it ended up as a smugglers' den, complete with sliding ceiling panels. Decorated with fine 15th-century carvings and wall paintings, the interior seems a veritable forest of English oak. The antique store teems with Victorian paraphernalia, stuffed birds, grandfather clocks, and other fascinating oddities—themselves worth the price of admission. (Open Mon.-Sat. 9:30am-5pm. Admission 80p.)

Pevensey's **tourist office** stands guard in Pevensey Castle Car Park, High St. (tel. (0323) 761 444; open Easter-Sept. daily 10:30am-4:30pm). For rail information in the area, call (0424) 429 325; for buses, (0424) 722 223.

To top off a tour of local castles, bus or hitch along the A268 to **Bodiam Castle.** Built in the 14th century, Bodiam conveys a sense of romance with its moat and its sweeping views of the sheep-dotted downs. Ah, those sheep-dotted downs. (Open April-Oct. daily 10am-6pm; Nov.-March Mon.-Sat. 10am-4pm. Admission £1.70.)

Brighton

> *In Lydia's imagination, a visit to Brighton comprised
> every possibility of earthly happiness. She saw with the
> creative eye of fancy, the streets of that gay bathing
> place covered with officers.*
> —Jane Austen, *Pride and Prejudice*

Garish Brighton is Queen Victoria and Liberace rolled into one. Here British
holiday-makers put away mounds of cotton candy, sneak a peek at the seedy side-
shows on Palace Pier, peel it off at England's first official nudist beach, and marvel
at the almost unbelievable gaudiness of the Royal Pavilion. From the anonymous
B&Bs amidst elegant Regency and Georgian squares to the reams of naughty postcards on the seafront, Brighton is the undisputed home of the "dirty weekend."

Orientation and Practical Information

Trains escape regularly from London to Brighton (at least 2 per hr., 1¼ hr., £9.70,
£9.90 day return). An express train leaves London's Victoria Station every 50 min.
(50 min., £9.70 single or day return.) To reach the tourist office, take a bus to Old
Steine from the train station, or walk straight down Queen's Rd. At the clocktower,
turn left onto North St. (not North Rd.), then right onto Old Steine (about a 15-
min. walk).

Tourist Information Centre: Marlborough House, 54 Old Steine (tel. 237 55). Open July-Aug.
Mon.-Fri. 9am-6:30pm, Sat. 9am-6pm; June and Sept. Mon.-Sat. 9am-6pm, Sun. 10am-6pm;
April-May Mon.-Fri. 9am-5pm, Sat. 9am-6pm, Sun. 10am-6pm; Oct.-March Mon.-Sat. 9am-
5pm, Sun. 10am-4pm. Accommodations service free (10% first night deposit). Map, guide
and accommodations list 25p. Historic town trail guides 10p.

Student Travel Office: Campus Travel in YHA Adventure Shop, 126 Queen's Rd., near
Church St. Open Mon.-Sat. 9:30am-5:30pm.

American Express: 66 Churchill Sq., BN1 2EP just off Western Rd., near the Queen's Rd.
clocktower (tel. 212 42). Open Mon. and Wed.-Fri. 9am-5pm, Tues. 9:30am-5pm, Sat. 9am-
4pm.

Currency Exchange: Major banks along North St., including Barclays at #139 (open Mon.-
Fri. 9:30am-5:30pm, Sat. 9:30am-12:30pm) and Lloyd's at #171 (open Mon.-Fri. 9:30am-
4:30pm, Sat. 9:30am-12:30pm).

Post Office: 51 Ship St. Open Mon.-Tues. and Thurs.-Fri. 9am-5:30pm, Wed. 9:30am-
5:30pm, Sat. 9am-1pm. **Postal Code: BN1 1AA.**

Telephone Code: (0273).

Train Station: (tel. 206 755), at the end of Queen's Rd. away from the front. To Portsmouth
(every hr., 1½ hr., £8.30, £8.30 day return) and Arundel via Ford (2 per hr., 30 min., £4.20,
£4.30 day return). London timetable tel. 278 23, Portsmouth timetable tel. 202 172.

Bus and Coach Stations: National Express services stop at the Pool Valley bus station at
the southern angle of Old Steine. Ticket and information booth at the south tip of the Old
Steine green. Open Mon.-Sat. 8:30am-5:15pm, Sun. 9:30am-5:15pm. For information call 674
881. Local bus information from One Stop Travel at Old Steine and St. James St. Open Mon.-
Fri. 8:15am-6pm, Sat. 9am-5pm, Sun. 9am-4pm. For information, call 206 666 (Brighton and
Hove Bus and Coach Co.) or Worthing 376 61 (Southdown Buses).

Bike Rental: Harmon Leisure Hire, 21-24 Montpelier Rd. (tel. 205 206). £5.75 per day, £16
per week; £50 deposit. Open Mon.-Fri. 8am-5:30pm, Sat. 8am-2pm.

Taxis: Streamline Taxis, tel. 242 45.

Laundromat: On the corner of St. James Ave. off St. James St. Wash £2, dry 20p. Open daily
from 7:30am, last wash 9pm.

Public Library: Church St. (tel. 691 197), next to the Royal Pavilion. In a fantastic Victorian building, with intriguing exhibits and a good café. King George IV guards the stairs to the reference library on the first floor. Open Mon.-Tues. and Thurs.-Fri. 10am-7pm, Sat. 10am-4pm.

Women's Center: 10 St. George's Mews (tel. 005 26). Pregnancy testing and advice. Open Mon. and Wed.-Thurs. 10:30am-3pm and 7-9pm, Sat. 11:30am-1:30pm.

Gay Switchboard: Tel. 690 825. Practical advice, counseling and information. Referral point for other gay groups. Open Mon.-Fri. 8-10pm, Sat. 6-10pm, Sun. 8-10pm.

Rape Crisis: Tel. 203 773. Open Tues. 6-9pm, Fri. 3-9pm, Sat. 10am-1pm.

Late Closing Day: Thurs., most shops open until 7pm.

Hospital: Royal Sussex County, Eastern Rd., parallel to Marine Rd. east of town. (tel. 696 955).

Police: John St. (tel. 606 744).

Emergency: Dial 999; no coins required.

Accommodations and Camping

Brighton (pop. 250,000) thrives on tourism, and prices for accommodations are predictably high (B&B rates hover around £17). The cheaper B&Bs snuggle in the **Kemp Town** area, on the streets perpendicular to the sea opposite the Palace Pier—Madeira Place and Dorset Gardens, for example. Test the beds and smell the dust before signing your night away. From the train station, follow Queen's Rd. until you reach the clocktower; turn left at the tower onto North St. and continue along North across Old Steine to St. James St. Look for Dorset Gardens on your left, and Madeira Place on your right, each about a 20-minute walk from the station.

IYHF Youth Hostel, Patcham Pl. (tel. 556 196), 4 mi. north on the main London road (the A23). Hitch or take Patcham bus #773 or 5A (from stop E) from Old Steine to the Black Lion Hotel. Big country house with rooms that look so new it's hard to believe it's 400 years old. Often full; call ahead in July-Aug. or show up around breakfast time. £7, ages 16-20 £5.90. Breakfast £2.30. Sleep sack hire 75p. Open Feb.-Dec.

Dorset Guest House, 17 Dorset Gdns. (tel. 694 646), on a quiet side street. 18th-century house covered in decidedly 20th-century pink paint. £14-£17 per person.

Almara Guest House, 11 Madeira Pl. (tel. 603 186), near the water and Palace Pier. Welcoming owner. £15-17.50 per person.

Pebbles Guest House, 8 Madeira Pl. (tel. 684 898). Tidy rooms with tea and coffee and TV. £15-18 per person.

Cavalaire Guest House, 34 Upper Rock Gdns. (tel. 696 899). Cheering good value, with TV, tea-making facilities, and assorted electrical appliances in each room. Doubles £28, with private bath £40.

Camping: Sheepcote Valley, Wilson Ave. (tel. 605 592), 1½ mi. from town center. Go east on Marine Parade, left on Arundel Rd., right on Roedan Rd., and left on Wilson Ave. Bus #1A runs directly to the campsite every ½ hr.; buses # 1, 3, and 37 follow the seafront—ask the driver where to get off. Open early March-late Oct. Tents £1.75 per person.

Food

Wander around "the Lanes," a jumble of narrow streets between North St. and Prince Albert St. where the Brighthelmstone fishermen once lived. The cheapest restaurants can be found up the hill between Western and Dyke Rd. Trendy American-style burger and pizza houses line up along Prince Albert St. Pick up fruit and vegetables at the open market on Saturday mornings on Upper Gardner St. Safeway is on St. James St.; Tesco is in Churchill Sq.

Food for Friends, 17a Prince Albert St. Cheap, well-cooked, well-seasoned vegetarian food in a breezy, relaxed atmosphere. Meals £2.50-3.50. Open Mon.-Sat. 9am-10pm, Sun. 9:30am-10pm.

Donatello, 3 Brighton Pl. New Italian café in the heart of the Lanes. Sumptuous salads £3.20, pizza £3.75-5. Open daily 11:30am-11:30pm.

Meeting House Restaurant, 9 Meeting House Lane, in the Lanes. Wide selection of good, inexpensive food for under £3.50. Look for the green awning. Open Mon.-Sat. 11am-6pm, Sun. 10am-6pm.

Ed's Easy Diner, corner of Meeting House Lane and Prince Albert St. 50s-style diner complete with a soda fountain and Elvis on the jukebox. Burgers—veggie or beef—£3.65. Open daily 11:30am-11:30pm.

Moon's Café, 42 Meeting House Lane. Bountiful sandwiches £3-4. Sussex cream tea £2.35. Open daily 11:30am-10pm.

Sights

Brighton's transformation from the sleepy village of Brighthelmstone to England's "center of fame and fashion" was catalyzed by the scientific efforts of one man and the whimsical imagination of another. In 1750, Dr. Richard Russell wrote a Latin treatise on the merits of drinking and bathing in sea water for the treatment of glandular disease. Until that time, bathing in the sea had been considered nearly suicidal. The treatment received universal acclaim, and seaside towns like Brighton began to prosper. In 1783, the Prince of Wales (later George IV) visited Brighton, adopted it as his own, and arranged construction of the **Royal Pavilion** from 1810-1815. It is mostly the work of John Nash, who almost singlehandedly created the Regency style. Such architecture tends to be sober and elegant; the Royal Pavilion is bold, elaborate, and eccentric. In the second half of the 19th century, the royal family visited the pavilion only sporadically, and during World War I it served as a hospital for Indian soldiers. The mansion has recently been restored; Persian carpets, bamboo furniture, and gold serpents grace the interior. The Royal Pavilion shimmers on Pavilion Parade, next to Old Steine. (Open June-Sept. daily 10am-6pm; Oct.-May 10am-5pm. Admission £3.10, students £2.30.) You can get a joint admission ticket (£5; high season only) for **Preston Manor** as well, a grand Georgian house on the A23. (Take same buses as for youth hostel, or #5, 5A, 5B. Open Tues.-Sun. 10am-5pm. Admission £2.)

Life in Brighton has always focused on the seashore. Few people actually swim along the pebbly beaches—most spend their time wilting in deck chairs or waddling along the stately promenade. The **Palace Pier,** 100 years old and recently painted, offers a host of amusements and every imaginable sort of entertainment, including a **museum of slot machines** between the piers under King's Road Arches (free). **Volk's Railway,** a three-foot-gauge electric train, Britain's first, shuttles back and forth along the waterfront. (Open April-Sept. Call 681 061 for times and information; 80p.) The **Brighton Sea Life Centre,** once the Victorian Aquarium, has recently liberated its dolphins: Missie and Silver are now living in the West Indies. The center, England's largest, showcases sea life in both 20th-century and Victorian style. (Open daily 10am-6pm. Admission £3.50.) The **Grand Hotel,** on the front on King's Rd., has been substantially rebuilt since the 1984 bombing that killed five but left Mrs. Thatcher unscathed. Farther west, the ghostly **West Pier** has most certainly not been rebuilt; its utter dilapidation seems almost alluring.

The local **Museum and Art Gallery,** around the corner from the Royal Pavilion, maintains a collection of paintings, English pottery, and some priceless art deco and art nouveau pieces, including a sofa designed by Salvador Dalí entitled *Mae West's Lips.* The fine **Willett Collection of Pottery** illustrates some of the more peculiar dimensions of English social life. (Open Tues.-Sat. 10am-5:45pm, Sun. 2-5pm. Free.)

Several churches consecrate Brighton's tacky shores. **St. Nicholas' Church,** Dyke Rd., dates from 1370 and contains a 12th-century baptismal font that some consider the best work of Norman carving in Sussex. You can also take bus #5, 5A, or 5B to visit **St. Bartholomew's Church** on Ann St. Originally called "The Barn" or "Noah's Ark," this little-known spurt of Victorian genius rises to a height of 135 feet, taller than Westminster Abbey.

The Lanes, a hodge podge of 17th-century streets—some narrower than three feet—are south of North St. and constitute the heart of Old Brighton. Guided walking tours leave from the tourist information center. (Tours April-Nov. Sun. at 3pm and Thurs. at 10am; £1.50, students £1.)

Entertainment

Brighton's nightlife may not rival London's in quantity, but in verve the city earns its nickname of "London-By-the-Sea." You can easily find pubs specializing in all musical genres, theatres both intimate and Olympian, outdoor concerts, and indoor outrages. Obtain the tourist office's list of activities or do some independent pub-crawling in The Lanes. A free local monthly called "The Punker" lists details on evening events. Check pubs, newsagents, and record shops.

Brighton Centre, King's Rd., and the **Dome,** New Rd., host Brighton's mammoth rock and jazz concerts. Tickets can be acquired at the Brighton Centre booking office on Russell Rd. (tel. 202 881; open Mon.-Sat. 10am-5:30pm) and at the Dome booking office at 29 New Rd. (tel. 674 357; open Mon.-Sat. 10am-5:30pm). Summer brings outdoor concerts and assorted entertainment (mime, juggling) to the pavilion lawn and the beach deck. Ask at the tourist office for a schedule of events. Numerous clubs with short lifespans cater to all sensibilities. Trendier types dance at **The Escape Club** (tel. 606 906), nearer to the pier on Marine Rd. **Night Fever,** Ship St. (tel. 284 39), has a gay disco on alternate Wednesdays despite its Saturday promise. By far the most popular spot for jazz is **The King and Queen,** Marlborough Pl. (tel. 607 207; jazz Wed.-Thurs., and Sun.). **The Marlborough** (tel. 570 028), opposite the Royal Pavilion, blends folk and rock (Wed. and Sat.), while **The Royal Oak,** 46 St. James St. (tel. 606 538) sticks mainly to Friday night folk. **The Old Vic,** on Ship St. in the Lanes (tel. 247 44), is a lively rock pub. The tourist office has comprehensive free lists of clubs and pubs with entertainment.

Plays and touring London productions take the stage at the **Theatre Royal,** New Rd., a Victorian beauty with the requisite red plush interior (gallery tickets £4-6, circles and stalls £7-14.50; student standbys from 10am on day of performance except Sat. evenings £6-7; box office tel. 284 88; open Mon.-Sat. 10am-8pm). The intimate **Nightingale Supper Theatre** (tel. 267 86) on Surrey St. offers a variety of productions (shows Sat.-Sun. 8pm; £7.50).

Just west of Brighton Marina, you can frolic at the outlandish naked bathing area. Be sure to stay within the limits. For a more clothed, indoor swim try the **Prince Regent Swimming Pool,** Church St. (tel. 685 692). (Open Mon. 10:30am-9:30pm, Tues.-Fri. 7am-10pm, Sat. 9am-6:30pm, and Sun. 9am-4:45pm. Swimming £1.85, solarium £2.90, towel rental 80p. Numerous sailing opportunities crop up in summer; check bulletin boards at the tourist office.

Arundel

Paul Weller never wrote a song about Arundel. With acres of forests, grassy knolls, and winding streams surrounding the town, Arundel is not the stuff of youthful rebellion. The town is squat and affable, its narrow streets lined with respectable second-hand bookstores and antique shops. The River Arun glides genteely through Arundel, and from a stately Norman castle perched on a hilltop, Death looks down upon the town.

Orientation and Practical Information

Trains leave London's Victoria Station for Arundel (pop. 3200) hourly (1¼ hr., £9.70 cheap day return). Most other train and bus routes involve connections at Littlehampton to the south or Barnham to the east. Bus #32 goes to Littlehampton hourly, stopping across from the Norfolk Arms on High St. Many hitch to and from Brighton along the A27.

To reach the center of town from the rail station, turn left onto the A27; it becomes the Causeway, Queen St. and then, as it crosses the river, High St. At the **tourist office** at 61 High St. (tel. 882 268 or 882 419), you can find useful brochures: pick up *A Walk Around Arundel* (25p). A local accommodations service (deposit 10%) is also available. (Open Mon.-Sun. 9am-6pm, off-season Mon.-Sat. 9am-1pm and 2-5pm.) **Currency Exchange** is possible at either of Arundel's two banks: Lloyd's, at 14-16 High St., or NatWest, at 57 High St. The **post office,** 2-4 High St., sorts at the corner of Mill Rd. near the river. (Open Mon. and Wed.-Fri. 9am-1pm and 2-5:30pm; Tues. 9:30am-1pm and 2-5:30pm; Sat. 9am-12:30pm.) Arundel's **postal code** is BN18 9AD; its **telephone code** is (0903).

Accommodations and Food

The most reasonable lodgings option in Arundel is the **Warningcamp Youth Hostel (IYHF)** (tel. 882 204), 1½ miles from town. From the train station, turn right onto the A27 and take the first left; after a mile, turn left at the sign and then follow the other signs (2 right turns). The hostel has kitchen facilities. It closes its doors from 10am to 5pm, and after 11pm. (Open late March to Sept. daily; Oct. Mon.-Sat., and Jan. to mid-March Tues.-Sat. £5.50, ages 16-20 £4.40. Sheet sack rental 75p.) Otherwise, prepare to pay at least £14 for B&B. The **Arden Guest House,** 4 Queens Lane (tel. 882 544), just off Queen St., has doubles with TV and tea-making facilities for £28, with bath £32. **The Bridge House and Cottage,** 18 Queen St. (tel. 882 142 or 882 779), has singles for £16-24, doubles for £28-36. The only budget campsite nearby is the **Ship and Anchor Site** (tel. Yapton 551 262), two miles from Arundel on Ford Rd. (Open April-Sept. £5 for tent and 2 people.)

Arundel's pubs and tea shops tend to fall on the dear side of reasonable. For great value, try **The Castle View,** 63 High St., which offers homemade lasagna (meat or veggie) for £3.60, as well as a cheap and filling selection of snacks. The display of wattle and daub construction in the right stall of the ladies' room is informative. (Open in summer daily 10am-5:30pm; in winter 10:30am-5pm.) The **Café Violette,** just up High St., has a flashy interior of frescoes, statuary, and the obligatory wax-soaked bottles, and serves light lunches, vegetable dishes (£4-5), and a delightful Sussex cream tea (£2.20). (Open daily 10am-11pm.) The **White Hart,** 12 Queen St., serves hearty pub grub (scampi and trimmings £5.50; food available daily noon-2:30pm and 7-9pm). **Trawlers,** across the way at 19 Queen St., fries up a wicked plaice and chips (£3). (Open Mon.-Sat. 11:30am-2pm, 4:45-9:30pm; Sun. noon-5pm.) For picnics or late-night snacks, the rather incongruous **Circle K,** 17 Queen St., stays open daily until 10pm.

Sights

Arundel Castle (tel. 883 136 or 882 173), the third oldest in Britain and the seat of the Duke of Norfolk, Earl Marshal of England, has been restored to near-perfect condition. The airy **baron's hall,** with its vaulted oak roof, contains handsome 16th-century furniture, and the art gallery unveils some fine Van Dycks and Gainsboroughs. Look for the four 18th-century French tapestries, which depict four continents (two are in the baron's hall, two on the grand staircase). The library houses some ancient family mementos, including ceremonial robes and mantles; a few personal possessions of Mary, Queen of Scots; and the graphically outlined death warrant served against one family member by good-natured Queen Elizabeth I. The grounds include an 11th-century keep, with a ripping view of the countryside, and the Catholic **Fitzalan Chapel,** which guards the ancient and exquisitely sculpted tombs of the Norfolk family. (Open June-Aug. Sun.-Fri. noon-5pm; Sept.-Oct. and April-May Sun.-Fri. 1-5pm; last admission 4pm; admission £3.55.) At the end of August, the castle hosts the **Arundel Festival,** a week of concerts, jousting, and plays.

Arundel's **Cathedral of Our Lady and St. Philip Howard** perches atop the town on London Rd.; its spire is visible behind the castle. The cathedral was designed by Joseph Hansom, the renowned inventor of the Hansom Cab. Upon serious reflection, you may conclude that the building is shaped rather like a car. The nave is high and long, the transept practically nonexistent; massive pillars obstruct most views of the rose window. (Open daily in summer 9am-6pm; winter 9am-dusk.)

The **Arundel Museum and Heritage Center,** 61 High St., chronicles over 2000 years of the town's history. (Open May-Sept. Mon.-Sat. 10:30am-12:30pm and 2-5pm, Sun. 2-5pm. Admission £1.)

The **Wildfowl and Wetlands Trust Centre** (tel. 883 355) embraces 55 acres of semi-natural habitat where you can watch over 12,000 birds from concealed observation enclosures. The reserve roosts about ¾ miles down Arundel's scenic Mill Rd. toward Swanbourne Lake. (Good facilities for the disabled. Open in summer daily 9:30am-6:30pm; winter 9:30am-5pm, last admission 1 hr. before closing. Admission £3, students £2, children £1.50.)

Petworth House, 10 miles from Arundel, is a treasure chest of works by J.M.W. Turner, covering the years 1802-1812 and 1827-1831. Run by the National Trust, this estate used to be the home of the third Earl of Egremont, a famous early 19th-century patron of arts and letters. Turner painted many of his best works in an old library that the earl let him use as a studio. The visitors' gallery, located on the ground floor, contains some 71 sculptures and 59 paintings (including two by William Blake). The grounds of the house, designed by Capability Brown, were once described as "something like a heavily timbered American forest." (House open April-Oct. Tues.-Thurs. and Sat.-Sun. 1-5pm. Extra rooms shown Tues.-Thurs. Grounds open 12:30-5pm. Deer park open year-round daily 9am-sunset. Disabled access to ground floor of house. Admission to house and grounds £3.30, deer park free.) Unfortunately, the closest you can get to Petworth by public transportation is Pulborough (a 10-min. train ride from Arundel); from there you can walk, hitch, or take a taxi the two miles to the house. Ask for directions at the Arundel tourist office.

A short train ride from Arundel in Amberley, the **Amberley Chalk-Pits Museum** (tel. (0798) 831 370) slaves away as the "industrial history center" of the south, six miles north of town on the A29. In a series of open-air displays, the museum energetically traces the development of typical industries of the southeast. (Open April-Oct. Wed.-Sun. and bank holidays 10am-6pm; late July to mid-Sept. daily 10am-6pm. Admission £3.70.) The museum can also be reached by river; boats leave Arundel for Amberley at 2pm (£4 return; children £3 return. Call 883 920 for details).

Portsmouth

> Don't talk to me about the naval tradition. It's nothing but rum, sodomy, and the lash.
> —*Winston Churchill*

Base of the D-Day armada, Portsmouth is the overlord of British maritime history. Henry VIII's **Mary Rose,** which sank in 1545 and was raised 437 years later (in 1982), crowns an incomparable array of naval heritage. Nowhere else would Nelson's triumphant flagship, **HMS Victory,** have to fight to gain top billing.

Orientation and Practical Information

Portsmouth (pop. 180,000) lies on the south coast 75 miles southwest of London. Trains from London Waterloo stop at both Portsmouth and Southsea station (the "town station") and Portsmouth harbor station (2 per hr., 1½ hr., £13.20 day return). National Express coaches (from London every 1½ hr., 2½ hr., £8.50 single or day return) stop at the Hard Interchange next to the harbor station. Two tourist offices are open year-round on the Hard and in town on Commercial Rd.; two more open during the high season.

Tourist Information Centres: The Hard (tel. 826 722), right next to entrance to historic ships; 102 Commercial Rd. (tel. 838 382), next to the town station. Open daily 9:30am-5:30pm. Seasonal offices at the Continental Ferry Port (tel. 838 635) and at the Pyramids Resort Centre, Clarence Esplanade, Southsea (tel. 832 464). Open July-Sept. daily 9:30am-5:30pm. A sea of free maps and leaflets. Free accommmoration list. Accommodation booking service (deposit of 10% of first night's cost, deducted from final payment). Currency exchange available sometimes (£2.50 min. commission).

Student Travel Office: Student and Youth Travel Centre, Portsmouth Polytechnic Union, Alexandra House, Museum Rd. (tel. 816 645). Open Mon.-Wed. and Fri. 10am-4pm, Thurs. 12:15-5:15pm.

Currency Exchange: Major banks cluster in Commercial Rd. shopping precinct just north of Portsmouth and Southsea station, including **Midland** (open Mon.-Fri. 9:30am-5pm, Sat. 9:30am-3:30pm) and **Barclay's** (open Mon.-Fri. 9:30am-5pm, Sat. 9:30am-noon). Currency exchange also available at tourist office (see above).

Post Office: Slindon St. (tel. 833 201), near the town station. Open Mon.-Thurs. 9am-5:30pm, Fri. 9:30am-5:30pm, Sat. 9am-12:30pm. **Postal Code:** PO1 1AA.

Telephone Code: (0705).

Train Stations: Portsmouth and Southsea station, Commercial Rd. Travel center open Mon.-Sat. 8am-8pm. **Portsmouth Harbor station,** The Hard, ¾ mi. away at the end of the line. To Cosham, for the hostel, every 20 min., £1.20, £1.40 day return. Trips between town and harbor cost 80p, day return £1. Call 825 771 for information.

Buses: The Hard Interchange, The Hard, next to the Harbor station. Local routes (enquiries tel. 738 570 or 815 452) and National Express services (tel. (0329) 230 023). National Express tickets sold at Sealink office (open July-Aug. daily 8am-5pm; Oct.-June Mon.-Sat. 8am-5pm).

Ferries: Isle of Wight passenger ferry leaves from Harbor station (every hr., every 30 min. in summer; 15 min.; £3.90, £5.40 day return; tel. 827 744). For continental services call 647 047.

Taxis: Streamline Taxis (tel. 811 111).

Hospital: Queen Alexandra Hospital, Southwick Hill Rd. (tel. 379 451).

Police: Tel. 321 111.

Emergency: Dial 999; no coins required.

Accommodations

Moderately priced B&Bs clutter Southsea, Portsmouth's contiguous resort town 1½ miles east along the coast from the Hard. Take Southdown Portsmouth bus #6, 43, or 44 to South Parade. Cheaper lodgings lie two or three blocks inland—Whitwell, Granada, St. Roman's, and Malvern Rd. all have a fair sprinkling.

IYHF Youth Hostel, Wymering Manor, Old Wymering Lane, Medina Rd., Cosham (tel. 375 661). The old home of Catherine Parr now houses those somewhat less likely to be the sixth spouse of a fat English monarch. Take bus #1, 12, or 22 from the Hard to Cosham post office and walk left on Medina Rd., or train to Cosham then right out of the station to the post office. Open July-Aug. daily; April-June and Sept. Mon.-Sat.; mid-Feb. to March and Oct.-Dec. Tues.-Sat. £5.90, ages 16-20 £4.70; July-Aug. £6.30, ages 16-20 £5.10.

Portsmouth Polytechnic Halls of Residence, Bellevue Terrace (tel. 843 178), overlooking Southsea common, 15 min. from the Hard. Single and twin rooms available July 10-Sept. 27. **Burwell House** has small modern rooms with puritanically narrow beds; older **Rees Hall** shows more signs of age and character. £12 per person.

Testudo House, 19 Whitwell Rd., Southsea (tel. 824 324). Comfortable rooms in quiet surroundings. Mrs. Parkes, the landlady, proudly displays her collection of American table mats. Singles £13. Doubles £26. Triples £31.

YMCA, Penny St. (tel. 864 341), 10 min. from the Hard. Basic worn rooms; those on higher floors look out over the sea wall to the Solent. Singles £10.25. Twins £18.50.

Camping: **Southsea Caravan Park,** Melville Rd., Southsea (tel. 735 070). At the eastern end of the seafront, 3 mi. from The Hard. Tent with 2 adults £9 in high season, £6 shoulder, £5-8 low season. Call in advance.

Food

Decent restaurants with a dash of style bunch along Osborne, Palmerston, and Clarendon Rd. in the Southsea shopping district (buses #6, 43, and 44 all stop at Palmerston Rd.). Standard fast-food joints abound around Commercial Rd. near the town station. The town is awash in pubs; try **The Gorge** at 85 Queen St. for a hearty fillet of plaice (£3).

Brown's, 9 Clarendon Rd. Solid English food in relaxed low-key surroundings. Steak, kidney, and Guinness pie £4, desserts 95p. Open daily 9:30am-9:30pm.

HMS Victory Buffet, in the Historic Dockyard. The only food to be had while boarding the boats. Clean and tidy with a nautical flair. No mealy pudding or salt beef here. Light meals and snacks 40p-£2.

Sights

Portsmouth overflows with engrossing ships, relics, and museums. Head first to the spectacular **Naval Heritage Centre,** in the Naval Base (entrance right next to the Hard tourist office; follow brown signs to Historic Ships.) The **Mary Rose** grabbed Britain's attention when she was raised from the Solent in 1982. Henry VIII's best-loved ship set sail from Portsmouth in July 1545 amidst much ballyhoo to engage the French fleet. In one of the greatest anti-climaxes in history, the overloaded vessel keeled over and sank in front of him. Centuries later, divers and underwater engineers raised up the starboard side. On display in a special **ship hall,** sprayed by chilled water to prevent crumbling, the hulk is an eerie, compelling sight.

An enthralling collection of Tudor artifacts, salvaged along with the wreck but displayed in a separate exhibition hall, give an unsurpassable picture of 16th-century life. The backgammon board and dice belie their age, although the horrific syringe used for urethral injections makes a clear statement about medical knowledge 400 years ago. An Elizabethan manicure set includes a natty little ear-wax remover. Ornate bronze and iron guns, including two fine Bastard Culverins, guard the exhibits. (Open March-Oct. daily 10:30am-5:30pm; Nov.-Feb. daily 10:30am-5pm. Last admission 1 hr. before closing—a general rule in Portsmouth. Admission £3.60, students and children £2.30. Ship hall is behind HMS Victory, 300 yd. from exhibition hall.)

Two 100-foot masts lead the way to Admiral Horatio Nelson's flagship **HMS Victory,** the oldest surviving Ship of the Line in the world. While winning the decisive Battle of Trafalgar against the French and Spanish in 1805, Nelson was shot in the fighting and died beneath deck—a small plaque marks the spot where he fell. Active sailors and marines conduct tours. The ship, 30% genuine Trafalgar vintage, conveys a vivid impression of the dismal cramped conditions for press ganged recruits—just eight toilets for 850 men. Some rich and strange equipment has been restored: versatile hammocks, variously used as sandbags, life jackets, or coffins; dummy wooden guns ("Quakers"), to fool the enemy; and bendy gun rammers for use in a tight spot. (Open March-Oct. daily 10:30am-5:30pm; Nov.-Feb. daily 10:30am-5pm. Admission £3.60, children and students £2.20. Tickets include entrance to Royal Naval Museum.)

HMS Warrior, somewhat eclipsed by its famous neighbors, nevertheless provides an intriguing companion to the Victory. The pride and joy of Queen Victoria's navy and the first iron-clad battleship in the world, Warrior has never seen battle. The restored innards (it took eight years to transform the ship from makeshift oil tank to pristine battleship) detail Victorian naval technology. (Open March-Oct. Mon.-Sat. 10:30am-5:30pm; Nov.-Feb. 10:30am-5pm. Admission £3.50, students and children £2.) The five galleries of the **Royal Naval Museum** fill in the gaps (historically) between the three ships; the collection of grotesque figureheads in the first gallery is the stuff of nightmares. (Open daily 10:30am-5pm. Admission £1.50, students and children £1.10. Admission to Victory includes free entry to museum.)

In the **D-Day Museum,** along Clarence Esplanade, the Overlord Embroidery, a latter-day Bayeux Tapestry, recounts the invasion of France. (Open daily 10:30am-5:30pm. Admission £3.10, children and students £1.90; low season £2.30, children and students £1.40.) Next door, the **Sea Life Centre** displays aquatic exhibits with a finful of verve. Look down, up, or across at tiddly sharks and sinister sting-rays. (Open daily 10am; tel. 734 461 for closing times. Admission £3.50, students £3.)

The **Royal Marines Museum,** in Eastney barracks, relentlessly traces the glory of the Navy's soldiers. The regimented ranks of the medal collection might overwhelm even the enthusiast. Archaic syringe fanatics will be satisfied with one particularly gruesome item. (Open Easter-Sept. daily 10am-5:30pm; Oct.-Easter 10am-4:30pm. Admission £2, students and children £1.) The **Eastney Industrial Museum,** three miles east from the Hard, on Bransburg Rd., steams up its two James Watt beam engines each weekend during summer and displays sundry polished metal. (Open April-Sept. daily 1:30-5:30pm, in steam on weekends; Oct.-March first Sun. in month 1:30-5:30pm in steam. Admission £1, students and children 60p (in steam); 60p, students and children 35p (non-steam).)

Charles Dickens was born in 1812 at 395 Old Commercial Rd., ¾ mile north of the town station. The house has been done up in the Regency style. Morbidly enough, the only authentic Dickens artifact is the couch on which he died. (Open March-Oct. daily 10:30am-5:30pm. Admission 80p, students and children 50p.)

Salisbury

Unlike many other English medieval cities, Salisbury did not grow haphazardly into a jumble of streets. Rather, the "City of New Sarum" was built according to a rectangular grid pattern (five streets running north to south and six running east to west) devised by Bishop Poore in the early 13th century. The heart of the city, despite its 20th-century commercial chaos, retains its 13th-century logic. Not far from the din and tumult of the city center, Salisbury Cathedral remains quiet and secluded, walled off from the clamor by the buildings around the close and wreathed in an expanse of green meadow.

Orientation and Practical Information

Salisbury (pop. 38,000) lies 80 miles southwest of London. Trains leave at 15 minutes past each hour from London's Waterloo Station (£15.10 cheap day return). National Express coaches run from Victoria (every 3 hr. 9am-6pm, 2½ hr., £11.25 day return). Wilts and Dorset service X4 runs from Bath, 40 mi. northwest of Salisbury (6 per day, 2 hr., £2.65). You'll find the Salisbury bus and coach station in the center of town; the train station is a 10-min. walk. To reach the tourist office from the train station, turn left out of the station onto South Western Rd., bear right onto Fisherton St. (which becomes Bridge St.), pass over the bridge, and cross High St. Walk straight ahead onto Silver St., which becomes Butcher Row and then Fish Row.

Tourist Information Centre: Fish Row (tel. 334 956), in the Guildhall in Market Sq. Extremely helpful. Accommodation service (10% deposit), book-a-bed-ahead service £2.10. List posted. Guided tours mid-April to mid-Oct. Mon.-Sat. at 11am; also June to mid-Sept. at 2:30pm and 8:30pm (£1). Currency exchange, commission £3. Open July-Aug. Mon.-Sat. 9am-7pm, Sun. 11am-5pm; June and Sept. Mon.-Sat. 9am-6pm, Sun. 11am-4pm; Oct.-May Mon.-Sat. 9am-5pm.

Currency Exchange: Barclay's, on the corner of High and Bridge St. Open Mon.-Fri. 9:30am-4:30pm, Sat. 9:30am-noon. **Thomas Cook,** 5 Queen St. Open Mon.-Tues. and Thurs.-Sat. 9am-5:30pm, Wed. 9:30am-5:30pm. **Lloyd's,** on Minster St. across from Market Sq. Open Mon.-Fri. 9:30am-5pm, Sat. 9:30am-1pm. **National Westminster,** on Blue Boar Rd. Open Mon.-Fri. 9:30am-4:30pm, Sat. 9:30am-1pm.

Post Office: 24 Castle St. (tel. 41 30 51), at Chipper Lane. Open Mon.-Tues. and Thurs.-Fri. 9am-5:30pm, Wed. 9:30am-5:30pm, Sat. 9am-1pm. **Postal Code:** SP1 1AB.

Telephone Code: (0722).

Train Station: South Western Rd. (tel. 275 91), west of town across the river. To Portsmouth (every hr., 1½ hr., £8.50). Information and ticket office open Mon.-Sat. 5:45am-9pm, Sun. 8am-8:45pm.

Bus and Coach Station: 8 Endless St. (tel. 336 855). It's not an end, it's a beginning. Booking office open Mon.-Fri. 8:15am-5:45pm, Sat. 8:15am-5:15pm. Explorer ticket £3.50, child £1.75; good on Wilts and Dorset, Hampshire bus, Provincial or Solent Blue. To Stonehenge (Mon.-Fri. 5 per day, Sat.-Sun. 4 per day, ½ hr., £3.05 return).

Taxis: Tel. 334 343. Taxi stands at train station (for Stonehenge) and New Canal (near the cinema).

Bike Rental: Hayball and Co., Rollestone St. (tel. 411 378). £5 per day, £25 per week; £25 deposit. Cash only. Open Mon.-Sat. 9am-5:30pm.

Public Library: Salisbury Library, Market Pl. (tel. 324 245). Open Mon., Wed., and Fri. 10am-7pm; Tue. 9:30am-7pm; Thurs. 10am-5pm; Sat. 9:30am-5pm.

Laundromat: Washing Well, 28 Chipper Lane. Drop-off Mon.-Fri. 8:30am-6pm. Wash, dry, and fold £3.30 per load. Open daily 8am-9pm.

Crisis: Samaritans, 42 Milford St. (tel. 233 55). 24 hrs.

Market Days: Tues. and Sat., in Market Sq. (roughly 6am-3pm).

Early Closing Day: Wed. at 1pm (small shops only).

Hospital: Salisbury General Infirmary, Fisherton St. (tel. 336 212), just over the bridge.

Police: Wilton Rd. (tel. 411 444).

Emergency: Dial 999; no coins required.

Accommodations and Camping

IHYF Youth Hostel, Milford Hill House, Milford Hill (tel. 327 572). From the tourist office, turn left on Fish Row, right on Queen St., left on Milford St., and walk ahead a few blocks under the overpass. A beautiful old house amid 2 acres of garden. Lockout 10am-1pm. Curfew 11:30pm. £6.60, ages 16-20 £5.40. Camping £3.30. Breakfast £2.30.

Ron and Jenny Coats, 51 Salt Lane (tel. 327 443), just up from the bus station. A welcoming and clean 400-year-old house. Hostel-type lodgings in mellow 3- and 6-bed rooms. Centrally located. £6.50, £8.30 with breakfast, 80p sleepsack rental, 10p for 2-min. shower.

Mrs. Spiller, Nuholme, Ashfield Rd. (tel. 33 65 92), 10 min. from the train station. Bear right out of station; cross the car park straight ahead; turn right onto Churchfields Rd. then turn right again onto Ashfield. Very friendly place run by an elderly woman who can recite Shakespeare over a cuppa. £11, students £10.

Camping: Hudson's Field of the **Camping Club of Great Britain,** Hudson's Field, Castle Rd. (tel. 320 713). On the way to Old Sarum. 100 pitches. Curfew 11pm. £3.70 per person. Open April-Oct.

Food and Pubs

From 6am to 3pm on Tuesdays and Saturdays the town center throbs with vendors hawking clothes, fresh local produce, and homemade jams. Satisfy your sweet tooth with tea and homemade chocolates at **Michael Snell's,** 5 St. Thomas Sq., near Bridge St. (open Mon.-Sat. 9am-5:30pm). Grocery stores include Tesco on Castle St. and Safeway in the Malting Shopping Centre.

Mo's, 62 Milford St., on the way to the youth hostel. Favored by locals for its tasty food at low prices. Carnivores can devour burgers (£4.05) or ribs (£5.40) while vegans can ruminate over lentil creations (£4.05) or veggie burgers (£4.05). Mo's milkshake is magnificent (£1.75). Open daily 11:30am-11pm.

The Golden Curry, 7 Minster St. Bargain 3-course lunch £4. Dinner a tad more pricey with £5 minimum. Open daily noon-2:30pm and 5:30pm-midnight.

Don Giovanni's, 44 St. Catherine St. Wide range of pasta dishes (£3.50-5.50). Open Mon.-Sat. 11:30am-2pm, 6-9:30pm.

The Old House Restaurant, 47 New St. A range of English favorites: bar lunches £3-5; cream teas £2; roast beef with Yorkshire pudding £4.50. Open Sun.-Mon. 11am-3pm, Tues.-Fri. 10am-5:30pm, and Sat. 10am-8pm.

With sixty-seven pubs in the city, you're sure to find one that suits you. The venerable **New Inn,** New St., was one of the first non-smoking pubs in Britain. Try also **Burke's Bar and Buttery,** New St., or **The Oddfellows Arms,** Milford St. Live music has been known to descend upon the **Cathedral Hotel,** Milford St. The **Haunch of Venison,** Minster St., a 600-year-old beauty, serves real ale, mostly to tourists. The pub displays a replica of a hand that was severed from the arm of a dishonest poker player and mummified for posterity. Salisbury's younger crowd hunts their game at **The Pheasant,** on Salt Lane.

Sights

Rising monolithically from its grassy close, **Salisbury Cathedral** ascends to the neck-breaking height of 404 feet. The bases of the marble pillars near the entrance to the choir are buckling under the strain of 6400 tons of limestone; if a pillar rings when you knock on it, you should probably move away. The flying buttresses supporting the tower both inside and out were added to ease the problem, and the inverted arches above the choir keep the walls from caving in. Despite these measures, nearly 700 years of use and weathering have left the cathedral in need of structural and aesthetic repair. (Sir Christopher Wren calculated that the spire leaned 29½ inches.) The spire, the tower, and the west front of the cathedral are shrouded in scaffolding. During guided tours in the summer and on Tuesdays you can ride up to the roof and the base of the spire on the outdoor contruction workers' elevator. Tour and hard hats are free. (Tours June-Aug. Mon.-Sat. at 11am, noon, 2pm, 3pm; March-May and Sept.-Oct. Mon.-Sat. at 11am, 2:30pm). The oldest working clock in Britain, dating from 1386, stands by the North Door. Several tombs of crusaders line the sides of the nave. The most colorful is that of William Longespée, bastard son of Henry II, who was instrumental in writing the *Magna Carta.* Longespée brought what is now one of four surviving copies of the famous document to Salisbury (two are stored in the British Museum, the fourth in Lincoln); today it rests in the cathedral's **Chapter House.** (Open Mon.-Sat. 9:30am-4:45pm, Sun. 1-4:45pm; Nov.-Feb. Mon.-Sat. noon-3:15pm, Sun. 1-3:15pm. Donation 50p.) The **cloisters** adjoining the cathedral somehow grew to be the largest in England, although the cathedral never housed any monks. Bump, nudge, and rub brass here (Mon.-Sat. 10am-5pm, Sun. 2-5pm). (Cathedral open Aug.-June daily 8am-6:30pm; July 8am-8:15pm. Donation £1, virtually mandatory; students 50p. Evensong Mon.-Sat. at 5:30pm.)

The open lawns of the **cathedral close** flank some beautifully preserved old homes, including **Malmesbury House,** where Handel once lived, and reputedly now haunts. (Open for guided tours April-Sept. Tues.-Thurs. every ½ hr. 10am-5pm. Admission £2, children £1.) **Mompesson House,** another sumptuous residence, has fine plaster-work, a Queen Anne interior, and an inspiring collection of 18th-century drinking glasses. (Open April-Oct. Sat.-Wed. 12:30-5:30pm. Admission £2.30.)

The **Salisbury and South Wiltshire Museum** is housed in the King's House, 65 The Close. Tantalizing exhibits trace the development of Salisbury, show aerial photographs of ancient cities and burial mounds, and present the latest crackpot theories on Stonehenge. (Open April-Sept. Mon.-Sat. 10am-5pm, Sun. 2-5pm; Oct.-March Mon.-Sat. 10am-4pm. Admission £1.80, students £1.20.)

Entertainment

Salisbury's repertory theatre company presents a variety of high-quality productions at the **Playhouse,** Malthouse Lane (tel. 320 333), over the bridge off Fisherton St. Tickets start at £5; student seats at £4.10 are available in advance for first nights, matinees, and Monday shows. (Rush seats at the same price available 5 min. before curtain.) The **Salisbury Festival** features dance exhibitions, music, and a separate wine tasting festival at the Salisbury library during the first two weeks of September. (Tickets from £2.50. Write to the Festival Box Office, Salisbury Playhouse, Malthouse Lane, Salisbury SP1 7RA; tel. (0722) 325 173.) The **Salisbury Arts Centre,** in St. Edmund's Church, Bedwin St. (tel. 321 744), promotes a wide range of events, including punk musicals, jazz bands, and Shakespearean tragedies. (Box office open Mon.-Sat. 10am-6pm, and evenings of most performances. Tickets from £2.50.)

Near Salisbury

The germ of Salisbury, **Old Sarum,** lies 1½ miles north of the town. Here, an Iron Age hill fort evolved into a Saxon town and then into a Norman fortress. In the 13th century, friction with Richard I goaded church officials into moving the settlement and building a new cathedral. Gradually, New Sarum replaced the old town as the prominent trading and religious center.

Deserted today, **Old Sarum** was the most notorious of the "rotten boroughs" eliminated by the Reform Act of 1832. Until then, it had continued to send two members to Parliament although no one had lived there for centuries; the MPs were chosen by the owner of the land. Today Old Sarum is a lonely windswept mound that is home to the bishop's palace, a castle, a Norman castle moat, the foundations of the original cathedral, and the ruins of the original fort. (Open April-Sept. daily 10am-6pm; Oct.-March Tues.-Sun. 10am-4pm. Admission 95p, students 75p.) Old Sarum is off the A345, on the way to Stonehenge. Buses #5-9 run every 15 minutes from the Salisbury bus station.

Declared by James I to be "the finest house in the land," **Wilton House,** three miles west of Salisbury on the A30, exhibits paintings by Van Dyck, Rembrandt, Rubens, and others, and has an impressive, almost outrageous interior design. The Double Cube Room is one of eight extraordinary 17th-century state rooms. (Open April to mid-Oct. Tues.-Sat. 11am-6pm, Sun. 12:30-6pm. Admission £4.20, students £3.50, grounds only £1.60.) Catch the bus outside Marks and Spencer (Mon.-Sat. every 10 min., Sun. every hr.).

Stonehenge

> You may put a hundred questions to these rough-hewn giants as they bend in grim contemplation of their fellow companions; but your curiosity falls dead in the vast sunny stillness that shrouds them and the strange monument, with all its unspoken memories, becomes simply a heart-stirring picture in a land of pictures.
>
> —Henry James

Stonehenge is a potent reminder that England seemed ancient even to the Saxons and Normans. Surrounded by imperturbable cows and swirled by winds exceeding 50mph, the much-touted stones, only 22 feet high, may initially be disappointing. Consider, however, that they were lifted by a simple but infinitely tedious process of rope-and-log leverage. Built over many lifetimes, Stonehenge represents an enduring religious and aesthetic dedication that defies modern explanation. Buffeted by nonsensical theories and ludicrous fantasies, Stonehenge has yielded none of its ageless mystery.

The most famous Stonehenge legend holds that the circle was built by Merlin, who magically transported the stones from Ireland. (Actually, the seven-ton Blue Stones are made of rock quarried in Wales.) Other stories attribute the monument to giants, Romans, Danes, Phoenicians, Druids, Mycenaean Greeks, and—most recently—to aliens. In any case, whether they traveled by land or water, the Bronze Age builders would seem to have possessed more technology than anthropologists can explain. Archeologists now date construction from approximately 2800 to 1500 BC, dividing the complex into three successive monuments. The relics of the oldest are the Aubrey Holes (white patches in the earth) and the Heel Stone (the isolated, rough block standing outside the circle). This first Stonehenge may have been a worship and burial site for seven centuries. The next monument consisted of about 60 stones imported from Wales around 2100 BC to mark astronomical directions. The present shape was formed by 1500 BC; it may once have been composed of two concentric circles and two horseshoes of megaliths, enclosed by substantial earthworks.

Many different peoples have worshipped at Stonehenge: from late Neolithic and Early Bronze Age chieftains to contemporary mystics. In 300 BC the Druids arrived from the Continent and claimed Stonehenge as their shrine. The true Druids have died out, but the Druid Society of London (ordinary folks who like to wrap themselves up in sheets) still honor the sun's rising over the Heel Stone on Midsummer's Day. The summer of 1988 saw a bizarre confrontation between hippie-pagan celebrants and police amid spotlighting, a haze of tear gas, and barbed wire. The finest view of the monument can be captured from Amesbury Hill, 1½ miles up the A303. On some winter Tuesdays and Fridays, in clear weather, the ropes around the monument are taken down to allow a closer view. (Stonehenge open daily April-Sept. 10am-6pm; Oct.-Easter 10am-4pm. Admission £1.90, students £1.50.)

Getting to Stonehenge takes little effort. Several buses run daily from the center of Salisbury and from the train station (£3.05 return). The first bus leaves Salisbury at 8:45am, and the last one leaves Stonehenge at 4:15pm (40 min.). A taxi to Stonehenge from Salisbury station costs £26. Amesbury is a short hitch along the A345 from Salisbury. The most scenic walking or cycling route to Stonehenge follows the **Woodford Valley Route** through Woodford and Wilsford. Go north from Salisbury on Castle Rd., bear left just before Victoria Park onto Stratford Rd., and follow the road over the bridge through Lower, Middle, and Upper Woodford. After about nine miles, turn left onto the A303 for the last mile to Stonehenge.

Bath

A visit to Bath remains de rigueur, even though this elegant Georgian city is now more of a museum than a resort. Immortalized by Fielding, Austen, and Dickens, Bath was at one time the second social capital of England. Aristocrats came here in search of something calmer than the metropolis and livelier than the country. Heavily bombed during World War II, Bath has since been painstakingly restored. Aristocratic patronage has graced the city with glorious buildings, a long roster of famous residents, and many minor artistic treasures.

Legend ascribes the founding of Bath to King Lear's leper father Bladud, who wandered the countryside bemoaning his banishment from court. He took work as a swineherd, but his pigs soon caught the affliction. The devoted and decomposing swine led their king to a therapeutic spring; out of gratitude, Bladud founded a city on the site of the healing waters. Tragically, Bladud's attempt to heal his faithful herd resulted only in a large amount of cold pork stew.

The Romans built an elaborate complex of baths here early in their occupation of Britain. The success of the spa was sealed when Queen Anne paid a visit in 1701. From then on, a parade of distinguished visitors and residents—Pitt, Burke, Johnson, Defoe, Austen, and innumerable bathing-beauty high-society types—came here to indulge themselves in the healing powers of the spa. Unfortunately, the baths were far from therapeutic for one 11-year-old girl who visited them a few years ago and contracted a fatal case of cerebral meningitis. Although much mystery surrounds the exact source of the disease, the baths have been reopened to visitors for viewing, although not for bathing.

Orientation and Practical Information

Bath (pop. 83,000) is served by direct rail service from London's Paddington Station (every hr., 1½ hr., supersaver return £23) and National Express coaches from Victoria coach station (every 2 hr., 3 hr., £16.50 return). Bristol is a 15-minute train ride (£3.50 return) or 50-minute coach ride from Bath aboard the Badgerline bus (£1.95 return). Bath is 107 miles west of London and 12 miles east of Bristol.

The Pulteney Bridge and North Parade Bridge span the **River Avon,** which runs through the city from the east. The Roman Baths, the Abbey, and the Pump Room are all in the city center. The Royal Crescent and the Circus lie to the northwest. The train and coach stations are near the south end of Manvers St., at the bend in the river. From either terminal, walk up Manvers St. to the Orange Grove roundabout and turn left to the tourist office in the Abbey Churchyard.

Tourist Information Centre: The Colonnades, (tel. 462 831 for information and accommodations). Exceptionally efficient staff, although the office gets crowded in summer. Reams of useful information. Accommodations service with 10% deposit, list free. Book-a-bed-ahead £2. Map and mini-guide 25p. Pick up a free copy of Bath Events. Open Mon.-Sat. 9:30am-7pm, Sun. 10am-6pm.

Tours: Several available. Excellent free 1¾-hr. guided walking tours leave from the Abbey Churchyard Mon.-Fri. at 10:30am and Sun. at 10:30am and 2:30pm; extra tours May-Sept. Tues. and Fri.-Sat. at 7pm and Wed. at 2:30pm; Oct. Wed. at 2:30pm. Bus tours of city (every ½ hr., 1 hr., 10am-5:30pm) cost £3, students £2.50.

Currency Exchange: Barclay's on Stall St. (tel. 462 521), behind the Abbey Churchyard, will exchange Visa checks for free. Open Mon.-Fri. 9:30am-4:30pm, Sat. 9:30am-noon. **Thomas Cook,** 20 New Bond St. (tel. 463 191), charges £2; open Mon.-Wed. and Fri. 9am-5:30pm, Thurs. 9:30am-5:30pm, Sat. 9am-5pm. **Lloyd's** on Milsom St. will exchange American Express checks for free. Open Mon.-Fri. 9:30am-4:30pm.

American Express: Bridge St. (tel. 444 767), just before Pulteney Bridge. Open Mon.-Wed. and Fri. 9am-5pm, Thurs. 9:30am-5pm, Sat. 9am-2pm, Sun. 10am-2pm.

Post Office: New Bond St. (tel. 825 211), at Broad St. Open Mon.-Fri. 9:30am-5:30pm, Sat. 9am-1pm. **Postal Code: BA1 1AA.**

Telephone Code: (0225).

Train Station: At the south end of Manvers St. (tel. 463 075). To: London (every hr., 1½ hr.,£23); Exeter (22 per day, 1¾ hr., £16); and Bristol (60 per day, 15 min., £3.50). Booking office open daily 6am-9:30pm.

Bus and Coach Station: Manvers St. (tel. 464 446). National Express to London (every hr., 3 hr., £16.50); to Oxford (6 per day, 2 hr., £11.50); to Salisbury (4 per day, 1½ hr., £4.15). **Badgerline Explorer** ticket (£3.90) gives unlimited travel for one day. Badgerline to Bristol (every ½ hr., 50 min., £1.95).

Taxis: Ranks near stations. Abbey Radio (tel. 465 843), Rainbow (tel. 460 606).

Bike Rental: Avon Valley Bike Hire, Railway Pl. (tel. 461 880), behind train station. £5-11 for 4 hr., £8-17 for 8 hr.; £15-50 deposit. Open daily 9am-6pm.

Boating: Bath Boating Company, Forester Rd. (tel. 466 407), about ½ mi. north of town. Punts £2.50 per person per hr., rowboats £3 per person per hr. £30 deposit required. One-hr. guided river tours from Pulteney Bridge £2.50, children £1.50.

Bookstore: George Gregory, 23 Mawes St. (tel. 466 000) in the basement. Established in 1845. Open Mon.-Fri. 9am-1pm and 2-5pm, Sat. 9:30am-1pm.

Public Library: Bath Central Library, 10 the Podium (tel. 428 144). Open Mon. 10am-6pm, Tues.-Fri. 9:30am-8pm, Sat. 9:30am-5pm.

Laundromat: Self Serve Laundry, George St. Open daily 8:30am-7:45pm. Wash £2, 10-min. dry 20p.

Pharmacy: Boots, Southgate St. Open Mon.-Wed. and Fri.-Sat. 9am-5:30pm, Thurs. 9am-8pm.

Crisis: Samaritans, tel. 429 222. Phone answered 24 hrs.

Gay and Lesbian Information: Gay West, tel. (0272) 425 927.

Police: Manvers St. (tel. 444 343), just up from the train and bus stations.

Emergency: Dial 999; no coins required.

Accommodations and Camping

Bath has traditionally catered to the well-heeled. Don't try to find a bargain basement room (some are quite frightening). Instead, dig deep, expect to pay £12-17, and enjoy Bath's gracious style. B&Bs cluster on **Pultney Road** and **Pultney Gardens.** From the stations, walk up Manvers St., which becomes Pierrepont St., right on to N. Parade Rd. and past the cricket ground to Pulteney Rd. For a more relaxed setting continue past Pultney Gdns. (or take the footpath from behind the rail station) to **Widcombe Hill**—a steep climb, with prices to match (from £14).

IYHF Youth Hostel, Bathwick Hill (tel. 656 74). From N. Parade Rd., turn left onto Pulteney Rd., then right onto Bathwick. A footpath takes the hardy up this steep hill to the hostel (20-min. walk). Badgerline "University" bus #18 (5 per hr. until 11pm, 75p return) runs from the bus station or the Orange Grove roundabout. The hostel crowd seems out of place in this gracious Italianate mansion overlooking the city. 112 beds, shower, TV, laundry. Curfew 11pm. Reception open 7:30-10am and 1-10:30pm. July-Aug. £7, ages 16-20 £5.90; Sept.-June £6.60, ages 16-20 £5.40.

YMCA International House, Broad St. Place (tel. 460 471). Walk under the arch and up the steps from Walcot St. across from Beaufort Hotel. Men and women allowed. More centrally located than IYHF hostel (3 min. from tourist office), with free hot baths or pulsating showers and no curfew. Heavily booked in summer. Singles £12. Doubles £21.50. Dorm rooms £9 per person. £5 key deposit. Continental breakfast included; hot breakfast 50p extra.

The Shearns, Prior House, 3 Marlborough Lane (tel. 313 587). Great location on west side of town beside Royal Victoria Park. Take bus #14 or 15 from bus station (every 15 min.). Far and away the best value in Bath. Warm, wonderful proprietors treat guests well. No singles. £12 per person. English breakfast included.

Mrs. Guy, 14 Raby Pl. (tel. 465 120). From N. Parade, turn left onto Pulteney Rd., then right. Comfortable rooms in an elegant Georgian house with light, cool interiors and superior views of the city. Fresh seasonal fruits and yogurts complement a generous English breakfast. No smoking indoors. Singles £14. Doubles £28.

Mrs. Rowe, 7 Widcombe Crescent (tel. 422 726). In the southeastern area, up the hill from the stations. The height of elegance—they don't make 'em like this anymore—and a view to match. Management quite particular, and atmosphere decidedly staid. Blissfully quiet neighborhood. Full bath and TV. Singles £14-16. Doubles £24-34.

Avon Guest House, 1 Pulteney Gdns. (tel. 313 009), at Pulteney Rd. Large rooms, each with full bath, color TV, and tea-making facilities. Friendly owners. £16 per person. Fine English breakfast included.

Pulteney Guest House, 14 Pulteney Rd. (tel. 460 991). Well-appointed rooms with a myriad of electrical conveniences. Singles £15-18, doubles £32-40.

Camping: Newton Mill Touring Centre, Newton St. Loe (tel. 333 909), 3 mi. west of city center off the A36/A39. Take bus #5 from bus station (5 per hr., 75p return) to Newton Rd. 105 sites. Laundry; free warm showers. £6.70 per pitch. £3 per person.

Food and Pubs

For budget-priced fruits and vegetables, visit the **Guildhall Market,** between High St. and Grand Parade. (Open Mon.-Sat. 9:30am-5:30pm.) **Harvest Wholefoods,** 27 Walcot St., stocks a tremendous selection of organic produce, including some exotic items. (Open Tues.-Sat. 9:30am-5:30pm, Mon. 11:30am-5:30pm.) **Seasons,** 10 George St. (tel. 697 30), has a small deli and also offers a good selection of natural foods. (Open Mon.-Sat. 9am-5:30pm.) Grab picnic fare at **Waitrose** in the Podium on High St. across from the Post Office.

Pub meals are a particularly good alternative on Sunday nights. For take-away, try **The Kitchen** (a.k.a. **Bake and Take**), on Upper Borough Walls near Barton St.—cheap, reliable, and open late (daily until 11pm). Splash out for an elegant cream tea (£4.25) in the **Pump Room**, Abbey Churchyard, a palatial Victorian restaurant (open Mon.-Sat. 10am-noon and 2:45-5pm).

Scoff's, corner of Monmouth and Westgate St. Memorable, freshly baked wholefood pastries and filling lunches served in a warm, woody dining room with high ceilings and a fine view of shady Kingsmead Sq. Take-away too. Big *tandoori* burger and salad £2.50. Open Mon.-Sat. 9am-5pm.

The Walrus and The Carpenter, 25 Barton St., uphill from the Theatre Royal. No cabbages or kings, just your basic bistro: carefully casual, cramped but intimate, candle-stuffed wine bottles, checked tablecloths, drowsy waiters . . . you know the rest. Good burgers with creative toppings £5-7. Smattering of vegetarian entrees £5-8. Open Mon.-Sat. noon-2pm and 6-11pm, Sun. 6-11pm.

Pasta Galore, 31 Barton St., just over from the Walrus and Carpenter. A big (albeit very good) franchise successfully masquerading as a cozy little Italian café with a walled garden off the back. Wide selection of homemade pastas and rich desserts. *Canneloni* with a choice of 3 sauces £5.40. Open Mon.-Thurs. noon-2:30pm, Fri.-Sat. 6-11pm.

Huckleberry's, 34 Broad St., down the street from the Y. Bath's only vegetarian restaurant, and it's good. Walls as green as the politics. Full meals from £3.50. Open Mon.-Thurs. 9am-4:30pm, Fri. 9am-9pm, Sat. 9am-5:30pm.

The Crystal Palace, 11 Abbey Green, behind Marks and Spencer. A sprawling, 18th-century pub-*cum*-restaurant with an outdoor patio. Ploughman's lunch 12 different ways (£3-4.50). Open Mon.-Thurs. 10:30am-2:30pm and 6-10:30pm, Fri.-Sat. 10:30am-2:30pm and 6-11pm, Sun. noon-2pm and 7-10:30pm.

Salamander Restaurant and Free House, 3 John St. Good pub grub at good pub prices. Paul Weller never wrote a song about this place. Open Mon.-Sat. noon-3pm and 6-11pm, Sun. noon-11pm.

Fagin's Restaurant, Queen St. A range of dishes with a twist. Mr. Bumble's bolognese £4, Dickens or Beadle burger £4, Toff's Chicken Curry £5.

Maxson's Diner, Argyle St. at Laura Pl. Beef burgers in a bebop joint (£4.50-5). Vegans should try the spinach and lentil lasagna (£5.40). Open daily noon-11pm.

Among Bath's many pubs, **The Grapes**, Westgate St., attracts an energetic student throng. The **Regency Bar**, Sawclose, complete with video screen, also draws a crowd. The Green Room at **The Garricks Head**, beside the Theatre Royal, is a calm, pleasant gay pub. The **Saracen's Head**, on Broad St., Bath's oldest dating from 1713, inspired Dickens to pen the *Pickwick Papers*.

Sights

As the Roman spa city of Aquae Sulis, Bath flourished for nearly 400 years, and the **Roman Baths** retain their prominence in the town center. Sewer-diggers first uncovered the site inadvertently in 1880, and recent intentional excavation has yielded a splendid model of advanced Roman engineering. Make your way through a maze of tunnels interrupted by dripping and fenced-off segments of the bath. Also on display within the corridors lurk a gilded bronze head of Minerva, a heap of Roman pennies tossed into the baths for good luck, and *ligulae,* bronze ear wax removers. (Open March-June and Sept.-Oct. daily 9am-6pm; July 9am-7pm; Aug. 9am-7pm and 8:30-10:30pm; Nov.-Feb. Mon.-Sat. 9am-5pm, Sun. 10am-5pm. Admission £3.60, ages 5-16 £1.70, under 5 free.) Excellent guided tours of the baths leave twice per hour from beside the main pool.

In 1703, professional gambler Richard "Beau" Nash, grabbing the opportunity of developing a luxury tourist trade in the area, promoted Bath as a status spa with resort facilities. The **Pump Room** above the Roman Baths (see Food and Pubs above) exemplifies the elegant atmosphere he created. The city's residential northwest corner is another, in which Nash's contemporaries John Wood, *père et fils,* transformed the Georgian row house into an element of design. Though bus tours run regularly from the bus station and from Kingsmead Sq. (see Practical Information above), you may want to stay on foot to see the city. Walk up Gay St. to **The Circus,** which has attracted illustrious residents for two centuries. Blue plaques mark the houses of Thomas Gainsborough, William Pitt, and David Livingstone. Proceed from there up Brock St. to **Royal Crescent** and its great upended saucer of a lawn. Note that there are precisely 114 giant Ionic columns. The interior of **No. 1 Royal Crescent** has been painstakingly restored by the Bath Preservation Trust to a near-perfect replica of a 1770 townhouse, authentic to the last teacup and butter knife. (Open March-Oct. Tues.-Sat. 11am-5pm, Sun. 2-5pm; Nov.-Feb. Sat.-Sun. 11am-3pm. Admission £2.50, children £1.50.) **Royal Victoria Park,** next to Royal Crescent, contains one of the finest collections of trees in the country, and its botanical gardens nurture 5000 species of plants from all over the globe. (Open daily 9am-sunset. Free.)

The famous **Assembly Rooms,** Bennett St., just east of The Circus, staged fashionable social events in the late 18th century. Royalty, musicians, and other self-absorbed characters frequented the balls and concerts held here. Although the ravages of World War II decimated the rooms, renovations duplicate the originals in fine detail. Between the Assembly rooms and the Baths, at the engaging **National Centre of Photography,** you can buy picture-perfect postcards, catch contemporary exhibits, and follow the history and growth of the camera. (Open Mon.-Fri. 10am-6pm, Sat. 10am-5pm. Admission £2.50, children £1.25.)

The 15th-century **Abbey Church** seems an anomaly among Bath's first-century Roman and 18th-century Georgian sights. Inside the church, tombstones cover the walls and floor (the center benches were added in the 1800s, covering the stones). A stone just inside the entrance commemorates Reverend Dr. Thomas Malthus (1766-1834), founder of modern demographics and inspiration to family planners everywhere. (Open Mon.-Sat. 9am-6pm, Sun. 1-2:30pm, 4:30-5:30pm. 50p donation.)

The **American Museum** (tel. 460 503), perched high above the city at Claverton Manor, houses a fascinating series of furnished rooms transplanted from historically significant homes in the United States. The exhibits reflect a wide range of period and regional styles of architecture; among the most impressive are a 17th-century Puritan Keeping Room, a Shaker Meeting House, an ornate Greek Revival dining room, and a cozy Revolutionary-War era tavern kitchen complete with a working beehive oven. The #18 bus (£1.20) can save you a steep two-mile trudge up Bathwick Hill. (Open Tues.-Sun. 2-5pm. Admission £4, students £3.25, children £2.50.)

Entertainment

Classical and jazz concerts enliven the **Pump Room** (see Food and Pubs above) during morning coffee (Mon.-Sat. 10:30am-noon) and afternoon tea (3-5pm). In summer, buskers (street musicians) perform in the Abbey Churchyard, and a brass band often graces the Parade Gardens. Beau Nash's old pad, the magnificent **Theatre Royal,** Sawclose (tel. 448 844), at the south end of Barton St., sponsors a diverse dramatic program (tickets £5-25, matinees £5-7; student discounts available). **The Tier Garten** (tel. 425 360), under Pulteney Bridge near Tilley's Bistro, has a good mix of local rock and jazz bands, comedy, and DJ nights (open nightly 9pm-2am; cover £3). **The Little Theatre,** St. Michael's Pl. (tel. 466 822), shows offbeat movies and oldies (tickets £2.70, seniors and children £1.60). High-energy dance tracks draw a young crowd to the **Players Club,** on the corner of Pierrepont and North Parade (open nightly 9pm-2am; cover £5).

The renowned **Bath International Festival of the Arts,** a 17-day program of concerts and exhibits, takes place all over town from late May to early June. The festival opens with the **Contemporary Art Fair,** including the work of over 700 British artists. Musical offerings range from major symphony orchestras and choruses to chamber music, solo recitals, and jazz. For a festival brochure and reservations, write to the Bath Festival Office, Linley House, 1 Pierrepont Pl., Bath BA1 1JY. The concurrent **Fringe Festival** celebrates music, dance, and liberal politics—and proves just as much fun as the established gala, with no advance booking required.

Wells

Named for the five natural springs at its center, the small town of Wells orbits a splendid Gothic cathedral. Its streets, lined with petite Tudor and golden sandstone shops, fade gently into quiet meadows.

Orientation and Practical Information

Rail routes don't get around to Wells (pop. 9000), but bus routes regularly do, from Bath, Bristol, Glastonbury, and Street. Buses stop in the **Princes Road depot**. To reach the tourist office in the Market Place, walk out to Market St. (ahead and to the left as you face the bus information window), then turn left onto Queen St. and right onto High St., which runs into the Market Place. The center of town is a rectangle bounded on the north by Chamberlain St., the south by High St., and the east by the cathedral and the Market Place.

Tourist Information Centre: Town Hall (tel. 672 552), in the Market Place, to the right as you face the cathedral grounds. Accommodations service £1, list 35p. Book-a-bed-ahead £1.85. Maps of Wells 5p, area bus timetables free. Open April-Oct. Mon.-Fri. 9:30am-5:30pm, Sat.-Sun. 10am-5pm; Nov.-March daily 10am-4pm.

Tours: Well's town crier, the fashionably-attired Freddy Gibbons, gives excellent hour-long guided tours of the city including the cathedral district, Thurs. at 3pm (£1). Groups leave from the tourist center. In addition, the knowledgeable Blue Badges lead 1¼ hr. tours July-Sept. Fri at 1pm (£1.50).

Currency Exchange: Barclay's, Market Place, next to the Conservative Club. Visa checks exchanged free, others for £2. Open Mon.-Fri. 9:30am-3:30pm. **Thomas Cook,** High St., near Market Place. Cook checks exchanged free, others for £3. Open Mon. 9:30am-5:30pm, Tues.-Fri. 9am-5:30pm, Sat. 9am-5pm. **Lloyd's,** High St., exchanges American Express checks for free. Open Mon.-Fri. 9am-4:45pm. **National Westminster,** High St. Open Mon.-Fri. 9am-5:30pm. **Midland,** High St. Open Mon.-Fri. 9:30am-3:30pm.

Post Office: Market Place (tel. 677 825). Open Mon. and Wed.-Fri. 9am-5:30pm, Tues. 9:30am-5:30pm, Sat. 9am-12:30pm. **Postal Code:** Somerset, BA5 2RA.

Telephones: Three phone boxes including a Phonecard phone in Market Place. Three more by the bus station. **Telephone Code:** (0749).

Buses: Badgerline buses from Avon and Somerset stop in the Princes Rd. depot. Call 673 084 or pick up a timetable at the tourist center. To Bath (#173 or 773; every hr. Mon.-Sat., every 3 hr. Sun.; 80 min; £3.30 return) and Bristol (#376 or 676; every hr. Mon.-Sat., every 3 hr. Sun.; 1 hr.; £3). Regular service (#376) to Glastonbury and Street. If you'll be rambling from place to place buy a day **Rambler** (£3.90).

Bike Rental: Wells City Cycles, 80 High St. (tel. 675 096). Three-speeds £4.50 per day, mountain bikes £9 per day; £25-50 deposit. Repairs too. Open Mon.-Tues. and Fri.-Sat. 9am-5:30pm, Wed. 9am-1pm.

Taxi: Wells Taxi (tel. 672 387).

Laundromat: Wells Laundrette, St. Cuthbert St. Wash £1.50, 10-min. dry cycle 20p. Open daily 8am-8pm. Last wash 7pm.

Early Closing: Wed., at 1pm. Not observed by many shops during tourist season.

Hospital: Cottage Hospital, St. Thomas St. (tel. 673 154).

Police Station: Glastonbury Rd. (tel. 673 481).

Emergency: Dial 999; no coins required.

Accommodations

The closest **IYHF youth hostels** are in Cheddar (10 mi.) and Street (6 mi.; see Glastonbury). During the summer, accommodations fill up early. A number of B&Bs (rates about £13-15) line **Chamberlain Street,** and others cluster on St. Andrews St., behind the cathedral.

IYHF Youth Hostel, Hillfield, Cheddar BS27 3HN (tel. (0934) 742 494), off the Hayes, three blocks from Cheddar bus stop (walk up Tweentown Rd.), and one mile from Cheddar Gorge. Frequent buses from Wells (#126-129, Mon.-Sat. every hr. until 5:40pm, £1.20). Stone Victorian house, a bit worn. Lockout 10am-5pm. Open July-Aug. daily; Sept.-Oct. and Feb.-March Tues.-Sat.; and April-June Mon.-Sat. £5.50, ages 16-20 £4.40. Breakfast £2.10, evening meal available.

Mrs. J. Ollis, 1 St. Thomas Terrace (tel. 675 361), across from St. Thomas Church. Immaculate, elegantly decorated rooms. Down comforters on every bed. Warm, accommodating proprietor. English breakfast to top it off. £12 per person.

The Old Poor House, 7a St. Andrew St. (tel. 675 052). One need not be a pauper to stay here. Mrs. Hazelwood is perfectly charming and the rooms are quite posh. £13.50 per person.

Bridge House, 5 St. John St. (tel. 677 074), near the bus station. A stony stream teeming with eel runs alongside this tranquil, 16th-century home. Ancient flagstone floors, working fireplaces, caring owners. Rooms come with color TV, tea-making facilities, firewood, and the blessing of an Anglican priest. No smoking indoors. Doubles only £24-26.

Richmond House, 2 Chamberlain St. (tel. 676 438). Large rooms and friendly proprietors. Vegetarian breakfast available. From £15.

Camping: In **Wookey Hole** and **Cheddar** (see Near Wells).

Food

Assemble a picnic at the Market Place (Wed. and Sat. 8:30am-4pm) or try **The Cheese Board,** at the top of High St. (open Tues.-Sat. 9am-5pm). Health-conscious **Holland & Barrett,** up the block, sells wholefood (open Mon.-Sat. 9am-5:30pm), while **Read's Bakery,** High St., specializes in fattening fare (open Mon.-Sat. 8:30am-5pm, Sun. 10am-4pm). Greengrocers flourish on busy Broad St. **Crispin's Fish and Chips,** at #17, is a popular, Tudoresque chippie serving up cheap, daily lunch specials (open Mon.-Thurs. 11:30am-11pm, Fri.-Sat. 9:30am-11:30pm). In the evening, you may want to step in on one of Well's many pubs; the best of the lot, **Bishop's Kitchen** and the **Penn Eating House,** near the Market Place, serve hot bar food until 9pm. Take-away pizza is available from **Toppings** (7-in. pizza £2.50, 14-in. £4.50; open Tues.-Thurs. noon-2pm and 5-10:30pm, Fri.-Sat. noon-2pm and 5pm-midnight, Sun. 7-11pm).

Sights

The 13th-century **Cathedral Church of St. Andrew** is one of the best surviving examples of a full cathedral complex: bishop's palace, vicar's close, and chapter house. Entering any of the medieval gateways, you will face the quiet western front, adorned with 293 of the original 400 medieval sculptures. Their bright colors now faded, the statues depict the nine angelic orders and the dozen apostles; notice their division into six tiers according to sacred and secular history. A thorough restoration effort involving sandblasting the front's blackened stone, has restored it to its proper golden shade. Each piece of stained glass has been removed, cleaned, and reinserted.

Inside, the magnificent scissor arches sweeping up from the time-worn flags to the vaulted ceilings of the nave encompass some of the most fluid masonry of medieval England. Massive yet graceful, these ingenious, hourglass-shaped structures were devised by some anonymous architect to displace the thrust of the central tower, relieving the cathedral's cracking foundation. Atop the fanciful 14th-century clock in the north transept, a pair of jousting, mechanical knights spur on their chargers and strike at each other every 15 minutes—the same unfortunate rider is unseated every time. Cradled in the arms of umber angels on the clockface below, the bodiless heads of the four winds hurl their breath into the corners of a confidently ordered universe; the moon is depicted in its proper cycle and the sun revolves around the earth. The gold sandstone pillar in the center spreads across the ceiling like a tree trunk crowned with interlacing branches. (Cathedral open daily 9:15am-8:30pm. Expert tour guides will educate you for free, daily at 10:30am, 11am, 11:30am, 2pm, and 2:30pm. Suggested donation £1.50, students 75p.) During term time (Sept.-April), the renowned **Wells Cathedral School Choir** gives evensong recitals weekdays (except Wed.) at 5:15pm and Sundays at 3pm in the cathedral.

The **Bishop's Palace** to the right of the cathedral (entrance from Market Place) evokes the power wielded by medieval bishops. One of the oldest inhabited houses in England, it has served as palace, castle, and country house. Bishop Ralph of Shrewsbury (1329-63), alarmed by village riots in the 14th century, built the moat and walls to protect himself. No fighting transpired, but when rioting Chartists destroyed the bishop's palace in Bristol in 1831, the bridge here was drawn up just in case. Today, with less to fear from the villagers, a cement walkway bridges the moat. (Open Easter-July and Sept.-Oct. Thurs. and Sun., Aug. daily 2-6pm. Admission £1.) The mute swans in the moat have been trained to pull a bell-rope when they want to be fed. A note asks that only brown or wholemeal—heavens, not white—bread be given to the new-age designer swans. **Vicar's Close,** behind the cathedral, is the oldest street of houses in Europe; the houses date from 1363, their chimneys from 1470.

Just north of the cathedral green, the **Wells Museum** displays plaster casts of the figures on the cathedral's west front. The shop of miniature antiques has every detail exquisitely reproduced. (Open April-Oct. daily 11am-5pm; Nov.-March Wed.-Thurs. and Sat.-Sun. 11am-4pm. Admission £1, children 50p.)

Near Wells

You need only venture a short distance from the simplicity and serenity of Wells to encounter crass commercialized settings. If you plan to see both Wookey Hole and Cheddar, save money and buy a **Day Rambler** ticket (£3.90).

Wookey Hole, only two miles northwest of Wells, is home to the **Wookey Hole Caves and Mill** (tel. (0749) 722 43; open May-Sept. daily 9:30am-5:30pm; Oct.-April 10:30am-4:30pm). The admission price of £4.50 (seniors £4, children £3), 50p cheaper at the tourist center in Wells, includes the subterranean caves, a tour of the working paper mill, and a spectacular collection of wooden carousel animals from Britain, the Continent, and the U.S. The gold lion is worth over $50,000. Steel yourself to the somewhat tawdry and distracting man-made elements, and appreciate the natural ones. **Camping** is available at **Homestead Park** (tel. (0749) 730 22) beside a babbling brook (£7 per tent and 2 people). For lunch, stop at the **Wookey Hole Inn.** (Open daily 10:30am-2pm and 7-10:30pm.)

Cheddar, as in the cheese, is an overcrowded mélange of touristy tea-shops and tired cheezwhizardry; a day trip here is justified only by the two mile-long **Cheddar Gorge,** formed by the River Yeo in the hills just northeast of town. The bus from Wells (every hr. Mon.-Sat., 20 min., £1.50) lets you off below the thicket of tourists at the gorge's mouth. From the bus stop follow the signs to Jacob's Ladder, a 322-step stairwell to the top (75p, seniors and children 50p). The unsullied view of the hills to the north and the broad expansive plain to the south rewards the climber. At the foot of the cliffs huddle the **Cheddar Caves,** the finest show caves in England. Note the different mineral colors of the stalagmites and stalactites: rust-red is iron; green is manganese; and grey is lead. (Caves open Easter-Sept. daily 10am-5:30pm, Oct.-Easter 10:30am-4:30pm. Admission to all caves, Jacob's Ladder, and museum £4, children £2.50.)

The Cheddar **tourist office** is located in the town library on Union St. (tel. (0934) 742 769; open Mon. and Wed. 10am-1pm and 2-5:30pm, Fri. 10am-1pm and 2-7:30pm, Sat. 10am-12:30pm). From June to September, there's another tourist information office at the base of Cheddar Gorge (tel. (0934) 744 071). **Camping** is available at **Froglands Farm** (tel. (0934) 742 058), just outside of town toward Wells (£3.50 for tent and 2 people). The town also boasts an **IYHF youth hostel** (see Accommodations in Wells).

In 1170 Henry II declared Cheddar cheese the best in England. Modern day wine and cheese enthusiasts can sate their appetite at the **Chewton Cheese Dairy,** just north of Wells on the A39. Take the bus toward Bristol and get off at Cheddar Rd., just outside Wells (tel. (076 121) 666; shop open April-Dec. Mon.-Fri. 8:30am-5pm, Sat.-Sun. 9am-5pm; Jan.-March Mon.-Fri. 8:30am-4pm, Sat.-Sun. 9am-4pm; cheese-making around noon, but call first). Ask at the Wells or Glastonbury tourist office about vineyard tours.

Glastonbury

The reputed birthplace of Christianity in England and the seat of Arthurian myth, Glastonbury has evolved into an intersection of Christianity and mysticism. According to ancient legend, Jesus traveled here with his merchant uncle, Joseph of Arimathea. Other myths hold that the area is the resting place of the Holy Grail; that Glastonbury Tor is the Isle of Avalon, with the bones of Arthur and Guinevere still beneath Glastonbury Abbey; and that the Tor contains a passage to the underworld. Grow your hair, suspend your disbelief, and join hands with Glastonbury's subculture of hippies, spiritualists, and mystics.

Orientation and Practical Information

Glastonbury lies six miles southwest of Wells on the A39 and 22 miles northeast of Taunton on the A361. Fast, frequent Badgerline buses come from Bristol (#376; every hr. Mon.-Sat., every 2 hr. Sun.; 1½ hr.; £3.45) and from Wells (#167, 168 or 378; 25 min.; £2). From Bath, change at Wells (£3.75).

Glastonbury is a compact town bounded by Manor House Rd. in the north, Bere Lane in the south, Magdelene St. in the west, and Wells Rd. in the east. Shopping and services are concentrated on High St.

Tourist Information Centre: Marchants Bldg., Northload St. (tel. 329 54), 1 block from the Market Cross (about 50 yd. down Northload St.) near the parking lot in a side alley (entrance through small archway). Accommodations service 60p. Free maps. Open April to mid-Nov. Mon.-Sat. 9:30am-5pm, Sun. 10am-4pm.

Currency Exchange: Barclay's, Midland, and **Natwest** cluster on the High St. Open Mon.-Fri. 9:30am-3:30pm.

Post Office: High St. (tel. 314 82). Open Mon.-Fri. 9am-5:30pm, Sat. 9am-1pm. **Postal Code:** BA6 9HS.

Telephones: In front of town hall, Magdelene St. **Telephone Code:** (0458).

Buses and Coaches: Badgerline (tel. (0749) 730 84) and **Southern National** (tel. (0823) 272 033). Both stop in front of the town hall on Magdelene St. National Express tickets are sold at the travel agency on High St.

Bike Rental: Pedlars Cycle Shop, 8 Magdelene St. (tel. 311 17). Repairs and rentals. Bikes £5 per day plus £20 deposit. Open Mon.-Sat. 9am-5:30pm.

Laundromat: Glastonbury Launderette, 46a High St. Wash £1.40; dry cycle 20p. Open daily 8am-9pm. Last wash 8pm.

Early Closing Day: Wednesday at 1pm.

Pharmacy: Andrew Bond, at the top of High St. Emergency prescriptions tel. 506 89. Open Mon.-Fri. 9am-1pm and 2-6:30pm, Sat. 9am-1pm.

Police: Benedict St. (tel. 321 12).

Emergency: Dial 999; no coins required.

Accommodations

Singles are hard to find in Glastonbury. Stop by the tourist information office for a free list. Some B&Bs are located in the hilly hinterlands of town.

IYHF Youth Hostel, The Chalet, Ivythorn Hill, Street BA16 OT2 (tel. (0458) 429 61), 2 mi. south from Street off the B3151. Take Badgerline bus #376, alight at Leigh Rd., and walk 1 mi. Swiss-style chalet with views of Glastonbury Tor, Sedgemoor, and Mendip Hills. Lockout 10am-5pm. Open March-Oct. Mon.-Sat. £5.50, ages 16-20 £4.40.

Tamarac, Mrs. Talbot, 8 Wells Rd. (tel. 343 27 or 320 36). A spiffy modern house on a central residential street. Plush, comfortable rooms with color TV and teapots. Primarily doubles, though families can get a lovely cottage out back. Generous breakfast. £11 per person.

The Bolthole, 32 Coursing Batch (tel. 328 00), opposite the Chalice Well. Bright, flowery rooms with basins, TVs, and teapots. Proprietor keeps healing well water on hand. Singles and doubles from £11 per person.

Mr. and Mrs. Knight, 1 Northload St. (tel. 310 39). Knock on the white door opposite the Tourist Information Center; if no one answers, inquire next door at Knight's Pub. Though larger, more expensive, and less intimate than many of the B&Bs outside of town, the central location, colorful rooms, and breezy rooftop terrace make Knight's an excellent choice for travelers on foot. Singles £15. Doubles £30.

Tor Down Guest House, Mrs. Parfitt, 5 Ashwell Lane (tel. 322 87), a steep mile from the town center, at the base of Glastonbury Tor. Sunny and spotless rooms, all with basins and tea-making equipment. Vegetarian breakfast available. Small but cheerful singles £12.50. Doubles £26.

Little Orchard, 2 Ashwell Lane (tel. 316 20), a short drive or 20-min. trudge from the center; access from Shepton Mallot as well. Luminous rooms with tall windows and fine views of the Vale of Avalon. Singles and doubles from £10 per person.

Camping: Ashwell Farm House, Ashwell Lane at Edgarley End (tel. 323 13). Take the first left after Ashwell Lane. Impeccably maintained sites with nothing but green void between you and Avalon. £2.50 per person. Electricity hookup £1.

Food

Try a picnic by the Tor; **Truckle of Cheese,** 33 High St., has a good selection of luncheon fare. (Open Mon.-Sat. 8:30am-5:30pm.) High St. also has greengrocers, two supermarkets, a wholefood store, a bakery, and reasonably priced restaurants. **Market day** is Tuesday from 8:30am to 5:30pm.

Rainbow's End, 17a High St. Whole-food buffet table on earthenware dishes in pleasant atmosphere. Try the ratatouille and garlic bread (£1.80) or pizza (£1.10). Wear your Birkenstocks. Open Mon.-Sat. 10am-4:30pm.

Market House Inn, 21 Magdalene St., near the town center. Huge helpings at bargain prices. Sweet and sour pork (£2.75); cottage pie with fresh veggies (£2.75). Open Mon.-Sat. 11am-11pm, Sun. noon-2pm. No meals Tues. nights.

Abbey Tea Room, Magdalene St. Quiet and correct lunch for under £3 and delicious cream teas with scones and jam for £1.75.

Deacon's Coffee House, 24 High St. Ploughman's lunch (£2.75) or Coronation chicken (£3). Roast beef with horseradish sauce £2.75. Skip lunch and feast on Somerset Cream tea (£2.30). Open Mon.-Fri. 10am-5:30pm, Sat. 9:30am-5:30pm, Sun. 11:30am-5:30pm.

Sights

Behind the archway on Magdalene St. lurk the ruins of **Glastonbury Abbey,** the oldest Christian foundation and once the most important abbey in England. It now consists of one steeple surrounded by green lawns marked with the outline of the old abbey. Joseph of Arimathea supposedly built the original wattle-and-daub church on this site in 63 AD; larger churches were successively raised over the next millenium. Erected in 1184, the stone abbey flourished until the Reformation. It sixth and last abbot, Richard Whiting, disobeyed Henry VIII's order that all Catho lic churches dissolve. Not known for his sense of humor, Henry had Whiting hanged, drawn, and quartered on Glastonbury Tor.

Two national patron saints, Patrick of Ireland and George of England, have been claimed by the abbey—Patrick is said to be buried here and George to have slain his dragon just around the corner. But King Arthur most captivates the legend-makers. In 1191, the monks dug up a coffin they claimed contained the remains of Arthur and Guinevere; in 1276, in the presence of King Edward I, they reinterred the pair before the high altar. (Abbey open daily 9am-6pm. Admission £1.50, children £1.)

The tower visible across Somerset's flatlands from miles away is **Glastonbury Tor** or, more properly, the remains of St. Michael's Chapel. Glastonbury Tor is the site of the mystical Isle of Avalon, where the Messiah is slated to reappear. From the top of the hill, you can survey the Wiltshire Downs, the Mendips and, on a clear day, the distant spires of Bristol Cathedral. To reach the Tor, turn right at the top of High St. and continue up Wellhouse Lane. Take the first right up the hill.

On the way down from the Tor, visit the **Chalice Well,** at the corner of Wellhouse Lane, the supposed resting place of the Holy Grail. Legend once held that the well ran with Christ's blood; in these post-Nietzschean days, rust deposits at the source turn the water red. The water gurgles from the well down through a tiered garden of hollyhocks, climbing vines, and dark, spreading yew trees. You can drink the water from the lion's head on the second tier. When the grounds are shut down, you can still get well water from a tap on the outside wall. (Open March-Oct. daily 10am-6pm; Nov.-Feb. daily 1-3pm. Admission 40p, children 20p.)

Take a short walk down Chilkwell St. to the 14th-century **Abbey Barn,** part of the **Somerset Rural Life Museum** (tel. 311 97). Exhibits depict the rural industries of Somerset, such as cider-making and peat-digging. Notice the elegant roof in the Abbey Barn; it supports 80 tons of stone tiles. (Open Easter-Oct. Mon.-Fri. 10am-5pm, Sat.-Sun. 2-6pm. Admission £1.20, seniors 80p, children 30p.)

Head down Bere Lane to Hill Head to reach **Wearyall Hill,** where legend has it that Joseph of Arimathea's staff bloomed and became the **Glastonbury Thorn.** The Thorn, a grove of trees native to Palestine, has grown on Wearyall Hill since Saxon times. The Thorn should, according to legend, burst into bloom in the presence of royalty. Horticulturists here and abroad (where offshoots of the thorn are planted) have wasted considerable time on making the trees bloom each time the Queen comes to visit.

Appendices

Opening Times of Sights

Bank of England Museum	Easter-Sept. Mon.-Fri. 10am-5pm, Sun. 11am-5pm; Oct.-Easter Mon.-Fri. 10am-5pm.
Banqueting House	Mon.-Sat. 10am-5pm.
HMS Belfast	April-Oct. daily 10am-5:20pm; Nov.-March daily 10am-4pm.
Bethnal Green Museum of Childhood	Mon.-Thurs. and Sat. 10am-6pm, Sun. 2:30-6pm.
British Museum	Mon.-Sat. 10am-5pm, Sun. 2:30-6pm.
Brompton Oratory	Daily 6:30am-8pm.
Burgh House	Wed.-Sun. noon-5pm.
Cabinet War Rooms	Daily 10am-6pm.
Carlyle's House	April-Oct. Wed.-Sun. 11am-5:30pm.
Chelsea Old Church	Daily 10am-6pm.
Chelsea Royal Hospital	Mon.-Sat. 10am-noon and 2-4pm, Sun. 2-4pm.
Chiswick House	April-Sept. daily 10am-6pm; Oct.-March daily 10am-4pm.
College of Arms	Mon.-Fri. 10am-4pm.
Commonwealth Institute	Mon.-Sat. 10am-5pm, Sun. 2-5pm.
Thomas Coram Foundation	Mon.-Fri. 10am-4pm.
Courtauld Institute	Mon.-Sat. 10am-6pm, Sun. 2-6pm.

Crosby Hall	Mon.-Sat. 10am-noon and 2:15-5pm.
Cutty Sark	Mon.-Sat. 10am-6pm, Sun. noon-6pm; in winter Mon.-Sat. 10am-5pm, Sun. noon-5pm.
Design Museum	Tues.-Sun. 11:30am-6:30pm.
Dickens House	Mon.-Sat. 10am-5pm.
Dulwich Picture Gallery	Tues.-Fri. 10am-1pm and 2-5pm, Sat. 11am-5pm, Sun. 2-5pm.
Eton College	Yard, cloisters and museums April and July-Sept. daily 10:30am-4:30pm; May-June and Oct.-March daily 2-4:30pm.
Fenton House	April-Oct. Sat.-Wed. 11am-6pm; March Sat.-Sun. 2-6pm.
Geffrye Museum	Tues.-Sat. 10am-5pm, Sun. 2-5pm.
Golders Green Crematorium	Daily 9am-5pm.
Guildhall	May-Sept. daily 10am-5pm; Oct.-April Mon.-Sat. 10am-5pm.
Greenwich Old Royal Observatory	Mon.-Sat. 10am-6pm, Sun. 2-6pm; in winter Mon.-Sat. 10am-5pm, Sun. 2-5pm.
Guildhall Clock Museum	Mon.-Fri. 9:30am-4:45pm.
Gypsy Moth IV	April-Sept. Mon.-Sat. 10am-6pm, Sun. noon-6pm; Oct. daily 10am-5pm.
Hampton Court	Mid-March to mid-Oct. daily 9:30am-6pm; mid-Oct. to mid-March daily 9:30am-4:30pm.
Harrods	Mon.-Tues. and Thurs.-Sat. 9am-6pm, Wed. 9am-8pm.
Highgate Cemetery	April-Oct. daily 10am-5pm; Nov.-March daily 10am-4pm.
Hogarth's House	April-Sept. Mon. and Wed.-Sat. 11am-6pm, Sun. 2-6pm; Oct.-March Mon. and Wed.-Sat. 11am-4pm, Sun. 2-4pm.
Imperial War Museum	Daily 10am-6pm.
Institute of Contemporary Arts	Daily noon-11pm.
Dr. Johnson's House	Oct.-April Mon.-Sat. 11am-5pm.
Keats' House	April-Oct. Mon.-Fri. 2-6pm, Sat. 10am-1pm and 2-5pm, Sun. 2-5pm; Nov.-March Mon.-Fri. 1-5pm, Sat. 10am-1pm and 2-5pm, Sun. 2-5pm.
Kensington Palace	Mon.-Sat. 9am-5:30pm, Sun. 11am-5:30pm.
Kenwood House	Mid-April to Sept. daily 10am-6pm; Oct. to mid-April daily 10am-4pm.
Kew Gardens	Feb.-Sept. Mon.-Sat. 9:30am-6:30pm, Sun. 9:30am-8pm; Oct.-Jan. daily 9:30am-4pm.
Kew Palace	Daily 11am-5:30pm.
Leighton House	Mon.-Sat. 11am-5pm.
Lloyd's Building	Visitors' Gallery Mon.-Fri. 10am-12:30pm.
London Toy and Model Museum	Tues.-Sat. 10am-5:30pm, Sun. 11am-5:30pm.
London Transport Museum	Daily 10am-6pm.
London Zoo	March-Oct. Mon.-Sat. 9am-6pm, Sun. 9am-7pm; Nov.-Feb. daily 10am-dusk.
Madame Tussaud's	June-Sept. daily 9am-5:30pm; Oct.-May daily 10am-5:30pm.
Marble Hill House	April-Sept. daily 10am-6pm; Oct.-March daily 10am-4pm.
The Monument	April-Sept. Mon.-Fri. 9am-6pm, Sat.-Sun. 2-6pm; Oct.-March Mon.-Sat. 9am-4pm.
Museum of London	Tues.-Sat. 10am-6pm, Sun. 2-6pm.
Museum of Mankind	Mon.-Sat. 10am-5pm, Sun. 2:30-6pm.
Museum of the Moving Image	June-Sept. daily 10am-8pm; Oct.-May Tues.-Sat. 10am-8pm, Sun. 10am-6pm.
National Army Museum	Daily 10am-5:30pm.
National Gallery	July-Aug. Mon.-Sat. 10am-8pm, Sun. 2-6pm; Sept.-June Mon.-Sat. 10am-6pm, Sun. 2-6pm.
National Maritime Museum	Mon.-Sat. 10am-6pm, Sun. noon-6pm; in winter Mon.-Sat. 10am-5pm, Sun. noon-5pm.
National Portrait Gallery	Mon.-Fri. 10am-5pm, Sat. 10am-6pm, Sun. 2-6pm.
National Postal Museum	Mon.-Thurs. 9:30am-4:30pm, Fri. 9:30am-4pm.
Natural History Museum	Mon.-Sat. 10am-6pm, Sun. 11am-6pm.
North Woolwich Old Station Museum	Mon.-Wed. and Sat. 10am-5pm, Sun. 2-5pm.
Old Bailey	Visitors' Gallery Mon.-Fri. 10am-1pm, 2-4pm.
Orleans House	April-Sept. Tues.-Sat. 1-5:30pm, Sun. 2-5:30pm; Oct.-March Tues.-Sat. 1-4:30pm, Sun. 2-4:30pm.
Osterley House	April-Oct. Wed.-Fri. 1-5pm, Sat.-Sun. 11am-5pm.
Parliament	House of Commons Visitors' Gallery Mon.-Thurs. 4-10pm, Friday 10am-3pm. House of Lords Visitors' Gallery Mon.-

	Wed. 2:30pm-late, Thurs. 3pm-late, Fri. 11am-late.
Percival-David Foundation	Mon.-Fri. 10:30am-5:30pm.
Planetarium	June-Sept. daily 10:20am-5pm; Oct.-May daily 12:20-5pm.
Pollock's Toy Museum	Mon.-Sat. 10am-5pm.
Public Records Office	Mon.-Fri. 10am-5pm.
Queen's Gallery	Tues.-Sat. 10am-5pm, Sun. 2-5pm.
Queen's House, Greenwich	Mon.-Sat. 10am-6pm, Sun. 2-6pm; in winter Mon.-Sat. 10am-5pm, Sun. 2-5pm.
Ranger's House, Greenwich	April-Sept. daily 10am-6pm; Oct.-March daily 10am-4pm.
Royal Academy	Daily 10am-6pm.
Royal Air Force Museum	Daily 10am-5:30pm.
Royal Courts of Justice	Mon.-Fri. 10:30am-4:30pm.
Royal Naval College	Fri.-Wed. 2:30-5pm.
St. Anne's, Limehouse	Sun. 3-4:30pm
St. Bartholomew the Great	Mon.-Thurs. 8am-4:30pm, Fri. 10:45am-4:30pm, Sun. 8am-8pm.
St. Bride's	Daily 8:15am-4:45pm.
St. Clement Danes	Daily 8am-5pm.
St. George's Chapel, Windsor	Mon.-Sat. 10:45am-4pm, Sun. 2-4pm.
St. John's Gate	Mon.-Fri. 10am-4:30pm, Sat. 10am-4pm.
St. Magnus Martyr	Tues.-Fri. 9am-4pm, Sat.-Sun. 9:30am-1pm.
St. Martin-in-the-Fields	Daily 7:30am-7:30pm.
St. Martin-within-Ludgate	Mon.-Fri. 10am-5pm.
St. Mary Abchurch	Thurs. 10am-4pm.
St. Mary Aldermary	Tues.-Fri. 11am-3pm.
St. Mary-le-Bow	Mon.-Fri. 8:15am-5:45pm.
St. Mary-le-Strand	Mon.-Fri. 11am-3:30pm.
St. Olave's	Mon.-Fri. 8am-3:30pm.
St. Paul's Cathedral	Mon.-Sat. 9am-4:15pm; ambulatory Mon.-Sat. 9:30am-4:15pm; crypt Mon.-Fri. 9:30am-4:15pm, Sat. 11am-4:15pm; galleries Mon.-Sat. 9:45am-4:15pm.
St. Paul's Church, Covent Garden	Mon.-Fri. 9am-4pm.
St. Stephen's Walbrook	Mon.-Fri. 9am-4pm.
Science Museum	Mon.-Sat. 10am-6pm, Sun. 11am-6pm.
Shakespeare Globe Museum	Mon.-Sat. 10am-5pm, Sun. 2-5:30pm.
Sir John Soane's Museum	Open Tues.-Sat. 10am-5pm.
Syon House	Easter-Sept. Sun.-Thurs. noon-5pm; Oct.-Easter Sun. noon-5pm.
Tate Gallery	Mon.-Sat. 10am-5:50pm, Sun. 2-5:50pm.
Temple Church	Oct.-July Mon.-Sat. 10am-4pm, Sun. 2-4pm.
Thames Barrier	Visitor Centre Mon.-Fri. 10:30am-5pm, Sat.-Sun. 10:30am-5:30pm.
Theatre Museum	Tues.-Sun. 11am-7pm.
Tower Bridge	April-Oct. daily 10am-5:45pm; Nov.-March daily 10am-4pm.
Tower of London	March-Oct. Mon.-Sat. 9:30am-5pm, Sun. 2-5pm; Nov.-Feb. Mon.-Sat. 9:30am-4pm.
Victoria and Albert Museum	Mon.-Sat. 10am-5:50pm, Sun. 2:30-5:50pm.
Wallace Collection	Mon.-Sat. 10am-5pm, Sun. 2-5pm.
Wellington Museum	Tues.-Sun. 11am-4:30pm.
Westminster Abbey	Thurs.-Tues. 8am-6pm, Wed. 8am-7:45pm.
Whitechapel Art Gallery	Tues. and Thurs.-Sun. 11am-5pm, Wed. 11am-8pm.
Windsor Castle	Grounds April-Sept. daily 10:15am-6:15pm; Oct.-March daily 10:15am-4:15pm; State Apartments April-Sept. Mon.-Sat. 10:30am-5pm, Sun. 12:30-5pm; Oct.-March Mon.-Sat. 10:30am-4pm, Sun. 12:30-4pm.

By Appointment Only

Some London sights require you to book in advance. Make reservations as far ahead of time as possible.

City Livery Companies	City of London Information Centre, St. Paul's Churchyard, EC4 (tel. 606 3030).
Docklands Development Corporation tour	Call 512 3000, ext. 3510 or 3513.

Fenton House Keyboard Instruments	**Warden, Fenton House, Windmill Hill, London NW3.**
Henry VIII's Wine Cellar	**Department of the Environment, St. Christopher's House, Southwark St., London, SE1.**
Houses of Parliament in session	**Write to your embassy in London; Brits can write to their MPs.**
Ceremony of the Keys	**Resident Governor, Tower of London, EC3.**
Lambeth Palace	**Lambeth Palace, Lambeth Palace Rd., SE1.**
National Theatre backstage tours	**South Bank, SE1.**
Postal box collection	**National Postal Museum, King Edward Building, King Edward St., EC1.**
Trooping the Colour	**Household Division HQ, Horse Guards, SW1.**

Royal London

Trooping the Colour. On the Queen's official birthday (a Sat. in early June). Get tickets for the Mall in advance from Household Division HQ, Horse Guards, SW1. Best view is on TV.

Changing of the Guard, Buckingham Palace. In summer daily at 11:30am; in winter on alternate days at 11:30am. To avoid the crowds, view from between Victoria Memorial and St. James's Palace.

Changing of the Guard, Horse Guards Parade. Mon.-Sat. at 11am, Sun. at 10am. On west side of Whitehall. Fewer crowds than at Buckingham Palace.

Changing of the Guard, Windsor Castle. Daily at 11am.

State Opening of Parliament. In early Oct. Queen rides to and from parliament via the Mall and Whitehall.

Remembrance Day Service. On the Sun. nearest Nov. 11. At the Cenotaph in Whitehall.

Maundy Money. On Maundy Thurs., the day before Good Fri. Location changes each year (can be outside London).

INDEX

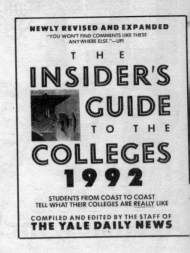